Essential
Statistics

Essential Statistics

for
Public Managers and
Policy Analysts

Second Edition

Evan M. Berman
Louisiana State University

CQ PRESS

A Division of Congressional Quarterly Inc.
Washington, D.C.

CQ Press
1255 22nd Street, NW, Suite 400
Washington, DC 20037

Phone: 202-729-1900; toll-free, 1-866-4CQ-PRESS (1-866-427-7737)

Web: www.cqpress.com

Cover design: Mike Grove, MG Design

☉ The paper used in this publication exceeds the requirements of the American National Standard for Information Sciences—Permanence of Paper for Printed Library Materials, ANSI Z39.48-1992.

Printed and bound in the United States of America

10 09 08 07 06   1 2 3 4 5

Library of Congress Cataloging-in-Publication Data

Berman, Evan M.
    Essential statistics for public managers and policy analysts / Evan M. Berman. — 2nd ed.
        p. cm.
    Includes index.
    ISBN-13: 978-0-87289-301-6 (alk. paper)
    ISBN-10: 0-87289-301-4
    1. Social sciences—Statistical methods.   I. Title.

HA29.B425 2007
519.5—dc22   2006020300

This book is dedicated to my wife, Dira, who brings light, which is the essence of this book.

It is also dedicated to the Lynch and White families, who generously provided refuge to us, evacuees from New Orleans during Hurricanes Katrina and Rita (2005).

CONTENTS

Tables, Figures, and Boxes

TABLES

FIGURES

"IN GREATER DEPTH" BOXES

PREFACE

This second edition of *Essential Statistics* continues the positive features of the
first edition: brevity, straightforward instruction, and hands-on application. Ever
mindful that instructors must balance comprehension of statistical concepts, the
development of data analysis skills, and the application of both to problems of
public management and policy analysis, I am hopeful that instructors who have
used the first edition will find that this revision improves on, but does not alter,
the strengths at the core of the book. *Essential Statistics* continues to offer a
conceptual understanding of statistics that can be readily applied to the real-life
challenges of public administrators and policy analysts. Key ideas are presented
in a concise manner, and data analysis skills are developed through computer-
based analysis, rather than by hand-based calculations. The brevity and clarity of
presentation promote flexibility so that professors can readily add or adjust
material to meet specific instructional needs.

The conceptual and hands-on approach followed in *Essential Statistics* is
consistent with ongoing developments in the field of quantitative methods. The
increasing availability of user-friendly and affordable statistical software limits
the rationale for doing hand calculations. On all but rare occasions, the text
restricts hand calculations to situations in which they strengthen and enhance
students' understanding of basic statistical concepts. The text presents the
assumptions, purposes, and applications of statistics, illustrated by real-world

examples and numerous tables, charts, and graphs. Learning objectives start off each chapter, and key terms are highlighted in the text and listed at the end of chapters for quick and easy review. And because students have limited time and demand a high degree of practical application, this book quickly gets to the point and shows them multiple applications they will need on the job. In addition, this edition incorporates new "Getting Started" boxes in the chapter text, which point students toward critical skills and insights that will help them master the material. Based on feedback from adopters, this second edition features a number of improvements:

- Almost all of the original eight chapters have been split to allow for more explanation of particular statistical techniques. As well, the book's new sixteen-chapter structure gives instructors flexibility when assigning reading over the course of an academic term.
- A wealth of examples have been added throughout the text to help clarify statistical concepts, offering students additional scenarios for seeing conceptual material in application.
- Three new chapters early in the book—covering research design, conceptualization and measurement, and data collection—help round out a more substantial section devoted to research methods, further laying out important foundational concepts.

This text is designed for courses that cover statistics in a separate, single term, as well as those that combine statistics with research methods. If the program requirement is for a separate course on statistics, the instructor may want to exclude some of the new material on research methods. Yet those early chapters may serve as a handy refresher on material for students. If the program requirement combines quantitative methods with research methods, then the section on research methods will likely be a welcome feature. Such courses may skip some of the later chapters in the book that address advanced topics on inferential statistics. The additional datasets and exercises help strengthen both types of courses.

A UNIQUE LEARNING PACKAGE

This textbook is part of a unique resource set consisting of several valuable teaching tools. Developed in tandem with one another, each piece has been crafted as part of a larger learning package to enhance and reinforce lessons learned in the classroom.

Exercising Essential Statistics

The accompanying workbook complements the textbook. Its aim is to strengthen students' learning and extend their ability to apply the material from the text, offering them opportunities to practice through carefully crafted exercises. The second edition of *Exercising Essential Statistics* contains even more exercises for students to work through, with an average of twenty-eight per chapter. Corresponding directly to the core text, workbook chapters cover the same learning objectives and consist of four parts that facilitate learning, testing, and application. The first part, "Q & A," identifies key learning points in a question-and-answer format to help students test their comprehension. The second part, "Critical Thinking," contains open-ended questions designed to stimulate students' thinking and deepen their insight. The questions carry the material one step further and are excellent for in-class teaching, discussion sections, and homework assignments. The third part, "Data-Based Exercises," includes computer-based applications that use the datasets provided on the CD-ROM included with the workbook. These exercises will help students get comfortable working with data. The fourth section, "Further Readings," lists other books, resources, and examples for anyone interested in further research. Workbook pages are perforated and three-hole punched so that students can easily turn in work for credit and later save them for reference.

The datasets reflect students' and professors' preferences for real-life data that shed light on important problems and issues that arise when working with data. The datasets cover experiences of the public and nonprofit sectors. They are based on employee and citizen surveys as well as environmental, welfare, and public safety data. This second edition includes new datasets, such as quality-of-life indicators for cities and data relevant to nonprofit organizations. In a few instances, plausible hypothetical data are used. The sets include both cross-sectional and time series data. They contain complete documentation, including survey instruments, which many readers will find useful. Data are provided in SPSS, Stata, SAS, and SYSTAT formats so that students can access these sets with a range of software programs. Recognizing the widespread use of SPSS, the workbook includes a chapter on using SPSS (chapter 17). Chapter 18 provides documentation for the datasets on the CD-ROM.

The workbook and datasets span a wide range of areas and are designed to support integration with other areas of study in master's degree programs in public policy and in public administration. The workbook covers many examples from human resource management, organizational behavior, budgeting, and public policy. The problems are written with those students in mind who have not yet taken these courses. In addition, the datasets are quite extensive, enabling professors to develop additional applications in the areas they choose to emphasize.

Instructor's Resources on CD-ROM

A new set of PowerPoint lecture slides highlight chapter concepts, lessen class prep time, and assist with teaching. The CD-ROM includes a solutions manual with answers to exercises and questions. Adopters should contact James Headley at jheadley@cqpress.com for their copy.

ACKNOWLEDGMENTS

As always, numerous people contributed to this project. I would like to thank Charisse Kiino (chief acquisitions editor, College division, CQ Press) for her unwavering support for this project; no author could wish for more support or a better technical team. Amy Marks provided some of the very best editing an author could have, and Lorna Notsch did a superb job with production. I thank David Laney for support in collecting data and assisting in the SPSS chapter of the workbook. I am grateful to Amy Davis (formerly of the City of Maitland) for developing the bonus PowerPoint presentation (on the CD), and Toby Comeaux and Edgardo Bustamante for their help with the new Community Indicators dataset.

I also wish to thank the numerous academic reviewers throughout the life of this project, including Gary Copeland (University of Oklahoma–Norman), David Coursey (Florida State University), Lucinda Deason (University of Akron), Anand Desai (Ohio State University), Kimberly Nelson (Southern Illinois University–Carbondale), Bruce Rogers (Tennessee State University–Nashville), and especially Michelle Piskulich (Oakland University), whose review comments were among the best that this author has ever received—nearly each strengthened the set in some way. As well, I'd like to thank Richard Feiock (Florida State University), who generously converted the datasets from SPSS into other formats that are now on the CD.

Despite all the help that I received, I reluctantly accept that any remaining errors are mine. In addition, I give special thanks to the faculty and administrators at my universities, past and present, as well as numerous practitioners with whom I have worked over the years, especially Michelle DelValle, Jorge Figueredo, Ben Hardcastle, and Dean Sprague. I remain impressed by their professionalism and commitment to public administration. I continue to be indebted to Professors Jonathan West and Bill Werther (both of the University of

Miami) for enriching my career in more ways than can be enumerated here. Finally, I want to thank hundreds and hundreds of former students who indirectly contributed to this book through their feedback. They have never been shy in expressing themselves.

Evan M. Berman
Baton Rouge and Metairie, Louisiana
berman@lsu.edu

Statistics Roadmap

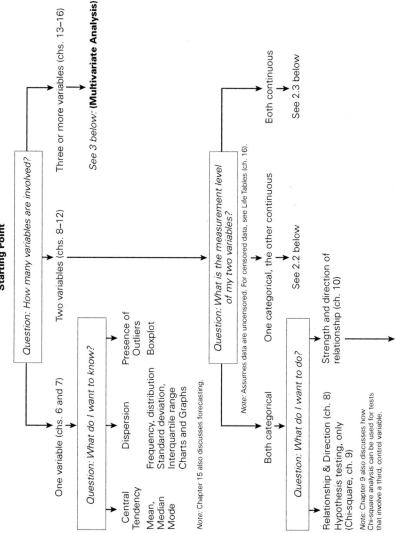

Starting Point

Question: How many variables are involved?

One variable (chs. 6 and 7)

Two variables (chs. 8–12)

Three or more variables (chs. 13–16)

See 3 below: **(Multivariate Analysis)**

Question: What do I want to know?

Central Tendency	Dispersion	Presence of Outliers
Mean, Median Mode	Frequency, distribution Standard deviation, Interquartile range Charts and Graphs	Boxplot

Note: Chapter 15 also discusses forecasting.

Question: What is the measurement level of my two variables?

Note: Assumes data are uncensored. For censored data, see Life Tables (ch. 16).

Both categorical

One categorical, the other continuous

See 2.2 below

Both continuous

See 2.3 below

Question: What do I want to do?

Relationship & Direction (ch. 8)
Hypothesis testing, only (Chi-square, ch. 9)

Strength and direction of relationship (ch. 10)

Note: Chapter 9 also discusses how Chi-square analysis can be used for tests that involve a third, control variable.

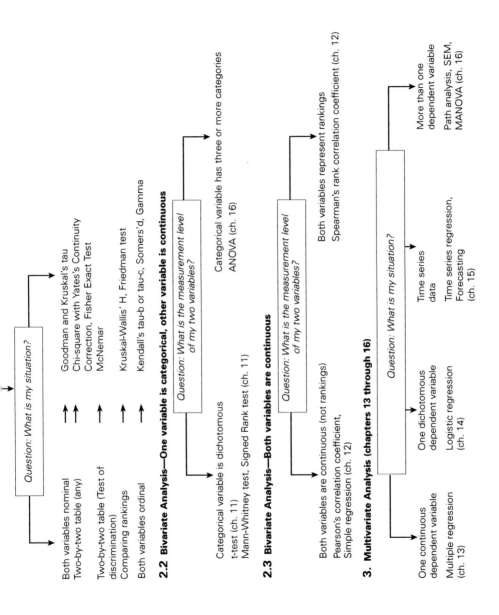

Question: What is my situation?

Both variables nominal	
Two-by-two table (any)	Goodman and Kruskal's tau
	Chi-square with Yates's Continuity Correction, Fisher Exact Test
Two-by-two table (Test of discrimination)	McNemar
Comparing rankings	Kruskal-Wallis' H, Friedman test
Both variables ordinal	Kendall's tau-b or tau-c, Somers'd, Gamma

2.2 Bivariate Analysis—One variable is categorical, other variable is continuous

Question: What is the measurement level of my two variables?

Categorical variable is dichotomous
t-test (ch. 11)
Mann-Whitney test, Signed Rank test (ch. 11)

Categorical variable has three or more categories
ANOVA (ch. 16)

2.3 Bivariate Analysis—Both variables are continuous

Question: What is the measurement level of my two variables?

Both variables are continuous (not rankings)
Pearson's correlation coefficient, Simple regression (ch. 12)

Both variables represent rankings
Spearman's rank correlation coefficient (ch. 12)

3. Multivariate Analysis (chapters 13 through 16)

Question: What is my situation?

One continuous dependent variable
Multiple regression (ch. 13)

One dichotomous dependent variable
Logistic regression (ch. 14)

Time series data
Time series regression, Forecasting (ch. 15)

More than one dependent variable
Path analysis, SEM, MANOVA (ch. 16)

SECTION

I

Introduction

For many professionals and students, past experiences with statistics often have been less than fully satisfying—perhaps nightmares best forgotten. This is both unfortunate and increasingly unnecessary. This book, now in a second edition, is guided by the underlying philosophy that statistics is an enterprise that is both practical and increasingly easy. Modern advances in computers and software have reduced the importance of hand calculations, allowing students to work readily with real-life applications. Conceptual understanding and application are central to statistics, not arithmetic and cumbersome calculations.

For public managers and analysts, this book shows how to apply the principles and practices of statistics to problems of public management and analysis. Whether through program evaluation; policy analysis; performance measurement; or program client, citizen, or employee surveys, statistics offers public managers and policy analysts ample opportunities for "speaking truth to power."[1] In doing so, these professionals inform public discourse and add value to democratic processes at all levels of government. The ability to analyze data will enhance students' skills and can help to further their careers.

This book is part of a set that consists of

- A textbook: *Essential Statistics for Public Managers and Policy Analysts*
- A workbook: *Exercising Essential Statistics,* which includes

- exercises with applications in public management and analysis
- a CD-ROM with datasets and presentations in various formats

All of these materials include various features that make it easier to understand statistics and to benefit from its application. The textbook is written in an accessible, direct, and economical style. A flow chart located in the front of the book, called the "Statistics Roadmap," is a quick reference tool that will help guide readers to choose the correct statistical method for their research. From there, sixteen chapters build upon each other, taking the reader from the very fundamentals of research design all the way through advanced statistics. Each chapter begins with a list of learning objectives— the skills and concepts students can expect to know when they have finished reading. Key terms are shown in bold italics and are listed at the end of each chapter for easy reference.

The workbook extends conceptual understanding through application of statistics principles, drawing on the practical problems of managers. Chapters 1 through 16 of the workbook correspond to the equivalent chapters in the textbook and are organized in five parts: "Q & A" reinforces key learning points and assists in test preparation; "Critical Thinking" stimulates insight into statistics principles; "Data-Based Exercises" emphasizes hands-on skill-building and additional applications; and "Suggested Readings" recommends books for further study in areas of interest. The workbook is an integral part of this set, and the articles and Web site are also recommended.

The datasets on the CD-ROM are based largely on real-life data and include employee and citizen surveys. They also cover topics of environmental, welfare, and public safety interest and are relevant to all levels of government. A new dataset of Community Indicators is included with this second edition. Complete documentation, including survey instruments that can be tailored to students' own situations, is found in Chapter 18 of the workbook. Data are provided in SPSS and other formats for use in other software packages. The workbook also includes a tutorial for using SPSS (Chapter 17). The CD-ROM has some useful bonus material, too, such as examples of reports.

The workbook, together with these datasets, teaches students how to apply statistics to practical problems in the real world. Students will also discover the principles that allow them to go beyond these examples to specific problems they encounter in the workplace. After using this learning package, readers will see not only how practical and easy statistics can be but also how the effective use of statistics can help them.

I'd like to hear from you. The textbook, the workbook, and the CD-ROM reflect decades of feedback from other professionals and students. Don't be shy. Let me know what features you like and what should be improved upon. Now, let's get started!

Evan M. Berman
Baton Rouge and Metairie, Louisiana
berman@lsu.edu

Note

1. This phrase is borrowed from the classic work of Aaron Wildavsky, *Speaking Truth to Power* (Boston: Little, Brown, 1979).

CHAPTER

1

Why Statistics for Public Managers and Analysts?

CHAPTER OBJECTIVES

After reading this chapter, you should be able to
- Appreciate the importance of using data in public management and analysis
- Identify levels of competency and proficiency in data analysis
- Describe strategies for increasing proficiency in data analysis
- Understand the importance of ethical principles in data analysis

ROLE OF DATA IN PUBLIC MANAGEMENT

Why research? Why statistics? The ethos of public management is to "go out and make a difference," not to sit behind a desk and crunch numbers. Public managers often join agencies because they seek to serve and help their communities and country. Not surprisingly, some managers are puzzled by the suggestion of engaging in research and statistics: research appears boring in comparison with developing and implementing new programs, and statistics seems, well, impossibly challenging with little payoff in sight.

In fact, analytical techniques involving research and statistics are increasingly in demand. Many decisions that public and nonprofit managers make involve data and analysis, one way or another. Consider the following common **uses of analysis and data**:

First, data and objective analysis often are used to *describe and analyze problems,* such as the magnitude of environmental disasters (for example, oil spills), the extent of social and public health problems (such as homelessness or the AIDS epidemic), the extent of lawlessness, the level of economic prosperity or stagnation, or the impact of weather-related problems such as brought on by hurricanes and snow storms. For example, it matters whether the illiteracy rate among 12 year olds is 3 percent or 30 percent, or somewhere in between. By describing the extent of these problems and their underlying causes accurately, managers are able to better formulate effective strategies for dealing with them. Policy analysis often begins by describing the extent and characteristics of problems and the factors associated with them.

Second, data are used to *describe policies and programs.* What are programs and policies expected to achieve? How many services are programs expected to provide? What are some milestones of achievement? How much will a program cost? These questions involve quantifiable answers, such as the number of national guardsmen that are brought in to assist with search and rescue efforts after a major hurricane, or the number of evacuees for whom officials expect to provide refuge. Policies and programs can be described in quite detailed ways, involving distinct program activities, the duration and geographic scope of activities, and staffing levels and area program budget data.

Third, programs produce much routine, administrative data that are used to *monitor progress and prevent fraud.* For example, hospitals produce a large amount of data about patient visits, who attended them, their diagnosis, billing codes, and so on. Schools produce vast amounts of data about student achievement, student conduct, extracurricular activities, support and administrative services, and so on. Regulatory programs produce data about inspections and compliance. In many states, gaming devices (such as slot machines) are monitored electronically to ensure that taxes are collected and that they are not tampered with. Administrative data assist in monitoring programs, and managers are expected to be familiar with these data.

Fourth, analysis is used to guide and *improve program operations.* Data can be brought to bear on problems that help managers chose among competing strategies. For example, what-if analysis might be used to determine the cost-effectiveness of alternative courses of action. Such analysis often is tailored to unique situations and problems. In addition, client and citizen surveys might be used to inform program priorities by assessing population needs and service satisfaction. Systematic surveys provide valid and objective assessments of citizen and client needs, priorities, and perceptions of programs and services. Systematic surveys of citizens and clients are used increasingly and are considered a valuable tool of modern management.

Fifth, data are used to *evaluate outcomes.* Legislatures and citizens want to know what return they are getting from their tax dollars. Did programs and policies achieve their aims? Did they produce any unexpected results? Most grant applications require public managers to be accountable for program outcomes. Public managers must demonstrate that their programs are producing effective outcomes and that they are doing so in cost-effective ways. This demand for outcome evaluation and monitoring far exceeds any requirement of proper funds management. Analysis can also be used to determine the impact of different conditions on program effectiveness, leading to suggestions for improving programs.

Data and analysis are omnipresent in programs and policies. They are there at every stage, from the inception of programs and policies, to their very end. Of course, decisions are also based on personal observation, political consensus, anecdotal and impressionistic descriptions, and the ideologies of leaders. Yet data and analysis often are present, too, one way or another.

Getting Started
How are these uses of data and analysis present in your area?

This is because analysis is useful. Specifically, quantitative analysis aids in providing an objective, factual underpinning of situations and responses. Analysis, along with data, helps quantify the extent of problems and solutions in ways that other information seldom can. Analysis can help quantify the actual or likely impact of proposed strategies, for example, helping to determine their adequacy. At the very least, a focus on facts and objective analysis might reduce judgment errors stemming from overly impressionistic or subjective perceptions that are factually incorrect. So managers are expected to bring data and analysis to the decision-making table.

COMPETENCY AND PROFICIENCY

Analysis requires competency and proficiency. The standards of accredited graduate programs in public administration and affairs recognize the importance of quantitative analysis. The accrediting organization for these programs, the *National Association of Schools of Public Affairs and Administration (NASPAA)*, requires that the "common curriculum components shall enhance the student's values, knowledge, and skills to act ethically and effectively in the application of quantitative and qualitative techniques of analysis." NASPAA further stipulates that such skills should be applied to policy and program formulation, implementation, and evaluation, as well as to other decision-making and problem-solving activities.

These uses of data and analysis imply the need for six **competencies for analysis,** which can be addressed through this course. First, managers and analysts will have to be *familiar with data sources* in their lines of business. They will need to know what data are available and to what uses they are commonly put. For example, are they used for monitoring? For estimating service needs? For determining program efficiency? For describing community conditions? Beyond this, managers will also need to be able to determine the validity of these data and understand their limits. They will need to know whether data have been collected in ways that do not induce additional bias. Finally, managers will need to be able to develop new uses of data, for dealing with situations and problems as they arise.

Second, managers and analysts need competencies to *gather their own data.* Simply, existing data do not always address important issues at hand. For example, they may not be adequate to determine client needs or evaluate programs. The ability to collect new data implies familiarity with and competencies in conducting different types of research, such as archival research, or in conducting scientific population or program client surveys. Many managers value the ability of their staff to conduct these types of research. Client and citizen surveys are increasingly a staple of public management.

Third, public managers and analysts need to be able to *analyze the data.* Without analysis, it is not possible to generate meaningful information about program efficiency and effectiveness, for assessing whether a program is on track and for determining and identifying new client needs. Analysis requires competency in statistics. Analysis must be done in ways that shine light on important problems. It must also be done in ways that are sound, defensible, objective, and consistent with current practice.

Fourth, public managers and analysts need to be able to *communicate* their results. Communication requires the ability to explain complex or abstract concepts in ways that are accessible to different audiences. Results should be explained in simple ways without oversimplifying. Communication also involves effective writing and presentation skills. Communication is often used to meet additional objectives of accountability and transparency, and thus also to seek out and engage different publics and stakeholders in order to enhance trust in public and nonprofit organizations and their programs and policies.

Fifth, analysts must be able to bring to their analysis *the theory and practice of management and policy analysis.* Understanding the specific and unique problems of public and nonprofit programs and their context informs analytical tasks to be carried out. The needs of homeless people in New York City are different from those in Louisiana, as are the priorities of stakeholders and affected publics. Analytical tasks must be infused, from the start, with a clear sense of the specific program and contextual issues; without context or purpose, analysis is a blind exercise in technique only, not connected to purpose.

Sixth, analysts must have a sound and strong sense of *ethics.* Technical skills alone are not enough to ensure soundness of analytical purpose and practice; analysis also requires a commitment to being truthful, complete, mindful and useful. Ethics affects how analysts and managers approach matters of analysis and communication and how they view the role of research and analysis in their field. Ethics affects which questions analysts and managers ask, and how they deal with them. Ethics is a hallmark of modern professionalism, and a key to public service; it is discussed in greater detail in the next section.

These six competencies are to varying degrees grounded in the canons of scientific research and statistics. **Scientific research** is the careful, systematic process of inquiry that leads to the discovery or interpretation of facts, behaviors, and theories. The methods used for scientific research include standards and procedures for gathering, analyzing, and reporting data such as through surveys, focus groups, or archival research, for example. Scientific research is distinguished from personal and other forms of research or inquiry by rather strict standards for accepting new facts and theories as knowledge, and by a process that includes other scientists in making such determinations. Science sets a high standard for what is considered to be valid knowledge. As a branch of science, **statistics** is the body of systematic knowledge and practice that provides standards and procedures for correctly analyzing one's data, which often are collected in the process of scientific research.

Research and statistics provide essential frameworks and language that inform the six competencies described here. Research and statistics provide guidelines for determining what to measure, how to collect data, and how to draw conclusions from data. These guidelines help managers, for example, to evaluate the scientific validity of data, whether they use existing data or gather their own. Indeed, public management data often are incomplete, biased, or inaccurate in some way, and managers need to know how to address these matters. Some problems are correctable, whereas others warrant caveats. Knowledge of these standards can also help managers and analysts avoid problems, such as when they plan to collect their own data. This is not to say that all knowledge or information used by managers meets or should meet scientific standards, but the above competencies, as well as previously mentioned uses of data and analysis, do require careful attention to these matters. Knowledge of scientific standards and research processes, discussed in this book, cannot be ignored without sacrificing credibility.

Students and managers seeking to improve these competencies often experience different ***stages of proficiency***. Respectively, these stages might be called the "know nothing," journeyman, technocrat, and sophisticated expert stages. Understanding these stages can help guide one's progress and development activity.

Know Nothing. Many people who are new to public and nonprofit management do not bring with them much background about data in their lines of business, or ways in which data might be used for improving program efficiency. This is not a problem but a fact. A good share of these students are reserved, skeptical, fearful, or even hostile about the uses of data and statistics. Then, they will need to acknowledge these feelings and work to become aware of ways in which data are usefully and correctly applied in management and policy analysis. To get beyond this stage, they will need to obtain a good foundation in research and statistics, and succeed in finding useful examples in each of the five areas of use described earlier.

Journeyman. People in this stage have worked for a few years in their lines of business. As such, they have usually seen some applications and are clear about the utility of data and analysis. They sometimes use data for monitoring program progress. However, lacking research and statistics skills, they often do not see themselves as being qualified to develop broader applications or even to analyze data in relatively simple ways. The purpose of this course is to provide readers with the necessary foundations and skills and to encourage the development of new uses of data and analysis in their lines of business. People at this level are often concerned about communicating their results and methods correctly, and this skill should also be focused on at this stage.

Technocrat. People in this stage have acquired varying levels of technical mastery of research and statistics. Some technocrats are highly skilled, whereas others have only a modest level of ability. A common problem is that technocrats are unable to integrate and guide their analysis with the substantive concerns of program and policies in their lines of business. They might even view themselves as statistics resource persons, rather than as managers and employees tied to specific programs and policies—the fifth competency (relating research and statistics to the theory and practice of management and policy analysis) is missing. The main challenge for technocrats is to learn how to put research and statistics in service of programs and policies. They need to put these substantive concerns on par with the technical analysis.

Sophisticated Expert. People at this stage have found the right balance between the development of policies and programs and the use of objective data and analysis to further decision making. They understand both.

Because they have spent several years in their lines of business, they are familiar with the relevant existing data, they know the strengths and weaknesses of these data, they are familiar with a range of applications, and they are able to develop new applications and collect original data. They are well-rounded in the use of data. Sophisticated experts often have a positive orientation toward continuing, professional education. They may challenge themselves by writing articles for scholarly journals and making presentations at conferences.

At whatever stage of proficiency you are at, think of how you can benefit from increased use of data and analysis. Data and analysis are increasingly used skills in public and nonprofit organizations. Whether positions are analytical, such as policy analysis, budgeting, or information technology, or people oriented, such as counseling, human resources, or social services, analytical skills are in demand for analyzing data, conducting surveys, and communicating quantitative findings to a broader audience. Program managers, city managers, and elected officials, too, require a solid grasp of analytical skills, for monitoring performance, detecting fraud, and improving productivity. Almost every department needs people with analytical skills, and jobs associated with analytical skills often command a salary premium.[1]

Getting Started
At which stage of competency do you see yourself today? Which competencies and uses of data and analysis would further your career? How will you attain these competencies?

ETHICS IN DATA ANALYSIS AND RESEARCH

The effectiveness of data and analysis in decision making depends on more than just technical competency; it also depends on the ethical integrity with which analysis is performed and presented. When questions surface about the ethics of an analysis, its credibility suffers, and people may be unwilling to give it much, if any, consideration. Specifically, there are three *areas of ethical concern*: (1) the integrity of purpose, (2) the integrity of the process of analysis and communication, and (3) the integrity of dealing with human subjects. When research and analysis are clear about these matters, and technically proficient, too, then the role of analysis in decision making and policy can be enhanced.

First, managers need to be clear about the purpose of their analysis. Analysis often has *dual purposes*: (1) to further programs and policies, such as by making them more efficient or effective, and (2) to establish factual, objective truths that meet standards of scientific evidence and that hold up under scrutiny. The first purpose causes analysis to focus on matters that are relevant to the agency and its mission; analysts need to be forthright in disclosing what questions they considered, and that which they did not—no analysis can cover everything. The second purpose implies that analysts should be open to all facts, whatever they are, and ensure that all facts comply fully with standards of scientific evidence. Analysts must disclose and issue caveats for instances in which this is not the case. Ethics in analysis requires full disclosure of the purpose of the analysis, and all the biases, trade-offs, and shortfalls encountered along the way.

These dual purposes can come into conflict, forcing ethical choices and decisions. For example, what is a manager to do when careful analysis shows his or her programs to be less effective than hoped for? Should pursuit of mission cause a blind eye to facts that are contrary? Such results may indicate the need for further research or to consider future program changes. Consider another example: Should the agency intentionally ignore questions or analysis that could strengthen the arguments of those who advocate against the program or agency? Agencies cannot totally ignore their fiduciary responsibilities to society at large and thus their broader impacts. Such counterarguments should be taken into consideration in some way. These tensions are quite common in practice, and they cannot be ignored or swept under the rug.

Second, managers need to consider the integrity of the analysis and communication process. Many of these considerations are based on the *guiding principles of scientific research*—to be honest, objective, accurate, and complete. Analysts should not hide facts, change data, falsify results, or consider only data that support a favored conclusion. For example, data may be sketchy and incomplete, and management judgment is that such information is better used than ignored. Then the poor quality of the information needs to be clearly stated and a caveat given. Analysts should also fully report the sources of their data, data collection methodologies, any possible gaps and shortfalls, and they should assess the impact of such shortcomings on their findings.

It is obvious that facts and findings should not be altered or manufactured in any way. That is outright lying, and people will be justly outraged to know that they have been deceived. Regrettably, each year cases of scientific misconduct and fraud make headlines. However, it is equally important that analysis be as meticulous and objective as possible in testing its own findings. Findings should be checked for errors and inaccuracy. Conclusions should be examined for the possibility of alternative or rival explanations. The impact of assumptions, gaps, and bias should be examined. Doing so is not only proper, but it also strengthens study findings by providing detailed knowledge about their validity and robustness. The more that is known about the data and results, the more confidence that others may have in them.

Communication in research matters, and results should be presented in straightforward and nonmisleading ways. For example, analysis should not adjust scales to give the appearance of a significant increase when the increase is in fact minor and insignificant. Such misrepresentations are considered the same as lying with statistics. Findings should be communicated in ways that are straightforward and easy to understand, for both experts and nonexperts, without oversimplification or deception. These ethical norms are not merely standards for evaluating analysis that has already been undertaken and presented; rather, these norms provide essential guidance to analysts throughout the entire analytical process, as they decide what to analyze, how to write up their findings, and how to present them.

Third, in recent years considerable attention has been given to the impact of research on the **well-being of human subjects** in research. Some key ethical principles in research involving people are that their participation should be voluntary and based on informed consent (that is, they should know what they are getting involved in), that information about them should be held confidentially, and that risks of harm to subjects should be minimized and reasonable in relationship to anticipated benefits. Concerns about the well-being of human subjects arose from various medical research experiments that intentionally misled patients and exposed them to great harm.

Some landmark examples of **scientific misconduct** in medicine include the Nazi war crimes during World War II, in which concentration camp prisoners were subjected to torture and poisonous injections to see how they would be affected. In the United States, the Tuskegee syphilis study (1930–1972) used as its subjects several hundred black males with untreated syphilis, without informed consent. Even after penicillin was found to be an effective antibiotic treatment in the 1940s, these black males were neither informed about nor offered treatment choices. In the Willowbrook study, 1963–1966, newly admitted children with mental handicaps were injected with hepatitis in order to track the natural history of the disease. Parents had to approve of the treatment, but approval was also necessary as a condition for admission into this overcrowded facility.

Regrettably, these cases do not stand alone. Instances of deceit and coercion, whether subtle or blatant, led to the development of the ethical principles mentioned earlier. There are many other examples of research misconduct, too. For example, in one case, public health workers lost a confidential file of known AIDS patients that was later sold in a local nightclub. Most human subject research is now overseen by institutional review boards (IRBs) to ensure that risks to subjects are reasonable, and that possible harm is identified and minimized. These boards are committees at universities and other research institutions composed of scientists who evaluate the protocols of proposed research. The point is that we confront ethical issues in research pretty much every time we do research, and we need to learn from past errors. For example, what ethical issues are involved in the push to have the

Table 1.1 ⸺∿⸺ Ethics of Research and Analysis

Be honest:
1. Do not hide facts, change data, falsify results, or use only data that support your conclusion.
2. Present results in straightforward and nonmisleading ways. For example, do not adjust scales to give the appearance of a significant increase when the increase is minor or insignificant. Also, do not suggest a level of precision that is not present.

Be complete:
3. Report all data and results that relate to a conclusion, not just those that support it.
4. Identify caveats and alternative explanations that may qualify your findings, even if no data exist to evaluate these caveats or alternative explanations.
5. Report the sources of your data, data collection methodologies, possible gaps and shortfalls, and impact on findings.
6. Be thorough, meticulous, and objective in your analysis, conclusions, and communications.

Be useful:
7. Try to produce information that can help your employer, other stakeholders, and the public interest.
8. Communicate information and results in ways that nonexperts can readily understand.

Be mindful:
9. Information is power; be aware of possible negative consequences. Address possible negative consequences of your analysis by considering further analysis, by considering the interests of affected parties, and by identifying relevant caveats in findings.
10. Respect the interests of human subjects whose data are being analyzed. They may have rights to privacy and "hold harmless" clauses. Obey research protocols.

Food and Drug Administration approve some drugs early, before they have been fully tested? The notions of research not causing unnecessary harm and being upfront with participants are now fully established ethical principles. If analysis involves access to confidential data, then steps must be taken to ensure that these data are protected. The impact of research on human subjects must be considered, and steps undertaken to minimize and address harmful impacts. Managers also need to be mindful of the negative impacts that their analysis can have. The interest of affected parties should be considered, for example, by ensuring that conclusions are accurate and fair. Table 1.1 provides an overview of important ethical principles.[2]

SUMMARY

Analysis and data are commonly used by public and nonprofit managers to support decisions. Analysis is useful because it helps provide an objective, factual underpinning to situations and programs and helps quantify the extent of problems and solutions. At the very least, a focus on facts and objective analysis can help reduce judgment errors that stem from impressionistic or subjective perceptions. Analysis and data often are used to describe problems, programs, and policies; to assist in monitoring programs and in making decisions that might make them more effective or efficient; and to evaluate outcomes.

The effective use of analysis and data requires competency in the following areas: knowing existing data sources, their applications, and their limitations; having an ability to gather one's own data; having an ability to analyze data; being able to communicate findings; being able to guide analysis by the specific, substantive program and policy interests; and being aware of ethics practices. Managers who seek to increase their competency often experience different stages of proficiency: "know nothing," journeyman, technocrat, and the sophisticated expert.

The effectiveness of data and analysis in decision making depends on more than just technical competency; however, it also depends on the ethical integrity with which research is performed. Areas of ethical concern involve the integrity of the research purpose, the integrity of its analysis and communication, and the integrity of dealing with human subjects. Analysis in public and nonprofit organizations often serves dual purposes, namely, to promote programs and policies and to establish factual, objective truths that meet standards of scientific evidence. Analysis should be forthcoming about the purposes that it serves and about the ways in which these purposes have affected it.

KEY TERMS

Areas of ethical concern (p. 10)
Competencies for analysis (p. 7)
Dual purposes (of analysis) (p. 10)
Guiding principles of scientific
   research (p. 11)
NASPAA (p. 6)

Scientific misconduct (p. 12)
Scientific research (p. 8)
Stages of proficiency (p. 9)
Statistics (p. 8)
Uses of analysis and data (p. 5)
Well-being of human subjects (p. 12)

Notes

1. To learn more about salaries in public and nonprofit administration, take a thorough look at salaries at www.bls.gov/oes/current/oessrci.htm

(for government, scroll down and select sector 92; for nonprofits, select NAICS 712100, museums, or NAICS 813300 and then the subgroup "community and social services." For an interesting look at careers, visit www.naspaa.org/students/careers/careers.asp. This site also offers salary information.

2. Table 1.1 deals with ethics in research and data analysis, but it is also useful to consider codes of professional conduct generally. Most professional organizations have such codes, such as the American Society for Public Administration (www.aspanet.org) and the International City/County Management Association (www.icma.org).

SECTION

II

Research Methods

This section examines research methods and their application to public and nonprofit management as well as to policy analysis. **Research methodology** is the science of methods for investigating phenomena. Research methods are used in almost every social science discipline. The chapters in this section provide an in-depth examination of the research methods that managers and analysts need to be familiar with, so that they can gain the competencies described in Chapter 1, such as to gather, analyze, and communicate facts and findings in their lines of work.

In this brief introduction, we offer a few distinctions that shape a useful perspective about research methods. First, research methods can be applied to problems found in many different fields, including the sciences and public and nonprofit management and analysis. Here, we examine research methods used to bring understanding to three important problems that public and nonprofit managers and analysts commonly face: (1) evaluating the past performance of programs and policies, (2) monitoring the present performance of programs and policies, and (3) forecasting the future of programs, policies, and community conditions. Each of these areas involves questions about facts, relationships, understanding, and more. These problems span questions about the past, present, and future and are relevant to many areas of public and nonprofit management.

Second, we can distinguish between two research purposes. Generally the purpose of *basic research* is to develop new knowledge about phenomena such as problems, events, programs, or policies, and their relationships. Here are some basic research questions in public and nonprofit management: What is the nature of citizen apathy? What is the nature of citizen voluntarism? Which factors affect voluntarism? What consequences does voluntarism have? Or, what are the activities and outcomes of programs or policies? And, why do some people have an aversion to statistics? These questions clarify the nature and relationships among phenomena by asking, generally, "What is this, and what consequences does it have?" This question can be asked with regard to events in the past, present, or future.

But research and analysis in public and nonprofit management also serve applied and highly practical purposes. *Applied research* is used to solve practical problems. Examples of applied research questions include the following: What can governments do to reduce citizen apathy? How can governments increase the use of certain programs? What can be done to minimize the impact of turnover among political appointees on program quality? What can be done to increase students' interest in statistics? These questions clearly have practical matters in mind. They often ask, "How can this be done or improved?"

Research begins by asking questions, and managers and analysts will encounter both basic and applied questions in their work. For example, program evaluation might involve basic research questions such as, "What is the program achieving?" Or it might involve applied research questions such as, "How can the program be made more effective?" Both kinds of questions are important, and research methods help managers and analysts formulate and address them. Indeed, questions about improving programs presume knowledge of what these programs do and what they have achieved.

Third, after raising questions, managers and analysts must choose among a broad range of research methods to answer their questions. Research methods often are classified as quantitative or qualitative in nature. *Quantitative research methods* involve the collection of data that can be analyzed using statistical methods. Such data typically are collected through surveys or compilations of administrative records, and they produce numbers used to describe (that is, to measure) the extent of societal problems (such as teenage violence or homelessness, for example), to monitor program operations, to determine program efficiency and effectiveness and to analyze by how much they can be improved, and to evaluate the impact of programs.

Qualitative research methods refer to the collection and analysis of words, symbols, or artifacts that are largely nonstatistical in nature. Such data often are collected through interviews, focus groups, and direct observation. Typically the purpose of qualitative research is to identify and describe new phenomena. Qualitative research provides a detailed, rich understanding of what is going on and why it matters to stakeholders, in their own words. Qualitative research is used to identify problems and the factors associated with these problems. It is also used to describe programs and policies, such as their priorities and methods of operation, as well as processes through which programs and policies affect outcomes. Qualitative research can also suggest ways in which programs might be improved.

Both quantitative and qualitative methods are indispensable in addressing questions of basic and applied research. Quantitative research requires solid knowledge of existing phenomena and how they are related to each other. Simply, before we measure something, we need to be certain that we know what we are measuring and that we are measuring the right thing. However, qualitative research does not provide much specific information about the magnitude of problems and phenomena, nor can it offer conclusive, statistical proof about the impacts of programs and policies. Hence, research in public management and analysis typically uses both quantitative and qualitative research methods.

Managers and analysts need a working familiarity with a range of basic and applied, quantitative and qualitative research methods. The chapters in this section reflect a diversity of purposes and methods, providing many examples of the distinctions described here. Chapter 2 introduces basic concepts of research and applies these concepts to program evaluation. Managers and analysts are often called upon to demonstrate the outcomes of public and nonprofit programs and policies. Program evaluation is an important method for holding people accountable, focusing on questions about how programs and policies performed in the past. The chapter explores experimental and quasi-experimental designs for evaluating programs and gives examples. Program evaluation demonstrates the use of both basic and applied research, and the need for both qualitative and quantitative research methods.

Chapter 3 addresses the problems of conceptualization and measurement that affect program evaluation and other research approaches in public management and policy analysis. For example, how are abstract concepts like democracy, apathy, safety, self-sufficiency, or congestion to be measured? The chapter discusses the problem of conceptualization, measurement validity, and the importance of measurement scales and levels.

Chapter 4 describes additional research methods for public managers and analysts. It deals with research on problems that involve the present (monitoring) and the future (forecasting). Specifically, it discusses performance measurement, which is increasingly used for program monitoring and to provide accountability. The chapter also applies criteria of validity, developed in Chapter 3, to the measures of performance measurement.

Chapter 4 also examines common research methods for forecasting. The discussion of these methods is concise but encompassing and includes examples.

Chapter 5 looks at data collection methods. An important competency for analysts and managers is familiarity with the data sources in their lines of work. This chapter discusses uses and challenges of secondary data, administrative and archival data, and survey data. It provides guidelines for conducting surveys, including sampling strategies and methods, and also notes the roles of qualitative data, such as interviews and focus groups. The workbook that accompanies this textbook includes many additional examples of the research methods and data collection strategies discussed in this chapter.

Finally, this book includes footnotes that serve a variety of purposes. Some of these notes provide additional clarification or examples, and others provide additional depth and detail that expand the material. Readers are encouraged to examine the footnotes. Also, because each social science has its own terminology, and interdisciplinary fields like public and nonprofit management draw professionals from many different sciences, readers will need to become familiar with the analogous terms and concepts they come across. Throughout the book, such analogous terms and concepts are clearly identified as such.

CHAPTER

Research Design

CHAPTER OBJECTIVES

After reading this chapter, you should be able to
- Distinguish between independent and dependent variables
- Describe the six steps of program evaluation
- Explain experimental and quasi-experimental designs
- Understand the importance of rival hypotheses
- Identify threats to validity in research design

This chapter introduces major concepts in social science research and applies them to program evaluation. Program evaluation, which helps managers and analysts to determine the outcomes of programs and policies, is an important and necessary skill for managers and analysts to have. This chapter also examines a variety of research designs commonly used in program evaluation.

INTRODUCING VARIABLES AND THEIR RELATIONSHIPS

Research is fundamentally about establishing the nature of things. For example, assume that we are responsible for managing a program to reduce high school violence or that we are otherwise interested in this topic. One of the first steps that we need to take is to gain a solid understanding of this phenomenon, high school violence, by examining the ways in which it is manifested. We would want to know about its various forms such as verbal and emotional abuse; its physical manifestations such as shoving, hitting, and the use of weapons; and its racial and sexual manifestations, too. Thereafter, we would want to know the magnitude of each manifestation, such as how many fist fights, gun fights, or rapes occur. And we might want statistics on specific types of injuries, such as broken bones or concussions. Indeed, the frequency of these phenomena often is a key target for management and public policy.

The same is true for many other phenomena such as community conditions (for example, poverty or economic growth), events (such as wildfires or toxic spills), as well as programs and policies shaping conditions and events. We will want to first establish the manifestations of a phenomenon and then learn something about their magnitude. If we are interested in environmental quality, for example, we will want to know facts about the state of the environment and how it varies in different ways and in different locations. If we are in health care management, we will want to know the incidence of different diseases. If we are interested in inflation, we will want to know its current level, which factors such as energy prices or housing costs are responsible for recent changes, and how inflation varies in different parts of the country. Once we decide what we are interested in, we will want to know more about its manifestations and variations.

Public and nonprofit management and policy typically involve phenomena that vary in some way. *Variables* are defined as empirically observable phenomena that vary. This is best illustrated by a few examples. "High school violence" is a variable because it is observable and varies across schools; violence is more common in some schools than in others, and we can observe the differences. "Environmental quality" is also a variable because it is observable and varies across locales, as do "diseases" and "inflation," for example. Variables are key to research, and they are everywhere. The number of students in classes is also a variable because different classes have

> **Getting Started**
> Can you identify important variables in your present or future line of work, such as services or program outcomes that vary in some way?

different numbers of students, and the number of students in each class can be observed. By contrast, in a study of only female students, the variable "gender" does not vary and is therefore called a *constant*. Constants are phenomena that do not vary.

Attributes are defined as the specific characteristics of a variable, that is, the specific ways in which a variable can vary. All variables have attributes.

For example, high school violence can be measured as being absent, sporadic, occurring from time to time, or ongoing—these are the attributes of the variable "high school violence." Another example is the variable "gender." Gender varies in the population, and the attributes of gender are "male" and "female." The variable "race" often has more than two attributes (Caucasian, African American, Native American, and so forth). The variable "income" can have few or a nearly infinite number of attributes if income is measured as specific dollar amounts. In surveys, often each survey item is treated as a separate variable, and the response categories for each question are the variable's attributes. For example, the question "What is your gender?" is considered a variable, and the response categories "male" and "female" are its attributes.

Research usually involves both *descriptive analysis* and the study of *relationships* involving variables. **Descriptive analysis** provides information about the nature of variables—such as whether a high school violence problem exists and the extent or level of it. The preceding section gave examples of descriptive analysis. In our high school violence example, descriptive analysis can be used to show the nature of the perpetrators, the geographic areas in which such violence most often occurs, and the extent to which it is perceived as a problem. Descriptive analysis is useful in public management and policy because managers need to know the state of the world that they are trying to shape. They need to know, for example, the number of teenagers who have been hurt by others at school. This is simply a number—such as 5 percent.

Managers also want to know the causes of problems and the effectiveness of interventions. This involves examining **relationships**, that is, specifying which variables are related to each other, and the ways in which they are related. Indeed, research is not only about establishing the nature of phenomena, but also about their relationships. For example, we might want to examine whether students who participate in anger management classes describe themselves as being less angry or less prone to acting out against others. Specifically, we want to know whether participation in anger management class decreases the extent of acting out by students. We might also examine the effect of other conditions—such as drug use or gang participation—on high school violence. By knowing how programs and conditions affect outcomes, managers can better recommend and pursue alternative courses of action. Most studies involve both descriptive analysis and an examination of relationships.

Relationships in social science are distinguished by whether they are *probabilistic* (occurring sometimes) or *deterministic* (occurring each time). For example, when we say that anger management reduces high school violence, we are not implying that this always occurs, for each student. Some students might even become more violent, perhaps learning new ways of expressing their anger. Rather, we mean that, *on average,* the number of violent incidents will decrease. The number of incidents will decrease for some students more than for others, and for still others it will not decrease at all; the relationship is probabilistic in nature. Many relationships in the social world are probabilistic.

When social scientists say that "anger management reduces high school violence," they typically mean that in most instances anger management reduces high school violence. They usually also have a standard in mind, such as anger management reducing high school violence at least 95 out of 100 times. Sometimes, social scientists adopt an even stricter standard, such as at least 99 out of 100 times. By adopting such standards, social scientists provide information about probabilistic relationships with a relatively high degree of confidence.[1]

Relationships also are distinguished as being either *causal* or *associational*. **Causal relationships** show cause and effect, such as the impact of anger management programs on high school violence, the impact of employee compensation on workplace productivity, or the impact of environmental policies on water quality. In these instances, one variable is assumed to affect another. By contrast, associations are relationships that imply no cause and effect. For example, it is said that in Sweden a relationship exists between the number of storks and the number of childbirths; both increase in the spring. Does this imply that storks really do bring babies, at least in Sweden? No, of course it doesn't. The appearances of storks and new babies are unrelated; they have no cause-and-effect relationship.[2]

> **Getting Started**
> Can you identify examples of causal relationships and associations in your area?

Among causal relationships, we further distinguish between *independent variables* and *dependent variables*. **Dependent variables** are variables that are affected by other variables (hence, they are dependent on them). **Independent variables** are variables that cause an effect on other variables but are not themselves shaped by other variables (hence, they are independent). For example, in a study of the impact of anger management on high school violence, anger management is the independent variable that affects high school violence, which is the dependent variable. Causal relationships are commonly thought of in the following manner:

Independent Variable(s) → Dependent Variable

An important step in any research is specifying the dependent and independent variables. Doing so brings clarity and direction to the research.

Although many studies examine several relationships, most evaluations focus on explaining only a few dependent variables. In our example, we wish to examine the impact of anger management on high school violence:

Independent Variable		*Dependent Variable*
Anger Management	$\rightarrow$	High School Violence

Of course, our evaluation needn't be limited to studying just this relationship, but specifying relationships in this manner helps concentrate our attention on (1) accurately determining the level of high school violence and (2) examining whether anger management is associated with it. We might also study the effect of gun control laws (independent variable) on this dependent variable, or other relationships such as the effect of homework assistance (independent variable) on academic performance (dependent variable). *Distinguishing between independent and dependent variables clarifies and sharpens one's thinking about which variables are being studied and how they are related to each other. It is a cornerstone of research, program evaluation, and policy analysis, and it is an essential skill that managers and analysts will want to practice.*

A literature review of scholarly (research) and professional articles can often help to further develop and clarify our thinking about independent and dependent variables. Oftentimes, managers and analysts are interested in a phenomenon, such as school violence, and perhaps one or two factors associated with it. Then, prior research can help to further develop this interest. Previous studies may suggest ways of measuring high school violence and perhaps provide a critical review of alternative measures. Researchers might have also taken different perspectives on the causes of high school violence, leading them to consider different independent variables. Research might have evaluated the effect of independent variables in different settings, though not necessarily yours. Research might have carried this interest further, examining the impact of high school violence on, for example, educational performance. In these different ways, prior research, as a reflection of careful and considered thought, can be used by managers and analysts in helping them to further develop their topic.

Program evaluation is often intended to stake a claim of *causation*. In our example, managers might want to argue that anger management has caused the decline in high school violence. You may have heard the expression "correlation does not prove causation." This is true. Causation requires both (1) *empirical (that is, statistical) correlation* and (2) *a plausible cause-and-effect argument*. These two **criteria for causality** must be present. Statistical analysis tests whether two variables are correlated, but causality also requires a persuasive argument (also called theory) about how one variable could directly affect another.[3] Regarding the impact of anger management on high school violence, a plausible theory might readily be written up. Anger management training teaches people how to identify anger and release it in ways that are nonviolent toward others. Thus, both statistical correlation and a persuasive theoretical argument are required to stake a claim of causation.

How difficult can it be to make a theoretical argument of cause and effect? Examining, say, the relationship between gender and high school violence, we have yet to make a plausible cause-and-effect argument. If we lack specific evidence (especially evidence that might persuade a skeptical audience) that gender, defined by reproductive organs and hormones, causes violence, then we best regard this relationship as a mere correlation, that is, an *association*. Empirical correlations remain mere associations until analysts have argued, in persuasive and exacting detail, how one variable can plausibly cause another.

Finally, relationships that have not yet been empirically tested (that is, established) are called *hypotheses*. For example, a study hypothesis might be that, on average, female teenagers are less prone to violence than males. Then, empirical data will need to be collected and analyzed in order to prove the hypothesis either true or false for the population from which these data are drawn. Subsequent chapters in this book discuss how to analyze data and draw conclusions about hypotheses. Academic research studies are usually quite explicit about which hypotheses are being tested and why they are relevant.

This brief introduction lays out important concepts that are used over and over again in research. Quite simply, when we do research, we see the world existing of variables and their relationships. We also identify the attributes of variables, and ask whether relationships are deterministic or probabilistic, causal or only associational, tested (established) or hypothesized.

> **Getting Started**
> Look around and identify some relationships. Then identify the independent and dependent variables in each relationship.

PROGRAM EVALUATION

Program evaluation can be defined as the use of social science research methods to determine whether, and in what ways, a program works. Program evaluation involves the description of programs, conditions, and events, as well as the analysis of relationships, such as the impact of programs on outcomes. Program evaluation uses both quantitative and qualitative methods to describe programs and analyze their relationships.

How difficult can it be to document program outcomes? There usually is more to program evaluations than meets the eye. Among the first challenges is to find out what the program is expected to accomplish. Consider the following example. In response to growing concerns about teen violence, many communities and states have created after-school programs. The idea, according to elected officials and supported by the public, is to get teenagers off the streets and into supervised environments. As a public manager, your job is to implement such a program. Funding guidelines require that you document the success of the program.

Now, you must figure out what the program is expected to accomplish. You might be surprised to learn that sometimes little thought has gone into identifying specific outcomes for such programs, or that some elected officials and experts have different views. Some advocates only want teenagers off the streets, but others expect them to learn something as well. Still others feel that anger management should be taught. Even if you are responsible only for program evaluation, oftentimes you will find yourself formulating program outcomes.

Next, assume that you and others agree that anger management is one of several appropriate activities for the after-school program. Specifically, the after-school program will teach students to recognize and deal with anger in appropriate ways. You might even try to target so-called high-risk students. How will you measure the success of your anger management efforts? Should you ask students whether they feel less angry? Should you ask their parents and teachers as well? Should you ask teachers to record the number of classroom incidents, such as student outbursts? Should you do all of this? If so, in what way?

Suppose you decide to ask teachers to track classroom incidents. Which incidents should be tracked? Is it appropriate to compare different classroom incidents across schools or classes? Should you develop baseline data, and if so, which? Also, how accurate do you think the teachers will be in their reporting and tracking? Are their responses likely to be biased in any way? Or suppose you decide to send a survey to parents. Do you need to send your survey to all parents? How many questions should you ask? What response rate is appropriate? How do you avoid biased questions?

Finally, consider the possibility that the number of classroom incidents drops during the course of your anger management program. How do you know that the drop is due to the anger management course? Could teachers and parents have become more involved in anger management themselves? What if some students who are known to be angry and violent were transferred out of the school? In short, how sure can you be that any changes are due to the after-school program?

These questions are hardly academic. Elected officials and senior managers expect others to have answers to such questions, regardless of whether they concern after-school programs, prison overcrowding, environmental protection, or national security. Determining which outcomes ought to be measured and measuring their attainment in credible ways are activities germane to all public programs and polices. Public departments need people with skills to assess program outcomes; program evaluation applies social science methods to these issues.[4]

> **Getting Started**
> Select a program in your area of interest (or workplace) that is a candidate for program evaluation. Which relationship(s) would you focus on?

Six Steps

Program evaluation usually involves six steps. The purpose of these steps is to help researchers and managers identify and address relevant concerns in an orderly manner. These steps help ensure that evaluation is done in objective and scientifically valid ways—evaluation findings must be credible and stand up under the light of public scrutiny—and that conclusions and recommendations are embraced by those who have the power to bring about change. Program evaluation must include opportunities for stakeholders to have input; study conclusions must be credible, relevant, and consistent with opportunities for change. The following *six steps of program evaluation* provide a strategic road map that combines these dual needs—to be both responsive and objective:

1. *Define the activity and goals that are to be evaluated.* What are the key objectives and constraints according to key decision makers? What are the main objectives and concerns according to program staff? How do clients and others outside the program view it? What is the key target population of these activities and goals?
2. *Identify which key relationships will be studied.* Which program outcomes does the evaluation measure? Which factors are hypothesized to affect these program outcomes? Which counter-explanations are considered?
3. *Determine the research design that will be used.* Will a control or comparison group be used? Is there a need for developing a baseline of current performance? Are periodic or follow-up measurements foreseen and, if so, over what time period?
4. *Define and measure study concepts.* Which study concepts require detail in measurement? Which concepts require little detail? Will existing data be used, and how accurate are they? Will new data be gathered through, for example, a survey or focus group? If so, who will undertake such a

project, and how long will it take? What statistical requirements must the data meet for subsequent analysis? What resources and expertise are needed for data collection and program evaluation? What suggestions do key decision makers and others have for improving measurement?

5. *Collect and analyze the data.* Which statistical techniques will be used for data analysis? What type of conclusions are researchers seeking from the data? Do the data meet the requirements of different statistical techniques?

6. *Present study findings.* How, and to whom, will conclusions be presented? Can presentations be part of other consensus and decision-making processes? Can preliminary feedback about tentative findings be obtained from key decision makers and others? Who requires a detailed analysis and presentation? Who requires only a brief overview of main findings? What should the final report look like, and to whom should it be sent?

Previously we dealt with some matters pertaining to the first two steps. In our example, the activity is anger management as an after-school program. This program will teach students to recognize and deal with their anger. At this point, we might further specify that the program targets high-risk students, though it may include other students as well. The preceding questions prompt us to make finer specification. Also, assume that after further interviewing school administrators, teachers, and students and their parents, additional program objectives are formulated, in addition to reducing high school violence. These additional objectives might be to keep students safe after school, to improve academic performance, to reduce disruptive classroom behavior, to reduce violent behavior outside school, and to provide opportunities for getting involved in other, "fun" activities such as sports and music. The latter might seem far removed from anger management objectives, but program clients sometimes view such activities as useful motivators for continued participation.

Regarding the second step, while participation in anger management is examined for its impact on the specified outcomes, it is recognized that other factors might play a role, too. For example, gang participation and drug use is likely to reduce the effect of anger management training as a result of strong countervailing peer pressures and addictive impulses. Also, a lack of parental interest in their children's education is a likely negative factor. On the other hand, being transferred to a low violence school might reduce violence. Thus, program evaluation will need to consider additional circumstances along with the impact of anger management training. Such circumstances are part of steps 2 and 3 and are discussed below. Step 4, the definition and measurement of study concepts, is discussed in Chapter 3.

Rival Hypotheses and Limitations of Experimental Study Designs

The purpose of research design is to help ascertain that outcomes, such as reduced high school violence, are occurring and plausibly related to the program and not to other factors. But what if, parallel to anger management, another program aims to reduce student access to weapons? Then it is conceivable that any reduction in school violence might be partly or entirely ascribed to this other program. Such alternative explanations for observed outcomes are called ***rival hypotheses***, and variables used to measure rival hypotheses are called ***control variables***. Control variables are empirical, just as dependent and independent variables are, but they get their name from their research role: to test whether relationships between independent and dependent variables hold up under the presence of alternative, rival explanations for the observed pattern of outcomes. They are sometimes also called confounding variables, referring to concomitant activities that also explain outcomes and, hence, complicate efforts to establish a causal effect of programs or policies on outcomes. In our example, the presence of a weapons access policy, a concomitant event, is certainly a control variable that the manager will want to take into account. Indeed, the credibility of research findings often rests on the extent to which pertinent rival hypotheses have been identified and incorporated into study designs.[5]

Rival hypotheses (and their associated control variables) can be dealt with through experimental design and statistical analysis. ***Experimental designs*** address rival hypotheses through the use of control groups, which are similar to the study group in all aspects *except* that members of the control group do not participate in the intervention. You may be familiar with control groups through literature that describes the effectiveness of medical treatments. In ***classic, randomized experiments***, participants are randomly assigned to either a control or an experimental (or study) group. The assignments are random to ensure that any observed differences between these two groups are due only to the treatment and not to any other factor. Random assignment ensures that the two groups are similar, and baseline data are used to further rule out any chance differences in the groups' respective starting conditions. Further, neither the participants of the control and study groups nor their doctors are told whether they are receiving the experimental treatment or the ineffective placebo (they both look alike), because doing so might cause patients or their doctors to alter their behavior. In short, everything is done to ensure that the *only* difference between the groups is that one gets the treatment and the other does not. The logical inference, then, is that any difference *must* be due to the experimental treatment. The research design rules out every other factor.

Programs and policies are the public management equivalent of clinical interventions. Unfortunately, classic, randomized experiments are notoriously difficult to implement in public administration and policy because it is generally legally and ethically impossible to deny citizens or jurisdictions programs and policies. In our example, we do not envision randomly assigning teenagers to after-school programs. Some parents would be outraged if their children were denied access to the anger management program. They might even sue. It is also unclear what the "placebo" intervention might be in our example; it is absurd to suggest that subjects might participate in an anger management program that is intentionally designed to be ineffective. The problems of rival hypotheses are real, but the classic, experimental design is seldom a feasible strategy for addressing this matter in public administration and public policy.

The fact that we are unable to conduct classic, randomized experiments in public programs does not mean that we cannot use comparison groups or baselines measurement. Indeed, doing so can add valuable information to our program evaluation. For example, it would be interesting to compare high school violence among schools, of which only some have anger management programs. The term *comparison group* rather than control group would then be used, because the comparison group is not similar in all ways to the experimental group but for the intervention; other differences may exist. Clearly we can no longer rely on the research design itself to rule out the presence of rival hypotheses; rather, we must use the **strategy of statistical control** to account for rival hypotheses. This strategy involves (1) identifying plausible rival hypotheses, (2) collecting data about them, and (3) using *statistical techniques* to examine their impact on high school violence, relative to anger management. Specifically, we ask, What is the impact of anger management on high school violence, controlled for these other factors? The statistical techniques for analyzing data in this way are discussed later in this book; however, this approach obviously requires that analysts identify relevant control variables and collect data about them prior to analysis. Hence, the need to identify relevant rival hypotheses is determined early in program evaluation, during step 3.

> **Getting Started**
> Identify control variables that are relevant in a program evaluation.

QUASI-EXPERIMENTAL DESIGNS IN PROGRAM EVALUATION

Comparisons between experimental and comparison groups that do not meet the standard of classic research designs are called **quasi-experimental designs**. These designs may lack randomization, baseline (or pretest) measurement, or a comparison group. However, comparison groups and baselines often provide important information that help evaluate the effectiveness of programs and policies. Comparison groups provide a useful reference, for example, when outcomes show a widening gap between groups. Without a baseline, it is harder to persuade others that a program has had an impact. These features should be considered as part of the research study whenever practicable.

It is useful to view quasi-experimental research designs as variations on the classic, randomized design. Box 2.1 provides a stylistic representation of such designs. Design A is the classic, randomized design, showing randomization, a control group, pretests, and posttests. The designs under B are all lacking in one or more ways. Specifically, they all lack randomization, and many also lack a pretest, a comparison group, or both. These are quasi-experimental designs. Designs B2, B3, and B4 are rather typical quasi-experimental designs in public and nonprofit management.

Sometimes policy analysts and managers want to assess the impact of a policy or program after it has been implemented, without taking steps to develop such an assessment prior to the intervention (design B2). Perhaps managers had not given prior consideration to conducting the outcome evaluation. Lacking systematic assessment prior to the intervention, after-the-fact designs often are limited to interviewing managers and participants about their subjective assessment of impacts, and gathering quantitative data that might provide insights about outcomes. Data from before the intervention may be available, such as through administrative records that are routinely gathered. However, such data vary in their pertinence to the intervention.

Sometimes a comparable comparison group is found (design B3). The art is to find such a group, such as a comparable school that does not have an anger management program. Analysts will have to argue that the comparison group is indeed a valid comparison group. In our example, they might find a school where students have similar test scores, similar socioeconomic backgrounds, similar academic and extracurricular programs, and similar arrest and felony rates among students. Then these data must be gathered and these variables used as control variables to statistically control for any differences that might exist. An example of such a design is discussed in Box 2.2.

In other instances, evaluation is planned prior to intervention. Sometimes evaluation of programs and policies is a requirement, which may spur such advance planning. Then, to supplement administrative data, additional baseline data are gathered, as well as information pertaining to rival hypotheses that might be considered (design B3). The design of before and after measures may vary. For instance, measurements may span several time periods, before and after the intervention. In our example, high school violence might be recorded on a monthly basis, 6 months prior to and perhaps up to 12 months after the intervention, producing time series data.

In Greater Depth...

Box 2.1   Research Designs

Research designs can be characterized using the following notation, where R = randomization, X = intervention, and O = measurement. The following is based on the enduring, classic work of Donald Campbell and Julian Stanley.

A. The classic, randomized design is depicted graphically as follows. Any significant program impact would be indicated when $(O2–O1) > (O4–O3)$. The placebo intervention is not shown, but if it existed it would be implemented between O3 and O4; it would be similar to X, except that it is intentionally ineffective.

	Pretest	Program	Posttest
Group 1:	R O1	X	O2
Group 2:	R O3		O4

B. Quasi-experimental designs vary from this design in several ways:

1. Research design with a nonrandomized comparison group:

	Pretest	Program	Posttest
Group 1:	O1	X	O2
Group 2:	O3		O4

2. One-group research design with posttest measure, only:

	Pretest	Program	Posttest
Group 1, only:		X	O2

3. Research design with comparison group and posttests, only:

	Pretest	Program	Posttest
Group 1:		X	O2
Group 2:			O4

4. One-group research design with pretest and posttest:

	Pretest	Program	Posttest
Group 1, only:	O1	X	O2

Source: Donald Campbell and Julian Stanley, *Experimental and Quasi-experimental Designs for Research* (Chicago: Rand McNally), 1963.

~~~~~~

In Greater Depth...

Box 2.2   **Program Evaluation in Practice**

Program evaluations are undertaken by many organizations, some of which emphasize and excel in this activity. The Government Accountability Office (GAO, formerly the General Accounting Office) of the U.S. Congress provides numerous assessments each year and is highly respected. Some GAO reports evaluate program outcomes. For example, a GAO study of 23 adult drug court programs found that recidivism rates were 10–30 percent lower among participants than among those in comparison groups (GAO-05-219). In this study, a comparison group was developed for each of the adult drug court programs. Some comparison groups were contemporaneous, that is, consisting of defendants who were eligible for the adult drug court program but who received conventional case processing. Other, historical comparison groups were developed from individuals who completed conventional case processing before the adult drug court was implemented. In each case, comparison group participants were selected to closely match characteristics of those in the adult court groups regarding substance abuse, socioeconomic status, demographic profile, and criminal justice history. However, recognizing the possibility of selection bias (matching is not perfect), the study used statistical methods to control for individual differences between adult court and comparison group members.

In another study, the GAO examined how long it took the Departments of State and Commerce to issue export licenses, which are required for exporting equipment and services that have military applications. The State Department issues licenses for items that have only military applications, and the Commerce Department issues licenses for items that have both military and commercial uses. Each year these agencies receive, respectively, 46,000 and 11,000 license applications (GAO-01-528). The study found little difference between these agencies; the State Department took 46 days to review an application, and the Commerce Department took 50 days. In making the comparison, the GAO was mindful to consider the nature and complexity of the application as a source of possible variation. Examples of GAO studies can be found at www.gpoaccess.gov/gaoreports/index.html.

However, many GAO reports are only descriptive, for example, providing information on what programs are doing, and focusing on issues of critical importance to the programs. For instance, a study of homelessness programs described what these programs do and examined the extent of coordination,

(continued)

> **Box 2.2** *(continued)*
>
> which the GAO concluded that agencies should increase (GAO RCED-99-49). In other instances, the GAO examines the nature of oversight and accountability maintained by agencies and suggests ways in which that might be improved. Sometimes GAO reports examine an agency's potential for evaluation and recommend that the agency do a better job of maintaining and gathering data to enable meaningful evaluation.
>
> The GAO is a good example of a government's ability to evaluate programs; reading a dozen or so of its reports can help increase your familiarity with program evaluation. However, as a government agency, the GAO is under considerable time pressure, too. Think-tanks such as the Urban Institute, the RAND Corporation, the Brookings Institution, and the American Enterprise Institute exemplify how program evaluation can be deeper and even more thorough when conducted by independent, nonprofit organizations dedicated to public policy research. Many of their evaluations, funded by government programs, are book length and sometimes use extensive methodologies. The websites of these organizations reveal the breadth of topics and programs that they have researched.

The efficacy of the intervention might be suggested by a change in trend after the sixth month, controlled for any intervening confounding variables, of course. One such possibility is suggested below:

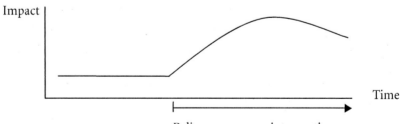

Policy or program intervention

The additional observations, before and after the start of the intervention, allow analysts to research important questions on the persistence of intervention impacts. In our example, the impact of anger management programs might reach a saturation point, beyond which further decreases in high school violence are not observed. This would indicate that some causes of high school violence are not related to anger. Or students might adopt new behaviors designed to mitigate or overcome the impact of anger management principles and practices. In this case, violence might begin to increase again after an initial decrease. Finally, how does the level of outcomes develop after the program ceases? Do students incorporate the new behaviors permanently, or do they go back to their old ways? A variety of such policy impact models can be examined toward the end of the intervention, when time series data are available.

The before-and-after design with a comparison group (design B1) combines features of designs B3 and B4 and resembles the classic, randomized experiment, except that subjects are not randomly assigned to the experimental and comparison groups. For example, in a study of innovative housing vouchers or mental health interventions, subjects with similar conditions might be assigned to different programs in similar cities that have similar neighborhoods. Some subjects might be followed who do not participate in any program; these subjects would make up the comparison group. Others might be assigned to a traditional program and others to one or more innovative programs. Outcomes would then be compared across these groups, controlling for rival hypotheses and differences that might exist among the different populations and local conditions. Such a design is obviously quite extensive and often expensive to undertake; it requires the development and coordination of programs. Few evaluations are of this kind, but they provide excellent insight into the rigors of evaluation methodology.

The models described here can help in developing designs for specific program evaluations; they draw attention to the roles of comparison groups and of baselines that might be used.

Finally, considerable thought exists about *types* of rival hypotheses. Rival hypotheses may still arise either from substantive matters of the program or from the use of quasi-experimental designs. While not all of the following concerns or categories are likely to be important in every situation, they assist analysts in identifying those concerns that are most salient as rival hypotheses in their specific situations. The following discussion draws attention to issues that might otherwise be overlooked.

Getting Started

Which quasi-experimental design might you use? Identify a control group or groups that might be used and any baselines, too.

Threats to external validity are defined as those that jeopardize the generalizability of study conclusions about program outcomes to other situations. For example, suppose we evaluate one anger management program in one school setting and, on the basis of that evaluation, wish to generalize our study conclusions to anger management programs in all schools? Such a generalization might be invalid if conditions in these other schools differ from conditions in the school that was studied. Or perhaps there is something unique about the study population or about the students in the other schools that makes generalization problematic. If generalization is a study objective, then such concerns should be considered during the study design phase; we would need to choose program settings that can be generalized to other settings.

Threats to internal validity are those that jeopardize the study conclusions about whether an intervention in fact caused a difference in the study population. These threats often question the logic of study conclusions. Many different types of such threats exist, which are sometimes referred to using the following categories. *History* refers to events that are not part of the intervention yet occur during the intervention and affect study outcomes. For example, a shooting rampage among high school students elsewhere might temporarily reduce violence in other schools as that event is discussed and digested. Hence, history might explain the study outcomes. *Maturation* refers to the natural development of subjects in ways that affect study outcomes but that are not affected by the intervention. For example, students may themselves learn to control their anger, apart from any anger management program. People do grow up. Did the program control for this possibility? *Testing* refers to subjects changing their behavior because they are being tested rather than because of the intervention. For example, if high school violence is measured partly by asking students how many episodes of anger they experienced recently (however defined), asking them this question may cause some students to view anger as a problem, and they might take steps to reduce it. Any reduction in violence is then caused by the act of being tested rather than by the intervention itself.

Instrumentation refers to changes in outcomes resulting from the way in which an instrument (such as a survey) measures the outcomes. Perhaps violence is measured partly by observation, and observers become more attuned to different forms of violence over time. This will inflate later (for example, post-intervention) measures of violence; the instrument (observation) measures more violence over time, regardless of whether more violence is occurring. *Statistical regression* refers to the fact that extreme scores tend to become less extreme over time; they regress toward the average. If we start out with students who all exhibit extreme violence of the worst kind, then it may not be possible for them to become any worse. Regardless of the intervention, the group is likely to improve. *Selection bias* refers to the problem that subjects may not be truly comparable between the experimental (intervention) and comparison groups. For example, the experimental group might have more at-risk students, as discussed earlier. *Mortality* refers to biases due to attrition of study subjects, for example, the transfer of angry students to other schools during the intervention. This event will reduce the incidence of violence, of course. *Imitation* occurs when some subjects in the comparison group learn of the intervention in the experimental group and begin imitating such behavior. In our example, students in classes that do not receive the anger management intervention might also see reductions in violence as a result of students talking with each other. *Rivalry* occurs when subjects in the experimental and comparison groups begin competing with each other. In our example, these students might compete with each other for being the least (or most!) violent.[6,7]

The point of the above discussion is to identify rival hypotheses that take away from the credibility of study conclusions later. These concerns need to be identified before program evaluation, so that program evaluation can be designed to address them. Most program evaluations involve at least a few of the above threats, as well as other rival hypotheses that relate to substantive matters of the research topic. Then analysts address these concerns either through program design or by gathering data about them so that they, as control variables, can later be accounted for through statistical techniques. Indeed, data often can be gathered about the above phenomena, such as behaviors that study subjects engage in during the program or the impact of intervening events. In short, analysts should identify important rival hypotheses and find ways to address them. By identifying and addressing rival hypotheses at an early stage, analysts can hope to increase the validity and acceptance of their work.[8]

SUMMARY

Social science research methods are often applied to many problems of management and analysis. Analysis typically involves a range of qualitative and quantitative research methods, and both basic and applied research focuses. Program evaluation is an example of such an application.

Variables, defined as observable phenomena that vary, represent a cornerstone concept in scientific research. Programs and policies usually attempt to affect variables in some ways (for example, by increasing or decreasing some social or economic conditions), and analysis often involves studying these changes.

Relationships in social science are distinguished by whether they are probabilistic (occurring sometimes) or deterministic (occurring each time). Relationships in social science are often probabilistic. Relationships are further distinguished as being either causal or associational. Causal relationships show cause and effect. When relationships are causal, independent and dependent variables can be distinguished. Independent variables are variables that cause an effect on other variables, and dependent variables are variables that are affected by other variables. Programs and policies are commonly conceptualized as independent variables causing changes in dependent variables, or outcomes.

The purpose of program evaluation often is to establish the effect of programs or policies on outcomes. A common concern is that other factors in addition to the program or policy (for example, events or processes) also affect outcomes. These alternative explanations for outcomes are referred to as rival hypotheses, and the variables associated with them are called control variables. The analytical task is to identify these rival hypotheses, collect data for the control variables, and use statistical methods to take their impact into account.

Program evaluation often uses quasi-experimental research designs. Such designs typically use comparison groups and baseline measurement in a variety of ways. The theory of quasi-experimental research design includes consideration of different types of rival hypotheses, which are distinguished as threats to internal or external validity. Familiarity with these categories can help analysts to identify rival hypotheses that are salient to their specific program evaluation.

KEY TERMS
(includes bolded terms in the Section II introduction)

Applied research (see section introduction) (p. 17)
Association (p. 25)
Attributes (p. 21)
Basic research (see section introduction) (p. 17)
Causal relationships (p. 23)
Classic, randomized experiments (p. 29)
Constant (p. 21)
Control variables (p. 29)
Criteria for causality (p. 24)
Dependent variables (p. 23)
Descriptive analysis (p. 22)
Experimental designs (p. 29)
Hypotheses (p. 25)
Independent variables (p. 23)

Program evaluation (p. 25)
Qualitative research methods (see section introduction) (p. 17)
Quantitative research methods (see section introduction) (p. 17)
Quasi-experimental designs (p. 30)
Relationships (p. 22)
Research methodology (see section introduction) (p. 16)
Rival hypotheses (p. 29)
Six steps of program evaluation (p. 27)
Strategy of statistical control (p. 30)
Threats to external validity (p. 35)
Threats to internal validity (p. 36)
Variables (p. 21)

Notes

1. Later, in Chapter 9, we provide a more specific, technical definition of level of confidence, in our discussion of statistical significance.
2. Consider another example. In Louisiana a relationship exists between the increase in population and the state's shrinking in size each year. Does

this mean that the weight of more people is causing the state to sink? No. The shrinking size is caused by erosion of coastal wetlands, not the weight of more people. These are unrelated events; the relationship is an association, only.

3. Two concerns are sometimes raised: (1) that the independent variable must precede the dependent variable in time and (2) that neither is caused by other variables; see the discussion of *spurious relationships* in note 5.

4. A variety of books address program evaluation. The leading text is Peter Rossi et al., *Evaluation: A Systematic Approach,* 7th ed. or later (Thousand Oaks, Calif.: Sage, 2003). See also *Exercising Essential Statistics,* the workbook that accompanies this textbook, for other references and exercises.

5. Control variables can affect the relationship between the independent and dependent variables in several ways. Different authors use different names to indicate these effects, but shown here is one approach. All three examples involve control variables. In the following graphic, moderating variables affect the way in which the independent variable affects the dependent variable, for example, sabotaging a class in which the instructor helps students learn to control their anger.

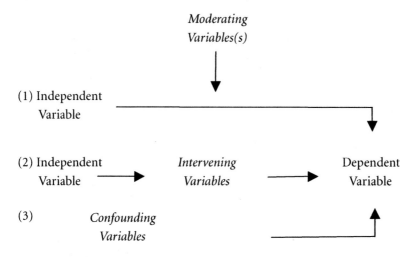

Sometimes a variable gives rise to two variables, when in fact no relationship exists between the two variables. This is called a spurious relationship, as is shown below. For example, the time of year (spring) is a spurious variable that gives rise to both storks and childbirths.

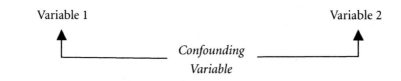

Bottom line: Regardless of how control variables affect variables, the point is to identify rival hypotheses (control variables) that may affect study conclusions.

6. A useful acronym for remembering these threats to internal validity is "Mis Smith:" maturation, instrumentation, selection, statistical regression, mortality, imitation, testing, and history. The classic source for these distinctions is Donald Campbell and Julian Stanley, *Experimental and Quasi-experimental Designs for Research* (Chicago: Rand McNally), 1963.

7. Even the classic, randomized research design is subject to some of these validity threats. Threats to external validity (generalizability) are a problem in any setting, and problems of history and mortality also may be present. It is not a given that the experimental and control groups experience the same intervening events (history), and they may have different rates of attrition (mortality). Testing might affect both groups, too. To address the problem of testing, a modification of the classic, randomized research design is the Solomon four-group design:

	Pretest	**Program**	**Posttest**
Group 1:	R O1	X	O2
Group 2:	R O3		O4
Group 3:	R	X	O5
Group 4:	R		O6

In this design, groups 3 and 4 allow the researcher to control for the impact of pretesting on groups 1 and 2.

8. For example, in a simple posttest design with no comparison group, the evaluation of anger management should consider whether any intervening effects (history) occurred that could have affected students' levels of anger and violence. Analysts will want to examine and account for possible maturation, statistical regression, and sample bias effects on the results. They also will want to assess subjects' knowledge of other efforts used elsewhere (which could give rise to imitation or rivalry) and ensure that the assessment method is accurate (minimizing effects of instrumentation).

CHAPTER

3

Conceptualization and Measurement

CHAPTER OBJECTIVES

After reading this chapter, you should be able to
- Appreciate the challenge of measuring abstract concepts
- Implement methods for measuring abstract concepts
- Distinguish between different levels of measurement
- Apply a variety of Likert scales
- Create index variables
- Understand criteria for assessing measurement validity

Measurement is a foundation of science and knowledge. How well phenomena are measured affects what we know about them, and rigor in measurement increases the validity of analytical work. This chapter discusses key concepts of measurement and shows how to apply these measurements in analytical work such as program evaluation. This chapter also shows how to make index variables.

MEASUREMENT LEVELS AND SCALES

A *scale* is defined as the collection of attributes used to measure a specific variable. For example, the variable "gender" is commonly measured on a scale defined by the specific attributes "male" and "female." Scales are important because they define the nature of information about variables. For example, we can measure incomes by asking respondents for their exact income or by asking them to identify their income using prespecified income brackets. Scales vary greatly—some are unique to the variables they measure, such as the Richter scale, which measures the strength of earthquakes; others are used for many different purposes, such as response scales found in survey questionnaires. Managers should be familiar with different types of scales so that they can adapt them to their needs.

Measurement scales are distinguished by their level of measurement. There are four levels of measurement: *nominal, ordinal, interval,* and *ratio.* A variable that has, for example, an ordinal-level measurement scale is commonly referred to as an ordinal-level variable or, simply, as an ordinal variable. The importance of the **measurement level** is threefold: (1) it determines the selection of test statistics (highly relevant to subsequent chapters), (2) it affects the amount of information collected about variables, and (3) it affects how survey and other types of questions are phrased.

A **nominal-level scale** exhibits no ordering among the categories. It provides the least amount of information. For example, the variable "gender" has a nominal scale because there is no ordering among the attributes "men" and "women." We cannot say that "men" are more than "women," regardless of any coding scheme that assigns numbers to these categories; they are nominal categories, only. "Region" is another common nominal scale: no ordering exists among the values of North, South, East, and West.

By contrast, an **ordinal-level scale** exhibits order among categories (hence, the name *ordinal*), though without exact distances between successive categories. "Order" means that categories can be compared as being "more" or "less" than one another. For example, assume that we measure teenage anger by asking adolescents whether they feel irritated, aggravated, or raging mad. Clearly someone feeling "raging mad" is more angry than someone who feels only "aggravated," who in turn is more angry than someone who feels "irritated." "Distance" means that we can measure how much more one category is than another. Ordinal scales lack distance. Although we can say that "raging mad" is more angry than "aggravated," we cannot say *how much* more angry "raging mad" is than "aggravated. Collectively, ordinal- and nominal-level variables are called **categorical** (or **discrete**) **variables.**

Likert scales are a common type of ordinal scale. Developed in 1932 by Professor Rensis Likert, these scales are now a staple in surveys that measure attitudes. The responses used on Likert scales come in many variations, such as Strongly Agree, Agree, Somewhat Agree, Don't Know, Somewhat Disagree, Disagree, and Strongly Disagree. Survey respondents are read statements (for example, "I feel safe at school") and are then asked, after each statement, to respond by selecting one of the responses. Likert scales demonstrate order and the absence of distance between categories: "strongly agree" is a higher level of agreeing than just "agree," but we cannot say how much more. Likert

---

In Greater Depth...

Box 3.1   Likert Scales

Likert scales are ordinal-level scales; several major variations are shown below. Five-point scales are identical to seven-point scales in the first three examples, except that they omit the categories of "somewhat." Some surveys (for example, some political polls) also lack the category "don't know" or "can't say," thereby forcing respondent answers. This approach is objectionable academically, because it fails to measure accurately the responses of those who genuinely "don't know" or "can't say" while overestimating adjacent categories.

1. Please indicate your agreement with the following statements, using the following scale:

   > 7 = Strongly Agree   3 = Somewhat Disagree
   > 6 = Agree   2 = Disagree
   > 5 = Somewhat Agree   1 = Strongly Disagree
   > 4 = Don't Know / Can't Say

   Students who are violent should be removed from class.   ①②③④⑤⑥⑦
   I would like us to have anger management classes.   ①②③④⑤⑥⑦
   There should be an after-school homework assistance program. ①②③④⑤⑥⑦

2. How important are the following items to you? Please use the following scale:

   > 7 = Very Important   3 = Somewhat Unimportant
   > 6 = Important   2 = Unimportant
   > 5 = Somewhat Important   1 = Very Unimportant
   > 4 = Don't Know / Can't Say

   Feeling safe in my neighborhood   ①②③④⑤⑥⑦
   Putting those who commit crimes in jail   ①②③④⑤⑥⑦
   Seeing more guards in school   ①②③④⑤⑥⑦

   (continued)

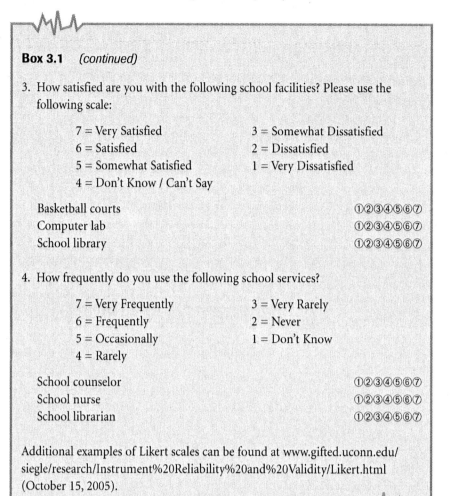

Box 3.1 *(continued)*

3. How satisfied are you with the following school facilities? Please use the following scale:

7 = Very Satisfied	3 = Somewhat Dissatisfied
6 = Satisfied	2 = Dissatisfied
5 = Somewhat Satisfied	1 = Very Dissatisfied
4 = Don't Know / Can't Say	

Basketball courts   ①②③④⑤⑥⑦
Computer lab   ①②③④⑤⑥⑦
School library   ①②③④⑤⑥⑦

4. How frequently do you use the following school services?

7 = Very Frequently	3 = Very Rarely
6 = Frequently	2 = Never
5 = Occasionally	1 = Don't Know
4 = Rarely	

School counselor   ①②③④⑤⑥⑦
School nurse   ①②③④⑤⑥⑦
School librarian   ①②③④⑤⑥⑦

Additional examples of Likert scales can be found at www.gifted.uconn.edu/siegle/research/Instrument%20Reliability%20and%20Validity/Likert.html (October 15, 2005).

scales are so popular because they have been widely tested and are easy to use and adapt. Box 3.1 provide further examples of these important scales.[1]

Interval- and *ratio-level scales* exhibit both order and distance among categories. We can say that someone who exercises daily does so seven times more often than someone who exercises only weekly. Someone who earns $75,000 per year makes exactly three times that of someone making $25,000. The *only* difference between interval and ratio scales is that the latter have a true "zero" (for example, income can be zero, but IQ cannot). The distinction between ratio- and interval-level variables is typically of little relevance to public and nonprofit administration and policy analysis. Variables with interval- and ratio-level scales are also called ***continuous variables***.[2]

In general, we strongly prefer having more information about variables than less. Therefore, continuous-level scales are preferred over ordinal-level

~~^^~~
In Greater Depth...

Box 3.2   Writing the Report

New researchers and analysts sometimes struggle to write up their methods and results in professionally appropriate ways. What must be written? How must it be written? How can the report be made to appear professional? The adage that practice makes perfect is true but of insufficient guidance. Here are some pointers and *tips on writing* that may help:

1. Collect 6–10 reports that are suitable examples of the kind of report you are looking to write. Subject matter is less important than the depth and nature of analysis, the report length, and its methodological sophistication. Study these reports very, very carefully. How is the report organized (table of contents)? What types of graphs and tables are presented? What do the appendices (if any) cover? Which of the issues mentioned in the chapters so far do they deal with? How do the reports deal with these issues? What aspects of these issues do they raise, and what language do they use in addressing them? Learn from these examples. Emulate them.
2. Develop an outline. The outline is your template, your strategy that tells you what you need to write. Therefore, draft an outline that is suited for you, modeled on the example reports. Decide what parts your report should have, and then write each part. The broad outline of many reports is as follows: executive summary, introduction, literature review, methods, results, conclusion, and appendices. Analytical reports are built piecemeal. Often, parts of different sections are generated in the research and analysis processes.

   The literature review is particularly helpful in that it brings to us what others have done before; even someone doing a comparables study for a local government labor negotiation wouldn't start from scratch. The traditional literature review is sometimes supplemented by reports and documentation reflecting the experiences of other jurisdictions and agencies.
3. Language matters. The words that come to you first may not be or sound very professional. Most analysts write several drafts; some write as many as 10 or 20. Ultimately you should write reports in the third person, using the active voice and present tense. Present your ideas clearly and concisely. Use short sentences rather than long and convoluted ones. Write down the thoughts and language that come to you, but then rework what you have written as often as necessary. Technical writing is very different from writing an English essay or fiction. Identify your audience, and write for it.
4. Details, details. Check the grammar. Format the report. Make it look professional. Double-check that you have made all of the arguments that need to be made. As you write, consult the example reports for additional ideas and arguments that you might make. Let others look over your work and make comments from which you can learn.

scales, which in turn are preferred over nominal-level scales. We also prefer ordinal and nominal scales that have more rather than fewer categories. Of course, a variable such as "gender" cannot be made ordinal or continuous, and it can have only two categories. Likewise, some variables can only be ordinal and cannot be continuous.[3]

The development of measures and scales is a precise task. We must avoid scales that are incomplete, ambiguous, or overlapping. An *incomplete scale* might omit "zero" as a response category when asking respondents how many fist fights they witnessed. An *ambiguous scale* is one that asks respondents to answer a question about the presence of violence "on a scale of 1 to 10" without defining each value. Respondents may have different definitions of any specific value, such as the value of "6." In an *overlapping scale,* at least one response is covered by more than one category. An example of such a scale is one that measures income with brackets $20,000–$40,000 and $40,000–$60,000. It is better to use $20,000–$39,999 and $40,000–$59,999. Another example is measuring "fist fights" and "scuffles" as separate categories.

Problems with measurement scales can affect the validity of one's findings. Measurement scales should be complete, unambiguous, and have unique categories for each response. Of course, other measurement challenges also exist, such as well-known problems of using leading (or biased) survey questions as well as samples that are biased or restricted in some way; these matters are discussed further in Chapter 5.[4] We now turn to another measurement topic, that of measuring abstract concepts.

CONCEPTUALIZATION

Many important matters of public and nonprofit management and analysis involve abstract concepts, such as notions of democracy, effectiveness, volunteerism, citizen satisfaction, and, yes, high school violence and anger. The rigor with which study concepts are defined (such as the level of anger or high school violence) enhances the validity of our efforts. *Measurement validity* simply means that something measures or reflects what it is intended to. This is identified as step 4 in the six-step model of program evaluation (see Chapter 2). A research task needs to be clear about what is being studied. For example, how should we measure the concept "high school violence?"

In this regard, variables must be distinguished from concepts. Whereas variables belong to the realm of directly observable phenomena, concepts belong to the realm of ideas. *Concepts* are abstract ideas that are observed indirectly, through variables. *Processes of concept measurement* typically have two steps. First we need to be clear about the meaning of the concept and, in particular, identify all of the relevant dimensions of the concept. This is called *conceptualization.* Then we need to identify and define the variable(s) that will be used to measure the concept and its dimensions. This is called *operationalization.*

This process is best explained through an example. Suppose we want to measure the concept "student anger." First we need to be clear about what "student anger" means. What is the essence of this concept?[5] How might we best define it in the context of our study? Because our program aims to reduce and control manifestations of anger and violence that can be disruptive, we might define "student anger" as "a strong emotion of displeasure by students that may be triggered by, or directed toward, specific or general grievances." Of course, this is not the only way to define student anger, and certainly some other definitions might be better. Perhaps you know of a better definition? We can justify this definition, however, through criteria that are commonly used for this purpose: consistency with generally understood meanings of the concept (here, anger), consistency with expert understandings and studies, and being relevant and central to the program and its evaluation.

Next, and still part of conceptualization, we need to ask whether any discernible, distinct dimensions of this concept should be considered and measured separately? Assume that we identify the following three dimensions to the concept "anger": (1) emotions of anger, (2) thoughts (cognition) of anger, and (3) physical rage. Each dimension stands alone and can be measured separately. For example, some students might have thoughts of anger but little emotion associated with these thoughts, and vice versa. Some may have rage and emotion but little cognition. These are different dimensions of anger. Only after the dimensions of "student anger" have been identified can the analytical task shift toward developing a process for measuring these dimensions (that is, operationalization).

It is not a given that this concept will or should always have these dimensions. Complex concepts and those that are key to the research design are usually conceptualized with greater rigor than those that are simple or less key to the program or evaluation. In the case of evaluating the anger management program, "student anger" is an important concept and one that managers and analysts will want to examine carefully. Yet this concept might not be of much importance in a study about, say, student achievement. Such a study might choose to measure "student anger" in only a cursory way, perhaps as just a single item (for example, "How angry do you usually feel?"). Decisions about study rigor and the importance of specific study concepts drive thoroughness.

When study concepts are conceptualized with rigor and thoroughness, analysts need to determine how many concept dimensions they will identify and measure. An imprecise guiding principle is that analysts should be true and comprehensive with regard to their concepts. Typically two to five dimensions are used in rigorous conceptualizations, usually based on (1) the consensus of past studies, (2) whether concept definitions include disparate facets or dimensions, (3) program needs that might suggest dimensions, and (4) practical constraints in the ability to collect data.[6] Our example of conceptualizing "student anger" reflects judgments that it is a key study concept requiring rigor, that the three identified dimensions reflect a comprehensive and appropriate understanding of the concept, and that the concept is relevant to program management.

Analysts must justify their choices about the conceptualization and operationalization of study concepts. An important perspective is that no correct number of dimensions or variables exists, only bad or lacking ones.[7]

Another example involves the conceptualization of "high school violence." Assume that after defining this concept, conducting a brief literature review, and talking with program officials, we reach a consensus that high school violence has three dimensions: (1) use of weapons, (2) inappropriate physical contact (occurring without weapons and not involving sanctioned physical contact during sports activities), and (3) verbal assaults. These are seen not as degrees of violence, but as three different dimensions (or types) of violence. Students can have physical contact without necessarily using weapons or involving verbal assault. These dimensions of violence can be measured separately.

OPERATIONALIZATION

As we discussed earlier, the development of specific measures is called operationalization. This process develops the specific variables that will be used to measure a concept. Three approaches to operationalization are (1) to develop separate measures for each dimension, (2) to develop a single set of measures that encompass the dimensions, or (3) to develop a single measure. These three strategies reflect a *declining* order of rigor.[8]

The *first* strategy is the most comprehensive approach—measuring each dimension separately. By way of example, Table 3.1 lays out the basic measurement strategy for conceptualizing and operationalizing the three dimensions of high school violence.

Whereas the table shows a mix of objective data and subjective assessments, this is not always the case nor is it always necessary. Student perceptions might be assessed through a survey in which students are asked to evaluate such statements. Typically 5–10 questions are used to measure each dimension. For example, the following questions might be used to assess student perceptions of inappropriate physical contact at school (dimension 2):

> Please tell me which of the following you experienced in or around school, during the last month, which were not part of any normal sports activity:

Table 3.1 ⎯⎯⎯⎯⎯⎯⎯‿⋀‿⋀‿⎯ Measuring High School Violence

Dimension	Measurement
1: Use of weapons	Number of students caught using weapons
	Student perception of presence of weapons (guns, knives, other)
2: Physical contact	Number of fights and scuffles reported to administrators
	Number of inappropriate physical contacts reported to administrators (sexual and nonsexual)
	Student perception of fights, scuffles, and inappropriate physical contact (sexual and nonsexual)
3: Verbal assaults and threats	Number of harassment allegations brought to administrators
	Student perception of verbal assaults and threats

I was involved in a fight or scuffle.
I was physically injured in a fight or scuffle.
I was pushed or tripped by someone who, I believe, tried to injure me.
I was touched sexually in ways that were unwanted by me.
I was struck by someone with an object (such as a stick or stone).
I was assaulted in some way but not injured.
I was physically hurt in some other way (please specify). . . .

This is certainly not the only way to assess student perceptions of inappropriate physical contact. Some assessments might ask different questions. Unwanted sexual contact is included as a form of violence. As indicated in the table, objective data might also be included for each dimension. In the same way, survey items would be developed to measure the other two dimensions, "use of weapons" and "verbal assaults and threats." The correct and complete development of study measures finishes the process of operationalization. Chapter 5 provides additional guidance on developing survey questions and collecting data.

The *second,* less rigorous (but still comprehensive) approach is to develop questions that each measure a different aspect of high school violence, without specifying and developing these questions into measures of the three dimensions. Such an approach might be necessary because of data limitations (for example, limited space on surveys) or because other study concepts are more important. Although less thorough than the first approach, the following question might be considered a measure of high school violence:

Please indicate whether you strongly agree, agree, don't know, disagree, or strongly disagree with each of the following statements:

At least one of my classmates has carried a gun to school.

Some students in my class regularly carry knives to school.

Students in my class regularly get involved in fights and scuffles.

There is inappropriate sexual contact or gesturing occurring in my class.

People try to hurt others in my class through tripping, pushing, or shoving.

People in my class threaten each other with physical violence.

People in my class vandalize each other's property.

People in my class regularly insult each other.

Note that the list encompasses the three dimensions identified earlier. Whether this measure suffices depends on the manager's needs for more specific information and on validation (discussed later in this chapter). Sometimes this second approach develops into the first approach as analysts give more careful consideration to the distinct dimensions of the concept.

The *third* approach is decidedly nonrigorous, using a single survey item to measure the concept. For our current example, such an item might read as follows:

Please indicate whether you strongly agree, agree, don't know, disagree, or strongly disagree with the following statement:

My high school is a violent place.

While not biased, this item does not provide any information about specific aspects of the phenomenon. As noted earlier, this approach is typically used when the concept is of quite minor importance to the program or evaluation. In our example, however, we want more information than would be obtained from this single item.

Getting Started
Identify an abstract concept, and practice conceptualizing it using these three strategies.

Finally, an important question is whether any best set of measures exists for measuring a concept. The *theorem of the interchangeability of indicators* states that if several measures are equally valid indicators of a concept, then any subset of these measures will be valid as well. In other words, there are many valid ways to measure a given concept. The analyst's task is to choose one approach and then justify that that approach is valid. The challenge of justification is discussed later in this chapter.

INDEX VARIABLES

An *index variable* is a variable that combines the values of other variables into a single indictor or score. For example, the consumer price index is a

Table 3.2 ——————〜〴〵〜—— Creating an Index Variable

Observation	Measure 1	Measure 2	Measure 3	Measure 4	Index
567	1	2	2	4	9
568	4	1	1	1	7
569	4	2	2	4	12
570	5	5	5	5	20
571	1	2	—	1	—
572	1	1	1	1	4

variable that combines the prices of common consumer goods and services into a single score. Index variables are common, for example, measuring the economic outlook, infant and child health, environmental quality, political stability, volunteerism and giving, culture in cities, and so on. Managers and analysts frequently encounter index variables in their work.

Index variables are also commonly used to empirically measure abstract concepts and multifaceted, encompassing phenomena. In the preceding sections, we developed a strategy for measuring different dimensions of high school violence. Some variables measure violence that involves weapons, other variables measure inappropriate physical contact, and still other variables measure verbal assaults and threats. How can these disparate measures be combined into one aggregate measure of high school violence?

The logic of index variable construction is simple: the values of the measurement variables are simply summed. The term *measurement variable* refers to the (observed) variables that make up the index; it has no bearing on any measurement scale or data collection strategy and is used to distinguish these variables from the index variable. When respondents score low on measurement variables, the resulting index score is also low, and vice versa. Table 3.2 shows how an index variable is created by simply adding up the values of the measurement variables that constitute the dimension or concept. Thus, when respondents score high on measurement variables, the resulting index score is high. When one or more of the measurement variables are missing from an observation, the value of the index variables for that observation is missing, too, as shown for observation 571. Note that whereas measurement variables might be ordinal (for example, measured on a five-point Likert scale), the resulting index variable often is continuous. In the example in Table 3.2, the index variable can range from a minimum of 4 to a maximum of 20. Of course, statistical software does the addition.

This logic is applied to other indexes, too. For example, the consumer price index is based on price changes for a bundle of goods. The sum of all prices is determined in each period, and the periods are then compared with each other. An index of municipal cultural activity might sum the number of performances, renowned organizations, and cultural facilities (museums, theaters, and the like).

To continue our example of high school violence, in our second approach we simply sum the values of each of the survey items and in this way construct an index measure of high school violence. The values of these items are summed for each observation, in exactly the same manner as in Table 3.2. But in our first, more rigorous approach, we follow a two-step process for creating the index measure. In the first step, we construct index variables for each of the three separate dimensions (use of weapons, inappropriate physical contact, and verbal assaults and threats). In the second step, we sum the values of these three index variables, for each observation, which then results in a new, "super" index of "high school violence." The latter index is clearly grounded in the three dimensions of high school violence.

A practical problem with index variables is that individual components sometimes have different scales or ranges. For example, if one variable can range from 0 (min) to 10 (max), and the other from 0 (min) to 1,000 (max), then the former will likely not have much impact on the aggregate measure, the index. Especially if most values of the latter variable are between, say, 300 and 800, then adding the values of the first variable, ranging between 0 and 10, will not much affect the aggregate score. To address this problem, analysts can rescale each of the variables being summed, so that each has the same range, such as 0 to 100. One way to do this, in the preceding case, would be to multiply each value of the first variable by 10 and divide each value of the second variable by 10. However, other approaches exist.[9]

Although index measures are not very difficult to make, a key issue is their validation. The resulting index variable must be established as a valid measure of the underlying concept being measured. The next section discusses how we go about doing that.

MEASUREMENT VALIDITY

It is always important to think about the validity of what we do. Earlier, in Chapter 2, we discussed validity with regard to drawing study conclusions; here, we discuss it narrowly with regard to measurement. Measures must be shown to be valid measures of the phenomena and concepts that they measure. Measurement validity simply means that variables really measure what they are said to measure. Considerable thought has gone into the different strategies that can be used to establish measurement validity. Analysts are not expected to use all or even most of these strategies, but they are expected to justify their variables in some way.[10]

An important form of validation is theoretical—a persuasive argument that the measures make sense. One argument is that the measures are reasonable, common-sense ways of measuring the underlying concept. This is called *face validity*. Measuring gender by asking respondents whether they are male or female is a reasonable, common-sense method. Some respondents may erroneously indicate the wrong gender, but such numbers will likely be few and not affect study conclusions in any material way. In the case of high school violence, however, the justification is more elaborate. But again we can argue that the measures used are reasonable, common-sense ways of measuring the specific variables and underlying concept.

Regarding index variables, another argument is that they should encompass a broad range of aspects. For example, variables measuring "physical exercise" should not be skewed in some biasing way, perhaps underemphasizing individual sports in favor of team sports. Whether "student anger" is measured in a comprehensive or simple way, it should not be biased against certain forms of student anger. This form of validity is called *content validity*. The very simple operationalization given earlier ("how angry do you usually feel?") avoids this problem by not specifying any specific form of anger. In the case of high school violence, we measure a broad range of aspects, especially those that ought to be included in such a study.

Empirical evidence can also be mustered in several ways. First, variables can be validated by comparing them with other measures or sources. For example, the measure "physical contact without weapons" might be triangulated by records of the school nurse (treatment of scrapes and bruises) and a student survey. Although such correlation does not prove that the measure is valid, certainly the lack of correlation would raise some eyebrows. Comparison with external sources is sometimes called *criterion (or external) validity* (not be confused with threats to external validity, discussed in Chapter 2). Some researchers also refer to this as *triangulation*. When the variable correlates as expected, additional validity is provided.

Second, we might ask respondents on the same survey about physical contact without weapons and compare that response with other responses, such as regarding physical injuries incurred at school. Such comparison against internal sources is called *construct (or internal) validity*. Although this comparison does not provide absolute proof (respondents may receive injuries at school for reasons unrelated to high school violence), it may provide some reassurance and, hence, a measure of validity. Certainly a lack of correlation would require further inquiry and explanation.

Third, regarding index variables, the variables used to measure a concept should be strongly associated (or correlated) with each other. This is

Getting Started
How can you validate your conceptualized measure?

because each index variable measures different but related dimensions. When variables are not highly related, analysts should consider whether, perhaps, one or more of the variables measure some other concept. The correlation of measurement variables is called **internal reliability** (or internal consistency, not be confused with "threats to internal validity," discussed in Chapter 2). **Cronbach alpha** (also called *alpha* or *measure alpha*) is a statistical measure of internal reliability that is often cited in research articles that use index variables.[11] Although you need not be concerned about the exact calculation of this measure,[12] alpha can range from 0 to 1, where a 1 indicates perfect correlation among the measurement variables, and a 0 indicates the lack of any correlation among the measurement variables. Values between 0.80 and 1.00 are desired, and they indicate high reliability among the measurement variables. Values between 0.70 and 0.80 indicate moderate (but acceptable) reliability. Alpha values below 0.70 are poor and should cause analysts to consider a different mix of variables. While index variables with alpha scores below 0.70 should be avoided, values between 0.60 and 0.70 are sometimes used when analysts lack a better mix of variables. Analysts usually collect a few more variables than are minimally needed because they cannot know, prior to reliability analysis, which variable mix will have a sufficiently high alpha score to lend empirical support for the index measure. This is especially relevant for one-dimensional measures of complex concepts, such as the less rigorous measure of high school violence discussed earlier in this chapter.

Finally, descriptive analysis is used to examine the range of values of (index) variables. If most values of a variable are "high," then little will be known about those who score "low." Being mindful of this problem helps analysts avoid inappropriate generalizations to categories (for example, subpopulations) about which little empirical information has been collected. For example, if most of our respondents indicate that high school violence is a serious problem, then little will be learned about factors associated with high school violence among those who perceive it to be low, including, quite possibly, strategies causing some schools to have low levels of high school violence. Descriptive analysis is also used to examine whether observations with missing values in their index variables create a pattern of bias, perhaps systematically excluding some group or groups of observations, for example, such as minorities or pregnant teenagers for whom some items may have been irrelevant or in some way troublesome.

In sum, a plethora of strategies exists for assessing measurement validity. Analysts are not expected to use all of these approaches, but they should use some strategies to justify their measures. In scientific research, this usually requires some up-front consideration because, after data have been collected, it may be too late to collect more observations as needed for validation.

An obvious and final question is this: what is an analyst to do if one or more of the strategies described in this chapter show variables to be less valid than hoped for? Perhaps the measures of internal and external validity provide mixed results, and the alpha measure is marginal at best. If this happens, the analyst needs to add a caveat to his or her results. However, with foresight and planning, analysts usually gather a broad range of variables so that adequate supporting evidence from face and construct validity are available.

SUMMARY

The four measurement levels of variables are nominal, ordinal, interval, and ratio. A general guideline is that measurement scales are preferred that give as much information as possible about variables. Nominal-level scales exhibit no order among attributes, ordinal-level scales exhibit order but no distance between attributes, and interval- and ratio-level scales exhibit both order and distance. Variables with interval- and ratio-level scales are sometimes called continuous variables, and variables with nominal- and ordinal-level scales are called categorical or discrete variables. A variable's measurement level is also important in the selection of statistical tests, discussed in later chapters. Likert scales are commonly used ordinal-level variables in surveys. There are many different types of Likert scales, assessing degrees of importance, satisfaction, agreement, and frequency, for example. Index variables sum the values of disparate variables and are used to measure concepts.

Rigor in measurement increases the validity of analytical work. When working with abstract concepts, analysts need to carefully identify the different dimensions of their concepts and then develop appropriate ways to measure each. Measures used by other studies can help guide analysts in this task, but they often must develop and validate their own measures.

Measures should be valid, and this chapter offers strategies for determining measurement validity. Four types of validity are face validity, content validity, criterion validity, and construct validity. Additionally, Cronbach alpha is used for index variables as a measure of their internal reliability. Analysts should examine their measures for validity and provide caveats to their results as necessary.

KEY TERMS

Categorical variables (p. 42)
Concepts (p. 46)
Conceptualization (p. 46)
Construct validity (p. 53)
Content validity (p. 53)
Continuous variables (p. 44)
Criterion validity (p. 53)

Cronbach alpha (p. 54)
Discrete variables (p. 42)
Face validity (p. 53)
Index variable (p. 50)
Internal reliability (p. 54)
Interval-level scales (p. 44)
Likert scales (p. 42)

Notes

1. Other types of ordinal-level scales exist, too, but they are much less common. For example, *Guttman scales* are based on a series of statements with increasing or decreasing intensity, for example, "I feel safe around my classmates," "I avoid classmates who are violent," and " I bring a knife to school to defend myself against my classmates." The scale assumes a consistent pattern in answering these statements. That is, those who agree with the last statement are unlikely to agree with the first statement too. A statistical coefficient is calculated that measures the extent to which such a consistent pattern exists. Guttman scales have become less popular in recent years, due to their rigidity and complexity. *Thurstone scales* use judges to assess and order a large number of such statements, from which a scale is then composed. The cumbersomeness of using panels also makes Thurstone scales unpopular.

   Somewhat more common are *semantic differential scales*, especially in psychological studies. These scales assume that people think in opposing pairs as they assess situations, such as "How do you feel about anger management classes as a method for reducing high school violence?" Respondents are asked to indicate a point on each line that indicates their feeling:

Good	------------------	Bad
Smart	------------------	Dumb
Respectful	-----------------	Disrespectful

2. Some texts refer to both interval and ratio scales as interval scales, which may cause confusion. Other texts refer to both as metric scales and often refer to nominal and ordinal variables as nonmetric variables. In this context, the term *metric* has no bearing on the metric system of measurement. We avoid using the terms *metric* and *nonmetric* here, to prevent any such confusion.

3. The following question is sometimes raised: how many categories must an ordinal-level variable have in order to be considered an interval variable? This question misses the point that the key theoretical distinction between ordinal and continuous variables is whether the distances between categories can be determined. Even so, in practice ordinal-level variables with seven or more categories are sometimes analyzed with

statistics that are appropriate only for interval-level variables. This practice has many critics, but it is done, because interval-level statistics more readily address control variables and also because ordinal-level statistics sometimes don't work well with large tables. Nonetheless, the practice is controversial and it is best to analyze ordinal variables with statistics that are appropriate for ordinal-level variables, discussed later.

4. Measurement validity is also discussed at the end of this chapter.

5. This can be regarded as an example of asking questions of basic research—see Section II introduction.

6. Many scientific studies in public administration and public policy use one to five dimensions per concept (thus some concepts have only one dimension), and operationalization is often limited to five to eight variables per dimension. A practical consideration is that, when working with existing data (also called secondary data), analysts often must use whatever variables are available. Conceptualization and operationalization may then be wanting, to say the least. Analysts must acknowledge study limitations (caveats) and argue that the analysis adds value and is the best available.

7. In addition to the strategies discussed here, empirical approaches such as *factor analysis* can be used to justify the number of dimensions (see Chapter 16).

8. Some researchers also use this term to include procedures for data collection, but these procedures are discussed in Chapter 5.

9. Variability is another factor. A better way of dealing with this factor is through standardization, a process discussed in Chapter 6.

10. Recall the other threats to internal and external validity discussed in Chapter 2. Some problems of validity deal with sample bias, such as a biased selection of administrative records or survey respondents. Other problems deal with testing and instrumentation, such as biased or leading questions on survey questionnaires. Guidelines for dealing with these problems are discussed in Chapter 5.

11. You can find such articles in public administration, for example, by Googling "cronbach" "public administration".

12. See note 8 in Chapter 12.

CHAPTER

4

Measuring Performance:
Present and Future

CHAPTER OBJECTIVES

After reading this chapter, you should be able to
- Develop performance measures for programs and policies
- Understand the logic model
- Distinguish between measures of efficiency and effectiveness
- Identify criteria for evaluating performance measures
- Distinguish data-based and expert-based approaches to forecasting
- Understand the role of statistical forecasting models

Performance measurement provides a real-time assessment of what a program or policy is doing, what resources it is using, and what it has accomplished recently. Whereas program evaluation focuses on the past (what has a program policy achieved?), performance measurement focuses on the present (what is a program or policy achieving?). Performance measurement assists management by providing information and analysis that shape current understanding and decisions, such as about the efficiency and effectiveness of program operations. In addition, performance measurement provides key indicators about activities and performance.

Managers also face questions about the future. What is the future expected to be like? What impact is the program or policy likely to have? A variety of methods are available to managers who are using forecasting to answer these questions. This chapter completes our discussion of research strategies for providing information about the past, present, and future of programs and policies.

PERFORMANCE MEASUREMENT

Performance measurement is defined as a process for assessing progress toward achievement of program goals. As an analytical process, it is designed to produce information on an ongoing basis to determine what a program or policy is doing and what results are being achieved. This process helps managers to improve program monitoring and accountability and, by focusing on measurable results, to improve program performance and stakeholder satisfaction, too.

Performance measurement is used increasingly. More and more grants require performance measurement. The United Way requires performance assessment in its funding process. The Government Finance Officers Association encourages the use of performance measurement in program budgets. The movement toward demonstrating that outcomes are achieved is occurring across sectors. Twenty years ago, organizations and their managers could merely report how many services were provided ("we provided services to 6,000 individuals in the previous year"), but this is not the case any longer. Funders, and that includes councils and boards, want to know what services were provided, and what differences these services made. This is a considerable shift, and one that demands heightened analytical skills for organizations and their managers.

Performance measurement developed from program evaluation.[1] Although program evaluation can be a thorough process, it often is quite cumbersome and may produce information that is neither ongoing nor timely for management purposes. By contrast, performance measurement aims to overcome this limitation and provide an up-to-date management information system. Performance measurement provides a system of *key indicators* of program activities and performance. These measures are based on systematic and quantitative information, thereby supplementing other, sometimes impressionistic sources of management knowledge. Performance measurement is not the sole basis for understanding programs and policies, but it provides a snapshot that integrates important, frequently quantitative information about programs and policies.

The Logic Model

Public and nonprofit organizations are increasingly using the *logic model* to conceptualize program performance. This model defines a way to describe relationships among resources, activities, and results, and it can be applied to any program:

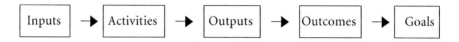

Performance measurement provides key indicators of the following components: inputs, activities, outputs, outcomes, and goals, and each program will have its own unique measures. Indicators should be chosen to reflect managers' and stakeholders' interests, and thereby to assist in meaningful monitoring and decision making. Programs and their managers are apt to vary in how they choose to measure inputs, activities, outputs, and outcomes. Standards and common practices for conceptualizing and operationalizing (that is, measuring) these indicators are not yet well established. Organizations are often encouraged by professional associations, by their boards, or by legislatures to develop their own measures. Some funding agencies may prescribe specific indicator measures, and even ways in which some data are to be collected, but organizations and their managers are still responsible for developing their performance measurement systems.

Some general criteria for performance measures are that they should be *relevant, understandable,* and *consistent* over time. Also, measures should be considered that are likely to be relevant for some time and thus become part of trend data over time. However, some performance measures typically reflect important but likely temporary concerns, too; these will likely not become part of any trend data. Beyond these standards, performance measures should also be *valid*; they should avoid problems of inaccurate and incomplete measurement, as discussed in Chapter 3. Clearly, snapshots are only as accurate and valid as their measures. Some information is based on existing data sources such as might be obtained from accounting or operations departments, but some indicators require new data collection.

Regarding the specific components of the logic model, *inputs* are defined as resources used by the program to produce its goods and services. Programs use financial, human, organizational, and political resources, but not all of these resources are quantifiable nor are they necessarily all key to program decision making. Inputs typically are measured as (1) total program costs, or subsets of costs, and (2) personnel costs or time involved in providing a service. Of course, personnel costs are a subset of total costs (that is, a partial measure), but they reflect key concerns related to service efficiency.

Input measures illustrate well the possibility of considerable measurement bias. First, inputs cover not just costs. They also include qualitative components such as organizational leadership and political commitment, which are essential and strategic for program success, and which managers should not take for granted. Second, cost measures are obtained from agency budgets and administrative records. These sources are usually agency-centric, that is, they do not take into account the sometimes-substantial services and in-kind contributions from other agencies. Third, costs are sometimes defined as costs to the agency and sometimes only as those budgeted to the program. As such, they exclude indirect and overhead costs, such as facilities and administrative services. These amounts can be significant. Managers need to be clear about what their costs data include and what they do not.

In our ongoing example of the anger management program, inputs might be measured as (1) total program costs, defined as (a) the direct cost of teachers and support staff administering the program, as well as (b) the costs of using school facilities beyond regular school hours, and (c) a markup of these costs that reflects customary indirect and administrative overhead charged by schools for after-school programs. The teacher and support staff costs can also be used as a separate, partial measure. Another partial input measure might be (2) the actual time spent by teachers on the anger management program; this includes preparing for and teaching the class and following up with students. Presumably these cost data can be collected frequently, which aids in monitoring. In this example, resources provided by community organizations are not included, such as guest speakers making presentations to students, which might be done pro bono or paid for by other grants.

Activities are defined as the processes, events, technologies, and actions that a program undertakes with its resources, to produce results. Examples include the number of police patrols, the number of permit applications that have been logged in and processed in some way, or the number of clients participating in a counseling program. These are clearly measures of effort. Activities performed are typically those that are key to furthering the principal missions and goals of the program. Indeed, programs are increasingly encouraged to think strategically, that is, to define their goals and then develop their activities from those goals. The main activities that are essential to furthering the missions of programs or agencies should be included. By contrast, incidental activities and the activities by other units supporting these key activities, such as fleet maintenance or information technology services, are excluded. These services are subject to their own performance measurement.

Some key measures of the activities of the anger management program are the number of hours that the anger management classes are taught and the number of students involved in these classes. These measures address different but key aspects of the overall activity. Additional measures might include special events conducted in connection with the program.

Outputs are defined as the *immediate, direct results of program activities.* The logic model recognizes that many public and nonprofit programs have long-term goals, such as ensuring public safety or achieving behavioral changes in a population of clients. These long-term goals are supported by immediate program results, such as arrests of delinquents, timely and accurate completion of permit applications, and successful completion of a course of treatment. These outputs are precursors to later outcomes. As key indicators, outputs often measure what are considered to be successful or desired immediate results of activities. Sometimes outputs are also designed to highlight and track possible problem areas in service delivery.

What might be useful output measures for our anger management program? Examples could include (1) the number of students who completed the anger management program, including any tests that might be administered, (2) the number of students who did not complete the program (obviously a possible problem area), (3) the percentage of the school's students who successfully completed the program, and (4) the percentage of the school's at-risk students who completed the program. Each of these measures provides managers with useful information. The first is a measure of success, the second a measure of failure; the third takes stock of the program's "footprint" on the school; and the fourth relates the program to its principal target group, students known to be prone to violence. Multiple output measures reflect different dimensions of program performance as well as managerial interest in these dimensions. Consistency among these measures may also provide a measure of validity regarding overall program performance.

Outcomes are defined as specific changes in behaviors or conditions that relate to program goals. *Goals* are commonly defined as the ultimate purposes of a program; outcomes are the specific measures of that attainment. Thus, if the goal is public safety, then outcomes might be measured as crime rates and public perceptions of public safety, for example. If the purpose of a counseling program is to help people increase their self-sufficiency by finding a job, then an outcome is likely the percentage or number of people who found a job. These are meaningful measures of such goals. Even though outcomes are presumed to be caused by outputs (see the logic model), they are conceptualized as measures that reflect goals: *outcomes are measures of goal attainment.*

In our example, a key goal of the anger management program is to reduce the level of high school violence. Chapter 3 conceptualized high school violence as involving the dimensions of violence through weapons,

Table 4.1 ⎯⎯⎯⎯⎯⎯ᴧᴧᴧ⎯ Anger Management Performance Measures

Performance component	Performance measure
Inputs	Total program costs
	Teacher and support staff costs
	Teachers' hours
Activities	Program hours
	Students enrolled in program
	Special events
Outputs	Students who completed the program
	Students who withdrew from the program
	Students who completed the program (%)
	At-risk students who completed the program (%)
Outcomes	Gun and knife incidents
	Fights and scuffles
	Sexual assaults and harassment
	Teachers' perception of school violence
	Students' perception of school violence
Goals	Reduce school violence
	Create a safe school environment

inappropriate physical contact, and verbal threats and assaults. Based on that conceptualization, measures of high school violence might include (1) incidents involving guns or knives reported to the administration, (2) fights and scuffles, not involving guns or knives, reported to the administration, (3) incidents of sexual assault and harassment reported to the administration, (4) teachers' perception of school violence, and (5) students' perception of violence. Obviously the first three measures need some guidelines to correctly measure incidents that involve, for example, both knives and sexual assault. School administrators will likely keep detailed records about such incidents, and this further informs management decisions. The last two measures are stakeholder assessments. Subjective assessments (such as through surveys) are commonly used to support objective data, and obtaining such assessments may provide a measure of external validation. However, whereas the objective data might be available on a monthly basis, subjective data might be gathered only once or twice yearly. Table 4.1 summarizes the anger management performance measures described here.

Getting Started
Develop performance measures for a program of your choice.

Further Examples

Performance measurement can be applied to many different programs. Here are some further examples and reflections:

Fundraising. Fundraising typically involves different activities and purposes: mass mailings and telethons for the purposes of recruiting first-time donors who usually contribute small amounts, galas and special events for regular donors who contribute modest amounts, and major giving campaigns among wealthier donors who may contribute large sums. Typical input measures are staff time and costs of fundraising activities, as well as volunteer time and expenses. Activity measures are the number and size of mass mailings, telethons, galas, and visits with potential major donors. Outputs are the immediate consequences of these events, including not just the pledges and moneys received during the events but also the number of first-time donors. Outcomes are measures of the goal, the total amount of money or in-kind contributions raised. This includes funds received that are not attributed to specific fundraising activities, such as annual donations that are routinely made.

Law enforcement. Law enforcement involves many different activities, each of which requires attention to performance measurement. For example, many local government police departments engage in preventive patrols, traffic enforcement, crime investigations, vehicle accident investigations, neighborhood and community activities (for example, neighborhood watches, school activities), 911 and emergency response activities, records management, and administrative services. Police departments usually maintain extensive activity reports and are required to report crimes, such as the number of murders, rapes, and robberies; even though these data assist in performance measurement, specific performance measures must nonetheless be designed. What are the outputs and outcomes of detective activity? Outputs are completed crime investigations, but outcomes must speak to both criminal convictions as well as other goals such as crime deterrence and creation of safe communities. These latter aspects, crime deterrence and community safety, may well require the subjective assessments of citizens. Because these latter outcomes are also shared with other law enforcement activities such as patrols and neighborhood watches (different activities contributing to the same goal), this example illustrates well that managers need to conduct their own, informal investigation into factors affecting performance.

Public works. Like law enforcement, public works involves many disparate activities. Public works may include road maintenance and repairs (including street sweeping and signage), drainage repairs and storm water management, fleet maintenance, plan review and permitting, lake management, code enforcement, grounds maintenance (for example, irrigation, mowing), and arbor care and beautification. It may also include parks management and water production, distribution, and billing activities. Typically, costs and activities are clearly defined, and outputs are measured by the successful and timely completion of these activities. For example, outputs of paved road repairs might include the number of repaired potholes, as well as the percentage of potholes filled within 48 hours. Similar measures could be readily developed for plan review or fleet maintenance.

Outcomes measure the goals of these activities, which often indicate community infrastructure conditions. For example, public works outcomes relating to roads might measure the percentage of roads that are paved; the condition of paved roads; or the percentage of roads that fall below standards for paving, cleanliness, signage, or beautification. This example illustrates that although performance measurement aims to provide up-to-date and timely information, in practice such assessments are probably undertaken only on an annual basis. Hence, outcome measurement may occur on a different cycle than other measurements. This is also the case when citizen surveys are involved. It may be argued that such outcomes do not change rapidly and require only annual measurement. Some time lag is a practical reality. Also, performance measurement may prompt jurisdictions to undertake a more extensive, accurate community assessment than they otherwise might do.

Global assessment. Many jurisdictions and agencies prepare performance measurement reports focusing on their entire agency or jurisdiction, rather than on distinct services. These reports develop measures of progress toward attaining strategic goals, and often incorporate performance measures of specific programs that were developed using the logic model. For example, a city might have as its goal that citizens feel safe and might measure attainment of this goal by citizen perceptions of safety, various crime rates (for example, murder, rape, burglary, arson), alcohol-related and other traffic accidents, community preparedness for disasters and emergency management, and neighborhood watch activities. These measures provide a broad perspective, though they do not always relate to activities and resources, or distinguish outputs from outcomes. Likewise, federal agencies often prepare performance reports identifying major goals and the milestones or activities that suggest progress made toward these goals.

EFFICIENCY, EFFECTIVENESS, AND MORE

Based on the measures described in the preceding section, other performance measures are developed as well. *Effectiveness* is simply defined as the level of results; to say that a program is effective is to point to one or more key results. Thinking about effectiveness forces managers to think about evidence of program performance that is compelling and, often, succinct. Effectiveness is typically measured by one or more output or outcome measures. The number of students who completed the anger management program might be considered as a measure of program effectiveness. The number of assaults in high schools might be considered a measure of the effectiveness of school efforts to reduce violence and provide a safe environment.[2]

In some instances, managers describe the "effectiveness" of their programs according to some standard, such as exceeding 95-percent on-time delivery or helping 60 percent of program clients to find a new job within six months. However, such standards fall outside the definition of the term *effectiveness*. They are more appropriately referred to as program or policy benchmarks. **Benchmarks** are standards against which performance is measured. In the case of the anger management program, standards might be set for a very low number of scuffles and fist fights, and gun- and knife-related incidents. Benchmarks might also be set for stakeholders' perceptions of safety and violence. Setting performance standards goes to the essence of "managing by the numbers."

Different types of benchmarks can be distinguished. *Internal* benchmarks are standards that organizations base on what their own prior programs have achieved, or on what they feel is appropriate, irrespective of what similar organizations or programs are achieving. *External* benchmarks are standards that are based on the performance of other organizations and programs. Acknowledging that not all organizations can be among the very best (say, in the top 5 percent), in recent years external benchmarks are increasingly based on comparison with the performance of *peer organizations* (those that are similar to or in the same class as the organization), *aspirant organizations* (those that are one step above the class of the organization and in the class to which the organization aspires), and *exemplary organizations* (those that are among the top 5 percent in the country). These distinctions are helpful for management purposes. A practical problem is knowing what these standards are. Often, this is determined based on discussions with members of such organizations. Sometimes published or national standards exist, such as related to mowing grass or drinking water quality. Readers might note an analogy between using external benchmarks and using comparison groups as discussed in Chapter 2. In recent years, benchmarking has sometimes become identified with determining best industry practices, but this is a limited application of the concept.

Efficiency is defined as the unit cost to produce a good or service. It is calculated as the output or outcomes over inputs, or O/I. Efficiency indicators can be calculated in many different ways and should be chosen to reflect program management concerns. Examples include the number of arrests per officer (arrests/officer), the number of completed permit application reviews per inspector (completed reviews/inspector), or the number of clients who successfully found jobs per counseling program (new jobs/program). In our example, some measures of efficiency might be the number of students who have successfully completed the anger management program per hour of teaching time (students passing program/hour of teaching), or the average total cost of successfully completing the anger management program per student (program cost/student passing program).

A useful measure of administrative efficiency might be faculty and staff time administering the program per student completion (administrative time or cost/student passing program). Obviously benchmarks can be set for efficiency measures, too.

> **Getting Started**
> Develop efficiency and effectiveness measures for your program.

A potential problem with measures of efficiency is that they may compete with those of effectiveness. In the preceding examples, efficiency can be increased by lowering standards for course completion or by reducing the quality of the course, both of which are undesirable for effectiveness. Efficiency measures need to be chosen and managed carefully. The earlier examples also avoid another problem—inaccurately ascribing outcomes to activities. Recall that performance measurement does not analyze the causes of performance. Calculating the cost of reducing assaults per hour of teaching the anger management program has little validity when, in fact, reducing high school violence involves other activities, too. Thus, efficiency measures often are based on calculating outputs per cost, rather than outcomes per cost. Efficiency measures are sometimes mistaken for cost-benefit measures, which are discussed in Box 4.1.

Efficiency also must be distinguished from workload ratio measures. *Workload ratios* are defined as the ratios of activities over inputs, or A/I. For example, a workload ratio is the number of students in anger management courses per teacher providing such courses. As many case managers know, distinguishing between workload ratios and efficiency measures is important: a high caseload of clients does not mean that they are being served well. Likewise, large class sizes do not mean that students are getting the attention they need. Therefore, efficiency measures—which are based on outcomes—may be more relevant. Many managers, however, mistake workload ratios for efficiency measures, for example, when they state that they are now teaching more students, or have larger class sizes, or are undertaking more patrols. These are not measures of efficiency but rather activities or workload ratios; they do not include accomplishments. In our example, an obvious workload measure is the number of students being taught anger management, or the number of such students per teacher. The former is a measure of the workload for the entire school, whereas the latter is a measure of the workload placed on the teachers.

In some jurisdictions, performance measurement is limited to developing measures of workloads, effectiveness, and efficiency, whereby the latter

In Greater Depth...

Box 4.1 Cost-Benefit Analysis

Efficiency measures are sometimes mistaken for those arising from cost-benefit analysis (CBA); however, CBA is fundamentally different from performance measurement. CBA uses a *comprehensive* approach to measurement; this means that *all* costs and benefits should be identified. One issue in undertaking such an analysis is the perspective that is taken. From the agency's perspective, costs borne by other agencies are not its costs. From society's perspective, these other costs are part of the total costs of providing goods or services and thus should be included. CBA typically provides a calculation of costs and benefits from both private and social perspectives. The term *private* connotes the perspective of a specific actor, such as a public or private agency; it is not used in any legal sense but rather is used to distinguish the agency from society as a whole.

CBA also deals with the thorny issue that not all costs and benefits are readily quantifiable. What are the benefits of an anger management program that provides as a benefit a safer environment for learning? How can we quantify this benefit of feeling safer? CBA uses some skillful approaches, such as trying to figure out how much parents might be willing to pay for a safer learning environment for their children, or trying to assess the cost differential of schools with different levels of safety. This is obviously no easy task.

The problem of assigning dollar values is illustrated in the familiar problem of putting a dollar value on the price of a human life. What is the dollar benefit of an environmental program or policy that saves lives? Some approaches use actuarial data of future earnings or life insurance policies, but many people find these approaches unsatisfying. When benefits are identified but not expressed in dollar values, the resulting analysis is usually called *cost-effectiveness analysis*. Also, CBA typically includes some costs and benefits that are identified but not quantified; these are assumed to have little effect on study conclusions even if they could be quantified.

CBA must also deal with the time-value of money. Often costs occur in the present and near future, but benefits accrue in the more distant future. CBA must discount future values, reflecting the depreciating effect of future inflation, but the rate used to discount future dollars can greatly affect conclusions about the cost-benefit of proposed programs and policies.

are based on outputs rather than outcomes. These limited measures serve the needs of managers. Outcomes are measured separately, sometimes at more aggregate levels such as through global assessments.

Equity measures are used to compare performance across different groups. For example, it is often useful to measure how different outcomes or activities affect different populations or target groups. In the matter of police patrols or arrest rates, for instance, it is useful to know whether these measures differ in particular sections of the jurisdiction or among members of different races. Equity measures can be analyzed for different groups of population, types of organizations, programs or services, and so on. These measures also relate to a fundamental public service value, namely, that public agencies often are required to serve entire populations, and cannot "cherry pick" customers or citizens that they would like to serve; by contrast, private organizations do not have this requirement. Because of the broad, all-encompassing nature of some public services, equity measures that compare service performance across districts or population groups can be especially salient.

Balanced scorecards are not really an application of the logic model but rather are a different way of providing a global assessment. Many balanced scorecards provide a descriptive focus on the organization's financial state, customer and stakeholder satisfaction, efficiency and effectiveness of delivery processes, and activities to promote learning and improvement within the organization. Some of these measures are typically provided through performance measurement efforts, but others, such as efforts to advance learning by organizational members, typically require additional measurement. When new concerns arise, managers and organizations readily adapt the notion of managing by key indicators to include these new measures.[3]

Given the many performance measures that are available, how does a manager choose which ones to use? Recall that performance measurement is a system of key indicators used to provide a snapshot description of activities and performance. There is no one or even best set of performance measures. The snapshot should be useful and valid, and it should involve measures that are used consistently over time. The selected measures are likely to be tailored to the availability of data, discussed further in Chapter 5. The manager's task is to construct such a system for measuring activity and performance. Box 4.2 provides an additional perspective on putting performance measurement to work.

PEERING INTO THE FUTURE: FORECASTING

How can we use information gathered from performance measurement and other sources to assist in answering questions about the future? Managers

In Greater Depth...

Box 4.2   Making Performance Measurement Work

Performance measurement is increasingly used in public and nonprofit organizations. Federal agencies are required to prepare annual performance and accountability reports, and many state and local governments require and strongly encourage their agencies to use performance measures, too. Many nonprofit organizations also use performance measurement. With so much usage, lessons have been learned about making performance measurement work.

Leadership is a critical factor. Leaders set expectations and show how performance measurement is an important and consequential management tool. Leadership also helps ensure adequate training and resources for implementation. When leaders do not understand performance measurement well, efforts are unlikely to go far or have much benefit for the organization.

Analytical capacity is a critical factor, too. Organizations that use performance measurement need staff with abilities to collect, evaluate, and analyze the necessary data. In recent years, staff have been recruited to oversee or manage performance measurement efforts. This involves using data from disparate information technology systems, as well as leading new data collection efforts that include valid stakeholder satisfaction surveys.

Lessons also have been learned from managing through performance measurement. You may be familiar with the saying "What gets measured gets done." When lower-level managers and employees know what senior managers are focusing on, they can focus on the same issues—this is an intended, positive outcome of performance measurement. However, managers may also experience unintended, harmful outcomes such as goal displacement, caused by the overzealous pursuit of narrow targets. For example, rather than focusing on reducing school violence broadly, managers may focus narrowly on selected targets such as reducing gun violence. Worse, staff might encourage students and faculty not to report incidents if doing so might make the school look bad.

All initiatives have the potential of unintended consequences and the corruption of good intentions. The challenge of all new efforts is to make them work. Managers obviously need to carefully manage the many sides of managing by the numbers.

and analysts are often called upon to provide information about some future state: How many babies are likely to be born next year? How much will our revenue be three, four, and five years from now? How many business start-ups will there be three years from now? What is the likely quality of air and water 10 years from now? Managers and analysts are also expected to fore-cast the impact of alternative policies. For example, how is air quality likely to be affected in future years if the city adopts stricter rules for new permit applications? Or, how is the anger management program likely to affect high school violence in coming years?

A *forecast* is defined as a prediction about the future. Sometimes called a projection or prognosis, forecasting is different from planning. Whereas forecasting discusses what the future will look like, planning provides a normative model of what the future should look like, such as a specific vision for a city or school in the future. Planning often begins with forecast-ing in order to establish what the future is likely to look like, so that alterna-tive futures or scenarios that might be preferred can be developed. Answers to the above questions require forecasting.

The problem of forecasting is, of course, that the future is somewhat unpredictable. Events are likely to happen that are beyond our scope or current vision. Thus, every forecast is caveated in that it is based on current information and assumptions about the future. The current information is based on whatever is known about past, present, and future events. Forecasts are intended to guide decision makers today; it is an endeavor that informs decisions, but it is not a guarantee of what will happen. Tomorrow, based on new information, may warrant a different forecast. We need to be clear and forthcoming about our data, limitations, and assumptions. The challenge of forecasting is significant.

Separate research methods have been developed to deal with forecasting. These methods are generally distinguished by whether they are based on *statistical analysis* of trends and conditions or on *judgments* about situations and events. Statistical methods typically describe and aim to extrapolate quantitative trends based on past and present data. Statistical analysis and extrapolation use techniques ranging from the very simple to the highly complex. Analysis can involve no more than the simple extrapolation of the past few data points, but it can also analyze complex cyclical patterns and model other variables affecting past and present levels. Many of these tech-niques are discussed further, in Chapter 15, and they include validation strategies, too.

Judgment-based methods often use experts to assess the likelihood of futures occurring. Experts can be brought together in groups, or as individ-uals. For example, the **Delphi method** is a forecasting method that asks experts to respond anonymously through written surveys using several rounds. After each round, summary opinions are provided, which is the basis for the next round, until, at last, one or more consensus-based opinions have materialized. A problem with this approach, however, is that it is quite time consuming, and experts may be disinclined to persist for more than just a few rounds. Experts can also be asked to create different scenarios for what may happen, and the probability of these scenarios can be evaluated or "guesstimated." Decision trees can structure complex choices and follow consecutive events through to final outcomes. Experts can also use analogies and make comparisons with other, contemporary or historical situations as a basis for forecasting what might occur in the present or future. In short, experts contribute a range of insights about what could occur, and they often are used in forecasting.[4]

Different approaches to forecasting are available. The following six principles and practices should guide forecasting efforts. First, forecasting should use multiple methods, because single methods of forecasting are subject to large errors. Specifically, statistical trend forecasting may overlook factors that have yet to occur in the future, and experts are known to have been widely off in their opinions. The strategy is to learn something credible about the future from different forecasting methods, and to combine them when possible; experts can help identify future events that trend forecasting may overlook. Thus, analysts do well not to merely extrapolate an upward or downward trend in their data, but also to identify future factors or circumstances that could affect these projections. Indeed, forecasting often should begin by identifying a full range of future scenarios and events that might be possible so that they don't overlook such factors. Then, consideration of these factors can lead to "what-if" scenarios and a range of probable forecasts that can inform decision making. This notion is captured in Figure 4.1.

Second, the longer the forecasting period, the more uncertain it is, as unforeseen events may occur and interactions among associated variables can have large effects. Thus, forecasts are thought to be more reliable for shorter periods, and the uncertainty of longer forecasts needs to be acknowledged. Third, all forecasts make assumptions and have limitations as to what factors are considered, and these assumptions and limitations should be stated clearly. Forecasts are only as good as the data and expert judgments going into them; both should be as up-to-date and accurate as possible. Forecasting should also note unusual past events that affect data and forecasts. Fourth, the accuracy of forecasts should be determined whenever possible. This can be done in several ways, such as by comparing predictions about the present against the observed reality of the present. It may also be possible to assess the accuracy of previous forecasts that use similar meth-

Figure 4.1 ————————∿∿∿— Outcomes under Alternative
Scenarios

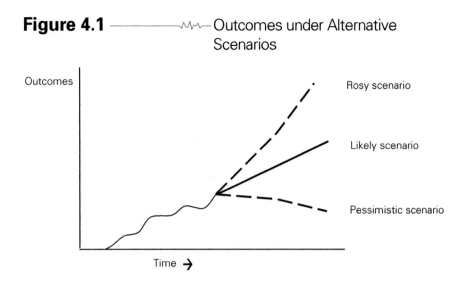

ods, and predicted scenarios might be compared against past experience
with similar conditions.

Fifth, forecasts that incorporate more information about the past, present, and future are preferred over those that provide less. However, experts
and judgmental methods may become overwhelmed by too much information, which is one reason quantitative, statistical methods are sometimes
preferred. Sixth, forecasts using more complex methods are not always more
accurate than ones made with simple methods. It is difficult to generalize
about the reasons for this; some events are difficult
to forecast, and complex methods may make
assumptions that turn out later to be invalid.
Indeed, a bias exists in favor of simple forecasting
methods that make full use of available information
about the past, present, and future.

Getting Started
How can you use your
performance measures
for forecasting?

In sum, forecasting is not to be taken lightly. It is good to have trend
data, but we need to think carefully about the future and not make rash
assumptions that it will necessarily unfold as it has in the past. In 2004, New
Orleans had not been flooded for almost 40 years; the last time was during
Hurricane Betsy in 1965. One year later, in 2005, New Orleans was flooded in
the wake of Hurricane Katrina, despite significant levee improvements. The
past is only prologue—no more, no less.

SUMMARY

Managers deal with a range of questions about the present and future. Some
questions deal with the current status of programs and polices, whereas

others deal with the future, including the impact of programs and policies on community and other conditions.

Performance measurement describes present activities and results of programs. It provides a system of key indicators of program inputs, activities, outputs, outcomes, and goals. These components are described by the logic model. Performance measurement provides a snapshot that integrates important, quantitative information about programs and policies.

Performance measures should be relevant, understandable, consistent over time, and valid. Inputs are defined as resources that are used by the program to produce its goods and services. Activities are defined as the processes, events, technologies, and actions that a program undertakes with its resources to produce results. Outputs are defined as the immediate, direct results of programs. Outcomes are defined as specific measures that assess progress toward changes or program goals, which are defined as the ultimate purposes of programs. The challenge of performance measurement is to develop measures that are key indicators of these components, that are valid, and that are useful to management.

Forecasting is about making predictions of the future. Forecasts are distinguished by whether they are based on statistical analysis of trends and conditions, or on judgments about situations and events. Forecasting should use multiple methods, and experts can provide input into statistical methods.

KEY TERMS

Activities (p. 61)

Balanced scorecards (p. 69)

Benchmarks (p. 66)

Delphi method (p. 71)

Effectiveness (p. 65)

Efficiency (p. 66)

Equity (p. 69)

Forecast (p. 71)

Goals (p. 62)

Inputs (p. 60)

Logic model (p. 60)

Outcomes (p. 62)

Outputs (p. 62)

Performance measurement (p. 59)

Workload ratios (p. 67)

Notes

1. Performance measurement was first developed in the late 1970s and was developed further in the 1980s. However, diffusion of performance measurement at all levels of government was greatly enhanced by the Government Performance and Results Act of 1993, which required its use in the federal government. Performance measurement became widely used by state and local governments, albeit with varying rigor, by the beginning of the twenty-first century.

2. This latter example illustrates well that "performance measurement does not analyze the causes of performance." It would be difficult to attribute the number of assaults in high schools to the anger management program alone; it is best described as a measure of the overall effort of the school to reduce violence, which may include other activities as well.

3. An example of a balanced scorecard, created by the Department of Energy, can be seen at professionals.pr.doe.gov/ma5/MA-5Web.nsf/ Business/Balanced+Scorecard?OpenDocument (or Google "DOE Balanced Scorecard"). A variation of scorecards are *dashboards*. For an example, see dashboard.virginiadot.org or Google "VDOT dashboard".

4. Another approach involves putting people in an artificial situation involving role playing, gaming, or prediction markets. In role playing, managers or actors are asked to play out roles, given specific scenarios and constraints. Role playing shines light on actions that individuals might take, and their considerations and dilemmas that shape these choices. Gaming is similar but places players in a competitive situation with predetermined standards for "winning." A problem with using role playing and gaming for forecasting is that actual conditions may vary, of course. Prediction markets ask people to place bets with real money on future events, similar to future markets for stocks. For example, a bet might pay out $1 if a future event occurs, and $0 if it does not. If the current price for this bet is, say, $.60, then the collective wisdom of people in this market is that the future event has a 60 percent chance of occurring. Bets could be placed on any future event, such as who might win the next presidency. The U.S. Defense Department created such a market for predicting the probability of future terrorist attacks but cancelled it after much public concern.

CHAPTER

5

Data Collection

CHAPTER OBJECTIVES

After reading this chapter, you should be able to
- Identify sources of data in your field
- Describe how data can be used for program evaluation, performance measurement, and forecasting
- Evaluate the availability and validity of data in your field
- Develop and implement a scientifically valid survey
- Understand the value of qualitative data
- Understand how to draw a random sample

The previous chapters discussed how managers and analysts can address questions about the past, present, and future of their programs and policies. These strategies require the availability of data, of course. What sources of data exist? What do these sources contain? How accurate are the data in these sources? If accurate data do not exist, can new data be collected and, if so, how? How should data be collected? In particular, what kinds of samples are available and how should the data be gathered?

This chapter deals with these questions of data collection. Managers and analysts are expected to be familiar with the data in their lines of business, and to be able to generate new data when existing data are unsatisfactory. As managers and analysts take inventory of the data in their fields and build skills in collecting new data, they are likely to find new and sometimes surprising uses of data. The first part of this chapter looks at data sources, and the second part looks at sampling from these sources.

SOURCES OF DATA

Administrative Data

Public and nonprofit managers have access to a considerable amount of data about their programs and policies. *Administrative data* are those that are generated in the course of managing programs and activities. There are many sources of administrative data:

- Activity logs and reports
- Error logs
- Inspection and repair reports
- Work orders
- Permit reviews and approvals
- Client requests and complaints
- Customer comments and complaints
- Accident reports
- Client accounts and information
- Litigation
- Progress and completion reports
- Mandated studies
- Financial monitoring and reporting
- Grant requests and reports
- Bank accounts
- External program reviews
- Ad-hoc and other special reports
- Inventory reports
- Time cards and program staffing data
- Absenteeism records

Programs vary greatly in their administrative data. Schools often have data about crimes and violent incidents that occur, which they may be required to report. They likely have data about their students' academic achievements from course work and standardized tests. They might have additional data on student participation in after-school activities (such as remedial language or math education), as well as information on students' special medical needs and psychosocial conditions such as problems at home, histories of violence, and so on. Schools also have other data concerning their teachers and staff, building and ground maintenance activities, and so on.

Among the first tasks of managers and analysts is to take inventory of available data and to determine the quality and uses of the data. Traditionally, administrative data have had three purposes: (1) to ensure that resources are not misused, (2) to determine the status of the organization's activities, and (3) to provide a record of what has been completed and accomplished. The first purpose often is associated with auditing and anti-corruption, such as being accountable for how money is spent. The second purpose helps managers gain control over present activities and set priorities. Activity logs might be a first step toward developing project progress and completion charts. The third purpose has legal and accountability ramifications, documenting that agreed-upon objectives have been accomplished (for example, roads have been repaired, the class has been taught). Client complaints and inspection reports provide additional documentation about activities meeting standards.

Administrative data vary in their usefulness for program evaluation and performance measurement; the variables may or may not be those that are needed. Administrative data often are not collected with these purposes in mind, and sources of these data often cover many input and activity measures but lack data for many important output and outcome measures. For example, administrative data from road repairs are likely to include information about the amount of funding for repairs (input), the number of repairs undertaken in any reporting period (activity), and the number and miles of completed repairs (output). But data might be missing about the timeliness of key repairs and certainly about the condition of the roadways (outcome).

Performance measurement usually requires that additional administrative data be collected. Doing so adds a fourth purpose: monitoring key outputs and outcomes. This purpose goes well beyond providing a record of what has been completed and accomplished. In the case of road repairs, it requires that data be collected about the timeliness and efficiency of repairs, too. It also requires a comprehensive, perhaps annual or quarterly, assessment of the condition of roadways; this assessment could be part of an ongoing system that monitors street conditions. Similarly, many of the measures listed in Table 4.1, regarding the anger management program, might not even be gathered by schools if not required as part of a performance measurement and management system. Although teachers and administrators might monitor individual at-risk students, they might not identify and track that cohort in any systematic way. Hence, organizations that are committed to performance measurement are likely to require additional administrative data.[1]

Administrative data may also suffer from some quality challenges that must be acknowledged or overcome. Data are sometimes (1) missing or incomplete, (2) inaccurately reported, (3) subject to definitions that have changed over time and therefore cannot be compared, (4) not linked to particular events or clients, or cannot be disaggregated in necessary ways, (5) confidential and unavailable for analysis, or (6) insufficiently available in electronic format. These problems will need to be identified and addressed. Analysts may also need to make reasonable adjustments that make it possible to relate data across time or cases. The rigor with which these problems are identified and addressed enhances the validity and credibility of administrative data. Recognizing that some problems are not easily or fully correctable (for example, past records may be irretrievable or incomplete), organizations may make the timeliness and quality of data collection a priority; many organizations are now investing in real-time, fully electronic ways of capturing their data. An objective of this activity is to ensure that data inaccuracies are inconsequential for purposes of validity and management. Some organizations take electronic collection a step further, using common enterprise software that makes administrative data from different departments available to senior managers throughout the organization. Overall, the availability and quality of administrative data have increased greatly during the past decade as a result of greater commitment to performance measurement and information technology applications.

Administrative data are also used in program evaluation and forecasting. Administrative data provide important descriptive information for program evaluation, but administrative data are generally not designed to provide adequate information about outcomes and factors affecting program outcomes (for example, rival hypotheses). Hence, program evaluation almost always requires data from additional sources, such as surveys, interviews, focus groups, and secondary sources (discussed later in this chapter). Administrative data can also be used in forecasting, though usually in combination with expert judgment and secondary data about community conditions. Finally, the administrative data of other organizations, when available, is sometimes used to identify external benchmarks.

In short, administrative data assist in the management of programs and policies. Such data are essential for program evaluation and performance measurement, though typically they are insufficient or inadequate in some way. Managers and analysts should know what data are available to them and be able to assess the uses and validity of these data. Often, administrative data are complemented with data from other sources.

> **Getting Started**
> Identify administrative data in your field. How relevant are these data for the five uses described in Chapter 1?

Secondary Data

A broad range of studies and statistics available from public and private organizations provide important information for managers and analysts. These are sometimes called *secondary data*, referring to the fact that they were collected for some other purpose. An extraordinary amount of secondary data are available, and they are increasingly available though the Internet. For example, *Fedstats* is a portal for statistics from many federal agencies, through which data can be accessed about health, education, incomes, housing, crime, agriculture, transportation, the environment, economic growth, and much more. These data are available at different levels of aggregation, such as at the state or city level. Nonprofit and other public organizations, including international organizations such as the United Nations and World Bank, also make secondary data available.[2]

An important task for managers and analysts is to know what specific data are available in their field, and how these data can help them. Secondary data are often used to describe communities in statistical terms (for example, how many crimes, how many cars), which in turn can contribute toward needs assessment, benchmarking, and outcome measurement. First, needs assessment involves determining the needs of members or organizations in a community. This activity also involves in-depth interviews and surveys of community members and leaders. Secondary data can buttress claims regarding widespread concerns about crime, low incomes, health, and so on. Second, secondary data can be used to compare or rank communities against each other on issues such as education, crime, or economic growth. Indeed, such benchmarking comparisons and rankings often are reported in newspaper and magazine articles. Third, some community-level data may be relevant to public organization outcomes, such as secondary data pertaining to illiteracy, juvenile crime, student-teacher ratios, and so on.

Obviously the nature of data varies greatly across fields. Some areas have long histories of data collection, sometimes mandated by the federal government, whereas others have less data available. Some secondary data are available at very disaggregated levels, for example, at the level of individuals. Similarly, public statistics may be available at the level at which they were collected, such as for individual hospitals, schools, or cities. In other instances, only aggregated data are available, such as for entire states or school districts. These aggregated data can still be relevant, for example, in comparing one organization against a city or state average. Sometimes, agencies are willing to make available their raw data. Some cities use secondary data to prepare *community indicators,* which are global assessments of how well their community is doing.

Secondary data are also used in scholarly studies, such as to study relationships (for example, juvenile crime and drug use) and the control variables and circumstances that affect these relationships (for example, household income). Such in-depth uses have contributed to understanding limitations of secondary data. First, secondary data seldom provide managers and analysts with all of their data needs for their community; secondary data were not created with these needs in mind. Managers and analysts will typically use other data sources, too. However, secondary data may be more readily available and cheaper than those you collect on your own; there is thus an obvious bias toward using them when available. Second, biases may be found in secondary data as a result of uneven sampling; for example, school data may miss out on some schools or children, and these schools or children may be disproportionately in poorer districts or come from poorer or non-English-speaking households. The U.S. Census is well known for undercounting minorities and undocumented aliens. The significance of these biases depends on the use and role of the data. Whereas in the aggregate the undercount is probably but a few percent, it is highly important to estimating the demand for services by these populations (see the discussion of sampling later in this chapter).

Third, data definitions may be unclear, unstable, or not suited for the study or management purpose. If unemployment is measured by those receiving unemployment compensation, this is likely an undercount because some people seeking employment do not file for unemployment compensation or even qualify for it. If we ask people whether they consider themselves unemployed, we might overestimate the amount of unemployment, because some people may not be sufficiently looking for employment. Likewise, whether or not a housing crisis exists depends on how it is measured: by the percentage of people living in a room (overcrowding), or by the percentage of income spent on rent or mortgage? Thus, we need to know the exact data definitions and ensure that they are reasonable for our purpose. No measure is perfect, but it might be embraced as an indicator.

Though secondary data may suffer from poor quality and problems of definition and sampling, managers and analysts are expected to know about and use the secondary data in their field.

> **Getting Started**
> Identify sources of secondary data in your field. Explore the data definitions for your program.

Surveys

Surveys collect information about the opinions and conditions of stakeholders. The most common forms are citizen, client, business, and employee surveys. Surveys provide important information about stakeholders that otherwise might be unavailable. For example, a survey of citizens or employees can identify concerns about the availability of child care services and after-school programs, and the quality of each. These may be important conditions that affect decisions, in this case about employment and child care. Knowledge of stakeholder preferences and conditions is often important in management decision making.

The argument for using surveys is that they provide systematic and objective information about stakeholder preferences and conditions. Managers usually know something about stakeholder problems and needs through their impromptu comments, calls, and complaints; through public hearings; or through comments made by elected officials. Although this information is valuable, it seldom provides comprehensive and unbiased information. Those who call or complain have a specific agenda in mind; they are seldom representative of all citizens, clients, businesses, or employees. Surveys provide the necessary antidote of objectivity and comprehensiveness; they help prevent perceptions from becoming reality.

Surveys also supplement administrative and secondary data; when these sources are inadequate, managers need to collect their own information. Surveys are varied, and the number and types of questions asked should depend on what you are trying to find out. Likert scales often are used (see Chapter 3), but other respond formats may be used depending on the information that is sought. Some surveys are short, others longer depending on the audience and the issues being explored. Surveys are commonly used in program evaluation research and, increasingly, performance measurement. They are also used to aid community leaders in establishing community priorities and to determine how to address community needs. For example,

Getting Started

How can a survey help managers in your area?

in a growing community, a survey might be used to lay the groundwork for determining which roads to widen to cope with increased traffic, to determine the level of support for moving to a single waste hauler, or to measure community perceptions of which intersections in the city are the worst.

Three types of surveys are mail, phone, and in-person surveys. Each has somewhat different advantages, and the manager's experience with each type may vary according to the specific conditions assessed (see Table 5.1). Phone surveys are increasingly used for citizen surveys because of cost and speed advantages. Data collection for phone surveys can often be completed in two to three weeks (unlike mail surveys, which may require multiple mailings) and are cheaper than mail or in-person surveys. Phone surveys also are used for client surveys. Although phone surveys are shorter than mail or in-person surveys, more than 50 items can be asked when questions are easy and asked in a similar format.[3] For example, a typical lead-in might be, "I am going to read you a series of statements. Please tell me for each whether

Table 5.1 ⎯⎯⎯⎯⎯⎯ Comparing Mail, Phone, and In-Person Surveys

Criterion	Mail	Phone	In-person
a. Response rate	Variable	Variable	High
b. Amount of data	Highest	Low to Medium	Low or High
c. Data collection	6–8 weeks	2–3 weeks	4–6 weeks
d. Cost per survey	Low to Medium	Medium to High	Very high
e. Interviewer bias	Low	Medium	Medium

you strongly agree, agree, . . ." after which a series of short statements follows. A great deal of information can be gathered by using this format. A relatively recent development is the use of voice recognition software to assist interviewers in capturing responses to open-ended responses. For example, the analysis of open-ended questions such as "What three things do you like most [or least] about the program" provides useful information with face validity. Internet surveys are increasingly used, too, and various software programs now make web surveys relatively easy to develop.[4] However, a practical problem is obtaining a valid, random sample of respondents; this sampling problem is discussed further below.

Employee surveys are frequently conducted using confidential pen-and-paper survey. To ensure both high response rates and anonymity, employees sometimes are asked to complete the surveys simultaneously and then return them in blank envelopes. In theory, employee surveys can be conducted using a company's internal computer network, if employees have adequate trust that responses will indeed be kept confidential and anonymous.

Mail surveys continue to be used, though their cost and time advantages relative to phone surveys probably make them increasingly less attractive. When mail surveys are used, the appearance of the instrument should reflect high levels of professionalism in design and customer orientation; the instrument should look attractive and be easy to use for respondents. To reduce intimidation—mail surveys often are lengthy—they often are presented in a small booklet format, such as by folding legal-size paper double. Mail surveys usually include a stamped return envelope, too. The idea is to make it easy for the respondent to complete the survey. In-person surveys are very expensive and seem to be increasingly rare. The U.S. Census uses them to conduct interviews that are extraordinarily lengthy, for example.

Surveys are typically carried out using the following steps: (1) obtaining permission and resources for conducting surveys, (2) interviewing stakeholders to fully understand the study context and to specify study objectives, (3) obtaining a sample of the study population for surveying, (4) designing, testing, and improving a pilot survey, (5) implementing the final survey instrument, and (6) analyzing and reporting findings.

It is obvious that biased questions are a threat to validity. In addition, questions should be clear (that is, unambiguous and specific) and answerable by respondents.[5] Furthermore, double-barreled phrasing, leading (or biased) phrases, and negative statements should be avoided. Consider the following examples. "Do you feel safe?" is ambiguous for the purpose of evaluating high school violence and should be clarified as, "How safe do you feel at school?" A leading question would be, "Could you ever think of hitting a classmate?" This question implies that it is undesirable or unacceptable to do so. A better question would be, "Have you thought about

<table>
<tr><td>

Getting Started
Formulate some initial
survey questions, and
then improve them.

</td><td>

hitting a classmate during the last seven days?"
An example of a double-barreled question is,
"Do you feel that guns should be barred from
school and that those who bring guns to school
should be punished?" These questions should be
asked separately.

</td></tr>
</table>

Regardless of the type of survey used, survey questions should be as
easy as possible for respondents to answer while providing researchers with
all the information they need. Formulating good questions is an art built on
practice and continuous improvement. Beyond this, some other guidelines
are that questions that deal with the same topic should be grouped together.
Likert scales greatly assist in survey development because the same response
scale can be used for many different items. The survey introduction should
state the purpose of the survey and how results will be used, and all interviewers should follow the same script, with no variation; neither the interviewers nor the script should introduce bias. Many surveys go through
numerous iterations and pilot testing before they are implemented. The
CD that accompanies the workbook, *Exercising Essential Statistics,* includes
examples of survey instruments, data, and reports. In short, surveys are
increasingly used in management and analysis. Surveys allow managers
and analysts to gather a considerable amount of information from their
stakeholders.

Other Sources

Four other sources of data are *observers, actors, experts*, and *focus groups.*
Observers are sometimes used to assess the condition of facilities and infrastructure, such as roads, public facilities, and park grounds. These assessments can be quite detailed, following extensive checklists and other structured reporting formats. For example, park grounds might be checked for
litter, unsafe objects, grass length and condition, weeds, sign markings, pathway safety, condition of benches and playgrounds, paint and rust, and so on.
Typically, considerable care is taken to ensure that all observers make their
observations in the same manner, and reliability checks are conducted from
time to time for this purpose. Observers should be carefully trained and
evaluated to ensure that they are consistent in their assessments.

Actors are observers who are actively involved in what they observe.
Role playing is sometimes used to assess frontline services, such as toll
collection or welfare application processing. Actors usually participate as
clients and assess services according to different conditions that they
describe or represent. For example, actors are used to ensure that services are
rendered irrespective of race or gender.

Experts are used when objective data and stakeholder opinions and
accounts alone are insufficient for making judgments about program

outcomes. For example, landfill maintenance, analysis of medical records, and evaluation of the quality of higher education programs require a balance of objective facts and subjective opinion. In these cases, experts provide important information. Chapter 4 explored the idea of using experts in the context of forecasting. Experts can work either alone or collectively in coming to a consensus.

Focus groups are purposive samples used to generate insights about program services and goals. For example, a citizen focus group on law enforcement might be asked about perceptions of police officers in a jurisdiction, as well as program needs and outcomes. Focus groups often are homogeneous, because different populations have different experiences and may drown each other out. For example, minorities and whites often have very different perceptions about law enforcement personnel. Although focus groups are valuable, the small number of focus group members (typically about 10–20) suggests that we cannot assume that the opinions of group members accurately reflect those of the larger group to which they belong. Generalization to the larger population is not possible. Also, focus groups do not provide much quantifiable data. Rather, focus groups are used to generate insights into the reasoning, priorities, and experiences of participants.[6]

SAMPLING

After the research design has been selected, variables defined, and data sources selected, questions arise about how information will be collected. Among these questions is the matter of the target population. Specifically, about which population is information to be gathered, and how many members of the population need to be reached? The latter question refers to getting information from a sample, that is, a subset of a population. In public management, samples of citizens, clients, or employees are quite common. Three frequently asked sampling questions are (1) When is a sample needed? (2) What is the best way to select the sample? and (3) How large should the sample be?

When Is a Sample Needed?

Although a *census* could be used to survey or count (tally) an entire group or population, such as all citizens in a jurisdiction or all program clients, doing so is often impractical. In these cases, a sample is used. Sometimes data collection aims to conduct a census, such as when all employees or all clients are surveyed in a small program. However, some employees or clients may not respond, in which case the resulting response group is considered to be a sample.[7]

A *sample* is a selection, such as of citizens, from an entire population. In most surveys, the purpose of a sample is to make a *generalization*, or a statement about one group that is applied to another group or to a broader group. A statement made about a sample is held to be valid for the population from which the sample was drawn. Indeed, we are interested in knowing how a population, not just the sample, assesses something; we must be able to draw conclusions about the population.

Only representative samples allow generalizations to be made about an entire population. A *representative sample* is one that has characteristics similar to those of the population as a whole. Surveys are valid reflections of the general population only when they are based on a representative sample; the strategy of conducting a valid survey requires that a representative sample be obtained. Unrepresentative samples have a biased (or skewed) mix of characteristics (for example, a greater proportion of females) and do not lend themselves to generalization.

How Should Samples Be Selected?

Random sampling is the most accurate way to obtain a representative sample. In this process, each population member has an equal chance of being selected for the study sample. The list from which a sample is drawn is called a *sampling frame,* and one of the first tasks in conducting a survey is to acquire the sampling frame from which a sample is to be drawn. A common approach is to select participants blindly, thereby minimizing any researcher-induced bias. Two popular methods of random sampling are to assign a number to each population member and use computer-generated random numbers to select the sample, or to use randomly dialed telephone numbers to select participants for phone surveys. Another sampling method, *systematic sampling,* involves selecting a random number from the sampling frame and then selecting every *n*th member from the sampling frame. Note that chance (random selection) implies that representative samples are similar but not identical to the population; slight differences will exist between the sample and the population with regard to age, gender, income, and so on. In historical or archival research, sometimes a random sample of records is chosen when the entire population of records is too large for study.

Some threats to validity for surveys are inadequate sampling frames and unrepresentative samples. Ideally the sampling frame should closely match the survey population, but discrepancies will exist in practice. For example, a phone survey of citizens will miss out on households that have no phone. Some households may have only cell phones, which generally are not included in the sampling frame. This inaccuracy might be of minor significance, but it should be acknowledged. In some cases, however, such an inaccuracy might be very significant, for example, in a survey that aims to assess or compare opinions of households that have only cell phones. Thus, analysts must be aware of discrepancies between the population and the sampling frame.

Unrepresentative samples are another threat to validity. Two examples of unrepresentative samples are those based on customer comment cards and responses to enclosures in mass mailings such as utility bills. Although these efforts provide important information, they cannot be relied on for generalization. Those who complete customer comment cards are usually heavily skewed toward clients with gripes, though they typically include a few clients who offer praise. We cannot assume that their opinions reflect all clients. Enclosures in utility bills and other mass mailings to which recipients respond may suffer from this problem, as well. Very few recipients return such enclosures, and we cannot assume that they are representative of all recipients. Community leaders typically want all citizens to receive a survey, but the resulting response sample often is a nonrepresentative sample based on self-selection. Rather, if generalization is the objective, then these methods should not be used and a random sample must be drawn.[8]

> **Getting Started**
> Develop a strategy for obtaining a representative sample of program clients.

Finally, in recent years, studies of "exemplary practices" have been conducted. Organizations selected for such studies are selected not randomly but purposively, because of their exemplary practices. *Purposive sampling* is used to produce further insight, rather than generalization. These are not random samples. Often, these are case studies that are not even generalizable to other exemplary organizations, but the insights of how things are done are of great importance and most useful in improving public management. Likewise, case studies of policy impacts often are very useful in identifying unintended outcomes and program innovations that otherwise might not come to light. Research based on purposive samples can yield important insights, but the results are not generalizable.

How Large Should the Sample Be?

Large random samples will more accurately reflect characteristics of the population from which they are drawn. The term *sampling error* is defined as discrepancies (errors) that occur because random sampling procedures may cause sample statistics to differ from (unknown) population statistics. In a population, 30 percent of students might have an A, but a random sample might show 35 percent, leading to the conclusion that, in the population of students, 35 percent of students rather than 30 percent have an A. Of course, in practice one seldom knows these population statistics; that is why a sample is taken.

The sampling error can be calculated for random samples as the range within which one can be 95 percent certain that the population estimate

Table 5.2 ⎯⎯⎯⎯⎯⎯⎯ Relationships between Sample Size and Sampling Error

Sample size	Sampling error (%)	Sample size	Sampling error (%)
100	± 9.8	500	± 4.4
200	± 6.9	800	± 3.5
300	± 5.7	1,200	± 2.8
400	± 4.9	2,000	± 2.2

falls. Larger samples better mirror the population from which they are drawn and thus have smaller sampling errors. Sampling errors reflect *reliability*, the extent to which repeated measurement produces the same result. The relationship between sample size and sampling error for samples drawn from populations over 20,000 is shown in Table 5.2. For example, the sampling error of a survey with a sample size (n) of 300 is ±5.7 percent; if a survey finds that 73.4 percent of respondents favor a new road, then you can be 95 percent certain that, in the population from which the sample was randomly drawn, between 67.7 percent [73.4% – 5.7%] and 79.1 percent [73.4% + 5.7%] favor the road. This assumes, of course, that the finding is not subject to other survey errors, such as asking biased questions or having unrepresentative samples.

For populations greater than 20,000, *sampling errors are independent of population size*. The same sampling error applies for a survey of a medium-sized jurisdiction of 40,000 as for the entire United States or the world![9] Another consideration is that gains in accuracy must be balanced against cost and effort. Accuracy gains on samples over 1,200 are seldom justified. Most samples range between 200 and 800. Larger samples are required only when analyses include many subsets (for example, many districts for which data must be reported separately).

Decisions on sampling can be aided by some further practical considerations. First, small populations (say, less than 100 or 200) do not require sampling; rather, the entire population should be surveyed. Second, sometimes sampling frames are lacking, such as when clients are served on a walk-in basis and no record is kept of names. In that situation, managers randomly select days and times at which anonymous walk-ins are surveyed. Third, when the population includes subgroups of small numbers (for example, small minority groupings), **stratified sampling** is used. Stratified sampling first divides the sampling frame according to each subpopulation to be surveyed and then samples randomly within each subgroup. This approach gives members from small groups a greater chance of participation than members of large groups. Of course, study results must later be weighted appropriately to ensure unbiased conclusions. Such weighting is discussed in Chapter 6. Fourth, nonrespondents must be accounted for by using a greater initial sample. If a 50-percent response rate is expected and 400 completed surveys are desired, then a random sample should be drawn of 800 participants.

Finally, generalization assumes that nonrespondents answer in the same manner as respondents. ***Nonresponse bias*** (also known as nonresponse error) is the extent to which views of nonrespondents differ from those of respondents, thus affecting generalizability from the sample to the population. Low response rates merit concern about nonresponse bias; this, too, is a validity concern for surveys based on enclosures in mass mailings. The problem of nonresponse bias is usually dealt with by comparing sample and population demographics. When differences exist (for example, phone surveys sometimes oversample females), researchers can statistically weight survey responses to account for over- or undersampling and may conclude that the likely, known effect of such oversampling is minor.[10] However, when the extent of over- or undersampling is large, the imbalance may reflect biases that cannot be overcoming by such weighting. Therefore, the best approach to this problem is to avoid over- and undersampling as much as possible. In the case of phone surveys, the solution may be to monitor participation rates of females and at some point survey only males. The same approach would apply to whites and older respondents, who also tend to be oversampled. Many surveys compare sample and population demographics and report these comparisons in their methods section (see Box 5.1). In other cases, caveats may be needed in reporting results.

PUTTING IT TOGETHER

Conducting research and analyzing data clearly involve many different aspects. The six steps of program evaluation, discussed in Chapter 2, provide an organized way to look at the different activities and considerations involved. Below is a summary proposal—for evaluating an after-school program—that integrates elements of the previous chapters in this book. In some ways, we can think of proposals as final reports that lack data analysis or conclusions.

Proposal for Evaluating an After-School Program
In recent years, new after-school programs have been implemented in our region. The purpose of this proposal is to outline a strategy for evaluation. Input has been sought and obtained from many sources, including county management, school administrators, teachers, and a panel of school psychologists. We also conducted two focus groups with school students. A consensus exists that school violence is an important

In Greater Depth...

Box 5.1   Writing Up Your Methods

The following excerpt is from a report of a citizen survey for a large county:

This study was conducted by the Florida Institute of Government and the Department of Public Administration at the University of Central Florida, on behalf of Orange County Government. The survey of Orange County residents focuses on government priorities, satisfaction with government services, and contact with public officials. Its purpose is to assist in updating the Orange County Strategic Plan.

The survey was developed with input from Orange County staff and includes items from an the earlier survey for the purpose of comparison. Calls were typically made between the hours of 1 PM and 6 PM on Saturdays and Sundays, and between 5:30 PM and 9:30 PM on Mondays through Thursdays. Some callbacks were made at other hours.

The survey protocol is provided in Appendix 4 [not shown here]. Random digit dialing was used to ensure a representative sample. This procedure involves selecting numbers at random from the appropriate exchanges in the Greater Orlando directory, and then substituting two randomly generated digits for the last two numbers. This allows the inclusion of new and unlisted numbers.

A total of 9,503 different telephone numbers were identified, and each phone number was dialed up to four times in order to contact potential interviewees. Of these 9,503 phone numbers, 3,669 (38.6 percent) were ineligible, because they were business or government offices, fax lines, disconnected or out of service numbers, or, in a few cases, exchanges with respondents living in nearby Seminole County. Some ineligible respondents occurred toward the end of the survey, when participation criteria were restricted to ensure demographic balance of the final sample. An additional 2,818 (29.7 percent) were never reached in four attempts. These were numbers at which no response, other than an answering message or a busy signal, was ever elicited. A total of 3,016 potential respondents were reached and asked to participate, which represents 31.7 percent of the total numbers selected and called. Of the 3,016 eligible respondents, 1,982 (65.7 percent) were unwilling or unable to complete the interview. The

(continued)

Box 5.1 *(continued)*

remaining 1,034 (34.3 percent) of eligible respondents participated and completed the interview.

The above procedures are designed to ensure a valid (that is, representative) sample of Orange County residents. A valid (or representative) sample is one that is adequate for generalizing study results to the entire population. In this regard, the following comparisons provide statistical evidence supporting the similarity between the sample and the Orange County population:

	Population	Sample
Age		
18–45	62.3%	62.8%
46–65	24.1	26.8
66+	13.6	10.4
Race		
White	81.5%	84.3%
Non-white	18.5	15.7
Gender		
Male	49.0%	43.9%
Female	51.0	56.1

The total sample size is 1,034 completed surveys. This implies a sampling error of no more than 3.2 percent. That is, we can be 95 percent certain that the population results are within ± 3.2 percent of the results reported in this study. The sample size was selected based on cost-effectiveness: to reduce the sampling error to, for example, 2 percent, requires a sample size of about 2,400, more than a doubling of effort.

problem and that an after-school program presents an opportunity to reduce it. However, many observers believe that the benefits of after-school programs extend beyond the current issue of school violence, and we were encouraged to evaluate other outcomes, too.

The main after-school activities whose outcomes we will evaluate are the homework assistance and anger management components.

Student participation in after-school programs often is voluntary, although many schools have made an effort to ensure that those teenagers participate who they believe are prone to violence, socially isolated, or academically at risk.

To better determine the impact of these after-school programs, we will include after-school programs that vary in their use of anger management and homework assistance. A few after-school programs provide only recreational activities, and we feel that those are an appropriate comparison group for these others programs. Although no baseline data have been gathered to date, we propose to gather such data as soon as the proposal is approved. Baseline data are important in evaluating the impact of these programs.

We will focus our efforts on a variety of well-targeted outcome measures. With regard to anger management, we will focus on students' knowledge of anger management principles, their ability to identify anger in themselves and others, the strategies they use to release anger in nonviolent ways, and their willingness to help others use such strategies. With regard to homework assistance, we will focus on the utilization of this service, the areas in which it is most often used, and perceptions of increased valuation of academics and study discipline. With regard to high school violence, we will assess violence with weapons, physical violence without weapons, and verbal assaults.

While after-school programs could affect violence and improve academic ability, other factors contribute to these outcomes as well. This evaluation acknowledges these other factors and will collect information about the following variables for purposes of statistical control: student access to weapons, student social isolation, peer pressure exerted by violence-prone groups, school enforcement of nonviolence policies, teacher awareness of teenage violence predictors, and teacher and staff commitment to reducing teenage violence. We will also consider student academic performance, composition of student household (number of parents and siblings living with student), gender, and race.

We will collect data from a variety of sources. School records track incidents of physical violence, though such records vary in accuracy regarding that which is recorded. Rather, the primary sources will be students and teachers. On a quarterly basis, teachers will be asked to participate in a survey about violence in their classes, and on the impact of the after-school programs on students who are in their classes. Also, students will be given a test of their knowledge of anger management principles, as well as an assessment of the usefulness and impact of homework assistance. The latter assessment is, of course, administered only to those who participate in such homework assistance. Both the teacher and student surveys include items regarding the other control variables mentioned above.

We intend to survey all teachers and a sample of students participating in these programs. We anticipate surveying about 100 teachers and a sample of 300 students (which has a sampling error of 5.6 percent). Detailed information about the measurements and survey instruments and protocols is provided in the appendix [not shown here].

SUMMARY

Managers and analysts can use several sources of data for program evaluation, performance measurement, and forecasting. These sources are administrative data; secondary data; survey research; and other sources such as observers, actors, experts, and focus groups. Managers and analysts are expected to be familiar with the data in their field and to be able to develop and integrate data from these different sources to meet their needs.

Sampling involves selecting a group for study from the population being examined. Studies that rely on generalizability (that is, most surveys) require representative samples. Such samples are obtained through random sampling, in which each population member has an equal chance of being selected. The size of the sample depends on the required sampling error; larger samples have smaller sampling errors and are thus more accurate. Some threats to validity are unrepresentative samples (for example, customer comment cards, enclosures in mass mailings) and low responses rates, which may also result in unrepresentative samples.

KEY TERMS

Actors (p. 84)

Administrative data (p. 77)

Census (p. 85)

Experts (p. 84)

Focus groups (p. 85)

Generalization (p. 85)

Nonresponse bias (p. 89)

Observers (p. 84)

Purposive sampling (p. 87)

Random sampling (p. 86)

Representative sample (p. 86)

Sample (p. 85)

Sampling error (p. 87)

Sampling frame (p. 86)

Secondary data (p. 79)

Stratified sampling (p. 88)

Three types of surveys (mail, phone, in-person) (p. 82)

Notes

1. In recent years, many managers and analysts have contributed to their organizations by helping them collect more or better data. Some

organizations have hired employees who are responsible for managing the organization's data needs for performance measurement.

2. Managers should be familiar with the following useful portals: www.fedstats.gov; www.worldbank.org/data; www.secondarydata.com (select "general sources"); and for state-level data, www.census.gov/sdc.

3. Examples of such lengthy and comprehensive phone surveys are shown on the CD that accompanies the workbook *Exercising Essential Statistics*. The workbook also provides further references (resources) for doing surveys.

4. For example, Survey Monkey is a popular tool that makes producing a web-based survey relatively easy.

5. Although respondents may have opinions about school safety, they are apt to be unfamiliar with specific options. Thus, "Do you want anger management programs?" may be unanswerable by those who are unfamiliar with such programs. It would be best to precede this question with, "How familiar are you with anger management programs?" Some of the best survey questions follow the K.I.S.S. rule: Keep It Simple, Stupid.

6. As noted by an anonymous reviewer, "One of my pet peeves is the tendency for community and nonprofit leaders to insist on a tool that is inadequate to the task. I have had people ask me to do randomly selected focus groups so they can generalize. This of course is not possible."

7. Although the term *census* is usually limited to a population, tallies are also taken of all program resources, activities, and results. Shortfalls in such counts are problematic, suggesting that the organization has achieved less than it really has. Organizations usually undertake considerable control to ensure that such important tallies are highly accurate and complete. Although gaps and inaccuracies can be estimated, analysts are conservative in making such guesses; they often are difficult to justify and may induce errors of their own. Recall that the ethics of research includes being objective and avoiding any appearance of tampering with data (see Chapter 1).

8. Of course, there are good reasons why elected officials would like all citizens to receive the survey: it is good public relations, and it gives every citizen the chance to speak up. Some interesting responses might be obtained, but we need to acknowledge that the sample is unrepresentative.

9. Small populations have smaller sampling errors. For results that vary by ±5 percent, populations of 5,000 require samples of 357; populations of 1,000 require samples of 278; populations of 500 require samples of 217; populations of 300 require samples of 168; and populations of 200 require samples of 132. Populations of 100 require samples of 79,

suggesting that a census would require only a modest amount of additional effort. Numerous Internet sites provide sample size–estimation tables. One such site is the DSS Research "Researcher's Toolkit," www.dssresearch.com/toolkit/secalc/error.asp. The sampling errors shown are maximum estimates, which are commonly used. Specifically, they are based on the assumption that 50 percent of respondents answer in a specific way.

10. In scholarly studies, samples of nonrespondents are sometimes obtained and nonrespondents contacted and surveyed; their responses can then be compared to those of the respondent group.

Descriptive Statistics

Descriptive statistics provide important summary information about variables, such as their average, frequency distribution, and other measures that describe variables in helpful ways. Descriptive statistics are used widely in public and nonprofit management and analysis. For example, knowing how much pollution is occurring, the percentage of citizens favoring improved parks, or the average rate of absenteeism is often meaningful information that affects public decision making. This descriptive information can also be used for subsequent comparisons against past performance, against the performance of other jurisdictions, and across respondent or jurisdictional characteristics such as gender or area incomes. Descriptive statistics are a staple of analysis.

This section discusses many useful descriptive statistics and shows how to use them. It recaps essential concepts from Section II, such as variables, attributes, and levels of measurement. In Section III, Chapters 6 and 7 describes strategies for analyzing single variables, also called *univariate analysis*. There are two basic types (or families) of univariate statistics. One tells us about *central tendency* (also known as averages), and the other discusses *dispersion,* such as is examined through frequency distributions. For example, we might want to know the average crime rate in the past months, and whether monthly rates vary a lot or a little. Univariate, descriptive statistics are sometimes also called *summary statistics.*

Chapter 8 discusses descriptive statistics for analyzing two or more variables. For example, we might want to compare the average crime rate among two or more high schools, or want to know whether violence varies by gender or age. The analysis of two variables is also called **bivariate analysis.** The approach described in Chapter 8 uses categorical variables to construct contingency tables (sometimes called cross-tabs), and a combination of categorical and continuous variables to construct pivot tables. Although tables are used widely for analysis, the use of descriptive statistics for analyzing such bivariate relationships has limits; the analysis of contingency tables is revisited and extended in Chapter 9 (Section IV).

The presentation of these chapters reinforces important tasks of analysts engaged in statistics. They must (1) understand the definition and purpose of a statistic, (2) ensure that a statistic is appropriate to the data and problem at hand, (3) understand and evaluate the test assumptions of a statistic, (4) apply the statistic to the problem at hand in ways that are mindful of the above, (5) draw correct conclusions, and (6) communicate results in ways that are appropriate for both professional and general audiences. These tasks are consistent with the competencies identified in Chapter 1.

The philosophy of this book is one of hands-on, computer-based application. The quality of results is only as good as the quality of the data that are used. Remember the expression "garbage in, garbage out?" Prior to analysis, analysts perform a series of tasks to ensure that their data are ready for analysis. Three tasks follow data collection: data coding, data input, and data cleaning, all of which precede data analysis. **Data coding** is the process of preparing data (from pen-and-paper surveys or from electronic or other sources) for input into statistical software programs. For example, analysts may need to decide which variable names and labels will be used to reference specific survey questions, how they will code different responses, and how they will deal with missing values. These are routine but necessary matters in getting the data ready for analysis by statistical software programs.[1]

Data input (also known as data entry) is the activity of recording these data in statistical software programs. This is sometimes a manual process, such as when data must be transcribed from pen-and-paper surveys or published statistical tables into electronic form. More often, this is a process of uploading a data spreadsheet into a statistical software program. This step usually requires some adjustments or recoding, and it requires careful attention to detail to ensure that the uploaded data are as intended. For example, data labels and strings (text, rather than numbers, as well as missing responses and data) must be appropriately recognized and read by the software program, and missing values must be addressed.

Data cleaning is the process of identifying and removing reporting and recording errors. Errors include mistyped values, errors that arise in the process of uploading, and other implausible values that have been recorded. Data cleaning is aided by univariate analysis, and examples are shown in Chapter 7. It is common practice to assume that unexamined data usually contain various errors that must be identified and removed. Without data cleaning, such errors may have a biasing effect on your results.

Data cleaning usually consists of several activities. First, analysts identify implausible values in their data that they then remove or correct. For example, a variable "age" that has a value of "999" certainly requires further investigation. This might be a coding error or it might be that the value is used to indicate a missing value, in which case analysts should ascertain that "999" is defined in their software program as a missing value for this variable. Analysts can examine the highest and lowest values of their variables and ascertain whether they are plausible. Second, analysts ascertain that their dataset is complete and accurate. To this end, the number of observations (records) in the dataset is verified against the number of records in the source (paper or electronic). In addition, a random sample of records in the statistical software is compared against corresponding records in the original data source; analysts will want to ensure that the data in these records match exactly. Analysts might also compare whether statistics (for example, the mean) are identical between variables in the statistical software program and the original data source. When this not the case, problems with variables or groups of observations may be indicated. Only *after* the analyst has determined that the data are complete and free from data-coding and data-entry errors can data analysis proceed further.

Note

1. The workbook that accompanies this text includes a manual with examples for data coding and data input into SPSS or any other statistical software program. The workbook also includes an SPSS user's guide.

CHAPTER

6

Central Tendency

CHAPTER OBJECTIVES

After reading this chapter, you should be able to
- Identify three statistics of central tendency
- Calculate the mean, median, and mode
- Know appropriate uses of the mean, median, or mode
- Address problems of missing data
- Know when and how to weight data
- Estimate measures of central tendency from grouped data

The first family of univariate analysis is ***measures of central tendency,*** which provide information about the most typical or average value of a variable. Although measures of central tendency are popularly referred to as averages, they are in fact three separate measures: the *mean, median,* and *mode.* Analysts frequently use these types of measure when reporting on, for example, high school violence, housing starts, pollution, and the like. Analysts should always indicate which measure is being used.

Chapters 2 and 3 introduced important research concepts. It is worth reviewing these concepts here, because the discussion that follows illustrates their relevance. Succinctly, ***variables*** are key to research and are defined as empirically observable phenomena that vary. High school violence, housing starts, and pollution are examples of empirical phenomena that vary. Management and policy is very much about changing or shaping variables in some way to make society better off—with a bit less high school violence, more affordable housing, less pollution, and so on. ***Attributes*** are defined as the characteristics of a variable, that is, the specific ways in which a variable can vary. For example, high school violence can be measured as being absent, sporadic, occurring from time to time, or ongoing; these are the attributes of the variable "high school violence." Gender has two attributes, namely, "male" and "female," and so on.

A ***scale*** is defined as the collection of specific attributes (or values) used to measure a specific variable. There are *four* levels of measurement scales: *nominal, ordinal, interval,* and *ratio*. Because many statistics require that variables have certain levels of measurement, managers and analysts must be able to determine the level of measurement for their variables. A ***nominal-level scale*** is one that exhibits no ordering among the categories. Gender is a nominal variable: we cannot say that "male" is more than "female" or vice versa. By contrast, an ***ordinal-level scale*** is one that exhibits order among categories but without exact distances between successive categories. Likert scales, which are common on surveys, are examples of ordinal scales. A typical example of a Likert scale is one with the following response categories: Strongly Agree, Agree, Don't Know, Disagree, and Strongly Disagree. Variables with nominal- and ordinal-level scales are referred to as ***categorical variables***.

Interval- and ***ratio***-level variables are those whose scales exhibit both order *and* distance among categories. For example, someone who earns $75,000 per year makes exactly three times that of someone making $25,000. The *only* difference between interval and ratio scales is that the latter have a true "zero" (for example, height can be zero, but IQ cannot). Variables with nominal- and ordinal-level scales are sometimes referred to as ***continuous variables***. *Variables, attributes,* and *measurement scales* are of critical importance in statistics. Readers are encouraged to review the more extensive discussions of these concepts found in Chapters 2 and 3.

THE MEAN

The ***mean*** (or arithmetic mean) is what most people call "the average," but analysts should use the word *mean* to avoid confusion with other types of averages. Mathematically, the mean is defined as *the sum of a series of observations, divided by the number of observations in the series*. The term is commonly used to describe the central tendency of variables, such as the mean number of crimes, public safety inspections, welfare recipients, abortions, roads under repair, and so on. The mean is appropriate for continuous variables. Mean calculations are essential to most analyses and are used in almost every report.

The following example shows how to calculate the mean. Although computers and hand calculators are typically used to calculate the mean, you should also understand how to do so by hand. Assume that a sample of eight observations of variable x has the following values (or data elements): 20, 20, 67, 70, 71, 80, 90, and 225 ($n = 8$). Obviously, variable x is just a name that could refer to anything, such as the level of violence, educational attainment, arrests, test scores, and the like. A series of values (such as 20, 20, 67, . . .) is also called an *array*. For the above values, the mean is calculated as follows:[1]

$$Mean = \sum_i x_i / n =$$
$$(20 + 20 + 67 + 70 + 71 + 80 + 90 + 225)/8 = 643/8 = 80.38.$$

This equation is probably not new to you, though the notation might be. As a second example, the mean of 15, 25, and 50 is [(15 + 25 + 50)/3 =] 30. The notation $\sum_i x_i$ means "the sum of all values of (variable) x," as shown above. In our example, this notation is shorthand for $\sum_{i=1}^{8} x_i$, which specifies adding the first eight values of x, in the order shown. In this example, $x_1 = 20$, $x_2 = 20$, $x_3 = 67$, and so on. Because our variable has only eight values, there is no need for the notation $\sum_{i=1}^{8} x_i$. Also, n is used to indicate that the observations are a sample. If the observations had constituted the entire population, we would have used a different notation: N (or $\sum_i x_i / N$). This is just a matter of notation, which affects neither the definition nor the calculation of the mean.

> **Getting Started**
> Practice calculating the mean using your statistical software program.

Calculating the mean is straightforward, indeed, but managers and analysts may encounter some practical issues that, for the most part, concern the data rather than the formula itself. These concerns are relevant to other statistics, too, and hence illustrate important general matters in statistics. First, variables often have missing data. For example, data may be missing for some clients, about some services, or for some years. We do not like to guess the values of these missing data because it is difficult to credibly justify such guesses. The most common approach is to exclude such observations from calculations; if we do not know x_5, then we generally do not guess it either. The incidental exclusion of a few observations from among many (say, hundreds) will usually not bias results in any material way; indeed, most analyses have a few missing observations. However, bias may occur when the proportion of missing data is large. Then analysts need to acknowledge that an extensive amount of data is missing and will need to add an appropriate caveat to their report. Obviously it is best to avoid using variables that have many missing values.[2]

Second, calculations of means usually result in fractions (for example, "the mean number of arrests is 8.52 per officer"). The presence of fractions implies that distances between categories are measured exactly, hence, that variables are continuous (that is, interval or ratio level). However, analysts frequently have ordinal variables, such as responses to survey questions that are based on a five- or seven-point Likert scale (see Box 3.1). Because fractions are not defined for ordinal scales, analysts should avoid writing, "On average, respondents provide stronger support for item A (3.84) than item B (3.23)." Rather, analysts might write, "On average, respondents provide stronger support for item A than item B. For example, whereas 79.8 percent agree or strongly agree that . . . , only 65.4 percent agree or strongly agree that. . . ." The latter phrasing is also easier for many readers to understand or relate to. Nonetheless, this recommendation is not always followed; fractional reporting of ordinal-level variables is commonplace in analytical reports and data tables.[3]

Third, caution should be used with time series data (discussed in depth in Chapter 15). Briefly, dollar values should typically first be expressed as constant dollars (that is, adjusted for inflation), before applying the formula to calculate the mean. Today's dollars do not have the same purchasing power as yesterday's dollars; thus, they first need to be made comparable. The mean assumes that data elements are measured in the same units, including the same kind of dollars.

Fourth, in some cases the mean can be misleading. For example, suppose that most hospital patients stay either one or five days after some type of surgery. Other patients stay other lengths of time, but these lengths are much less frequent. Then we could say that the most common lengths of stay are one and five days. The mean leads us to a single value (say, maybe about three days), which is a poor measure of central tendency in this case because of the two values that occur most often. Though this is not a common situation, awareness of such possibilities may lead analysts to consider the distribution of variables as well (see Chapter 7) and not rely only on measures of central tendency for summarizing and describing their variables.

Finally, in some cases it may be necessary to use a **weighted mean**, which is defined as a mean for which the observations have been given variable weights. The assignment of weights usually reflects the importance or contribution of each observation relative to other observations. This approach is often taken when measures are based on different population sizes. For example, consider the central tendency of a crime rate of 2.3

percent in city A, with a population of 500,000, and a crime rate of 4.5 percent in city B, with a population of 250,000. Then the mean can be expressed as either [(2.3% + 4.5%)/2 =] 3.4 percent across cities, or as [{(2.3%*500,000) + (4.5%*250,000)}/(500,000 + 250,000) =] 3.0 percent in the region encompassing the populations of cities A and B. The latter is the weighted mean, reflecting the importance of each rate relative to the overall population.[4] Rather than asking which mean is best, it is important to understand the conceptual differences and choose accordingly. Weighted means are also used for adjusting over- and undersampling in surveys. For example, when minorities are undersampled, we might want to weight each of their responses more heavily in order to reflect their actual proportions in the population. Box 6.1 illustrates these calculations. Weighted data can be used to calculate other statistics, too. Each of the eight observations discussed earlier was weighted equally (20 + 20 + 67 + . . .), so using the weighted mean was not necessary.

The issues described here may or may not be germane in every situation. The essential lesson is to be mindful before applying any statistical formula. You need to understand your data and the purposes, definitions, and assumptions of statistical formulas (such as for the mean), and then critically examine summary statistics that result. By taking this approach, you will have increased confidence in the calculated results.

THE MEDIAN

A limitation of the mean is that its usefulness is greatly affected when the data include a few very large or very small values, relative to other values. In the earlier example, if x_8 (the eighth observation in the above sequence, which is 225) had been 950, then the mean for the array would be 171—more than double its initial value! A realistic example of this problem arises when calculating the mean household income in the small hometown of Bill Gates, one of the world's richest people. In that case, the mean is a poor summary statistic of the average household income in that jurisdiction.

The **median** is defined as *the middle value in a series (or array) of values.* Its value is, by definition, unaffected by a few very large or small values. *The median should always be used when a few very large or very small values affect estimates of the mean.* Indeed, most summary income statistics of populations report both means and medians because they can be so different. The median is appropriate for both continuous- and ordinal-level variables. The interpretation of the median is that *half of the observations lie above the median, and the other half lie below it.* To find the median, the data must be ordered from low to high and then the value of the middle observation determined. If the number of observations is uneven, the median is the

In Greater Depth...

Box 6.1   Weighting Your Data

Weighted means are easily calculated. The formula for weighted means is $\sum_i w_i x_i / \sum_i w_i$, which means "identify the weights, then multiply each weight with the value of each observation, then add these values and, finally, divide this number by the sum of all weights. Confused? The following example demonstrates this process:

Value	Weight	Weighted Value
2	0.5	1
2	1.0	2
3	2.0	6
3	2.0	6

The unweighted mean is (10/4) = 2.50, and the weighted mean is (15/5.5) = 2.73. Weighted means have many applications, including in survey research. Nonresponse bias is the bias that occurs because survey samples seldom match the population exactly: nonrespondents might have answered differently from respondents. Perhaps the best approach is to conduct a separate survey of nonrespondents and compare their responses with those of the initial respondents. But this method often is expensive and complicated. A second best approach, then, is to compare weighted responses against the actual responses (called unweighted responses). The weighted responses are those that would have been obtained if the sample distribution had perfectly matched that of known population demographics. Typically, census and other sources provide information about age, race, and gender. Consider the following demographics, reported in the workbook *Exercising Essential Statistics*:

Age	Population(%)	Sample(%)
18–45	62.3	62.8
46–65	24.1	26.8
66+	13.6	10.4

Race	Population(%)	Sample(%)
White	81.5	84.3
Nonwhite	18.5	15.7

(continued)

Box 6.1 *(continued)*

Gender	Population(%)	Sample(%)
Male	49.0	43.9
Female	51.0	56.1

Clearly, residents over 66 years of age are undersampled: their responses should be weighted by (13.6/10.4) = 1.308. Given the above information, the weight assigned to every white female respondent of age 45–65 years is [(81.5/84.3)* (51.0/56.1)*(24.1/26.8)] = 0.790. (A few extra decimal places are given here to avoid introducing bias.) Similarly, weights are assigned for all other groupings. For example, the weight assigned to every non-white male respondent over 66 years is [(18.5/15.7)*(49.0/43.9)*(13.6/10.4)] = 1.720. (While this is a large value, there are few such respondents in the sample.) Then analysts can compare weighted and unweighted responses to determine the extent of nonresponse bias, if any (see workbook). Keep in mind that weighted means are best-guess estimates, and they should not be used instead of survey data.

value of the middle observation. If the number of observations is even, the median is the mean of the two observations that are nearest to the middle location of the array. This location is found through visual inspection or the formula $(n + 1)/2$, where n is the number of observations.

> **Getting Started**
> Find examples of the mean and median in your area.

In our earlier example, variable x has an even (eight) number of observations, which have already been arrayed from low to high. The two middle values are 70 and 71 (at locations 4 and 5); so the median is 70.50 (at location [(8 + 1)/2 =] 4.50). If a ninth observation is added to variable x, for example, $x_9 = 275$, the median becomes 71. Note that these estimates are unaffected by the values of the highest or lowest values. If $x_9 = 875$, the median is still 71, because the value of this variable does not affect the value of the middle observation in the series. Note that having few very large or very small values can also be caused by data entry errors, for example, coding x_8 as 1,225, when it should be 225. This property of the mean is yet another reason for taking data cleaning seriously.

Examples of the median are common in demographic studies of income, in which a few individuals or households typically have very large incomes. Other examples include studies of average jail time served by inmates (some people serve very long sentences!), average wait times for tax returns or class registration, and average jury awards (some people have received huge sums). A rule of thumb is that when the mean and median are considerably different, analysts should report both. For example, the U.S. Census reports both the mean and median incomes of U.S. households; in 1999 these were, respectively, $56,644 and $41,994, which are considerably different. When the mean and median are similar, it suffices to report only the mean. The measure of what constitutes a "considerable difference" is a judgment call informed by the magnitude of the difference and the study's context. Of course, the earlier cautions about missing data, fractional reporting, time series data, and weighted samples apply when calculating medians, too.

Finally, sometimes analysts only have access to already published, tabulated data tables, rather than having the actual observations as the basis for their calculations. Then, the data have already been grouped, such as by age or income categories. Census data often come in this format, for example. The appendix to this chapter describes how to calculate measures of central tendency for data that have already been grouped.

THE MODE

The *mode* is defined as *the most frequent (typical) value(s) of a variable.* The mode is appropriate for all levels of variable measurement. In our example, the mode of variable x is the value 20; it occurs twice in the array. Another example is that the mode of people living in households is two. Perhaps the mode of assaults on school grounds is five annually. The mode is used infrequently, but an advantage of the mode is that it can also be used with *nominal*-level data, which is not possible for calculating the mean and median.[5] However, when the mode is used as a measure of central tendency for nominal-level data, managers frequently turn to *measures of dispersion,* discussed in Chapter 7, to express the frequency with which the mode occurs. For example, a manager who is analyzing choices of clients or respondents among a range of program options (a nominal variable) will state the number or percentage of clients or respondents who most often chose the most popular program option (that is, the mode).

SUMMARY

Descriptive statistics of the average are commonly used by public managers and analysts. After managers and analysts have verified the accuracy of their data, they may wish to calculate measures of central tendency. There are three such measures: the mean, median, and mode. The most commonly used of these measures is the mean, defined as the sum of a series of observations, divided by the number of observations in the series. Weighted means reflect the importance or contribution of each observation relative to other observations or can be used to account for over- or undersampling. Caution should be exercised in using means with ordinal-level variables.

The median is defined as the middle value in a series (or array) of values. The median should always be used when a few very large or very small values affect estimates of the mean. The mode is defined as the most frequent (or typical) value(s) of a variable. Analysts should always indicate which measure is being used, rather than referring to any of these measures simply as the "average."

The mean is appropriate for continuous-level variables, whereas the median is appropriate for both continuous- and ordinal-level variables. The mode is appropriate for all levels of measurement. Managers and analysts should be mindful when variables are missing a great deal of data or involve time series data.

KEY TERMS

(includes bolded terms in the Section III introduction)

Attributes (see also Chapter 3) (p. 100)

Bivariate analysis (see section introduction) (p. 97)

Categorical variables (see also Chapter 3) (p. 100)

Continuous variables (see also Chapter 3) (p. 100)

Data cleaning (see section introduction) (p. 98)

Data coding (see section introduction) (p. 97)

Data input (see section introduction) (p. 97)

Descriptive statistics (see section introduction) (p. 96)

Grouped data (see appendix to this chapter) (p. 108)

Interval-level scales (see also Chapter 3) (p. 100)

Mean (p. 100)

Measures of central tendency (p. 99)

Measures of dispersion (see also Chapter 7) (p. 106)

Median (p. 103)

Mode (p. 106)

Nominal-level scale (see also Chapter 3) (p. 100)

Ordinal-level scale (see also Chapter 3) (p. 100)

Ratio-level scales (see also Chapter 3) (p. 100)

Scale (see also Chapter 3) (p. 100)

Univariate analysis (see section introduction) (p. 96)

Variables (see also Chapter 2) (p. 100)

Weighted mean (p. 102)

APPENDIX

Using Grouped Data

The calculations described in this chapter have assumed that the analyst has data for each observation. This is the assumption used in statistical software programs. However, analysts sometimes have published data only in tabular format, or in a similar format. *Grouped data* refers to observations that have already been grouped in different categories. An example is shown in Table 6.1. The column labeled "Interval of variable *x*" could be almost anything, such as the groupings of city sizes, students' test scores, motorists' speeds through toll booths with electronic collection, or regional water quality ratings. The ranges show the values of each category. Ranges are sometimes shown as footnotes to tables, which then show only categories and frequencies. The "Frequency" column counts occurrences. For example, there are 12 cities in category 1, 5 cities in category 2, and so on. The column *Cumulative frequency* shows the running total of frequencies of each category and may be absent from some grouped data tables.

Calculations of means and medians of grouped data are *best-guess estimates* and should be used *only when individual observations are unavailable.* Unfortunately, few computer programs can read tabular formats of grouped data, in which case calculations must be done by hand. *Note that your ability to make these calculations will not affect your understanding of other material in this book.*

The *mean of grouped data* is calculated in two steps. First, the mean of the categories is calculated using the formula $\sum_i w_i r_i / \sum_i w_i$, where r is the row number and w is the number of observations in each row. Applying the data shown in Table 6.1, we find that the weighted mean of categories is $[\{(12*1) + (5*2) + (18*3) + (36*4) + (14*5)\}/(12 + 5 + 18 + 36 + 14) = 290/85 =]$ 3.412.[6]

Second, the *variable value* associated with this group mean value is determined. This requires interpolation in the following manner: The mean of the grouped data, 3.412, lies somewhere between categories 3 and 4. The

Table 6.1 ——— Illustration of Grouped Data

Category	Interval of variable *x*	Frequency	Cumulative frequency
1	1–5	12	12
2	6–10	5	17
3	11–15	18	35
4	16–20	36	71
5	21–25	14	85

estimate of the average variable value associated with category 3 is defined as the midpoint of its range, or [(11 + 15)/2 =] 13, and the midpoint of the value associated with category 4 is [(16 + 20)/2 =] 18. Then the variable value associated with the category location of 3.412 (which is 3.000 + 0.412) is defined as the midpoint estimate of the range associated with category 3 (that is, 13) *plus* 0.412 of the difference of these category midpoints, or [18 – 13 =] 5. Hence, the estimated value of the variable mean is [13 + (0.412*5) =] 15.06 (with rounding). An equivalent expression is that 3.412 "lies 41.2 percent from category 3 toward category 4," which is shown graphically below:

Variable value:	13	← 2.06 → |	18
Category value:	3	3.412	4

The *median of grouped data* is estimated in an analogous way. The sample has a total of 85 observations; the median is defined by the value of the forty-third [(85 + 1)/2] observation when values are ordered. Examining the cumulative frequencies, we find that the median falls somewhere between the third and fourth categories:

Variable frequency:	12	17	35	43	71	85
Category value:	1	2	3 ← 0.222 → |		4	5

The value of the forty-third observation lies [(43 – 35)/(71 – 35) =] 0.222 from category 3 toward category 4, with a category value of 3.222. Using the same method of interpolation described for the group mean, we calculate the corresponding variable value of category location 3.222 as [13 + 0.222*(18 – 13) =] 14.11. Note the difference between the estimated group mean and median. The linear interpolation used for calculating grouped means and medians assumes defined distances between categories, hence, a continuous level of variable measurement.

The *mode of the grouped data* is the most frequent observation. This is category 4, which has a midpoint value of 18. The mode of these grouped data is thus 18.

Notes

1. Additional examples can be found in the workbook. Also, as a matter of nomenclature, we distinguish between attributes (introduced in Chapter 2) and values. The term *value* refers to the actual, observed responses or

measures of a variable, whereas *attributes* refers to the range of values that a variable can have. For example, the variable "gender" has three attributes (male, female, and unknown), even if none of the respondents state that they are male. A variable has as many values as observations, and as many attributes as the different values that a variable *can* have. However, when these terms are used synonymously, confusion can result.

2. On surveys, missing data may indicate a problem with how the question was phrased, indicating a problem with survey validity.

3. Some analysts feel that the mean should not be used with ordinal-level variables, but it does provide useful information. However, the mean is especially inappropriate for nominal-level variables. For example, we cannot say that the average region is 2.45, on a scale of 1 = Northeast, 2 = South, 3 = Midwest, and 4 = West. When working with nominal variables, we should describe response frequencies, such as "23.7 percent of employees live in the Northeast, 19.8 percent live in the West," and so on.

4. We can also express the formula in the text as $(2.3*0.67 + 4.5*0.33) = 3.0$.

5. The mode might be useful in the following instance: Consider the number of violent incidents in which all high school students are involved. The mode may well be 0, and the mean 0.2, for example. If only those who have experienced an incident are included, then the mode might be 2 and the mean 4.2, for example. In this case, the mode is used as a precursor to a better understanding of the distribution of the data.

6. Often, we report values to two decimal places, by default. However, on occasion we may wish to report values to more or fewer decimal places. Here, we report the result to three decimal places to avoid rounding errors that would become evident in the next paragraph.

CHAPTER

7

Measures of Dispersion

CHAPTER OBJECTIVES

After reading this chapter, you should be able to

- Make frequency distributions and report results
- Distinguish between a histogram and a stem-and-leaf plot
- Create line charts, pie charts and other visual aids
- Use boxplots for data cleaning
- Identify and address problems of outliers
- Understand the normal curve and standard deviation

This chapter examines *measures of dispersion*, which provide information about how the values of a variable are distributed. These measures are the second family of univariate statistics (the first family is *measures of central tendency*, as discussed in Chapter 6). A common measure of dispersion in public and nonprofit management is the frequency distribution. Knowing what percentage of clients or employees score above a specific value is often a prelude to decision making. Such frequency distributions can then be used to make comparisons or create rankings. Frequency distributions often are reported in tabular form, but they are also the basis of many graphs—such as bar charts, pie charts, and line graphs used in presentations.

Measures of dispersion are also used in preliminary data analysis, such as for data cleaning and for generating a first understanding of one's data. The boxplot is a useful tool for data cleaning and is used in this chapter to discuss outliers (that is, unusually large or small values). Analysts need to know how to identify and deal with outliers. An interesting paradox is that knowing the mean or median often invites further questions about the distribution of variables (calling for the use of measures of dispersion), but preliminary analysis of variables' distribution often precedes the analysis of central tendency to ensure that data are clean and appropriate. As a result, analysts commonly first use boxplots for data cleaning, then analyze means and medians, and then examine frequency distributions. This is an important sequence to remember.

This chapter also provides an introduction to the normal distribution, which is relevant for continuous variables. Many continuous variables, such as height and IQ, are normally distributed. Such variables have certain characteristics and terminology with which managers and analysts need to be familiar. In addition, many of the statistical tests discussed in later chapters assume that continuous variables are normally distributed. Those chapters also describe tests for examining this assumption and strategies for dealing with situations when this assumption is not met.

FREQUENCY DISTRIBUTIONS

Frequency distributions describe the range and frequency of a variable's values. They are easy to create and understand, and they often are a prelude to generating data tables and attractive graphics. First we discuss frequency distributions for categorical (nominal or ordinal) variables, and then we look at frequency distributions for continuous variables.

The categories of ordinal or nominal variables often are used in frequency distributions. For example, if a variable is measured on a five-point Likert scale, then we can count, or determine the frequency of, the data elements for each category. Table 7.1 shows a common type of typical frequency distribution; it gives the number of respondents and the frequency of responses (as a percentage) for each item in an employee survey.[1] For example, 81.3 percent [22.8% + 58.5%] of the 969 respondents who answered this question agree or strongly agree that they are satisfied with their job. Likewise, percentages can be determined for other items, and comparisons made across items, too. For example, more respondents agree or strongly agree that they are satisfied with their jobs than agree or strongly agree that each individual is treated with dignity (81.3% versus 42.3%). Frequency distributions are often found in the main bodies of reports and

Table 7.1 ——————〜〜〜—— Frequency Distribution: Employee Survey

Statement	Mean[a]	Strongly agree (%)	Agree (%)	Don't know (%)	Disagree (%)	Strongly disagree (%)	n
I am satisfied with my job at Seminole County	3.88	22.8	58.5	5.5	10.7	2.5	969
Seminole County is a good place to work compared with other organizations	3.64	15.4	53.6	14.1	13.1	3.8	969
Each individual is treated with dignity	3.02	8.1	34.2	18.6	29.6	9.5	967

[a] 5 = Strongly agree; 4 = Agree; 3 = Don't know; 2 = Disagree; 1 = Strongly disagree.

sometimes are used in the statistical appendices of reports, showing the distributions of all survey items.

Table 7.1 also shows the number of observations for each item (n). Because of incidental missing responses, this number may be different for each item. If all items have the same number of observations, then this number can be reported just once, such as at the top or bottom of a table. Table 7.1 also shows the mean of each response. Frequency distribution tables commonly include mean item responses, and this additional information is sometimes used for ordering (ranking) the items, based on their mean responses. Of course, items can also be ordered on the basis of those who agree or strongly agree with an item. Either approach results in the same ordering of the three items in Table 2.2.[2]

Frequency distributions are readily calculated by statistical software programs. However, when variables are continuous, analysts will have to construct their own categories, because otherwise the frequency distribution will likely have a large number of frequency table categories with just one or a few observations. A practical question is how wide each category should be. Although no hard-and-fast rules exist, analysts should avoid recoding in ways that mislead. To avoid perceptions of lying with statistics, a rule of thumb is that categories should be based on *category ranges of equal length,* unless compelling reasons exist that are clearly explained in the text of the report.[3]

Many computer programs produce **stem-and-leaf plots**, which assist in category construction.[4] These plots seldom appear in final reports; rather they are tools that aid in analysis, and analysts should know how to read

Figure 7.1 ───────〜〜〜─Stem-and-Leaf Plot

```
00   23589
01   0012344589
02   1123367
03   01134456889
04   00111223445567889
05   011233455568899
06   12223444445566778999
07   001235556899
08   01112234444
09   112334556
10   00233
11   035
```

them. Stem-and-leaf plots show the frequency distribution of continuous variables. The categories are computer generated, based on the values of observations. The stem-and-leaf plot shown in Figure 7.1 was generated for a continuous variable that has 124 observations. In a stem-and-leaf plot, these observations are shown ordered from low to high. The left column is called the stem, and the right column is called the leaves. The values are found by combining each stem with its leaves: the stem is composed of the first figures of any number, and the leaves are the figures added onto it. In this case, the lowest number of the series is 002 followed by 003, 005, 008, 009, 010, 010, 011, 012, and 013, and so on. The five highest values are 103, 103, 110, 113, and 115. The median value is at location [(124 + 1)/2 =] 62.50, and is 058 (the sixty-second and sixty-third values, starting from lowest value 002 and counting forward, are both 58). Based on Figure 7.1, an analyst might decide to construct following four categories, of equal width: 0–29, 30–59, 60–89, and 90–120. Or perhaps more categories might be created, such as in widths of 10: 0–9, 10–19, 20–29, 30–39, and so on. Once an analyst decides which category widths he or she wants to use for recoding, statistical software programs contain procedures for recoding the data values.

Frequencies can also be shown in a *histogram*, as shown in Figure 7.2. A histogram is similar to a stem-and-leaf plot but differs in that it shows the number of observations in each category. Unlike stem-and-leaf plots, histograms are commonly seen in reports. A histogram is useful because it provides a quick visual representation of the extent and nature of dispersion. Unlike the stem-and-leaf plot, a histogram allows the analyst to see how many observations are present in each category, although it does not show the value of each observation; many analysts use histograms rather than stem-and-leaf plots. Software programs often automatically generate category

Figure 7.2 ⎯⎯⎯⎯⎯⎯⟋⟍⟋⟍⎯ Histogram

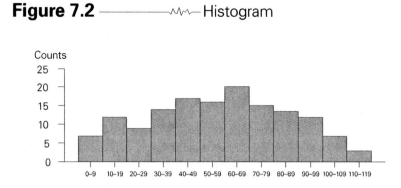

widths (shown in Figure 7.2 in increments of 10, the default used by SPSS for these data), but software users can also define these widths.[5]

Frequency distributions are a staple of analysis. Managers and analysts need to be able to describe them in plain terms that are readily understood by a broad audience. It's not a bad idea to practice making them until you are comfortable doing so. This matter is discussed in Box 7.1.

Graphical displays often aid in highlighting key results. Tables of frequency distributions, like the one shown in Table 7.1, can be used as the basis of displays that highlight important conclusions. Statistical software programs readily generate these graphs, which can be copied into other programs for further editing and word processing. Managers and analysts need to know how to create attractive graphical displays for their reports and presentations. *Bar charts* are graphs that show the frequency of occurrences through stacks (Figure 7.3); they are used with categorical data. Bar chart A shows options for three-dimensional effects and shading. Bar chart B is also called a Pareto chart, an ordering of categories according to their frequency or importance. This is a visually useful way of drawing attention to that which is important, as well as to the unimportance of other categories that, cumulatively, add very little to our understanding of the problem. Sources 5 through 7 seem barely worth debating. As a convention, bar charts are used with categorical variables, and the bars in such charts should not touch each other. Histograms are used with interval- and ratio-level variables, and their bars should touch each other, suggesting that these data are continuous (see Figure 7.2).

Pie charts typically are used to focus on equality: who gets the most (or the least) of what? Pie charts are used with categorical (often nominal) data, and they can be shown in various ways; Figure 7.3 shows a pie chart with a slice that has been pulled out. *Line charts* are used with continuous data,

In Greater Depth...

Box 7.1   Writing It Up . . .

Effective communication of statistical findings is very important. People expect results to be written in a professional manner; otherwise, statistical analysis may well fall on deaf ears. New analysts often want and need to know how to write up their results.

In one sense, writing up statistical results is no different from any other writing. First, you need to know what you *want to say*. Second, you need to know what you *need to say about what you want to say*. Finally, you need to know *how to say it*. Regarding the first point, what you want to say often is either the result of an analysis or an argument that you wish to back up with statistical analysis. For example, you might want to inform an argument about education policy with an analysis of educational attainment. With a histogram or frequency distribution, you probably want to say something about the percentage of observations in one or more categories.

Second, people need to know that your conclusions are based on valid data and analysis. Thus, you will need to tell them what data you used, how they were collected, what they can be used for, and any known shortcomings. You also need to briefly state your analytical methods and show through your analysis that you are conversant with any issues or limitations that are pertinent to specific methods. Sometimes variables can be constructed or analyzed in different ways, and you might want to present a range of possible answers. In the case of a histogram or frequency distribution, in addition to matters of data validity, you might note if a large number of values were missing or if different ways of constructing categories might have led to different interpretations.

Third, you need to know how to say things. Generally you should state the facts as they are. It suffices to say, for example, that "53.4 percent of respondents disagree or strongly disagree with. . . ." Leave interpretations to the conclusion and discussion sections, where they should be clearly noted as such. As suggested in Box 3.2, it is useful to find several examples of write-ups that you like and then try to adapt the specific language to your needs. Then double-check the language to ensure that it is professional (using third person, present tense, and active voice) and that the report looks professional, too.

Figure 7.3 ———————⋏⋏⋏—Graphical Displays

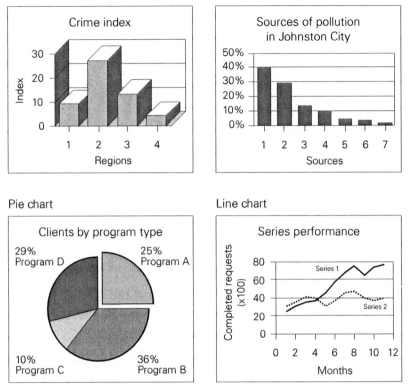

partly to avoid displaying a very large number of bars. In Figure 7.3 the lines show averaged occurrences each month. In this figure, two variables are shown in a way that highlights important trend differences.

Visual representation is important for analysis and in the communication of study findings to a broader audience. Graphs and charts help draw out differences and inform analytical decisions about differences that matter. For audiences, graphs and charts succinctly summarize and communicate study conclusions, and demonstrate visually why they matter. Analysts are increasingly expected to use visual representations in their reports and oral presentations; they are typically an important and essential part of PowerPoint presentations.

Getting Started

Practice making a frequency distribution and a bar chart with data in your area.

BOXPLOTS

A *boxplot* is a graphical device that shows various measures of dispersion. Boxplots are useful for obtaining a quick, visual, preliminary understanding of data. They assist analysts with their data cleaning and are seldom found in final reports. The boxplot is a quick and nicely visual tool, and computer programs readily provide boxplots for any number of variables. Though analysts also use other tools for their data cleaning, the boxplot offers much useful information, such as identifying outliers, which, for example, histograms or frequency distributions do not. Boxplots are appropriate for both continuous- and ordinal-level variables. The following calculations are shown only for purposes of conceptual understanding, given that software programs typically calculate the following values. We use the same array as in Chapter 6, namely, 20, 20, 67, 70, 71, 80, 90, and 225.

Boxplots show statistics that are calculated on the basis of the location of data, such as the median. Figure 7.4 shows the boxplot for our example array. Because our example has eight observations, the median is defined as the value at location $[(n + 1)/2 =]$ 4.50 (see Chapter 6), that is, the mean of the values of the fourth and fifth observations, when all observations are ordered from the lowest to the highest values. This value is 70.50. The *first quartile* is simply the lowest quartile score (*it is not a range*). That location is defined as half the location of the median, hence, $[4.50/2 =]$ 2.25. The variable value associated with this location (2.25) is defined as the value of the second observation plus one-quarter of the distance between the second and third observations. In our example, that value is calculated as $[20 + 0.25^*(67 - 20) =]$ 31.75. The *third quartile* is the third quartile score, or location $[4.50 + 2.25 =]$ 6.75. The value is $[80 + 0.75^*(90 - 80) =]$ 87.50. Most computer programs also produce a statistic called the *midspread* (or *interquartile range*, IQR). The midspread is defined as the difference between the first quartile and the third quartile, hence, $[87.50 - 31.75 =]$ 55.75. The *range* is simply the difference between the highest and lowest values, or $[225 - 20 =]$ 205. Again, even though statistical software programs will calculate these values, you need to have a clear understanding of what these concepts mean.

The boxplot also shows a singular observation with a value of 225 that is labeled "outlier." As mentioned at the beginning of this chapter, *outliers* are extremes, or analyst-defined observations with unusual values relative to other values in the data. Outliers may be the result of data-coding errors (which should be either fixed or removed), or they may reflect actual but unusual values in the sample. Such outliers matter because many public decisions are based on average behavior, rather than the unusual behavior of a few.[6] Thus, it makes good sense to distinguish *usual observations from unusual ones*. An important task of data cleaning and preliminary analysis is to iden-

Figure 7.4 ────────〰〰── Boxplot

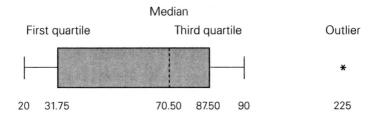

tify outliers and to decide whether they should be retained. Our position is that observations flagged as outliers generally should be retained when they are not coding errors, when they are plausible values of the variable in question, and when they do not greatly affect the value of the mean (of continuous variables). However, when outliers are present, their effect on final results should be studied. Analysts should also report any observations (outliers) that have been dropped from the analysis, along with reasons for doing so.

Boxplots also help analysts to calculate cut-off points beyond which any observations are statistically considered as outliers. These cut-off points are called, respectively, the inner and outer fences. The ***inner fence*** is an imaginary value that lies 1.5 times the midspread *below* the first quartile. For the data in our example, the inner fence is [31.75 − (1.5*55.75) =] −51.88. All of our data are greater than the value of the inner fence; thus, our data show no outliers on this lower end. The ***outer fence*** is an imaginary value that lies 1.5 times the midspread *above* the third quartile. It is calculated as [87.5 + (1.5*55.75) =] 171.13. Our data has one observation that exceeds this value, $x_8 = 225$, which is therefore labeled an outlier.[7] Analysts might consider omitting x_8 from further analysis. Doing so greatly affects the mean, reducing it from 80.38 to 59.71. As expected, omitting x_8 does not much change the median, which goes from 70.5 to 70.0; the loss of the observation merely redefines the location of the middle observation. As discussed earlier, the decision to drop an observation from analysis should be based on argument. If the observation is deemed to be representative of the population from which it is drawn, then it should be retained. If it is thought to be unrepresentative, then it should be excluded. Whatever the decision (retention or deletion), the case must be argued and its impact on further analysis noted.

The boxplot further shows two ***whiskers*** extending out from the first and third quartiles. The end points of these whiskers are *the lowest and highest values of the variables that are not outliers.* These values differ from the lowest and highest values of the data only when there are outliers. Together with the box (shown as the "area" between the first and third quartiles), these whiskers give analysts a quick visual image of the spread of the data. If the whiskers and box are relatively short, then the variable varies little in the sample. If the whiskers and box are long, there is more variation to talk about.

In short, boxplots are a great tool for preliminary data analysis and are easily produced by computer. They help identify outliers and provide valuable information about the distribution. Imagine the analyst who rushes head-long into producing detailed tables and reports, only to redo this work after outliers (and perhaps other problems, too) have been discovered in the data!

STANDARD DEVIATION

When variables are continuous, the question "How widely are the data dispersed around the mean?" is especially salient because continuous vari-ables often have a large number of values that can be narrowly or (very) widely dispersed. By contrast, many ordinal-level variables have only a few different data values (for example, a five-point Likert scale) and thus may have a limited range. The *normal distribution* refers to the distribution of a variable that resembles a bell-shaped curve (Figure 7.5). The left and right sides of the curve mirror each other; they are symmetrical. Many variables are normally distributed, such as student scores, IQ scores, average crop yields, or counts of lightning flashes over time. However, in practice, almost no data are *exactly* normally distributed. Many analysts rely on *visual inspec-tion* to determine distribution, supplemented with the statistics described in this section and in subsequent chapters. The sample data are not expected to match a theoretical bell-shaped curve perfectly because, given that they represent a sample, deviations due to chance selection should be expected.[8]

The *standard deviation* is a measure of dispersion that is calculated based on the values of the data. The standard deviation has the desirable property that, when the data are normally distributed, 68.3 percent of the observations lie within ±1 standard deviation from the mean, and 95.4

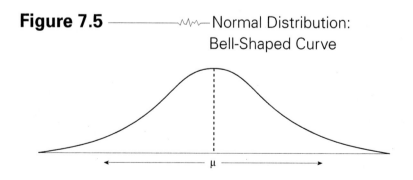

Figure 7.5 ———⋀⋀⋀— Normal Distribution: Bell-Shaped Curve

Figure 7.6———————Small and Large
Standard Deviation

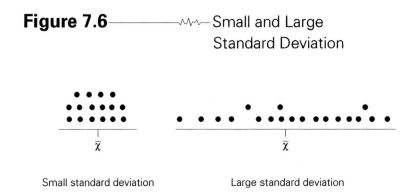

| Small standard deviation | Large standard deviation |

percent lie ±2 standard deviations from the mean, 99.7 percent lie ±3 standard deviations from the mean. A key qualifier of the following discussion is that it applies only *when the data are normally distributed*. Although you can use computer programs to calculate the standard deviation, for explanatory purposes we note that the *standard deviation* is defined as[9]

$$ s = \sqrt{\frac{\sum (x_i - \bar{x})^2}{n-1}} $$

Thus, when an observation lies far from its mean, $(x_i - \bar{x})^2$ is large, and when an observation lies close to the mean, $(x_i - \bar{x})^2$ is small. Likewise, when *most* observations are scattered widely around the mean, $\sum (x_i - \bar{x})^2$ is large, and when *most* observations are scattered narrowly around the mean, $\sum (x_i - \bar{x})^2$ is small. Thus, data that are widely spread around the mean will have a larger standard deviation than data that are closely clustered around the mean. This is shown in Figure 7.6.[10] Computer programs also calculate s^2, called the *variance* of a variable. However, this measure has no particularly important properties and is provided as information only.[11]

For the data shown in the stem-and-leaf plot (see Figure 7.1), the computer will calculate that the mean is 56.39 and the standard deviation is 27.43. Thus, when the data are normally distributed, about two-thirds of the observations will lie between 28.96 and 83.82. About 95 percent lie between the values of 1.53 and 111.25.

The distributional properties of the standard deviation can also be used to determine what percentage of values lie above or below a given value. For example, what is the percentage of caseloads in which female welfare clients have more than 2.6 children, if the mean number of children in such caseloads is 2.20, the standard deviation is 0.44, and the variable is normally

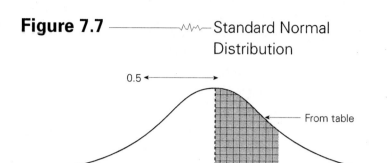

Figure 7.7 ⎯⎯⎯⎯⎯⎯ Standard Normal Distribution

distributed? To answer such questions, we need to compare our values against a table showing such percentages for the standard normal curve, which is defined as a normal distribution that has a mean of 0 and a standard deviation of 1. Appendix A shows values for areas under the standardized normal distribution. Shown also in Figure 7.7, the area under this curve is 1.00, which means that an observation has a probability of 1.00 of being somewhere under the curve.[12] Note that the areas to the left and right of the midpoint ($z = 0$) are both 0.50, as the curve is symmetrical. All data can be standardized by using the formula $z = (x_i - \bar{x})/s$, and the resulting values are called **z-scores** (or standardized values). Variables whose values have been standardized are called **standardized variables**, and computers can readily calculate them.

For any given z-score, the question is what percentage of observations have values greater or smaller than it. We plug the above information into the z-score formula and find a standardize value of [(2.60 − 2.20)/0.44 =] 0.91. Appendix A shows areas to the left of the midpoint; for $z = 0.91$, that area is shown as 0.3186. Thus, 81.86 percent [50% + 31.86%] of cases have a value less than the value that gave rise to this z-score (2.60), and 1 minus 0.8186, or 18.14 percent, have a larger value. Note that negative z-scores indicate a probability less than 0.50. For example, the z-score of caseloads with 1.65 children among female welfare clients in the same sample is [(1.65 − 2.20)/0.44 =] −1.25. The area associated with 1.25 in Appendix A is 0.3944 (only positive values are shown), but negative z-score values indicate areas to the left of the mean, and so [0.5 − 0.3944 =] 10.56 percent of caseloads have fewer than 1.65 children, and [0.5 + 0.3944 =] 89.44 percent of caseloads have more than 1.65 children.

The standard deviation is also used to identify outliers in normally distributed variables. When variables are normally distributed, values that lie more than ±3 standard deviations from the mean are often considered outliers. Thus, for the data of Figure 7.1, values greater than [56.39 +

(3*27.3) =] 138.68 or smaller than [56.39 – (3*27.3) =] –25.90 would be considered outliers. No such values are present in Figure 7.1. Of course, outliers can also be identified using boxplots (see the earlier section on boxplots as a method for dealing with outliers).[13]

The standard deviation is also used to calculate the **confidence interval**, defined as the range within which a statistic is expected to fall on repeated sampling. This is also used to estimate population means from samples. Random samples are often used to estimate population characteristics (see Section II), and statisticians have long worked on the problem that different random samples will yield somewhat different results. A confidence interval also expresses how certain we can be that the real, but unknown population parameter falls within an interval. By convention, the term *parameter* refers to a population characteristic, whereas *statistic* refers to a sample characteristic.

The formula for calculating a 95 percent confidence interval of the mean (that is, the range within which the mean will fall in 95 of 100 samples) is $\bar{x} \pm 1.96*s / \sqrt{n}$. The measure, $s / \sqrt{n}$, is also called the *standard error of the mean*. The value 1.96 is the z-value corresponding with 95 percent of the area under the standard normal distribution (0.475 on both sides) in Appendix A, and is discussed more fully in Section IV. For the data in Figure 7.1, using this formula, we expect the population mean to lie between [56.39 ± (1.96*27.43) / $\sqrt{124}$ =] 51.56 and 61.22. The formula for calculating a 99 percent confidence interval is $\bar{x} \pm [(2.58*s) s / \sqrt{n}$. See Box 7.2 for further information about confidence intervals.

The above formula has considerable utility for managers and analysts. It provides a measure of how accurate the estimate of the mean is without having to consider or draw other samples; it is based only on the single sample at hand. It also prevents the manager and analyst from having to stake his or her conclusions on a single number, such as 56.39. If the mean of data taken from some other sample or data in the next period is, say, 52.59, this value would still within the realm of current findings.

Getting Started
Identify uses of the standard deviation in your area of interest, and verify calculations in the text on a computer.

Finally, computers also calculate two measures that assist in determining whether data are normally distributed. These measures are used in conjunction with visual inspection efforts. **Skewness** is a measure of whether the peak is centered in the middle of the distribution. A positive value indicates that the peak is "off" to the left, and a negative value suggests that it is off to the right. **Kurtosis** is a measure of the extent to which data are concentrated in the peak versus the tail. A positive value indicates that data are concentrated in the peak; a negative value indicates that data are concentrated in the tail (giving the curve a "fat tail"). Values of skewness and kurtosis have little inherent meaning, other

In Greater Depth...

Box 7.2   Confidence Intervals

Pollsters typically use the term *sampling error* to indicate a 95 percent confidence interval. Thus, if survey results report that 79.5 percent of program clients are satisfied with a program, with a sampling error of, say, 3 percent, then the analyst is stating that he or she is 95 percent certain that between 76.5 percent and 82.5 percent of all clients are satisfied with the program. The probability of the estimate falling within the confidence interval, here 95 percent, is also called the *confidence level*.

The formula for calculating the 95 percent confidence interval for a *proportion*, *p*, such as from *categorical* variables, and based on a large sample ($n > 100$), is as follows:

$$p \pm 1.96^* \sqrt{[p(1-p)/n]}.$$

Sampling errors, such as those shown in Table 5.2, are usually calculated for $p = .500$, which produces the largest possible confidence interval. For example, the 95 percent confidence interval for $n = 124$ and $p = .500$ is $.5 \pm .088$, and for $p = .795$, it is $.795 \pm .071$.

The formula for calculating confidence intervals in small samples ($n < 100$) of continuous and normally distributed variables is analogous, but it uses the so-called "t-distribution" (discussed further in Chapter 11) to determine the constant. Appendix C shows that this value for a 95 percent confidence interval increases from 1.96 for a large sample to 2.086 for $n = 20$. For our sample, with mean $= 56.39$ and $s = 27.43$, we can be 95 percent certain that the population mean lies between $56.39 \pm [2.086^*(27.43 / \sqrt{20})] = 43.60$ and 69.18. This larger interval than that shown in the text, or $n = 124$, reflects less certainty in our estimates because we have fewer observations. The theoretical underpinnings of confidence intervals involve inference and hypothesis testing (see Section IV).[14]

than that large values indicate greater asymmetry. A rule of thumb is that the ratio (absolute value) of skewness to its standard error, and of kurtosis to its standard error, should be less than two (these statistics are calculated by the computer). Large ratios indicate departure from symmetry. The respective ratios of skewness and kurtosis of our data, as calculated by the computer, are | –0.06/0.22 | and | –0.73/0.43 |, which are both well below 2.0. Thus, our data are well centered; the tail is a little fat but not enough to cause us to worry about the normality of our data.[15]

Many computer programs can also superimpose a curve over a histogram to help tell analysts if their data are normally distributed. If this curve looks close to a perfect bell-shaped curve, the data are considered normally distributed. Many statistical tests discussed in Chapter 11 and beyond assume that variables are normally distributed; we return to this important matter in subsequent chapters.

SUMMARY

Measures of dispersion provide important information about the distribution of a variable's values, and they also help with data cleaning. Frequency distributions show the percentage of observations (for example, clients or employees) that score in or above a certain category. Frequency distributions often are reported in tabular form, and are very common in reports. They are also used to generate graphs that are used in reports and presentations; such graphs are essential in helping analysts to communicate their findings to a broader audience.

The boxplot is a useful tool for data cleaning. In particular, it helps to detect outliers, or extreme values. Outliers generally should be retained when they are not coding errors, when they are plausible values of the variable in question, and when they do not greatly affect the value of the mean. Analysts commonly first use boxplots for data cleaning, then analyze means and medians, and finally examine frequency distributions.

Finally, this chapter also examines the normal distribution. Many variables are normally distributed. When variables are normally distributed, the standard deviation is a measure of the spread of the data value around the mean, and confidence intervals can be calculated that express the range within which a statistic is expected to fall. Such information provides an appropriate sense of the accuracy of calculated means.

KEY TERMS

Bar charts (p. 115)

Boxplot (p. 118)

Confidence interval (p. 123)

First quartile (p. 118)

Frequency distributions (p. 112)

Histogram (p. 114)

Inner fence (p. 119)

Interquartile range (p. 118)

Kurtosis (p. 123)

Line charts (p. 115)

Measures of dispersion (p. 111)

Midspread (p. 118)

Normal distribution (p. 120)

Outer fence (p. 119)

Outliers (p. 118)

Pie charts (p. 115)

Range (p. 118)

Skewness (p. 123)

Standard deviation (p. 120)

Standardized variables (p. 122)

Stem-and-leaf plots (p. 113)

Third quartile (p. 118)

Whiskers (p. 119)

Z-scores (p. 122)

Notes

1. These data are from the Employees Attitudes dataset, which can be found on the CD that accompanies the workbook, *Exercising Essential Statistics.*

2. Both approaches are found in practice. As noted in Chapter 6, analysts should be mindful that fractional values (means) are not defined for ordinal variables. The write-up should report the percentages of data values in relevant categories.

3. Table 6.1 (see appendix to Chapter 6) shows how data for a continuous variable might be recoded into five categories. For example, categories for the data in Table 6.1 could have been created with unequal intervals (such as category 1 with range 1–14, category 2 with range 15–17, and category 3 with range 18–25) that would lead to a different conclusion.

4. For example, in SPSS, stem-and-leaf plots are produced by the "Explore" routine (Analyze → Descriptive Statistics → Explore).

5. In SPSS, category widths are often defined after the default histogram is generated; the editing options allow category widths (called "bin sizes") to be changed.

6. For example, decisions about educational programs are based on the mean attainment of students in those programs, expressed as "on average, enrolled students improved their XYZ ability by x percent more than students who did not enroll in the programs." Of course, irregular behavior draws attention in its own right, and public laws are often passed to address that. In addition, a lot can be learned from case studies of infrequent behavior.

7. Some computer programs, including SPSS, distinguish between outliers and extreme values. Then, outliers are defined as observations that lie 1.5 times the midspread from the first and third quartiles, whereas extreme values are observations that lie 3 times the midspread from the first and third quartiles.

8. But if the sample is consistent with a bell-shaped curve and if we had an infinite number of drawings, the sample would eventually look normal. This matter is taken up in Chapter 11.

9. To calculate the standard deviation for a population, divide by N.

10. Standard deviations can also be calculated from grouped data, Chapter 6 (Appendix), using the following revised formula:

$$s = \sqrt{\frac{\sum w_i(\bar{x}_i - \bar{x})^2}{n-1}}$$

where the i's indicate the group categories. Consider an example. Referring to the data in Table 6.1, we first calculate the estimated group means of each category and then subtract these values from the previously calculated group mean. The estimated category means are 3, 8, 13, 18, and 23, respectively. Subtracting the value of the overall mean of 15.1, we get −12.1, −7.1, −2.1, 2.9, and 7.9. Then we take the squared difference of each, which is 146.4, 50.4, 4.4, 8.4, and 62.4, and weight each of these values by the number of observations in each category. Thus, the value for the first category is [12*146.4 =] 1,756.8, and subsequent values are 252.0, 79.2, 302.4, and 873.6. We add these numbers, get 3,264, and divide by 85, which is 38.4, and then take the square root, which is 6.2.

11. However, in Chapter 12 we will see that *variance* is used to explain the amount of variation in a variable.

12. A curve in which the area is 1.00 is also called a *density curve*.

13. Because boxplots do not assume variables to be normally distributed, they have broader use as a tool for data cleaning. However, boxplots cannot be used for constructing confidence intervals, and so both tools have their place.

14. Standard deviations also underlie the development of control charts, which are used in assessing production and service delivery processes. Control charts help managers determine the likelihood that unusually high or low performance is caused by chance. The upper and lower critical limits of control charts are defined as $UCL = \bar{x} + 3(s / \sqrt{n})$ and $LCL = \bar{x} - 3(s / \sqrt{n})$:

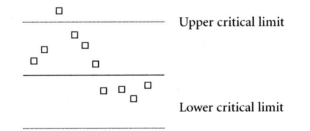

15. Another rule of thumb is that both of the following measures should be less than ±1.96: *skewness*/$\sqrt{6/n}$ and *kurtosis*/$\sqrt{24/n}$. In our case, the respective values are −0.27 and 1.66.

CHAPTER

8

Contingency Tables

CHAPTER OBJECTIVES

After reading this chapter, you should be able to
- Create, interpret, and analyze contingency tables
- Understand the concept of a statistical relationship
- Discuss relationships in contingency tables
- Explain how pivot tables differ from contingency tables
- Generate pivot tables
- Transpose variables in pivot tables

   After individual variables have been analyzed and results reported, analysts often turn to questions about relationships between variables. The study of relationships between two variables is called *bivariate statistics.* Some of these relationships aim at a better understanding of the effectiveness of programs and policies, whereas others help illuminate conditions under which programs and policies operate. For example, we might want to know whether participation in a teen anger management program is associated with lower rates of high school violence. If we have data on both variables, then we can examine the nature of the relationships between them.

Similarly, we might examine whether participation in a teen pregnancy prevention program is associated with lower teen pregnancy rates. Gathering empirical information about relationships is a key step in determining program effectiveness.

We can also look at relationships across cities, rather than using program-level data. For example, we can ask whether average incomes are associated with different health problems, such as diabetes, hypertension, and HIV/AIDS. We can also use relationships to better understand characteristics of populations with which managers work. For example, if data are available on the economic status of program clients (such as annual household income or participation in food stamp programs), and also on their health conditions (such as hypertension or diabetes), then we can study quantitatively whether, for example, such diseases are more prevalent among clients with lower incomes. An understanding of this relationship may affect how programs are delivered, for example, ensuring that adequate transportation and funding is available for treatment.

Managers benefit from knowledge about relationships; it helps them improve program operations and understand program outcomes. It can help managers and policy makers by determining how, and which, variables affect key outcomes. This chapter introduces contingency tables, and subsequent chapters examine additional important statistics that managers and analysts need to consider.

CONTINGENCY TABLES

A *contingency table* expresses the relationship between two *categorical* variables. One variable is shown in rows and the other in columns. Each row and column shows the frequency of observations with specific values for both variables. Typically, row and column totals also are present. An example is given in Table 8.1 for data on the gender and year of promotion of employees. In this case, the manager or analyst wants to examine whether a relationship exists between gender and rate of promotion.

Regarding the anatomy of contingency tables, the term *data cell* is commonly used to refer to table cells that show the counts or percentages based on the values of the two variables.[1] For example, Table 8.1 shows that 14 male employees and 8 female employees received promotions within the first year. Each of these numbers is entered in a separate data cell. Table 8.1 also shows the row and column totals, which are called the *marginal totals*; they are located in the margins of the table. The number of 95 total employees in the lower right-hand corner is called the *grand total*. The table also has clear column and row headings and a succinct but clear title, which

Table 8.1 ⎯⎯⎯⎯⎯⎯⎯ Year of Promotion
by Gender

| Year | Gender | | Total |
	Male	Female	
1	14	8	22
2	16	14	30
3	7	22	29
4	6	8	14
Total	43	52	95

avoids ambiguity. You should practice making contingency tables that are similar to this one in appearance (that is, neat and clear).

The placement of the variables in contingency tables depends on the nature of the relationship. In Chapter 2 we distinguished between causal relationships and associations. Causal relationships show cause and effect, whereby one variable affects another. The dependent variable is defined as the one that is affected (or caused) by the other, which is called the independent variable. When a relationship is causal (as determined by the analyst), the dependent variable is conventionally placed in the rows and the independent variable in the columns.[2] When two variables are only associated (with no causality implied), no preference exists regarding the location of variables.

We now examine how rates of promotion vary between men and women, that is, the relationship between these two variables. The absolute frequency counts in Table 8.1 do not tell us much. No conclusion can be drawn from the fact that 14 males and 8 females were promoted in the first year, because the sample has an unequal number of men and women. Rather, we need to compare the percentages of men and women promoted in each year. *Column percentages* are calculated by dividing each frequency by the column total. For example, [14/43 =] 32.6 percent of men and [8/52 =] 15.4 percent of women were promoted in the first year, and so on for subsequent years, too. The result is shown in Table 8.2. Note that each column adds up to 100 percent.

The examination of relationships in contingency tables is usually based on comparisons of column percentages or groups of rows. From Table 8.2 we see that men were indeed promoted at a faster rate than women. About 69.8 percent [32.6% + 37.2%] of men were promoted in the first two years, compared with only 42.3 percent [15.4% + 26.9%] of women. Conversely, a majority of women were promoted in the last two years, namely, 57.7 percent compared with only 30.2 percent of men. The conclusion is clear. Many software programs can produce both frequency counts and column percentages in the same table, hence, aiding analysis.

Table 8.2 ⸺⸺⸺⌇⌇⸺ Year of Promotion by Gender: Column Percentages

	Gender		
Year	Male	Female	Total
1	32.6%	15.4%	23.2%
2	37.2	26.9	31.6
3	16.2	42.3	30.5
4	14.0	15.4	14.7
Total	100.0	100.0	100.0
(n)	(43)	(52)	(95)

Table 8.3 ⸺⸺⸺⌇⌇⸺ Row and Total Percentages

A: Row Percentages				B: Total Percentages			
	Gender				Gender		
Year	Male	Female	Total	Year	Male	Female	Total
1	63.6%	36.4%	100.0%	1	14.7%	8.4%	23.1%
2	53.3	46.7	100.0	2	16.8	14.7	31.5
3	24.1	75.9	100.0	3	7.4	23.2	30.6
4	42.9	57.1	100.0	4	6.3	8.4	14.7
Total	45.3	54.7	100.0	Total	45.3	54.7	100.0
(n)	(43)	(52)	(95)				

A point of possible confusion is that computers can also calculate row percentages and total percentages. *Row percentages* show the percentages of men and women promoted within each year. For example, [14/22 =] 63.6 percent of employees promoted in the first year were men and [8/22 =] 36.4 percent were women. This is shown in Table 8.3. Likewise, [16/30 =] 53.3 percent of employees promoted in the second year were men, and [14/30 =] 46.7 percent were women. When row percentages are calculated, each row adds up to 100 percent. In our example, row percentages show the gender composition of each of the cohorts. Because we wish to know the cohort composition of each of the genders, we use column percentages. Analysts must be clear about what it is they are comparing; the row versus column placement convention described previously is designed partly to avoid this confusion. Tables in published reports usually show column percentages; row percentages are far less common.

Total percentages show frequencies as a share of all observations. For example, [14/95 =] 14.7 percent of all employees in the sample are males who were promoted within the first year, [22/95 =] 23.2 percent of all

Table 8.4 ～～～ Gender by Year of Promotion

Gender	Promotion (Year) 1	2	3	4	Total
Male	63.6%	53.3%	24.1%	42.9%	45.3%
Female	36.4	46.7	75.9	57.1	54.7
Total	100.0	100.0	100.0	100.0	100.0
(n)	(22)	(30)	(29)	(14)	(95)

employees in the sample are females who were promoted within the third year, and so on. Such frequencies are sometimes useful when describing the sample, but they do not help address the question of whether differences in the rate of promotion exist across gender. Note that when total percentages are calculated, only the grand total adds up to 100 percent.

The preference for column percentages often affects the placement of variables. Typically, when analysts want to know the demographic distribution of a variable (for instance, gender composition of each cohort in our example), preferences for displaying column percentages will cause the demographic variable (such as gender, age, location, and the like) to be placed in rows and the other variable in the columns. Then column percentages show the demographic distribution of that variable. In our case, if we wish to show the demographic (gender) make-up of the promotion cohorts, and use column percentages, then we should show gender in the rows, as in Table 8.4. Confused? It is simply a matter of being clear about what the analyst wants to know, and then typically using column percentages to obtain that information.

Finally, in Chapter 2 we noted that "correlation does not prove causation." As with all statistical techniques, contingency table analysis sheds light on whether variables are empirically associated, but it does not address whether an explanation exists that establishes causality; this requires an additional cause-and-effect argument. Hence, if gender is causally related to promotion, then analysts will need to explain how that occurs. If gender is only associated with promotion rates, then no further explanation of cause and effect is required. Analysis often results in a thorough consideration of these matters.

Getting Started
Replicate Tables 8.1 and 8.2 on your computer.

RELATIONSHIP AND DIRECTION

When analysts state that a relationship exists between variables, what exactly do they mean? The *relationship* is sometimes broadly defined as two variables being associated with each other, possibly as one causing the other (see

Chapter 2), but in statistics, relationships are defined in specific, technical terms. A ***statistical relationship*** means that as one variable changes, so too does another. Thus, if a relationship exists between gender and the rate of promotion, then the rate of promotion must change when the value of gender changes; males will have a different rate of promotion than females. If no relationship exists between gender and the rate of promotion, then the rate of promotion does not differ between males and females. Differences in the rate of promotion might be measured by mean rates of promotion, the percentage of employees promoted in first years, or in some other way.[3]

Relationships involving ordinal or continuous variables are characterized as having a positive or negative direction. A positive relationship means that large values of one variable are associated with large values of the other variable *and* that small values of one variable are associated with small values of the other variable. A negative relationship implies the opposite: large values of one variable are associated with small values of the other variable *and* vice versa. The idea of relationship did not arise in the earlier example because gender is a nominal variable. It makes no sense to say that the relationship between gender and promotion is positive or negative.

However, if we were to look at promotion rates by age, then we could talk about a positive or negative relationship. For example, if it takes older workers more time to be promoted than younger workers, then we can say that a positive relationship exists between the age and the number of years that it takes to be promoted.

The direction of a relationship refers to whether it is positive or negative. To determine the direction of a relationship in a contingency table (that is, whether it is positive or negative), we can focus on the distribution of column percentages. In a ***positive relationship***, small values of the column variable are associated with small values of the row variable, and large values of the column variable are often associated with large values of the row variable. This is shown in Table 8.5, part A by focusing on the corner cells of the contingency table. When a relationship is positive, the relative frequencies (percentages) of the cells in the upper left and lower right corners will be large. Conversely, a ***negative relationship*** means that small values of the column variable are often associated with large values of the row variable, and vice versa. In Table 8.5, part B, which shows a negative relationship, the

Table 8.5 ⎯⎯⎯⎯⎯⎯ Positive and Negative Relationships

A: Positive Relationship			B: Negative Relationship		
	LO	HI		LO	HI
LO	65%	29%	LO	31%	62%
HI	35	71	HI	69	38

relative frequencies (percentages) of the cells in the upper right and lower left corners are large.

The direction of a relationship can be difficult to determine in large tables through visual inspection alone. Studying the corner cells may be inconclusive; the pattern may be unclear. Several statistics are available that provide quantitative measures of relationships and of their direction. These statistics that do not rely on visual inspection are discussed in Chapters 10 and 12.[4] Positive values of these test statistics indicate a positive relationship, and negative values indicate a negative relationship. These statistics also establish statistical grounds for establishing whether relationships exist.

In addition to the direction of relationships, it is also important to consider the **strength of relationships,** that is, the extent to which differences occur. In the previous example, are men promoted a lot or only a little faster? One way to express a sense of difference is to ask how much longer it takes women to get promoted than men. Applying the descriptive techniques in Chapter 2, we find that the mean promotion rate is 2.12 years for men and 2.58 years for women. So, on average, men are promoted about 0.46 years faster than women. We can also state that it takes women [(2.58 − 2.12)/2.12 =] 21.7 percent longer to be promoted than men.

We can flesh out this idea a little more. For example, comparing medians, we find that half of the men are promoted within two years, as compared with three years for women. We can also examine the percentile distributions. Whereas 25 percent of men were promoted within one year, the same percentage of women were promoted in two years. Or, using cumulative frequencies, we can say that whereas 69.8 percent of men were promoted within two years, only 42.3 percent of women were promoted within two years, as shown in Figure 8.1. Whether or not these differences are practically relevant ultimately rests with managers and elected officials; it is probably important whether men are promoted 4 percent faster, or 40 percent faster, and in what year these differences most often occur.

Searching for practical relevance and presenting results may involve some decisions regarding ethics. The data in Table 8.2 can be presented in ways that indicate a large difference ("the rate of promotion is much faster for men than women; twice as many men get promoted than women in the first year") or a minute difference ("while men are promoted faster than women, the differences are quite small in the fourth year: 14 percent of men are promoted in the second year, as are 15 percent of women"). Both statements are based on but parts of the data in Table 8.2. Consistent with Table 1.1 ("Ethics of Research and Analysis"), results should be presented in a complete and objective way. The task of the analyst is to be complete and to inform. Given the facts presented in Table 8.2, the analyst might better state something like this: "Men are promoted faster than women; 69.8

Figure 8.1 —————⋀⋀—Promotion Rates

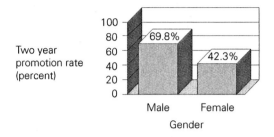

Two year
promotion rate
(percent)

percent of men were promoted in the first two years, compared to 42.3 percent of women. More women were promoted in the third year (42.3% versus 16.2%), and both genders were promoted at nearly equal rates in the fourth year." We should present the facts as they are, complete and without bias or an attempt to spin.

PIVOT TABLES

Pivot tables take contingency tables a step further in an important way. They are used to analyze continuous variables, in addition to categorical variables. The contingency tables described earlier in this chapter are used to analyze only categorical variables.[5] Although *pivot tables* may appear to be similar to the earlier tables, they show statistics of one or more continuous variables for one or more categorical variables in the data cells. Consider the following example. Assume that in addition to data about employees' gender and year of promotion, we also have for each employee a performance evaluation score. The score is a continuous variable that ranges from 1 (low) to 10 (high). Table 8.6 shows the mean performance score for the combination of gender and year of promotion.[6]

Table 8.6 shows that mean performance scores are higher for both males and females who were promoted sooner than for those who were promoted later. For example, the mean score of males who were promoted in the first year is 8.986, compared with 8.769 among those promoted in the second year, 8.514 among those promoted in the third year, and 7.683 in the fourth year. The mean performance scores of females show a similar decreasing pattern for promotions in later years. Moreover, the performance scores of males and females are quite similar in each year of promotion.

Statistics reported in the data cells of pivot tables are not limited to means, of course. Statistical software programs can provide the full range of univariate statistics for continuous variables, such as median, standard

Table 8.6 ⎯⎯⎯⎯⎯⎯ Mean Performance Scores by Gender and Year of Promotion

Year	Gender		Total
	Male	Female	
1	8.986	9.150	9.045
2	8.769	8.757	8.763
3	8.514	8.555	8.545
4	7.683	7.663	7.671
Total	8.647	8.563	8.601
(n)	(43)	(52)	(95)

deviation, range, minimum, maximum, skewness, and kurtosis. Pivot tables can calculate several of these statistics in the same table. Note that when categorical variables are reported in the data cells, continuous-level statistics are calculated, too. For example, if year of promotion is considered a variable to be reported in data cells, then pivot tables calculate continuous-level statistics, such as means, for this variable. The mean year of promotion is then shown as 2.12 for males, 2.58 for females, and 2.37 for the combined sample of male and female employees.

The term *pivot* is derived from the handy property that row and column variables can be readily transposed. *Transposing* means interchanging the locations of these variables; column variables become row variables, and vice versa. In addition, two or more variables can also be used in the same column or row, thereby creating a grouping structure as shown in Table 8.7. This can also be done in contingency tables. A *layer variable* is one that

Table 8.7 ⎯⎯⎯⎯⎯⎯ Mean Performance Scores by Gender and Year of Promotion

Year	Gender	Location		Total
		A	B	
1	Male	9.150	8.767	8.986
	Female	9.140	9.167	9.150
2	Male	8.760	8.783	8.769
	Female	8.760	8.750	8.757
3	Male	8.750	8.200	8.514
	Female	8.617	8.531	8.555
4	Male	7.300	7.760	7.683
	Female	7.150	7.757	7.663
Total		8.830	8.435	8.647
(n)		(45)	(50)	(95)

defines the subset of data used for subsequent data tables.[7] In this case, year of promotion is the layer variable. For illustrative purposes, assume that we have further data on the location of employees, in site A or B.

Note that gender is now grouped within each year of promotion. Table 8.7 shows, for example, that the mean performance score of females promoted within the first year in site A is 9.140. This is nearly identical to that of males, 9.150. Note also that marginal totals show the mean performance scores for each gender by year; these are the same means shown in Table 8.6. Pivot tables can be used to quickly "drill down" your data, and many software programs allow users to graphically move around variables. With very little effort we can also group year of promotion within gender, or move both to the column. It also possible to create tables for only selected values of data; for example, we might produce a table like Table 8.6 for the A site only, or like Table 8.7 for female employees only. Pivot tables offer considerable flexibility, and an examination of the ease of constructing pivot tables in your software program is instructive.[8]

Be aware, however, that creating more data cells (compare Tables 8.6 and 8.7) implies that observations in the sample are distributed over more cells. This increases the possibility that some cells have very few observations. In our case, which involves a relatively small dataset, the number of men promoted in year 4 in site A is only 1 (not shown in Table 8.7)! Surely, managers will not want to base policy decisions on just a single or a few observations. Larger tables do require larger datasets. Although no hard-and-fast rule exists regarding the minimum number of observations in each data cell, it is good practice to avoid creating tables in which any column or row has a large percentage of cells with fewer than five observations.[9] If this happens, the analyst should add a caveat to his or her findings or consider combining categories to eliminate cells with sparse counts. In Table 8.7, the categories of the third and fourth years of promotion might be combined to avoid a small number of frequencies in the fourth year by gender.

> **Getting Started**
> Develop a pivot table using one continuous and two categorical variables in your area.

Pivot tables and contingency tables can be used for many analytical tasks. Box 8.1 examines how the univariate and bivariate techniques discussed in Chapters 6–8 are used to analyze community indicators.

The ease with which variables can be analyzed in so many different ways using pivot tables is highly appealing. But it also means that analysts need to know which calculations or comparisons they are looking for, rather than randomly trying out different analyses of variables. While blind analysis may reveal interesting and even important facts, eventually these facts must be understood and placed into context. The analytical process is usually a

In Greater Depth...

Box 8.1   Community Indicators

Many jurisdictions now report *community indicators* about conditions in their community. Indicators include general population characteristics—such as population size, age, and race—as well as indicators about literacy, housing, incomes, crime (for example, murder, rape, burglary), juvenile crime, health (various diseases such as AIDS) and exercise (walking, bicycling, swimming), educational attainment (test scores), environmental quality (air, water, and other pollution), transportation (road construction, accidents, commuting times, use of public transportation), and so on. These indicators track changes and improvements, and they help analysts to compare jurisdictions. Public and nonprofit organizations often use these data, for example, for program development.

Community indicators can be analyzed using the statistical techniques described in Chapters 6–8. For example, if indices are compared across jurisdictions, an index of overall community conditions might be developed that compares jurisdictions within a region. For example, measures such as average household income, educational attainment, crime rates, water quality, and commuting time might be compared by ranking one jurisdiction against others (see Chapter 3). The sums of these disparate ranks can be summed and evaluated against other jurisdictions. Comparisons also can be made over time to show improvement (or lack thereof), or against other, comparable jurisdictions in other parts of the country.

Within a given measure such as crime we can also calculate the mean and median levels of crime, expressed as either absolute (for example, number of crimes) or relative measures (for example, crimes per capita). We can also calculate standard deviations and percentiles. You may be able to determine in which percentile of crime, pollution, or income your jurisdictions falls.

We can also examine relationships between indicators, for example, whether income is associated with health problems, home ownership, illiteracy, or transportation. We might find that some expected relationships hold up and others do not. Among those relationships that hold up, we might find many exceptions, for example, jurisdictions with low mean incomes that also have low levels of disease and crime. Such findings will prompt analysts to seek to better understand the specific conditions of these jurisdictions. Through all of these uses, community indicators are increasingly used to inform decision making and public policy debates.

back-and-forth between empirical and theoretical inquiry. By way of example, Table 8.2 shows that males are promoted faster than women. We now
ask: why is this so? Suppose that we entertain the rival hypothesis (see Chapter 2) that the promotion rate is different because men are more productive
than women. That is, there is no gender discrimination per se. Regardless of
your purposes, you will need to examine this possibility: either show that
productivity differences (if any) do not explain gender discrimination
(hence, gender discrimination really does exist), or show that the alleged
gender discrimination is but an artifact of productivity differences.

Such reasoning underlies the construction of Table 8.6. As we already
saw, Table 8.6 shows that the productivity scores of men and women are
quite similar in years in which they are promoted. Hence, it might be that
men are promoted faster based on their scores. However, reaching such a
conclusion does not end the analytical inquiry. We might ask why men
receive higher scores than women. Although discrimination might exist in
how the productivity scores are assigned, a further hypothesis is that productivity scores might differ across work sites. Table 8.7 bears this out; the mean
productivity score in site B is indeed lower than in site A (8.435 versus
8.830). Moreover, further analysis (not shown) indicates that women are
more likely than men to work in site B (57.8 percent versus 46.5 percent).
Perhaps then, there is something about site B that is problematic. . . . And so
it goes. Empirical inquiry might not answer all questions, but it can answer
some. This kind of reasoned inquiry, rather than mindless calculation or
analysis, eventually brings analytical, quantitative insight to problems of
management and policy. In short, analysis is the pursuit of understanding.[10]

SUMMARY

Contingency tables are used to analyze the relationships between two or
more categorical variables. They help managers examine the impact of
programs or policies; one variable is the policy or program, and the other is
the outcome. Managers can also use contingency tables to examine how
conditions differ among clients, employees, or jurisdictions. In this case, one
variable is the condition and the other is a categorical variable describing
clients, employees, or jurisdictions.

Contingency tables are used to calculate differences across categories,
such as how employees vary in their rates of promotion, or how cities vary on
community indices, or how clients vary in their program outcomes. Often,
analysts calculate column percentages as a basis for making comparisons.
Whether such differences are practically relevant depends on the judgment of
analysts and managers. Contingency tables are also used to determine
whether the relationship between ordinal variables is positive or negative.

Pivot tables are helpful extensions of contingency tables; they allow statistics to be calculated for continuous variables. These statistics are shown in the data cells of tables. The term *pivot* is based on the property that row and column variables can be readily transposed and grouped together. A limitation of tables that have many data cells is that they may require larger datasets. Contingency and pivot tables are essential and widely used to study relationships between variables.

KEY TERMS

Column percentages (p. 130)
Contingency table (p. 129)
Data cell (p. 129)
Grand total (p. 129)
Layer variable (p. 136)
Marginal totals (p. 129)

Negative relationship (p. 133)
Pivot tables (p. 135)
Positive relationship (p. 133)
Statistical relationship (p. 133)
Strength of relationships (p. 134)
Transposing (p. 136)

Notes

1. In website programming, the term *data cell* describes all table cells, including row and column attributes and labels. In other instances, the term *data cell* is limited to cells at the intersections of row and column attributes, hence, excluding marginal and grand totals. We use the term here to refer to all cells that contain, well, data.
2. This convention often is violated, hence, making it a weak convention. Nonetheless, following it makes the analysis of tables easier when column percentages are used, as is commonly the case. Note that this convention is rather different from placing the dependent variable on the Y-axis in scatterplots and graphs, as discussed in Chapter 12.
3. The idea of variables varying together in some way is also expressed by terms such as *covary* and *correlate*. The prefix co- means together or jointly. Variables that are related to each other covary (when variable X varies, then variable Y varies in some way, too) and are thus correlated.
4. Kendall's tau-c (described in Chapter 10) is an example of such a statistic.
5. Whether one considers a pivot table as a type of contingency table or as something different is a matter of opinion. At this point in our discussion, we treat them as being different for illustrative purposes.
6. The terminology of *pivot tables* is not adopted uniformly or consistently. SPSS calls these tables "OLAP cubes," or On-line Analytical Processing (Analyze → Reports → OLAP Cubes). However, once these tables are created, analysts can edit and modify them by selecting graphical commands from the Pivot menu (Pivot → Pivoting Trays).

7. A layer variable is sometimes called a nesting variable. In this case, Table 8.6 would be called a nested table. However, this term is best reserved for statistical techniques (factorial designs) with which the term is traditionally associated.

8. See footnote 6. In Microsoft Excel, pivot tables are created by selecting from the menu bar Data → PivotTable and PivotChart Report.

9. It may be impossible to avoid all cells having sparse counts. Hence, the tenet concerns *most* cells in any one row or column.

10. Whether one calls this approach reasoned inquiry or post-hoc story-telling is a matter of perspective and opinion. In the end, truth must be told and supported by the facts.

Inferential Statistics

This section examines the family of statistics commonly called *inferential statistics*. As the name implies, these statistics allow inferences to be made about characteristics of the population from which the data were drawn. Inferential statistics address several problems that managers and analysts face, but the key question is determining whether or not a relationship exists. Inferential statistics provide statistical evidence for answering this important question. Only if a relationship exists does it make sense to provide further description of its direction and magnitude or impact. When no relationship exists, these later matters are irrelevant. Indeed, determining whether a relationship exists is the unresolved problem in Chapter 8.

Different statistical tests are available for addressing this question. The rather broad range of tests reflects, in large measure, that different measurement levels of variables and specific questions require different statistics. Statistics also have assumptions that affect test selection. Therefore, a key task in inferential statistics is to select the correct, or appropriate, statistic. The statistics roadmap provided at the beginning of this book assists in this matter. The differences in these tests also underlie the sequence of chapters in this section. Specifically,

- When two variables are *categorical,* tests based on contingency tables should be used (Chapters 9 and 10).

- When one variable is *dichotomous* (for example, gender) and the other is *continuous,* the t-test should be used (Chapter 11).
- When both variables are *continuous,* simple regression analysis should be used (Chapter 12).
- When three or more variables are analyzed, multivariate techniques should be used (Chapters 13–15).

The statistics discussed in this section are used widely in research. Analysts must be conversant with them in order to undertake their analyses, and they are expected to know whether sufficient statistical evidence exists for the relationships on which they report. Even if these statistics are not included in final reports and presentations, analysts are expected to be able to explain the tests they used if called upon to do so. Being familiar with a broad range of statistics is also necessary for comprehending the professional research literature in one's field; it is essential statistical literacy. The chapters include many footnotes containing detailed explanations that guide and further inform; readers are encouraged to examine these notes.

Chapter 9 defines essential statistical concepts involved in determining whether a relationship exists: hypothesis testing, statistical significance, critical values, degrees of freedom, test assumptions, confidence intervals, and other statistical terms. The chapter is the foundation for subsequent chapters. Chapter 9 shows how to test whether a relationship exists, and it does so using a practical example involving two categorical variables. The example uses the chi-square test statistic in a discussion of hypothesis testing.

Chapter 10 discusses measures of association that provide information about the direction and strength of relationships. Many of these measures also have tests of statistical significance associated with them; they are useful alternatives to chi-square. Further, these statistics help address additional problems that managers and analysts might encounter, such as evaluating whether programs meet performance standards, dealing with problems of evaluation rankings, and determining the equivalency of samples. This chapter provides such additional statistics for working with categorical data, including a variety of nonparametric test statistics that can be used both to test hypotheses and to provide information about the direction and strength of relationships. Nonparametric statistics are characterized by having few or no test assumptions, which makes them relatively easy to use.

Chapter 11 discusses a variety of t-tests, which are used to analyze relationships between one continuous and one dichotomous variable. Although t-tests involve some cumbersome test assumptions, they are popular because they are relatively robust against violations of these assumptions. The chapter discusses the assumptions in detail and indicates how violations might be addressed. Because analysts sometimes want to use other tests, the chapter also provides nonparametric alternatives. However, if one variable is categorical with three or more categories, and the other variable is continuous, then analysis of variance (ANOVA) should be used (see Chapter 16, in Section V).

Chapter 12 examines the analysis of relationships between two continuous variables. Such relationships are tested primarily with Pearson's correlation coefficient, as well as with simple regression. Simple regression uses tests of the regression slope to determine whether a relationship exists. Many terms introduced in this chapter are essential to understanding subsequent chapters.

Chapter 13 transitions readers to the use of multivariate statistics, for relationships involving three or more variables. Multiple regression is used widely to test rival hypotheses. This method offers essential advantages over the layering approach discussed in Chapter 8, and it can also be used to examine the impact of policies across jurisdictions or subjects. The chapter discusses the essential approach of a nomothetic explanation as well as the importance of various test assumptions of multiple regression.

Chapter 14 examines logistic regression, the technique used when the dependent variable is dichotomous. This method overcomes an important limitation of multiple regression, namely, the requirement that the dependent variable be continuous. Dichotomous dependent variables are quite common in political science, for example, when studying election outcomes or the occurrence of war. These events are seen as dichotomous; either something happens or it doesn't. Logistic regression can then be used to estimate the probability of these events occurring.

The chapters in this section provide a comprehensive selection of essential statistics. The final section in this book examines times series analysis and offers a survey of advanced statistics that managers and analysts might encounter.

CHAPTER

9

Hypothesis Testing with Chi-Square

CHAPTER OBJECTIVES

After reading this chapter, you should be able to
- Understand the process of hypothesis testing
- Define and apply the concept of "statistical significance"
- Test relationships among categorical variables
- Evaluate chi-square test assumptions
- Discuss how sample size affects statistical significance
- Consider tests involving control variables

Descriptive analysis goes only so far. An important task of statistics is to provide statistical evidence for determining whether relationships exist. This is essential to public policy, for example, establishing whether a program or policy had any impact, such as whether an anger management program affected classroom violence. It is also essential to science, establishing whether or not two variables are related. This chapter discusses general procedures for testing whether a relationship exists. This is also called *hypothesis testing*. Different statistical tests for hypothesis testing are used for different measurement levels of variables involved in relationships. This chapter, using chi-square, shows how to test for relationships between two categorical variables, but the process as described here is valid for other measurement levels, too. This chapter focuses on hypothesis testing, whereas the next chapter discusses statistics that are used to describe the direction and strength of relationships. Only after the existence of any relationships has been established does it make sense to describe them; this is done using measures of association (see Chapter 10).

WHAT IS CHI-SQUARE?

Chi-square (pronounced "ky-square") is a quantitative measure used to determine whether a relationship exists between two categorical variables. The Greek notation for chi-square is χ^2, which can be used interchangeably with its Latin alphabet spelling, chi-square. Many statistics quantify the relationship between variables in some way. We continue here with the example from Chapter 8 to illustrate the process of calculating chi-square and determining whether a relationship exists, but you are also encouraged to identify categorical variables in your field of interest.

In Chapter 8 we examined the relationship between two categorical variables, namely, gender and the year of promotion for a sample of employees. Managers are concerned that employees are promoted at unequal rates based on gender, raising the possibility of gender discrimination in the workplace. The data are shown again, in Table 9.1. We want to establish whether a relationship exists between gender and year of promotion. Table 9.1 shows both frequency counts and column percentages (in parentheses).

Table 9.1 ⎯⎯⎯∿∿⎯⎯ Year of Promotion by Gender: Frequencies and Percentages (frequency counts in parentheses)

Year	Gender Male	Female	Total
1	32.6%	15.4%	23.2%
	(14)	(8)	(22)
2	37.2	26.9	31.6
	(16)	(14)	(30)
3	16.2	42.3	30.5
	(7)	(22)	(29)
4	14.0	15.4	14.7
	(6)	(8)	(14)
Total	100.0	100.0	100.0
	(43)	(52)	(95)

Table 9.2 ⎯⎯⎯⎯⎯⎯ Year of Promotion by Gender: Expected Frequencies

| | A: Percentages | | | B: Counts | |
| | Gender | | | Gender | |
Year	Male	Female	Total	Male	Female
1	23.2%	23.2%	23.2%	10.0	12.1
2	31.6	31.6	31.6	13.6	16.4
3	30.5	30.5	30.5	13.1	15.9
4	14.7	14.7	14.7	6.3	7.6
Total	100.0	100.0	100.0	43.0	52.0
(n =)	(43)	(52)	(95)		

Chi-square provides a quantitative measure of the relationship between two categorical variables, first, by determining what the distribution of observations (frequencies) would look like if *no* relationship existed and, second, by quantifying the extent to which the observed distribution (such as in Table 9.1) differs from that determined in the first step. This section explains the calculation of chi-square, which is used in the next section for hypothesis testing (that is, determining whether a relationship exists).

What would the relationship in Table 9.1 look like if no relationship existed between gender and year of promotion? When no relationship exists between gender and the year of promotion, then men and women, by definition, do not differ in promotion rates. The column percentages in Table 9.1 will then be identical for men and women; they will not differ from the aggregate sample of all men and women. This distribution is shown in the right-hand, "Total" column. When no relationship exists between men and women, both men and women will be promoted at those rates. Hence, 23.2 percent of both men and women will be promoted in their first year, 31.6 percent will be promoted in their second year, 30.5 percent will be promoted in their third year, and 14.7 percent will be promoted in their fourth year.

The frequencies associated with these rates when no relationship exists are called **expected frequencies**. Table 9.2 shows these expected frequencies. For example, when no difference in promotion rates exists between men and women, 30.5 percent of 43 men, or 13.1 men, would have been promoted in their third year. Similarly, 30.5 percent of 52 women, or 15.9 women, would have been promoted in their third year. The other expected frequencies are calculated in similar fashion in Table 9.2.

Clearly, when the data indicate that no relationship exists between these variables, the values of observed and expected frequencies must be identical. Also, the greater the relationship, the greater the difference between the observed and expected frequencies. The *chi-square* statistic (χ^2) measures

Table 9.3 ⌁⌁⌁ Calculating Chi-Square

	Male			Female			Total
Year	Obs.	Exp.	χ^2	Obs.	Exp.	χ^2	χ^2
1	14	10.0	1.60	8	12.1	1.39	2.99
2	16	13.6	0.42	14	16.4	0.35	0.77
3	7	13.1	2.84	22	15.9	2.34	5.18
4	6	6.3	0.01	8	7.6	0.02	0.03
Total	43	43.0	4.87	52	52.0	4.10	8.97

Note: Obs. = Observed Frequency; Exp. = Expected Frequency

the difference between the expected and observed frequencies and is thus a quantitative measure of this relationship. Chi-square is defined in the following manner:

$$\sum_i \frac{(O_i - E_i)^2}{E_i}$$

where O_i is the observed frequency in a cell and E_i is the expected frequency in a cell. As is readily seen, when $E_i = O_i$, the chi-square value for that cell is zero. Using the frequencies shown in Tables 9.1 and 9.2 (part B), we find that the chi-square value of the first cell is $[(14 - 10)^2/10 = 4^2/10 = 16/10 =]$ 1.60. Calculating chi-square for all of the cells yields 8.97, as shown in Table 9.3. *Of course, the value of chi-square is usually calculated by computer.*[1]

In short, when no relationship exists between the variables, chi-square equals zero. The greater the relationship, the greater the value of chi-square. Finally, note also that chi-square is always positive and that it provides no information about the direction of the relationship.[2]

HYPOTHESIS TESTING

We now use chi-square to determine whether a relationship exists between gender and promotion. This is called *hypothesis testing.* In our example, the hypothesis is that a relationship exists between gender and the rate of promotion; a hypothesis is a tentative statement about some relationship or condition that is subject to subsequent verification. The ***purpose of hypothesis testing*** is, simply, to determine whether a relationship exists. Specifically, we ask, "What is the probability that the above distribution of promotion rates among 95 men and women is consistent with a distribution in which men and women are promoted at *equal* rates?" That is, is a chi-square value of 8.97 sufficiently large to conclude that men are promoted at a faster rate than women? A *key task* in statistics is to determine how large any measure of a relationship must be in order to say that it is "statistically significant." This part of hypothesis testing involves

- The null hypothesis
- The concept of statistical significance
- Critical values
- Steps to determine statistical significance

These issues are relevant to all statistical tests, such as chi-square tests, t-tests, and others discussed in this book.

The Null Hypothesis

Since statistics is a careful and cautious discipline, we presume that no relationship between variables exists and that any relationship that is found may have been obtained purely by chance. The **null hypothesis** states that *any observed pattern is due solely to chance* and that, hence, no relationship exists. Thus, the null hypothesis (that is, that no relationship exists) is assumed, and an objective of statistical testing is to examine whether the null hypothesis can be rejected. This idea is similar to the court of justice in which individuals are presumed innocent until proven guilty beyond a reasonable doubt. In our example, we presume that no relationship exists between gender and the rate of promotion.

In statistics the specific concern is that we may find a relationship in our sample when in fact none exists in the population. This may occur because of a fluke in our random sample. We endeavor to disprove this possibility. Another way of looking at this issue is that if we assume that a relationship does exist, we might be guilty of not trying hard enough to prove that it doesn't exist. By assuming that a relationship doesn't exist, we need only satisfy the standard of "reasonable evidence" in order to claim that it does exist. That standard is that it should be *very unlikely to find a relationship among variables* (that is, a test-statistic value such as chi-square) *of a certain (large) magnitude when in fact no relationship exists in the population.*

The null hypothesis is stated as follows:

H_0: No relationship exists between gender and the rate of promotion.
H_A: A relationship exists between gender and the rate of promotion.

H_0 is the null hypothesis, and H_A is called the *alternate hypothesis*. H_0 is also sometimes called the straw man because we endeavor to "strike it down" or disprove it. The **alternate hypothesis** is the logical opposite of the null hypothesis; all possibilities must be accounted for between the null hypothesis and the alternate hypothesis.

In most instances, the null hypothesis is that *no relationship exists* between two variables, and the alternate hypothesis is that *a relationship does exist* between two variables. However, if the researcher has a priori information that a relationship can exist only in one direction (for example, that men can be promoted faster than women but that women cannot be promoted faster than men), then it is appropriate to state the null hypothesis as "men are not promoted faster than women" and the alternate hypothesis as "men are promoted faster than women." However, because, as is often the case, we cannot a priori rule out the direction of the relationship (it could be that women are promoted faster than men), we use the customary approach indicating that no relationship exists. If a relationship exists, we later can determine its direction.

Many scholars prefer to state these hypotheses as follows:

H_0: No relationship exists between gender and the rate of promotion in the population.

H_A: A relationship exists between gender and the rate of promotion in the population.

This usage clearly indicates that we are using sample data to draw inferences about relationships in the population. Indeed, we are not interested in our sample, per se. Who cares about the preferences of, say, 500 citizens? We care about them only to the extent that their opinions *represent* those of the entire population. In the end, we want to know how the population, not merely a sample of it, thinks about something. We use a sample to infer conclusions about the population. To distinguish conclusions about the sample from those of the population, we use Greek letters to refer to the population. Then, the hypotheses are also written as follows:

$$H_0: \mu_m = \mu_f$$
$$H_A: \mu_m \neq \mu_f$$

where μ is the rate of promotion in the population, and the *m* and *f* subscripts stand for "male" and "female," respectively.

Statistical Significance

The phrase *statistically significant* often carries considerable weight in public discourse. To say that something is statistically significant is tantamount to throwing the weight of science behind a statement or fact. But what exactly does the phrase mean? *Statistical significance* simply refers to the probability of being wrong about stating that a relationship exists when in fact it doesn't.

The phrase *level of statistical significance* refers to the level of that probability—in other words, *how often* we would be wrong to conclude that a relationship exists when in fact none exists, or how often we would incorrectly reject the null hypothesis when in fact it is true. One reason we might wrongly reject the null hypothesis is that our data are a random sample; had we drawn a different sample, we might have concluded otherwise.

The statistical standard for significance is 5 percent in the social sciences; we are willing to tolerate a 1-in-20 chance of being wrong in stating that a relationship exists (that is, concluding that the null hypothesis should be rejected when in fact it shouldn't). Many researchers also consider a 1-in-100 (1 percent) probability of being wrong as an acceptable standard of significance. The latter is a stricter standard. We are less likely to be wrong stating that a relationship exists (when in fact it doesn't exist) when it is significant at the 1 percent level than when it is significant at only the 5 percent level.

We could set the bar even higher—for example, by choosing a level of significance of one-tenth of 1 percent—but doing so may cause us to conclude that no relationship exists when in fact one does. A standard of less than 1 percent is thus thought to be too risk averse. Why not settle for a 10 percent level of significance? If we did so, we would be accepting a 10 percent chance of wrongfully concluding that a relationship exists when in fact none does. Usually, that is thought to be too risky.[3]

By convention, 5 percent is usually thought to be the uppermost limit of risk that we accept. Thus, relationships that are significant at more than 5 percent (say, 6 percent) are said to be *not significant.* Only relationships that are significant at 5 percent or less are considered significant, and relationships that are significant at 1 percent or less are said to be *highly significant.* Another convention is that most relationships are reported as being significant only at the 1 percent or the 5 percent level. Thus, a relationship that is statistically significant at the 3 percent level is reported as being significant at the 5 percent level but not at the 1 percent level. A relationship that is significant at one-tenth of 1 percent is reported as being significant at the 1 percent level.

Finally, the phrase *level of significance* should not be confused with the term *confidence level.* The confidence level refers to the probability that an unknown population parameter falls within a range of values calculated from the sample (see Box 7.2). Sometimes the phrase *level of confidence* is taken as being synonymous with 100 percent minus the level of statistical significance; for example, a 5 percent level of significance is said the be the same as a 95 percent confidence level. However, the phrase *level of significance* should be used in connection with matters of hypothesis testing.

The Five Steps of Hypothesis Testing

Recall the question asked earlier: How large should chi-square be so that we can conclude that a statistically significant relationship exists between gender and year of promotion or, in other words, so that we can reject the null hypothesis and accept the alternate hypothesis? All statistical tests follow the same *five steps of hypothesis testing*:

1. State the null hypothesis (in Greek letters).
2. Choose a statistical test.
3. Calculate the test statistic (t.s.) and evaluate test assumptions.
4. Look up the critical value (c.v.) of the test.
5. Draw a conclusion:

> If | t.s. | $<$ c.v., do not reject the null hypothesis.
> If | t.s. | $\geq$ c.v., reject the null hypothesis.

We already discussed the first item and mentioned the second item in the introduction to Section III. Readers also may wish to consult the Statistics Road Map at the beginning of this book for more detailed guidance on selecting test statistics. We have seen how to calculate the chi-square test statistic. Most statistical tests make assumptions about variables: we will soon address those of the chi-square test statistic. Now we discuss critical values. The **critical value** is the minimum value that a test statistic must be in order to rule out chance as the cause of a relationship. Technically, the critical value is the value above which the test statistic is sufficiently large to reject the null hypothesis at a user-specified level of significance.

The following discussion is provided to enhance conceptual understanding because, again, computers do most of the work. The *critical value* of any test statistic is determined by two parameters: (1) the desired level of statistical significance and (2) the number of degrees of freedom (df). As stated earlier, by convention, analysts are interested in rejecting the null hypothesis at the 1 percent and 5 percent levels. The **degrees of freedom** address the practical, statistical problem that the magnitude of most test statistics is affected by the number of observations or categories. For example, the formula for calculating the chi-square test statistic requires us to calculate a value for each cell and then add them all up. All things being equal, the larger the number of cells, the larger the value of this test statistic. The degrees of freedom statistic controls for this problem.[4] (This also means that it is generally meaningless to compare the values of different chi-square test statistics based on tables of unequal sizes and, as we will soon see, unequal numbers of observations.)

Each type of statistical test has its own way of calculating degrees of freedom. The degrees of freedom for any chi-square test are defined by the formula $(c-1)(r-1)$, where c = the number of columns in a contingency table and r = the number of rows. In Table 9.1, df = $(2-1)*(4-1) = 3$. If our table had six rows and four columns, the number of degrees of freedom would be $(6 - 1)*(4 - 1) = 15$, and so on.

To determine the critical value of our test, we turn to a table of chi-square critical values (see Appendix B). The table shows the levels of significance in columns and the degrees of freedom in rows. Assume that we wish to test whether our previously calculated χ^2 test statistic (8.97) is statistically significant at the 5 percent level. The critical value at this level of significance and three degrees of freedom is shown to be 7.815. Thus, applying the very last step in the method for testing hypotheses, we evaluate the absolute value of 8.97 as indeed larger than the critical value. The absolute value is stated in step 5 because some test statistics, but not χ^2, can have negative values, and because the critical value is always positive. So, we conclude that *a relationship exists between gender and the rate of promotion at the 5 percent level of significance.* Alternatively, we can write that *a statistically significant relationship exists between gender and the rate of promotion* ($\chi^2 = 8.97$, p $<$ .05). This important language is found in most analyses.

But is this relationship also significant at the 1 percent level? The critical value of this chi-square test at the 1 percent level and three degrees of freedom is 11.341. We evaluate that the absolute value of 8.97 is less than the critical value at this level of significance, and so we conclude that the relationship between gender and years of promotion is significant at the 5 percent level but not at the 1 percent level. We should always identify the highest level of significance, which in this instance is the 5 percent level. But if the test statistics had also been greater than the critical value at the 1 percent level, then the 1 percent level would be concluded.[5]

Getting Started
Replicate these results on your computer.

Note some features of the table of chi-square critical values in Appendix B. First, at any given level of significance, the value of the chi-square critical values increases as the degrees of freedom increase. This is consistent with the problem mentioned earlier: contingency tables with more rows and columns will have larger test statistics simply as a result of having more cells. The degrees of freedom "compensate" for this fact. Second, at any given number of degrees of freedom, the value of the chi-square critical values increases as the level of significance decreases. This, too, makes sense because a 1 percent level of significance will have a higher threshold than a 5 percent level.

Statistical software programs calculate test statistics and report the level of statistical significance at which the test statistic is significant. For example, software output might have shown "p = .029," which indicates that the test statistic is statistically significant at the 5 percent level but not at the 1 percent level. The probability "p = .000" means that the relationship is highly significant, at better than the 1 percent level. The probability "p = .1233" or "p = .9899" indicates that the relationship is not significant. Software programs do not ordinarily report critical values at the 1 percent and 5 percent levels; rather, they show the level of significance at which test statistics are significant. Looking up critical values is a valuable exercise that increases conceptual understanding but one that you will need to do only sporadically.

Chi-Square Test Assumptions

Nearly all test statistics make *assumptions* about the variables that are used. *Violation of test assumptions invalidates any test result.* There are three **chi-square test assumptions**. First, the variables must be categorical, which applies to our variables. Second, the observations are independent, as ours are. Independent samples are those in which each observation is independent of other observations in the sample. The concept of dependent samples is discussed more fully in Chapter 10, and typically involves such experimental situations as before-and-after measurement. Third, all cells must have a minimum of five expected observations. When this condition is not met, it is usually because the contingency table contains a large number of rows and columns relative to the number of observations. That is, the data are spread too thinly across too many cells. To correct this problem, simply redefine the data categories (that is, combine adjacent rows or columns) to create a smaller number of cells. Examination of Table 9.2 shows that our data meet this third assumption, too. The smallest expected frequency count is 6.34. If our data had violated this assumption, we would have combined rows or columns, recalculated results, and reported the revised conclusions. Some analysts, however, feel that this third assumption is too strong.[6]

Although chi-square is useful for testing whether a relationship exists, we have also noted some limitations: chi-square provides no information about the direction or strength of the relationship, and the third assumption may be problematic at times. For this reason, analysts often consider an alterative statistic, Kendall's tau-c, which offers information about significance, direction, and strength, without concern for the third assumption. Tau-c is discussed in Chapter 10. Chi-square is widely used and easy to calculate, and thus it is better used in the illustrative example in this chapter.

> **Getting Started**
>
> Test whether a relationship exists between two variables of your choice. Apply the above steps, verify chi-square test assumptions, and interpret your results.

Statistical Significance and Sample Size

Most statistical tests are also affected by **sample size**, which has implications for the likelihood of finding statistically significant relationships. Specifically, it is easier to find statistically significant relationships in large datasets than in small ones. This is more than a statistical artifact; rather, it reflects that having more information makes us more confident of our conclusions, and

Table 9.4 ⎯⎯⎯⎯⎯⎯ᴧ⅄ᴧ⎯ Year of Promotion by Gender: Observed and Expected Counts

| | A: Observed counts | | | B: Expected counts | |
| | Gender | | | Gender | |
Year	Male	Female	Total	Male	Female
1	140	80	220	100	121
2	160	140	300	136	164
3	70	220	290	131	159
4	60	80	140	63	76
Total	430	520	950	430	520

vice versa. The sample size affects the statistical significance of many widely used test statistics, including chi-square.

For example, assume we had a sample of 950 employees, rather than 95 employees, with the same relative distribution as shown in Table 9.1 (see Table 9.4). It is easy to verify that the data in Table 9.4 are distributed in the same exact manner as shown in Table 9.1. But the added observations affect the calculation of the chi-square test statistic. The value of the chi-square test statistic in the first cell is $(O_i - E_i)^2/E_i$, or $[(140 - 100)^2/100 =]$ 16. This is exactly *10 times* that of the previously calculated value. Indeed, each cell value is 10 times larger, as is the chi-square test statistic, which now becomes 89.7. Yet, the chi-square critical value is still defined as $(c - 1)(r - 1)$. The critical value for rejecting the null hypothesis at the 1 percent level is still 11.345. Whereas previously we could not reject the null hypothesis at this level, we now succeed in doing so by virtue of *having more observations*. This phenomenon occurs with many other widely used test statistics, too.

Of course, the opposite is also true: if we had tried to test for significance using only, say, 20 observations (instead of 95), we would have failed to reject the null hypotheses at even the 5 percent level. This reflects our having too little information to be sufficiently confident in our conclusions. By convention, many researchers prefer to test their null hypotheses on sample sizes of about 100 to a few hundred (say, 400). This is only a rough guideline. One implication is that analysts are neither surprised to find statistically significant relations in large samples, nor are they surprised to find the lack of statistical significance in small samples. Another implication is that, when working with large samples, analysts can find minute differences between groups to be statistically significant, even when the differences have very little practical relevance. Bigger samples are not necessarily better: they merely increase the importance of questions about the practical significance of findings. Box 9.1 discusses statistical power, which often is used to determine a minimum sample size.

In Greater Depth...

Box 9.1 Power and Sample Size

The level of statistical significance indicates how often we would be wrong to reject the null hypothesis when in fact it is true. However, another possible testing error occurs when we fail to reject the null hypothesis when in fact we should. The former is called a Type I (or α) error, wrongfully concluding that a relationship exists. The later is called a Type II (or β) error, wrongfully concluding that a relationship does *not* exist.

A typical reason for Type II errors is that the sample size is too small relative to the relationships or differences for which we are testing. We just don't have enough statistical evidence to reject the null hypothesis.

If β is the probability of wrongfully concluding that a relationship does not exist when in fact it does (Type II error), then $1 - \beta$ is the probability of correctly rejecting the null hypothesis when we should. This probability, $1 - \beta$, is called **statistical power**. The relationships between these concepts are summarized below:

		Decision	
		Reject	Accept
Null Hypothesis	True	Type I (α) error	Correct
	False	Correct (Power, $1 - \beta$)	Type II (β) error

It has been suggested that the power of tests should be at least .80. When the power is too small, analysts may fail to reject the null hypothesis when they should. The purpose of analyzing power is usually to determine *minimum sample size*. Formulas for calculating power vary from test to test; they depend on the sample size, the level of statistical significance (α), and the effect size (a measure of the strength of a relationship). Effect size, too, is defined differently for different tests; for example, for testing whether two continuous variables have different mean scores, the effect size is the standardized difference of means.[7] Typically, analysts use tables or power calculators, many of which are

(continued)

Box 9.1 *(continued)*

now available on the Internet (search "statistical power calculator").[8] Calculations of power require that analysts *ex ante* specify the expected effect size, hence, postulating expected means and standard deviations for continuous variables, or percentages for categorical variables. Analysts err on the side of caution by postulating small effect sizes (such as small differences between means or large standard deviations), thereby indicating a need for larger samples.

Finally, recall from Chapter 8 that once statistical significance has been established, analysts must turn to the task of establishing practical relevance. Some key questions concern the direction and strength of the relationship. Are the differences between categories large or small? Are they large enough to warrant interest from policy makers? Are they large enough to conclude that programs and policy have a salient impact on society? This is the essential task that must follow up after statistical hypothesis testing. The descriptive techniques described in Chapter 8 regarding the analysis of contingency tables and the use of column percentages are essential to providing these answers, as are the statistics discussed in Chapter 10.

RIVAL HYPOTHESES: ADDING A CONTROL VARIABLE

We now extend our discussion to deal with *rival hypotheses*. The following is but one approach, and we provide many other approaches in subsequent chapters. Rival hypotheses were first mentioned in Chapter 1. They are alternative, plausible explanations of findings. We established earlier that men are promoted faster than women, and in Chapter 8 (see "Pivot Tables") we raised the possibility that the promotion rate is different between men and women because men are more productive than women. We can now begin to examine this hypothesis formally using chi-square. Again, managers will want to examine this possibility as one of several.

Assume that we somehow measured productivity. Variables associated with rival hypotheses are called control variables. The control variable "productivity" is added to our dataset. To examine the rival hypothesis, we divide the sample into two (or more) groups, namely, employees with high productivity and those with low productivity. For each of these groups, we make a contingency table analysis by gender. If it is true that productivity, and not gender, determines the rate of promotion, then we expect to find no

Table 9.5 ·········∿∿∿···· Year of Promotion by Gender: Controlling for Productivity

	Low productivity		High productivity	
	Gender		Gender	
Year	Male (%)	Female (%)	Male (%)	Female (%)
1–2 Years	47	22	85	52
3+ Years	53	78	15	47
Total	100	100	100	100
(n =)	(17)	(18)	(26)	(34)

differences in the rate of promotion within the *same* level of productivity (high or low) because the differences exist across levels of productivity, and not by gender. Next, we construct a table (see Table 9.5). Note that the control variable "goes on top." We still have a total of 95 employees, 43 of whom are men and 52 of whom are women. For simplicity, and to avoid violating chi-square test assumptions (we must maintain a minimum of five expected frequencies in each cell), the variable "year of promotion" has been grouped, although this needn't be done in other instances. The relevant hypotheses are now as follows:

H1_0: No relationship exists between gender and rate of promotion among employees with high productivity.

H1_A: A relationship exists between gender and rate of promotion among employees with high productivity.

H2_0: No relationship exists between gender and rate of promotion among employees with low productivity.

H2_A: A relationship exists between gender and rate of promotion among employees with low productivity.

Chi-square test statistics are calculated for *each* of the two different productivity groups. We could find that one or both relationships are now statistically significant. When both relationships are not statistically significant, the result is called an **explanation** of the initial findings; that is, the statistically significant result has been explained away. Sometimes it is said that the previous relationship has proven to be *spurious*. When both relationships are statistically significant, the result is called a **replication** of the initial findings. When only one of the relationships is statistically significant, the result is called a **specification** of the initial findings. We would want to further examine the relationship that is not explained away. Finally, rarely does using a control variable result in uncovering statistically significant relationships that are otherwise insignificant. When this does occur, however, the result is called a ***suppressor effect***. That is, the existing relationship is suppressed in the absence of the control variable.

Through our data, we obtain the following results. The chi-square test statistic for the relationship between gender and year of promotion among employees with low productivity is 2.39, which is not statistically significant (p = .117). Thus, we conclude that gender does *not* discriminate in the rate of promotion among employees with low levels of productivity. But the chi-square test statistic for the relationship between gender and year of promotion among employees with high productivity is 6.65, which is statistically significant at the 1 percent level (p = .010). Gender differences continue to explain differences in the rate of promotion among employees with high levels of productivity. This type of finding is called a *specification*.[9]

Although this approach allows us to test rival hypotheses, two limitations may be noted: results are sometimes inconclusive (for example, in the case of specification), and the added cells require a larger number of observations. Table 9.5 acknowledges this problem; rows were combined. In Chapter 13 we discuss multiple regression as an alternative for continuous dependent variables. Although this approach isn't applicable here, analysts need to be familiar with it.

SUMMARY

When researchers assess the existence and nature of relationships between two variables, hypothesis testing and chi-square applications are invaluable tools. Hypothesis testing is an important step in data analysis because it establishes whether a relationship exists between two variables in the population, that is, whether a relationship is statistically significant. Processes of hypothesis testing involve

1. Stating the null hypothesis
2. Choosing the appropriate test statistics
3. Ensuring that data meet the assumptions of the test statistics
4. Calculating the test statistic values
5. Comparing the test statistic values against critical values and determining at what level a relationship is significant (or relying on the computer to calculate test statistics and to state the level at which they are statistically significant)

When analysts are confronted with two categorical variables, which can also be used to make a contingency table, chi-square is a widely used test for establishing whether a relationship exists (see the statistics roadmap at the beginning of the book). Chi-square has three test assumptions: that variables are categorical, that observations are independent, and that no cells have fewer than five expected frequency counts. Remember, violation of test assumptions invalidates any test result. Chi-square is but one statistic for testing a relationship between two categorical variables; others are discussed in Chapter 10.

Once analysts have determined that a statistically significant relationship exists through hypothesis testing, they need to assess the practical relevance of their findings. Remember, large datasets easily allow for findings of statistical significance. Practical relevance deals with the relevance of statistical differences for managers; it addresses whether statistically significant relationships have meaningful policy implications.

KEY TERMS

Alternate hypothesis (p. 149)
Chi-square (p. 146)
Chi-square test assumptions
  (p. 154)
Critical value (p. 152)
Degrees of freedom (p. 152)
Expected frequencies (p. 147)
Explanation (p. 158)
Five steps of hypothesis testing
  (p. 152)
Level of statistical significance
  (p. 151)

Null hypothesis (p. 149)
Purpose of hypothesis testing
  (p. 148)
Replication (p. 158)
Rival hypotheses (p. 157)
Sample size (and hypothesis testing)
  (p. 154)
Specification (p. 158)
Statistical power (p. 156)
Statistical significance (p. 150)
Suppressor effect (p. 159)

Notes

1. The CD accompanying the workbook *Exercising Essential Statistics* replicates these calculations on an Excel spreadsheet, called "Chi-Square." The computer-calculated value of chi-square is slightly higher, 9.043, due to rounding errors in calculating the expected frequency counts. This same result is achieved when using expected frequency counts with three decimal places. The expected frequency counts are then, for men: 9.976, 13.588, 13.115, and 6.321; for women: 12.064, 16.432, 15.860, and 7.644. Of course, maintaining three decimal places is more labor intensive for the illustrative, manually calculated example in the text, which retains only one decimal place in calculating the expected frequencies.

2. See Chapter 8 for a discussion of the direction of relationships.

3. Such a level might be acceptable at times in administration, and scientists occasionally report a 10 percent level, too.

4. The concept of degrees of freedom is not easy to explain. Some texts explain it as the number of calculations that are not predetermined after others have already occurred. Succinctly, if an array (or column) has four data elements, and the sum total is also known, then after choosing the first three elements, the fourth element is predetermined: hence, we are free to choose only three elements, and the array is said to have three degrees of freedom, or $c - 1$.

5. For example, if the test statistic of our data had been, say, 15.0, then $p < .01$ rather than $p < .05$ would be concluded and reported. This is not the case here, though.

6. The rationale is to ensure that chi-square calculations are not unduly affected by small differences in cells with low counts: note that the expected frequency is in the denominator of the chi-square formula. Some analysts feel that the standard of no cells with expected frequencies below five is too strict. They feel that (1) all cells should have greater expected frequency counts than 1.0 and (2) that no more than 20 percent of cells should have expected frequency counts lower than 5.0. The standard adopted in the text is more conservative. The point is, of course, that test statistics should not be affected by a few sparse cells.

7. This is defined as $(\mu_1 - \mu_2)/\sigma_{pooled}$, whereby $\sigma_{pooled} = \sqrt{[(\sigma_1^2 + \sigma_2^2)/2]}$. Small effect sizes are defined as those for which $\mu_1 - \mu_2$ is about $.2\ \sigma_{pooled}$, medium effect sizes are about $.5\ \sigma_{pooled}$, and large effect sizes are $.8\ \sigma_{pooled}$. For a chi-square test, effect size is defined as the *Phi coefficient*, ϕ, for two-by-two tables, $\sqrt{(\chi^2/N)}$, and as the contingency coefficient, C, for larger tables, $\sqrt{[\chi^2/(\chi^2 + N)]}$. Some of these measures are discussed in later chapters.

8. For example, see www.dssresearch.com/toolkit/spcalc/power.asp or calculators.stat.ucla.edu/powercalc/.

9. This approach is rather inefficient: note that we had to combine categories in order to preserve an adequate number of observations in each cell. In subsequent chapters, we will examine approaches that are more efficient and more conclusive. Of course, when productivity is found to cause explanation or specification, you subsequently want to report on the bivariate relationship between the rate of promotion and productivity. That, of course, is a different relationship from the one discussed here.

CHAPTER

10

Measures of Association

CHAPTER OBJECTIVES

After reading this chapter, you should be able to:
- Understand the concept of "proportional reduction in error"
- Determine the strength and direction of relationships
- Know why Kendall's tau-c is increasingly used for tests involving two ordinal variables
- Test whether program or policy outcomes meet norms
- Test for relationships involving very small samples
- Test whether two or more evaluators agree in their rankings

Although chi-square is widely used for testing the statistical significance of relationships, it provides no information about the direction and strength of those relationships. Measures of association provide information about the direction and strength of relationships, and many of these measures also have tests associated with them for hypothesis testing; hence, they are very useful for analysis. This chapter discusses such statistics for two categorical variables. Many of these tests are referred to as *nonparametric statistics*, a name derived from the fact that these test statistics involve very few parameters or test assumptions. These statistical tests are easy to use, which makes them quite popular.

This chapter differs from Chapter 9 in that it covers a fairly broad range of statistics and situations. Some are alternatives to chi-square, and others are designed for specific situations such as testing significance in small samples. Working through the examples in this chapter will increase your familiarity with the process of hypothesis testing. Analysts and managers need to be familiar with the types of situations in which each of these statistics is used so that they can apply the appropriate statistics. Chapter 11 discusses additional nonparametric test statistics that can be used as alternatives to the test statistics discussed here.

THREE NEW CONCEPTS

We now introduce three concepts that extend the discussion of chi-square from Chapter 9: (1) Proportional reduction in error (PRE) is used to quantify the strength of relationships that involve categorical variables, (2) paired cases are used to measure the direction of such relationships, and (3) when dependent samples are involved, responses from one subject or observation are linked to the responses of another. It is assumed that readers will use computers to calculate statistics; the following formulas are provided only to enhance conceptual understanding.

PRE: The Strength of Relationships

Proportional reduction in error (PRE) is defined as *the improvement, expressed as a fraction, in predicting a dependent variable due to knowledge of the independent variable.* Frequently analysts want to know with how much certainty the knowledge of one variable can be used to predict another variable. For example, we may know that receiving welfare is statistically associated with having a low income, but to what extent is having a low income a good predictor of receiving welfare? If we know that a subject has low income, how certain can we be that that subject also receives welfare? PRE is used as a measure of the **strength of a relationship** between two variables, that is, the extent to which one variable is a good predictor of the other.

PRE can be calculated in several ways. The following example is purely illustrative because, in practice, computers are used. Assume that in a sample of 160 people, 90 people are not on welfare and 70 are on welfare (Table 10.1). If we guess that each person is *not* on welfare, we will be wrong 70 times. If we guess that each person is on welfare, we will be wrong 90 times. Hence, the mode (the most frequent category) is our best guess, because it results in fewer wrong guesses. However, *when the level of income is also*

Table 10.1 ⎯⎯⎯ᴧᴧᴧ⎯ Welfare and Income

Receiving Welfare	Income		Total
	Low	High	
No	40	50	90
Yes	60	10	70
Total	100	60	160

known, as well as the number of welfare recipients at each level of income, we make even fewer wrong guesses (or errors). If we know that welfare program participants have low income, we make 40 errors when we guess that everyone with low income in the sample receives welfare. Likewise, if we guess that the people with high income are not on welfare, we make 10 wrong guesses. Thus, the total number of mistakes when taking income into account is now 50, slightly less than the earlier 70 wrong guesses. The proportional reduction in errors (wrong guesses) can be defined as follows:

$$\frac{\text{Errors without knowledge of the independent variable} - \text{Errors with knowledge of the independent variable}}{\text{Errors without knowledge of the independent variable}}$$

Applying this equation to our example, we find a PRE of $[(70 - 50)/70 =]$ 0.2857, or 28.6 percent, with rounding. In other words, as a result of knowing respondents' incomes, we are able to improve our guesses of their welfare situation by 28.6 percent.

PRE fractions range from 0.00 (no association or improvement in prediction) to 1.00 (perfect association or prediction). Although there are no absolute standards for PRE scores, many analysts regard scores of less than 0.25 as indicating a weak association, scores between 0.25 and 0.50 as indicating a moderate association, and scores above 0.50 as indicating a strong association. Thus, our calculated value of 28.6 percent is said to indicate a *moderate* association between these two variables.[1]

Paired Cases: The Direction of Relationships

Analysts often want to know the ***direction of a relationship***. For example, public managers may know that student participation in anger management classes is significantly associated with classroom violence, but is the association positive or negative? Teachers may hope that the relationship is statistically significant and negative, that is, that increased participation decreases violence (but then, who knows what students learn and apply?). Some methods for calculating PRE use an approach based on the concept of ***paired*** *cases.* This method distinguishes among similar, dissimilar, and tied pairs and is used to determine the direction of relationships. *Similar pairs* are pairs of observations that rank similarly low (or high) on both variables: both observations score high or low on both variables. *Dissimilar pairs* are pairs of observations that have reverse ranking on two variables—one observation scores high and the other low, and vice versa, on both variables. *Tied pairs* are those that rank similar on one variable and dissimilar on the other variable. The direction of relationships is determined by comparing the number of similar pairs against the number of dissimilar pairs. When there are more similar pairs than dissimilar pairs, the relationship is said to be positive. When there are more dissimilar pairs than similar pairs, the relationship is negative.[2]

Computers calculate the number of similar, dissimilar, and tied pairs, of course. For illustrative purposes, the number of similar pairs in Table 10.1 is calculated as 40*10 = 400. The number of dissimilar pairs is [50*60 =] 3,000. The number of tied pairs on "Receiving Welfare" is [40*50 + 60*10 =] 2,600, and the number of tied pairs on "Income" is 40*60 + 50*10 =] 2,900. When the table is organized to show causal relationships, the number of tied pairs on "Receiving Welfare" is also called "the number of tied pairs on the dependent variable" (Ty), and the number of tied pairs on "Income" is called "the number of tied pairs on the independent variable" (Tx). The calculations for larger tables follow the same logic but are more complex.[3]

Different statistics, discussed later in this chapter, make different uses of similar, dissimilar, and tied pairs in calculating PRE and the direction of relationships. However, all statistics have the following expression in their numerators: (number of similar pairs) – (number of dissimilar pairs). Hence, a positive value indicates a positive relationship between the variables, and a negative value indicates a negative relationship between the variables. In our example, the expression is negative (400 – 3,000), indicating a negative relationship between income and welfare. PRE statistics based on paired cases have a range of –1.00 to +1.00, which also provides information about the strength of the relationship. For example, a PRE test statistic based on paired cases with a value of –0.57 indicates a strong, negative relationship between two variables.

Dependent Samples

So far, the examples used in the text have involved independent samples. *Independent samples* are those in which the selection of one group (or sample) of subjects has no effect on the selection or responses of the other group (or sample) of subjects. For example, in a random sample of male and female employees, the selection of male employees has no effect on the selection of female employees, nor does it affect their responses. The sample thus consists of independent observations. ***Dependent samples*** (also called *related* samples) are those in which the selection of one subject in a sample does affect the selection of subjects in another group. For example, in before-and-after experiments, measures of subjects are taken at two points in time; those who belong to the first group necessarily also belong to the second group. The samples are thus necessarily linked though the same subjects. Moreover, the two measurements of each subject (before and after) are tied (or related) together; they are not independent observations. Such linkage violates the assumptions of many statistical tests that require independent samples.

Separate statistical tests exist for dependent samples. By convention, the following three situations constitute dependent samples: (1) the before-and-after test scores of subjects in (quasi-) experimental situations (including other repeated measures of subjects), (2) subjects who have been matched (or paired, that is, chosen as having similar characteristics), and (3) the ratings of evaluators. Matched subjects are necessarily linked across groups. When a group of evaluators rates the same set of items, the ratings of each item by different evaluators are regarded as repeated measures. Generally, *samples are assumed to be independent, except when the preceding scenarios are present, or when samples are necessarily correlated for other reasons.*[4] This chapter discusses, a bit later, some tests for dependent samples.

PRE ALTERNATIVES TO CHI-SQUARE

Data analysis often involves two ordinal variables, such as when citizen and client survey questions use five- or seven-point Likert scales. Measures of association that have PRE interpretations and tests of statistical significance associated with them are useful alternatives to chi-square, providing information about statistical significance as well as strength and direction. A broad range of such measures have been developed, however, and many are routinely provided by computers along with other calculations. Analysts will thus want to be familiar with some of the more common ones, and this chapter provides guidance in choosing among them.

In analyses of relationships among two ordinal-level variables, four frequently calculated PRE-based statistics are ***gamma*** (γ), ***Somers' d***, ***Kendall's tau-b*** (τ_b), and ***Kendall's tau-c*** (τ_c). These statistics differ chiefly in the manner in which ties are taken into account, resulting in different estimates of PRE. Of these tests, tau-c is typically most conservative in estimating PRE and is therefore used widely.

Examination of the formulas for these statistics provides a sense of the differences. The following discussion is for illustrative purposes only, as computers calculate the statistics, of course. Gamma is defined as (Ns –

$Nd)/(Ns + Nd)$, where Ns is the number of similar pairs and Nd is the number of dissimilar pairs. Gamma does not take tied pairs into account. By contrast, Somers' d is defined as $(Ns - Nd)/(Ns + Nd + Ty)$, where Ty represents ties on the dependent variable. Because Ty is in the denominator, the value of Somers' d is less than γ; thus Somers' d is a more conservative estimate of the PRE. Somers' d is a *directional measure*, which means that the value of Somers' d depends on which variable is identified as the dependent variable; statistical software programs compute Somers' d for both possibilities. Tau-b is defined as $(Ns - Nd)/\sqrt{(Ns + Nd + Ty)(Ns + Nd + Tx)}$. It is symmetrical (that is, it does not depend on which variable is identified as dependent)[5] and is even more conservative than Somers' d. However, tau-b is appropriate only for square tables, which is an important limitation. Tau-c is developed from tau-b and designed for nonsquare tables.[6] It is defined as $2m(Ns - Nd)/N^2(m - 1)$, where m is the smaller number of rows or columns, and N is the sample size. Tau-c makes an adjustment for the number of cases, as well as rows or columns, rather than for the number of pairs. These adjustments result in even more conservative estimates.

Computer programs provide a range of statistics in part because, depending on the unique features of one's data, the above generalizations may not always hold up. In some cases, the value of Somers' d may be less than that of tau-c, for example. Also, some analysts prefer the conceptual clarity of gamma, which does not make adjustments for ties. Nonetheless, Kendall's tau-c is widely used and reported as an alternative to chi-square for ordinal-level data; it is among the most conservative estimates, and many scientists have become familiar with it.[7] Also, unlike chi-square, these measures do not make assumptions about the number of expected frequencies, which further increases their ease of use.[8]

The use of these measures of association is shown in the following example. A human resources manager wants to know whether perceptions of the county as an employer are associated with feelings of fairness, especially in the area of work rewards. An employee survey is administered. The lead-in question is this: "Please evaluate the following statements by indicating whether you strongly agree, agree, disagree, or strongly disagree with the following statements. You may also state that you don't know." Two items are "I am satisfied with my job in Seminole County" and "The people who get promoted are the best qualified for the job." The results are shown in Table 10.2.

The results show that job satisfaction is *significantly, moderately,* and *positively* associated with this measure of fairness for each of the test statistics. Table 10.2 also shows that tau-c has indeed the smallest PRE value and that all statistics are evaluated at the same level of statistical significance. A contingency table can be examined to determine practical significance (not shown here). Among employees who agree or strongly agree that the best

Table 10.2 ⟶ Comparing Ordinal-Ordinal PRE Measures of Association

Statistic		Value	Approx. Sig.
Chi-square		253.17	0.000
Somer's d	Symmetric	0.323	0.000
	Dep = job satisf.	0.285	0.000
	Dep = promoted	0.372	0.000
Gamma		0.470	0.000
Kendall's tau-b		0.326	0.000
Kendall's tau-c		0.275	0.000

Note: Dep = dependent variables; sig. = significance.

people get promoted, 93.3 percent also agree or strongly agree that they are satisfied with their jobs; by comparison, only 69.1 percent of employees who disagree or strongly disagree that the best people get promoted also agree that they are satisfied with their jobs. Disagreeing that the best people get promoted also increases job *dis*satisfaction: 35.4 percent of employees who disagree or strongly disagree that the best people get promoted are dissatisfied with their jobs, as compared with only 3.2 percent of employees who agree or strongly agree that the best people get promoted.

When two variables are *nominal* level, **Goodman and Kruskal's tau** (τ_{yx}) is a test statistic with PRE interpretation. See Table 10.3 for an example of its use. Perhaps the analyst wants to know whether skill type affects job type, or vice versa. Because Goodman and Kruskal's tau is a directional measure, statistical software packages produce two measures of Goodman and Kruskal's tau that vary according to which variable is designated as the dependent variable. Goodman and Kruskal's tau is always positive (the question of direction is moot for nominal variables). For the data shown in Table 10.3, Goodman and Kruskal's tau is 0.016 (p = .579 > .05) when "Job" is the dependent variable and 0.016 (p = .584 > .05) when "Skills" is

Getting Started
Collect data for two ordinal-level variables, and calculate tau-c on a computer.

Table 10.3 ⟶ Job Applied For by Skills of Recipient

	Skills of Welfare Recipient			
Job	Word processing skills	Public speaking	Spread-sheets	Total
Clerk	14	5	10	29
Office assistant	15	10	20	45
Messenger	5	5	5	15
Total	34	20	35	89

the dependent variable. Thus, the relationship between these two variables is not significant. The accompanying footnote discusses some other nominal-level measures that, though used less often, are provided by statistical software programs.[9]

BEATING THE STANDARD?: THE GOODNESS-OF-FIT TEST

We now examine some tests for dealing with diverse situations that managers and analysts may encounter. For example, managers and analysts sometimes need to know whether a program or policy exceeds a standard or norm. The chi-square test discussed in Chapter 9 can also be adapted for this purpose. Assume we test 400 cars and find a 6 percent failure rate. Is that any different from a norm of 8 percent? You can readily think of other applications. For example, we might compare students who pass a test versus a stated norm, or clients who succeed in a treatment against a stated norm. We might look at water samples, housing, or anything else against a stated norm.

Regarding the chi-square test, program or policy outcomes are seen as observed frequencies, and the norm is used for calculating expected frequencies. Then we can examine whether a relationship exists between these variables. Such a test is a *goodness-of-fit test*, a test of whether one distribution is similar to another. The two distributions for the cars example are shown in Table 10.4. The left data column shows the actual frequencies, and the right column shows the expected frequencies that would exist if the actual distribution was exactly consistent with the norm. Specifically, the actual frequencies are [0.06*400 =] 24 failed cars and [0.94*400 =] 376 passed cars. The expected frequencies are [0.08*400 =] 32 failed cars and 368 passed cars. This definition and method of calculating expected frequencies is quite different from the test shown in Chapter 9.

The null hypothesis is that the two distributions are similar, and the alternate hypothesis is that they are dissimilar. Using the chi-square formula, $\Sigma(O_i - E_i)^2/E_i$, we calculate chi-square as $(24 - 32)^2/32 = 2.000$ for the failed category and as $(376 - 368)^2/368 = 0.174$ for the passed category. Thus, the chi-square test statistic is [2.000 + 0.174 =] 2.174. The degrees of freedom for this test is defined as rows − 1, or [2 − 1 =] 1. From Appendix B, the chi-square critical value at the 5 percent level and df = 1 is 3.841. Because the

Table 10.4 ⌁⌁⌁ Test Failure Rates

	Actual (Observed)	Norm (Expected)
Passed	376	368
Failed	24	32

Table 10.5 ~~~~~~ U.S. Census Response by Age Groups

Age	U.S. Census (%)	Survey sample (%)
18–45	62.3	62.8
46–65	24.1	26.8
66+	13.6	10.4

test statistic is less than the critical value, |t.s.| < c.v., we fail to reject the null hypothesis. Hence, we conclude that the failure rate is *not different* from the prespecified norm of 8 percent. The failure rate is neither higher nor lower than the standard; it meets the standard.

The above example can be expanded by considering more than just two response categories such as pass or fail. Assume that we just completed a citizen survey yielding 1,034 valid responses. We next want to know whether the age distribution of these respondents is consistent with that of the U.S. Census for the area. The lack of consistency may suggest problems of under- or oversampling and, thus, possible bias that we might want to know about. Hence,

H_0: The age distribution of the sample is consistent with that of the population.
H_A: The age distribution of the sample is inconsistent with that of the population.

The results are shown in Table 10.5. Here, the census population frequencies are the expected frequencies, and the sample frequencies are the observed frequencies. With 1,034 completed survey responses, the expected frequency of the 18–45 age category is [1,034*0.623 =] 644. The expected frequencies of the other two categories are, respectively, [1,034*0.241 =] 249 and [1,034*0.136 =] 141; similarly, the observed (actual) frequencies are 649, 277, and 108. Using the usual chi-square formula, we find that the chi-square value for the first category (age 18–45) is [(649 – 644)^2/644 =] 0.039. The values for the second and third categories are calculated similarly and are, respectively, 3.149 and 7.723. Thus, the chi-square test statistic is 10.91 (with rounding). The number of degrees of freedom is $r - 1$, or [3 – 1 =] 2. The critical value at the 5 percent level of significance with df = 2 is 5.991 (see Appendix B); thus we conclude that the sample *is significantly different* from the population. Note that if the sample had consisted of only 300 completed responses, then the chi-square would have been 3.16, which is not significant.

Further inspection of Table 10.5 suggests that the researchers undersampled older respondents and that they thus may want to reweight their findings to examine the effect, if any, of this undersampling on their conclusions. Note also that these calculations can be used to determine the number of surveys among those 66 years and older that should have been collected in order to avoid this problem. Perhaps researchers can continue surveying among that group. You can verify, by redoing the preceding calculations (using a spreadsheet), that completing another 12 surveys among the 66+ group (increasing the sample size to 1,054) reduces the chi-square test statistic to 5.955, which provides a sample that no longer is significantly different from that of the population.

DISCRIMINATION AND OTHER TESTS

A rather different kind of problem is faced by managers when they want to test for discrimination. In a typical scenario, assume that we want to test whether program staff is discriminating against minority clients by failing to provide them with services that are provided to other, white clients. To examine this possibility, we match up pairs of minority and white clients; each pair has similar equivalent conditions and are trained to provide similar responses to questions. Their main difference is race. This strategy is also used for testing discrimination in employment interviews or in bank lending practices. Pairs of majority and minority job (or loan) seekers are sent to interviews (or to apply for loans), intermingled with other candidates.

This scenario involves a *dependent sample* because the responses are linked to matched subjects. This scenario is also interesting in that we want to examine whether a pattern exists among dissimilar outcomes, only. The **McNemar test** determines the level at which dissimilar outcomes are statistically significant. For example, consider Table 10.6, in which each count compares the employment outcomes of the paired testers. The McNemar test compares whether the eight instances in which a white but not minority applicant received a job are significantly different from the one instance in which the minority candidate, not the white one, received the job. The test for these data is significant ($p = .039 < .05$), which means that this disparate outcome cannot be attributed to chance alone. The McNemar test ignores similar outcomes; thus, the same test result is obtained by examining the nine dissimilar outcomes, only. It ignores similar outcomes in which both testers are hired, such as when employers hire multiple candidates through the same interview process.[10]

Table 10.6 ～～ Employment Discrimination Test

Minority Applicants	White applicants		Total
	Hired	Not hired	
Hired	0	1	1
Not hired	8	2	10
Total	8	3	11

The McNemar test is an example of a test designed for small samples. For *independent samples,* a variety of small sample tests exists, often adaptations of chi-square. Although chi-square and Goodman and Kruskal's tau can be used for two-by-two tables with independent observations, some researchers argue that when analysts have small samples they should use *chi-square with the Yates' continuity correction.* Small samples (that is, those with small frequency counts) bias the expected frequencies slightly upward; this bias is "corrected" by subtracting 0.50 from the difference of expected and observed frequencies, thus producing a more conservative test statistic. However, others argue that this correction overcorrects.[11] The *Fisher exact test* is used for two-by-two tables with small samples. It compares the observed table with all other possible tables that have the same marginal counts (that is, row and column totals). Based on this comparison, the test calculates the probability that the two variables are related.[12]

As an example, consider the following scenario. You are a senior staff member at a drug treatment center. Drop-out (discontinuation) rates among those undergoing treatment is an important problem. One of your contractors has proposed a new method that promises to reduce discontinuation. To test whether the system works, you implement it among a small sample of clients and want to compare the results with those who get the traditional method. The analytical task is clearly to align this problem with some method of statistical testing. Consider the outline of Table 10.7 as a way of structuring this problem. The right column shows clients using the new system; the left column shows outcomes among clients using the traditional treatment. Designed in this way, these are independent samples, and we can use tests that are appropriate for two-by-two tables and involve small samples. Note that although Table 10.7 appears similar to Table 10.6, this treatment scenario does not involve a dependent sample, nor are we interested in comparing only dissimilar outcomes.

Assume that the initial results are as shown in Table 10.7, which indicate that discontinuation decreased from [8/15 =] 53.3 percent to [5/15 =] 33.3 percent. Is this sufficient evidence to conclude that the decrease is statistically significant? The Goodman and Kruskal's tau test statistic for this test is 0.41 ($p = .277$), chi-square with continuity correction is 0.543 (df = 1, $p = .461$), and the Fisher exact test shows $p = .462$. Thus, the decrease is *not*

Table 10.7 New Treatment Test Results

| | Uses New Treatment System | |
	No	Yes
No discontinuation	7	10
Discontinuation	8	5

statistically significant. Is this a problem for the manager or consultant? Probably not. Although we can ask how large the decrease has to be for it to be statistically significant,[13] a better managerial response is to acknowledge the decrease as "sizable" and ask how many more clients have to be involved for the difference as shown to be statistically significant. To this end, the raw data used to generate this table can readily be multiplied (copied and pasted) in statistical software programs, and we then conclude that about a fourfold increase, to 60 clients in each group, will show statistically significant results for these differences.[14] Then, Goodman and Kruskal's tau is 0.41 (p = .028), chi-square with continuity correction is 4.11 (df = 1, p = .043), and the Fisher exact test shows p = .042. Hence, the managerial response is thus to continue the alternative method, getting therapists' assessment and input into the new treatment; closely monitor continuation rates; and then reassess the alternative intervention for statistical evidence at a later date after more clients have been involved.

DO THE EVALUATORS AGREE?

Evaluators often are used to assess program or agency performance by providing qualitative judgments. *Kruskal-Wallis' H* assesses whether programs differ in their ratings. Assume that 15 evaluators are each asked to evaluate one of three programs, and an index score is constructed of their evaluations. This is a test for *independent samples*; each evaluator evaluates only one program. The null hypothesis is that, on average, each program receives the same average ranking. The data are shown in Table 10.8 (for presentation, the variables are in separate columns; these data are entered in statistical software programs as one table with 15 observations and two variables). The group variable identifies the program. Note that the rating variable is shown as a continuous variable. Kruskal-Wallis' H assigns ranks to the rating variable, thus creating an ordinal variable from the continuous variable. Specifically, it does so by ranking the collective observations of all groups from high to low and then testing whether the means of the ranks of

Table 10.8 ———⌁⌁⌁— Ratings of Three Programs

Group	Rating	Rank	Group	Rating	Rank	Group	Rating	Rank
1	2.5	3	2	3.4	7.5	3	4.8	13
1	2.9	4	2	3.3	6	3	5.0	14.5
1	4.0	10.5	2	4.0	10.5	3	5.0	14.5
1	3.2	5	2	3.9	9	3	3.4	7.5
1	1.2	1	2	2.1	2	3	4.2	12
Mean		4.7			7.0			12.3

Table 10.9 ━━━━━〜〜〜━━ Actual Ratings of Three Evaluators

Item	Rater 1	Rater 2	Rater 3
1	5	3	4
2	4	2	2
3	3	3	3
4	2	4	3
5	1	1	1

the groups are significantly different. Kruskal-Wallis' H has a chi-square distribution. The H test statistic for the data in Table 10.8 is 7.636 (df = 2, p = .022 < .05).[15] That is, the three programs vary in their mean ranking of evaluation scores. Information provided with this result shows that the mean rankings are, respectively, 4.70, 7.00, and 12.30.

Samples that involve evaluators often are dependent, however. Typically, a few evaluators assess different program items, and we want to know whether evaluators agree in their ratings. This occurs in program reviews, when outside experts assess programs or facilities such as hospitals or parks departments in connection with accreditation. It also occurs in regulatory inspections (do two or more inspectors or assessors agree?) and in the evaluations of trained observers. By convention, we assume that ratings are necessarily correlated because raters are typically consistent in their ratings. The data must be ordinal. The **_Friedman test_**, developed by the well-known economist Milton Friedman, uses data in the format shown in Tables 10.9 and 10.10 and has a chi-square distribution. The Friedman test ranks the evaluations of the three raters for each item (5 = highest). Table 10.9 shows that Rater 1 has the highest ranking of Item 1. The relative ranking of Item 1 across the three raters is 3, 1, and 2 (Table 10.10) because Rater 1 gives Item 1 a higher rating than Rater 3, who, in turn, gives Item 1 a higher rating than Rater 2. The ratings for Item 2 are tied between the second and third raters. The ranked ratings for Item 2 are 3.00, [(1 + 2)/2 =] 1.50, and 1.50. The ranked ratings for Item 3 are 2.00, 2.00, and 2.00 (they are all tied), and so

Table 10.10 ━━━━━〜〜〜━━ Relative Ratings of Three Evaluators

Item	Rater 1	Rater 2	Rater 3
1	3	1	2
2	3	1.5	1.5
3	2	2	2
4	1	3	2
5	2	2	2
Mean rank	2.2	1.9	1.9

on. Based on these rankings, the mean ranked ratings for each evaluator are determined, as shown in Table 10.10. The Friedman test statistic for these data is 0.545 (df = 2, p = .761 > .05). Thus, we conclude that the ratings of the evaluators are not different; *the evaluators agree with each other.* When columns and rows are reversed, the Friedman test assesses whether differences exist among the mean rankings of items. This test can also be used to examine test score changes in before-and-after situations. Then, the rows are subjects and the columns are the subjects' before-and-after scores.[16]

> **Getting Started**
> Discuss how these statistics can be used in your area.

SUMMARY

Analysts are frequently confronted with categorical data. For example, many surveys (of employees, citizens, or program clients) involve categorical data, such as gender or income (when measured in brackets). Surveys also involve ordinal assessments, such as the extent to which respondents agree or disagree with certain statements. To analyze the extent and manner in which two variables are related to each other, analysts often use the PRE and nonparametric statistics discussed in this chapter. PRE-based statistics provide information about the statistical significance of relationships, as well as their strength and direction and are thus preferred to chi-square for testing relationships of categorical variables. Nonparametric statistics are used for rather special situations, such as comparing the ratings of two evaluators, significance testing that involves very small samples, and dependent samples (samples in which observations are correlated).

A plethora of PRE and nonparametric statistics exists. It would be a true challenge to memorize all of the statistics discussed in this chapter. Rather, the task is to be familiar with the types of problems they address. Recognizing particular situations and problems will help analysts to know when to use each test. As bewildering as the array of tests might seem, clearly, the tests themselves are not particularly difficult to use. Indeed, they are rather straightforward:

- When both variables are ordinal, Kendall's tau-c is a commonly used PRE statistic for testing the significance, strength, and direction of the relationship between these two variables.
- When both variables are nominal, Goodman and Kruskal's tau is a PRE statistic used for testing the significance and strength of the relationship.
- When the sample is very small, statistics specifically designed for that purpose are used, such as the Fisher exact test.
- When a test of discrimination is needed, the McNemar test is used.

- When one variable is ordinal and the other is nominal, the scenario may involve a comparison of evaluators' rankings. Then, Kruskal-Wallis' H is used for independent samples, and the Friedman test is used for dependent samples.

This short list is an important resource for you as you learn to identify the particular situations that warrant the use of specific tests.

KEY TERMS

Chi-square with the Yates'
   continuity correction (p. 172)
Dependent samples (p. 166)
Directional measure (p. 167)
Direction of a relationship (p. 164)
Dissimilar pairs (p. 165)
Fisher exact test (p. 172)
Friedman test (p. 174)
Gamma (p. 166)
Goodman and Kruskal's tau (p. 168)
Goodness-of-fit test (p. 169)
Independent samples (p. 165)

Kendall's tau-b (p. 166)
Kendall's tau-c (p. 166)
Kruskal-Wallis' H (p. 173)
McNemar test (p. 171)
Paired cases (p. 164)
Proportional reduction in error
   (PRE) (p. 163)
Similar pairs (p. 165)
Somers' d (p. 166)
Strength of a relationship (p. 163)
Tied pairs (p. 165)

Notes

1. Some authors suggest that values below 0.20 indicate weak relationships; between 0.20 and 0.40, moderate relationships; between 0.40 and 0.60, strong relationships; and above 0.60, very strong relationships. We suggest erring on the side of caution and thus using a higher standard.
2. This extends the earlier discussion about Table 8.5.
3. For example, see Chava Frankfort-Nachmias, *Social Statistics for a Diverse Society,* 2d ed. (Thousand Oaks, Calif.: Pine Forge Press, 1999), chap. 7. Many books provide similar calculations. The example is provided for conceptual understanding only; the computer calculates test statistics.
4. Independent observations are also called independent samples, and dependent samples are also called paired or matched observations. The concept of paired observations should *not be* confused with that of paired cases, discussed as part of PRE.
5. Gamma, tau-b, and tau-c are symmetrical measures; only Somers' d is directional.
6. While tau-c is designed for nonsquare tables, many scientists use tau-c for tables of any size. This reflects a bias toward more conservative estimates, and the fact that p-values of tau-b and tau-c are identical.

7. Tau-c can also be used when one variable is ordinal and the other is continuous, or when one variable is ordinal and the other dichotomous. When used with continuous variables, the estimates of tau-c may result in somewhat higher p-values, relative to statistics discussed in later chapters. For mixed ordinal-nominal level data, analysts can consider the Mann-Whitney test described in Chapter 11, or the Friedman and Kruskal-Wallis' tests, discussed later in this chapter.

8. In addition to the statistics discussed here, many computer programs will produce additional measures of chi-square, but these often have little additional utility. The linear-by-linear association is the square of the Pearson's drop-out (discontinuation) rates correlation coefficient (see Chapter 12), multiplied by the sample size, minus one. The likelihood ratio is used for n-way tables, in which a third variable is added to the contingency table. See B. G. Tabachnick and L. S. Fidell, *Using Multivariate Statistics,* 3d ed. (New York: HarperCollins), chap. 7.

9. SPSS produces a large range of statistics for nominal variables. Lambda is calculated using the PRE formula provided in the text. However, this results in a computational quirk that limits its usefulness; the value of lambda is zero when all of the category modes of the independent variable occur on the same category of the dependent variable, regardless of any association that may exist. Goodman and Kruskal's tau overcomes this computational problem by calculating association in a different way. *Cramer's V* is a chi-square-based measure that is corrected for the problem that χ^2 increases with sample size the number of cells. Cramer's V ranges from zero (no association) to one (perfect association) and is defined as

$$\sqrt{\frac{\chi^2}{n*(rows-1,columns-1)}}.$$

Although not calculated as a PRE statistic, Cramer's V values below 0.25 are considered to indicate weak relationships, values between 0.25 and 0.50 to indicate moderate relationships, and values over 0.50 to indicate strong relationships. Many computer programs also produce the *contingency coefficient, C* (also called Pearson's coefficient of contingency), which is calculated as

$$\sqrt{\chi^2/(\chi^2+n)}$$

C is calculated similar to V but has the disadvantage that its maximum value can be less than 1.0. Cramer's V overcomes this problem and is thus preferred. The *uncertainty coefficient, U,* is a measure that is quite similar to lambda and does not offer many advantages in this context. A formula for this statistic can be found in R. A. Cooper and A. J. Weeks, *Data, Models, and Statistics Analysis* (Oxford: Philip Allan, 1983), and other general statistics books.

10. The McNemar test statistic is defined as $\chi^2_{McNemar} = (|f_{0,1} - f_{1,0}|)^2 / (f_{0,1} + f_{1,0})$.

11. The chi-square statistic with Yates' continuity correction is defined as

$$\sum_i \frac{(|O_i - E_i| - 0.5)^2}{E_i}$$

12. The following measures may also be considered. Phi (ϕ) is defined as $\sqrt{\chi^2/n}$, and ranges from zero to one for two-by-k tables ($k \geq 2$). Phi-squared (ϕ^2) has a "variance-explained" interpretation; for example, a ϕ^2 value of 0.35 (or $\phi = 0.59$) means that 35 percent of the variance in one variable is explained by the other. Yule's Q is a measure of association with a PRE interpretation but without a test of statistical significance. Yule's Q is defined as follows. Assume the following two-by-two table:

A	B
C	D

Then, Yule's Q is $\frac{(AD) - (BC)}{(AD) + (BC)}$.

13. With the sample sizes of Table 10.7, the discontinuation rate of the alternative treatment would have to drop further to 13.3 percent (2 of 15 clients). Then, Goodman and Kruskal's tau is .180 (p = .022), chi-square with continuity correction is 3.750 (p = .53), and the Fisher exact test shows p = .50.

14. Another approach is to calculate power (see Box 9.1). Using the above continuation rates and $n = 60$ for each group, we find power to be 71.8 percent, which is indeed close to 80 percent.

15. The formula for H is

$$\frac{12}{n(n+1)} \left(\frac{T_1^2}{n_1} + \frac{T_2^2}{n_2} + \ldots \right) - 3(n+1),$$

where T_i is the sum of ranks in Group 1, and so on.

16. The Friedman test is quite sensitive to the number of items; it is best to have at least 10 rows.

CHAPTER

11

The T-Test

CHAPTER OBJECTIVES

After reading this chapter, you should be able to

- Test whether two or more groups have different means of a continuous variable
- Assess whether the mean is consistent with a specified value
- Evaluate whether variables meet test assumptions
- Understand the role of variable transformations
- Identify t-test alternatives

When analysts need to compare the means of a continuous variable across different groups, they have a valuable tool at their disposal: the t-test. T-tests are used for testing whether two groups have different means of a continuous variable, such as when we want to know whether mean incomes vary between men and women. They could also be used to compare program performance between two periods, when performance in each period is measured as a continuous variable.

The examples in this chapter differ from those in Chapters 9 and 10 in that in this chapter's examples one of the variables is continuous and the other is categorical. Many variables are continuous, such as income, age, height, case loads, service calls, and counts of fish in a pond. Moreover, when ordinal-level variables are used for constructing index variables (see Chapter 3), the resulting index variables typically are continuous as well. When variables are continuous, we should not recode them as categorical variables just to use the techniques of the previous chapters. Continuous variables provide valuable information about distances between categories and often have a broader range of values than ordinal variables. Recoding continuous variables as categorical variables is discouraged because it results in a loss of information; we should use tests such as the t-test.

Statistics involving continuous variables usually require more test assumptions. Many of these tests are referred to as *parametric statistics*; this term refers to the fact that they make assumptions about the distribution of data and also that they are used to make inferences about population parameters. Formally, the term "parametric" means that a test makes assumptions about the distribution of the underlying population. Parametric tests have more test assumptions than nonparametric tests, and most typically that the variable is continuous and normally distributed (see Chapter 7). These and other test assumptions are also part of t-tests.

This chapter focuses on three common t-tests: for independent samples, for dependent (paired) samples, and the one-sample t-test. For each, we provide examples and discuss test assumptions.

This chapter also discusses nonparametric alternatives to t-tests, which analysts will want to consider when t-test assumptions cannot be met for their variables. As a general rule, a bias exists towards using parametric tests because they are more powerful than nonparametric tests. Nonparametric alternatives to parametric tests often transform continuous testing variables into other types of variables, such as rankings, which reduces information about them. While nonparametric statistics are easier to use because they have fewer assumptions, parametric tests are more likely to find statistical evidence that two variables are associated; their tests often have lower p values than nonparametric statistics.[1]

T-TESTS FOR INDEPENDENT SAMPLES

T-tests are used to test whether the means of a continuous variable differ across two different groups. For example, do men and women differ in their levels of income, when measured as a continuous variable? Does crime vary between two parts of town? Do rich people live longer than poor people? Do high-performing students commit fewer acts of violence than do low-performing students? The t-test approach is shown graphically in Figure 11.1, which illustrates the incomes of men and women as boxplots (the lines in the middle of the boxes indicate the means rather than the medians).[2]

Figure 11.1 ———————⌇⌇⌇— The T-Test:
Mean Incomes by Gender

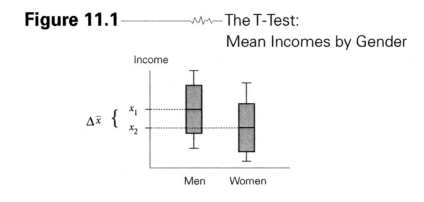

When the two groups are independent samples, the t-test is called the
independent-samples t-test. Sometimes the continuous variable is called a
"test variable" and the dichotomous variable is called a "grouping variable."
The t-test tests whether the *difference of the means* ($\Delta \bar{x}$, or $\bar{x}_1 - \bar{x}_2$) *is significantly different from zero,* that is, whether men and women have different
incomes. The following hypotheses are posited:

H_0: Men and women do not have different mean incomes (in the
    population).
H_A: Men and women do have different mean incomes (in the population).

Alternatively, using the Greek letter μ to refer to differences in the population, H_0: $\mu_m = \mu_f$, and H_A: $\mu_m \neq \mu_f$. The formula for calculating the t-test
test statistic (a tongue twister?) is

$$t = \frac{\bar{x}_1 - \bar{x}_2}{\sqrt{s_p^2 \left(\frac{1}{n_1} + \frac{1}{n_2} \right)}}$$

As always, the computer calculates the test statistic and reports at what
level it is significant. Such calculations are seldom done by hand. To further
conceptual understanding of this formula, it is useful to relate it to the
discussion of hypothesis testing in Chapter 9. First, note that the difference
of means, $\bar{x}_1 - \bar{x}_2$, appears in the numerator: the larger the difference of
means, the larger the t-test test statistic, and the more likely we might reject
the null hypothesis. Second, s_p is the pooled variance of the two groups, that
is, the weighted average of the variances of each group.[3] Increases in the
standard deviation decrease the test statistic. Thus, it is easier to reject the
null hypotheses when two populations are clustered narrowly around their
means than when they are spread widely around them. Finally, more observations (that is, increased information or larger n_1 and n_2) increase the size
of the test statistic, making it easier to reject the null hypothesis.

The test statistics of a t-test can be positive or negative, although this depends merely on which group has the larger mean; the sign of the test statistic has no substantive interpretation. *Critical values* (see Chapter 3) of the t-test are shown in Appendix C as *(Student's) t-distribution.*[4] For this test, the *degrees of freedom* are defined as $n - 1$, where n is the total number of observations for both groups. The critical value decreases as the number of observations increases, making it easier to reject the null hypothesis.

The t-distribution shows one- and two-tailed tests. *Two-tailed t-tests* should be used when analysts do not have prior knowledge about which group has a larger mean; *one-tailed t-tests* are used when analysts do have such prior knowledge. This choice is dictated by the research situation, not by any statistical criterion. In practice, two-tailed tests are used most often, unless compelling a priori knowledge exists or it is known that one group cannot have a larger mean than the other. Two-tailed testing is more conservative than one-tailed testing because the critical values of two-tailed tests are larger, thus requiring larger t-test test statistics in order to reject the null hypothesis.[5] Many statistical software packages provide only two-tailed testing. The above null hypothesis (men and women do not have different mean incomes in the population) requires a two-tailed test because we do not know, a priori, which gender has the larger income.[6] Finally, note that the t-test distribution approximates the normal distribution for large samples: the critical values of 1.96 (5 percent significance) and 2.58 (1 percent significance), for large degrees of freedom (∞), are identical to those of the normal distribution.

> **Getting Started**
>
> Find examples of t-tests in the research literature.

T-Test Assumptions

Like other tests, the t-test has various *test assumptions* that must be met to ensure test validity. Statistical testing always begins by determining whether test assumptions are met before examining the main research hypotheses. This section discusses these tests, as well as ways in which tests and variables are adapted to meet test assumptions. *Four t-test test assumptions* must be met to ensure test validity:

- One variable is continuous, and the other variable is dichotomous.
- The two distributions have equal variances.
- The observations are independent.
- The two distributions are normally distributed.

The *first assumption,* that one variable is continuous and the other dichotomous, usually does not present much of a problem. Some analysts use t-tests with ordinal rather than continuous data for the testing variable. This approach is theoretically controversial because the distances among ordinal categories are undefined. This situation is avoided easily by using nonpara-

Figure 11.2 ⎯⎯⎯⎯⎯⎯⎯⎯ Equal and Unequal Variances

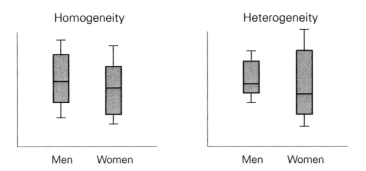

metric alternatives (discussed later in this chapter). Also, when the grouping variable is not dichotomous, analysts need to make it so in order to perform a t-test. Many statistical software packages allow dichotomous variables to be created from other types of variables, such as by grouping or recoding ordinal or continuous variables.

The *second assumption* is that the variances of the two distributions are equal. This is called ***homogeneity of variances***. The use of pooled variances in the earlier formula is justified only when the variances of the two groups are equal. When variances are unequal (called ***heterogeneity of variances***), revised formulas are used to calculate t-test test statistics and degrees of freedom.[7] The difference between homogeneity and heterogeneity is shown graphically in Figure 11.2. Although we needn't be concerned with the precise differences in these calculation methods, all t-tests *first* test whether variances are equal in order to know which t-test test statistic is to be used for *subsequent* hypothesis testing. Thus, every t-test involves a (somewhat tricky) two-step procedure. A common test for the equality of variances is the ***Levene's test***. The null hypothesis of this test is that variances are equal. Many statistical software programs provide the Levene's test along with the t-test, so that users know which t-test to use—the t-test for equal variances or that for unequal variances. The Levene's test is performed first, so that the correct t-test can be chosen.

The term ***robust*** is used, generally, to describe the extent to which test conclusions are unaffected by departures from test assumptions. T-tests are relatively robust for (hence, unaffected by) departures from assumptions of homogeneity and normality (see below) when groups are of approximately equal size. When groups are of about equal size, test conclusions about any difference between their means will be unaffected by heterogeneity.

The *third assumption* is that observations are independent. (Quasi-) experimental research designs violate this assumption, as discussed in Chapter 10. The formula for the t-test test statistic, then, is modified to test whether the *difference* between before and after measurements is zero. This is called a **paired t-test**, which is discussed later in this chapter.

The *fourth assumption* is that the distributions are normally distributed. Although normality is an important test assumption, a key reason for the popularity of the t-test is that t-test conclusions often are robust against considerable violations of normality assumptions that are not caused by highly skewed distributions. We provide some detail about tests for normality and how to address departures thereof. Remember, when nonnormality cannot be resolved adequately, analysts consider nonparametric alternatives to the t-test discussed at the end of this chapter. Box 11.1 provides a bit more discussion about the reason for this assumption.

A combination of visual inspection and statistical tests is always used to determine the normality of variables. Two tests of normality are the **Kolmogorov-Smirnov test** (also known as the K-S test) for samples with more than 50 observations and the **Shapiro-Wilk test** for samples with up to 50 observations. The **null hypothesis of normality** is that the variable *is* normally distributed: thus, we *do not* want to reject the null hypothesis. A problem with statistical tests of normality is that they are *very sensitive* to small samples and minor deviations from normality. The extreme sensitivity of these tests implies the following: whereas failure to reject the null hypothesis indicates normal distribution of a variable, rejecting the null hypothesis does not indicate that the variable is not normally distributed. It is acceptable to consider variables as being normally distributed when they visually appear to be so, even when the null hypothesis of normality is rejected by normality tests. Of course, variables are preferred that are supported by both visual inspection and normality tests.

Remedies exist for correcting substantial departures from normality, but these remedies may make matters worse when departures from normality are minimal. The *first* course of action is to identify and remove any outliers that may affect the mean and standard deviation. The *second* course of action is **variable transformation**, which involves transforming the variable, often by taking $\log(x)$, $\sqrt{x}$ or x^2 of each observation, and then testing the transformed variable for normality. Variable transformation may address excessive skewness by adjusting the measurement scale, thereby helping variables to better approximate normality.[8] Substantively, we strongly prefer to make conclusions that satisfy test assumptions, regardless of which measurement scale is chosen.[9] Keep in mind that when variables are transformed, the units in which results are expressed are transformed, as well. Examples of variable transformation are provided below.

Typically, analysts have different ways to address test violations. Examination of the causes of assumption violations often helps analysts to better understand their data. Different approaches may be successful for addressing

In Greater Depth...

Box 11.1 Why Normality?

The reasons for the normality assumption are twofold: First, the features of the normal distribution are well-established and are used in many parametric tests for making inferences and hypothesis testing. Second, probability theory suggests that random samples will often be normally distributed, and that the means of these samples can be used as estimates of population means.

The latter reason is informed by the ***central limit theorem***, which states that an infinite number of relatively large samples will be normally distributed, *regardless of the distribution of the population*. An infinite number of samples is also called a sampling distribution. The central limit theorem is usually illustrated as follows. Assume that we know the population distribution, which has only six data elements with the following values: 1, 2, 3, 4, 5, or 6. Next, we write each of these six numbers on a separate sheet of paper, and draw repeated samples of three numbers each (that is, $n = 3$). We record the mean of each sample. Our first sample might consist of the numbers 2, 4, and 5; hence, we record the mean of $[(2 + 4 + 5)/3] = 3.67$. The next sample might be 1, 2, and 6, and so we then record the mean value 3.00. After we have taken about 30 or so samples (not quite an infinite number of samples, but getting there. . .), the histogram of recorded means will resemble a normal distribution with a mean of about 3.5. This number is also the population mean, namely, $[(1 + 2 + 3 + 4 + 5 + 6)/6] = 3.5$.

This theorem is important because it shows that we do not need to know the population distribution to estimate the mean of the population. Note that the population is not normally distributed; each value occurs just once, but the distribution of sample means is normally distributed. Further, although in practice we have only one sample, the central limit theorem states that we can use the normal distribution to create expectations about any sample mean. Our discussion of confidence intervals, in Chapter 8, demonstrates this point.

In short, parametric tests such as the t-test are based on these properties for their inferences and hypothesis testing and require variables to be normally distributed. Although nonparametric statistics do not require variables to be normally distributed, a bias exists toward using parametric tests because they are more powerful than nonparametric tests. Nonparametric alternatives to parametric tests often transform continuous testing variables into other types of variables, such as rankings, which reduces the information available about them.

test assumptions. Analysts should not merely go by the result of one approach that supports their case, ignoring others that perhaps do not. Rather, analysts should rely on the weight of robust, converging results to support their final test conclusions.

Working Example 1

Earlier we discussed efforts to reduce high school violence by enrolling violence-prone students into classes that address anger management. Now, after some time, administrators and managers want to know whether the program is effective. As part of this assessment, students are asked to report their perception of safety at school. An index variable is constructed from different items measuring safety (see Chapter 3). Each item is measured on a seven-point Likert scale (1 = Strongly Disagree to 7 = Strongly Agree), and the index is constructed such that a high value indicates that students feel safe.[10] The survey was initially administered at the beginning of the program. Now, almost a year later, the survey is implemented again.[11]

Administrators want to know whether students who did not participate in the anger management program feel that the climate is now safer. The analysis included here focuses on 10th graders. For practical purposes, the samples of 10th graders at the beginning of the program and one year later are regarded as independent samples; the subjects are not matched. Descriptive analysis shows that the mean perception of safety at the beginning of the program was 4.40 (standard deviation, $SD = 1.00$), and one year later 4.80 ($SD = 0.94$). The mean safety score increased among 10th graders, but is the increase statistically significant? Among other concerns is that the standard deviations are considerable for both samples.

As part of the analysis, we conduct a t-test to answer the question of whether the means of these two distributions are significantly different. First, we examine whether test assumptions are met. The samples are independent, and the variables meet the requirement that one is continuous (the index variable) and the other dichotomous. The assumption of equality of variances is answered as part of conducting the t-test, and so the remaining question is whether the variables are normally distributed. The distributions are shown in the histograms in Figure 11.3:[12]

Are these normal distributions? Visually, they are not the textbook ideal—real-life data seldom are. The Kolmogorov-Smirnov tests for both distributions are insignificant (both $p > .05$). Hence, we conclude that the two distributions can be considered normal. Having satisfied these t-test assumptions, we next conduct the t-test for two independent samples. Table 11.1 shows the t-test results.

The top part of Table 11.1 shows the descriptive statistics, and the bottom part reports the test statistics. Recall that the t-test is a two-step test.

Figure 11.3 ——————∿∿—Perception of High School Safety among 10th Graders

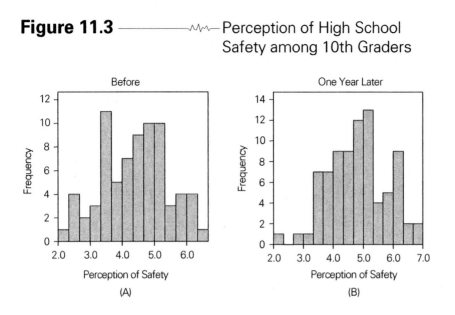

Table 11.1 ⋯⋯⋯⋯∿∿⋯ Independent-Samples T-Test: Output

Group Statistics

Group	N	Mean	SD
One year later	82	4.805	0.962
Before	74	4.399	1.008

	Step 1: Levene's test for equality of variances			Step 2: T-test for the equality of means		
Variable	F	p		t	df	p (2–tailed)
High school safety	0.177	0.675	Equal variances assumed	2.576	154	0.011
			Equal variances not assumed	2.570	150.57	0.011

Note: SD = standard deviation.

We first test whether variances are equal. This is shown as the "Levene's test for the equality of variances." The null hypothesis of the Levene's test is that variances are equal; this is rejected when the p-value of this Levene's test statistic is less than .05. The Levene's test uses an F-test statistic (discussed in Chapters 13 and 16), which, other than its p-value, need not concern us here. In Table 11.1, the level of significance is .675, which exceeds .05. Hence, we accept the null hypothesis—the variances of the two distributions shown in Figures 11.3 are equal.

Now we go to the second step, the main purpose. Are the two means (4.40 and 4.80) significantly different? Because the variances are equal, we read the t-test statistics from the top line, which states "equal variances assumed." (If variances had been unequal, then we would read the test statistics from the second line, "equal variances not assumed."). The t-test statistic for equal variances for this test is 2.576, which is significant at p = .011.[13] Thus, we conclude that the means are significantly different; the 10th graders report feeling safer one year after the anger management program was implemented.

Working Example 2

In the preceding example, the variables were both normally distributed, but this is not always the case. Many variables are highly skewed and not normally distributed. Consider another example. The U.S. Environmental Protection Agency (EPA) collects information about the water quality of watersheds, including information about the sources and nature of pollution. One such measure is the percentage of samples that exceed pollution limits for ammonia, dissolved oxygen, phosphorus, and pH.[14] A manager wants to know whether watersheds in the East have higher levels of pollution than those in the Midwest.

An index variable of such pollution is constructed. The index variable is called "Pollution," and the first step is to examine it for test assumptions. Analysis indicates that the range of this variable has a low value of 0.00 percent and a high value of 59.17 percent. These are plausible values (any value above 100.00 percent is implausible). A boxplot (not shown) demonstrates that the variable has two values greater than 50.00 percent that are indicated as outliers for the Midwest region. However, the histograms shown in Figure 11.4 do not suggest that these values are unusually large; rather, the peak in both histograms is located off to the left. The distributions are heavily skewed.[15]

Because the samples each have fewer than 50 observations, the Shapiro-Wilk test for normality is used. The respective test statistics for East and Midwest are .969 (p = .355) and .931 (p = .007). Visual inspection confirms that the Midwest distribution is indeed nonnormal. The Shapiro-Wilk test statistics are given only for completeness; they have no substantive interpretation.

We must now either transform the variable so that it becomes normal for purposes of testing, or use a nonparametric alternative. The second

Figure 11.4 ⎯⎯⎯⎯⎯⎯⎯⎯〰⎯Untransformed Variable:
Watershed Pollution

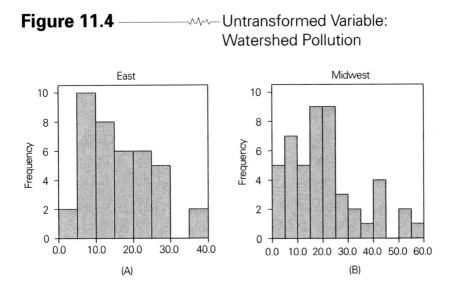

(A)   (B)

option is discussed later in this chapter. We also show the consequences of ignoring the problem.

To transform the variable, we try the recommended transformations, $\log(x)$, $\sqrt{x}$, or x^2, and then examine the transformed variable for normality. If none of these transformations work, we might modify them, such as using $x^{1/3}$ instead of $x^{1/2}$ (recall that the latter is $\sqrt{x}$).[16] Thus, some experimentation is required. In our case, we find that the $x^{1/2}$ works. The new Shapiro-Wilk test statistics for East and Midwest are, respectively, .969 (p = .361) and .987 (p = .883). Visual inspection of Figure 11.5 shows these two distributions to be quite normal, indeed.

The results of the t-test for the transformed variable are shown in Table 11.2. The transformed variable has equal variances across the two groups (Levene's test, p = .119), and the t-test statistic is −1.308 (df = 85, p = .194). Thus, the differences in pollution between watersheds in the East and Midwest are not significant. (The negative sign of the t-test statistic, −1.308, merely reflects the order of the groups for calculating the difference: the testing variable has a larger value in the Midwest than in the East. Reversing the order of the groups results in a positive sign.)

For comparison, results for the untransformed variable are shown as well. The untransformed variable has unequal variances across the two groups (Levene's test, p = .036), and the t-test statistic is −1.801 (df = 80.6, p =.075). Although this result also shows that differences are insignificant, the level of significance is higher; there are instances in which using nonnormal variables could lead to rejecting the null hypothesis. While our finding

Figure 11.5 ⎯⎯⎯⎯〰️⎯ Transformed Variable: Watershed Pollution

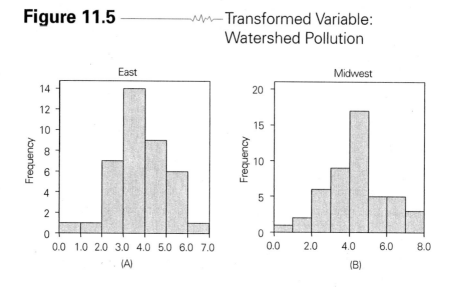

(A)   (B)

Table 11.2 ⎯⎯⎯⎯〰️⎯ Independent-Samples T-Test: Output

Variable: watershed pollution

	Step 1: Levene's test for equality of variances			Step 2: T-test for the equality of means		
	F	*p*		*t*	df	*p* (2–tailed)
Transformed	2.479	0.119	Equal variances assumed	−1.308	85	0.194
			Equal variances not assumed	−1.347	80.6	0.182
Untransformed	4.537	0.036	Equal variances assumed	−1.723	85	0.089
			Equal variances not assumed	−1.801	80.6	0.075

of insignificant differences is indeed *robust*, analysts cannot know this in advance. Thus, analysts will need to deal with nonnormality.

Variable transformation is one approach to the problem of nonnormality, but transforming variables can be a time-intensive and somewhat artful activity. The search for alternatives has led many analysts to consider nonparametric methods.

TWO T-TEST VARIATIONS

Paired-Samples T-Test

The paired t-test often is used when using before-and-after tests to assess student or client progress. Paired t-tests are used when analysts have a *dependent* rather than an independent sample (see the third t-test assumption, described earlier in this chapter). The **paired-samples t-test** tests the null hypothesis that the mean difference between the before and after test scores is zero. Consider the following data from Table 11.3:

Table 11.3 ⎯⎯⎯⎯⎯⎯ Paired-Samples Data

Before	After	Difference
3.2	4.3	1.1
3.2	4.3	1.1
4.0	3.8	-0.2
2.4	3.5	1.1
3.0	3.3	0.3
4.0	4.4	0.4
4.3	4.2	-0.1
3.8	3.3	-0.5
2.9	3.9	1.0
3.8	4.2	0.4
2.5	3.8	1.3

The mean "before" score is 3.39, and the mean "after" score is 3.87; the mean difference is 0.48. The paired t-test tests the null hypothesis by testing whether the means of the difference variable ("Difference") is zero. The paired t-test test statistic is calculated as

$$t = \frac{\overline{D}}{s_D/\sqrt{n}},$$

where D = the difference between before and after measurements, and s_D is the standard deviation of these differences. Regarding t-test assumptions, the variables are continuous, and the issue of heterogeneity (unequal variances) is moot because this test involves only one variable, D; no Levene's test statistics are produced. We do test the normality of D and find that it is normally distributed (Shapiro-Wilk = .925, p = .402). Thus, the assumptions are satisfied.

We proceed with testing whether the difference between before and after scores is statistically significant. We find that the paired t-test yields a t-test statistic of 2.43, which is significant at the 5 percent level (df = 9, p = .038 < .05).[17] Hence, we conclude that the increase between the before and after scores is significant at the 5 percent level.[18]

One-Sample T-Test

Finally, the **one-sample t-test** tests whether the mean of a single variable is different from a prespecified value (norm). For example, suppose we want to know whether the mean of the before group in Table 11.3 is different from the value of, say, 3.5? Testing against a norm is akin to the purpose of the chi-square goodness-of-fit test described in Chapter 10, but here we are dealing with a continuous variable rather than a categorical one, and we are testing the mean rather than its distribution.

The one-sample t-test assumes that the single variable is continuous and normally distributed. As with the paired t-test, the issue of heterogeneity is moot because there is only one variable. The Shapiro-Wilk test shows that the variable "Before" is normal (.917, p = .336). The one-sample t-test statistic for testing against the test value of 3.5 is –0.515 (df = 9, p = .619 > .05). Hence, the mean of 3.39 is *not* significantly different from 3.5. However, it is different from larger values, such as 4.0 (t = 2.89, df = 9, p = .019).

Finally, note that the one-sample t-test is identical to the paired-samples t-test for testing whether the mean $D = 0$. Indeed, the one-sample t-test for $D = 0$ produces the same results (t = 2.43, df = 9, p = .038).

NONPARAMETRIC ALTERNATIVES TO T-TESTS

The tests described in the preceding sections have nonparametric alternatives. The chief advantage of these tests is that they do not require continuous variables to be normally distributed. The chief disadvantage is that they are less likely to reject the null hypothesis. A further, minor disadvantage is that these tests do not provide descriptive information about variable means; separate analysis is required for that.

Nonparametric alternatives to the independent samples test are the **Mann-Whitney** and **Wilcoxon tests.** The Mann-Whitney and Wilcoxon tests are equivalent and are thus discussed jointly. Both are simplifications of the more general Kruskal-Wallis' H test, discussed in Chapter 10.[19] The Mann-Whitney and Wilcoxon tests assign ranks to the testing variable in the exact manner shown in Table 11.4. The sum of the ranks of each group is computed, shown in the table. Then a test is performed of the statistical significance of the difference between the sums, 22.5 and 32.5. Although the Mann-Whitney U and Wilcoxon W test statistics are calculated differently, they both have the same level of statistical significance: p = .295. Technically,

Table 11.4 ――――― ᰧᐧ᰷ᐧᰧ― Rankings of Two Groups

Group	Rating	Rank	Group	Rating	Rank
1	2.5	3	2	3.4	7
1	2.9	4	2	3.3	6
1	4.0	9.5	2	4.0	9.5
1	3.2	5	2	3.9	8
1	1.2	1	2	2.1	2
Sum		22.5	Sum		32.5

this is not a test of different means but of different distributions; the lack of significance implies that Groups 1 and 2 can be regarded as coming from the same population.[20]

For comparison, we use the Mann-Whitney test to compare the two samples of 10th graders discussed earlier in this chapter. The sum of ranks for the "before" group is 69.55, and for the "one year later group," 86.57. The test statistic is significant at p = .019, yielding the same conclusion as the independent-samples t-test, p = .011. This comparison also shows that nonparametric tests do have higher levels of significance. As mentioned earlier, the Mann-Whitney test (as a nonparametric test) does not calculate the group means; separate, descriptive analysis needs to be undertaken for that information.

> **Getting Started**
> Calculate a t-test and a Mann-Whitney test on data of your choice.

A nonparametric alternative to the paired-samples t-test is the **Wilcoxon signed rank test**. This test assigns ranks based on the absolute values of these differences (Table 11.5). The signs of the differences are retained (thus, some values are positive and others are negative). For the data in Table 11.5, the are seven positive ranks (with mean rank = 6.57) and three negative ranks (with mean rank = 3.00). The Wilcoxon signed rank test statistic is normally distributed. The Wilcoxon signed rank test statistic, Z, for a difference

Table 11.5 ――――― ᰧᐧ᰷ᐧᰧ― Wilcoxon Signed Rank Test

Before	After	Difference	Signed rank
3.2	4.3	1.1	8.5
4.0	3.8	−0.2	−2.0
2.4	3.5	1.1	8.5
3.0	3.3	0.3	3.0
4.0	4.4	0.4	4.5
4.3	4.2	−0.1	−1.0
3.8	3.3	−0.5	−6.0
2.9	3.9	1.0	7.0
3.8	4.2	0.4	4.5
2.5	3.8	1.3	10.0

between these values is 1.89 (p = .059 > .05). Hence, according to this test, the differences between the before and after scores are not significant.

Again, nonparametric tests result in larger p-values. The paired-samples t-test finds that p = .038 < .05, providing sufficient statistical evidence to conclude that the differences are significant. It might also be noted that a doubling of the data in Table 11.5 results in finding a significant difference between the before and after scores with the Wilcoxon signed rank test, Z = 2.694, p = .007.

The Wilcoxon signed rank test can also be adapted as a nonparametric alternative to the one-sample t-test. In that case, analysts create a second variable that, for each observation, is the test value. For example, if in Table 11.5 we wish to test whether the mean of variable "Before" is different from, say, 4.0, we create a second variable with 10 observations for which each value is, say, 4.0. Then using the Wilcoxon signed rank test for the "Before" variable and this new, second variable, we find that Z = 2.103, p = .035. This value is larger than that obtained by the parametric test, p = .019.[21]

SUMMARY

When analysts need to determine whether two continuous variables differ in their means, the t-test is the tool of choice. This situations arises, for example, when analysts compare measurements at two points in time or the responses of two different groups. There are three common t-tests, for independent samples, for dependent (paired) samples, and the one-sample t-test.

T-tests are parametric tests, which means that variables in these tests must meet certain assumptions, notably that they are normally distributed. The requirement of normally distributed variables follows from how parametric tests make inferences. Specifically, t-tests have four assumptions:

- One variable is continuous, and the other variable is dichotomous.
- The two distributions have equal variances.
- The observations are independent.
- The two distributions are normally distributed.

The assumption of homogeneous variances does not apply to dependent-samples and one-sample t-tests because both are based on only a single variable for testing significance. When assumptions of normality are not met, variable transformation may be used. The search for alternative ways for dealing with normality problems may lead analysts to consider nonparametric alternatives.

The chief advantage of nonparametric tests is that they do not require continuous variables to be normally distributed. The chief disadvantage is that they yield higher levels of statistical significance, making it less likely that the null hypothesis may be rejected. A nonparametric alternative for the independent-samples t-test is the Mann-Whitney test, and the nonparametric alternative for the dependent-samples t-test is the Wilcoxon signed rank test.

T-tests and their nonparametric alternatives provide information about whether two group means are significantly different. Analysts will need to further assess the magnitude of these differences, and to determine whether they are practically significant. Chapter 16 discusses analysis of variance, or ANOVA, which can be used when means are compared across three or more groups, rather than the two groups of a dichotomous variable.

KEY TERMS

Central limit theorem (p. 185)
Four t-test test assumptions (p. 182)
Heterogeneity of variances (p. 183)
Homogeneity of variances (p. 183)
Independent-samples t-test (p. 181)
Kolmogorov-Smirnov test (p. 184)
Levene's test (p. 183)
Mann-Whitney test (p. 192)
Null hypothesis of normality
   (p. 184)
One-sample t-test (p. 192)

One-tailed t-tests (p. 182)
Paired-samples t-test (p. 191)
Paired t-test (p. 184)
Robust (p. 183)
Shapiro-Wilk test (p. 184)
Student's t-distribution (p. 182)
T-tests (p. 180)
Two-tailed t-tests (p. 182)
Variable transformation (p. 184)
Wilcoxon signed rank test (p. 193)
Wilcoxon test (p. 192)

Notes

1. Some research suggests that nonparametric tests may not be as robust as thought when variances of groups of rankings are substantially unequal.
2. Boxplots are shown for ease of presentation. It is more appropriate, theoretically, to show two normal distributions, but that clutters the presentation. In any event, continuous data can be presented in boxplots.
3. The formula for the pooled variance is

$$s_p^2 = \frac{(n_1-1)s_1^2 + (n_2-1)s_2^2}{n_1+n_2-2}.$$

When $s_1 = s_2$, the value of s_p is affected by the relative number of observations in each group, that is, n_1 and n_2. The computer calculates the pooled variance, of course. For more on this topic, see David Howell, *Statistical Methods for Psychology,* 3d ed. (Belmont, Calif.: Duxbury Press, 1992), 181–187.
4. The name *Student's t* is derived from W. S. Gossett, who used "Student" as a pseudonym in the early twentieth century to protect his identity. Legend has it that Gossett was concerned that his employer, an

agro-industrial company, might want to protect the formula as a trade secret because of competitive advantages: the t-test enables very efficient testing of samples.

5. See Box 9.1. The decision to require a higher critical value is not without cost; it could increase Type II errors. However, many analysts prefer to err on the side of caution.

6. Even though studies have shown that men typically have higher incomes than women, this need not always be the case. In any specific setting, in any specific industry, at any point in time, women could have higher incomes.

7. The revised formula for calculating the t-test when variances are unequal is

$$t = \frac{\bar{x}_1 - \bar{x}_2}{\sqrt{\dfrac{s_1^2}{n_1 - 1} + \dfrac{s_2^2}{n_2 - 1}}}.$$

See Howell, *Statistical Methods for Psychology*, for the revised formula for calculating degrees of freedom.

8. Students often want to know how they can transform variables. In most software packages it is simply a matter of specifying something like: newvar = sqrt(oldvar) or newvar = lg10(oldvar). Students also ask what transformation works best. This is largely unknown. It is a matter of trial and error.

9. Some students initially consider variable transformation to be "playing with the data." However, we need to consider that the ancient development of the common measurement scale (1, 2, 3, 4, 5. . .) is as arbitrary as any other scale that might have been chosen (such as 1, 4, 9, 16, 25. . .). The fact that the common measurement scale is frequently useful from the perspective of satisfying test assumptions should not lead us to assign supreme considerations to it or to be reluctant to try other measurement scales that work better in other situations. It is far more important to ensure that the variables are normally distributed for the purpose of test validity.

10. With a Cronbach alpha measure of 0.79, the analyst concludes that the index measure has adequate reliability (see Chapter 3).

11. The data in this example are real, but the reported scenario is fictitious.

12. SPSS readily produces these plots as part of the Analyze → Descriptive Statistics → Explore routine.

13. Software output may also include the 95 percent confidence interval for estimates of the difference. When t-tests are insignificant, the interval will include the value zero, indicating that no difference between the means can be ruled out. When t-tests are significant, the interval will not include the value zero.

14. For more information about this measure, visit www.epa.gov/iwi.
    See also the Watershed dataset on the CD accompanying the workbook
    Exercising Essential Statistics to replicate the results given here. The index
    variable is called "conpolut" in the dataset.
15. This conclusion is further indicated by the measures of skewness: East
    (.519) and Midwest (.912). Based on the test described in Chapter 7,
    skewness/se(skewness) for the two regions is, respectively, [.559/.378 =]
    1.48 and [.912/.343 =] 2.65, which confirms the considerable departure
    from zero for Midwest. The measures of kurtosis are −.113 and .406.
16. This conclusion is consistent for a wide range of root variable transfor-
    mations that result in a normal distribution (for example, using $x^{.35}$, not
    shown, rather than the root variable $\sqrt{x}$.
17. In paired tests, degrees of freedom are defined as $n-1$ (where n is the
    number of *pairs* or, equivalently, difference scores).
18. In many t-tests the output includes a 95 percent confidence interval of
    the difference. This is the range within which we can be 95 percent
    certain that the population difference lies. For this test, the range is
    between .032 and .927. Although this is a considerable range, it excludes
    the value zero, or, no difference of the means.
19. The formula for calculating the Mann-Whitney U test statistic is

$$n_1 n_2 + \frac{n_1(n_1+1)}{2} - T_1,$$

    where T_1 = the sum of ranks for Group 1, n_1 = the number of observa-
    tions in Sample 1, and n_2 = the number of observations in Sample 2.
    The relationship between U and the Wilcoxon W test statistic is

$$U + W = \frac{m(m+2n+1)}{2}.$$

    where m = the number of observations in the group that has the smaller
    number of observations, and n = the number of observations in the
    group that has the larger number of observations.
20. By contrast, the p-value for comparing Groups 1 and 3 in Table 10.8 is
    .016. We may note that using the Kruskal-Wallis' H test for these two
    groups yields the exact same level of significance.
21. Another, less powerful alternative is the sign test. It is conducted in the
    same manner as described in the text, but it compares only the number
    of positive and negative signs rather than the differences of the mean
    ranks. It is a very crude test that is generally not preferred. In the exam-
    ple in the text, the sign test finds p = .070, indicating that the mean
    "Before" score is not significantly different from 4.0.

CHAPTER

12

Simple Regression

CHAPTER OBJECTIVES

After reading this chapter, you should be able to
- Use simple regression to test the statistical significance of a bivariate relationship involving one dependent and one independent variable
- Use Pearson's correlation coefficient as a measure of association between two continuous variables
- Interpret statistics associated with regression analysis
- Write up the model of simple regression
- Assess assumptions of simple regression

This chapter completes our discussion of statistical techniques for studying relationships between two variables by focusing on those that are *continuous*. Several approaches are examined: simple regression; the Pearson's correlation coefficient; and a nonparametric alterative, Spearman's rank correlation coefficient.

Although all three techniques can be used, we focus particularly on simple regression. Regression allows us to predict outcomes based on knowledge of an independent variable. It is also the foundation of time series analysis, which is useful for budgeting and planning, and it is the essential foundation for studying relationships among three or more variables. Such relationships are examined in subsequent chapters and include control variables, which were introduced in Chapter 9. We begin with simple regression.

SIMPLE REGRESSION

Simple regression is used to analyze the relationship between two continuous variables. For example, we might study the relationship between productivity and job satisfaction when both variables are measured on a continuous scale. Continuous variables assume that the distances between ordered categories are determinable.[1] In simple regression, one variable is defined as the dependent variable and the other as the independent variable.

Scatterplot

The relationship between two continuous variables can be portrayed in a *scatterplot*. A scatterplot is merely a plot of the data points for two continuous variables, as shown in Figure 12.1 (without the straight line). By convention, the dependent variable is shown on the vertical (or Y-) axis, and the independent variable on the horizontal (or X-) axis. The relationship between the two variables is estimated as a straight line relationship. The line is defined by the equation $y = a + bX$, where a is the intercept (or constant), and b is the slope. The slope, b, is defined as $\Delta y / \Delta x$, or $(y_2 - y_1)/(x_2 - x_1)$. The line is mathematically calculated such that the sum of distances from each observation to the line is minimized.[2] By definition, the slope indicates the change in y as a result of a unit change in x. The straight line is also called the *regression line*, and the slope (b) is called the *regression coefficient*.

A positive regression coefficient indicates a positive relationship between the variables, shown by the upward slope in Figure 12.1. A negative regression coefficient indicates a negative relationship between the variables and is indicated by a downward-sloping line.

Test of Significance

The *test of significance of the regression coefficient* is a key test of hypothesis regression analysis that tells us whether the slope (b) is statistically different from zero. The slope is calculated from a sample, and we wish to know whether it is significant. When the regression line is horizontal ($b = 0$), no relationship exists between the two variables. Then, changes in the

Figure 12.1 ⎯⎯⎯⎯⟋⟍⟋⟍⎯ Scatterplot

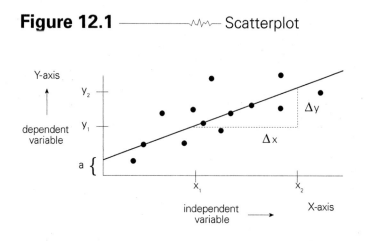

independent variable have no effect on the dependent variable. The following hypotheses are thus stated:

H_0: $b = 0$, or the two variables are unrelated.
H_A: $b \neq 0$, or the two variables are (positively or negatively) related.

To determine whether the slope equals zero, a t-test is performed. The test statistic is defined as the slope, b, divided by the standard error of the slope, $se(b)$. The standard error of the slope is a measure of the distribution of the observations around the regression slope, which is based on the standard deviation of those observations to the regression line:

$$\frac{b}{se(b)}.$$

Thus, a regression line with a small slope is more likely to be statistically significant when observations lie closely around it (that is, the standard error of the observations around the line is also small, resulting in a larger test statistic). By contrast, the same regression line might be statistically insignificant when observations are scattered widely around it. Observations that lie farther from the regression line will have larger standard deviations, and hence larger standard errors. *The computer calculates the slope, intercept, standard error of the slope, and the level at which the slope is statistically significant.*

Consider the following example. A management analyst with the Department of Defense wishes to evaluate the impact of teamwork on the productivity of naval shipyard repair facilities. Although all shipyards are required to use teamwork management strategies, these strategies are assumed to vary in practice. Coincidentally, a recently implemented

Table 12.1 ～～ Simple Regression Output

Model Fit		
R	R-square	SEE
0.272	0.074	0.825

Dependent variable: Productivity

Coefficients

Model	Unstandardized coefficients		t	Sig.
	b	SE		
Constant	4.026	0.213	18.894	0.000
Teamwork	0.223	0.044	5.053	0.000

Note: SEE = standard error of the estimate; SE = standard error; Sig. = significance.

employee survey asked about the perceived use and effectiveness of team-work. These items have been aggregated into a single index variable that measures teamwork. Employees were also asked questions about perceived performance, as measured by productivity, customer orientation, planning and scheduling, and employee motivation. These items were combined into an index measure of work productivity. Both index measures are continuous variables. The analyst wants to know whether a relationship exists between perceived productivity and teamwork. Table 12.1 shows the computer output obtained from a simple regression. The slope, *b*, is 0.223; the slope coefficient of teamwork is positive; and the slope is significant at the 1 percent level. Thus, perceptions of teamwork are positively associated with productivity. The t-test statistic, 5.053, is calculated as 0.223/0.044 (rounding errors explain the difference from the printed value of *t*). Other statistics shown in Table 12.1 are discussed below. The appropriate notation for this relationship is shown below. Either the t-test statistic or the standard error should be shown in parentheses, directly below the regression coefficient; analysts should state which statistic is shown. Here, we show the t-test statistic:[3]

$$\text{PRODUCTIVITY} = 4.026 + 0.223^{**}\text{TEAMWORK}$$
$$(5.05)$$

$^{**} p < .01; \, ^* p < .05$

The level of significance of the regression coefficient is indicated with asterisks, which conforms to the p-value legend that should also be shown. Typically, two asterisks are used to indicate a 1 percent level of significance, one asterisk for a 5 percent level of significance, and no asterisk for coefficients that are insignificant.[4]

Table 12.1 also shows R-square (R^2), which is called the **coefficient of determination**. R-square is of great interest: its value is interpreted as *the percentage of variation in the dependent variable that is explained by the independent variable*. R-square varies from zero to one, and is called a goodness-of-fit measure.[5] In our example, teamwork explains only 7.4 percent of the variation in productivity. Although teamwork is significantly associated with productivity, it is quite likely that other factors also affect it. It is conceivable that other factors might be more strongly associated with productivity and that, when controlled for other factors, teamwork is no longer significant. Typically, values of R^2 below 0.20 are considered to indicate weak relationships, those between 0.20 and 0.40 indicate moderate relationships, and those above 0.40 indicate strong relationships. Values of R^2 above 0.65 are considered to indicate very strong relationships. R is called the *multiple correlation coefficient* and is always $0 \le R \le 1$.

To summarize up to this point, simple regression provides three critically important pieces of information about bivariate relationships involving two continuous variables: (1) the level of significance at which two variables are associated, if at all (*t-statistic*), (2) whether the relationship between the two variables is positive or negative (*b*), and (3) the strength of the relationship (R^2).

The primary purpose of regression analysis is hypothesis testing, not prediction. In our example, the regression model is used to test the hypothesis that teamwork is related to productivity. However, if the analyst wants to predict the variable "productivity," the regression output also shows the SEE, or the **standard error of the estimate** (see Table 12.1). This is a measure of the spread of *y* values around the regression line as calculated *for the mean value of the independent variable, only, and assuming a large sample*. The standard error of the estimate has an interpretation in terms of the normal curve, that is, 68 percent of *y* values lie within one standard error from the calculated value of *y*, as calculated for the *mean* value of *x* using the preceding regression model. Thus, if the *mean* index value of the variable "teamwork" is 5.0, then the calculated (or predicted) value of "productivity" is [4.026 + 0.223*5 =] 5.141. Because SEE = 0.825, it follows that 68 percent of productivity values will lie ±0.825 from 5.141 when "teamwork" = 5. Predictions of *y* for other values of *x* have larger standard errors.[6]

Assumptions and Notation

Simple regression assumes that the relationship between two variables is *linear*. The linearity of bivariate relationships is easily determined through visual inspection, as shown in Figure 12.2. In fact, all analysis of relationships involving continuous variables should begin with a scatterplot. When variable relationships are nonlinear (parabolic or otherwise heavily curved), it is not appropriate to use linear regression. Then, one or both variables must be transformed, as discussed in Chapter 11.

Simple regression also assumes that the *linear relationship is constant* over the range of observations. This assumption is violated when the relationship is "broken," for example, by having an upward slope for the first half of independent variable values and a downward slope over the remaining values. Then, analysts should consider using two regression models each for these different, linear relationships. The linearity assumption is also violated when no relationship is present in part of the independent variable values. This is particularly problematic because regression analysis will calculate a regression slope based on all observations. In this case, analysts may be misled into believing that the linear pattern holds for all observations. Hence, regression results always should be verified through visual inspection.

Linear regression also assumes that the variables are continuous. In Chapter 13, we will see that regression can also be used for nominal and dichotomous independent variables. The dependent variable, however, must be continuous. When the dependent variable is dichotomous, logistic regression should be used (Chapter 14).

Finally, the following notations are commonly used in regression analysis. The predicted value of y (defined, based on the regression model, as $y = a + bX$) is typically different from the **observed value of y**. The **predicted value of the dependent variable y** is sometimes indicated as $\hat{y}$ (pronounced "y-hat"). Only when $R^2 = 1$ are the observed and predicted values identical for each observation. The difference between y and $\hat{y}$ is called the regression *error* or **error term** (e). Hence the expressions

$$\hat{y} = a + b^*x \text{ and}$$
$$y = a + b^*x + e$$

are equivalent, as is $y = \hat{y} + e$. Certain assumptions about e are important, such as that it is normally distributed. When error term assumptions are violated, incorrect conclusions may be made about the statistical significance of relationships. This important issue is discussed in greater detail in Chapter 13 and, for time series data, in Chapter 15. Hence, the above is a pertinent, but incomplete list of assumptions.

Getting Started
Conduct a simple regression, and practice writing up your results.

PEARSON'S CORRELATION COEFFICIENT

Pearson's correlation coefficient, r, measures the association (significance, direction, and strength) between two continuous variables; it is a measure of

Figure 12.2 ⎯⎯⎯⎯⎯⎯⎯⎯ ⟋⟍⟋⟍ ⎯Three Examples of *r*

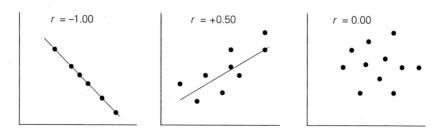

association for two continuous variables. Also called the Pearson's product-moment correlation coefficient, it does not assume a causal relationship, as does simple regression. The correlation coefficient, *r*, indicates the extent to which the observations lie closely or loosely clustered around the regression line. The coefficient *r* ranges from –1 to +1. The sign indicates the direction of the relationship, which, in simple regression, is always the same as the slope coefficient. A "–1" indicates a perfect negative relationship, that is, that all observations lie exactly on a downward-sloping regression line; a "+1" indicates a perfect positive relationship, whereby all observations lie exactly on an upward-sloping regression line. Of course, such values are rarely obtained in practice because observations seldom lie exactly on a line. An *r* value of zero indicates that observations are so widely scattered that it is impossible to draw any well-fitting line. Figure 12.2 illustrates some values of *r*.

It is important to avoid confusion between Pearson's correlation coefficient and the coefficient of determination. For the two-variable, simple regression model, $r^2 = R^2$, but whereas $0 \le R \le 1$, *r* ranges from –1 to +1. Hence, the sign of *r* tells us whether a relationship is positive or negative, but the sign of *R*, in regression output tables such as Table 12.1, is always positive and cannot inform us about the direction of the relationship. In simple regression, only the regression slope, *b*, informs us about the direction of the relationship. Statistical software programs usually show *r* rather than r^2. Note also that the Pearson's correlation coefficient can be used only to assess the association between two continuous variables, whereas regression can be extended to deal with more than two variables, as discussed in Chapter 13. Pearson's correlation coefficient assumes that both variables are normally distributed.

When Pearson's correlation coefficients are calculated, a standard error of *r* can be determined, which then allows us to test the statistical significance of the bivariate correlation. For bivariate relationships, this is the same level of significance as shown for the slope of the regression coefficient. For the variables given earlier in this chapter, the value of *r* is .272 and the statistical significance of *r* is p ≤ .01. Use of the Pearson's correlation coefficient assumes that the variables are normally distributed and that there are no significant departures from linearity.[7]

Comparing the measures *r* and *b* (the slope) sometimes causes confusion. The key point is that *r* does not indicate the regression slope but rather the extent to which observations lie close to it. A steep regression line (large *b*) can have observations scattered loosely or closely around it, as can a shallow (more horizontal) regression line. The purposes of these two statistics are very different.[8]

SPEARMAN'S RANK CORRELATION COEFFICIENT

The nonparametric alternative, *Spearman's rank correlation coefficient* (ρ, or "rho"), looks at correlation among the ranks of the data rather than among the values. The ranks of data are determined as shown in Table 12.2 (adapted from Table 10.8):

Table 12.2 ⎯⎯⎯⎯⎯⎯ Ranks of Two Variables

Observation	Variable 1 Value	Variable 1 Rank	Variable 2 Value	Variable 2 Rank
1	2.5	2	3.4	3
2	2.9	3	3.3	2
3	4.0	5	4.0	5
4	3.2	4	3.9	4
5	1.2	1	2.1	1

Because Spearman's rank correlation coefficient examines correlation among the ranks of variables, it can also be used with ordinal-level data.[9] For the data in Table 12.2, Spearman's rank correlation coefficient is .900 (p = .035).[10] Spearman's p-squared coefficient has a "percent variation explained" interpretation, similar to the measures described earlier. Hence, 90 percent of the variation in one variable can be explained by the other. For the variables given earlier, the Spearman's rank correlation coefficient is .274 (p < .01), which is comparable to *r* reported in preceding sections.

Box 12.1 illustrates another use of the statistics described in this chapter, in a study of the relationship between crime and poverty.

SUMMARY

When analysts examine relationships between two continuous variables, they can use simple regression or the Pearson's correlation coefficient. Both

‍In Greater Depth...

Box 12.1   Crime and Poverty

An analyst wants to examine empirically the relationship between crime and income in cities across the United States. The CD that accompanies the workbook *Exercising Essential Statistics* includes a Community Indicators dataset with assorted indicators of conditions in 98 cities such as Akron, Ohio; Phoenix, Arizona; New Orleans, Louisiana; and Seattle, Washington. The measures include median household income, total population (both from the 2000 U.S. Census), and total violent crimes (FBI, Uniform Crime Reporting, 2004). In the sample, household income ranges from $26,309 (Newark, New Jersey) to $71,765 (San Jose, California), and the median household income is $42,316. Per-capita violent crime ranges from 0.15 percent (Glendale, California) to 2.04 percent (Las Vegas, Nevada), and the median violate crime rate per capita is 0.78 percent.

There are four types of violent crimes: murder and nonnegligent manslaughter, forcible rape, robbery, and aggravated assault. A measure of total violent crime per capita is calculated because larger cities are apt to have more crime. The analyst wants to examine whether income is associated with per-capita violent crime. The scatterplot of these two continuous variables shows that a negative relationship appears to be present:

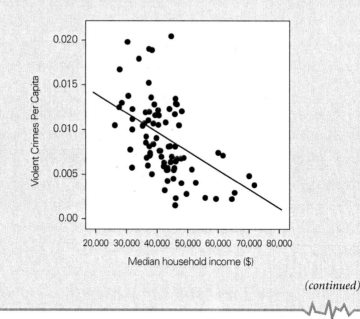

(continued)

Box 12.1 *(continued)*

The Pearson's correlation coefficient is $-.532$ (p $<.01$), and the Spearman's correlation coefficient is $-.552$ (p $<.01$). The simple regression model shows $R^2 = .283$. The regression model is as follows (*t*-test statistic in parentheses):

$$\text{Violent Crime Per Capita} = .020 - 2.54*10^{-7}**\text{Household Income}$$
$$(-5.72)$$

** p $<.01$.

The regression line is shown on the scatterplot. Interpreting these results, we see that the R-square value of .283 indicates a moderate relationship between these two variables. Clearly, some cities with modest median household incomes have a high crime rate. However, removing these cities does not greatly alter the findings. Also, an assumption of regression is that the error term is normally distributed, and further examination of the error shows that it is somewhat skewed. The techniques for examining the distribution of the error term are discussed in Chapter 13, but again, addressing this problem does not significantly alter the finding that the two variables are significantly related to each other, and that the relationship is of moderate strength.

With this result in hand, further analysis shows, for example, by how much violent crime decreases for each increase in household income. For each increase of $10,000 in average household income, the violent crime rate drops 0.25 percent. For a city experiencing the median 0.78 percent crime rate, this would be a considerable improvement, indeed. Note also that the scatterplot shows considerable variation in the crime rate for cities at or below the median household income, in contrast to those well above it. Policy analysts may well wish to examine conditions that give rise to variation in crime rates among cities with lower incomes.

measures show (1) the statistical significance of the relationship, (2) the direction of the relationship (that is, whether it is positive or negative), and (3) the strength of the relationship.

Simple regression assumes a causal and linear relationship between the continuous variables. The statistical significance and direction of the slope coefficient is used to assess the statistical significance and direction of the relationship. The coefficient of determination, R^2, is used to assess the strength of relationships; R^2 is interpreted as the percent variation explained. Regression is a foundation for studying relationships involving three or more variables, such as control variables. The Pearson's correlation coefficient does not assume causality between two continuous variables.

A nonparametric alternative to testing the relationship between two continuous variables is Spearman's rank correlation coefficient, which examines correlation among the ranks of the data rather than among the values themselves. As such, this measure can also be used to study relationships in which one or both variables are ordinal.

KEY TERMS

Coefficient of determination, R^2 (p. 202)
Error term (p. 203)
Observed value of y (p. 203)
Pearson's correlation coefficient (p. 203)
Predicted value of the dependent variable y, $\hat{y}$ (p. 203)
Regression coefficient (p. 199)

Regression line (p. 199)
Scatterplot (p. 199)
Spearman's rank correlation coefficient (p. 205)
Standard error of the estimate (p. 202)
Test of significance of the regression coefficient (p. 199)

Notes

1. See Chapter 3 for a definition of continuous variables. Although the distinction between ordinal and continuous is theoretical (namely, whether or not the distance between categories can be measured), in practice ordinal-level variables with seven or more categories (including Likert variables) are sometimes analyzed using statistics appropriate for interval-level variables. This practice has many critics because it violates an assumption of regression (interval data), but it is often done because it doesn't (much) affect the robustness of results.
2. The method of calculating the regression coefficient (the slope) is called *ordinary least squares*, or OLS. This method estimates the slope by minimizing the sum of squared differences between each predicted value of $a + bX$ and the actual value of y. One reason for squaring these distances is to ensure that all distances are positive.
3. No consistent preference exists about what is shown in parentheses. The current practice in many political science journals is to report the standard error, but many public administrations report the t-test.
4. Some authors also identify other levels of significance, such as $p < .001$ or $p < .10$, but this does not affect study conclusions, of course.

5. The formula for R^2 is presented in Chapter 13, in our discussion of the F-test.

6. For predictions not based on the mean of x, the standard error of y is larger than the SEE, according to the following formula:

$$SEE' = SEE\sqrt{1+\frac{1}{N}+\frac{(x_i-\bar{x})^2}{(N-1)s_x^2}},$$

where s_x^2 is the variance of x, that is, $\Sigma(x-\bar{x})^2/(N-1)$. As can be seen, $SEE' = SEE$ only when N is large and the predicted values of y are calculated for the mean value of x (that is, $x_i = \bar{x}$). Graphically, the relationship between SEE' and x is as follows:

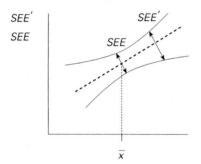

7. Based on visual inspection, these two variables are normally distributed. In addition, the Kolmogorov-Smirnov test (see Chapter 11) for the variable "teamwork" shows p = .084.

8. Pearson's correlation coefficient is also the basis for calculating Cronbach alpha, the measure of internal reliability discussed in Chapter 3. The formula for alpha is $\alpha = N*\bar{r}/[1 + (N-1)*\bar{r})]$, where $N =$ the number of variables and $\bar{r}$ is the mean of the correlations among all of the different pairs of variables that make up the measure. This formula clearly shows that alpha is bounded by zero and one: when $\bar{r} = 1$, then $\alpha = 1$, and when $\bar{r} = 0$, then $\alpha = 0$.

9. Spearman's rank correlation coefficient would also be used when assumptions of normality are violated, or when variables are related in nonlinear ways.

10. The formula for Spearman's rank correlation coefficient is as follows:

$$r_s = 1 - \frac{6\Sigma d^2}{n(n^2-1)}$$

where d is the difference between ranks in each observation (x,y). For the data shown in Table 12.2, consider the following calculation:

Observation	Variable 1 Rank	Variable 2 Rank	d	d^2
1	2	3	−1	1
2	3	2	1	1
3	5	5	0	0
4	4	4	0	0
5	1	1	0	0

Hence, the value of $r_s = 1 - [(6{*}2)/5(25 - 1)] = 0.9$.

CHAPTER

13

Multiple Regression

CHAPTER OBJECTIVES

After reading this chapter, you should be able to

- Understand multiple regression as a full model specification technique
- Interpret standardized and unstandardized regression coefficients of multiple regression
- Know how to use nominal variables in regression as dummy variables
- Explain the importance of the error term plot
- Identify assumptions of regression, and know how to test and correct assumption violations

Multiple regression is one of the most widely used multivariate statistical techniques for analyzing three or more variables. This chapter uses multiple regression to examine such relationships, and thereby extends the discussion in Chapter 12. The popularity of multiple regression is due largely to the ease with which it takes *control variables* (or rival hypotheses) into account. In Chapter 9, we discussed briefly how contingency tables can be used for this purpose, but doing so is often a cumbersome and sometimes inconclusive effort. By contrast, multiple regression easily incorporates multiple independent variables. Another reason for its popularity is that it also takes nominal independent variables into account.

However, multiple regression is no substitute for bivariate analysis. Indeed, managers or analysts with an interest in a specific bivariate relationship will conduct a bivariate analysis first, before examining whether the relationship is robust in the presence of numerous control variables. And before conducting bivariate analysis, analysts need to conduct univariate analysis to better understand their variables. Thus, multiple regression is usually one of the last steps of analysis. Indeed, multiple regression is often used to test the robustness of bivariate relationships when control variables are taken into account.

The flexibility with which multiple regression takes control variables into account comes at a price, though. Regression, like the t-test, is based on numerous assumptions. Regression results cannot be assumed to be robust in the face of assumption violations. *Testing of assumptions is always part of multiple regression analysis.* Multiple regression is carried out in the following sequence: (1) model specification (that is, identification of dependent and independent variables), (2) testing of regression assumptions, (3) correction of assumption violations, if any, and (4) reporting of the results of the final regression model. This chapter examines these four steps and discusses essential concepts related to simple and multiple regression. Chapters 14 and 15 extend this discussion by examining the use of logistic regression and time series analysis.

MODEL SPECIFICATION

Multiple regression is an extension of simple regression, but an important difference exists between the two methods: multiple regression aims for **full model specification**. This means that analysts seek to account for *all of the variables that affect the dependent variable*; by contrast, simple regression examines the effect of only one independent variable. Philosophically, the phrase identifying the key difference—"all of the variables that affect the dependent variable"—is divided into two parts. The *first part* involves identifying the variables that are of *most* (theoretical and practical) *relevance* in explaining the dependent variable. In social science, this is called a **nomothetic mode of explanation**—the isolation of the most important factors. This approach is consistent with the philosophy of seeking complete but parsimonious explanations in science.[1] The *second part* involves addressing those variables that were not considered as being of most relevance.

Regarding the first part, the specification of the "most important" independent variables is a judicious undertaking. The use of a nomothetic strategy implies that a range of plausible models exists—different analysts may identify different sets of "most important" independent variables. Analysts should ask which different factors are likely to affect or cause their dependent variable most, and they are likely to justify, identify, and operationalize their choices differently. Thus, the term *full model specification* does not imply that only one model or even a best model exists, but rather refers to a family of plausible models. Most researchers agree that specification should be driven by theory, that is, by persuasive arguments and perspectives that identify and justify which factors are most important, and inform why the set of such variables is regarded as complete and parsimonious. In practice, the search for complete, parsimonious, and theory-driven explanations usually results in multiple regression models with about 5–12 independent variables; theory seldom results in less than 5, and parsimony and problems of statistical estimation, discussed further, seldom result in models with more than 12.

The search for parsimonious explanations often leads analysts to first identify different categories of factors that most affect their dependent variable. Then, after these categories of factors have been identified, analysts turn to the task of trying to measure each, through either single or index variables. As an example, consider the dependent variable "high school violence," discussed in Chapter 2. We ask: "What are the most important, distinct factors affecting or causing high school violence?" Some plausible factors are (1) student access to weapons, (2) student isolation from others, (3) peer groups that are prone to violence, (4) lack of enforcement of school nonviolence policies, (5) participation in anger management programs, and (6) familiarity with warning signals (among teachers and staff). Perhaps you can think of other factors. Then, using the strategies discussed in Chapter 3—conceptualization, operationalization, and index variable construction—either single variables or index measures are used as independent variables to measure each of these factors. This approach provides for the inclusion of programs or policies as independent variables, as well as variables that measure salient rival hypotheses.

The strategy of full model specification requires that analysts not overlook important factors. Thus, analysts do well to carefully justify their model, and consult past studies and interview those who have direct experience with, or other opinions about, the research subject. Doing so might lead analysts to include additional variables, such as the socioeconomic status of students' parents. Then, after a fully specified model has been identified, analysts often include additional variables of interest. These may be variables of lesser relevance, speculative consequences, or variables that analysts want to test for their *lack* of impact, such as rival hypotheses. Demographic variables, such as the age of students, might be added. When additional variables are included, analysts should identify which independent variables constitute the nomothetic explanation, and which serve some other purpose. Remember, all variables included in models must be theoretically justified. Analysts must argue how each variable could plausibly affect their dependent variable.

The *second part* of "all of the variables that affect the dependent variable" acknowledges all of the other variables that are not identified (or included) in the model. They are omitted; these variables are not among "the most important factors" that affect the dependent variable. The cumulative effect of these other variables is, by definition, contained in the error term, described later in this chapter. The **assumption of full model specification** is that these other variables are justifiably omitted *only when* their cumulative effect on the dependent variable is zero. This approach is plausible because each of these many unknown variables may have a different magnitude, thus making it possible that their effects cancel each other out. The argument, quite clearly, is not that each of these other factors has no impact on the dependent variable—but only that their *cumulative effect is zero.* The validity of multiple regression models centers on examining the behavior of the error term in this regard. If the cumulative effect of all the other variables is not zero, then additional independent variables may have to be considered. The specification of the multiple regression model is as follows:

$$y = a + b_1 x_1 + b_2 x_2 + b_3 x_3 + b_4 x_4 + \ldots + error$$

Dependent = Independent Variables in Model   Variables Not in Model
Variable   ("most important factors")   ("all excluded factors")
                                      +
                          ("other included factors")

Thus, multiple regression requires two important tasks: (1) specification of independent variables and (2) testing of the error term. An important difference between simple regression and multiple regression is the **interpretation of the regression coefficients in multiple regression** (b_1, b_2, b_3, . . .) in the preceding multiple regression model. Although multiple regression produces the same basic statistics discussed in Chapter 12 (see Table 12.1), each of the regression coefficients is interpreted as its effect on the dependent variable, *controlled for the effect of all of the other independent variables included in the regression.* This phrase is used frequently when explaining multiple regression results. In our example, the regression coefficient b_1 shows the effect of x_1 on y, controlled for all other variables included in the model. Regression coefficient b_2 shows the effect of x_2 on y, also controlled for all other variables in the model, including x_1. Multiple regression is indeed an important and simple alternative to the approach discussed in Chapter 9 for analyzing control variables.

Note also that the model given here is very different from estimating separate simple regression models for each of the independent variables. The regression coefficients in simple regression *do not control* for other independent variables, because they are not in the model.

The word *independent* also means that each independent variable should be relatively unaffected by other independent variables in the model. To ensure that independent variables are indeed independent, it is useful to think of the distinctively *different types* (or categories) *of factors* that affect a dependent variable. This was the approach taken in the preceding example. There is also a statistical reason for ensuring that independent variables are as independent as possible. When two independent variables are highly correlated with each other ($r^2 > .60$), it sometimes becomes statistically impossible to distinguish the effect of each independent variable on the dependent variable, controlled for the other. The variables are statistically too similar to discern disparate effects. This problem is called *multicollinearity* and is discussed later in this chapter. This problem is avoided by choosing independent variables that are not highly correlated with each other.

A WORKING EXAMPLE

Previously, the management analyst with the Department of Defense found a statistically significant relationship between teamwork and perceived facility productivity (p < .01). The analyst now wishes to examine whether the impact of teamwork on productivity is robust when controlled for other factors that also affect productivity. This interest is heightened by the low R-square ($R^2 = 0.074$) in Table 12.1, suggesting a weak relationship between teamwork and perceived productivity.

A multiple regression model is specified to include the effects of other factors that affect perceived productivity. Thinking about other categories of variables that could affect productivity, the analyst hypothesizes the following: (1) the extent to which employees have adequate technical knowledge to do their jobs, (2) perceptions of having adequate authority to do one's job well (for example, decision-making flexibility), (3) perceptions that rewards and recognition are distributed fairly (always important for motivation), and (4) the number of sick days. Various items from the employee survey are used to measure these concepts (as discussed in the workbook documentation for the Productivity dataset). After including these factors as additional independent variables, the result shown in Table 13.1 is obtained. Comparison with Table 12.1 shows that R-square has increased greatly; it is now 0.274. Hence 27.4 percent of the variation in the dependent variable,

Table 13.1 ·······∿∿∿····· Multiple Regression Output

Model

R	R-square	Adjusted R^2	SEE
0.524	0.274	0.263	0.735

Dependent variable: Productivity

ANOVA Table

Model	Sum of squares	df	Mean square	F	Sig.
Regression	64.239	5	12.848	23.809	0.000
Residual	169.980	315	0.540		
Total	234.219	320			

Coefficients

Model	Unstandardized coefficients		Standardized coefficients		
	b	SE	Beta	t	Sig.
Constant	2.064	0.301		6.850	0.000
Teamwork	0.166	0.040	0.202	4.166	0.000
Knowledge	0.267	0.050	0.263	5.391	0.000
Authority	0.200	0.035	0.288	5.804	0.000
Days sick	−0.011	0.020	−0.026	−0.543	0.587
Fairness	0.076	0.033	0.113	2.284	0.023

Note: SEE = standard error of the estimate; SE = standard error; Sig. = significance.

"productivity," is now explained by the five independent variables in the model.

Regarding these independent variables, teamwork *remains statistically significant* ($p < .01$) *when controlled for all of the other variables in the model* (ability, authority, inducement, and fairness). The results also show that having adequate knowledge and authority are, statistically, positively associated with productivity (both $p < .01$). Perceptions of fairness in rewards and recognition are also associated with productivity at the 5 percent level of significance. The considerable increase in R-square reflects the addition of these significant variables. The number of sick days is not associated with productivity, when controlled for other variables. Note that the sign of the significantly associated variables is positive, as expected. We would have been piqued if it had been negative. We need not be concerned about the negative slope of sick days because this variable is insignificant (not significantly different from zero).

Figure 13.1Dependent Variable: Productivity

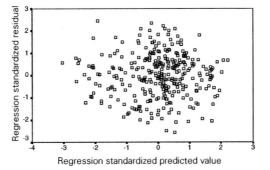

However, a key question is whether the model is fully specified. If the net effect on the dependent variable of all variables excluded from the model is not zero, then perhaps some other variable should be included that might affect our findings. The error term is examined to determine this possibility.

Recall that the net effect of all variables not included in the model is contained in the error term. When the net effect of such variables on the dependent variable is zero, *no relationship* exists between the error term and the predicted dependent variable. This relationship will be random, without pattern or shape. It is customary to plot the standardized error term (or residual) against the standardized predicted value of the dependent variable. This is called an ***error term plot***. The concept of standardization is discussed in Chapter 7 and involves transformation such that variables have a mean of zero and a standard deviation of one. Then, if no relationship exists between these two variables, the scatterplot should be random and clustered around (0,0), as shown in Figure 13.1. This figure is *prima facie evidence* that the net effect of variables not included in the model is zero because the data points are randomly scattered. Later in this chapter, we discuss other violations of regression assumptions, and strategies for examining and remedying such assumptions. Then we extend the preceding discussion and will be able to conclude whether the above results are valid.

Getting Started
Find examples of multiple regression in the research literature.

Again, this model is not the only model that can be constructed but rather is one among a family of plausible models. Indeed, from a theoretical perspective, other variables might have been included, too. From an empirical perspective, perhaps other variables might explain more variance. Model specification is a judicious effort, requiring a balance between theoretical and statistical integrity. Statistical software programs can also automatically select independent variables based on their statistical significance, hence, adding to R-square.[2] However, models with high R-square values are not necessarily better; theoretical reasons must exist for selecting independent variables, explaining why and how they might be related to the dependent variable. Knowing which variables are related empirically to the dependent variable can help narrow the selection, but such knowledge should not wholly determine it. We now turn to a discussion of the other statistics shown in Table 13.1.

FURTHER STATISTICS

Goodness of Fit for Multiple Regression

The model R-square in Table 13.1 is greatly increased over that shown in Table 12.1: R-square has gone from 0.074 in the simple regression model to 0.274. However, R-square has the undesirable mathematical property of increasing with the number of independent variables in the model. R-square increases regardless of whether an additional independent variable adds further explanation of the dependent variable. The ***adjusted R-square*** (or $\bar{R}^2$) controls for the number of independent variables. $\bar{R}^2$ is always equal to or less than R^2. The above increase in explanation of the dependent variable is due to variables identified as statistically significant in Table 13.1.

Adjusted R-square is often used to evaluate model explanation (or fit). Analogous with simple regression, values of $\bar{R}^2$ below 0.20 are considered to suggest weak model fit, those between 0.20 and 0.40 indicate moderate fit, those above 0.40 indicate strong fit, and those above 0.65 indicate very strong model fit. Analysts should remember that choices of model specification are driven foremost by theory, not statistical model fit; strong model fit is desirable only when the variables, and their relationships, are meaningful in some real-life sense. Adjusted R-square can assist in the variable selection process. Low values of adjusted R-square prompt analysts to ask whether they inadvertently excluded important variables from their models; if included, these variables might affect the statistical significance of those already in a model.[3] Adjusted R-square also helps analysts to choose among alternative variable specifications (for example, different measures of student isolation), when such choices are no longer meaningfully informed by theory. Empirical issues of model fit then usefully guide the selection process further. Researchers typically report adjusted R-square with their regression results.

Standardized Coefficients

The question arises as to which independent variable has the greatest impact on explaining the dependent variable. The slope of the coefficients (b) does not answer this question because each slope is measured in different units (recall from Chapter 12 that $b = \Delta y/\Delta x$). Comparing different slope coefficients is tantamount to comparing apples and oranges. However, based on the regression coefficient (or slope), it is possible to calculate the **standardized coefficient** (β, or "beta"). *Beta* is defined as the change produced in the dependent variable by a unit of change in the independent variable when both variables are measured in terms of standard deviation units. Beta is unit-less and thus allows for comparison of the impact of different independent variables on explaining the dependent variable. Analysts compare the relative values of beta coefficients; beta has no inherent meaning. It is appropriate to compare betas across independent variables in the same regression, not across different regressions.

Based on Table 13.1, we conclude that the impact of having adequate authority on explaining productivity is [(0.288 − 0.202)/0.202 =] 42.6 percent greater than teamwork, and about equal to that of knowledge. The impact of having adequate authority is two-and-a-half times greater than that of perceptions of fair rewards and recognition.[4]

F-Test

Table 13.1 also features an analysis of variance (ANOVA) table. The **global F-test** examines the overall effect of all independent variables jointly on the dependent variable. The null hypothesis is that the overall effect of all independent variables jointly on the dependent variables is statistically insignificant. The alternate hypothesis is that this overall effect is statistically significant. The null hypothesis implies that none of the regression coefficients is statistically significant; the alternate hypothesis implies that *at least one* of the regression coefficients is statistically significant. The F-test test statistic, 23.809, is statistically significant: hence, the overall effect of all independent variables jointly on the dependent variables is statistically significant. Analysts needn't rely on the global F-test for this information: the "Sig." (significance) column in the table of coefficients shows not only that at least one coefficient is statistically significant, it also shows which ones.[5]

As a point of information, the term *regression sum of squares* is a measure of the explained variation, $\Sigma (\hat{y}_i - \bar{y})^2$, and the *residual sum of squares* is a measure of the unexplained variation, $\Sigma (y_i - \hat{y}_i)^2$. These measures are shown graphically in Figure 13.2. Total sum of squares is defined as the sum of these measures. These measures are the basis for calculating R-square. Specifically, $R^2 = 1 - $ (residual sum of squares/total sum of squares). These values are shown in Table 13.1, from which we calculate R^2

Figure 13.2 ———————ᴡᴡ— Regression and Residual Sum of Squares

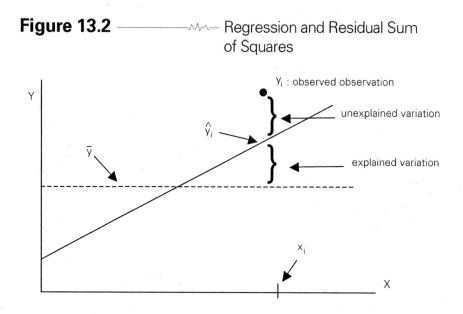

as $1 - (169.980/ 234.219) = 0.274$, which is shown as the value of R^2 in Table 13.1.[6]

USE OF NOMINAL VARIABLES

Multiple regression easily incorporates nominal variables as independent variables. However, a little transformation is required because the assumption of linearity suggests that it is not appropriate to regress a nominal variable against a dependent variable. Consider, for example, a nominal variable such as "Region" that is coded as West = 1, Northeast = 2, South = 3, and Midwest = 4. In this case, it would be incorrect to conclude that a predicted *y* value involving Midwest is four times that of West. Clearly, no such ordering exists among the values of this variable.

This difficulty is overcome by *recoding* the "Region" variable, creating *separate variables* for each of the response categories (except one, discussed below). Each new variable is dichotomous, having the value of one when it identifies the appropriate group, and zero otherwise. Such variables are called ***dummy variables*** because they take on only the values of zero and one. The recoding approach is shown in Table 13.2. Thus, for example, when Region = 1, the new variable West = 1, and West is zero in all other instances. Similarly, when Region = 2, the new variable Northeast = 1, and this new variable is zero in all other instances. The number of dummy variables is equal to the *number of categories minus 1*. This relationship results because the introduction of a variable representing the last category

Table 13.2 ‒‒‒‒‒‒‒‒⌇⌇‒‒‒ Recoding of Variables

Old	New		
Region	West	Northeast	South
1	1	0	0
2	0	1	0
3	0	0	1
4	0	0	0

(Midwest) creates a perfect linear relationship among the independent variables: West + Northeast + South + Midwest = 1. For mathematical reasons, when such perfect relationships exist among independent variables, it is not possible to calculate the regression coefficients.[7]

The implication of not including a variable identifying one of the categories is that results are interpreted as the effect on the dependent variable controlled for all independent variables in the model *plus the omitted category*. In our example, when the dummy variables are added to the model in Table 13.2, the regression coefficient of West shows its effect on productivity controlled for all other independent variables, including the effect of the Midwest, which is not entered into the regression.[8]

The corresponding regression model is then written as follows:

$$y = a + b_1 Northeast + b_2 South + b_3 West_3 + b_4 x_4 + b_5 x_5 + \ldots + error,$$

where $Northeast = 1$ when the observation is located in the Northeast; $Northeast = 0$ when the observation is located in the South, Midwest, or West; $South = 1$ when the observation is located in the South; $South = 0$ when the observation is located in the Northeast, Midwest, or West; $West = 1$ when the observation is located in the West; and $West = 0$ when the observation is located in the Northeast, South, or Midwest.

This interpretation is similar to considering the effect of gender on productivity, when the variable "gender" is coded as 0 = male and 1 = female. In that case, the regression coefficient of gender shows the effect of being female on productivity controlled for all other independent variables, including the effect of being male. There is no need to add a separate dummy variable for "male."

Dummy variables can also be used to identify control groups (for example, "exp" = 0) and experimental groups ("exp" = 1). Dummy variables are also useful for identifying observations at different time periods, for example, Time = 0 (before intervention) and Time = 1 (after intervention). This approach allows us to distinguish between two or more different groups and to determine whether belonging to a group (for example, getting treatment or not) has a statistically significant effect on the dependent variable. For example, a model might be specified as follows:

$$y = a + b_1x_1 + b_2x_2 + b_3x_3 + b_4x_4 + \ldots + error,$$

> **Getting Started**
>
> Develop your own multiple regression model.

where $x_1 = 1$ if the observation belongs to the treatment group, and $x_1 = 0$ if the observation belongs to the control group. Dummy variables are also used in time series analysis to model the impact of policies over time (see Chapter 15).

TESTING ASSUMPTIONS

Multiple regression is a powerful tool, but the technique includes assumptions that must be met. Many regression assumptions involve a test of the error term, which can help reveal problems with the model or data. Ideally, the relationship between the error term and the predicted dependent variable, shown in an *error term plot,* should be random (see Figure 13.1). However, several problems can occur that cause this pattern *not* to be random. The art of testing assumptions involves the analysis of these patterns.

Outliers

Outliers are observations with uncommon values, with regard to both single variables as well as combinations of variables. For example, although students with both high grade point averages (GPAs) and scholastic awards are not uncommon, any such student who commits frequent acts of school violence would likely be an outlier even among students who commit crimes. Outliers are common in multiple regression, and they are of concern because they may affect the statistical significance of regression coefficients.

This problem of outliers is shown graphically in Figure 13.3. Regression line A is estimated based only on the observations indicated with black dots.

Figure 13.3  Impact of Outliers

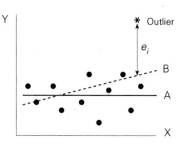

Figure 13.4 ———⌇⌇⌇— Outlier Detection

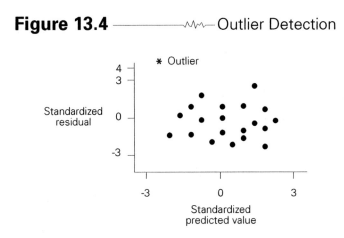

It is calculated without the uncharacteristic outlier, shown as the single starred observation; the regression slope is not significantly different from $b = 0$. Line B is the recalculated regression line that now includes the starred observation. The additional observation alters the direction of the regression line such that $b > 0$, leading to the conclusion that the independent variable is significantly associated with the dependent variable. Conclusions that are affected so strongly by just one or a few observations are not robust.

Detection. Outliers are commonly identified by the size of their residual. Note that the residual (or error, e_i, defined as $y_i - \hat{y}_i$) is larger for the additional starred observation than for any of the dotted observations in Figure 13.3. Outliers are usually first identified when the error term plot is examined (see Figure 13.4). Observations are defined as outliers when their residuals exceed ± 3 standard deviations; clearly, such observations are unusual relative to others. Statistical software packages can flag residuals that exceed a user-specified value (such as three standard deviations) and produce error term plots.[9]

How to resolve. The effect of outliers on regression conclusions is examined by removing outliers, reestimating the model, and then examining conclusions for substantive robustness. Statistical software packages allow users to save residuals associated with each observation. These residuals are then used to remove from subsequent analysis any observations that are outliers. The primary concern is with significant coefficients that become insignificant, and vice versa. Change in the direction (sign) of regression coefficients is also of concern. The final reported results should be robust; hence, they should exclude outliers that substantively affect conclusions.

Figure 13.5 ⎯⎯⎯⎯⎯⎯〰〰⎯Multicollinearity

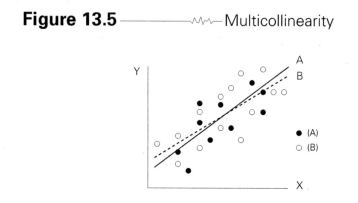

Multicollinearity

The problem of ***multicollinearity*** (pronounced "multi-KOH-li-nee-air-i-tee") is that two independent variables may be correlated to such a high degree that their effects on the dependent variable are indistinguishably similar. For example, in a study of high school violence, the variables "off-campus crimes" and "off-campus misdemeanors" might be highly correlated. In this case, the regression coefficients of these two independent variables might be statistically insignificant because, net of the other(s), they have little or no residual effect on the dependent variable, "high school violence." This problem is shown graphically in Figure 13.5. The black and white observations produce regression lines so similar that, given their respective standard errors, they are statistically indistinguishable.

Detection. Multicollinearity is more likely to occur as more independent variables are entered into the model. The more independent variables entered, the more likely that some will be highly correlated with each other. Multicollinearity is usually first suspected when the regression coefficients of independent variables in a multiple regression are statistically insignificant, even though in bivariate relationships they are known to be highly significant (for example, $r^2 > .60$). Computers readily calculate correlation matrices, which show these correlations for all pairs of variables. Computers also calculate the *variance inflation factor* (VIF) for each regression coefficient;[10] VIF is a measure of the effect of all other independent variables on a regression coefficient.[11] Values greater than 5 or 10 indicate multicollinearity; values of variables that do not exhibit multicollinearity are usually between 1.0 and 2.0. VIFs are routinely calculated by statistical software packages.

How to resolve. To correct for multicollinearity, researchers need to remove the collinear variables from the model. When the variables are substantively related, they might be combined to create a new index variable. For instance,

Figure 13.6 ———〰️—Curvilinear Relationship with Regression Line

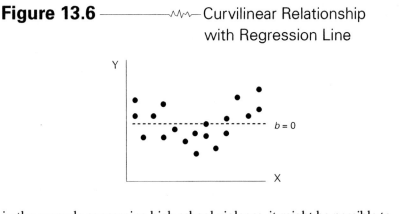

in the example concerning high school violence, it might be possible to combine the variables "off-campus crimes" and "off-campus misdemeanors" into a single, new index variable. When variables are not substantively related to each other, analysts should consider substituting one of the collinear variables for a similar measurement that is less highly correlated with the other variables.

Linearity

Multiple regression estimates a *straight* regression line; it assumes that independent variables are *linearly* correlated with the dependent variable. *Curvilinear* relationships are relationships that are not linear, such as $y = \sqrt{x}$ or x^2. For example, certain forms of pollution have curvilinear relationships with population density. In these cases, a straight regression line is a poor fit, and regression coefficients underestimate the significance of the relationship. In the worst cases, the regression coefficient will be estimated as being insignificant when it is not; this extreme problem is shown in Figure 13.6. Linear estimation is a poor fit for any curvilinear relationship.

Detection. Diagnosis of curvilinear relationships centers on examining the curvilinear pattern of error terms, as shown in Figure 13.7. Subsequent bivariate analysis is then used to identify *which* independent-dependent variable relationship is curvilinear. Many statistical packages also produce so-called *partial residual plots,* which show the relationship between the dependent variable and each independent variable, when controlled for other independent variables.[12] Using such plots, analysts decide whether the relationship is linear, curvilinear, or simply not present.

How to resolve. Curvilinearity is typically corrected by transforming the independent variable; square root, quadratic, and logarithmic transformations are used (see Chapter 11). For example, if a curvilinear relationship

Figure 13.7 ———— Detecting Curvilinearity

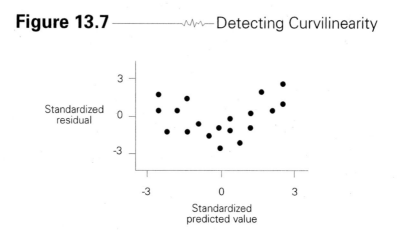

exists between the dependent variable and independent variable x_1, then the initial relationship might be transformed in the following manner:

$$\text{Initial relationship: } y = a + b_1x_1 + b_2x_2 + \dots.$$
$$\text{Transformed relationship: } y = a + b_1\sqrt{x_1} + b_2x_2 + \dots.$$

Of course, any other transformation of x_1 that results in a linear relationship between y and this independent variable is acceptable. In rare instances, it may be necessary to transform the dependent variable when it is curvilinearly related to all or most independent variables.[13]

Heteroscedasticity

Heteroscedasticity (pronounced "heh-troh-SKUH-das-ti-ci-tee") is the problem of unequal variances of the error term. For example, when expenditures are examined by unit size, the residuals of larger units will vary more than those of a smaller size because larger jurisdictions and households with larger incomes usually have more discretion in their spending patterns than do those of smaller size. The extent to which heteroscedasticity occurs in public management and policy varies with the nature of one's data or problems. Unequal variances of the error term are a violation of random distribution of the error term, and they cause the statistical significance of regression coefficients to be underestimated. Heteroscedasticity usually occurs when data include heterogeneous subunits, such as households with greatly varying levels of income or jurisdictions of vastly different populations.

Heteroscedasticity is detected graphically by examination of the error term plot for unequal variance, as shown in Figure 13.8. The figure shows a trumpet-like distribution of the error terms, but the heteroscedasticity can

Figure 13.8 ──────∿∿∿─Heteroscedasticity

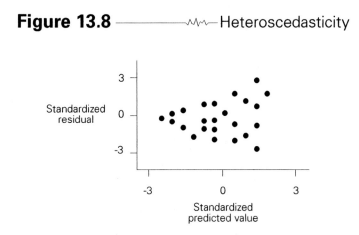

also occur to the left or even in the middle if that is the range in which error terms have relatively larger variances. When heteroscedasticity is suspected, the error terms (e) may also be plotted against each independent variable ($x_1, x_2, \ldots$) in order to determine *which* dependent-independent variable relationship is heteroscedastic.[14]

How to resolve. Heteroscedasticity is overcome by transforming one or more variables. The scale adjustment reduces the sizes of differences between variables, minimizing unequal variance. Often, a logarithmic transformation of *both* the dependent and the independent variables sufficiently corrects for the problem:

$$\text{Initial relationship: } y = a + b_1 x_1 + b_2 x_2 \ldots.$$
$$\text{Transformed relationship: } \ln(y) = a + b_1 \ln(x_1) + b_2 \ln(x_2) + \ldots.$$

The log transformation is useful when large error terms are associated with large values of the (in)dependent variables because the log transformation reduces large values much more than small values. However, this approach may fail when heteroscedasticity is caused by a more complex relationship between the error term and one or more variables. *Weighted least squares* (WLS) is a procedure that mathematically calculates the requisite transformation based on the observed variance and its relationship to a specific variable. WLS is available in most statistical software packages.[15] Box 13.1 illustrates the assumption testing carried out for the regression model examined earlier in this chapter.

Getting Started
Verify your understanding of regression assumptions.

In Greater Depth...

Box 13.1   Assumption Testing in Multiple Regression

Earlier in this chapter we discussed the example of a workplace productivity analysis, the results of which are shown in Table 13.1. In that example, perceived productivity is the dependent variable, and teamwork, job knowledge, authority, sick days, and fairness are independent variables. Table 13.1 shows that $\bar{R}^2 = 0.263$, and teamwork, job knowledge, and authority are significant at the 1 percent level. Fairness is significant at the 5 percent level. How do we test for assumptions?

The first step is to plot the error terms against the predicted values. Figure 13.1, shown at the beginning of this chapter, is that error term plot. The error term plot does not show the presence of any outliers, which would have been indicated by values of the regression standardized residual (shown on the Y-axis) smaller than –3 or greater than +3. We do note that one observation has a value that is close to –3. To examine its impact on regression results (as we would have done for all observations with standardized residuals smaller than –3 or greater than +3), we remove this observation from the sample and rerun the regression model to test for robustness. We then observe that removing this observation does not affect the reported levels of statistical significance, which hence are robust for outliers.

We also test for multicollinearity. The reported values of the variance infla-tion factors (VIFs) are 1.025 for teamwork, 1.074 for job knowledge, 1.074 for authority, 1.011 for sick days, and 1.056 for fairness. These VIFs are well below the threshold of 5; thus, we conclude that multicollinearity does not affect the statistical significance of the independent variables. This result is reflected by the Pearson's correlation coefficients of the bivariate correlations among the inde-pendent variables. The largest bivariate correlation coefficient, r, is a mere 0.202, occurring between the variables "fairness" and "authority."

Although the scatterplot shown in Figure 13.1 does not suggest heteroscedasticity (there is no obvious trumpet-shaped pattern), the Park test (see note 14) does find evidence of slight heteroscedasticity between the error term and the variable authority (t-test statistic 2.69, $p < .01$). Using the weighted least squares procedure, we rerun the model with "authority" as the weight variable. Adjusted R-square is now slightly lower (0.237), but the levels of statistical significance reported earlier remain unchanged.

Finally, we see no evidence of curvilinearity in the plot. This is verified further by examining the partial regression plots of each of the independent variables. In all, then, we conclude that the previously reported results are robust. They are not affected by any of the potential problems noted.

Figure 13.9 ———————— Autocorrelation

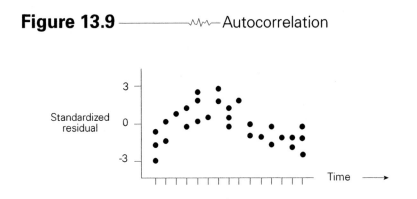

Autocorrelation

Autocorrelation is the problem that successive observations are correlated with each other; they are not independent. This is a frequent problem with time series data, because values at t = T are often good predictors of subsequent values at t = T + 1, which are then good predictors of other values at T + 2, and so on. This feature also causes error terms to be correlated with each other, when plotted in their time-ordered sequence, as shown in Figure 13.9. This is a violation of the assumption of the random distribution of error terms.

One problem of autocorrelation, which is also called *serial correlation,* is that it severely exaggerates the statistical significance of variables, leading to the erroneous conclusion that variables are statistically associated when they are not. Tests for detecting and addressing autocorrelation are discussed in Chapter 15. Typically, analysts do well to assume that problems of autocorrelation are likely to occur when working with time series data. For example, panel data collected and analyzed across different time periods are likely to have the problem of autocorrelation. By contrast, cross-sectional data rarely involve successive observations that are correlated with each other and, hence, autocorrelation.

Measurement and Specification

Multiple regression further assumes (1) that the model does not omit important variables, (2) that the model does not include irrelevant variables, and (3) that the variables are measured accurately. Unlike the assumptions discussed earlier in this chapter, detection and resolution are based largely on theoretical rather than empirical grounds. These problems are important and frequent threats to the validity of models.

As mentioned earlier in this chapter, full model specification allows for a family of plausible models. Random distribution of the error term does not imply that a given set of independent variables is the only plausible set;

relevant, independent variables may have been excluded. *Specification error* involves both the omission of relevant variables and the inclusion of irrelevant ones. The effect of *omitting a relevant variable* is to inflate the value of t-test statistics of independent variables that are included. Analysts should ask whether any theoretically relevant (control) variable has been excluded from the model. Indeed, adding a relevant control variable may affect the observed levels of statistical significance. Excluding relevant variables also biases the estimate of the intercept, which may affect prediction. To avoid these problems, analysts need to give full, theoretical consideration to the broadest possible set of relevant variables when they are building statistical models.

The effect of *including irrelevant variables* is the opposite of that of omitting a relevant value; namely, it understates the importance of other independent variables. Analysts should ask whether all variables included in the model are theoretically sound. The problem of including irrelevant variables often arises as analysts verify how existing models hold up under the impact of a broader range of variables. Generally, irrelevant variables should not be included because they reduce the level of statistical significance of other variables, increase the possibility of multicollinearity, and work against model parsimony. Also, theoretically irrelevant variables cannot be justified, no matter how statistically significant they may be. Thus, a guarded stance regarding irrelevant variables is usually appropriate.[16]

Measurement error is defined as inaccurate measurement of the underlying study concept; variables that have measurement error are substantively invalid or have systematic biases. Measurement validity was discussed earlier as part of validating index variables (see Chapter 3). Accurate measurement is especially important for the *dependent* variable because inaccurate measurement may render it impossible for independent variables to achieve requisite levels of statistical significance. For example, inaccurate measurement of the dependent variable can occur when there are few categories, such as when using a dependent variable with a five-point Likert scale. This typically causes an upward or downward sloping pattern of the error terms. To improve measurement, an index variable, which increases the range of values and improves substantive relevance (by encompassing more dimensions of the concept), should be used. Researchers usually give heightened importance to measurement of the dependent variable.

SUMMARY

Multiple regression is a powerful and popular technique for taking control variables (rival hypotheses) into account. It uses two or more independent variables. Multiple regression can also use nominal, independent variables, which are transformed as so-called dummy variables. Analysts frequently encounter multiple regression in research articles. Multiple regression is a full model specification technique; that is, the technique seeks to account for all effects on the dependent variable. The popularity of multiple regression is due largely to its ability to control for all other independent variables in the model when estimating the relationships between each independent variable and the dependent variable.

Although multiple regression is quite powerful, it does not substitute for developing a thorough understanding of the bivariate relationships in which analysts are interested. Both before and after multiple regression is used, the nature, strength, and practical significance of bivariate relationships should be examined. Indeed, analysts often turn to multiple regression because they want to learn more about a previously discovered, significant bivariate relationship. They want to know whether a specific bivariate relationship remains significant when controlled for other variables. Thus, multiple regression usually follows bivariate analysis.

Finally, although multiple regression is used widely, it also has various test assumptions that must be met. Models should be specified correctly and variables measured without error. In addition, assumptions pertaining to the error term are that there should be no outliers, heteroscedasticity, multicollinearity, autocorrelation, or curvilinearity.

KEY TERMS

Adjusted R-square (p. 218)
Assumption of full model
  specification (p. 214)
Autocorrelation (p. 229)
Curvilinear (p. 225)
Dummy variables (p. 220)
Error term plot (p. 217)
Full model specification (p. 212)
Global F-test (p. 219)
Heteroscedasticity (p. 226)

Interpretation of the regression
  coefficients in multiple
  regression (p. 214)
Measurement error (p. 230)
Multicollinearity (p. 224)
Nomothetic mode of explanation
  (p. 212)
Outliers (p. 222)
Specification error (p. 230)
Standardized coefficient (beta)
  (p. 219)

Notes

1. Nomothetic explanations are contrasted by *idiographic* explanations, which identify all factors affecting a dependent variable. Idiographic models are quite difficult in multiple regression because the number of factors that affect dependent variables often is very large, including unique factors that affect only a small subset of observations. Because empirical data about all of these factors are typically missing, nomothetic strategies are used instead.

2. SPSS and other programs offer a range of selection approaches. Some methods select the variables that are the most significantly associated with the dependent variable ("forward selection"), other methods remove the variables that are least significantly associated with the dependent variable ("backward selection"), and still other methods use a combination of forward and backward selection strategies until no more variables can be either added or removed ("stepwise selection").

3. Some phenomena are quite complex to explain, and models that have these as dependent variables will have a low model fit. For example, it can be very difficult to explain last-minute voting decisions, especially in a parsimonious way. Also, many phenomena include random elements, and there are also measurement errors that affect model fit.

4. Statistical software packages can also produce part and partial regression coefficients. *Partial correlation* examines the correlation between the dependent variable and one independent variable, controlled for correlations that each has with the other independent variables in the model. *Part (or, semipartial) correlation* examines the correlation between the dependent and one independent variable, controlled for the correlation that only the dependent variable has with the other independent variables in the model. Part correlations show the incremental or unique impact of an independent variable. *Zero-order correlations* are simply the bivariate correlation coefficients of each independent variable with the dependent variable.

5. Although the global F-test is not particularly useful, one variation is the *partial F-test.* Here, the analyst wants to know whether including other independent variables adds to the explanation of the dependent variable. The initial model is called the restricted model (R), and the model with additional independent variables is called the unrestricted model (UR). The *F* statistic for testing the statistical significance of the additional variables is defined as follows:

$$F = \frac{[(R_{UR}^2 - R_R^2)/m]}{[(1 - R_{UR}^2)/(N-k)]},$$

where N = the number of observations, k = the number of variables in the unrestricted model, and m = the number of variables in the unrestricted model minus the number of variables in the restricted model. To test this statistic, the denominator degrees of freedom (df) is defined as $(N-k)$ and the numerator degrees of freedom (df) is defined as m.

6. The formula for adjusted R-square shows the adjustment for the number of independent variables: $1 - [(\text{residual sum of squares})(n-1)/$

(total sum of squares)$(n - p - 1)$], where n = number of observations (here, 321) and p = number of independent variables. From Table 13.1, we calculate $1 - [(169.980*320)/(234.219*315)] = 0.263$.

7. Statistical software packages vary in their response to this problem. SPSS automatically deletes one variable that causes the perfect correlation, whereas other programs report error messages.

8. For example, if we thought that performance were also affected by region, we could specify the model in Table 13.2 as follows: productivity = f(teamwork, ability, authority, inducement, fairness, Northeast, South, West), where f indicates that productivity is a function of the variables between parentheses. Note that use of a dummy variable assumes that the regression models are statistically similar among all groups. If differences are suspected, analysts may also wish to run regression models for each separate group.

9. Other approaches exist for detecting influential observations. See any advanced text for a discussion of measures such as Cook's D. Measures of Cook's D greater than 1.0 may signal influential observations.

10. In SPSS, Analyze → Regression → Linear → Statistics: Collinearity Diagnostics.

11. VIF = 1/Tolerance, where Tolerance = $1 - R^2$, and R^2 is calculated for the model in which an independent variable is predicted by all of the other independent variables.

12. Technically, partial residual plots show the relationship between the error term of the independent and dependent variables, when each is regressed against all of the other independent variables. Partial residual plots differ from partial regression plots, which are used to identify influential observations such as outliers.

13. A special instance occurs when the dependent variable is a fraction p, ranging from 0.0 to 1.0. Then, a so-called logit transformation, which is defined as $\ln[1/(1 - p)]$, is recommended.

14. Some analysts believe that this graphical approach can sometimes fail to detect heteroscedasticity. They suggest analyzing the relationship between e^2 and each independent variable. This is the *Park test*. Squaring of the error term causes a positive relationship to occur with the independent variable if heteroscedasticity is present (see the figure, below). To determine whether a relationship exists between e^2 and x, the following simple regression is used. The log transformation is used to ensure that the relationship is linear, rather than curvilinear, which may occur because of the squaring:

$$\ln e^2 = a + b_1 \ln(x).$$

When the slope (b_i) is significant, a heteroscedastic relationship exists between the error term and the independent variable:

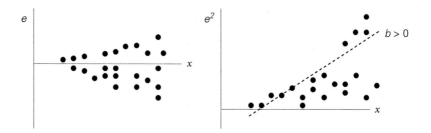

15. A thorough discussion of WLS is beyond this text. For a discussion and example of WLS, see SPSS, *Regression Models 10.0* (Chicago: SPSS, Inc., 1999 or latest edition), or Damodar Gujarati, *Basic Econometrics*, 3d ed. (New York: McGraw-Hill, 1999).

16. Some analysts also consider as a criterion whether adjusted R-square increases as a result of adding a variable. Increases in adjusted R-square imply that more variance of the dependent variable is explained. However, the ultimate basis for including or excluding variables should be theoretical; it cannot be based solely on empirical considerations.

Logistic Regression

CHAPTER OBJECTIVES

After reading this chapter, you should be able to
- State why logistic regression is used when the dependent variable is dichotomous
- Estimate the probability of an event
- Identify and test assumptions of logistic regression
- Address assumption violations

This chapter discusses logistic regression, a technique used when the dependent variable is dichotomous. Logistic regression is often used in political science, for example, when analysts try to understand the probability of a dichotomous event such as winning or losing an election. Logistic regression is in many ways analogous to multiple regression, but the former uses different statistics and estimation methods, hence requiring separate discussion in this short chapter.

THE LOGISTIC MODEL

Logistic ("loh-GIS-tic") *regression* deals with situations in which the dependent variable is dichotomous. Examples of dichotomous variables

Figure 14.1 ——————Logistic Curve

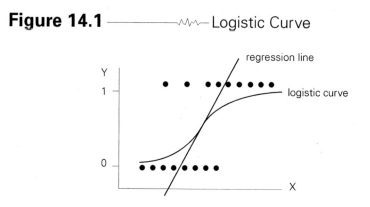

include winning a political election, receiving a death penalty, and having an abortion. In these instances, the dependent variable is dichotomous by nature because it is impossible to win half an election or to be somewhat put to death.

The dichotomous nature of the dependent variable violates an assumption of multiple regression, discussed in Chapter 15, that the dependent variable should be continuous. The dichotomous dependent variable creates a statistical problem, namely, that the linear regression line is poorly suited to predict the dichotomous variable. This situation is shown graphically in Figure 14.1. When the straight regression line is used, predicted values of the dependent variable can be less than zero and greater than one. This is problematic if we want to interpret the predicted values as the probability that the dependent variable event occurs. Obviously, the chance of winning an election can neither be negative nor greater than one. To resolve this problem, an S-shaped curve (also called a logistic curve) is fitted to the observations. The values of this curve always lie between zero and one.

The shape of the curve is defined by the following equation:

$$\text{Prob(event)} = 1/(1 + e^{-Z}),$$

where $Z = a + b_1 x_1 + b_2 x_2 + \ldots$. In this model, Prob(event) is the probability of the event occurring. For example, if a dichotomous variable "war" is defined as going to war (war = 1) or not going to war (war = 0), then the formula calculates the probability of going to war. Z is also called the **logit**.

In addition to using a different estimation equation, logistic regression uses a different method for estimating the logistic curve. In multiple regression, coefficients are estimated by minimizing the sum of squared differences of observed and predicted values of each observation, or $\Sigma(y_i - \hat{y}_i)^2$ of each observation (see Chapter 12). This method is called ordinary least squares (OLS), and it produces the closest fit of the observations around the regression line. In logistic regression, the coefficients are estimated such that the likelihood of correctly predicting the observed events is maximized. An iterative process is used, called maximum likelihood estimation (MLE), in which successive models are evaluated until further improvements in correctly predicting observed events are no longer significant. This estimation method results in statistics that differ from those in multiple regression.

The different estimation method also causes logistic regression to have fewer assumptions than multiple regression. Logistic regression does not assume normally distributed error terms, and the dichotomous dependent variable makes homogeneity a moot point. However, it does assume that outliers are not present, and it also assumes full model specification, that the variables are measured and specified without error, and that no autocorrelation or multicollinearity is present. Logistic regression also assumes large samples. Recommendations vary but often suggest minimum sample sizes of at least 50 observations, and more when models include many independent variables.

A WORKING EXAMPLE

Assume, hypothetically, that data exist about teenagers who have been involved in incidents of classroom violence. We do not know how many incidents they have been involved in, only that they have been involved. Hence, the dependent variable is dichotomous. Assume further that we want to know whether gender, grade level, and scholastic attainment (grade point average, or GPA) are predictors of classroom violence. Data are available for 30 students who have been involved in such incidents, as well as for an additional random sample of 50 students who have not been involved. The population is drawn only from high school students. The results shown in Table 14.1 are obtained. This output yields many new statistics because the estimation methodology is different from that used in multiple regression.

The top row of Table 14.1 shows a variety of goodness-of-fit statistics. The first statistic, the *log likelihood value* (–2LL),[1] is analogous to the global F-test in regression (see Chapter 13). It assesses whether the model with independent variables is significantly better in predicting observed events than a model with no independent variables. The absolute value (66.001) has no interpretation, but the level of significance shows that this model with three variables is significantly better than the base (or null) model that lacks these variables. This is hardly a surprise, given that all three independent variables are statistically significant.

The Cox and Snell R^2 is analogous to R^2 in multiple regression, but it cannot reach a value of 1.0. The *Nagelkerke R^2* is a modification that

Table 14.1 ⸺〰⸺ Logistic Regression Output

Model Fit

	-2 log likelihood (-2LL)				Hosmer and Lemeshow test	
Model	Sig. (base model)	Cox and Snell R²	Nagelkerke R²		Chi-square	Sig.
66.001	0.000	0.392	0.535		8.397	.396

Dependent variable: Student classroom incident

Coefficients

Model	Unstandardized coefficients		Wald chi-square	Sig.
	b	SE		
Constant	-7.405	5.202	2.027	0.155
Gender	-4.464	1.319	11.450	0.001
Education	1.558	0.544	8.212	0.004
GPA	-2.716	0.722	14.140	0.000

Classification Table

Observed		Predicted		
		Violence		Percent
Variable	Group	0	1	correct
Violence	0	44	6	88.0
	1	11	19	63.3
Overall percentage				78.8

Note: Sig. = significance; GPA = grade point average; SE = standard error.

overcomes this problem. The interpretation of the results shows that 53.5 percent of the variance in students involved in classroom incidents is explained by the model. The classification table at the bottom of Table 14.1 supports this finding. A ***classification table*** shows the percentage of corrected predicted observations. The minimum is 50 percent, indicating the lack of any useful prediction. Typically, standards of 80–85 percent indicate "good" model prediction. Our model falls somewhat short (78.8 percent correct); we acknowledge the desirability of a better model. Another goodness-of-fit statistic is the *Hosmer and Lemeshow test,* which compares the observed and predicted values. A good model fit has close correspondence between observed and predicted values and, hence, an insignificant chi-square value for this test. This is also shown in Table 14.1.

In addition to the above statistics, residuals can be calculated that measure the difference for each observation between the predicted probability of an event occurring and the observed probability (that is, group membership). This approach is analogous to calculation of the error term in multiple regression. Standardized residuals can be calculated,[2] and analysts can assess the effect of an observation whose standardized residuals exceed the absolute value of 2.58. Beyond this, logistic regression, like multiple regression, can flag other observations whose influence on coefficients and model fit can be examined.[3] In our case, further analysis shows that two observations might be classified as outliers, but removing them does not substantively alter or much improve the above results; hence, they are retained.

In short, a variety of statistics can be used to assess the overall goodness of fit. The classification table is a basic but very useful tool for understanding the predictive ability of the model. Regarding other assumptions, when working with time series data (which the above data are not), analysts need to follow the remediation processes described in Chapter 15. The possibility of multicollinearity is examined through the correlation matrix and the relationships of independent variables with the dependent variable as discussed in Chapter 13; no VIF test is available for logistic regression. Finally, a problem with logistic regression is that adding too many variables may result in solutions that are unstable, or regression coefficients that are inappropriate or no longer significant. Such problems may indicate *overfitting*, a term used in statistics to refer to models that have too many variables for the amount of data. When such estimation problems occur, analysts often need to use a model with fewer variables. (This problem is also relevant to multiple regression, but in practice it seems to occur far more often in logistic regression.)

Calculating Event Probabilities

The results in Table 14.1 show that all three variables are statistically significant. Gender, education (grade level), and GPA are all predictors of a student's becoming involved in a violent classroom incident. **Wald chi-square** is the test statistic used to determine the statistical significance of logistic regression coefficients. This statistic is analogous to the t-test, $b/se(b)$, in multiple regression. The Wald chi-square is defined as $[b/se(b)]^2$, and each variable has one degree of freedom.

The formula given earlier for the logistic curve can be used to calculate the probability of an event occurring. Using this formula, we can calculate the probability of a student's becoming involved in a violent incident for different levels of the independent variables. These calculations are readily performed on a spreadsheet (see Table 14.2), allowing for interesting what-if analyses. Positive logistic regression coefficients imply that probabilities increase, and negative logistic regression coefficients imply that probabilities decrease. For example, the negative coefficient of GPA means that increases

Table 14.2 ⎯⎯⎯⎯⎯⎯ Calculating Event Probability

Variables					Probability
Gender	Education	GPA	$a + bx + \ldots$	$e^{-(a + bx + \ldots)}$	$1/(1 + e^{-(a + bx + \ldots)})$
0	10	3.0	0.027	0.973	0.507
1	10	3.0	−4.437	84.521	0.012
0	10	2.0	2.743	0.064	0.939
0	10	4.0	−2.689	14.717	0.064
1	12	3.0	−1.321	3.747	0.211

Note: GPA = grade point averages; 0 = male; 1 = female.

in GPA are associated with lower probabilities of the event occurring, being involved in classroom incidents.

The results for 10th-grade students show that classroom violence is associated primarily with being male; for students with a GPA of 3.0, the probability of being involved in a violent classroom incident is much lower. The probability for the two groups are, respectively, 50.7 percent for males and 1.2 percent for females. Among 10th-grade males, the probability of being involved in a violent incident is affected greatly by school perfor-mance: for male students with a GPA of 2.0 the chance is 93.9 percent, but for those with a 4.0 GPA the chance is only 6.4 percent. Further analysis shows that the chance of violence increases with grade level; it is highest in the 12th grade. In partic-ular, 12th-grade females with a 3.0 GPA have a 21.1 percent probability of being involved in a violent incident.

Getting Started
Verify these calculations.

Finally, the ratio of P(event)/P(no event) is called an ***odds ratio***. The odds ratio is used to compare the probability of something occurring, as compared to it not occurring. This definition is not akin to the ordinary meaning of the word *odds* as it relates to probability. Rather, the odds ratio shows how much more likely it is that an event will occur than it will not occur. The odds ratio is calculated as follows:

$$P(\text{event})/P(\text{no event}) = e^Z,$$

where $Z = a + b_1x_1 + b_2x_2 + \ldots$.

This measure may be used to observe how the odds ratio changes when only one independent variable is changed, such as by one unit. For example, when GPA decreases by 1, Z increases by 2.716 (note the negative sign of this coefficient in Table 14.1), and the odds ratio is $e^{2.716} = 15.12$. This means that a decrease in GPA greatly increases the chances of being involved in a classroom incident. It bears repeating that these are hypothetical data. Box 14.1 discusses other uses of logistic regression.

~~~~

In Greater Depth...

Box 14.1   Logistic Regression in Research

A variety of research situations prompt analysts to use logistic regression. For example, political scientists frequently use logistic regression to examine the adoption of voting practices, to analyze specific voting decisions, and to look at turnover among presidential advisors. Specifically, we could try to predict whether or not citizens vote, how they choose between two candidates, and whether or not presidential advisors are retained from one year to the next.

Another line of research examines factors involved in whether or not jurisdictions adopted specific policies, laws, or practices, such as clean air policies, domestic violence legislation, lottery policies, or even whether they were awarded empowerment zones for urban economic development by the federal government. Other studies look at the adoption of innovative policies and practices by states. Indeed, in this way, researchers can study many differences across cities, counties, states, or countries.

Still other uses include researching factors that explain recidivism among offenders, whether municipal bonds are issued with insurance, whether or not highly qualified employees want to work for government, and whether or not wars occur (and how long they last). Other studies explain whether or not respondents are likely to adopt conservative or liberal attitudes.

In short, logistic regression can be used on many and varied occasions.

~~~~

A final thought. Logistic regression extends multiple regression by considering a dichotomous dependent variable. But what if the dependent variable has more than two categories, yet it is still not continuous? The dependent variable might be nominal with three or more categories. For example, we might want to predict parents' choice of a school voucher program out of three or more types. Or the dependent variable might be ordinal, such as a five-point Likert scale. Techniques for dealing with these situations are discussed briefly in Chapter 16.

Getting Started
Find examples of logistic regression in the research literature.

SUMMARY

Logistic regression is used when the dependent variable is dichotomous. It allows researchers to estimate the probability of an event occurring. The statistics used in logistic regression are somewhat analogous but nevertheless different from those used in multiple regression. A variety of statistics, such as the classification table, help researchers to assess logistic regression models. The most defining application of logistic regression is, however, the ability to predict the probability of an event occurring.

KEY TERMS

Classification table (p. 238)

Logistic regression (p. 235)

Logit (p. 236)

Log likelihood value (p. 237)

Nagelkerke R^2 (p. 237)

Odds ratio (p. 240)

Wald chi-square (p. 239)

Notes

1. The log likelihood is calculated as $-2*\log(\text{likelihood})$, hence, $-2LL$. The likelihood is a measure of how well observed values can be predicted. Better fitting models have smaller values of $-2LL$.
2. The standardized residual is defined as residual$/\sqrt{[p(1-p)]}$.
3. These measures include, for example, Cook's D. Measures of Cook's D greater than 1.0 may signal influential observations.

SECTION
V

Further Statistics

This section examines additional statistical techniques of interest to public managers and analysts. Here we discuss advanced techniques with three important purposes in mind. First, familiarity with advanced techniques makes research articles and reports more accessible for managers and analysts. Managers and analysts are expected to keep abreast of state-of-art research in their fields, and they will want and need to know how to read these statistics. No one can be an expert in all techniques, but some comprehension is expected. To assist, we offer summaries that focus on a few key aspects of these techniques: What is the purpose of these techniques? What statistics are commonly reported in applications? What assumptions pertain to these techniques? What are some typical applications of these techniques? These are the key questions to ask when first encountering statistical techniques.

A second purpose of these chapters is to lay the groundwork for those who might want to pursue these techniques further. The initial discussion of important purposes and measures can assist and stimulate more advanced study. Finally, a third purpose is to help readers understand how to apply these techniques; hence, some discussions include considerable detail, such as the discussion on time series regression and non-regression based forecasting. Indeed, some courses might highlight techniques beyond those discussed in Section IV, and the material covered in this section will help toward that end.

Chapter 15 discusses time series analysis. First, we extend the discussion of multiple regression to time series data. In particular, this chapter addresses unique issues pertaining to regression assumptions associated with such data. It demonstrates how to use time series regression in the assessment of policy and program impacts, adding to the strategies discussed in Section IV. Second, we examine the regression-based approaches to forecasting. Forecasting helps managers make decisions about future events (see Chapter 4). Some regression-based approaches rely solely on extrapolation of single variables, whereas others incorporate the impact of independent variables. Regression-based forecasting typically requires at least 20 observations; when these observations are not available, managers and analysts will want to use spreadsheet-based methods of forecasting. Third, we examine non-regression-based methods of forecasting, which are quite common in budgeting, for example.

Chapter 16 summarizes a broad range of statistical techniques. The first part discusses analysis of variance (ANOVA), which is useful when the independent variable is nominal and has three or more categories. This method extends the t-test. A bit more detail is provided, along with examples, because managers and analysts are likely to encounter this method in fields that typically have such data (for example, experimental research in medicine and agriculture, and education). The second part looks at path analysis. This technique is used when relationships between the dependent and independent variables are complex. This section also notes techniques that are used when feedback loops are present. The third part examines survival analysis, which is used when researchers want to study the decay of samples over time, such as factors that might cause students to drop out of educational programs over time. The fourth and final part examines some techniques for exploratory data analysis. It emphasizes factor analysis, which is often used in social science research. However, it also briefly notes some other methods, such as discriminant analysis.

The chapters contained in this final section provide a broad survey of advanced techniques. It is hoped that this discussion will provide a useful reference for managers and analysts to use when they encounter these statistical methods in research articles and reports.

CHAPTER

15

Time Series Analysis

CHAPTER OBJECTIVES

After reading this chapter, you should be able to
- Identify different techniques for analyzing time series data
- Test assumptions of time series regression, and address violations
- Use dummy variables to assess the impacts of policies in time series data
- Understand the uses of different regression-based forecasting techniques
- Undertake forecasts that are based on a few observations

This chapter presents an overview of techniques used in time series analysis, in three parts: (1) multiple regression of time series data, (2) regression-based forecasting, and (3) non-regression-based forecasting. Each part provides an overview of techniques, emphasizing major purposes, statistics, and applications. Some techniques are discussed in a bit more detail, providing readers with skills aiding in application.

TIME SERIES DATA IN MULTIPLE REGRESSION

Managers and policy analysts frequently use data that have been collected over time. Examples of these data include administrative data, such as activity logs, customer complaints, budget data, and inspection reports that have been completed or gathered in different periods, as well as survey data that are completed on a regular basis, such as client, citizen, and business surveys.

Time series data can be used with multiple regression, which is then called time series regression. The principles that apply to multiple regression—full model specification and the judicious selection of independent variables—also apply to time series regression. The same assumptions apply, as well: the dependent variable must be continuous; independent variables must be continuous or dichotomous (that is, dummy variables); and the error terms must meet the same assumptions as stated in Chapter 13 with regard to normality, homoscedasticity, and the absence of outliers. Independent variables must be linearly related to the dependent variable and not exhibit problems of multicollinearity.[1] The unique feature of multiple regression with time series data is the likely violation of error term assumptions in a new way, through autocorrelation (also called serial correlation). The discussion of multiple regression with time series data centers around detecting and correcting this problem.

Autocorrelation

With time series data, the assumption of random distribution of error terms is usually violated. This is because the adjacent, time-ordered values of observations are highly correlated with each other: knowledge of today's value is a good predictor of tomorrow's. *Autocorrelation*, also called *serial correlation*, reflects correlation in the order (or series) in which observations are measured. The error term plot, when plotted against the sequence of time-ordered observations, typically exhibits a "snake-like" pattern, as shown in Figure 15.1. Note that the figure examines the residuals against time (the order in which the observations are made) rather than the (standardized) predicted dependent variable $\hat{y}$. Plotting the error term against $\hat{y}$ will *not* show the pattern of Figure 15.1. The problem with autocorrelation is that it can severely exaggerate the statistical significance of variables, leading to the erroneous conclusion that variables are statistically associated when they are not.

Serial correlation is usually anticipated when working with time series data. It can be detected visually through the graph shown as Figure 15.1 or by calculating the *Durbin-Watson test statistic*. Statistical software packages do not always easily produce such a figure, and many analysts rely on the Durbin-Watson statistic. Values of the Durbin-Watson test statistic range from 0 to 4. Values close to 2 indicate the lack of serial correlation; values closer to 0 and 4 indicate serial correlation. Values less than 2 indicate positive serial correlation, whereas values greater than 2 indicate negative serial correlation. Positive serial correlation occurs when successive error terms are

Figure 15.1 ———————〜〜〜Autocorrelation

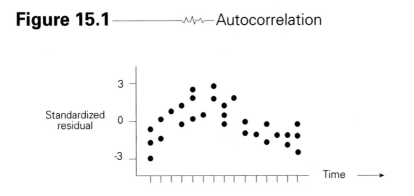

positively correlated with each other, which is most common. Negative serial correlation implies the opposite.

Durbin-Watson critical values differ from other test statistics in two ways: each critical value has an upper and a lower limit, and the statistic tests for both positive and negative serial correlation. Software packages do not always produce the level at which the test statistic is statistically significant; analysts need to refer to the table of critical values in Appendix D. Critical values are determined by the number of observations (n) and number of independent variables (k). For example, when $n = 30$ and $k = 2$, the lower critical value (d_l) is 1.28 and the upper critical value (d_u) is 1.57 ($p = .05$). Values less than d_l and greater than $4 - d_l$ indicate the presence of correlation, but values between d_l and d_u, and $4 - d_l$ and $4 - d_u$, are considered inconclusive in determining serial correlation. These are critical values at the level of 5 percent significance. Figure 15.2 shows the critical regions for this test statistic. Thus, in the preceding example, values less than 1.28 and greater than 2.72 indicate autocorrelation; values between 1.57 and 1.28 and between 2.43 and 2.72 are inconclusive. Values between 1.57 and 2.43 indicate the absence of autocorrelation.

> **Getting Started**
> Practice reading the
> Durbin-Watson table.

Figure 15.2 ———————〜〜〜Durbin-Watson Critical Values

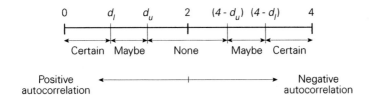

Correcting Autocorrelation

Two strategies are available for correcting serial correlation: the first strategy is to add a trend variable to the model, and the second strategy is to examine the relationship in so-called first-order differences.

The rationale for adding a trend variable is to control for the fact that over time many variables increase; the trend variable controls for growth over time and, hence, any spurious correlation between the dependent variable and independent variables. A **trend** (or counter) **variable** is simply a variable that records the order in which observations appear $(1, 2, 3, 4, 5, \ldots,$ shown as the variable "time" in Table 15.1). When adding a trend variable, we find that the relationship is changed in the following manner:

$$\text{Initial relationship: } y = a + b_1 x_1 + b_2 x_2 + \ldots$$
$$\text{Transformed relationship: } y = a + b_1 x_1 + b_2 x_2 + \ldots + b_n \text{Time}$$

A second strategy is to use **first-order differences.** These are the differences between successive observations, as shown below. The rationale for first-order differences (also called first-differences) is the logical proposition that if it is true that (the levels of) two variables are correlated with each other over time, then their increases also should be correlated over time. For example, the value of Δy for Time = 2 in Table 15.1 is the difference between the value of "vary" in Time = 2 and Time = 1, or $25 - 23 = 2$. The first observation is always lost because of the differencing. Statistical packages routinely calculate first-order differences. Thus, the relationship is transformed as follows:

$$\text{Initial relationship: } y = a + b_1 x_1 + b_2 x_2 + \ldots$$
$$\text{Transformed relationship: } \Delta y = a + b_1 \Delta x_1 + b_2 \Delta x_2 + \ldots .$$

Relationships in first-difference form often eliminate problems of serial correlation because differenced data exhibit far more variability than do

Table 15.1 ———〜〜〜—— Calculating First-Order Differences

TIME	VARY	VARX1	VARX2	ΔY	ΔX1	ΔX2
1	23	1	5	.	.	.
2	25	2	8	2	1	3
3	27	4	10	2	2	2
4	29	5	13	2	1	3
5	31	6	18	2	1	5
6	30	8	16	−1	2	−2
7	33	9	14	3	1	−2
8	34	11	14	1	2	0

levels data. This is clearly shown in Table 15.1, in which the differenced data do not show the upward bias that the levels data do.

Comparing these two strategies, we see that the regression of first-order differences is considered a far more stringent test than adding a trend variable and is therefore preferred. Adding a trend variable is a prophylactic strategy that attempts to control for the problem. Regressing first-order differences is a preventive strategy that aims to avoid the problem.

Policy Evaluation

Time series data are excellent for evaluating the impact of a policy or program. Levels of performance or service utilization are tracked and compared with the moment or period in which a policy is implemented. Time series data are fundamental to the use of (quasi-) experimental designs in public management and policy, as discussed in Chapter 1.

Policy variables measure when and how policies affect the dependent variables. Policy variables are dummy variables that indicate when the policy has caused an effect. These variables can be modeled in different ways, as shown in Figure 15.3. The initial zeroes indicate the pre-policy time period, the first "1" indicates the first period in which the policy or program is implemented, and so on. These variables are easily added to any dataset, with values as shown in Figure 15.3.

The *pulse* and *period* variables reflect a policy or program that is used for only a limited time. For example, these policy variables might be used to measure, respectively, a one-time or limited-period intervention, such as a one-night or month-long effort by roadway police to apprehend drunken drivers. The period after the policy or program is terminated is called the post-policy period. By contrast, the *step* and *increasing impact* variables signify an ongoing policy or program. (By definition, no post-policy periods are asso-

Figure 15.3 ————〜〜—Policy Variables

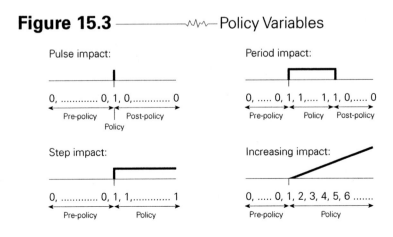

Pulse impact:

0, ... 0, 1, 0,............. 0
Pre-policy | Post-policy
Policy

Step impact:

0, ... 0, 1, 1,............. 1
Pre-policy | Policy

Period impact:

0, ... 0, 1, 1,.... 1, 1, 0,..... 0
Pre-policy | Policy | Post-policy

Increasing impact:

0, ... 0, 1, 2, 3, 4, 5, 6 ....
Pre-policy | Policy

ciated with these ongoing programs or policies.) These variables differ only with regard to the level of impact over time. For example, some programs are plausibly hypothesized to have a near-constant effect over time, such as a permanent increase in the speed limit. However, benefit programs, such as after-school services, often have an increasing effect over time as more and more beneficiaries are affected by the policy or enrolled in the program. It is typically a matter of empirical trial-and-error as to which policy form best approximates the actual impact of the policy. To examine for policy impacts, the relationship without policy impacts is modified in the following way:

Without policy impacts: $\Delta y = a + b_1 \Delta x_1 + b_2 \Delta x_2 + \ldots$
With policy impacts: $\Delta y = a + b_1 \Delta x_1 + b_2 \Delta x_2 + \ldots + b_r P_r + b_s P_s + \ldots,$

> **Getting Started**
>
> Find examples of time series regression in the research literature.

where $b_r P_r, \ldots$ are alternative specifications of the policy impact, shown in Figure 15.3. The model can include different policy impact variables; P_r might model the pulse impact, P_s might model the step impact, and so on. A significant coefficient of any policy variable signifies that the policy has had an impact on the outcome, Δy. This model can also be written in levels form with an added trend variable.

Consider the following hypothetical example. In response to growing concern about classroom violence, discussed in Chapter 1, a high school has begun an anger awareness and management program. Teachers are asked to record the number of incidents that involve physical contact. The total number of weekly incidents is tallied. There are eight weeks of data from before the anger management program began and eight weeks of data since it began. The following data (average number of classroom incidents) are available on a per-classroom basis: 6.3, 6.4, 6.8, 7.0, 7.2, 7.3, 7.1, 7.5, 6.6, 6.5, 6.2, 6.0, 5.8, 5.5, 5.2, and 4.9. Is the decline sufficient to conclude that the program has a statistically significant impact? Table 15.2 shows the regression output. The dataset has 16 observations, one for each week. Values for the variable "trend" are 1, 2, 3, . . . 14, 15, 16. Values for the variable "step impact" are 0, 0, 0, 0, 0, 0, 0, 0, 1, 1, 1, 1, 1, 1, 1, 1, and the values for the variable "increasing impact" are 0, 0, 0, 0, 0, 0, 0, 0, 1, 2, 3, 4, 5, 6, 7, 8. It also shows the results for the dependent variable in levels form with a trend variable. The first order of business is to determine whether the model violates regression assumptions. The Durbin-Watson test statistic is 1.597. With three explanatory variables and 16 observations, $d_l = 0.86$ and $d_u = 1.73$. Hence, the Durbin-Watson statistic is in the inconclusive range, and we decide that there is insufficient evidence of serial correlation. We also examine the error term plot and determine that no outliers are present. The

Table 15.2 ⎯⎯⎯⎯⎯~٠٨٨٠~⎯⎯⎯ Time Series Regression Output

Model Fit

R	R-square	Adjusted R-square	SEE	Durbin-Watson
0.989	0.979	0.973	0.125	1.597

Dependent variable: Violent classroom incidents (Level)

Coefficients

Model	Unstandardized coefficients		t	Sig.
	b	SE		
Constant	6.221	.097	63.916	0.000
Trend	.162	.019	8.399	0.000
Step impact	−0.570	.126	−4.511	0.001
Increasing impact	−0.408	.027	−14.979	0.000

Note: SE = Standard error, Sig. = Significance

results in Table 15.2 show that the program, modeled as both a step and an increasing impact, is significantly associated with the reduction in classroom incidents. It shows that the anger management program reduces classroom incidents, and that this reduction increases over time. These results are plausible, as behavioral programs often have effects that increase over time.

The results find support in first-order difference form. Then, the Durbin-Watson statistic is 2.801, which is again in the inconclusive range. T-test test statistics are shown in parentheses:

$$\Delta \text{Incidents} = 0.171 - 0.668^{**}\text{Step} + 0.0038 \text{ Increase}$$
$$(-3.43) \qquad (1.10)$$

** p < .01; * p < .05.

This result is consistent with the earlier one because the dependent variable measures differences; the significance of the "step" variable suggests that the change in the number of incidents is constant; hence, the number of incidents decreases from one period to another.[2]

Lagged Variables
A *lagged variable* is one whose impact on the dependent variable is delayed. Even though a policy is implemented on a certain date, it sometimes takes time before measurable effects on the dependent variable occur. For example, the impact of the anger management program on classroom incidents might be delayed a little, perhaps because it requires a few time periods for

the anger management program to be implemented fully, or because it takes students a few weeks before they begin to apply anger management. Thus, we wish to lag the effect of the program variable.

x_2	0	0	0	1	2	3	4	5	6	7
$x_{2,t-1}$	.	0	0	0	1	2	3	4	5	6
$x_{2,t-2}$	.	.	0	0	0	1	2	3	4	5

Statistical software packages can readily lag variables. For example, consider lagging the "increased impact" variable, identified as x_2. To indicate that the effect of this variable is lagged one time period, for example, the relationship "$y = a + b_1 x_1 + b_2 x_2 + \ldots$" becomes $y = a + b_1 x_1 + b_2 x_{2,t-1} + \ldots$. The notation "$t-1$" indicates the one-period lag. For illustration, x_2, $x_{2,t-1}$, and $x_{2,t-2}$ are shown above. An empirical question concerns the length of the lag: should x_2 be lagged one, two, three, or even more periods? Analysts can determine this on a trial-and-error basis. When effects are lagged, regression coefficients (and t-test statistics) often show a nice bell-shaped (or inverted-V) pattern for successive lags. For example, the regression coefficients of x_2 when lagged three through seven periods might be –2.25, 11.50, 73.89, 35.32, –1.83, suggesting that a lag of five is most appropriate, hence, $x_{2,t-5}$.[3]

On occasion, the dependent variable might be lagged, too: $y = a + b_1 y_{t-1} + b_2 x_2 + \ldots$. This signifies that the dependent variable is affected by its own immediate past: perhaps, juvenile delinquency is seen as feeding on itself. The specification of a lagged dependent variable is called autoregression and further reduces problems of serial correlation. The Durbin-Watson statistic is not appropriate for autoregressive models. Instead, the Durbin h statistic is used.[4]

Regarding the preceding example, we find no evidence of lagged effect. For instance, the t-test statistics of the "increasing impact" variable are as follows: –14.979 (no lag), –12.869 ($t-1$), –11.680 ($t-2$), and –5.466 ($t-3$). These results are obtained by running the model separately for each lag. Thus, the impact of this variable is strongest when there is no lag. Similarly, the t-test statistics for the "step" variable are, respectively, –4.511, –0.873, –0.055, and –1.051. This, too, does not show a lagged impact.

STATISTICAL FORECASTING METHODS: A PRIMER

As discussed in Chapter 4, analysts and managers often face questions about the future: How many clients are we likely to have? What will their needs most likely be? How much revenue can the city expect? And so on. These questions are fundamental to the public and to nonprofit organizations.

Figure 15.4 ———————⌇⌇⌇—Workload

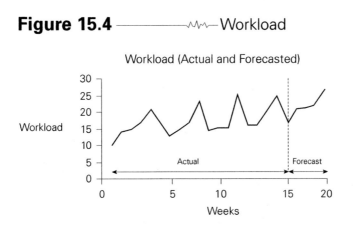

Workload (Actual and Forecasted)

Chapter 4 also distinguished between statistical and nonstatistical approaches for addressing these questions. The principles and best practices of forecasting suggest that analysts should use a range of different approaches and that shorter forecasting periods are likely to be more accurate.

Here, we provide a brief primer on statistical forecasting methods. Quite simply, **statistical forecasting methods** use data about the present and past for forecasting. The simplest method is to forecast the immediate future as a replica of the past and present; what happened today and yesterday might happen tomorrow, too. This is a reasonable approach when events are well established. For example, if you normally drink coffee in the morning, you might do that tomorrow and in the immediate future, too. We might expect the level of high school violence tomorrow to be the same as today.

A problem with forecasting tomorrow based on today is that it does not take into account patterns of past trends. If there is a generally upward pattern, then the forecast for tomorrow might be revised upward, especially for a few time periods beyond tomorrow. The technique of **trend extrapolation** analyzes the pattern of past trends. Specifically, it analyzes (1) the presence of a general upward or downward pattern, (2) whether variations in the upward or downward pattern are cyclical (for example, seasonal fluctuations), probabilistic, or random in nature, and (3) uncharacteristic values that do not seem part of the trend. Thus, trend forecasting might note that I usually drink coffee (say, an 80 percent chance) and more often in the winter (a cyclical variation). In the case of high school violence, trend analysis might reveal such variations; perhaps school violence is more common on certain days (for example, Tuesdays), or in certain months of the year. Figure 15.4 shows an example of a forecast with upward and cyclical patterns of a program's workload. When policy makers and managers are aware of such trends, they can better anticipate and manage the future.

A limitation of trend extrapolation is that it is uninformed by factors that give rise to the trend and is ignorant of incidental factors that might have affected or will affect it. Thus, trend forecasts are usually limited to but a few periods into the future, as shown in Figure 15.4. The accuracy of statistical forecasts may be enhanced further by considering other variables that affect trends. For example, local government revenues can be forecast not only as an extrapolation of past revenues but also by taking into account future changes in the taxable inventory of residential and commercial real estate; new office buildings or residential developments might soon be completed, for example, which add to the tax base. Similarly, future changes in the size of student cohorts associated with violence would shift the projected trend upward or downward. Analysts can adjust their trend forecasts based on these additional considerations, though some trend forecasting techniques can take such factors into account, as well. Obviously, some forecasts take into account several factors that are known to affect future trends.

Forecasting can also consider the impact of conditions that might occur, giving rise to a variety of what-if scenarios. The analysis of local government revenues might take into account the possibility of different assessment (tax) rates that might be considered as policy adoptions by council. The impact of economic conditions might be considered, too. These factors can then be used to identify a range of possible forecasts based on rosy, likely, and pessimistic scenarios. Revenue forecasts of the federal government typically involve such alternative scenarios (see Figure 4.1). Likewise, rosy, likely, and pessimistic scenarios can be identified for the impact of the anger management program. Again, experts can be used to help define such scenarios. All forecasting methods should acknowledge limitations of factors that are not considered. For example, even pessimistic scenarios for local tax revenues might need to acknowledge, through a caveat, that a catastrophic hurricane, or some other unforeseen event, might eliminate real estate and require temporary tax breaks.

Statistical modeling aims to forecast phenomena based on variables that significantly explain the phenomena in the present and past. When knowledge about likely future values of these explanatory variables exist, or can be guessed reliably, the future values of the phenomena can be predicted, too. This approach focuses on the dynamics giving rise to phenomena, rather than on trend extrapolation. These models are often statistically complex and some of them (for example, causal models) are discussed here and in Chapter 16. For example, a statistical model might identify 5 to 15 of the most important factors that explain changes in high school violence, and use statistical methods to determine the impact of each of these variables. By estimating future values of these variables, a manager can then estimate future levels of high school violence. A practical limitation of this approach is that the impact of policies and new conditions in the future must be estimated through the variables already included in the model; otherwise, they must be determined through the use of experts or past research studies, for example.

REGRESSION-BASED FORECASTING

Frequently, public managers and analysts are called upon to forecast. In this section, we provide some useful statistical forecast methods. To avoid confusion, the term *forecast* refers to predicted observations in the *future*. By contrast, the predicted values of *known* observations are called predicted values, ŷ, not forecasts. Readers may also wish to familiarize themselves with Chapter 4, which discusses principles and general limitations of forecasting.[5]

Multiple regression often is of limited use for statistical forecasting because *future* values of independent variables are unknown. At best, when all of the independent variables are lagged, some near-term forecasts are possible, based on known values of independent variables. Rather, simple regression is then used to make forecasts in which "time" is the (sole) independent variable. Various advanced, statistical regression techniques estimate time series that take into account *trends* and *periodic* (for example, seasonal) fluctuations.[6] These advanced techniques are often used in financial forecasting, but they have found little application in public management and policy to date. There are four types of *regression-based forecasting* techniques: forecasting with leading indicators, curve estimation, exponential smoothing, and ARIMA (autoregressive integrated moving average).

Validation is critical in any forecasting. Generally, the first step in forecasting is ascertaining that the model accurately predicts current values. We cannot place much credence in forecasting a model that does a poor job of predicting today's known values. To this end, the models are recalculated based on a smaller sample that excludes recent observations. Recent observations are then used to compare the predicted and actual values. If the model is found to make accurate predictions of recent known values, which is usually determined by visual comparison of the actual and predicted values, then existing values are included and predictions are made of future conditions.

A limitation of regression-based approaches to forecasting is that they often require more observations than are available to managers; few managers have 20 or more time-based observations. Also, long series may include the effects of events that have since seized. As a result, long trend series may not always be better for predicting the future. Hence, only a brief overview of each technique is provided here; later in this chapter, we examine spreadsheet-based approaches that do not require many observations.

Forecasting with Leading Indicators

Forecasting with leading indicators involves regression with independent variables that are all lagged (leading indicators). When independent variables are lagged, it is possible to forecast near-term observations by using the known, present values of the lagged independent variables to predict future values of the dependent variable. If the current predicted and observed values are close, then the forecasted values should be reasonably accurate. The usefulness of this approach is limited to forecasts that are no longer than the shortest of the lagged periods. Leading indicators are well-known in some fields, such as economics and business, where some indicators are seen as harbingers of future market changes. For example, manufacturing orders, building permits, and architecture billings are indicators of future construction activity. Leading indicators are used in other areas: environmental water quality is a leading indicator of certain fish stocks, for example, and student application requests are a leading indicator of student enrollment. It is useful to think of leading indicators in your line of work.

Curve Estimation

Curve estimation estimates the shape of a trend variable and makes forecasts based on it. Curve estimation is available in many statistical software packages. Typically, various linear, quadratic, and logarithmic models are estimated (fitted), where "time" is the sole independent variable. Thus, for example, a quadratic function is estimated as $y(t) = a + b_1 t + b_2 t^2$, and a logarithmic function is estimated as $y(t) = a + b_1 \log(t)$. Although R-square values are reported for each model, models should be selected that seem to best fit the observed curve. These models provide for level and trend but not for periodic effects (seasonality). If the analyst believes that a model fits accurately, then model parameters can be used as a basis for making forecasts. An example is shown in Figure 15.5. The figure shows linear, logarith-

Figure 15.5  Curve Estimation I

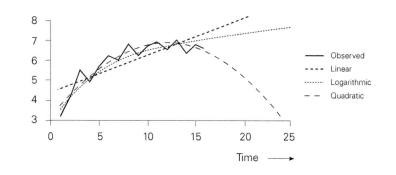

Figure 15.6 ——————〰️—Curve Estimation II

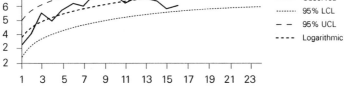

95% Confidence Intervals

mic, and quadratic model results in vastly different forecasts. This is quite common with such estimations. Although the R^2 values of these models are quite respectable (respectively, 0.455, 0.747, and 0.895), both the linear and quadratic models seem way off the mark for even near-term predictions.

Curve estimation procedures can also be used to calculate confidence intervals. Confidence intervals are somewhat smaller for known values and become larger for forecasts that lie farther into the future. For the curves in Figure 15.6, the 95 percent level confidence intervals are considerable, varying from ±0.87 to ±2.31 for each of the estimated curves. Figure 15.5 shows the 95 percent confidence interval for the logarithmic curve.

Exponential Smoothing

Exponential smoothing is a technique that estimates the dependent variables based on their level, trend, and seasonality: $y(t) = f$ (level, trend, seasonality). The estimation methodology involves an iterative testing of alternative parameters that define level, trend, and seasonality components. There are four parameters: alpha (specifying the relative weight given to recent observations in calculating the current level), gamma (specifying the relative weight given to recent observations in determining the trend), and delta (specifying the relative weight given to recent observations in determining seasonality). In addition, some models also have a parameter phi, which specifies the extent to which the trend is dampened (that is, dies out) over time.

The computer conducts a so-called grid search, which is iterative testing of combinations of parameters to minimize the *sum of squared errors* (SSE, not to be confused with SEE; see Chapter 12), defined as the squared differences between actual and predicted values. The model with the lowest SSE best fits the observations. Predictions with exponential smoothing often rely heavily on recent observations. Then, forecasted values closely resemble the most recent observations, modified according to any trend that is present in the most immediate observations, and any seasonality that is present. This is

Figure 15.7 ———————〰〰〰—Exponential Smoothing

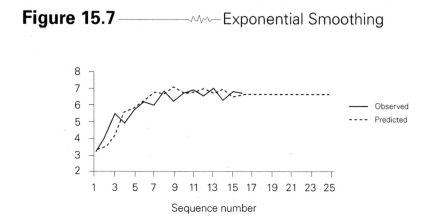

shown in Figure 15.6. The forecasted values closely match the last observation. Note that the most recent observations are also devoid of any trend. Figure 15.7 does not include a seasonality component. If seasonality had been specified and present, the forecast would have been modulated to reflect the estimated seasonality. The model can also be made to give more weight to past observations. Then the forecasted values will show an upward trend. However, based on the criterion of choosing a model with the lowest SSEs, the above model is preferred. In this instance, the predicted observations do not always closely match the actual observations; the predicted values seem to follow actual observations by about one period. In fact, manually lagging the predicted values further reduces the SSE.[7]

ARIMA

Autoregressive integrated moving average (ARIMA) is a highly advanced technique often used for financial forecasting (for example, in stock markets), but it has found little application in public management and policy to date. ARIMA models require users to specify the nature of moving averages, autoregression, and seasonality. When the purpose is only prediction (not forecasting), independent variables can be used, too. The first step in ARIMA modeling is to make the data stationary, that is, to ensure that the variable has the same mean and variance across the entire range. This typically is achieved by taking first-order differences (described earlier in this chapter). The second step involves determining the nature of parameters through myriad diagnostics that are part of ARIMA procedures. The third step is estimation and evaluation of the model by comparing actual and predicted values (see the discussion of validation earlier in this chapter). Following these procedures, we came up with predicted values and forecasts, as shown in Figure 15.8. We used first-order differences and no seasonality.

Figure 15.8  ARIMA

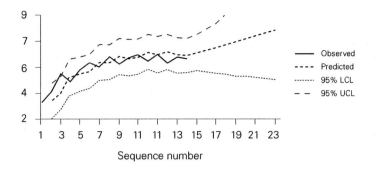

In comparison, ARIMA gives more weight to past observations than does exponential smoothing, resulting in the upward trend shown in Figure 15.8. ARIMA also produces confidence intervals. Forecasts that are farther into the future are more uncertain and thus have larger confidence intervals. The forecast methods described in the next section also give more weight to recent observations and increases; the smoothing of recent fluctuations quickly results in a constant forecast of about 6.7—the last observation, similar to the exponential smoothing forecast shown in Figure 15.7.

NON-REGRESSION FORECASTING WITH FEW OBSERVATIONS

Managers are frequently asked to make forecasts on the basis of few previous observations. This problem sometimes is encountered when managers are asked to forecast budget expenditures on the basis of just a few years or months of prior data. The lack of an adequate number of observations makes the use of time series regression impractical. When one is working with expenditures and revenues, it is common to use constant dollars, that is, to remove inflationary growth from other sources of growth. Hence, expenditures are deflated before forecasts are made. Assume that annual inflation rates are as shown in Table 15.3 (in percentages). All data are first recalculated in constant year T dollars, which are then forecasted. This is shown in the table.[8] Inflation rates affect the current year's expenditures.

Table 15.3 ~~~ Annual Inflation Rates: Percentages

Year	T–5	T–4	T–3	T–2	T–1	T	T+1	T+2	T+3
Inflation rate (%)	2.8	3.1	4.0	2.7	3.3	.			
Budget (current $s)	52.1	50.5	52.5	54.3	57.5	60.4			
Budget (constant $s)	60.9	57.4	57.9	57.6	59.4	60.4			

Table 15.4 ·····∿∿···· Forecasted Budget Using PMA

Year	T–5	T–4	T–3	T–2	T–1	T	T+1	T+2	T+3
Predicted budget (constant $s)	.	.	.	58.7	57.6	58.3	59.1	59.6	59.7

Hence, $57.5 in $T-1$ is equivalent to [$57.5*1.033 =] $59.4 in time period T. The amount $54.3 in Table 15.3 is equivalent to [$54.3*1.027 * 1.033 =] $57.6 in time period T. Any forecasted expenditures will now be net of any inflation. The result shows that despite the overall increase in current dollars, budget expenditures have been about level for most of the period; expenditures at time T are in fact less than at $T-5$, when both are expressed in constant $t = T$ dollars.

Several approaches to forecasting data exist. Each approach has its own bias. A conservative approach is the use of ***prior moving averages*** (also called PMAs). In this approach, the average of the current preceding observations is used to predict the following period. The problem with this widely used approach is that it *under*estimates future values by basing forecasts on the average of the recent past. Typically, a time span of three periods is used; hence, the three most recent periods are used to predict the next period. At the end of existing observations, predicted observations become part of the series used to predict the next period, and so on. Whenever possible, actual rather than predicted values should be used. The results are shown in Table 15.4. For example, the predicted value of the budget in the $T-2$ period is the mean of $60.9, $57.4, and $57.9, which is $58.7 (see Table 15.3). Similarly, the predicted value for the $T-1$ period is the mean of $57.4, $57.9, and $57.6, which is $57.6. The forecasted value of the budget in period $T+1$ is the mean of $57.6, $59.4, and $60.4, which is $59.1. Note that the values used to forecast the budget in $T+1$ are the actual numbers, not the predicted numbers. The forecasted value in $T+2$ is the mean of $59.4, $60.4, and $59.1, which is $59.6. Here, the value of $T+1$ is the forecasted value because no actual value exists. Comparing predicted against actual values for purposes of validation, we see the downward tendency for T and $T-1$.

A second approach, which we call ***prior moving changes***, forecasts on the basis of *changes* in preceding periods. Often the average of the last three increases is used to predict the next period. Then future values are defined as the immediate past level plus the average of the last three increases. The idea is that future changes in expenditures should resemble past increases. Using the average increases of three prior years, we obtain the results shown in Table 15.5. For example, the change from $T-5$ to $T-4$ is [$57.4 – $60.9 =] $–3.50. The average of changes in the three periods prior to $T-1$ is the mean of $–3.5, $0.5, and $–0.3, which is $–1.1. Hence, the predicted value

Table 15.5 ·········~⋏⋏~··· Forecasted Budget Using Average Changes

Year	T–5	T–4	T–3	T–2	T–1	T	T+1	T+2	T+3
Change from prior period		–3.5	0.5	–0.3	1.8	1.0	0.8	1.2	
Average change				–1.1	0.7	0.8	1.2	1.0	
Actual budget (constant $s)	60.9	57.4	57.9	57.6	59.4	60.4			
Predicted/forecasted budget (constant $s)					56.5	60.1	61.2	62.4	63.4

for $T-1$ is the actual budget of $T-2$, or \$57.6 – \$1.1, which is \$56.5. The other values are calculated similarly. For example, the forecasted value of $T+1$ is calculated as the value of T, \$60.4, plus the average of the last three increases (\$–0.3, \$1.8, and \$1), or \$0.83, which is \$61.2. This is [\$61.2 – \$60.4 =] \$0.8 higher than in time period T. (We prefer to use actual rather than predicted values whenever possible; hence, we use the actual value of \$60.4 rather than the predicted value of \$60.1.) This information is used to calculate the average increases for forecasts in the next time period, $T+2$, and so on. Comparing these two approaches, we find that forecasts based on average increases are far less conservative than those based on PMAs.[9] From the perspective of validation, we find that the predicted values of $T-1$ and T are slightly better than those using PMAs.

> **Getting Started**
> Verify these calculations.

These results can sometimes be improved, or at least validated, through a third approach, which forecasts expenditures based on known **forecast ratios**. Tests involve other variables, such as work orders, client requests, or populations. Assume, for example, that expenditures are known to be related to the population size, the source of service requests. These forecasts can be triangulated by forecasts of population growth, shown below for $T+1$ and beyond. These forecasts are made as shown in Table 15.6. The average ratio is 0.227. Hence, the predicted budget for $T+1$ is [275*0.227 =] \$62.4. These values seem consistent with the forecasting approach based on prior moving changes. If the ratios of only the last three periods are used, whose mean is 0.222, then the forecasted values are somewhat lower. Of course, the credibility of these forecasts hinges on the constancy and theoretical justification of the ratio. If credible, the forecasted values heighten the importance of incorporating estimated demand in expenditure forecasts.

Forecasting with Periodic Effects

A rather different problem involves forecasting when data exhibit **periodicity** (or **seasonality**), that is, systematically fluctuating (or modulating)

Table 15.6 ⌁⌁ Predicted Budget: Forecast Ratio

Year	T–5	T–4	T–3	T–2	T–1	T	T+1	T+2	T+3
Budget (constant $s)	60.9	57.4	57.9	57.6	59.4	60.4			
Population	250	253	258	260	266	273	275	280	282
Ratio	0.244	0.227	0.224	0.221	0.223	0.221			
Forecasted budget (constant $s) Mean of all ratios							62.4	63.6	64.0
Forecasted budget (constant $) Mean of last three ratios							61.1	62.2	62.6

values. Some examples of these problems are daily activities that exhibit lower workloads on Mondays and weekly activities that exhibit more activity toward the end of the month. Table 15.7 lays out an example of such data. When only PMAs are used, the last three values of Month 4 will greatly overestimate the value of Week 1 in Month 5. This is because the three prior observations (the last three weeks in Month 4) fail to take into account that, on average, Week 1 activity levels are low for all months. The strategy of forecasting Month 5, Week 1, requires that we take this information into account. The methodology is a straightforward, albeit cumbersome, three-step process. First, average workloads are calculated for each period, on the basis of which a forecast is made for the entire Month 5. Specifically, we forecast an average for Month 5 as the average of Month 4 plus the mean increase of preceding months. Second, the mean deviations are determined for each week of the preceding months. Third, these deviations are used to adjust the weekly forecasts in Month 5. The calculations are done as follows:

The "Mean monthly activity" column clearly shows an upward trend. Because these are not expenditures, we do not deflate them. The first step is to forecast all of Month 5. To this end, we calculate the *mean increase* from month to month. For example, the increase from Month 1 to Month 2 is [16.75 – 15.00 =] 1.75. In this manner, the mean increase is the mean of 1.75, 1.25, and 1.25, which is 1.42. Thus, it seems reasonable to forecast the average activity in Month 5 as 19.25 (the mean of Month 4) plus 1.42, which is 20.67.

Second, we calculate the deviations for each week and average them. For example, the mean deviation across all Week 1s (for each month) is the mean of –5.00, –4.75, –4.00, and –3.25, shown in italics, or –4.25. Similarly, mean deviations are calculated for other weeks. Third, the forecasted mean value for Month 5 is adjusted for these weekly deviations. For example, Week 1 in Month 5 is [20.67 – 4.25 =] 16.42. Values for other periods in Month 5 are calculated similarly. The results are shown in Table 15.7 and Figure 15.4.

Table 15.7 ⎯⎯⎯⎯⎯⎯⎯⎯⎯~⋏⋏⋏~ Weekly and Monthly Activity: Forecasted Values

Month	Week	Activity	Mean monthly activity	Deviation from mean	Predicted activity for week 5
1	1	10		−5.00	
1	2	14		−1.00	
1	3	15		0.00	
1	4	21	15.00	+6.00	
2	1	12		−4.75	
2	2	15		−1.75	
2	3	17		+0.25	
2	4	23	16.75	+6.25	
3	1	14		−4.00	
3	2	16		−2.00	
3	3	16		−2.00	
3	4	26	18.00	+8.00	
4	1	16		−3.25	
4	2	16		−3.25	
4	3	20		+0.75	
4	4	25	19.25	+5.75	
Forecasted:					
5	1		20.67	−4.25	16.42
5	2		20.67	−2.00	18.67
5	3		20.67	−0.25	20.42
5	4		20.67	+6.50	27.17

SUMMARY

A vast array of statistical methods are available for analyzing time series data. Analysts use multiple regression when they need to understand the causes of past or present events. Although time series data and results must meet the same assumptions as discussed in Chapter 13, a principal concern is with autocorrelation, which is tested using the Durbin-Watson test statistic. Autocorrelation often is overcome by adding a trend variable or transforming the data into first differences. This chapter also discusses how policies can be modeled using dummy variables.

Analysts have many techniques available to them for making forecasts; Chapter 4 discusses the importance of combining statistical and nonstatistical methods in forecasting. Regarding statistical methods, the basic choice is between using regression-based and non-regression-based methods. The former often are based on trend extrapolation, with or without other, independent variables. Techniques differ in how they deal with periodic fluctuations and with how much weight they give to recent rather than past observations.

Non-regression-based methods of forecasting typically use spreadsheets and are designed to deal with smaller numbers of observations. These forecasts, too, vary in how much weight they give to present or past observations, and whether they make forecasts that are related to other variables. In the business of making forecasts, analysts and managers do well to heed the principles of forecasting discussed in Chapter 4, and to rely on a range of plausible forecasts, rather than on any single approach.

KEY TERMS

Autocorrelation (p. 246)
Autoregressive integrated moving average (ARIMA) (p. 258)
Curve estimation (p. 256)
Durbin-Watson test statistic (p. 246)
Exponential smoothing (p. 257)
First-order differences (p. 248)
Forecast (p. 255)
Forecasting with leading indicators (p. 256)
Forecast ratios (p. 261)
Lagged variable (p. 251)

Periodicity (p. 261)
Policy variables (p. 249)
Prior moving averages (p. 260)
Prior moving changes (p. 260)
Regression-based forecasting (p. 255)
Seasonality (p. 261)
Serial correlation (p. 246)
Statistical forecasting methods (p. 253)
Statistical modeling (p. 254)
Trend extrapolation (p. 253)
Trend variable (p. 248)

Notes

1. Some time series data are also more likely to exhibit problems of multicollinearity because, over time, many variables show similar upward or downward sloping patterns.
2. Durbin-Watson h may fail to detect auto correlation when time series data are strongly seasonal or when a lagged dependent variable is used as an independent variable.
3. Statistical packages often have a cross-correlation function (CCF), which examines lags between two variables. This function is used to estimate the number of lags. The CCF should be used only when variables are stationary, that is, when they exhibit a stable mean and variances over time. This is typically accomplished by taking first-order differences. The discussion of CCF is beyond the scope of this text. See, for example, SPSS, *SPSS Trends 10.0* (Chicago: SPSS, Inc., 1999 or later editions).

4. Durbin $\hbar$ is defined as

$$(1-0.5DW)\sqrt{\frac{N}{1-N[se(b_{y_{t-1}})]^2}},$$

where N = sample size, DW = Durbin-Watson statistic, and $[se(b_{y_{t-1}})]^2$ is the squared standard error of the regression coefficient of the lagged dependent variable (that is, b_1, in the model $\Delta y = a + b_1 \Delta y_{t-1} + b_2 \Delta x_2 + \ldots$). Durbin $\hbar$ is normally distributed; hence, values greater than $|\hbar| > 1.96$ indicate serial correlation.

5. The methods discussed here concern statistical forecasting only and do not address the judgmental forecasting mentioned in Chapter 4.

6. Seasonal variation can also be modeled in multiple regression through dummy variables, for example, using dummy variables for spring, summer, and fall, or for different months.

7. In this regard, exponential smoothing with seasonal trend nearly identically matches the predicted observations shown in Figure 15.4. The mean discrepancy between these forecasts is 2.4 percent. Without seasonality, the fitted model merely shows the general trend.

8. For ease of calculation, only one decimal place is retained in the following data and tables. Actual results (such as when using a spreadsheet) will vary slightly due to rounding.

9. Some analysts might prefer using the average of prior expenditures, rather than the last expenditure, as the basis for future prediction. This approach, of course, has a downward effect on prediction. For example, the prediction for $T-1$ is the average of T through $T-2$, or $57.6, $59.4, and $60.4, which is $59.1, plus the average increase of $T-1$ through $T-3$, $0.67, or $59.8. This value falls between the two approaches discussed in the text.

CHAPTER

16

Survey of Advanced Techniques

CHAPTER OBJECTIVES

After reading this chapter, you should understand
- How ANOVA is used when dependent variables are nominal and have three or more categories
- How path analysis uses multiple dependent variables
- How survival analysis deals with events that have not yet occurred
- How factor analysis is used for exploratory purposes
- Other advanced, statistical techniques

This chapter provides an overview of several advanced statistical techniques. Each of these multivariate techniques expands on previous techniques in ways that help managers to work with some rather special situations. Four techniques are examined in some depth, and other advanced techniques are summarized more briefly. The four techniques described in some detail are ANOVA, path analysis, survival analysis, and factor analysis. Managers and analysts are apt to come across these techniques in the research literature.

ANALYSIS OF VARIANCE

Whereas the t-test is used for testing differences between two groups on a continuous variable (Chapter 11), **ANOVA (analysis of variance)** is used for testing means of a continuous variable across more than two groups. For example, we may wish to test whether income levels differ among three or more different ethnic groups, or whether the counts of fish vary across three or more lakes. Situations for using ANOVA often arise in medical and agricultural research, in which treatments are given to different groups of patients, animals, or crops. The F-test statistic compares the variances within each group against those that exist between each group and the overall mean:

$$F = \frac{s_b^2}{s_w^2}.$$

The logic of this approach is shown graphically in Figure 16.1. The overall group mean is $\bar{\bar{x}}$ (the mean of means). The boxplots represent the scores of observations within each group. (As before, the horizontal lines indicate means, $\bar{x}$, rather than medians.) Recall that variance is a measure of dispersion. In both parts of the figure, w is the within-group variance, and b is the between-group variance. Each graph has three within-group variances and three between-group variances, although only one of each is shown. Note in part A that the between-group variances are larger than the within-group variances, which results in a large F-test statistic using the above formula, making it easier to reject the null hypothesis. Conversely, in part B the within-group variances are larger than the between-group variances, causing

Figure 16.1———∿∿∿—ANOVA: Significant and Insignificant Differences

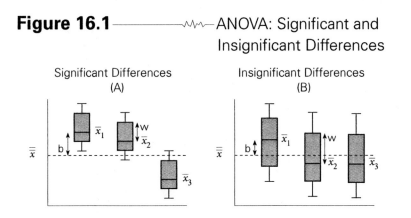

a smaller F-test statistic and making it more difficult to reject the null hypothesis. The hypotheses are written as follows:

H_0: No differences between any of the group means exist in the population.
H_A: At least one difference between group means exists in the population.

Note how the alternate hypothesis is phrased, because the logical opposite of "no differences between any of the group means" is that at least one pair of means differs. H_0 is also called the *global F-test* because it tests for differences among any means.

The formulas for calculating the between-group variances and within-group variances are quite cumbersome for all but the simplest of designs.[1] In any event, *statistical software calculates the F-test statistic and reports the level at which it is significant.*[2]

When the preceding null hypothesis is rejected, analysts will also want to know which differences are significant. For example, analysts will want to know which pairs of differences in watershed pollution are significant across regions. Although one approach might be to use the t-test to sequentially test each pair of differences, this should not be done. It would not only be a most tedious undertaking but would also inadvertently and adversely affect the level of significance: the chance of finding a significant pair by chance alone increases as more pairs are examined. Specifically, the probability of rejecting the null hypothesis in one of two tests is $[1 - 0.95^2 =]$ .098, the probability of rejecting it in one of three tests is $[1 - 0.95^3 =]$ .143, and so forth. Thus, sequential testing of differences does not reflect the true level of significance for such tests and should not be used.

Post-hoc tests is the name given to tests that test all possible group differences and yet maintain the true level of significance. Post-hoc tests vary in their methods of calculating test statistics and holding experiment-wide error rates constant. Three popular post-hoc tests are the Tukey, Bonferroni, and Scheffe tests. The Scheffe test is the most conservative, the Tukey test is best when many comparisons are made (when there are many groups), and the Bonferroni test is preferred when few comparisons are made. Often, these post-hoc tests support the same conclusions.[3]

Eta-squared (η^2) is a measure of association for mixed nominal-interval variables and is appropriate for ANOVA. Its values range from zero to one, and it is interpreted as the percentage of variation explained. It is a directional measure, and computer programs produce two statistics, alternating specification of the dependent variable.

Finally, ANOVA can also be used for testing interval-ordinal relationships. We can ask whether the change in means follows a linear pattern that is either increasing or decreasing. For example, assume we want to know whether incomes increase according to the political orientation of respondents, when measured on a seven-point Likert scale that ranges from very liberal to very conservative. If a linear pattern of increase exists, then a linear relationship is said to exist between these variables. Most statistical software packages can test for a variety of progressive relationships.

ANOVA Assumptions

The assumptions of ANOVA are essentially the same as those of the t-test: (1) one variable is continuous, and the other is ordinal or nominal, (2) the group distributions have equal variances, (3) observations are independent, and (4) the variable is normally distributed in each of the groups. The assumptions are tested in a similar manner.

Relative to the t-test, ANOVA requires a little more concern regarding the assumptions of normality and homogeneity. First, like the t-test, ANOVA is *not robust* for the presence of outliers, and analysts examine the presence of outliers for each group. Also, ANOVA appears to be less robust than the t-test for deviations from normality. Second, unlike the t-test, ANOVA does not provide alternative test statistics when variances are heterogeneous. Our main concern with homogeneity is that there are no *substantial* differences in the amount of variance across the groups. However, the test of homogeneity is a strict test, testing for *any* departure from equal variances. In practice, groups may have neither equal variances nor substantial differences in the amount of variances. In these instances, a visual finding of no substantial differences suffices. Other strategies for dealing with heterogeneity are variable transformations and the removal of outliers, which increase variance, especially in small groups. Such outliers are detected by examining boxplots for each group separately.

A Working Example

The U.S. Environmental Protection Agency (EPA) measured the percentage of wetland loss in watersheds between 1982 and 1992, the most recent period for which data are available (government statistics are sometimes a little old). An analyst wants to know whether watersheds with large surrounding populations have suffered greater wetland loss than watersheds with smaller surrounding populations.

Most watersheds have suffered no or only very modest losses (less than 3 percent during the decade in question), and few watersheds have suffered more than a 4 percent loss. The distribution is thus heavily skewed toward watersheds with little wetland losses (that is, to the left) and is clearly not normally distributed.[4] To increase normality, the variable is transformed by twice taking the square root, $x^{.25}$. The transformed variable is then normally distributed: the Kolmogorov-Smirnov statistic is 0.07 (p = .10 > .05). The

Table 16.1 ⎯⎯⎯⎯⎯⎯ Variable Transformation

| Population | N | Untransformed variable | | Transformed variable | |
		Mean (%)	Standard deviation	Mean (%)	Standard deviation
Small	31	2.52	4.30	0.97	0.50
Medium I	32	1.77	1.68	1.06	0.28
Medium II	30	2.79	6.80	1.07	0.38
Large	27	3.21	3.54	1.26	0.27

variable also appears visually normal for each of the population subgroups. There are four population groups, designed to ensure an adequate number of observations in each.

Boxplot analysis of the transformed variable indicates four large and three small outliers (not shown). Examination suggests that these are plausible and representative values, which are therefore retained. Later, however, we will examine the effect of these seven observations on the robustness of statistical results. Descriptive analysis of the variables is shown in Table 16.1. Generally, large populations tend to have larger average wetland losses, but the standard deviations are large relative to (the difference between) these means, raising considerable question as to whether these differences are indeed statistically significant. Also, the untransformed variable shows that the mean wetland loss is less among watersheds with Medium I populations than in those with Small populations (1.77 versus 2.52). The transformed variable shows the opposite order (1.06 versus 0.97). Further investigation shows this to be the effect of the three small outliers and two large outliers on the calculation of the mean of the untransformed variable in the Small group. Variable transformation minimizes this effect. These outliers also increase the standard deviation of the Small group.

Using ANOVA, we find that the transformed variable has unequal variances across the four groups (Levene's statistic = 2.83, p = .41 < .05). Visual inspection, shown in Figure 16.2, indicates that differences are not substantial for observations within the group interquartile ranges, the areas indicated by the boxes, do not resemble the heterogeneity of Figure 11.2); the differences seem mostly caused by observations located in the whiskers of the Small group, which include the five outliers mentioned earlier. (The other two outliers remain outliers and are shown.) For now, we conclude that *no substantial differences* in variances exist, but we later test the robustness of this conclusion with consideration of these observations (see Figure 16.2).

We now proceed with the ANOVA analysis. First, Table 16.2 shows that the global F-test statistic is 2.91, p = .038 < .05. Thus, at least one pair of

Figure 16.2 ⎯⎯⎯⎯⎯⎯⎯⎯⎯⁓⎯ Group Boxplots

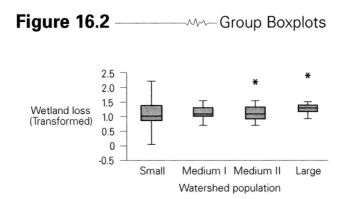

means is significantly different. (The term *sum of squares* is explained in note 1.)

Second, which pairs are significantly different? We use the Bonferroni post-hoc test because relatively few comparisons are made (there are only four groups). The computer-generated results (not shown in Table 16.2) indicate that the only significant difference concerns the means of the Small and Large groups. This difference (1.26 − 0.97 = 0.29 [of transformed values]) is significant at the 5 percent level (p = .028). The Tukey and Scheffe tests lead to the same conclusion (respectively, p = .024 and .044). This result is consistent with a visual reexamination of Figure 16.2, which shows that differences between group means are indeed small. The Tukey and Scheffe tests also produce "homogeneous subsets," that is, groups that have statistically identical means. Both the three largest and the three smallest populations have identical means. The Tukey levels of statistical significance are, respectively, .73 and .17 (both > .05).

Third, is the increase in means a linear increase? This test is an option on many statistical software packages that produces an additional line of output in the ANOVA table, called the "linear term for unweighted sum of squares" with appropriate F-test. Here, that F-test statistic is 7.85, p = .006 < .01, and so we conclude that the apparent linear increase is indeed significant: wetland loss is linearly associated with the increased surrounding population of watersheds.[5]

Table 16.2 ⎯⎯⎯⎯⎯⎯⎯⁓⎯ ANOVA Table

	Sum of squares	df	Variance (s^2)	F-test	p
Between groups	1.203	3	0.401	2.907	.038
Within groups	16.002	116	0.138		
Total	17.205	119			

Fourth, are our findings *robust*? One concern is that the statistical validity is affected by observations that statistically (although not substantively) are outliers. We find that removing the seven outliers identified earlier does not affect our conclusions. The resulting variable remains normally distributed, and there are no (new) outliers for any group. The resulting variable has equal variances across the groups (Levene's test = 1.03, p = .38 > .05). The global F-test is 3.44 (p = .019 < .05), and the Bonferroni post-hoc test similarly finds that only the differences of the Small and Large group means are significant (p = .031). The increase remains linear (F = 6.74, p = .011 < .05). Thus, we conclude that the presence of observations with large values does not alter our conclusions.

We also test the robustness of conclusions for different variable transformations. The extreme skewness of the untransformed variable allows for only a limited range of root transformations that produce normality. Within this range (power 0.222 through 0.275) the above conclusions are fully replicated. Natural log and base-10 log transformations also result in normality and replicate these results, *except* that the post-hoc tests fail to identify that the means of the Large and Small groups are significantly different. However, the global F-test is (marginally) significant (F = 2.80, p = .043 < .05), which suggests that this difference is too small to detect with this transformation. A single, independent-samples t-test for this difference is significant (t = 2.47, p = .017 < .05), suggesting that this problem may have been exacerbated by the limited number of observations. In sum, we find converging evidence for our conclusions. As this example also shows, statistics frequently requires analysts to exercise judgment and to justify their decisions.[6]

Finally, what is the practical significance of this analysis? The wetland loss among watersheds with large surrounding populations is [(3.21 − 2.52)/2.52 =] 27.4 percent greater than among those surrounded by small populations. It is up to managers and elected officials to determine whether a difference of this magnitude warrants intervention in watersheds with large surrounding populations.[7]

Beyond One-Way ANOVA

The approach described in the preceding section is also called *one-way ANOVA*. This scenario is easily generalized to accommodate more than one independent variable. These independent variables are either discrete (called factors) or continuous (called covariates). This is called *n*-way ANOVA or ANCOVA (the "C" indicates the presence of covariates). This scenario is even further generalized to allow for testing on two or more *dependent* variables. This is called *MANOVA,* or multiple analysis of variance. MANOVA, like ANOVA, has its own vocabulary of tests that is quite different from regression. Historically, it has often been used in medical research. Both

ANOVA and MANOVA allow for users to specify "contrasts" (that is, differences among treatments) in which they are especially interested. Although many analysts feel that ANOVA and regression are largely equivalent, the advantage of MANOVA is that it deals with multiple variables. Both *n*-way ANOVA and MANOVA are quite sensitive to departures from test assumptions. We can depict MANOVA graphically in the following way:

Figure 16.3 ⸺⟋ᴟ⟍⸺ MANOVA

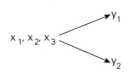

PATH ANALYSIS

Path analysis is a technique for estimating models with complex interrelationships among variables. Regression analysis does a poor job of modeling complex reality. Linear regression assesses the impacts of all variables on one dependent variable; what if reality allows for indirect effects? Consider the following hypothetical scenario from a welfare employment agency. Unemployed persons are provided the opportunity to participate in job training, which includes training in job interview techniques as well as some remedial education. The question is whether the job training is successful. Managers suspect that job training affects employment (that is, whether a job seeker secures employment within a certain time) in the manner shown in Figure 16.4. Job training is hypothesized to increase the employment of job seekers, but it also causes them to participate in more job interviews because part of the job training includes interviewing skills. This, in turn, also increases employment. Thus, the hypothesized effect of job training is both direct and

Figure 16.4 ⸺⟋ᴟ⟍⸺ Path Analysis

Relationship between Job Training, Job Interviews, and Employment

Figure 16.5 ———————∿∿∿— Path Analysis

Relationship between Job Training, Job Interviews, and Employment
with Effects of Dependents and Substance Abuse

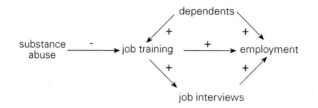

indirect. Figure 16.4 can be elaborated further by including the effects of
having dependents and substance abuse problems (see Figure 16.5).

Path analysis is a causal modeling technique for estimating such
complex models. However, an important limitation of path analysis is that it
may not be used when feedback loops are present. Feedback loops are relationships in which two or more variables are directly or indirectly caused by
each other; no such relationships are present in Figure 16.5. (Feedback loops
would have existed *if* additional paths had been added that go from "job
interviews" to "job training," or from "job interviews" to "having dependents." Of course, these additional paths make little theoretical sense in our
model.)[8] Models without feedback loops are called ***recursive models***. When
no feedback loops are present, each path can be estimated with ordinary
least squares (OLS) regression.[9] Specifically, in this example, the following
regression models are estimated:

Employment = a_1 + b_1 Job Interviews + b_2 Job Training + b_3 Dependents + e_1
Job Interviews = a_2 + b_4 Job Training + e_2
Job Training = a_3 + b_5 Dependents + b_6 Substance Abuse + e_3

Note that in causal models, the terminology of independent and dependent
variables often is inconclusive: the variable "Job interviews" is both an independent variable (causing employment) and a dependent variable (caused
by job training, having dependents, and substance abuse). Then, causal
modeling distinguishes between ***exogenous variables***, which are variables
that are unaffected by other variables in the model (such as substance
abuse), and ***endogenous variables***, which are affected by other variables
(such as employment and job interviews).

Figure 16.6 ———∿∿∿— Path Analysis Results

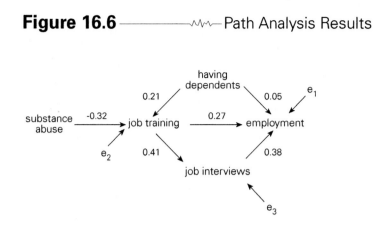

For each model, the impact of each variable is stated by the beta coefficient. Assume that the results in Figure 16.6 are available. The numbers along the arrows are the beta coefficients. The error terms that are shown are sometimes calculated as $\sqrt{1 - R^2}$.[10] Then, direct and indirect effects of the variables are calculated in Table 16.3. **Direct effects** are simply the beta coefficients of the variables that immediately affect another variable. **Indirect effects** are calculated as the product of beta coefficients of each pathway. Note that the variables "Dependents" and "Substance abuse" have two indirect pathways to "Employment" (see Table 16.3). The results shown in the table are interesting because they show that, although interviewing has a greater direct effect on employment than training, the indirect effects of training are substantial. The total effect of job training exceeds that of interviewing. If only multiple regression had been used (with "Employment" as a dependent variable), this indirect effect would have gone undetected. The results also show that the variables "Substance abuse" and "Having dependents" have less impact on "Employment" than do the other two variables.

Table 16.3 ——⌁⌁⌁—— Calculating Direct and Indirect Effects on Employment

| Variable | Effects | | |
	Indirect	Direct	Total
Job training	0.41*0.38 = 0.16	0.27	0.43
Job interviews	—	0.38	0.38
Dependents	0.21*0.27 + 0.21*0.41*0.38 = 0.09	0.05	0.14
Substance abuse	−.32*.27 + −0.32*0.41*0.38 = −0.14	—	−0.14

Path analysis is a relatively simple extension of multiple regression. The standards for its proper use are as follows:

- The model must be theory based. Although many different models can be constructed from even a modest number of variables, the relationships that they depict must make sense (have face validity). Typically, analysts specify a family of plausible models, and even though only one model might be reported, all models should have similar substantive conclusions.
- There are no feedback loops and all models satisfy standard regression assumptions. Thus, problems of outliers, heteroscedasticity, linearity, autocorrelation, and multicollinearity should be identified and addressed.
- All error terms should be uncorrelated with all exogenous variables. The correlation of an error term with an exogenous variable suggests that that variable has an effect on the endogenous variable associated with the error term. In such a case, another path should be drawn that reflects the impact of the exogenous variable with the endogenous variable. The absence of such correlation does not prove that the model is specified correctly, only that it is not specified incorrectly.

> **Getting Started**
> Find examples of the techniques of this chapter in your area.

Beyond Path Analysis

Path analysis is limited to models that have no feedback loops. When feedback loops are present, error term assumptions are violated. Causal models with feedback loops are called *nonrecursive* models. *Two-stage least squares* (known as 2SLS) is an econometric technique (that is, a statistical method used in economic research) for estimating two regression models that have feedback loops such as the following:

(1) $$x_{10} \leftarrow x_{11}, x_{12}$$
(2) $$x_{11} \leftarrow x_{13}, x_{14}, x_{10}$$

In model 1, x_{11} is endogenous and x_{12} is exogenous. The basic strategy of 2SLS is to use a modified version of x_{11} in model 1 that does not violate error term assumptions. The name *two stage* indicates a two-step process for estimating such systems of models. The purpose of the first step is to estimate the modified variable, here, x_{11}. Typically, x_{11} is predicted by other variables that are, hence, called instrumental variables. The predicted variable x_{11} is denoted $\hat{x}_{11}$. In the second stage, $\hat{x}_{11}$ is used to predict the dependent variable x_{10}, hence, $x_{10} = f(\hat{x}_{11}, x_{12})$.

Figure 16.7 ———————— SEM Model

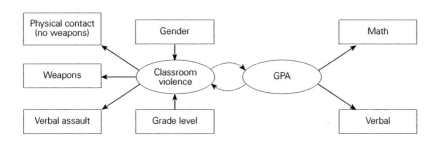

In recent years, advances in software interfaces have increased the popularity of *structural equation models* (SEMs). These are models that simultaneously estimate (1) the relationship between observed variables and their factor constructs and (2) relationships among variables and constructs that involve feedback loops. Estimation requires specific software such as LISREL or AMOS (now integrated as an add-on module with SPSS). Figure 16.7 shows an example of a SEM model. In the model, classroom violence is composed of measures of physical contact, weapons, and verbal assaults. GPA is measured through math and verbal scores. The impact on classroom violence is predicted through the same variables as in the logistic regression example in Chapter 14, namely, gender, grade level, and GPA. However, this model also, and simultaneously, examines the impact of classroom violence on GPA. The estimation methodology is quite complex, and analysts test for robustness and validity in ways that are dissimilar from those used in multiple regression.

SURVIVAL ANALYSIS

Another limitation of regression is that it assumes that complete information is available about all observations. *Survival analysis* deals with techniques that analyze information about events that is not yet available.[11] Assume that a welfare manager in our earlier example (see discussion of path analysis) takes a snapshot of the status of the welfare clients. Some clients may have obtained employment and others not yet. Clients will also vary as to the amount of time that they have been receiving welfare. Examine the data in Table 16.4. It shows that neither of the two clients, who have yet to complete their first week on welfare, has found employment; one of the three clients who have completed one week of welfare has found employment. *Censored observations* are observations for which the specified

Table 16.4 ⸺〰⸺ Censored Observations

Obs	Week	Emp	Obs	Week	Emp	Obs	Week	Emp
1	0	0	6	2	0	11	4	1
2	0	0	7	2	0	12	4	0
3	1	1	8	3	1	13	5	1
4	1	0	9	3	0	14	5	1
5	1	0	10	4	1	15	5	0

Note: Obs = observations (clients); Emp = employment; 0 = has not yet found employment; 1 = has found employment.

outcome has yet to occur. It is assumed that all clients who have not yet found employment are still waiting for this event to occur. Thus, the sample should not include clients who are not seeking employment. Note, however, that a censored observation is very different from one that has missing data, which might occur because the manager does not know whether the client has found employment. As with regression, records with missing data are excluded from analysis. A censored observation is simply an observation for which a specified outcome has not yet occurred.

Assume that data exist from a random sample of 100 clients who are seeking, or have found, employment. *Survival analysis* is the statistical procedure for analyzing these data. The name of this procedure stems from its use in medical research. In clinical trials, researchers want to know the survival (or disease) rate of patients as a function of the duration of their treatment. For patients in the middle of their trial, the specified outcome may not have occurred yet. We obtain the following results (also called a *life table*) from analyzing hypothetical data from welfare records (see Table 16.5). In the context shown in the table, the word *terminal* signifies that the event has

Table 16.5 ⸺〰⸺ Life Table Results

Start time	# Entering interval	# Terminal events	Cum. prop. surviving until end of interval	Probability density
0.0	100.0	0.0	1.0000	0.0000
1.0	91.0	2.0	0.9762	0.0238
2.0	75.0	5.0	0.9055	0.0707
3.0	58.0	6.0	0.7979	0.1076
4.0	37.0	9.0	0.5867	0.2112
5.0	22.0	14.0	0.1304	0.4563

Note: The median survival time is 5.19.

Figure 16.8 ————————⋏⋏⋏⋏⋏— Probability Density

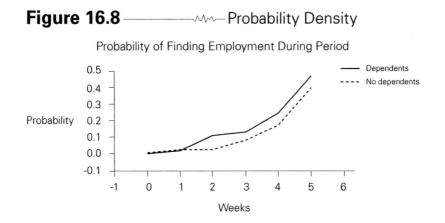

Probability of Finding Employment During Period

occurred. That is, the client has found employment. At start time zero, 100 cases enter the interval. During the first period, there are no terminal cases and nine censored cases. Thus, 91 cases enter the next period. In this second period, 2 clients find employment and 14 do not, resulting in 75 cases that enter the following period. The column labeled "Cumulative proportion surviving until end of interval" is an estimate of probability of surviving (not finding employment) until the end of the stated interval.[12] The column labeled "Probability density" is an estimate of the probability of the terminal event occurring (that is, finding employment) during the time interval. The results also report that "the median survival time is 5.19." That is, half of the clients find employment in 5.19 weeks.

Survival analysis can also examine survival rates for different "treatments" or conditions. Assume that data are available about the number of dependents that each client has. Table 16.5 is readily produced for each subset of this condition. For example, by comparing the survival rates of those with and those without dependents, the **probability density** figure, which shows the likelihood of an event's occurring, can be obtained (Figure 16.8). This figure suggests that having dependents is associated with clients' finding employment somewhat faster.

Beyond Life Tables

Life tables require that the interval (time) variable be measured on a discrete scale. When the time variable is continuous, *Kaplan-Meier survival analysis* is used. This procedure is quite analogous to life tables analysis. *Cox regression* is similar to Kaplan-Meier but allows for consideration of a larger number of independent variables (called covariates). In all instances, the purpose is to examine the effect of treatment on the survival of observations, that is, the occurrence of a dichotomous event.

FACTOR ANALYSIS

A variety of statistical techniques help analysts to explore relationships in their data. These exploratory techniques typically aim to create groups of variables (or observations) that are related to each other and distinct from other groups. These techniques usually precede regression and other analyses.

Factor analysis is a well-established technique that often aids in creating index variables. Earlier, Chapter 3 discussed the use of Cronbach alpha to empirically justify the selection of variables that make up an index. However, in that approach analysts must still justify that variables used in different index variables are indeed distinct. By contrast, factor analysis analyzes a large number of variables (often 20 to 30) and classifies them into groups based on empirical similarities and dissimilarities. This empirical assessment can aid analysts' judgments regarding variables that might be grouped together.

Factor analysis uses correlations among variables to identify subgroups. These subgroups (called factors) are characterized by relatively high within-group correlation among variables and low between-group correlation among variables. Most factor analysis consists of roughly four steps: (1) determining that the group of variables has enough correlation to allow for factor analysis, (2) determining how many factors should be used for classifying (or grouping) the variables, (3) improving the interpretation of correlations and factors (through a process called rotation), and (4) naming the factors and, possibly, creating index variables for subsequent analysis. Most factor analysis is used for grouping of variables (R-type factor analysis) rather than observations (Q-type). Often, discriminant analysis is used for grouping of observations, mentioned later in this chapter.

The terminology of factor analysis differs greatly from that used elsewhere in this book, and the discussion that follows is offered as an aid in understanding tables that might be encountered in research that uses this technique. An important task in factor analysis is determining how many common factors should be identified. Theoretically, there as many factor as variables, but only a few factors account for most of the variance in the data. The percentage of variation explained by each factor is defined as the eigenvalue/number of variables, whereby the eigenvalue of a factor is the sum of correlations (r) of each variable with that factor. This correlation is also called *loading* in factor analysis. Analysts can define (or "extract") how many factors they wish to use, or they can define a statistical criterion (typically requiring each factor to have an eigenvalue of at least 1.0).

The method of identifying factors is called principal component analysis (PCA). The results of PCA often make it difficult to interpret the factors, in which case the analyst will use rotation (a statistical technique that distributes the explained variance across factors). Rotation causes variables to load higher on one factor, and less on others, bringing the pattern of groups better into focus for interpretation. Several different methods of rotation are commonly used (for example, Varimax, Promax), but the purpose of this procedure is always to understand which variables belong together. Typically, for purposes of interpretation, factor loadings are considered only if their values are at least .50, and only these values might be shown in tables.

Table 16.6 shows the result of a factor analysis. The table shows various items related to managerial professionalism, and the factor analysis identifies three distinct groups for these items. Such tables are commonly seen in research articles. The labels for each group (for example, "A. Commitment to Performance") are provided by the authors; note that the three groupings are conceptually distinct. The table also shows that, combined, these three factors account for 61.97 percent of the total variance. The table shows only loadings greater than .50; those below this value are not shown.[13] Based on these results, the authors then create index variables for the three groups. Each group has high internal reliability (see Chapter 3); the Cronbach alpha scores are, respectively, 0.87, 0.83, and 0.88. This table shows a fairly typical use of factor analysis, providing statistical support for a grouping scheme.

Beyond Factor Analysis

A variety of exploratory techniques exist. Some purely seek to classify, whereas others seek to create and predict classifications through independent variables.

Multidimensional scaling and *cluster analysis* aim to identify key dimensions along which observations (rather than variables) differ. These techniques differ from factor analysis in that they allow for a hierarchy of classification dimensions. Some also use graphics to aid in visualizing the extent of differences and to help in identifying the similarity or dissimilarity of observations. *Network analysis* is a descriptive technique used to portray relationships among actors. A graphic representation can be made of the frequency with which actors interact with each other, distinguishing frequent interactions from those that are infrequent.

Discriminant analysis is used when the dependent variable is nominal with two or more categories. For example, we might want to know how parents choose among three types of school vouchers. Discriminant analysis calculates regression lines that distinguish (discriminate) among the nominal groups (the categories of the dependent variable), as well as other regression lines that describe the relationship of the independent variables for each group (called classification functions). The emphasis in discriminant

Table 16.6 ⸺⸺ Factor Analysis

Factor Analysis of Items of Managerial Commitment			
"in our city, most managers. . ."	Factor1	Factor2	Factor3
A. Commitment to Performance			
Embrace professional standards	.837		
Are committed to improving effectiveness and efficiency	.826		
Exhibit a lot of energy and personal drive	.752		
Would rather overcome obstacles than accept them	.711		
Set high standards for their programs	.708		
Know nationally recognized 'best practices'	.600		
B. Commitment to Accountability			
Conduct thorough program evaluations		.767	
Use performance measurement effectively in most programs		.745	
Provide detailed accountability about their programs		.675	
Regularly conduct performance audits		.667	
Receive training in ethics principles and practices		.622	
Ensure that all employees are aware of ethics standards and requirements		.552	
C. Commitment to Public Participation			
Seek frequent input from community leaders in defining program goals			.826
Solicit feedback from community leaders about our performance			.799
Have regular discussions with community leaders on city problems			.795
Seek citizen input to assess program performance			.787
Encourage public participation processes in decision making			.750
Are effective in building community consensus			.579
SSL (sum of squared loadings)	4.084	3.836	3.236
Variation explained (%)	22.69	21.31	17.98
Total variation explained (%)	22.69	44.00	61.97

Note: Factor analysis with Varimax rotation.

Source: E. Berman and J. West. (2003). "What Is Managerial Mediocrity? Definition, Prevalence and Negative Impact (Part 1)," *Public Performance & Management Review*, 27 (December): 7–27.

analysis is the ability of the independent variables to correctly predict values of the nominal variable (for example, group membership). Discriminant analysis is one strategy for dealing with dependent variables that are nominal with three or more categories.

Multinomial logistic regression and *ordinal regression* have been developed in recent years to address nominal and ordinal dependent variables in logic regression. Multinomial logistic regression calculates functions that compare the probability of a nominal value occurring relative to a base reference group. The calculation of such probabilities makes this technique an interesting alternative to discriminant analysis. When the nominal dependent variable has three values (say, 1, 2, and 3), one logistic regression predicts the likelihood of 2 versus 1 occurring, and the other logistic regression predicts the likelihood of 3 versus 1 occurring, assuming that "1" is the base reference group.[14]

When the dependent variable is ordinal, ordinal regression can be used. Like multinomial logistic regression, ordinal regression often is used to predict event probability or group membership. Ordinal regression assumes that the slope coefficients are identical for each value of the dependent variable; when this assumption is not met, multinomial logistic regression should be considered. Both multinomial logistic regression and ordinal regression are relatively recent developments and are not yet widely used. Statistics, like other fields of science, continues to push its frontiers forward and thereby develop new techniques for managers and analysts.

SUMMARY

A vast array of additional statistical methods exists. In this concluding chapter, we summarized the most common of these methods (ANOVA, path analysis, survival analysis, and factor analysis) and briefly mentioned other related techniques. This chapter can help managers and analysts become familiar with these additional techniques and increase their access to research literature in which these techniques are used. Managers and analysts who would like more information about these techniques will likely consult other texts or on-line sources.

In many instances, managers will need only simple approaches to calculate the means of their variables, produce a few good graphs that tell the story, make simple forecasts, and test for significant differences among a few groups. Why, then, bother with these more advanced techniques? They are part of the analytical world in which managers operate. Through research and consulting, managers cannot help but come in contact with them. It is hoped that this chapter whets the appetite and provides a useful reference for managers and students alike.

KEY TERMS

ANOVA (p. 267)
Direct effects (p. 275)
Endogenous variables (p. 274)
Exogenous variables (p. 274)
Factor analysis (p. 280)
Indirect effects (p. 275)

Loading (p. 280)
Path analysis (p. 273)
Post-hoc tests (p. 268)
Probability density (p. 279)
Recursive models (p. 274)
Survival analysis (p. 277)

Notes

1. The between-group variance (s_b^2) is defined as $\sum_k (\bar{x}_k - \bar{\bar{x}})^2 / k - 1$, where the subscript k identifies groups, $\bar{x}_k$ = each of the group means, $\bar{\bar{x}}$ = the overall group mean (the mean of the means), and k = the number of groups. The within-group variance (s_w^2) is defined as $\sum_k \sum_i (\bar{x}_i - \bar{x}_k)^2 / (n-1)$ for each group, where $\bar{x}_i$ = group observations and n = the total number of observations (across all groups). The terms $\sum(x_i - \bar{x}_i)^2$ are called "sums of squares." See also Table 16.2. Many textbooks provide examples of calculating these values.

2. F-test critical values are defined by two types of degrees of freedom: the degrees of freedom for the numerator is $k - 1$, where k = number of groups. The degrees of freedom for the denominator is $n - k$, where n = number of observations. For example, if there are 4 groups and 76 observations, then df (numerator) = 3, and df (denominator) = 72. Based on the F distribution (see Appendix E), the critical value of $F(3,72) = 2.74$ at the 5 percent level of significance (estimated based on table).

3. In SPSS, these tests are found through Analyze → Compare Means → One Way ANOVA → Post-Hoc.

4. The Kolmogorov-Smirnov test statistic is 0.28, $p = .000 < .01$. Skewness is 5.42, with a standard error of 0.22. This ratio greatly exceeds a value of 2.

5. The term *unweighted* simply means that all means are weighted equally, regardless of the number of observations in each group. This reflects our purpose. The weighted linear term, which weights the group means according to the number of observations in each group, should not be used.

6. These results are replicated for the untransformed variable, but only when numerous observations are removed that are identified as outliers for each group. The remaining untransformed variable is not normal for any group, but it does have homogeneous variances. The text findings for the transformed variables strengthen our conclusion that we

should regard the stated differences as significant, not as a special case of the nonnormal, untransformed variable.

7. When only "typical" wetland losses are considered (that is, the removal of watersheds that are characterized as outliers in the example analysis), the mean wetland losses of watersheds with small and large surrounding populations are, respectively, 1.73 percent and 2.52 percent, suggesting a 49.2 percent greater wetland loss among watersheds with large populations. The question is whether this categorization of "typical" losses has any traction in public discourse.

8. Two types of feedback loops are illustrated as follows:

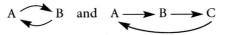

9. When feedback loops are present, error terms for the different models will be correlated with exogenous variables, violating an error term assumption for such models. Then, alternative estimation methodologies are necessary, such as two-stage least squares and others discussed later in this chapter.

10. Some models may show double-headed arrows among error terms. These show the correlation between error terms, which is of no importance in estimating the beta coefficients.

11. In SPSS, survival analysis is available through the add-on module in SPSS Advanced Models.

12. The functions used to estimate probabilities are rather complex. They are so-called Weibull distributions, which are defined as $h(t) = \alpha\lambda(\lambda t)^{\alpha - 1}$, where α and λ are chosen to best fit the data.

13. Hence, the SSL is greater than the squared loadings reported. For example, because the loadings of variables in groups B and C are not shown for factor 1, the SSL of shown loadings is 3.27 rather than the reported 4.084. If one assumes the other loadings are each .25, then the SSL of the not reported loadings is [12*.25² =] .75, bringing the SSL of factor 1 to [3.27 + .75 =] 4.02, which is very close to the 4.084 value reported in the table.

14. Readers who are interested in multinomial logistic regression can consult on-line sources or the SPSS manual, *Regression Models* 10.0 or higher. The statistics of discriminant analysis are very dissimilar from those of logistic regression, and readers are advised to consult a separate text on that topic. Discriminant analysis is not often used in public affairs.

APPENDIXES

Appendix A
Normal Distribution

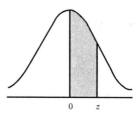

z	.00	.01	.02	.03	.04	.05	.06	.07	.08	.09
0.0	.0000	.0040	.0080	.0120	.0160	.0199	.0239	.0279	.0319	.0359
0.1	.0398	.0438	.0478	.0517	.0557	.0596	.0636	.0675	.0714	.0753
0.2	.0793	.0832	.0871	.0910	.0948	.0987	.1026	.1064	.1103	.1141
0.3	.1179	.1217	.1255	.1293	.1331	.1368	.1406	.1443	.1480	.1517
0.4	.1554	.1591	.1628	.1664	.1700	.1736	.1772	.1808	.1844	.1879
0.5	.1915	.1950	.1985	.2019	.2054	.2088	.2123	.2157	.2190	.2224
0.6	.2257	.2291	.2324	.2357	.2389	.2422	.2454	.2486	.2517	.2549
0.7	.2580	.2611	.2642	.2673	.2704	.2734	.2764	.2794	.2823	.2852
0.8	.2881	.2910	.2939	.2967	.2995	.3023	.3051	.3078	.3106	.3133
0.9	.3159	.3186	.3212	.3238	.3264	.3289	.3315	.3340	.3365	.3389
1.0	.3413	.3438	.3461	.3485	.3508	.3531	.3554	.3577	.3599	.3621
1.1	.3643	.3665	.3686	.3708	.3729	.3749	.3770	.3790	.3810	.3830
1.2	.3849	.3869	.3888	.3907	.3925	.3944	.3962	.3980	.3997	.4015
1.3	.4032	.4049	.4066	.4082	.4099	.4115	.4131	.4147	.4162	.4177
1.4	.4192	.4207	.4222	.4236	.4251	.4265	.4279	.4292	.4306	.4319
1.5	.4332	.4345	.4357	.4370	.4382	.4394	.4406	.4418	.4429	.4441
1.6	.4452	.4463	.4474	.4484	.4495	.4505	.4515	.4525	.4535	.4545
1.7	.4554	.4564	.4573	.4582	.4591	.4599	.4608	.4616	.4625	.4633
1.8	.4641	.4649	.4656	.4664	.4671	.4678	.4686	.4693	.4699	.4706
1.9	.4713	.4719	.4726	.4732	.4738	.4744	.4750	.4756	.4761	.4767
2.0	.4772	.4778	.4783	.4788	.4793	.4798	.4803	.4808	.4812	.4817
2.1	.4821	.4826	.4830	.4834	.4838	.4842	.4846	.4850	.4854	.4857
2.2	.4861	.4864	.4868	.4871	.4875	.4878	.4881	.4884	.4887	.4890
2.3	.4893	.4896	.4898	.4901	.4904	.4906	.4909	.4911	.4913	.4916
2.4	.4918	.4920	.4922	.4925	.4927	.4929	.4931	.4932	.4934	.4936
2.5	.4938	.4940	.4941	.4943	.4945	.4946	.4948	.4949	.4951	.4952
2.6	.4953	.4955	.4956	.4957	.4959	.4960	.4961	.4962	.4963	.4964
2.7	.4965	.4966	.4967	.4968	.4969	.4970	.4971	.4972	.4973	.4974
2.8	.4974	.4975	.4976	.4977	.4977	.4978	.4979	.4979	.4980	.4981
2.9	.4981	.4982	.4982	.4983	.4984	.4984	.4985	.4985	.4986	.4986
3.0	.4987	.4987	.4987	.4988	.4988	.4989	.4989	.4989	.4990	.4990

Source: Adapted from Table II of R. A. Fisher and F. Yates, *Statistical Tables for Biological, Agricultural, and Medical Research,* 6th edition, Longman Group, Ltd., London, 1974. (Previously published by Oliver & Boyle, Ltd., Edinburgh). Used with permission of the authors and publishers.

Appendix B
Chi-Square (χ^2) Distribution

Degree of Freedom (df)	0.10	0.05	0.01	.001
1	2.706	3.841	6.635	10.827
2	4.605	5.991	9.210	13.815
3	6.251	7.815	11.341	16.266
4	7.779	9.488	13.277	18.467
5	9.236	11.070	15.086	20.515
6	10.645	12.592	16.812	22.457
7	12.017	14.067	18.475	24.322
8	13.362	15.507	20.090	26.125
9	14.684	16.919	21.666	27.877
10	15.987	18.307	23.209	29.588
11	17.275	19.675	24.725	31.264
12	18.549	21.026	26.217	32.909
13	19.812	22.362	27.688	34.528
14	21.064	23.685	29.141	36.123
15	22.307	24.996	30.578	37.697
16	23.542	26.296	32.000	39.252
17	24.769	27.587	33.409	40.790
18	25.989	28.869	34.805	42.312
19	27.204	30.144	36.191	43.820
20	28.412	31.410	37.566	45.315
21	29.615	32.671	38.932	46.797
22	30.813	33.924	40.289	48.268
23	32.007	35.172	41.638	49.728
24	33.196	36.415	42.980	51.179
25	34.382	37.652	44.314	52.620
26	35.563	38.885	45.642	54.052
27	36.741	40.113	46.963	55.476
28	37.916	41.337	48.278	56.893
29	39.087	42.557	49.588	58.302
30	40.256	43.773	50.892	59.703

Source: Adapted from Table IV of R. A. Fisher and F. Yates, *Statistical Tables for Biological, Agricultural, and Medical Research*, 6th edition, Longman Group, Ltd., London, 1974. (Previously published by Oliver & Boyd, Ltd., Edinburgh). Used with permission of the authors and publishers.

Appendix C
T-Test Distribution

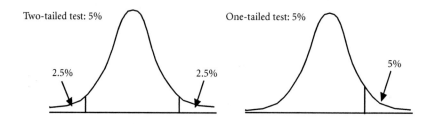

	Alpha Level for One-Tailed Test					
	.10	.05	.025	.01	.005	.0025
Degree of	Alpha Level for Two-Tailed Test					
Freedom (df)	.20	.10	.05	.02	.01	.005
1	3.078	6.314	12.706	31.821	63.657	127.32
2	1.886	2.920	4.303	6.965	9.925	14.089
3	1.638	2.353	3.182	4.541	5.841	7.453
4	1.533	2.132	2.776	3.747	4.604	5.598
5	1.476	2.015	2.571	3.365	4.032	4.773
6	1.440	1.943	2.447	3.143	3.707	4.317
7	1.415	1.895	2.365	2.998	3.499	4.029
8	1.397	1.869	2.306	2.896	3.355	3.833
9	1.383	1.833	2.262	2.821	3.250	3.690
10	1.372	1.812	2.228	2.764	3.169	3.581
11	1.363	1.796	2.201	2.718	3.106	3.497
12	1.356	1.782	2.179	2.681	3.055	3.428
13	1.350	1.771	2.160	2.650	3.012	3.372
14	1.345	1.761	2.145	2.624	2.977	3.326
15	1.341	1.753	2.131	2.602	2.947	3.286
16	1.337	1.746	2.120	2.583	2.921	3.252
17	1.333	1.740	2.110	2.567	2.898	3.222
18	1.330	1.734	2.101	2.552	2.878	3.197
19	1.328	1.729	2.093	2.539	2.861	3.174
20	1.325	1.725	2.086	2.528	2.845	3.153
21	1.323	1.721	2.080	2.518	2.831	3.135
22	1.321	1.717	2.074	2.508	2.819	3.119
23	1.319	1.714	2.069	2.500	2.807	3.104
24	1.318	1.711	2.064	2.492	2.797	3.091
25	1.316	1.708	2.060	2.485	2.787	3.078

(continued)

Degree of Freedom (df)	Alpha Level for One-Tailed Test					
	.10	.05	.025	.01	.005	.0025
	Alpha Level for Two-Tailed Test					
	.20	.10	.05	.02	.01	.005
26	1.315	1.706	2.056	2.479	2.779	3.067
27	1.314	1.703	2.052	2.473	2.771	3.057
28	1.313	1.701	2.048	2.467	2.763	3.047
29	1.311	1.699	2.045	2.462	2.756	3.038
30	1.310	1.697	2.042	2.457	2.750	3.030
40	1.303	1.684	2.021	2.423	2.704	2.971
60	1.296	1.671	2.000	2.390	2.660	2.915
120	1.289	1.658	1.980	2.358	2.617	2.860
∞	1.282	1.645	1.960	2.326	2.576	2.807

Source: Adapted from Table III of R. A. Fisher and F. Yates, *Statistical Tables for Biological, Agricultural, and Medical Research,* 6th edition, Longman Group, Ltd., London, 1974. (Previously published by Oliver & Boyd, Ltd., Edinburgh). Used with permission of the authors and publishers.

Appendix D
Durbin-Watson Distribution
Five percent significance points of d_l and d_u for Durbin-Watson test[†]

N	k = 1		k = 2		k = 3		k = 4		k = 5	
	d_l	d_u	d_l	d_u	d_l	d_u	d_l	d_u	d_l	d_u
15	1.08	1.36	0.95	1.54	0.82	1.75	0.69	1.97	0.56	2.21
16	1.10	1.37	0.98	1.54	0.86	1.73	0.74	1.93	0.62	2.15
17	1.13	1.38	1.02	1.54	0.90	1.71	0.78	1.90	0.67	2.10
18	1.16	1.39	1.05	1.53	0.93	1.69	0.82	1.87	0.71	2.06
19	1.18	1.40	1.08	1.53	0.97	1.68	0.86	1.85	0.75	2.02
20	1.20	1.41	1.10	1.54	1.00	1.68	0.90	1.83	0.79	1.99
21	1.22	1.42	1.13	1.54	1.03	1.67	0.93	1.81	0.83	1.96
22	1.24	1.43	1.15	1.54	1.05	1.66	0.96	1.80	0.86	1.94
23	1.26	1.44	1.17	1.54	1.08	1.66	0.99	1.79	0.90	1.92
24	1.27	1.45	1.19	1.55	1.10	1.66	1.01	1.78	0.93	1.90
25	1.29	1.45	1.21	1.55	1.12	1.66	1.04	1.77	0.95	1.89
26	1.30	1.46	1.22	1.55	1.14	1.65	1.06	1.76	0.98	1.88
27	1.32	1.47	1.24	1.56	1.16	1.65	1.08	1.76	1.01	1.86
28	1.33	1.48	1.26	1.56	1.18	1.65	1.10	1.75	1.03	1.85
29	1.34	1.48	1.27	1.56	1.20	1.65	1.12	1.74	1.05	1.84
30	1.35	1.49	1.28	1.57	1.21	1.65	1.14	1.74	1.07	1.83
31	1.36	1.50	1.30	1.57	1.23	1.65	1.16	1.74	1.09	1.83
32	1.37	1.50	1.31	1.57	1.24	1.65	1.18	1.73	1.11	1.82
33	1.38	1.51	1.32	1.58	1.26	1.65	1.19	1.73	1.13	1.81
34	1.39	1.51	1.33	1.58	1.27	1.65	1.21	1.73	1.15	1.81
35	1.40	1.52	1.34	1.53	1.28	1.65	1.22	1.73	1.16	1.80
36	1.41	1.52	1.35	1.59	1.29	1.65	1.24	1.73	1.18	1.80
37	1.42	1.53	1.36	1.59	1.31	1.66	1.25	1.72	1.19	1.80
38	1.43	1.54	1.37	1.59	1.32	1.66	1.26	1.72	1.21	1.79
39	1.43	1.54	1.38	1.60	1.33	1.66	1.27	1.72	1.22	1.79
40	1.44	1.54	1.39	1.60	1.34	1.66	1.29	1.72	1.23	1.79
45	1.48	1.57	1.43	1.62	1.38	1.67	1.34	1.72	1.29	1.78
50	1.50	1.59	1.46	1.63	1.42	1.67	1.38	1.72	1.34	1.77
55	1.53	1.60	1.49	1.64	1.45	1.68	1.41	1.72	1.38	1.77
60	1.55	1.62	1.51	1.65	1.48	1.69	1.44	1.73	1.41	1.77
65	1.57	1.63	1.54	1.66	1.50	1.70	1.47	1.73	1.44	1.77
70	1.58	1.64	1.55	1.67	1.52	1.70	1.49	1.74	1.46	1.77
75	1.60	1.65	1.57	1.68	1.54	1.71	1.51	1.74	1.49	1.77
80	1.61	1.66	1.59	1.69	1.56	1.72	1.53	1.74	1.51	1.77
85	1.62	1.67	1.60	1.70	1.57	1.72	1.55	1.75	1.52	1.17
90	1.63	1.68	1.61	1.70	1.59	1.73	1.57	1.75	1.54	1.78
95	1.64	1.69	1.62	1.71	1.60	1.73	1.58	1.75	1.56	1.78
100	1.65	1.69	1.63	1.72	1.61	1.74	1.59	1.76	1.57	1.78

[†]N = number of observations; k = number of explanatory variables (excluding the constant term).

Source: Reprinted with permission from J. Durbin and G. S. Watson, "Testing for Serial Correlation in Least Squares Regression," *Biometrika*, vol. 38, 1951, pp. 159–177.

Appendix E
F-Test Distribution $\propto$ = .05

Degree of freedom (df) within groups [denominator]

Degree of freedom (df) between groups [numerator]

	1	2	3	4	5	6	7	8	9	10	12	15	20	24	30	40	60	120	∞
1	161.4	199.5	215.7	224.6	230.2	234.0	236.8	238.9	240.5	241.9	243.9	245.9	248.0	249.1	250.1	251.1	252.2	253.3	254.3
2	18.51	19.00	19.16	19.25	19.30	19.33	19.35	19.37	19.38	19.40	19.41	19.43	19.45	19.45	19.48	19.47	19.48	19.49	19.50
3	10.13	9.55	9.28	9.12	9.01	8.94	8.89	8.85	8.81	8.79	8.74	8.70	8.66	8.64	8.62	8.59	8.57	8.55	8.53
4	7.71	6.94	6.59	6.39	6.26	6.16	6.09	6.04	6.00	5.96	5.91	5.86	5.80	5.77	5.75	5.72	5.69	5.66	5.63
5	6.61	5.79	5.41	5.19	5.05	4.95	4.88	4.82	4.77	4.74	4.68	4.62	4.56	4.53	4.50	4.46	4.43	4.40	4.36
6	5.99	5.14	4.76	4.53	4.39	4.28	4.21	4.15	4.10	4.06	4.00	3.94	3.87	3.84	3.81	3.77	3.74	3.70	3.67
7	5.59	4.74	4.35	4.12	3.97	3.87	3.79	3.73	3.68	3.64	3.57	3.51	3.44	3.41	3.38	3.34	3.30	3.27	3.23
8	5.32	4.46	4.07	3.84	3.69	3.58	3.50	3.44	3.39	3.35	3.28	3.22	3.15	3.12	3.08	3.04	3.01	2.97	2.93
9	5.12	4.26	3.86	3.63	3.48	3.37	3.29	3.23	3.18	3.14	3.07	3.01	2.94	2.90	2.86	2.83	2.79	2.75	2.71
10	4.96	4.10	3.71	3.48	3.33	3.22	3.14	3.07	3.02	2.98	2.91	2.85	2.77	2.74	2.70	2.66	2.62	2.58	2.54
11	4.84	3.98	3.59	3.36	3.20	3.09	3.01	2.95	2.90	2.85	2.79	2.72	2.65	2.61	2.57	2.53	2.49	2.45	2.40
12	4.75	3.89	3.49	3.26	3.11	3.00	2.91	2.85	2.80	2.75	2.69	2.62	2.54	2.51	2.47	2.43	2.38	2.34	2.30
13	4.67	3.81	3.41	3.18	3.03	2.92	2.83	2.77	2.71	2.67	2.60	2.53	2.46	2.42	2.38	2.34	2.30	2.25	2.21
14	4.60	3.74	3.34	3.11	2.96	2.85	2.76	2.70	2.65	2.60	2.53	2.46	2.39	2.35	2.31	2.27	2.22	2.18	2.13
15	4.54	3.68	3.29	3.06	2.90	2.79	2.71	2.64	2.59	2.54	2.48	2.40	2.33	2.29	2.25	2.20	2.16	2.11	2.07
16	4.49	3.63	3.24	3.01	2.85	2.74	2.66	2.59	2.54	2.49	2.42	2.35	2.28	2.24	2.19	2.15	2.11	2.06	2.01
17	4.45	3.59	3.20	2.96	2.81	2.70	2.61	2.55	2.49	2.45	2.38	2.31	2.23	2.19	2.15	2.10	2.06	2.01	1.96

(continued)

Appendix E Continued
F-Test Distribution ∝ = .05

	Degree of freedom (df) between groups [numerator]																		
Degree of freedom (df) within groups [denominator]	1	2	3	4	5	6	7	8	9	10	12	15	20	24	30	40	60	120	∞
18	4.41	3.55	3.16	2.93	2.77	2.66	2.58	2.51	2.46	2.41	2.34	2.27	2.19	2.15	2.11	2.06	2.02	1.97	1.92
19	4.38	3.52	3.13	2.90	2.74	2.63	2.54	2.48	2.42	2.38	2.31	2.23	2.16	2.11	2.07	2.03	1.98	1.93	1.88
20	4.35	3.49	3.10	2.87	2.71	2.60	2.51	2.45	2.39	2.35	2.28	2.20	2.12	2.08	2.04	1.99	1.95	1.90	1.84
21	4.32	3.47	3.07	2.84	2.68	2.57	2.49	2.42	2.37	2.32	2.25	2.18	2.10	2.05	2.01	1.96	1.92	1.87	1.81
22	4.30	3.44	3.05	2.82	2.66	2.55	2.46	2.40	2.34	2.30	2.23	2.15	2.07	2.03	1.98	1.94	1.89	1.84	1.78
23	4.28	3.42	3.03	2.80	2.64	2.53	2.44	2.37	2.32	2.27	2.20	2.13	2.05	2.01	1.96	1.91	1.86	1.81	1.76
24	4.26	3.40	3.01	2.78	2.62	2.51	2.42	2.36	2.30	2.25	2.18	2.11	2.03	1.98	1.94	1.89	1.84	1.79	1.73
25	4.24	3.39	2.99	2.76	2.60	2.49	2.40	2.34	2.28	2.24	2.16	2.09	2.01	1.96	1.92	1.87	1.82	1.77	1.71
26	4.23	3.37	2.98	2.74	2.59	2.47	2.39	2.32	2.27	2.22	2.15	2.07	1.99	1.95	1.90	1.85	1.80	1.75	1.69
27	4.21	3.35	2.96	2.73	2.57	2.46	2.37	2.31	2.25	2.20	2.13	2.06	1.97	1.93	1.88	1.84	1.79	1.73	1.67
28	4.20	3.34	2.95	2.71	2.56	2.45	2.36	2.29	2.24	2.19	2.12	2.04	1.96	1.91	1.87	1.82	1.77	1.71	1.65
29	4.18	3.33	2.93	2.70	2.55	2.43	2.35	2.28	2.22	2.18	2.10	2.03	1.94	1.90	1.85	1.81	1.75	1.70	1.64
30	4.17	3.32	2.92	2.69	2.53	2.42	2.33	2.27	2.21	2.16	2.09	2.01	1.93	1.89	1.84	1.79	1.74	1.68	1.62
40	4.08	3.23	2.84	2.61	2.45	2.34	2.25	2.18	2.12	2.08	2.00	1.92	1.84	1.79	1.74	1.69	1.64	1.58	1.51
60	4.00	3.15	2.76	2.53	2.37	2.25	2.17	2.10	2.04	1.99	1.92	1.84	1.75	1.70	1.65	1.59	1.53	1.47	1.39
120	3.92	3.07	2.68	2.45	2.29	2.17	2.09	2.02	1.96	1.91	1.83	1.75	1.66	1.61	1.55	1.50	1.43	1.35	1.25
∞	3.84	3.00	2.60	2.37	2.21	2.10	2.01	1.94	1.88	1.83	1.75	1.67	1.57	1.52	1.46	1.39	1.32	1.22	1.00

(continued)

Appendix E Continued
F-Test Distribution ∝ = .01

Degree of freedom (df) within groups [denominator] / Degree of freedom (df) between groups [numerator]

[denominator]	1	2	3	4	5	6	7	8	9	10	12	15	20	24	30	40	60	120	∞
1	4052	4999.5	5403	5625	5764	5859	5928	5981	6022	6056	6106	6157	6209	6235	6261	6287	6313	6339	6366
2	98.58	99.00	99.17	99.25	99.30	99.33	99.36	99.37	99.39	99.40	99.42	99.43	99.45	99.46	99.47	99.47	99.48	99.49	99.50
3	34.12	30.82	29.46	28.71	28.24	27.91	27.67	27.49	27.35	27.23	27.05	26.87	26.69	26.60	26.50	26.41	26.32	26.22	26.13
4	21.20	18.00	16.69	15.98	15.52	15.21	14.98	14.80	14.66	14.55	14.37	14.20	14.02	13.93	13.64	13.75	13.65	13.56	13.46
5	16.26	13.27	12.06	11.39	10.97	10.67	10.46	10.29	10.16	10.05	9.89	9.72	9.55	9.47	9.38	9.29	9.20	9.11	9.02
6	13.75	10.92	9.78	9.15	8.75	8.47	8.26	8.10	7.98	7.87	7.72	7.56	7.40	7.31	7.23	7.14	7.06	6.97	6.88
7	12.25	9.55	8.45	7.85	7.46	7.19	6.99	6.84	6.72	6.62	6.47	6.31	6.16	6.07	5.99	5.91	5.82	5.74	5.65
8	11.26	8.65	7.59	7.01	6.63	6.37	6.18	6.03	5.91	5.81	5.67	5.52	5.36	5.28	5.20	5.12	5.03	4.95	4.86
9	10.56	8.02	6.99	6.42	6.06	5.80	5.61	5.47	5.35	5.26	5.11	4.96	4.81	4.73	4.65	4.57	4.48	4.40	4.31
10	10.04	7.56	6.55	5.99	5.64	5.39	5.20	5.06	4.94	4.85	4.71	4.56	4.41	4.33	4.25	4.17	4.08	4.00	3.91
11	9.65	7.21	6.22	5.67	5.32	5.07	4.89	4.74	4.63	4.54	4.40	4.25	4.10	4.02	3.94	3.86	3.78	3.69	3.60
12	9.33	6.93	5.95	5.41	5.06	4.82	4.64	4.50	4.39	4.30	4.16	4.01	3.86	3.78	3.70	3.62	3.54	3.45	3.36
13	9.07	6.70	5.74	5.21	4.86	4.62	4.44	4.30	4.19	4.10	3.96	3.82	3.66	3.59	3.51	3.43	3.34	3.25	3.17
14	8.86	6.51	5.56	5.04	4.69	4.46	4.28	4.14	4.03	3.94	3.80	3.66	3.51	3.43	3.35	3.27	3.18	3.09	3.00
15	8.68	6.36	5.42	4.89	4.56	4.32	4.14	4.00	3.89	3.80	3.67	3.52	3.37	3.29	3.21	3.13	3.05	2.96	2.87
16	8.53	6.23	5.29	4.77	4.44	4.20	4.03	3.89	3.78	3.69	3.55	3.41	3.26	3.18	3.10	3.02	2.93	2.84	2.75
17	8.40	6.11	5.18	4.67	4.34	4.10	3.93	3.79	3.68	3.59	3.46	3.31	3.16	3.08	3.00	2.92	2.83	2.75	2.65
18	8.29	6.01	5.09	4.58	4.25	4.01	3.84	3.71	3.60	3.51	3.37	3.23	3.08	3.00	2.92	2.84	2.75	2.66	2.57
19	8.18	5.93	5.01	4.50	4.17	3.94	3.77	3.63	3.52	3.43	3.30	3.15	3.00	2.92	2.84	2.76	2.67	2.58	2.49

(continued)

Appendix E Continued
F-Test Distribution ∝ = .01

Degree of freedom (df) within groups [denominator]	Degree of freedom (df) between groups [numerator]																		
	1	2	3	4	5	6	7	8	9	10	12	15	20	24	30	40	60	120	∞
20	8.10	5.85	4.94	4.43	4.10	3.87	3.70	3.56	3.46	3.37	3.23	3.09	2.94	2.86	2.78	2.69	2.61	2.52	2.42
21	8.02	5.78	4.87	4.37	4.04	3.81	3.64	3.51	3.40	3.31	3.17	3.03	2.88	2.80	2.72	2.64	2.55	2.46	2.36
22	7.95	5.72	4.82	4.31	3.99	3.76	3.59	3.45	3.35	3.26	3.12	2.98	2.83	2.75	2.67	2.58	2.50	2.40	2.31
23	7.88	5.66	4.76	4.26	3.94	3.71	3.54	3.41	3.30	3.21	3.07	2.93	2.78	2.70	2.62	2.54	2.45	2.35	2.26
24	7.82	5.61	4.72	4.22	3.90	3.67	3.50	3.36	3.26	3.17	3.03	2.89	2.74	2.66	2.58	2.49	2.40	2.31	2.21
25	7.77	5.57	4.68	4.18	3.85	3.63	3.46	3.32	3.22	3.13	2.99	2.85	2.70	2.62	2.54	2.45	2.36	2.27	2.17
26	7.72	5.53	4.64	4.14	3.82	3.59	3.42	3.29	3.18	3.09	2.96	2.81	2.66	2.58	2.50	2.42	2.33	2.23	2.13
27	7.68	5.49	4.60	4.11	3.78	3.56	3.39	3.26	3.15	3.06	2.93	2.78	2.63	2.55	2.47	2.38	2.29	2.20	2.10
28	7.64	5.45	4.57	4.07	3.75	3.53	3.36	3.23	3.12	3.03	2.90	2.75	2.60	2.52	2.44	2.35	2.26	2.17	2.06
29	7.60	5.42	4.54	4.04	3.73	3.50	3.33	3.20	3.09	3.00	2.87	2.73	2.57	2.49	2.41	2.33	2.23	2.14	2.03
30	7.56	5.39	4.51	4.02	3.70	3.47	3.30	3.17	3.07	2.98	2.84	2.70	2.55	2.47	2.39	2.30	2.21	2.11	2.01
40	7.31	5.18	4.31	3.83	3.51	3.29	3.12	2.99	2.89	2.80	2.66	2.52	2.37	2.29	2.20	2.11	2.02	1.92	1.80
60	7.08	4.98	4.13	3.65	3.34	3.12	2.95	2.82	2.72	2.63	2.50	2.35	2.20	2.12	2.03	1.94	1.84	1.73	1.60
120	6.85	4.79	3.95	3.48	3.17	2.96	2.79	2.66	2.56	2.47	2.34	2.19	2.03	1.95	1.86	1.76	1.66	1.53	1.38
∞	6.63	4.61	3.78	3.32	3.02	2.80	2.64	2.51	2.41	2.32	2.18	2.04	1.88	1.79	1.70	1.59	1.47	1.32	1.00

Source: Adapted from Table II of R. A. Fisher and F. Yates, Statistical Tables for Biological, Agricultural, and Medical Research, 6th edition, Longman Group, Ltd., London, 1974. (Previously published by Oliver & Boyd, Ltd., Edinburgh). Used with permission of the authors and publishers.

INDEX

To Susie, Alex and Megan, my everlasting love.

PROLOGUE

S HE TOLD ME TO WRITE IT DOWN.

The nightmare is always the same. I start by climbing a dirt path with cedar trees on either side, the sky shockingly bright. It hasn't rained in a long time, and the trees are dry. The wind is blisteringly hot, and a tree bursts into flames. More trees catch fire, and I start running up the path, becoming winded.

Finally I reach the top and before me, erected on the dirt-and-stone bluff, is a crude scaffold. It's a beautiful spring day, and the fires have faded away, changing into a light breeze. Three women in party dresses and bare feet hang by the neck from a wooden beam above the scaffold. They call to me for help; the first is Rose, the second Gwen, and the third that poor ballerina.

I sprint to Rose but cannot reach her. Her cries die out and she swings quietly, hands tied behind her back, feet twitching. At one side of the scaffold is a ladder to the beam, and I begin climbing, my eyes glued to the still faces of the women. In my hand is a straight razor; I must cut them down. At the top I crawl across the beam. Rose is the first in line, but as I come closer the rope that holds her disappears.

The landscape below me has changed. The women are gone, and I'm crawling on a log across the San Marcos River, twenty feet above

clear aquamarine water. I could easily jump in and float to safety. The razor in my hand has changed into the Smith and Wesson, and a man's voice directs me: "Shoot him now." The command comes again. Scanning both banks of the river, I see no one; no one is there but me.

I slip on the log and fall as the water recedes a mile below. Day turns to dusk. As I fall, office building windows rush by. Sometimes I wake then, but usually I keep falling until I land in the water. Opening my eyes, all around me I see red. It's blood. The blood comes into my nostrils and seeps through my clothes to my skin; it's thick and slippery. I am deep in the river of blood and can't find the surface. The blood flows into my mouth and slowly drowns me.

I sit up in bed, sweating, heart pounding, eyes aching, with a man's scream in my ears.

She told me to write all that happened, from the beginning. She said if I write everything down it would help me sleep in peace. So I'm trying to remember everything, to write it all down.

CHAPTER 1

"TELL ME ABOUT THE MONEY AGAIN," Rose said, as she came out the patio door with frozen mango daiquiris. She put one in my hand, tiptoed to give me a warm kiss, and sat in a deck chair.

The mahimahi fillets sizzled and smelled of lemon and olive oil as I flipped them on the grill. Our girls, Chandler, seven, and Callie, five, were playing in the stone hot tub. A boat engine revved, and a wakeboarder stood up on Lake Austin, a quarter mile down the hill. He was a beginner and immediately fell back in the water.

I never tired of talking about the money.

"In a year to eighteen months we'll take the company public with a billion-dollar valuation, maybe higher. That will make our option worth eight million."

We had bought a five-thousand-square-foot house in West Austin so I could become the chief financial officer of Connection Software, one of the hottest private companies in town. The patio was the primary reason we had selected the house. The backside of the pool was framed with large desert-brown boulders and a waterfall. Over the edge of the pool the view of evergreen live oaks and cedars ran clear to the lake. It was winter, but it was also sunny and seventy degrees, so we had turned on the hot tub for the kids.

My new job would start the next day. It was January of 1999, the last year of the millennium, and the NASDAQ was on a roll.

"If the market keeps going up and the company continues to grow, we could personally bank forty or fifty million."

Rose raised her eyebrows and stood, five feet, six inches, one hundred and twenty pounds. She'd been pregnant in her early twenties, but a thousand workouts had long since toned the muscle and tightened the skin. She was thin but had inviting curves in the hips and up top and wasn't afraid to use them against me. Sauntering over, she put her arms around my neck and asked, "What are we going to do with all that money?"

"Whatever the hell we want to," I answered, putting my hand in the back pocket of her capris.

"You want to quit work?"

"Oh, I'll figure out something to do." I played with the back of her T-shirt.

"Professional boxer maybe?" She took two steps back and mimicked a ring announcer: "Ladies and gentlemen, in this corner at six feet, six inches—"

"Six-four," I corrected her.

"Weighing in at a hefty two hundred and forty pounds . . . ."

"Two-twenty."

"With dirty-blond curls, golden eyes, a Roman nose, and fast hands, it's Fighting Joe Robbins!"

"My boxing days are over, babe. Wakeboard instructor, how's that?"

"You'll have to learn how to wakeboard first."

"Details . . . don't bore me with details."

A splash of water landed at our feet, and we glanced over to the hot tub. Chandler held a water cannon while Callie giggled. Rose went to get the girls ready for dinner.

Two buzzards circled lazily in the air above the forest.

It's not that I wanted to do nothing with my career, just that I was tired of doing what I was doing. I was on a treadmill, and with a wife and two kids there was no end to the workout; it ended only with retirement or death.

Unless—and that had become a key word for me—unless I could join an outfit like Connection Software and win a ticket off the treadmill. I had a plan: Get rich so I could do what I wanted to do, forever.

Down on the lake the wakeboarder stood up and fell down again. How hard could it be?

. . .

AFTER DINNER AND SOME TELEVISION I put the girls to bed with a story and joined Rose in the great room. The kitchen and family room were combined to form one large living space. The floor was hardwood, and the ceiling angled up to an oak beam twenty feet high.

Sitting in a leather chair with my feet on a rustic table, I flipped back and forth between sections of a book titled *Getting Ready to Go Public*. Rose read a novel beside me. At some point, while I was reading, she got up and walked back to the bedroom wing.

The IPO notebook I kept was a third full and growing. Just as I finished the chapter and closed the book, Rose came out wearing a see-through teddy and nothing else. Straddling my lap, she asked, "What do you feel like doing now?"

. . .

A SMALL BEDSIDE LAMP provided the only light in the room. The four-poster bed rocked gently with our movements but made little sound. Rose had already enjoyed herself aplenty and was working to excite me by playing a porn actress.

She was completely naked on her knees and elbows before me, my upper legs making a rhythmic smacking sound against the backs of her thighs. Centered between her shoulder blades was a yin-yang tattoo colored red and green. Rose's head was collapsed on a pillow, turned to the side, her face partially covered by hair.

"Spank me again, Joey," she urged.

With an open palm I slapped each of her round cheeks in turn. Her ass was turning a light shade of pink and jiggled each time we made contact. The ceiling fan above clicked as it turned and pulled the sweat from our bodies.

"Oh . . . yes . . . do me hard. . . ."

I grabbed her around the hips and pounded away with gusto.

She raised her head off the pillow, turned back, and implored me, "Harder, baby. Harder!"

That did it. I pushed into her one last time, light-headed with euphoria.

From a bedroom down the hall came an insistent cry: "Mommy!"

Before I was even finished, Rose's natural instincts kicked in; she switched gears and tried to pull away from the grip I had on her hips.

"Let go. . . ."

She spun up to break free from my grasp, disengaging and bounding off the bed. Within seconds she had pulled on panties and a T-shirt and left the room.

A few minutes later I ventured into Chandler's room wearing pajamas. The adjoining bathroom door was ajar, and a muted light crept in. Rose lay on the bed and listened carefully as Chandler snuggled, played with her mommy's hair, and related the nightmare.

"And then the mean man came running after me, only now he looked like Daddy, but with long hair and a beard."

Rose smiled at me and said, "Uh-huh, and then what happened?"

"Then the mean Daddy killed the good Daddy, and I woke up."

"Well, the good Daddy's right here and he's still alive. See?"

I knelt by Chandler's side and gave her a kiss.

"I'm so glad you're alive, Daddy."

"Me too, sweetheart. Me too."

CHAPTER 2

I T WAS A FINE DAY TO START A NEW CHAPTER in my career: sunny, a crisp fifty-two degrees, and the lightest of breezes. My new office was a ten-minute commute: a simple climb out of the Eight Oaks neighborhood, followed by a meandering five-mile drive through the hill country. There were few cars on Bee Caves Road at seven thirty, a vast improvement from fighting traffic on the freeways of Dallas.

The road wound up, down, and around limestone cliffs. Although it was winter, the hills were green from the cedars and live oaks. At the tops of the hills I glanced to the left and saw Lake Austin snaking its way toward town.

As I approached Highway 360 my office building appeared on the left, seven stories of new reflective glass and stone rising up from the highest hill for miles. I pulled into the turn lane and noticed in the mirror a white BMW 323i convertible with the top down. The young woman behind the wheel played the music loud.

I turned into the driveway, curved up through the landscaped grounds and drove into the parking garage on the right. Inside the garage I hesitated, and the BMW zoomed around me to slip into a spot beside the walkway exit. I parked my Lexus next to her.

When I opened the door the woman was already standing.

"Sorry if I cut you off," she said.

I grabbed my briefcase from the backseat. "Don't worry about it. I wasn't sure where to park."

She wore gray wool slacks and a white dress shirt. Her blond hair was in a bob, parted on the left, slicked back from her forehead and tucked behind her right ear. Her lips ran on a diagonal, a little higher on the left side of her face, a little lower on the right. When she smiled, as she did when she realized who I was, the result was crooked, but charming.

"You're Joe Robbins, the new CFO." She shook my hand with conviction.

"Pleasure."

"Gwen Raleigh, VP of marketing. We were supposed to meet during the interview process, but I was always out of town."

"Sure. I remember."

Her eyes were royal blue, her nose straight and just a tad long. She had the body of an athlete, standing a couple inches shy of six feet, with squared shoulders and strong arms, a tennis player maybe, or a rower.

"I look forward to working together," she said. "Come on. I'll take you to your office."

"Nice ride," I said, looking at the BMW.

"You like it? It's totally impractical, but once I saw it I had to have it."

Gwen strode ahead, and I had to hustle to keep up. It was a strong, purposeful walk, not overly feminine. Once inside we rode the elevator with a kid in his early twenties who wore jeans shorts, a leather jacket, and Albert Einstein hair. He got off on the fifth floor.

"You might be a bit overdressed," Gwen said, looking at my sport coat.

"Was he an engineer?"

"I think he works for you, actually, in the collections group."

I looked down at my shoes, shined to perfection, and felt a little self-conscious.

The elevator stopped at the seventh floor.

"Do you have time for a coffee?" I asked. "I'd like to hear about how you run marketing."

"Rain check? I've got a meeting with my staff in a few minutes."

"Sure. We'll do it later."

Gwen dropped me off at my new office in the executive suite and disappeared down the hall.

A minute later I met Zola Conti, my new assistant. "Dang it," she said. "Nobody told me you were so tall."

Zola was half Asian, about a foot shorter than me, and shapely. She wore nice jeans and a black pullover blouse with frilly sleeves. We toured the top three floors, which were filled with cubicles for six hundred employees. The bottom floors of the building were empty, held in reserve to accommodate growth. Once back in my office, we sat down to get acquainted.

"Oh, here's a good tip for you," she said. "No one calls it Connection Software. Around here, everyone just calls it 'the Connection.'"

"Okay."

"And don't expect anyone to come to work at eight a.m. Many don't show up until ten o'clock, but then they'll work until midnight. Isn't that funny?"

"It will take some getting used to."

"So long as they get the work done I guess it doesn't matter when they work."

"I guess not."

Zola's Asian features, almond-shaped eyes, and round face were complemented with thick hair and a Latin complexion. She wore lots of jewelry: hoop earrings, multicolored bracelets, and several rings.

She looked down at her list of orientation topics. "Let's see. Oh yes, Webb told me to put you on the 'core team' e-mail group list."

"The core team? Who's on the core team?"

"Well, of course, there's Webb."

"Sure." Webb Elliot was the English-born CEO of the company.

"And Gwen Raleigh."

"Yep."

"Henry Jiwanlal and Tommy King. You've already met them, haven't you?"

"Yes, we had dinner during the recruiting process."

"And now you. That's it. Five of the senior executives make up the core team."

"I got it. Thanks."

Zola carefully consulted her notes again. "That's about it for now."

"Can I get on Webb's calendar today?"

"He's not in yet. Sometimes he doesn't get here until ten o'clock either. I'll check when he comes in."

After Zola left I surveyed my new office; it was huge, twice as big as the one I had at Liberty Air, my previous employer. A floor-to-ceiling window overlooked Highway 360 and hundreds of acres of undeveloped forest. Looking across the hills to the east I spotted the Texas Capitol building downtown and the University of Texas campus.

Two hours later I was busy on the computer, learning how to navigate the intranet, when Webb Elliot breezed into my office with Gwen Raleigh in tow. His voice boomed as he reached out to shake my hand.

"Brilliant! Excellent! I'm so glad you're here."

Webb looked like he walked off the cover of *Vanity Fair*. He was six feet tall and moved gracefully and quickly. He had the strong face and chin of an aristocrat, with a full head of glossy brown hair, cropped short and parted on the side. His eyes were arresting, dark

blue, almost violet. He dressed expensively casual: designer jeans, a pastel yellow dress shirt, and two-tone brown saddle shoes.

Like many CEOS, Webb always seemed to be in a hurry.

"Right. Got everything you need? Zola taking care of you? Good, good. Well, I need to spend some time with Gwen going over a new marketing strategy. Did you meet Gwen? Excellent."

While he was talking, his eyes darted from here to there, taking in everything: my clothes, briefcase, pens on the desk, notes on the whiteboard, the screen view on the monitor, the sky outside, and Gwen's reaction to the interaction with me.

"Good. This is what we'll do. After lunch I'll stop by, and we'll spend a couple hours together. Does that work for you? See you then."

In an instant he was gone.

It wasn't easy to sell multimillion-dollar software deals to corporations, and it wasn't easy to steal hot young talent from big companies either. Webb Elliot excelled at both.

Our courtship had been lengthy; I'd had a hundred questions about the risk of trading a hard-won career at Liberty Air for an equity stake in the Connection. Of course, Webb needed to assess me as well, and he put me through a series of interviews. Early on I sensed that he wanted me to join the team, but he never offered me the job. He knew instinctively the hard sell would not work with me. So he kept answering questions, and brought Rose down for a house-hunting trip, and answered more questions. His approach was soft and easy all the way, until I was convinced I wanted the job. He waited for me to say I wanted to work for him. That's how Webb Elliot closed the deal on me.

CHAPTER 3

I DID NOT SETTLE INTO MY NEW JOB. I arrived like Dorothy arrived in Oz, bedazzled by the new surroundings. There was nothing sinister about it, no Wicked Witches, but I definitely wasn't in Kansas anymore.

On my third day we caught an engineer stealing a DVD player from a marketing closet. The evidence was irrefutable, his brazen overnight theft captured on the security camera, but instead of firing the employee, as I proposed, which would have been standard practice at Liberty Air, Webb settled for having Tommy King, the engineer's boss, give him a lecture.

In my second week, Zola Conti, my executive assistant, made a pass at me. She had taken to wearing low-cut blouses and bending over frequently to give me a friendly view. I ignored the first couple of dips but then called her on it. She confessed and admitted that office romance had not worked for her in the past. I gave her a warning and told her to wear more conservative attire.

To top all that off I learned that the CEO, Webb Elliot, frequently dated Connection employees. It was a practice that would not be tolerated at a public company like Liberty Air, but the Connection was a private software company, and Webb owned seventy percent of the stock.

It was all a bit unnerving, and I had begun to think it was a mistake to join the Connection, but then something showed me that even though I was in a different world, there were intrinsic rewards that couldn't be had at a large company.

Late on Friday of my second week Gwen Raleigh came by my office. She wore white jeans and a black sweater.

"Webb wants to have a special meeting of the core team."

"Okay, where?"

"Not here. It's a short drive. You can follow me."

We drove north on Highway 360 for five miles and came upon the Pennybacker Bridge, which crossed Lake Austin. The rust-colored bridge was dominated by an arched steel span that ran a thousand feet from shore to shore. Sheer rock cliffs rose from the lake on the other side.

Two hundred yards past the bridge we made a U-turn and parked in a small dirt lot, next to a red Ford F-250. We were at the bottom of the hill that formed the rock cliffs on the edge of the lake. Gwen began to change into running shoes.

"Are we going for a jog?" I asked. "I'm not exactly dressed for a workout."

"No, it's a quick walk up the hill." She looked at my khakis and loafers. "You'll be fine, but these heels aren't suitable."

"Seems like an odd place for a meeting."

"I'm sure Webb's got something special in mind. We used to come here all the time when we were in the old office nearby."

She led the way to a small dirt path and set a fast pace, stepping surely around stray rocks. She held her head high as she walked, with shoulders back, arms swinging at her sides.

There were hardwood trees at the base of the hill, but as we climbed they grew scarcer until only the scrawny cedars remained. The hill was not steep, and the path carried us straight up. In a few

minutes we were on top of the cliff, looking out over Lake Austin and the hill country.

We faced south, and the lake ran east to west a hundred feet below. Purple and red cirrus clouds ran across the lowest quarter of the sky to the west. Across the lake lay the Austin Country Club golf course, where a few late players hurried to finish.

Henry Jiwanlal, the VP of business development, sat on a boulder not far from the edge of the cliff, taking in the view and drinking an Amstel Light. Henry was diminutive: small hands, small feet, and small in stature. He was from Toronto, and the first East Indian I ever met who spoke with an American accent, albeit Canadian.

"Where's Tommy?" Gwen asked.

"I'll show you." He picked up a half dozen pebbles and lobbed them over the side.

"Hey!" came a shout from below. "Cut it out."

Gwen and I scampered over to the edge. There was a lip at the top that curved in, and when I first looked I didn't see anyone, only the lake directly below. After a few seconds a huge hand and wrist came into view on the right, twenty feet down. Tommy King climbed surely and in another minute he had scrambled to the top and paused to catch his breath.

"Isn't that dangerous?" I asked.

He ignored me and walked over to get more Amstels out of a cooler at Henry's feet.

"He's been climbing that wall for years," Gwen told me.

Tommy handed me a beer and offered one to Gwen.

"No, thanks," she said. "I'm working out after."

In contrast to Henry, Tommy was massive, six-eight or six-nine, and close to three hundred pounds. He was a Texan, raised in Belmont, just sixty miles from Austin, and was VP of technical presales.

"Where's Webb?" Tommy finally spoke.

"Can't you be still for one damn minute?" Henry said. "We're witnessing a majestic sight, and you're in a hurry. Just sit your fat ass down and enjoy it."

Tommy shrugged and sat next to Henry; Tommy was twice as big. Henry was wrapped in a parka to protect his skinny frame from the chill. Tommy wore only a polo shirt.

A lone ski boat motored under the bridge. To our left the lake meandered toward downtown, miles in the distance. To our right it disappeared around a curve a half mile upstream. There was no breeze, but it was cool, and I was glad to be wearing a windbreaker.

Ten minutes later Webb came up the hill carrying a small cooler and a brown sack. He wore a brushed-leather bomber jacket and aviator sunglasses. When he reached us he pulled chilled bottles of Dom Pérignon from the cooler.

"You brought the good stuff," Henry said, rubbing his hands and bouncing with excitement.

"It's a special day for our merry band, Henry." Webb opened a bottle and poured it into five crystal flutes.

"What's the occasion?" asked Gwen.

"We're here to formally welcome Joe to the core team," said Webb. He turned toward me. "It was only the four of us for a long while, ever since Slim left."

"Who is Slim?" I asked.

"Never mind that," said Henry. "We don't want to spoil the moment."

Webb raised his glass in my direction. "Of course, we need your help with the IPO, but that is not the top priority."

"Damn right," said Henry.

"You curse too much," said Tommy.

"The point is," Webb said, "the four of us are focused on growth." He indicated Gwen, Henry, Tommy, and himself. "Joe, you will give

us balance, monitor our progress, and keep us moving in the right direction. You will help the Connection achieve its true potential."

Gwen winked at me and smiled her crooked smile. I wondered if they had all known the purpose of the special meeting.

"To Joe." Webb lifted his glass to me in toast. "Welcome to the family."

"To Joe," the small chorus responded in unison.

It surprised me. At Liberty Air I seldom heard expressions of personal warmth. Webb walked to the edge and took in the view. He turned to address us all.

"Let's be honest," Webb said. "We're egotists. We believe that with the right team we can accomplish anything, more than anyone else. We know this to be true."

Henry and Tommy stood stock still, mesmerized. Gwen bit her lip and watched closely.

"That is a special feeling. We have to pause, at times like this, and cherish it."

The four of them had spent eight long years together, laboring through the grueling process of birthing a company, nurturing it, correcting it, giving it their lives until finally it grew into a thriving business. I had joined much later, after the birthing pains were over, but still, I was now a part of it, a critical player on the core team, and the feeling of belonging bubbled within me like the champagne in the flute.

I raised my glass. "To the Connection."

"To the Connection!" the chorus sounded.

We were the core team of Connection Software, the darling of Austin, and we were invincible, on a rapid trajectory to greatness, and for an hour, I forgot I was in it for the money.

We sat on boulders and watched the sun set. The golfers and boaters had turned in. The western horizon grew pale yellow, and the first stars appeared. A hawk circled below, scanning the lake for an

evening meal. We sat without talking for a long while, no one wanting to end the moment.

Finally Henry spoke. "We few . . . eh, Webb?"

"We happy few," Webb replied.

* * *

THE SUN HAD SET by the time I got home. When I entered the house from the garage Chandler and Callie shouted, "Daddy, Daddy, Daddy!" and ran the length of the hall to spring into my arms. They had the faces of sisters, with the same oval shape and small noses of their mom. Chandler had Rose's dark Hispanic complexion and hair, while Callie was blond, with golden eyes like mine.

I carried both girls into the kitchen and put them down to give Rose a kiss. I buried my face in her neck; no perfume, only the residue of sweat from her afternoon workout. She wore a T-shirt and stretch pants, topped with an apron.

We exchanged news of our respective days while she finished sautéing mushrooms and spinach.

"I heard something today," I said, "an expression. 'We few, we happy few.' Do you know it?"

Rose had a Bachelor of Arts in English from Southern Methodist University, and I thought the saying might be a literary reference.

She cocked an eyebrow and repeated the line. "'We few, we happy few.'" She said the line several more times while searching through memories from a decade ago.

"It's Shakespeare," she said finally. "It's from a monologue in one of the histories, King John maybe, or a Henry."

I made a mental note to check the quote on the Internet, but then forgot about it.

CHAPTER 4

THE LIMO DROPPED US AT THE BRAZOS STREET ENTRANCE of the Driskill Hotel. It is the oldest fine hotel in Austin, with brick sidewalks surrounding the façade, arches over the windows, and Texas and American flags flying above the entrance.

Rose wore a little black dress purchased for the occasion, and I wore a rented tux. A short line of similarly attired employees and their dates waited to get past the reception committee. Webb had told me the annual Connection Ball would be the best party Austin had ever seen.

"Joe Robbins is here," announced one of the company's recruiters as we reached the front of the line. She wore a teal evening gown and pinned a boutonniere on my lapel. "You must be Rose," she said, with a welcoming smile. She gave Rose a corsage while another recruiter checked our names off a list.

Webb stood in the tile entryway, eager to greet us, looking regal in a fine-point black tuxedo and gold bow tie. He leaned in to give Rose a kiss on the cheek and ignored me completely. "I'm so glad you've come." He clung to her hand and looked directly into her eyes. "I know Joe's work schedule is a strain on you and the girls. Thank you for that sacrifice, and please, please . . . do have a grand evening."

He left Rose a little flustered and motioned urgently to a hotel assistant who was standing by. "Tony, Tony, get Joe and Rose a drink. Right away. I don't want them to wait a minute." He turned to greet the next guest in line.

"*¡Híjole!*" Rose declared as she began to follow Tony. "That Webb Elliot could sell anything to anybody."

"Told you."

The T-shaped lobby was grandiose, decorated in a luxurious Southwestern style, with white columns and ornate furniture. Centered in the ceiling at the top of the T was an inverted stained-glass dome, decorated with soft reds and yellows and carefully placed white Lone Stars.

Tony walked us up a half flight of stairs to the Longhorn Bar and asked us to wait.

Fifty-odd employees and their dates, in tuxedos and party dresses, talked all at once. A solo pianist played lively jazz, and small groups sat in low leather chairs around heavy wooden tables. The carpet was plush and the artwork all western action scenes. Tony soon returned with the drinks.

I had been at the company for three months, and this was the first event where Rose could meet employees. I sipped on the Maker's Mark, a double with lots of ice. The noise was borderline deafening.

"Are you ready for this?" I asked, scanning the bar for a place to start.

Rose took a gulp of her cosmopolitan. "Now or never."

Tommy King made his way through the crowd toward us with Henry Jiwanlal in tow. Tommy was pinched tight into a tuxedo two sizes too small. Henry wore formal tails with jeans, sneakers, and a T-shirt. The shirt had a bow tie and vest pattern on the front.

"Joe Robbins!" said Henry. He put one arm on my shoulder. His

other hand held a drink and he panned it across the room. "Isn't this awesome?"

"It certainly is. Henry, Tommy, meet my wife, Rose."

"Nice to meet you," said Rose, offering her hand.

"My God, it's nice to meet *you*," said Henry. He took her hand and kissed it formally. "'What's in a name? That which we call a rose by any other name would smell as sweet.'"

Rose smiled.

"Sorry," said Henry. "Never met a Rose before. I'm a bit of a Shakespeare nut and couldn't resist."

"You're such a clown," said Tommy. "You even look like a clown with that T-shirt."

"Well, look at you. You're wrapped tighter than a golf ball."

"It was the biggest size they had."

Henry positioned himself between Rose and me, facing the room. He looked out across the crowd, a huge grin on his dark face. He was shorter than Rose by a couple inches. "Hey," he said. "Joe . . . Rose . . . did you check out the models?"

"Excuse me?" said Rose.

"Look at all these gorgeous women."

It was true. There were a dozen stunning women in party dresses scattered throughout the bar.

"See that one?" Henry said, nodding at a redhead in a silver dress. "She was in Victoria's Secret."

She looked vaguely familiar, with high cheekbones, a perfect nose, and lustrous shoulder-length locks. Throughout the room engineers with bad haircuts were drinking and chatting with the women of their dreams.

"There's nothing worse than a party with a bunch of dateless geeks. You remember that incidentals line on the party budget?" Henry said.

"Oh . . ." I said, beginning to comprehend.

"A quarter million will lure of lot of models to a party."

Rose burst out laughing. "You hired models to be dates at the party?"

"Of course," said Henry. "Nothing is too good for the Connection Ball. And speaking of money, Rose, how does it feel to know you're going to be rich?"

"It feels good," said Rose, getting into the spirit. "Really good."

"Doesn't it?" he said. "We're going to make so much fucking money."

"You curse too much," said Tommy.

"Don't worry about it."

I interrupted their banter. "The market's still headed in the right direction."

"It sure is," said Tommy. "The NASDAQ closed at 2484 yesterday. It's up thirteen percent this year." Tommy was a keen observer of the stock market, and he always knew exactly how the theoretical value of the company affected his own stock options.

Tommy was tall enough to see over everyone. He looked toward the entryway of the bar. "Oh . . . there goes Sanjay. Come on, Henry. He's headed upstairs."

"What? Oh, yeah." Henry turned to me. "You know Sanjay Kumar, don't you?"

"Sure." I turned to Rose. "Sanjay's one of our best presales engineers."

"It's kind of embarrassing," said Henry. "We're giving him this huge award tonight for the Chartwell deal, and now he's told us he's leaving to join another company."

"Ouch . . ." I said. "That hurts."

It was a recurring and serious problem. There wasn't enough talent in Austin to fuel the growth needs of all the high-tech companies, so a recruiting war had broken out.

"Don't worry," said Henry. "We'll save him. See you two later."

We watched the two of them move toward the entrance of the bar. They made it only ten feet before Henry was distracted by someone else and stopped to talk. Tommy pulled on his arm until he broke Henry away.

"Henry's so funny," said Rose. "They make an odd pair."

"Yeah, they are funny-looking, but they've been a huge help to me. They've taught me a ton about the company and the industry. Tommy's articulate about technical issues, and Henry has great insight into how people think."

I noticed a bright flash of color on my left and turned to see a blonde standing alone next to us. She was attractive enough to be one of the models, but wasn't. Amanda Sorenson was one of the company recruiters and, like the others, she was young, smart, and enthusiastic. I had seen her with Webb Elliot once, driving out of the garage in his Porsche. I thought they might be dating.

Amanda's eyes darted through the crowd, stopping at different people for only an instant. She wore a midlength azure dress with a plunging neckline, and a single strand of pearls. Her pumps were the same color as the dress, as was her fingernail polish.

Rose leaned toward me and nodded her head in Amanda's direction. "Who's that? One of the paid models?"

"No. She's a recruiter."

"Introduce us."

"Hey, Amanda," I said, loud enough to get her attention.

"Oh . . . hi."

"This is my wife, Rose."

"It's a pleasure," said Rose.

"Hi . . . nice to meet you . . . too." Amanda kept searching the crowd.

"Can I get you a drink?" I asked.

"No, thank you, I'm supposed to talk to someone." She smiled tightly, bit her lip, and turned to scan the bar once more, her eyes

flitting from face to face. Turning back to us, she said, "Maybe he's upstairs in the ballroom. I'd better go check."

When Amanda was out of earshot Rose turned to me. "She seemed anxious. Don't you think?"

"Yes."

"And so young . . ."

"Less than a year out of college. She's probably twenty-three."

"This must be exciting for her, all this glamour and money. When I was her age we were already married, and Chandler was an infant."

Rose seemed a little disappointed, like maybe she had missed out. She looked down into the glass; there was a quarter left.

"None of these women come close to you, babe."

"I'd better not catch any of *them* putting the moves on *you*."

"No one would dare."

"It wouldn't be pretty."

Rose had a jealous streak. I had never told her that Zola Conti made a pass at me at the office. It would have created a tension I didn't need; besides, since that day Zola had been an excellent assistant.

The bar had begun to thin as more people walked upstairs. Rose swallowed the rest of her drink. "Okay. What's next?"

· · ·

WE JOINED THE MIGRATION of the crowd up to the mezzanine level. As we climbed the wide stairs, energizing music rushed down to greet us. Employees talked in loud, excited voices.

Upstairs, spread across the wide carpeted lobby, hundreds of employees and guests were taking in the spectacle. They were clustered in small groups, talking and laughing and drinking. At the center of the lobby stood three majestic ice sculptures: a stallion, a lion, and an eagle. The sculptures faced outward on the sides of a square. At the

fourth side two attendants served Veuve Clicquot from chilled bottles. Waiters in formal short coats and high-waisted trousers served hors d'oeuvres. Well-stocked open bars were scattered throughout, and I picked up fresh drinks.

As we sipped at them I looked at the people immediately around us. I recognized most of the employees but didn't know all their names. The engineers looked uncomfortable in their tuxedos, but the models were at ease in their party attire. Oh . . . there was someone I knew.

"Come this way, Rose," I said. "I want you to meet Jack O'Shea."

Jack wore a white tuxedo with black trim and a green bow tie. His hair was prematurely gray and cropped short; his face was tanned with sharp features. His wife, Sheri, was in a red cocktail dress, with blond curls and a painted-on Marilyn mole. Her eyes flitted around the room as Jack told a joke.

"The post office just recalled their latest stamps. They had pictures of lawyers on them, and people couldn't figure out which side to spit on."

The couple standing next to Jack and Sheri laughed politely. The man was a short, stocky salesman named Benny. His date was busty, a brunette in an off-white dress. We did quick introductions.

"Jack was just telling us how much he loves lawyers," said Benny.

"I think five lawyer jokes in a row are enough," said Sheri as she turned to Jack. "Don't you?"

"Six would be better. What happens when you cross a pig with a lawyer? Nothing—there are some things a pig won't do."

"Okay," said Sheri, now irritated. "That's enough."

"I can't help it," said Jack. "All lawyers are scumbags." He took another gulp of his martini. "I mean it. Gregor Smolnik almost killed the Chartwell deal over some bullshit damages terms."

I gave Rose some background. "Jack just closed a fourteen-million-dollar software deal with Chartwell Insurance."

"I don't like to brag," said Jack, "but it is the biggest deal in the company's history."

"*And* the biggest commission in the company's history," said Benny.

Sheri looked bored and continued to scan the crowd.

"The market's hot," said Jack. "It's there for the taking."

"You make it sound easy," said Rose.

"Not easy . . . no. I worked on that deal for a year, but big deals are available. What a great world. All the object code, documentation, and training materials were delivered by a link in an e-mail. Fourteen million dollars for an e-mail. It's a beautiful thing."

"Who's Gregor Smolnik?" asked Rose.

"He's a scumbag," said Jack.

"Gregor's on the board of directors," I said, "but he's also an attorney who helps out with the big deals."

"He's the one you don't like, right?" said Rose.

The others heard her say it, and I cringed. I didn't need anyone thinking I was critical of a director, but when I looked at Jack, he had a smile on his face.

"Don't worry. No one likes Gregor Smolnik."

Benny shared Jack's smile and said, "No one."

We chatted a few minutes more, and they went to get refills, leaving Rose and me in the middle of the floor.

◦ ◦ ◦

WE WORKED OUR WAY AROUND THE ROOM, and I introduced Rose to a half dozen married employees and their spouses. Many of the spouses were friends with one another, and they welcomed Rose into the extended Connection family.

There was a break in the action, and we stood to watch the roomful of people.

"Look," said Rose, "there's Amanda. She must have found who she was looking for."

They were in a corner of the foyer, Amanda and Slim Bohls, a man I had met only once. Slim's hair was the color of tarnished copper and sprang straight up from his forehead in a pompadour. His face was long, his chin square. He wore a burnt-red smoking jacket with black lapels.

"He's a friend of Webb's," I said. "Slim used to manage R&D for the Connection but he left to start his own Internet video company."

My initial impression of Slim had not been favorable. He struck me as someone who said the right things but never meant them. He was talking fast, and Amanda had a frown on her face. She shook her head. He reached out as if to touch her elbow gently, but she pulled her arm away.

"She doesn't seem to like him much," said Rose.

"No."

The exchange between Amanda and Slim struck me as odd, out of place at a festive occasion, particularly since I thought she might be dating Webb.

The dinner buffet was high-end Texan, with broiled redfish from the Gulf, grass-fed prime rib, grilled vegetables, and three dessert stations. The wait staff whisked empty plates away and kept our wineglasses full. After dinner, there was a brief ceremony to recognize exceptional employees, and then the disco ball began to spin.

An all-girl rock band, the Prom Queens, cranked up the party with a solid cover of The Go-Go's tune "We Got the Beat." Professional dancers in four floating cages jumped and jerked to the music.

Rose moved her shoulders to the beat and looked longingly at the dance floor. It was beginning to fill with engineers and their "dates."

"Come on, babe." She grabbed at my arm. "Let's dance."

"You know I'm not into dancing." I stood still, resisting.

"Well, too bad for you, because *I'm* dancing . . . and *not* by myself."

I was about to acquiesce when Zola stood up from several tables away and walked in our direction. She wore a ruby-colored dress with thin straps and sparkling sequins. Zola had acted professionally ever since I rejected her overture, but I was still nervous about introducing her to Rose. Zola didn't wait for me.

"You must be Rose," she said, as they shook hands. "I'm Zola—Joe's assistant. He talks about you and the girls all the time, but he never said you were gorgeous."

"Oh . . . hi . . ."

"Look at that dress! You're redefining the LBD."

"Thanks. You look great in that color—so festive."

Zola cast a quick smile in my direction and immediately turned her attention back to Rose. Zola was moving to the sound of the drums and the driving guitar. The chorus of "We Got the Beat" began again.

"Don't you love this song?" she asked.

"I do love it," said Rose.

Zola looked me up and down. "As tall as you are, I'm guessing you're not much of a dancer."

"No."

Zola looked back at Rose. "Do you mind dancing with another woman?"

A grin slowly spread across Rose's face. "Not at all."

"Let's party."

I watched them boogie their way to the dance floor. Zola had saved the day.

I walked back out to the foyer. The music was muted by the ballroom doors. About half the attendees had left their dinner tables to mingle in the open space of the mezzanine. Across the room, Gwen Raleigh stood talking with Webb Elliot. She wore a navy blue dress with a metallic sheen that went well with her blond hair. She was tall

but naturally graceful, confident. Webb said something, and Gwen laughed and shook her head.

In the next moment she saw me and then turned back to Webb to say something. Webb looked at me and responded to Gwen. He smiled as he talked, but Gwen wore a studious look. She shook her head slightly, and Webb chuckled. Gwen turned her back to me and talked while Webb listened intently.

I had a strange feeling they were talking about me. I walked toward them, but as I approached Gwen walked away, giving me a quick smile and a nod.

"Enjoying the party?" Webb asked.

"Uh . . . yes." My gaze followed Gwen as she crossed the room. "I'm having a great time."

"I think it's going well. Don't you?"

"It's a big success. Employees' spirits are high."

"Excellent! That's what it's all about really, boosting morale. Many of our engineers work seventy-hour weeks, longer even. The least we can do is to throw them a good party."

Gwen had stopped next to a group of marketing employees. A short man in a tuxedo talked excitedly, and the group burst into laughter. There was a free popcorn station nearby, and the man had a bag in his hand. He began tossing pieces high in the air for his colleagues to catch. The first two people missed, but Gwen caught hers easily.

"Gwen and I were just talking about the new marketing program," Webb said.

The remark grabbed my attention.

Webb took a sip from a glass of water. "She's quite concerned you're going to ask her to cut spending."

"It occurred to me. Marketing expenses are up over a hundred percent in the last year."

Webb's eyes were absorbing the crowd as we talked, darting from group to group. He waved and nodded at someone across the room and then turned back to me.

"You know that old cliché, 'You have to spend money to make money'? Well, in this case it might be true. If we can get this Internet marketing program to work, it will reduce our distribution costs dramatically."

"Hypothetically, I'm sure it's okay, but in the meantime we're spending a fortune on lead generation."

"I'm not telling you to ignore it. You should review the spending closely. That's your job. But conceptually I'm on board with the program. I told Gwen to share the plan with you. If her logic is sound, I'm sure you'll want to proceed."

"Okay. I just want to make sure we've got the proper controls in place."

"Of course. All right, that's enough talk about work."

Webb's attention was drawn away. Jack O'Shea's wife, Sheri, the one with the Marilyn Monroe look, walked past us and smiled. Her gaze lingered on Webb, and for a moment I thought she was going to stop, but she kept going, swinging a small purse at her side. She was hard to ignore; Webb and I watched as she walked by. At one end of the foyer were doors that led to an open-air balcony overlooking Sixth Street. Sheri pushed through the doors and went outside.

Webb turned to me. "I'm so glad that you and Rose could come tonight. Is she having a good time?"

"Definitely. Right now she's dancing with Zola."

"Really? That's tremendous. Did Rose meet some new people?"

"You bet. Many employees . . . and some spouses. She's already gotten an invitation to lunch."

"Excellent! Now, if you'll excuse me, I need to mingle a bit."

"Sure thing. I'll see you later."

I picked up a beer and ambled around the party for a while, stopping to chat with finance employees. I had focused on Rose for most of the party and needed to show my team some attention. When the beer was finished I headed back toward the ballroom.

On the way I saw Sheri O'Shea walk in from the balcony. She glanced from left to right and headed straight for the ladies' room. I slowed my pace. Her hair was mussed, and the hemline of her red dress rode higher on one leg. She paused to adjust it.

I looked across the foyer to see Jack O'Shea chatting with some of his sales buddies. Uh-oh . . .

As soon as Sheri entered the restroom, Webb walked in through the same door from the balcony. I turned my head quickly so he wouldn't see that I had noticed him coming in after Sheri. In another moment he crossed my field of vision, hurrying to talk with someone else. For the first time I had actual data to back up the rumors; in addition to being a brilliant software executive, Webb was a ladies' man.

It was a bizarre reality of my new world. Building the Connection had required unique powers of persuasion, the ability to sell software, attract investors, and recruit executives. Apparently, Webb also used those powers to seduce women. So be it. As long as it didn't interfere with the business, it was not my affair.

Back in the ballroom I found Rose and Zola standing by our table. Zola had come to the ball alone but was still having a good time. She talked nonstop and laughed at the engineers who tried to keep pace with models on the dance floor.

Scouting around the room, I saw Amanda Sorenson again, this time standing alone next to one of the ballroom exits. Her shoulders were slumped, and her arms hung listlessly by her sides. She dabbed a tissue at her eyes, then wiped her nose and turned to leave the room. Zola looked in her direction just as Amanda walked out.

"Is she involved with Webb?" I asked.

"Amanda Sorenson? No. Nobody dates Webb Elliot long-term." Zola took a sip from her wine. "They may have gone out a few times, though." She moved from side to side as the Prom Queens played a slow song. "Yeah, a lot of girls have dated Webb, off and on."

There was something in Zola's tone that warned me not to press for more details.

* * *

Rose and I decided to tour Sixth Street before calling the limo to take us home. Her words had gotten a little slurry; fresh air would help revive her. As we crossed the tiled lobby, Rose walked ahead and exaggerated her sway for my benefit.

Connection employees and their dates sat at small tables in the lobby, having coffee and quiet conversation.

As we walked through the front door, the clip-clop of a horse-drawn carriage drew near. We stepped down to the brick sidewalk and turned left. In the middle of the sidewalk, just outside the entrance to the hotel, was an azure pump with a three-inch heel lying on its side.

"Look at that," Rose said. "Someone's lost her shoe. It's like Cinderella." She turned to look at the carriage. "Where is she?"

Just then the shoe's twin dropped on the sidewalk, almost hitting Rose. At first I thought someone on the balcony above us was throwing their clothes over the side, but when Rose turned to look, she drew a quick breath. The smile on her face disappeared, instantly replaced by fear.

I hurried to look, my pulse quickening.

Above the sidewalk in front of the Driskill was the large balcony that extended out from the ballroom-level floor. Above that, a second balcony extended from a master suite on the fourth floor. Standing on

the concrete rail of that higher balcony, in her azure dress and bare feet, was Amanda Sorenson.

I stared at her without blinking. I raised my hands, palms open, every muscle in my body tense.

She stared straight ahead and took the ballerina's first position, her arms circled in front. She did a plié and then lifted her right leg straight up in a stretch; her raised hand touched the heel of her foot. She had replaced the strand of pearls around her neck with a thick, dark choker.

My heart pounded at my ears.

"Amanda!" I shouted, stepping closer. "Get back from there. It's dangerous."

She must be drunk, but no . . . she didn't appear drunk; her movements were sure, but at the same time dreamlike.

The carriage behind us stopped, and concerned voices talked in whispers. Passersby pointed. For the first time Amanda noticed that others were nearby. She looked down at Rose and me and smiled.

"Step back!" I shouted again. My throat was dry, my voice hoarse. "Amanda! Step back."

But she didn't. She smiled at me again, gave the slightest wave, and jumped. As she began to fall her dress floated around her thighs.

I lunged forward with arms outstretched, as if to catch a child.

A sickening snap sounded, like a flag blowing in a stiff breeze, only lower and dull. The woman in the carriage screamed. Amanda Sorenson hung between the two balconies; what I thought was a choker around her neck was actually a rope. An acid feeling rushed through me. The pounding in my ears moved to my brain and pressed against my skull. The sound I had heard was the rope snapping taut.

She made a grim spectacle in the light from a nearby lamp. Her feet quivered a few seconds and were still. Those pretty white arms

hung to the side. Her blond hair covered her face. Inanely, I wondered if her toenails were painted the same azure color as her dress and shoes and fingernails.

More screams came from the street, and people ran toward us. Rose was on her knees, her face buried in her hands, rocking. I reached for her arm, pulled her up and into the lobby and sat her down in a chair.

"Stay here," I said.

Her face was a blank. "What?"

I leaned in close. "Stay here!"

She blinked and nodded.

I grabbed the concierge, and we ran to the elevator. As the doors were closing, Gwen Raleigh rushed in.

"What's going on?" she asked. "I heard screams."

"Amanda Sorenson hanged herself." My voice was shaky.

"What? No! What are you talking about?"

"We've got to do something . . . maybe . . . maybe we can do something."

When the elevator doors opened, the three of us sprinted down the hall. The suite was unlocked; it was set up as a party room. Inside, the door to the balcony was open. Wispy curtains on the left swayed in the breeze. The curtains on the right were tied back with a thick rope.

Outside on the balcony the concierge and I hauled on the rope together. After three pulls I reached over the rail, wound my arms behind Amanda's back and under her armpits.

People watched from the street below. My cheek brushed against her ear; her hair was soft, like a child's, her perfume subtle and flowery. A siren sounded nearby. With a heave we fell in a pile on the balcony. Amanda's dress was above her waist, exposing a black thong and a rose tattoo on the outside of her hip. The red petals and green leaves were bright; they glistened like fresh paint. The rose had been recently inked.

I loosened the rope around her neck as Gwen pulled Amanda's dress down to cover her knees. As I looked at Amanda's lifeless body I almost froze, overwhelmed. I blinked twice and took a deep breath.

Together we performed CPR for the seven minutes it took the EMS team to arrive and take over. They called the vehicle to get the AED ready and hauled Amanda away.

Gwen and I stared at each other.

"My . . . oh my . . .," the concierge said. "This is awful. This is just awful."

"It's horrible," said Gwen. "Why would she do that?"

I shook my head. I had no answers, and there were no more actions to take.

CHAPTER 5

LIEUTENANT RICO CARRILLO was in his early forties, of medium height, and in good shape. His skin was light brown, and his hair wiry and black with a tinge of gray around the temples.

He arrived fifteen minutes later and was all business. He sealed the room and called for a forensics team. He questioned the uniformed police and sent them to find witnesses on the street. He spent five minutes with the concierge, ten with Gwen, and then came to see me.

"Good evening, Mr. Robbins. I'm sorry to keep you so late." Carrillo spoke English with no discernible accent.

"This is a terrible thing. I want to help in any way I can."

"You are a quick thinker, Mr. Robbins. I commend you for your actions. Unfortunately, Ms. Sorenson was pronounced dead at the hospital."

"I was afraid of that."

"Why?" Carrillo was quick with his questions.

"The rope was tied securely, and she fell eight or ten feet."

"Did you find a note of any kind or anything else in the room?"

"No, I already told the other policeman that."

Carrillo looked up from his notes. His eyes surprised me; they were pale, almond colored, and the left was flawed, with a black wedge

that ran from the pupil to the outer edge of the iris. My cousin has a similar flaw in his eye and explains it to me every time we meet; it's called a sectoral heterochromia.

"Sometimes witnesses remember details after some reflection," Carrillo said.

"Of course."

"What is your role at the company?"

"I'm the chief financial officer."

"How long have you worked for Connection Software?"

"Just three months."

"Where were you before?"

"I worked for Liberty Airlines, in Dallas."

"Did you know Amanda Sorenson well?"

"No, not really. She was one of the cheerleaders."

"Cheerleaders?"

"Sorry, I mean recruiters. At the Connection we call the recruiters 'cheerleaders' because they also work to boost the morale of the employees."

"I see."

Carrillo asked for what else I thought might be relevant, and I described the various times I had seen Amanda during the course of the evening.

"So you saw Ms. Sorenson three times tonight: first in the Longhorn Bar where she was looking for someone, second in the lobby of the mezzanine talking with Mr. Bohls, and the last time alone, when she might have been crying."

"Yes."

"Do you know what her relationship was with Mr. Bohls?"

"No. No idea."

"Okay, Mr. Robbins, that's all I need for now. Can you give me your phone number? In case we have follow-up questions."

I recited my contact information.

"Here," he said. "Take my card as well. In a suicide investigation we work to verify the motive. Call me if you hear anything useful."

"Sure."

As we rode home, Rose and I spoke in low voices. The buoyant atmosphere of the party had been shattered. It was cool in the limo, and she leaned against me.

"What could drive her to do such a thing?" Rose asked.

"I don't know."

"She was so young. She took such care to look nice for the party. Why would she kill herself?"

"I'm sure we'll learn something soon."

* * *

"I THOUGHT NOTHING BAD WOULD EVER HAPPEN," Webb said.

It was early Monday morning, and I found him in his office dressed in his standard uniform: crisp blue jeans, an expensive dress shirt. His hair was immaculate, his face clean shaven. He sat straight up in the chair, staring at a blank whiteboard on the opposite wall, his eyes red from crying.

"Are you all right?" I sat down tentatively.

He glanced at me and shook his head. "We hire these young people, brilliant and wonderful. I never expected it—something like this. We're building something new, something great, but still . . . we encounter tragedy."

"Have you heard anything from Lieutenant Carrillo?"

He stood and walked to the window overlooking Highway 360, and then, just as quickly, he returned to the desk and sat down again.

"Nobody knows why she did it," he said, frustrated. "Henry gave

her a difficult performance review last week. Her father has prostate cancer. It might even have been me."

"What do you mean?"

"She and I went out a few times, socially. I told her up front that I don't get serious with anyone, and she seemed to accept that condition. But who knows, really, what a person is thinking."

He seemed disappointed with himself, as if he should have been able to read Amanda's mind.

⁂

I MET WITH AMANDA'S PARENTS a week later in a small conference room to go through some paperwork. They were second-generation Swedish-American: tall, slender, with angular faces and blond hair.

They were deflated, as if all the energy had been drained of their bodies. Like most successful couples they were used to removing obstacles to their happiness, but here was the worst thing that could happen, and it had no solution.

Eric Sorenson said little. He sat in the corner and studied me, listening to every word of the conversation I had with his wife.

Krystyn's approach suggested her primary goal was to get through the meeting in one piece. She tried to make it an administrative task, with items to be checked off. We discussed the company-provided life insurance, 401(k) account information, and tax forms. They had boxed up Amanda's personal things from her cubicle and also artifacts from the shrine employees erected. There was one more item on my list.

"Have you heard anything from Lieutenant Carrillo?"

Krystyn sat back in the chair, eyes open wide, unable to respond. She picked up her purse and pulled out a packet of tissues, even though a box was on the table before her.

Eric finally leaned forward. "Mr. Robbins."

"Please call me Joe."

There was a catch in his throat, and he paused to clear it. "You seem like an honest man, so let me tell you the truth."

Krystyn hunched down with the tissue, sobbing quietly.

Eric put an arm around her and continued. "Something is not right here. We know our daughter. We know Amanda. Amanda was strong."

I nodded respectfully and kept silent.

"Amanda did not take her own life because of a poor performance review. She did not kill herself because I have cancer. And she did not commit suicide because she was jilted by the CEO. Something is not right here."

Krystyn was unable to sit; her shoulders sank to the side, and her legs started sliding out from the chair. Her face lost form, scrunching up impossibly. She emitted small, whimpering noises, and Eric reached to support her.

He repeated himself. "Something is not right here."

Eric's conviction was disturbing. I had not slept well since the suicide. My dreams had been invaded by images and sounds: Amanda stepping off the rail, her dress floating around her thighs, and the snap of the rope pulling taut.

CHAPTER 6

IT WAS DARK AND COOL in the bowling alley. Eighties disco music played over the speakers. I stood at the top of the lane and stared down at the tenpins at the other end. If I threw the ball hard enough, and fast enough, it would shatter them into oblivion. Three quick steps, wind the fourteen-pound ball all the way back, and hurl it in the air. It sailed fifteen feet, pounded the hardwoods, and rushed to hit the head pin dead on, creating a small explosion. Two pins remained standing, an impossible split.

I turned around to see Henry Jiwanlal grinning. Tommy King shook his head. My next try followed the same trajectory and hit no pins.

"You know," said Tommy, as he stood up to take his turn, "the goal is not to see how far the ball can fly."

The overhead screen showed my final tally: eighty-seven. I didn't care about the score. It had been two weeks since Amanda Sorenson's suicide, and I had been haunted by the specter of her fall and the meeting with her parents.

Tommy calmly stood at the top of the lane and eyed the pins over the ball he held before him. He was tall but he was also strong;

muscles bulged in his arms and legs. Tommy's was not a typical bowler's physique.

He took three small steps, then two long steps. His arm swung out to the side, and his hand twisted up as he released, creating action on the ball. Hopping on his left leg, he watched the ball careen in and create a flurry of flying pins that knocked one another down, a strike. On his next try he missed one pin and then he quickly picked up the spare.

"It's your turn, Henry," Tommy said.

"Why don't you bowl for me? It will certainly help my score."

"That wouldn't be honest."

"Shit, I didn't want to come anyway."

In contrast to Tommy, Henry was weak and lacked coordination. He walked over to the return, picked up an eight-pounder, and threw two gutter balls in quick succession. On the way back he shook his head.

"What a stupid game," he said, "fucking waste of time."

"Stop cursing so much," said Tommy, looking over his shoulder. "There are children in here."

It was eleven o'clock on a Saturday morning. The alley was half-full with soccer moms and kids who had come to celebrate birthdays. Henry looked at the group two lanes away; seven boys, about ten years old, were pushing one another to get their hands on slices of pizza.

"Shit. Those kids curse more than I do."

"That's the last frame," said Tommy, looking up at the screen. He had scored two twenty-three and Henry had a thirty-four; we were a lopsided group. "You guys ready for another game?"

"Go ahead," said Henry. "We're going to the snack bar for a beer."

"All right. I want to see if I can break two fifty. I'll be up in fifteen minutes."

They were about as different as two men could be. Henry's ears stuck out, and his eyes were small and bright behind glasses. Tommy's

eyes protruded from deep holes in his skull and were a dull gray, the eyelids naturally half-shut. Tommy seldom spoke and sat resolutely still for long periods of time, while Henry jabbered and bobbed next to him.

Before Webb had hired him, Henry had studied theater at Carnegie Mellon; eight years later he was running the Connection's business development group. Tommy was an engineering graduate of MIT and ran technical presales. Henry was the idea man, the dreamer, while Tommy brought the ideas to life. Together their teams created the demand that fed the sales executives.

Henry and Tommy had taught me everything I knew about our product: customer relationship management (CRM) software. They were polar opposites, a corporate duo who complemented each other in every way. Whenever I saw one of them, I also saw the other. Their staunch support of the Connection was legendary inside the company and had even earned them a nickname: employees called them the Zealots.

At the combo bar and grill, Henry ordered two Shiners. The air smelled of old hot dogs and popcorn. Every few seconds another bowling ball crashed into the pins.

"Look at that," said Henry. "He's gotten another strike. You wouldn't think a genius like Tommy could bowl. Did you know he got a perfect sixteen hundred on the SAT?"

"Someone mentioned that to me." There were many such stories of brilliance at the Connection, but I didn't want to talk about geniuses. I was preoccupied with Amanda's suicide.

I had two daughters of my own. To lose Chandler or Callie was unthinkable; to not know why would be a pain beyond comprehension, but there was even more to concern me than the Sorensons' loss. In the back of my mind there was a nagging sensation that something sinister had propelled Amanda's action, something to do with the Connection.

Lieutenant Carrillo had asked me to call with anything useful, but I had nothing to report. For the first week the suicide was all anyone could talk about at the office, and I paid close attention. By the second week the talk began to quiet down. I found myself raising the subject with Amanda's friends to see what they had learned, but there was nothing new. After a few days, I sensed that even they wanted to move on, but I couldn't let it go. More than once Zola found me sitting in my office staring out the window.

"Why do you think Amanda did it?" I asked Henry, for the third time.

"I don't think we'll ever know."

"There must have been a reason. If you could have seen her parents . . . they were devastated. They were so sure of her."

"How can you get inside the head of a dead girl?"

"If only I had the right data, I could figure it out. Maybe that would help the Sorensons handle their grief. Are you sure it had nothing to do with the feedback you gave her?"

"No chance. She wasn't that concerned about it. If anything she was apathetic. She gave me a halfhearted response, said she appreciated the constructive criticism, and then got up and left."

"I can't imagine it was her father's illness," I said. "Prostate cancer is not usually terminal. Maybe it had something to do with dating Webb."

"Look, we went over this before. They only dated a few times, eh, and then Webb ended it. He never stays with anyone for long, and she knew that."

"There is a reason. I just haven't figured it out yet."

After he finished his game, Tommy came up and got a beer. He immediately began watching a fishing show on the television mounted on the wall.

I had talked to employees who knew Amanda, but there was one person I hadn't seen.

"What about Slim Bohls?" I asked Henry.

Tommy interrupted. "Slim Bohls is an asshole." It was unusual for him to curse, but his eyes flashed anger. His upper body was tense, and his hands clenched into fists.

"It's okay," said Henry. "Joe was asking *me* about Slim. I got it."

Tommy took a large gulp of beer and turned his attention back to the television.

Henry looked at me and lowered his voice. "Tommy hates Slim. In the early days of the Connection the two of them went after the same girl. Neither of them succeeded, but Slim did something that irked Tommy, and he still harbors a grudge."

Tommy sat hunched over the bar. His polo shirt was stretched across thick back muscles. He was the wrong kind of guy to piss off.

"What did you want to know about Slim Bohls?" Henry asked.

"There is something about how he touched Amanda the night of the ball that keeps nagging me. Do you think he had something going with her?"

"You mean like intimacy?"

"Yeah, like that."

"Fuck, no!"

The bartender looked up from wiping the counter on the other side of the snack bar.

"Dude," he said. "Keep it down, will you? We get kids in here on Saturday morning."

"Sure. Sorry about that." Henry lowered his voice. "There's no way Slim was screwing Amanda Sorenson. Chicks call him the Slime Ball. They all find him disgusting. Even strippers won't get naked for him."

"Well, he was talking to her about something."

"It wasn't their sex life; I guarantee you that. The only way a woman would have sex with Slim is if he put a gun to her head."

It was frustrating. I believed in logic and numbers, cause and effect. People don't kill themselves randomly.

On the other side of Henry, Tommy watched a professional angler haul up a huge bass.

Henry looked up at the television. "Damn," he said, "look at the size of that fish."

"It's a bass," Tommy said. "They're on Lake Conroe, outside of Houston. Hey, maybe we should . . ."

Their conversation receded into background noise. I stared at the empty beer glass before me. I closed my eyes and watched as Amanda Sorenson did her ballet moves on top of the balcony; she took first position, did the plié, and then stepped off the rail. Over and over again I heard the sickening snap of the rope.

"Joe . . . Joe!" Henry shook my arm.

"What?"

"You sort of faded out on us. Come on. We're taking off."

We walked out of the alley into the bright sunshine. The three of us stopped, and Henry put his hand on my shoulder.

"You've got to let this go, buddy," he said. "It's not healthy."

I looked from one of them to the other.

"There's got to be a reason," I said.

"I'm sure there is," Henry said, "and maybe someday you will figure it out. In the meantime you have a lot of people counting on you."

I knew he was right. My work at the office was piling up: hundreds of e-mails, dozens of calls.

Henry continued. "You're the CFO. You've got reports to review, deals to sign, and numbers to crunch. If we're going to get this IPO off the ground we need your head in the game one hundred percent."

I looked over at Tommy. He nodded slowly. "The Connection needs you."

We each went to our respective cars. There was no shade in the parking lot, and inside my Lexus it was over ninety degrees. I sat and waited for the AC to kick in.

Yes, Henry was right. I had to let it go and focus on the work. We had a company to run and an IPO to manage.

Bad things happen, but the corporate train rolls on, and I still wanted the money.

CHAPTER 7

I HIT A BUTTON on the laptop, and the summary slide appeared on the screen.

"Revenues totaled fifty-five million for the quarter and were up sixty percent year over year."

It was the third Friday in July. Webb had asked me to begin our weekly executive meeting with a review of quarterly results. Eight of us were in a conference room on the seventh floor. In addition to the core team, the directors for product development, customer service, and human resources also attended the meeting.

"Profits climbed sixty-five percent, and cash flow was strong," I continued. "Those numbers are excellent."

"Hot damn," Henry interrupted. "Let's go public next month."

"I agree," said the director of customer service. "We should strike while the iron is hot."

Several people around the table spoke up, all in agreement, and I lost control of the conversation. Webb let the chaos reign, but only for a few seconds.

"Please, please," he said. "Everyone is talking at once." The room quieted instantly. "Our year-on-year performance was solid. There's

no question about that, but let Joe tell us how we did versus the first quarter."

I clicked to the next slide.

"The Chartwell deal closed in the first quarter. At fourteen million dollars it was our biggest deal ever, but it has resulted in an irregular top line. Revenues were down ten percent from the first quarter to the second, and profits were down twenty-five percent."

The group's enthusiasm waned.

"And what do the bankers have to say about that?" Webb asked me.

"We interviewed six investment banks to lead the IPO, and they all said the same thing. Because of our history of lumpy revenue we need two to three quarters of sequential growth before we can launch a home-run IPO."

I had everyone's attention again.

"Wait a minute," Henry said. "Define home run."

I couldn't keep the grin off my face. "North of a two-billion-dollar valuation."

Tommy whistled. Everyone in the room immediately reached for their laptops, except Henry, who began punching buttons on the calculator function of his cell phone. I knew what they were doing: calculating their personal net worth at a two-billion valuation.

Webb didn't need to. His math was easy: Seventy percent of two billion is one-point-four billion dollars. I had run my own numbers two weeks earlier—after the banker meetings. At two billion my grant was worth eighteen million. The other executives had built their own spreadsheets long ago and were hunched over their laptops, contemplating the results. All except Henry, who became increasingly frustrated.

"Damn it," he swore. "Who's got a calculator?"

He was sitting next to Tommy, who stared at his screen. Henry grabbed at Tommy's machine. "What is that? Let me see that."

Webb burst out laughing. Everybody looked up and gradually realized they were all doing the same thing. Gwen grinned sheepishly. Henry started giggling, and soon we were all enjoying a raucous celebration of our own greed. When the noise subsided, Webb took control of the meeting again.

"Team, you're all going to make piles of money. That's brilliant. Nothing would please me more. But first we have to put together some great quarters. So let's move on. And by the way, let's deliver twenty great quarters, not just three or four. The IPO is not the end goal. It's just a milestone."

Everyone was on the same page, so we got down to work. We reviewed the sales pipeline, the product road map, and the latest attrition figures.

"How is Sanjay Kumar?" Webb asked Tommy. "Did the new equity grant re-energize him?"

Sanjay Kumar had personally constructed the demo that won the Chartwell deal. He was from India and had a reputation for playing poker when he wasn't writing software. When Sanjay had threatened to resign, Henry and Tommy had convinced him to stay, but it had taken a sizable option grant.

"He's like a new man," Tommy said. "Works around the clock."

"No more talk of leaving?" Webb asked.

"None. He's here to stay."

"Good. Good. Gwen, give us the latest results on the new marketing campaign."

Gwen stood to give her presentation. She wore navy slacks and a white sleeveless crewneck. I was momentarily distracted. For the first time I realized I was physically attracted to Gwen. She and Rose were so different; Gwen was less curvy, more athletic, and had short blond hair, but the combined elements were compelling.

Concentrate! You're married.

There was something wrong with the presentation. All of Gwen's charts emphasized the positives, the up arrows. There was no mention of the exorbitant cost.

"How is the program's spending versus plan?" I asked.

"Um, just a second."

She fumbled with pieces of paper on the table before her.

"I'll tell you," I said. "Program spending is a million dollars above plan for the first six months."

She quit trying to find the numbers and stood up straight.

"Are you challenging the marketing strategy?" she said.

"No, I'm saying you don't have control over spending."

The room became quiet. Gwen stared at me, her breathing uneven. I could have let it go at that, but the CFO has a job to do.

"Did the extra cost result in more leads than forecast?" I asked.

"Not really," she confessed. "But the price for advertising on the Web was higher than we projected."

"Then the cost to generate a lead is more than was in your model. Isn't it?"

Gwen glared at me, not answering.

I kept the pressure on. Out-of-control costs would be a red flag to potential investors. We needed to cut the marketing spend. "Does the model still generate lower distribution costs than our current sales process?"

"Actually, it's a little higher," she said, "but we're generating more volume."

"The plan's not working," I concluded. "We have to change something."

Gwen's face turned red. She squared her shoulders in my direction.

"What do you know about it?" she fired back.

"I know the spending is too high, and it's going to stick out when we try to go public."

"Don't be an idiot."

"He's right, Gwen," Webb said, interrupting us. He paused a few seconds to let her cool down. "The inside sales strategy is showing promise, but the distribution cost is too high, and the price points on the deals are too low. You have to revise the plan."

"We could change the product configuration," offered Henry.

"We'll never make deployments successful at low prices," said Tommy.

"We should reduce spending in the meantime," I said.

"Enough . . . please." Webb cut us off. "We're wandering all over the place. Gwen, you have the action item. Work with your team and come back with a revised strategy. And work with Joe to get control over expenses."

. . .

AFTER WORK THAT DAY, an ad hoc group asked me to join them downtown for dinner and drinks. These invitations came frequently, and I usually declined. I was working sixty-hour weeks and tried to reserve weekends for Rose and the kids; however, the quarter-end pace had been frantic as we scrambled to get all the deals signed and the books closed. A night off to socialize with the team was overdue.

I called Rose from the car.

"Hey, babe," she answered. "You on the way home?"

"Ah, what do you think of me having dinner in town tonight?"

"Shoot. I thought we'd watch a movie after the kids go to bed."

"We could still do that. I'll just have a couple drinks. Be home by nine o'clock."

"I doubt that. Last time it was after midnight."

"I don't have to go. I can come straight home." I waited for her response; if she really needed me at home, she would tell me.

"No. You go ahead, but you owe me a nice dinner."

"You got it, and I'll be good tonight. I promise."

"Take a taxi if you drink much."

"Love you."

"Love you too."

. . .

AFTER DINNER WE WENT TO BUFFALO BILLIARDS on Sixth Street, a combination pool hall and drinking spot for an eclectic singles crowd. We headed straight for the oval-shaped bar. Half the room was dedicated to pool tables lit with old-fashioned hanging lamps.

A group of Connection employees was drinking heavily, with Webb leading the way. He was usually cautious with the booze but must have felt like partying, because he kept buying rounds. Webb asked if I wanted a shot, but I declined and sipped on a Grey Goose martini instead. My goal was to get home before Rose went to sleep.

Four young engineers, fresh out of college, sat next to me at the bar and argued about the quality of top-tier universities. One kid bragged that MIT's computer science program was better than Carnegie Mellon's. They were a highly intelligent group; I could tell by the level of discourse and the speed of the back-and-forth. Even when they were bullshitting among themselves I had to pay attention to keep up. A strange thought occurred to me as I looked from face to face; I had the lowest IQ of the group, by a fair margin.

They noticed I was listening.

"Where did you go to school, Joe?" an engineer asked.

My alma maters were third- or fourth-tier, but there was no point in dodging the question.

"UT at Arlington for undergrad. I got my MBA at the University of Dallas."

The kid who asked nodded, as if that were interesting, and the conversation moved on to something else.

The rowdy crowd kept doing shots for a while, and then most of the group trudged upstairs to continue the party.

I was about to gulp down the martini when I scanned the bar and saw Slim Bohls standing on the other side. I hadn't seen him in three months. He wore skinny jeans, boots, and a dude cowboy shirt. His tarnished copper pompadour jutted up from his forehead. In my mind I saw Amanda Sorenson yank her arm free from his grasp. I walked over.

As I sat down, he drained his beer, nodded at me, and stood to leave. I held him lightly by the arm; it was thin and weak.

"Let me buy you a beer," I said. "I want to ask you something."

"No, thanks. I was just heading out."

I didn't let go of his arm. Slim turned and saw I was serious. He hesitated and then sat down again. He wore a single diamond stud earring. "What's up?"

I took a sip of the martini. It wasn't hard to see why women called him the Slime Ball. There was something innately unappealing about him; his face was handsome enough, but the cocky pompadour matched his demeanor. Every time Slim spoke I got the feeling he thought he was in control of what would happen.

"You remember the night of the Connection ball, the night Amanda Sorenson committed suicide?"

"Sure."

"I noticed you talking to Amanda, and her shaking her head, early on in the evening."

Slim eyed me casually, as if I were asking about his utility bill.

"Yeah, so?"

"What were you two talking about?"

His eyes were the darkest brown, almost black. They studied me

only briefly. "I already talked to Carrillo four times about that." Slim got up to go, but I grabbed his arm again, tighter this time.

"Please humor me," I asked politely. "I had a rough meeting with her parents, and that image of you arguing with Amanda has been weighing on my mind. I'd like to know what it was about."

Customers continued to come in and add to the noise level. Slim looked at a cute bartender as she walked by to fetch a drink.

"Listen." He lowered his voice and leaned closer. "This is confidential, okay?"

I nodded.

"I was covering for Webb at the ball. You know, trying to keep her occupied so she'd stay away from him. He and Amanda dated for about a month, maybe six weeks. Webb banged her a few times and then told her it was over. She knew that was coming but couldn't accept it. I was trying to help Webb, and Amanda, by talking her through it."

"That's it?"

"Pretty much. I wish there was more I could tell you." Slim hung his head in disappointment. "She was a cute girl," he said. "She had a terrific future. To tell you the truth—and I told Carrillo this—I think she jumped because of Webb." He searched my eyes for a reaction.

I ran my finger over a rough spot on the bar. "I can't believe she would do that. Her parents were so sure of her."

"I'm telling you, man. Webb's got that effect on women. They'll do anything for him." Slim looked at me expectantly.

"You're sure that's all there was to it?"

He shrugged and waited. I couldn't think of anything else to ask. He made to leave, and I did nothing to stop him. Turning to go, he leaned in and whispered, "Remember now, confidential."

Slim weaved around customers and glided out of the room like a reptile.

I was no closer to understanding the pain that drove Amanda to suicide. Maybe no one would ever figure it out.

At Liberty Air my mentor taught me about business—not the stuff you learn in school, but practical information, like corporate politics. One time he told me that mysteries occur in any business. On a random Tuesday, passenger loads might be ten points higher than forecast, or you'll go a week with maintenance log items twenty percent below normal. You analyze the data, trying to determine cause and effect, until your eyes go bleary, but nothing explains it. "Remember that data point," he told me. "Something will happen six months later, or a year. You'll get another piece of data, another piece of the puzzle, and if you follow it up you'll learn something new about your business."

I would heed my mentor's advice by quietly and patiently monitoring the random data for a piece to the puzzle of Amanda's suicide.

I took a sip of the martini, nice and dry. I munched on one of the three speared olives—salty. Rose awaited me at home, but I had trouble overcoming my inertia. The conversation with Slim had left me with a sense of unfinished business.

When I looked up, Gwen Raleigh was standing at the door. She wore a loose-fitting mauve shirt and jeans. I waved. She frowned but walked over.

"Thanks," she said, "for making me look like a dumb shit in front of Webb today."

"I apologize."

"You should. We're supposed to be on the same team."

"It was wrong. I should have waited to talk to you one-on-one."

Gwen bit the lower corner of her lip. Her royal blue eyes looked at me without blinking. She wore a gold chain necklace with a turquoise stone that hung in the hollow of her neck.

The hard look softened. "I guess I need your help to figure out the numbers."

"You bet." I waved at the bartender, and Gwen ordered a draft beer. The bar was full, so I gave her my seat and leaned in to hear as we started to talk through it.

"My team's great on the creative side," she said, "but they can't add two and two." She got foam on her lip from the beer and wiped it off with a napkin before continuing. "I can read a spreadsheet fine, but don't know how to structure the initial analysis."

"I can help you with that stuff. No problem."

"And I obviously need help managing the spending."

"Obviously!" I exaggerated.

Gwen laughed and the tension between us melted away. We talked through some aspects of the model and agreed to get together at the office to go through the details. The conversation hit a lull.

"Hey," I said. "How about a game of pool?"

"I'm not much of a pool player."

"Me neither. We don't have to keep score."

There were a dozen tables spread out across the room and about half were occupied. I racked the balls, and Gwen neatly scattered them when she broke, dropping one in a corner pocket.

"Why do I get the feeling you're hustling me?" I asked.

"Never played the game before," she said. "Should we make a friendly wager?"

"No chance."

Gwen sank two more balls before missing, and I took a turn. When we finished the game I racked the balls again. As Gwen bent to take a shot, I noticed a disturbance a few tables away.

There were three bikers, and one of them was huge. The big guy walked with an exaggerated swagger. As he passed a table he reached out and pushed one of the balls hard enough to send it bouncing around, knocking into other balls. One of the players at the table was about to say something when his friend held him back.

I hate bullies, always have. I learned that in middle school, when most of the kids were bigger than me.

The two other bikers were medium height and pulled on their buddy's arm to move him along. The big guy made faces at people as he walked in our direction. He was about my height and weighed two fifty or more, with lots of facial hair and angry tattoos from his wrists all the way up his arms.

I leaned over the table to take a shot, and when I stood up the big guy bumped into my shoulder on purpose.

"Excuse me," I said sarcastically.

"Yeah."

Gwen was standing on the same side of the table, and the biker stopped next to her. "Hey, cutie," he said. "You're looking sweet . . . a real tight package. Nice." He glanced at me. "Why don't you shake this loser and come with us?"

I took a step toward him, and Gwen moved to stop me. "No, thanks," she said. "I'm good."

"Hey, Jimmy," one of the smaller bikers called from two tables away. "Over here. We got a table."

"Just a minute."

Jimmy looked hard at me and walked up close to Gwen. I moved toward them again, and Gwen pushed my chest to keep me away. Jimmy ran his finger up the side of her arm.

"Friend," I said, "you're about two seconds from me cracking this pool cue over your head."

"You feeling froggy . . . fancy boy?" He stood away from Gwen and backed up toward an open area between tables. "Come on. Let's see what you got."

Gwen shook her head and tried to hold me back, but it was too late. My blood was up.

"Stay out of this, Gwen." I pulled her behind me and started toward the biker. She held my arm.

"Let's get the hell out of here. He's an asshole."

"He'll just pick on somebody else."

I pulled my arm free and stepped toward Jimmy. We had a good open space, about fifteen feet on a side, a little smaller than a standard-size ring but enough to move around.

"What's it going to take to get you to leave?" I asked, tossing the pool cue on a nearby table. A few of the patrons had stopped playing and were watching. One look told me their money was on Jimmy.

He grinned at me. He had attractive facial features, a long nose and sharp eyes, but the effect was marred by overgrown sideburns and matted hair.

"How about a hundred bucks?" I asked. "Will that get you to leave?"

"Choirboy," he snarled, "nothing could get me to leave now."

"Are you sure?"

His laugh was a cruel sound.

I turned to give him less of a target but kept my hands down by my sides, waiting to see what he knew. His stance wasn't bad, and he brought his fists up well, but he stayed too far out of range, and his foot movement was all wrong. I breathed in deep through my nose and tried to relax.

He came at me aggressively with a straight right, but showed his lack of training by telegraphing the punch when he cocked his arm. I slipped outside the punch easily and countered with a straight right to his body, followed by a left hook, neither of which was blocked.

I came back up and threw two jabs at him, real quick, in the face. They barely made contact. I was still gauging him, sizing him up to see whether there were hidden strengths. He was a bit winded from the body punches but still quite determined.

I angled in and out a couple times to see what he would do next. He put everything into a left hook, but again he telegraphed the punch. I rocked back out of the way easily and countered with a straight right that hit his cheek solidly. I followed that immediately with a left hook that smashed his ear.

His fists were still up, but the fingers were loose. A look of concern replaced the smile on his face. I threw a powerful right-hook-into-left-hook combination at his head. He didn't even try to block the punches.

Jimmy dropped his hands and shook his head like an old dog.

According to Isaac Newton, for every force there is an equal and opposite force. I loaded up the right side and pivoted on my right foot. As I pushed down into the floor, the floor pushed back, generating power. The power transferred off the floor through my legs and waist to my shoulder, arm, and fist. I threw the right uppercut into the bottom of his chin; it nearly lifted him off the floor. His eyes went dull, and he took one little step before his knees gave out, and he fell in a heap on the floor.

It was a clean knockout; Jimmy would need more than a ten-count to get up. I stepped back and inspected my hands—nothing broken. My adrenaline was cranking full speed.

The onlookers were in shock, staring at either the biker on the floor or at me.

The downed biker's buddies walked over in no particular hurry. They both had hairy faces and tattooed skin but displayed no aggression.

I tried to look menacing. "You boys want to continue this nonsense?"

The blond one looked me over. "You're a boxer. Ain't ya?"

"I was, at one time."

"I thought so." He shook his head and looked at the biker on the floor. "Fucking Jimmy. Every time we come to town he wants to 'kick some high-tech ass.'"

The other biker took a swig of his beer. "Yep," he said. "It was just a matter of time."

The first biker rubbed the back of his hand across his face. "Come on, Todd," he said. "Let's haul him out of here before the cops show up."

Todd got a little grin on his face. He took a last pull on the beer and prodded at Jimmy with his boot toe. "Maybe we can just leave him here."

"Jesus Christ, we can't leave him here. He'll wake up in jail. We'd have to listen to him whine for a month. Come on."

"Shee-it," said Todd. "I didn't want to come to Sixth Street anyways. I wanted to go to the titty bar."

The three of us managed to half drag and half carry Jimmy out the door. By that time he was starting to wake up, so his buddies stumble-walked him around the corner.

I turned back toward the bar to check on Gwen and saw her standing on the sidewalk, shaking her head.

"What the fuck, Robbins?" she said. "Where did you learn to fight like that?"

"Frankie's boxing gym."

She gave me a puzzled look.

"I grew up in a small middle-class neighborhood in south Dallas where most of the kids went to private school. We didn't have the money, so I went to Sunset High, a public school for all the poor kids. My father said the experience would build character, but he didn't want me pummeled in the process. The first time I got beat up he paid for boxing lessons."

"No shit. Boxing lessons . . . at a gym called Frankie's."

"Yep . . . for three years. I had visions of becoming a professional boxer. Then I lost to a fighter in the ring who was faster and stronger. That put an end to my pugilistic aspirations."

"Are you going back in the bar?" she asked.

"No, I'm headed home."

"Where are you parked?"

"A block down San Jacinto."

"I'm that way too."

We started walking east on Sixth Street.

"A boxing cfo," she said. "Who would have thought it possible?"

"It's not that big a deal. A lot of kids in south Dallas studied self-defense . . . boxing . . . martial arts."

"You studied martial arts?"

"Not really. A little judo."

We stopped at the corner near where my car was parked.

I touched her bare arm above the elbow. "Are you okay?" The muscle was well toned, and the skin smooth on the inside.

"I'm fine."

I was about to say good night when a strange sight caught my eye. Across the street was a souvenir store called Texas Treasures. Out front were two cigar-store Indians, a brave and a squaw. Standing there, wearing designer jeans and a dress shirt, was Webb Elliot.

"Is that Webb?" I asked.

She turned to look. "Oh, my God."

As we crossed the street we could hear him talking to the squaw.

"She never really loved me. None of them love me. They only do things for me . . . things I ask them to. I can talk to you, though, honestly. You don't care for money. I just want someone, someday, to care about me. . . ."

Gwen approached him carefully. "Webb, what are you doing?"

"Who is it?" He jerked around.

I didn't know how he managed to stand. His eyes were red slits. His upper body swayed and made sudden adjustments as delayed signals reached his brain.

"Webb," she called, loud enough to get through. "It's Gwen."

"Gwen? Is that you? You care. Don't you?"

She turned to me. "He's completely wasted. *Gone* gone."

"What do you want to do?"

She looked at my face carefully. "I'll take him to his house and throw him in bed . . . make sure he's okay."

I looked north on San Jacinto and signaled for a cab.

"Need any help?"

"No, I got it." She took another look at Webb, who had turned back to the squaw. "Not exactly our CEO's finest hour." She helped Webb into the cab and they took off.

I looked both ways on Sixth Street and San Jacinto, relieved to find that no one else had noticed Webb's conversation with the squaw. It was the sort of incident best forgotten. I had never before seen Webb lose control, but every leader has his flaws, even a genius.

CHAPTER 8

"I T'S A DAMN FIASCO if you ask me," said Gregor Smolnik.

I looked at Henry Jiwanlal and knew he was considering a smart-ass remark, something like, *Nobody asked you.* I hoped he would refrain so we could avoid an argument in the boardroom. The most important thing I needed from the board was a date for going public, but we were stuck talking about Chartwell Insurance.

Four directors attended the meeting in a conference room on the top floor of the Connection's office building. Webb, as majority owner, was chairman. Mike Franzinni and his younger partner, Dan Chiu, represented Central Texas Ventures and their twelve percent stake. Gregor Smolnik, an obese attorney who had counseled the Connection for years, was the fourth director.

The outside view was of the hill country, with downtown Austin visible five miles to the east. Central air-conditioning and thick windows kept the hundred-degree heat at bay, but it still felt plenty hot in the boardroom.

Tommy King was standing by the screen, giving the presentation. "We've slipped our dates about three months, but the team feels we're back on track."

"The team was confident three months ago," Gregor sniped. "They obviously don't have a clue what's happening."

For once I agreed with Gregor. Chartwell was the second-largest life insurance company in the United States. The implementation was not going well, and key players were starting to point fingers at the Connection.

"Our estimate was good for the initial set of deliverables," said Tommy, "but the Chartwell project leadership has changed the specifications twice."

"A big company like Chartwell doesn't want to hear excuses like that. They want results."

"Don't worry," said Henry. "We just put two more engineers on the project. We have a team of superheroes now."

"Yeah," Gregor said cynically, "a superhero team. You always overestimate the value of a strong team."

"It's not possible to overestimate this team," said Henry. "They can do anything."

"Not if Chartwell keeps moving the goalposts," said Mike Franzinni. "You've got to get them to agree to a fixed set of specifications."

"It's like trying to squeeze Jell-O," said Tommy. "Every time we start coding to a set of specs, another Chartwell VP shows up and points us in a different direction."

"Then we're screwed," Mike declared. "We'll never successfully deploy the solution."

Tommy was silent; his huge hands nervously uncapped and capped a dry-erase marker.

To win the fourteen million dollar deal we had sold Chartwell a vision of linking their thousands of brokers into a single network that would make Chartwell faster than the competition. Their own analysts predicted it would double their profits, but if we couldn't stand up the system, there would be zero benefit.

"What is your recommendation?" Webb asked Mike. "If, as you say, 'we're screwed,' then what should we do?"

"I'm not sure," Mike said.

"Maybe we should give Chartwell back the fourteen million? Is that what you think?"

Nobody answered. It was an unspoken rule in the world of software: You never gave the money back to the customer. We had recognized the fourteen million in revenue when they signed the deal and paid us the cash. Refunding Chartwell's license fee would invalidate our entire revenue accounting policy.

Webb spoke again. "Well, what do you say? Gregor? Dan? Should we give them back their money?" He turned to me. "What would that do to the timing of the IPO?"

"The auditors would make us restate our financials," I said, "for the last two years, at least. It would set back the IPO a year, maybe longer."

"We can't refund their money," said Mike. He was slim and in his mid-forties. He colored his hair a dark chocolate and had intelligent eyes. "That's not an option."

"Then what should we do?" asked Webb again.

Webb waited patiently on the three directors. He looked as if he honestly wanted them to make a suggestion. Gregor looked down at his pad and said nothing. Mike held Webb's gaze, and his expression slowly changed into one of understanding.

"Well?" Webb asked.

"We'll have to learn how to squeeze Jell-O," Mike finally said. "Tommy, tell us more about this great team you have."

As they discussed Chartwell further, my thoughts wandered back to the IPO. In the six months since I had joined the Connection, the NASDAQ had risen eighteen percent. The market was ready, but the Connection was not.

A project like an IPO needs a deadline. A deadline would focus the resources and allow me to build a detailed plan with many tasks, each of which had start dates and completion dates and was linked to its dependencies. But despite my best efforts, and the best efforts of Henry, Tommy, and Gwen, Webb had so far refused to set a specific date; he had said only that we would go public when we were ready.

I preferred being aggressive with the deadline and believed we could go public in the first quarter of 2000. I had no ability to force Webb to change his mind, but the other directors might. The problem was that the meeting agenda didn't even mention the IPO. The Chartwell implementation was the last agenda item, and I was afraid the IPO wouldn't be addressed at all, but when the discussion ended, the directors asked me to remain in the room and excused the rest of management.

Before walking out, Henry leaned over and whispered in my ear, "Remember the deal—we drive the growth, and you get the directors on board." He smiled. "And I mean *all* the directors."

It wasn't like I had any real say in the decision; I was not a voting member of the board of directors. The best I could hope for was to influence the conversation.

"What's the schedule on the IPO?" asked Mike Franzinni. His eyes were eager, and his voice pitched up. He looked back and forth between Webb and me. Webb sat at the head of the table, doodling on the pad in front of him. I was on his right, with the three directors across from me.

"We've been focused on foundation work," I said. "We haven't exactly fleshed out a schedule."

"That's idiotic," said Gregor. "How do you expect to get it done without a schedule?"

Gregor never passed on an opportunity to make me look stupid. His head was enormous and covered with tight red curls; he wore

cheap clunky glasses with big lenses. An extra layer of fat sagged below his chin.

Before I joined the Connection, Gregor and I had negotiated my compensation package, and it had been a rough ride. He didn't want to budge on any major points, and twice I forced him to get more negotiating authority. Gregor hated to concede anything, but I guess the board, or maybe Webb alone, had wanted me enough to be flexible.

I glanced at Webb. He continued to doodle.

"How soon could you be ready to go?" asked Mike.

"Conservatively, the second quarter of next year," I said.

"What's the aggressive schedule?" asked Mike.

"It's possible we could go in the first quarter. We'd have to run like hell."

Webb looked up from his pad. "It's better to wait longer. It's important to be sure the company is ready. I'd say the second quarter is too aggressive. Better to wait for the third or fourth quarter."

Dan Chiu said, "There is an argument to be made that we should take the risk and go public as soon as we can."

Webb slowly rose and walked around the table behind the directors. He placed his hands on Dan's shoulders. "Of course, you could make that argument, Dan, but it strikes me as a rather short-term perspective. What is the primary objective, ensuring the long-term health of the company or cashing out? I hope you're not just focused on cashing out."

Dan looked nervous. "Wh-what's the downside to going out earlier?"

Webb backed away from Dan and walked to the window behind the directors, forcing them to swivel in their chairs to look at him.

"The downside is we go public when we're not ready and wind up with a broken company. Our primary goal is not to take the money and run."

"But the market is hot now," Gregor said. "It could fall." He seldom spoke against Webb, but he held one percent of the company. Gregor wanted to cash out his shares as badly as I did.

"That could happen in the short term," Webb admitted, "but a short-term swing doesn't concern me. In the long term the market would go up again. So long as the company continues to grow, we will be there when the market is ready."

"What about the employees?" Mike asked. "Many of them would like to take some money off the table. They've been waiting for years. We owe them some consideration."

"They will wait," Webb said.

"They won't wait forever," Mike said.

"No, but they will certainly wait awhile longer. Besides that, once we go public some of the employees will cash out and leave. From a long-term perspective it's better if we wait. It will give us more time to prepare for the inevitable attrition."

"What do you think?" Mike asked me.

"It's possible that we could go in January, but we will be in better shape with three more months to prepare."

Gregor turned his giant head to fix his gaze on me. He was wedged so tightly into the chair his sides spilled over the armrests. "And what if we don't get three quarters of growth? What if revenues falter? What then?"

"Then we shouldn't go public," Webb said matter-of-factly. He walked back to his chair and sat. "If we fall apart in the next few quarters, then we aren't ready."

Mike leaned into the table, toward Webb, and said, "I get the feeling you don't want to go public at all, and *that* wasn't our agreement. You said we would take the Connection public when the time was right."

"I never committed to a time line."

"I'm asking you to commit to one now. When do you think we'll be ready?"

Webb didn't answer. He started doodling on the pad again. Mike looked frustrated. The outside directors clearly all favored a faster timetable, as I did. Perhaps I could finesse the conversation with an alternative.

"We could gear up for a January date," I said, "and then hold off if it looks like the company needs more time."

Mike's face lit up. "Now you're talking! Let's get aggressive."

"Good idea," said Gregor.

"No!" said Webb. "I want to wait."

"Then when?" Mike asked.

For a second I thought Webb was going to start doodling again. As majority owner he could do what he wanted, but there was a lot of pressure on Webb, and not just from the directors. All the employees who held stock options wanted to go public, and soon.

"All right," he said finally. "We'll target the IPO for the second quarter . . . if we're ready."

"Thank you," said Mike.

I looked down at the table to hide a smile. We had a deadline. My goal was within reach. I could feel it.

CHAPTER 9

T HAT NIGHT, after dinner and some television, I told the girls a story. "'Sheila Learns to Climb,'" Callie insisted. "I want to hear 'Sheila Learns to Climb.'"

The three of us were piled in Chandler's bed, the girls in their pajamas with clean faces and teeth. I used to read stories to them from children's books, but at some point they grew tired of that; they wanted original stories. So I invented Sheila Wright, a young girl growing up in the early nineteen hundreds. Once Sheila came to life that was all they wanted.

"We've heard that a hundred times," Chandler complained.

It was true; they had heard the story many times before, but despite her complaints, I knew Chandler liked it too, so I told them "Sheila Learns to Climb" again.

In that story, Sheila is eighteen months old and wakes from her nap one day to find her brother Tim choking on a toy in her room. In the climactic moment, Sheila climbs out of her crib and summons her mother's help through the open window.

As always, at the end of a story, the girls sat mesmerized, transported to an earlier time.

"Oh, that was a good Sheila story," Chandler said.

"I was scared!" shouted Callie. "What if Tim died this time?"

"Don't be silly," Chandler scolded. "Sheila always saves Tim."

"I climbed out of my crib one time. Didn't I, Daddy?"

"Yes, you did."

Chandler sat up and looked straight at me, disappointment on her face. "Daddy," she said, "you missed my soccer game today."

"I know darling. I'm sorry, but I had to work." I brushed her hair back from her face.

"You used to come to soccer practice too, but you haven't been in a long time."

"I know."

My working hours were longer than when I was at Liberty Air. The Connection was a small company with few resources, and there was always something important to do. With the ipo cranking up it would only get worse. I hated to miss the girls' activities, but I rationalized it: For so much gain there had to be some pain.

"You didn't work so hard when we lived in Dallas," Callie said. She was the happy-go-lucky sister, with rarely a complaint, but her eyes were downcast, and her lips made a frown.

"You're right." My arm was around Callie, and I gave her an extra squeeze. "It's just that for a while I have to work longer hours . . . on a special project."

"You mean the ipo?" said Chandler. She pronounced the initials as if they were a secret code. "Mommy says once the ipo is done you won't have to work so hard."

"That's right."

"When will the ipo be done?" said Callie.

"This time next year."

"Will you come to soccer practice then?" said Chandler. "After the ipo?"

Both of their faces were hopeful.

"Yes, I'll have lots of time then."

CHAPTER 10

Gwen breezed into my office at ten after seven in the evening. She wore a black sleeveless top, a knee-length beige skirt, and black sandals.

"Sorry I'm late. I stopped by Siena for a glass of wine with the team. We do that whenever there's a birthday in the group."

We had met twice before to review the details of the Internet marketing program. Our goal was to increase the program's effectiveness while simultaneously reducing the cost.

Her blond locks were mussed, and her face was tired. I knew she was working ridiculous hours, because her car was always in the garage, both when I arrived in the morning and when I left at night.

"Do you still want to do this now?" I asked.

"Sure. I only had one glass. What are we covering tonight?"

We sat side by side at my office table and looked at the laptop screen.

"To understand what's driving the cost overruns we need to analyze past invoices. I asked the accounts payable clerk to pull every invoice since the program's inception and download them into an Excel file."

When they had started the program, Gwen's team had emphasized speed and ignored cost controls. They had hired vendors and told them to "get moving." The work started at a feverish pace, and the vendors

sent their invoices directly to Gwen's analysts. As the bills piled up, Gwen's analysts took them to accounts payable, but AP wouldn't pay them because there were no purchase orders to match them against. When the vendors didn't get paid, they threatened to quit.

To avoid that crisis, Gwen had gone to the controller, Randy Harlan, and convinced him to pay the invoices if she approved them manually with her signature. To accommodate the situation, accounting had created purchase orders themselves instead of requiring marketing to do it. The vendors were now getting paid, but there was still insufficient control; it was all after the fact. Gwen had no idea beforehand how to forecast costs for a given month.

"First we need to validate the data," I said. "I want you to look at the suppliers and spending as I scan the file. If anything seems out of order we'll drill down."

I looked over. Gwen's eyes were closed. After the wine she'd had, sitting and staring at a spreadsheet had made her drowsy. I watched while she lingered on the edge of sleep. The bob haircut curled just under her ear. She wore a black pearl necklace and earrings. Soft, fine hairs arranged themselves perfectly on the nape of her neck. The skin on her shoulders was tanned and smooth. She wore no perfume, but still I could smell her, the aroma of healthy woman after a long day. I touched her arm.

"Let's break now."

She jerked her head. "I'm fine."

"No, you're falling asleep in the chair. I'll e-mail the file, and you can look at it tomorrow."

"You're right. I'm tired." She suppressed a yawn and reached for her purse. We both stood up and pushed back from the table.

"Good night, Joe," she mumbled, and put her hand on my shirt-front, fingers flat. She leaned up and kissed me, eyes closed. Her lips were full, moist, and hinted of red wine. A tingling sensation began

at my lips; it quickly traversed the nervous system to my midsection. My right hand traveled of its own accord to rest on her hip.

Gwen opened her eyes, half-surprised, half-sleepy. She snapped out of it. "Did I just do that?" She stepped back and hurried to the door. "God, I'm so exhausted . . . I don't know what I'm doing. Sorry." She walked down the hall and out of the executive suite.

I pulled my chair next to the window. My office was on the seventh floor, and our building was constructed on a hill. I watched the traffic on Bee Caves and 360 hundreds of feet below. A few minutes later Gwen's BMW cruised through the intersection and turned left onto 360.

It must have been an absentminded slip caused by her exhaustion. I touched my lips, the memory of hers still fresh.

Forget it.

I had never strayed from Rose before and wasn't about to start then.

. . .

GWEN AND I PRETENDED IT NEVER HAPPENED. The next afternoon she came by my office and dropped a printout of the spreadsheet on the desk.

"Everything checks out except these vendors," she reported, pointing to four lines that had been highlighted in orange. "I've never heard of them."

I studied the outliers carefully; the first was Smart Web Hits LLC, and the other names were similarly related to Internet marketing.

"Are you sure? They look like companies your team would hire."

"I'm sure. They know better than to bring on a firm before reviewing it with me."

"Okay. It's about a hundred thousand bucks. We can pull them out of the data set, but before we do let's look a little closer. Have you got a few minutes?"

"Sure."

As Gwen pulled a chair over, my mind was racing ahead. Fraud is rampant in the corporate world. In a well-run shop you install checks and balances to make it more difficult, but a determined mind on the inside will find a way.

Fraud can be hard to uncover, but there is always a piece of evidence left behind, like a picture frame on the wall that is slightly askew. A good CFO pays attention to everything, and investigates when something looks out of place. Often it means nothing, an accounting error or a bad forecast. But sometimes it's fraud.

"As CFO I have access to all the detailed financial systems. I can pull up an invoice from one of the vendors you didn't recognize to see who authorized payment."

I double-clicked the record for a payment to Smart Web Hits and accessed the image of the invoice. Handwritten words across the bottom read, "Okay to Pay, Gwen Raleigh."

"Shit!" she said. "That's my signature."

"So it is your vendor."

"No, it's not. I mean, that looks like my signature, but I didn't sign that invoice."

"Let's look at one of your genuine signatures and compare the two."

I printed the Smart Web Hits invoice and then pulled the image from one of the vendors Gwen had recognized and printed that also. We compared the two. Gwen pulled her chair in closer and her shoulder edged against me. I detected a citrus fragrance. The tingling sensation from the night before returned, and I did my best to ignore it.

"It looks just like my signature."

"It does. Notice that the two are very similar but not identical. That's because no one signs their name the same way twice."

"Maybe I'm going crazy."

"Wait a minute. Let's look at a few more."

I printed another half dozen invoices from the suspect vendors, and we compared them. They were all signed by Gwen, and the signatures were all perfect replicas and in exactly the same place on every page.

"Someone has imposed an electronic copy of your signature on these invoices. Actually, it was probably the other way around. They lifted a copy of your signature from another document and printed the invoice on a piece of paper that already had the fraudulent signature on it."

"Damn." Her eyes flashed with anger. "Some bastard stole my signature," she said. "But why do all that just to pay a bill?"

"Hold on. I want to check something else."

I pulled up the database of authorized suppliers and looked up the suspect vendors.

"Look. All four vendors have business addresses with P.O. boxes here in Austin."

"That seems strange, but I still don't understand," she said.

"In the dummy-company fraud scheme, the perpetrator creates a new company, like Smart Web Hits, and generates a fake invoice for services that were never rendered. The fake invoice, complete with the falsified authorizing signature, is then dropped in the in-box of the accounts payable clerk to be paid. If everything else looks correct, the clerk will cut a check and mail it to the address on the invoice."

"Okay . . . then what?"

"The perpetrator deposits the Connection's check into Smart Web Hits' bank account and writes a check to himself or an accomplice on Smart Web Hits' check stock."

"So someone used my signature to steal from the company?"

"Let me check one more thing." I pulled up the purchasing module. "Before the clerk would pay the bill, there would need to be a clear match with an existing purchase order. There it is."

I scanned down the purchase order on the screen.

"It says Sam Houston was the authorizer," she said. "Is that a joke?"

"It's the dummy name accounting uses when they create a purchase order. We do that for recurring charges like rent and utilities. Someone used it to create POs to make the fraud scheme work."

Gwen pushed her chair back and crossed her legs. The right one rocked slowly; the calf muscle was well toned.

"Why did they use my signature?"

"This type of scheme only works when it's run through a cost area that's not being closely monitored."

"Like my marketing program."

"Apparently."

"Who did it?"

"I can't figure that out with the data I have. I'll have to get some help from the police to access records at the post office."

"We never would have figured it out if you hadn't forced me to dig deeper into the numbers."

"We got lucky. Do me a favor: Don't mention this to anyone else. I don't want word leaking out until I've had a chance to find the perpetrator."

"Sure thing." She stood and straightened her skirt.

My eyes unconsciously drifted down.

"Are we done for today?" she asked.

"What? Yeah, that's it. I'll let you know once I've done more analysis on the genuine spending."

After Gwen left I took a deep breath to clear my head. I had worked close to attractive women before; it was inevitable in the corporate world, but I had learned to block the base instincts and focus on the task at hand. I would do the same with Gwen.

I thought about the next move in my investigation. There were seven or eight people in the finance group who knew enough to orchestrate the scheme, starting with me and cascading down to the accounts payable

clerk. The police could help me pinpoint the culprit, but I preferred to do it myself so Webb could decide how to handle the thief.

I went back to the accounts payable module to review the outstanding invoices. There was a fifty-five-hundred-dollar payment for a fraudulent vendor scheduled to go out Friday. The mail would reach the local post office overnight. It was a long shot, but I could camp out in the post office parking lot on Saturday to see whether someone came by for the check.

⁎ ⁎ ⁎

THE WESTLAKE POST OFFICE is in a strip center on Bee Caves Road, surrounded by small retail stores and restaurants. Across the parking lot is a locally owned coffee shop. On Saturday, at seven a.m., I picked up a tall latte and sat in Rose's SUV.

On weekends I always cooked a big breakfast for the family. Rose had been perturbed when I left the house at six, skipping the breakfast ritual, but she was mollified when I explained the reason and promised to return in time for Chandler's soccer game.

I had already located the relevant P.O. box and could see it through the plate-glass window. I waited for more than two hours. At nine twenty a Toyota Camry that looked familiar pulled up. Twin boys, about five years old, got out of the car and raced to the door. They were followed closely by Randy Harlan, my controller. I knew Randy was divorced but didn't realize he had kids. He wore shorts and a T-shirt. He was built like a soccer player, with thick, muscular legs. As he walked back out of the post office he opened the envelope. He inspected it quickly, loaded the kids back in the car, and drove away.

Damn. I had trusted Randy, but there he was, stealing from the company. The bastard.

It would be difficult to replace him. Despite his apparent lack of integrity, Randy was a skilled controller. He knew how to keep the books and how to manage the back office. I silently wished him a good weekend, because Randy's world would change on Monday.

I called Webb on the way back to the house.

"Are you absolutely sure?" he asked.

"Positive." I recounted the steps of my investigation.

"Randy's been with us for six years now," he said. "When he first joined I was tracking numbers on a spreadsheet. In those days we managed the company strictly on a cash basis—no accrual accounting at all. He literally created the back office, every bit of it. Why risk so much for just . . . how much was it?"

"Ninety-eight thousand. I'm sure Randy has a justification. Fraud perpetrators always do."

"I can't believe it."

"Should I bring in the police?"

"No. No. I want to think about that. We'll talk to him on Monday."

° ° °

On Monday I brought Randy into Iago, the small conference room adjoining Webb's office, under the pretext of discussing the IPO. Webb was sitting at one end of the table, drawing with pen on paper. He scarcely looked up when we came in.

The room was brightly lit with overhead fluorescents. Randy sat on Webb's left, facing away from the window. He had grown up in Buda, studied accounting at Texas State in San Marcos, and cut his teeth at a regional CPA firm in Austin. He wore his dark hair short and had light brown eyes.

I sat across from Randy. Webb didn't say a word, and Randy

started to fidget. I watched cars on Bee Caves Road below. A wall clock hummed softly as the second hand revolved.

After two minutes Randy couldn't take the silence. "What did you want to talk about?"

"Shut up," Webb commanded, and continued to draw.

Randy looked at me and rolled his eyes. I rested my arms on the table and raised my eyebrows to suggest it was a mystery to me also. Randy opened a folder and pulled out some loose sheets of paper. He looked at each one quickly and laid it onto a new pile. When he was through, he took the reordered stack and put it back in the folder.

Finally Webb turned the paper around so Randy could see it. He had spelled "CONNECTION" in simple block letters, but after the first "N" the letters tumbled down to the right until the final "N" was upside down on the bottom of the sheet.

"You've been stealing from me." Webb leaned in while Randy stared at the letters on the page. Webb's eyes showed no anger, only cold dispassion. Randy looked from Webb to me, and I gave him a quick nod.

"We know about the scam," I said. "Almost a hundred thousand."

Randy's shoulders slumped. His face fell, and he pulled his hands into his lap.

"Why did you do it?" Webb asked. "I gave you everything. When you came here you were making less than fifty thousand. Your salary exceeds twice that now."

"It isn't enough. Everyone else is going to get rich, and I'm still making a paltry hundred thousand."

"So you decided to steal from me?"

"You promised me stock." Randy lifted his head. He straightened up, and his eyes narrowed. "You gave options to all the engineers but didn't give any to me."

"I tried to, but the board disapproved the grant." Webb shot me a glance of justification. "They maintain that controllers are easy to find, while engineering talent is impossible."

"I had that money coming to me," Randy accused Webb. His face grew red. His jaw was clenched, and he breathed loudly through his nose.

Randy looked like he might explode. It was like watching the fuse burn on a firecracker. I eased my chair back.

"The board wouldn't let me," said Webb.

"That's bullshit! You own the fucking company." Spittle flew from Randy's lips.

"Take it easy," I cautioned him.

"You stay out of it!" Randy shouted, his whole body shaking. "You've only been here a few months. I've been slaving away for six years."

"I couldn't give you stock," Webb reasoned. "That's why I gave you that ten percent increase."

Randy launched himself over the corner of the table at Webb, arms outstretched, aiming for the neck. His powerful legs generated enough force to push Webb backward out of his chair onto the floor. They scrambled, with Randy kicking and hitting, and Webb trying to get away. I took three steps, reached down for one of Randy's arms, and yanked him up. Crazed, he turned and clawed at me, scratching my skin just beneath the left ear. I hit him with a solid punch in the side, and he fell to his knees, coughing.

Webb backed away on the other side of the table. He straightened his shirt and combed his hair with his fingers, eyes wild and chest heaving. Randy stayed down, and I stood off to the side. The scratch stung. I put my finger to it and felt blood, but it was only a trickle.

Webb waited until he caught his breath and then walked the long way around the table to me.

"Just get rid of him. No police—and he can keep the cash." Looking at Randy on the floor, he added, "We'll consider it severance pay."

After Webb left, Randy continued to struggle to pull himself together. I felt no sympathy for him; he brought it all on himself and was getting off easy. I couldn't figure out why Webb was so generous about it. If I'd had my way, Randy would have paid back the money and probably gone to jail.

. . .

THAT NIGHT, as we were getting ready for bed, Rose cleaned the scratch carefully in our bathroom. We stood together next to my sink; she wore only bikini briefs, and I wore boxers.

"I can understand why Webb let Randy keep the money," she said.

"Really? Explain it to me."

"He worked hard for Webb for many years."

"But Randy was well paid for his efforts. He stole from the company."

"Randy also has a family, and Webb cares about people."

I leaned down to kiss her.

"I care about people too, but Randy is a thief, plain and simple."

"You're so tough." Her breasts kept pressing against my bare chest. "I can't tell if you're a CFO or a bouncer."

"We offer many career paths at the Connection."

As she shifted position to apply antiseptic, her hip nudged my crotch.

"Are you trying to seduce me?" I asked.

"Absolutely." Her hand reached under the waistband. "Is it working?"

"Absolutely."

CHAPTER 11

AS CONTROLLER, Randy had been my number one manager. After we fired him, all the work fell back to me, and I worked every day, including weekends, in September, October, and November. I'd get up before the kids, drive to the office, work fourteen or fifteen hours, and when my eyes no longer focused, I'd drive home again. My dreams became filled with numbers, spreadsheets, conference calls, and endless meetings.

In November the NASDAQ soared. Over the next two months the index climbed thirty-seven percent to close at 4069 on December 31. We signed scores of deals, and the company continued to grow; we had more than a thousand employees and hired more every week. As my workload increased, the pain it caused grew, but so did the value of my option grant.

On a perfect Sunday in January, Rose and I took the kids for a picnic in Zilker Park. We ate lunch at a wooden table in a grove of live oaks, next to a huge field of brown grass. Afterward, Chandler and Callie pestered me to help them fly a kite.

"You girls get started," I said. "Let Mommy and I relax a few minutes, and then I'll join you."

I kept an eye on their progress while Rose brought me up to speed

on the latest "Connection Plus" outing. Some of the spouses, including Rose, had formed their own support group. They went out once a month to have fun and compare notes on life as a Connection spouse. The night before, they had been to an upscale Mexican restaurant.

"Webb Elliot made an appearance," she said.

"Really? Does he always come to Connection Plus events?"

"Every couple months he shows up to buy a round and work the crowd. Last night he had us all try Gran Patrón Platinum, straight up."

The girls were trying to launch the kite in a gentle breeze. Chandler held the string while, from forty feet away, Callie held the kite upside down.

"Tequila? How was it?"

"Surprisingly good. We didn't do shots, though—just sipped it. It's much smoother than the cheap stuff."

"Well . . . we'll have to trade up. Did you talk with Webb?"

"Yes. I told him you were working too hard."

I looked at Rose. Her expression was perfectly serious. "You didn't really say that—not to the boss."

"He agreed with me. Said he's worried about everyone's workload, but he hopes the pace slows down after the ipo."

Chandler had shown Callie how to hold the kite upright, but now Callie was standing crosswind. Every time she launched the kite it immediately crashed.

"You know," said Rose, "Webb was awfully familiar with some of the spouses. I wouldn't be surprised if he's had an affair with one or two."

I remembered Jack O'Shea's wife adjusting her dress at the Connection ball after spending time outside with Webb.

"I've heard rumors to that effect," I said, "but I can't understand why the women would do that."

"Maybe their husbands are working too hard."

Rose tried to keep a straight face but couldn't manage; her lips turned up into a broad grin, and I laughed.

"I can understand the physical attraction," I said. "He's tall, handsome face. . . ."

"Those eyes . . . don't forget the violet eyes."

"And I gather some women go for the British accent."

"They certainly do. Plus, he's rich. All in all he's quite a package."

"I guess so."

"Believe me, honey. If you were hit by a beer truck, and Webb called on me, I'd have a hard time saying no."

"Well," I said, trying to match her wit. "In *that* case, I'll look both ways before stepping off the curb."

She smiled again, but only for an instant; then her eyebrows and lips turned down. "Are you sure this is worth it?"

"What's that?"

"All the work? This is the first day we've had together in a month."

I scooted closer on the bench.

"Listen, babe, we just finished a kick-ass quarter. In three months, when we're public, our grant will be worth twenty million with a *lot* of upside. It is definitely worth it."

She pressed her lips tightly together. "Joey, I trust you, but we are ready for the hours to come down . . . all of us."

My workload was putting pressure on her as well. Rose had always wanted a career but was too busy supporting me and the kids. In the past I had helped her by putting the girls to bed, taking them to activities on weekends, and doing the dishes, but for the last five months I had been no help at all.

I brushed a rogue strand of hair from her face and traced the contours of her ear. I massaged the lobe with thumb and forefinger.

"Why don't you take a break?" I said.

"What do you mean?"

"A girls' trip . . . a few days for yourself. You could visit friends in Dallas."

"How can I do that with you working seven days a week?"

"I'll make it happen. We'll arrange for babysitting coverage, and I'll take some time off."

"Do you think that's realistic?"

"Yes."

"A few Connection spouses are talking about a trip to San Miguel."

"Do it."

"They asked me, but I didn't think it was possible."

"Call them back."

Her pouty lips were irresistible. I leaned in for a kiss.

"Are you sure?" she said.

"Promise. I'll make it work." I kissed her again, quickly, and ran to assist the kite fliers.

. . .

IN JANUARY we hired Franklin Reynolds, a bulge bracket firm, as our investment bankers, and then focused on the most grueling part of the IPO process: putting together a registration statement.

We had daily meetings with our advisers: the lawyers, auditors, and bankers. We reviewed financial statements ad nauseam, checked and double-checked every number. We debated sentence structure and word choices over and again. We took out commas, only to reinsert them two days later. I read and reread the document until I imagined problems that didn't exist. More than once I fell asleep at my desk, long after everyone else had left the building. Finally, in late February, we filed the registration statement with the SEC.

On March 9 the NASDAQ broke 5000 for the first time. The index had doubled in the fourteen months since I had joined the Connection.

By the first week of April everything had been checked off the project plan except for the road show, a grueling three-week trip to pitch the Connection to potential investors. It had taken fifteen months and thousands of hours of work, but we were ready to go public.

. . .

"I'VE ALWAYS BEEN NERVOUS about Webb and this road show," Gwen said.

"Why?" I asked.

Webb, Gwen, and I were in New York to practice the pitch as a warm-up before the real show began in Europe the following week.

Gwen and I were walking to the New York Hilton, a few blocks from the restaurant. We had just finished dinner with Hugh Crandall, the partner from Franklin Reynolds who was leading our deal team; Webb had skipped the dinner part, claiming a prior commitment with a friend.

"Webb's such a private person," Gwen said. "He's fine selling to senior executives, but he abhors publicity . . . any kind of attention."

"The road show's not that big a deal. Most of these presentations are with small groups."

"I'm not talking about the presentations. Webb will be fine with those. It's the disclosures, the public scrutiny. Frankly, I was surprised he agreed to go through with the IPO at all."

"Well, he's going through with it now." I stated it as fact. "There's no turning back."

We wore overcoats to block the chill from a late-season cold front. I had a light buzz from the cocktails and wine. We turned on Sixth Avenue and walked briskly, our breath visible in the air. At Fifty-third Street we stopped for traffic. When the light turned, we crossed the street to the hotel and walked through the revolving door.

The lobby bar was at full speed, inviting us with the sound of happy customers.

Gwen opened her coat and shook her head. She had let her hair grow the last six months, and it hung loosely about her shoulders. Her delicate throat disappeared into the leopard-print scarf wrapped around her neck. She wore a black long-sleeved sweater, checked skirt, black tights, and suede pumps.

"How about a nightcap?" she said.

It wasn't a good idea. I remembered our inadvertent kiss in my office and the feel of her hip under my palm. I was a happily married man and had no business drinking with an attractive woman like Gwen. Still, it was only one drink, and I'd been killing myself preparing for the IPO. I deserved to cut myself some slack.

"Sure."

We sat at the bar and had a drink, and then another.

She wanted to know about my kids and their activities, and I wanted to know about her life before the Connection.

She was a swimmer, which explained the strong upper body, and had gone to Berkeley on an athletic scholarship, although her parents could certainly afford the tuition: Her father was an attorney, high on the food chain at a powerful firm in New York. Her two brothers were also attorneys, apparently on the same track as the old man. But her mother was an actress, or rather, she had been a Broadway actress early on, before the children came.

"I guess that's where I got my stubborn streak," she said.

"From your mother?"

"No. Not from her directly—more from my perception of her history. You see, my mother could have been a star. She had the talent, the potential, and a good head start. But then she married my father, started having kids, moved to Connecticut, and her career ended, just like that."

I took a sip of Beringer cabernet port. Over the top of the glass Gwen's royal blue eyes were downcast, her mouth in a frown. She looked up and continued her story.

"My dad wants the same thing for me . . . keeps introducing me to the right investment bankers. The last time, I told him if he ever did it again, I'd never return to Greenwich."

"Sounds like you two get along fine."

"He's a nice person, I guess, but he keeps trying to tell me what to do, and I hate that! You know what he said when I applied for the Berkeley scholarship?"

I shook my head.

The sad eyes came alive with angry fire, her strong shoulders thrown back, ready for combat.

"He said, 'Why bother? Why don't you go to Yale or Princeton, or Brown like your mother?' I wanted to tell him to fuck off. I got the scholarship, and I went to Berkeley, because it was as far away as I could get."

"Touché."

"When Webb wanted to hire me, my father said it was a terrible idea. He said the company would fail, and I was wasting my time."

"You should feel good about yourself. Your father was wrong."

"I do. I feel good about my accomplishments. Anyway, that's how I got my stubborn streak."

"I think 'determined' is a better word."

Gwen drank from her glass and sat back on the bar stool. She had tensed up while talking about her past, but now she took a deep breath and shook her hands to fling off the stress. She smiled her crooked smile.

The conversation had gotten personal, a little flirtatious. I recognized that, but it was fun, harmless fun.

"Sorry for getting so intense," she said. "Sometimes I just can't help it."

"No worries. Tell me more about yourself."

"Like what?"

"What will you do once you're rich?" I asked. "What's your dream?"

"You'll laugh at me." Gwen's eyes were hesitant, and she nibbled the corner of her lower lip.

"No, I won't. I promise."

"I want to get out of software. Move to Southern California."

Gwen spun slightly in the chair, and her leg brushed against mine. A trace of excitement ran up my thigh.

"You don't like software?"

"It's been good to me. I won't deny that, but now I hate it. I have no idea what the product does, or how it does it, and that drives me crazy. I want to do something real. I want to be right in the middle of the production process."

"In California?"

"Yes, like in entertainment."

"You mean Hollywood."

"Maybe."

There's an old saying about LA and broken dreams, but I wouldn't count Gwen out early. I had seen her determination with the marketing program.

"You can have that," I said.

"I'm glad you think so." She sounded doubtful, like perhaps she was reaching too far.

"I mean it. There's no reason you can't. It will be tough, sure. From what I've read, the industry's brutally competitive. But you're bright, creative. You can do anything you want."

"You really think so?"

"Sure, why not?"

"I appreciate your vote of confidence. It means a lot."

"Anytime. My vote of confidence is yours for free."

She looked directly at me and her voice dropped lower. "What about you?" she asked. "What's your dream?"

"I have no idea."

"Surely there must be something." She leaned toward me and rubbed her finger on the rim of my glass. I wondered whether her lips would taste as good as they had in my office.

"Well, yes, there is. First, I want to make enough so I don't have to worry about money. Then I can step back and figure out the dream."

Gwen frowned at my explanation.

"What's wrong?" I asked.

"That sounds backward. Usually people follow their dreams first and then get rich. You know?"

"But what if I never achieve my dream? What if I end up broke? I can't afford a dream . . . not with a family."

"I never thought about that."

The conversation had gotten heavy, so we switched subjects. It was late, and I had a ten-o'clock flight in the morning. After another round we headed for the elevator banks. We walked side by side, a tad wobbly, rubbing shoulders around the corners. I wondered about the protocol for ending a half date between a married man and a single woman. When we reached her floor, I stepped off the elevator to say good night. The hall was empty. Gwen stood straight, two feet away, leaving me the next move.

I scanned from the blond locks past the shoulders, the high breasts, the flat stomach and narrow hips, all the way past the shapely legs to the suede pumps. I watched as she breathed; her chest rose and fell.

Then we were in each other's arms, kissing. She opened her mouth,

and I tried to consume her. I held her head in my hands and ran my fingers through her hair, the sound of heavy breathing in my ears. I tasted her lips and smelled her skin. My hands caressed her from the strong shoulders down her back to the bottom of her spine, while she played with the hair on my neck. Losing control, I let my hands creep to the front, up along her stomach, to feel her breasts. She reached for the small of my back and pulled me toward her.

"Let's go to my room," she whispered.

The voice of conscience was weak, barely audible.

This is wrong.

In desperation, I tore myself away and backed up to press the elevator button. She stood before me, sweater and hair askew, hands on hips, eyes glued to mine. The bell rang, and I stepped in to push the button for my floor. Her look of frustration followed me long after the door had closed.

• • •

THE NEXT MORNING I was of two minds about the encounter with Gwen. I was mad at myself for kissing another woman *and* for putting Gwen in that position, but at the same time, I was relieved we had not slept together. That sort of guilt I could not bear.

In the taxi to LaGuardia I was hungover and put on sunglasses to dim the light. When I called Gwen's cell phone, she picked up immediately.

"Gwen, I can't do this."

There was a long pause on the other end of the line. "I know."

"You're wonderful . . . but I'm married, and want to stay married."

"I know."

"And I'm sorry about leading you on."

"You should be. You're a real tease. I thought only women did that."

"It was totally my fault. I hope we can ignore it and still work together."

"I'll try. . . ."

"Me too."

CHAPTER 12

THAT NIGHT, after my return from New York, I stayed home, while Rose went out with the spouses who had gone on the San Miguel trip. I tucked the kids into bed with a Sheila story and read the paper in the family room. The door to the patio was open for fresh air. Outside, a lone cricket sang.

My mind kept wandering back to the moment of kissing and fondling Gwen in the hall. With my busy schedule, Rose and I hadn't found time to make love in weeks. Tonight she would be drinking wine with her friends and would come home in a good mood, so I was hopeful.

At eleven I heard the garage door opener engage, and her SUV pull in. Rose entered the room humming a party tune and dropped her keys on the side table next to the couch. She took off her jean jacket and let it fall to the floor. Underneath she wore a pink long-sleeved sweater and jeans with half boots. On the way over she undid the top two buttons of the sweater, exposing a delicious amount of cleavage. Pressing against my chest, she said, "How about a little fun time, Joey?"

We kissed with open mouths; Rose's tongue darted in to toy with mine, sharing a taste of mint and a hint of red wine. I kissed

her earlobe. Rose started unbuttoning my shirt, and I ran my hands down to her ass.

Being close to Rose, after weeks without intimate contact, was like feeding an addiction. The physical attraction combined with the emotional longing concocted a promise of heaven.

She pushed her breasts hard against me, and we kissed again. I hugged her tight and buried my nose in her hair; it smelled of jasmine and something else, an unpleasant odor from long ago.

"Have you been smoking?" I asked.

She froze. In college we both smoked, but we had quit together when Rose got pregnant.

With her hands on my chest, she traced small circles with one finger. Rose looked down sheepishly. "I might have had a couple with some of the girls after dinner."

"But you quit. We quit."

"I just had a couple."

"That's how it starts, with just a couple."

Rose pushed away from me. "You don't have to get all freaked out about it."

Instinct told me to shut up, but I wanted an answer.

"I'm not freaked out, just disappointed. I thought we were done smoking."

Her eyes went from uncertain to resolute. She walked to the kitchen side of the great room, around the counter, and got a water glass from the cabinet. She filled it at the refrigerator door. This was an evening ritual, her last move in the big room before going to bed.

"Guess what," she said. "While you're flying off to steak dinners in New York, I'm here laundering, cooking, and carting kids all over the damn place."

"So you start smoking?"

"No, damn it. I'm just trying to cope—to have a little fun!"

She'd come back from San Miguel refreshed and relaxed, but that was more than a month ago. The renewed grind of caring for the kids and managing the big house, with no support from me, had worn her down. Her face still held beauty, but it was fatigued. There were circles under her eyes the makeup couldn't hide.

I stepped close and tried to hug her again. She tightened up.

"It won't be long now," I said. "The road show starts Sunday."

"Yeah, and you'll be traveling for three weeks."

I leaned down to kiss her lips. They were cold.

"Come on, babe. Let's not fight."

"Shit . . . you started it by getting all sanctimonious over two cigarettes."

"I'm sorry."

"I'm not feeling it, Joey. I'm tired. You're on your own tonight."

CHAPTER 13

A CHAMPAGNE CORK POPPED from the forward part of the cabin. Hugh Crandall appeared in the aisle with the bottle, a broad grin on his face.

We were at thirty thousand feet, sampling caviar on mini toasts. The Hawker 750 cabin quieted most of the engine noise, leaving only a high-pitched hum and the hiss of recirculating air. The plush interior seated six comfortably. Webb was to my right. Across from Webb sat Peter Walstoncroft, a manager from Franklin Reynolds.

"Refill?" asked Hugh.

"Please," I answered.

He leaned over, tipped the Bollinger in my direction, and then sat in the seat across from me.

I felt good all over. They had loved us in Milan, Amsterdam, and Paris. Webb was brilliant. With each repetition his pitch got better. The European leg of the trip was supposed to be practice for the big U.S. show, but after every presentation real investors lined up to place real orders for shares of Connection Software.

The flight attendant walked the few feet back to our seats.

"Is there anything else I can get you, gentlemen?"

"Do you have any more of those crab claws?" asked Hugh. "They were delicious."

"Of course, sir. Just a moment."

She turned and walked toward the galley, but paused on the way to flirt with the two junior analysts from Franklin Reynolds. The three of them laughed.

Webb read the *Financial Times*, the glass of champagne next to him untouched.

Walstoncroft looked at his cell phone. "The market is off again today," he said.

It was Tuesday night, and we were flying from Paris to Frankfurt for another show in the morning. The NASDAQ had risen most of the previous week, but had fallen a full six percent the day before.

"Don't be a buzz kill," said Hugh.

"I apologize."

"The index will bounce right back."

"How much is the NASDAQ off?" asked Webb, looking up from his paper.

"About fifty points," answered Peter.

"It's been quite volatile lately," said Webb. "There's a chap here in the *Times* who believes the market is poised for a major correction."

"Talk about a buzz kill," I said.

"Nothing to worry about," said Hugh. "You guys are on a rocket ship. Keep in mind the NASDAQ hit five thousand last month. It's up over a hundred and forty percent in the last eighteen months. It was overheated; a mild correction is healthy for a long bull market."

Hugh Crandall was the picture of an investment banker: crisply laundered white shirt with gray pinstripes, burgundy silk tie, cuff links, neat blond hair, and clear, keen eyes.

"Is the champagne satisfactory, Webb?"

"It's fine." Webb took a small sip.

"If you don't like it we have an excellent Châteauneuf du Pape on board to go with the veal."

"It's fine."

"Investors are never as eager as they were today in Paris," said Hugh. "Did you see the fat guy in the back with the sunglasses? Pascal Lombard—he manages ten billion in Middle East money. He wasn't even scheduled to come . . . called at the last minute to see if we had room. He wants ten percent of the whole deal."

There was more laughter from up front as the French flight attendant continued to charm the young bankers. Hugh looked perturbed.

"What will happen if the stock market keeps falling?" asked Webb.

"It won't," said Hugh. "Even if it does, we'll be fine. The Connection is the hottest deal I've seen in years."

"I hope you're right."

There was another round of laughter from the younger group.

"Where are those damn crab claws?" Hugh stood and stepped forward in the cabin.

I was supremely confident. When I started at the Connection the NASDAQ was at 2348. So what if the index had slipped a bit? It was still up almost eighty percent. Webb was right: The market was volatile, but every time it went down it came right back up.

* * *

THE MEETING ROOM of the Westin in Frankfurt had tall windows with sheer drapes and enough seats for fifty people. We had finished giving the presentation to the German investors and were well into the Q&A.

A tall, gray-haired man in a dark suit and skinny tie raised his hand. He was seated toward the back of the room.

"How concerned are you about the frailty of the stock market?"

We had heard most of the questions before, but this was a new twist.

Webb answered, "We like to stay focused on the business of selling software and leave the stock market vagaries to the experts."

The man's brows remained furrowed; he was not so easily brushed off. I stepped up to the microphone.

"We have a solid business at the Connection. As long as we continue to develop great software, and grow revenues and profits, our shareholders will realize long-term gains regardless of the short-term swings."

"Yes, but the market is off twenty percent from the high, and nine percent in the last two days. Isn't that the definition of a bear market?"

"Well, technically that's true," I said. "Obviously we can't control what happens to the stock market at large. What we can do is manage our business. So long as our performance is strong, the Connection will be an attractive investment even in the midst of modest headwinds."

"Of course, I agree with you, but isn't it possible that a weak stock market could affect the attitude of your buyers? In and of itself, that could put a damper on sales."

"I suppose that is theoretically possible, but it seems unlikely."

There were a few murmurs from the room. Hugh Crandall jumped in to help.

"I'd like to remind the group that Webb and Joe are running a very successful software company. They are not here to field questions about the stock market, so if we could steer the conversation back to the business, that would be great."

We got two more questions, but the mood had changed; energy seeped out of the room like air from a punctured tire.

In the limo to the airport, Webb and I sat in the backseat, across from Hugh. Webb didn't say anything, but he kept looking at Hugh, then out the window, then back at Hugh. He didn't bother to check his voice mail. Instead he held on to the ceiling handle, and finally settled on looking out the window.

"Don't be concerned with comments about the stock market," Hugh counseled. "A couple strong days and all that will disappear."

"I hope you're right," said Webb.

* * *

WE FLEW TO ROME to give another presentation and then rushed back to the charter plane. By the time we got to Edinburgh, the NASDAQ had closed at 3770, down another seven percent.

Up to that point Hugh's enthusiasm had been unshakable: "They loved you. You rocked the house. This is going to be a blowout."

But when we landed in Edinburgh, and the reality of a fifteen percent decline in three days sank in, Hugh's coaching began to change. Instead of pumping us up, he tried to provide comfort: "We'll be fine. These swings are temporary. No matter what happens in the market, the Connection is still a great business."

On Thursday morning we pitched to a polite but quiet Scottish crowd and then flew to London, our final stop in Europe. Less than a dozen showed up for the presentation. All the questions were about the stock market, and the meeting ended early.

"The market is down again today," Hugh said after the room had emptied. "I hope you guys don't mind if I catch the Concord back in an hour. That will give me a full day in New York tomorrow."

"You go ahead," Webb said, looking out the window at traffic. "We'll manage to find our way back to Austin."

"If the market is strong tomorrow we'll be fine. Let's have a call when you get back . . . to check status."

"Sure."

Hugh picked up his briefcase and hurried from the room, the Franklin Reynolds entourage close behind.

Webb watched them go. "Is it my imagination or was Hugh supposed to take us to dinner and a show tonight?"

"He was," I answered.

"I'm sure he has problems of his own. After this week Franklin's clients must be getting nervous about pending deals, acquisitions and so forth."

"Let's have a drink."

It was busy in the hotel bar; well-heeled business travelers jockeyed for the bartender's attention. My height gave me an advantage, and we soon carried pints over to a stand-up table.

"Bollocks!" said Webb. "This whole thing is a bad deal."

"What's that?"

"Think about it. You've worked like a slave on this IPO for over a year. And the rest of us . . . we've been at it almost ten years now. After all that, here we sit, the outcome completely out of our control. I detest that . . . that loss of control."

"We might still be okay. The market could be up big tomorrow."

"You're right, of course, but I'm not optimistic."

"What's the worst that could happen?" I asked. "Demand for high-tech stock goes soft. We shelve the deal for a few months and then come back."

Webb looked at me like I'd said something important, and then I lost him. He had a faraway look in his eyes. "What was that you said just now?" he asked, still not completely there.

"We shelve the deal for a few months and then come back."

"No, no, the first thing . . . What was the question you asked?"

"What's the worst that could happen?" I was puzzled. It wasn't profound.

"Yes, that's it. What's the worst that could happen?" He seemed to ponder the question while he sipped on his beer.

"What?" I asked.

"Nothing. Forget it. What should we do for dinner?"

After that, he was in a great mood. We went for an expensive dinner and a show.

. . .

THE FOLLOWING DAY, while we flew west over the Atlantic, the NAS-DAQ fell another ten percent. Since the preceding Friday the index had fallen from 4446 to 3321, more than twenty-five percent. It was the biggest weekly decline in NASDAQ history.

. . .

"AAAAAAAAAAAAAHHHHHHHHHHH." I stood on our patio and screamed down the hill for the fifth time.

It was well after dark, and the kids were asleep.

Months before I had bought a bottle of Knappogue Castle, a single-malt Irish whiskey, intending to drink it when the Connection went public. I had decided to open it early. I drank the whiskey neat; the strong flavor and alcohol warmed my throat.

Earlier that day, when we landed back on American soil, Hugh Crandall told us we had no choice but to shelve the IPO; no investors wanted to make a move until they knew where the market was headed.

The outline of the boulders rimmed our pool in the dark. The sky was clear. The stars tried to comfort me with their permanence. Down on the lake the running lights of a bass boat glided upstream.

I tried to think about anything but the IPO. Despite the effort my thoughts always came back to it, and I began to calculate the months and hours of work. My dream had been so close, but now it was months away again. When the calculations and thoughts churned me up inside, I stood and screamed to chase them away.

What if I had made a mistake coming to the Connection? What if the market never came back? I had bet my career on it.

Rose came out wearing jeans and a sweater. She sat in a chair with a glass of wine and pulled her legs under.

"I wish you'd stop that yelling. The neighbors will call the police."

"Sorry."

"I don't blame you for being upset. You worked harder on that deal than ever before."

"It was in the palm of my hand, babe. I could almost feel it. It was that close."

I reached over to the side table and poured another shot of the whiskey. A cool breeze blew up from the lake. It was late spring, and soon the summer would arrive.

"So what happens now?" she asked.

"We're on hold."

"For how long?"

"Hard to say. Hugh Crandall thinks the market will bounce back quickly. Once it does, we'll dust off the presentation and hit the road again."

"In the meantime do we have enough money, personally?" She asked as if she wasn't sure whether to be concerned or not. It was the first time Rose had asked about our finances in years, but it was a

reasonable question. Our living expenses were outpacing my salary by five thousand a month, and we had only thirty thousand left in savings.

But I didn't want to bother Rose with those troubles. If the NAS-DAQ hadn't faltered we would be drinking champagne. The fact that we weren't was bad enough; I didn't want to admit that I had allowed us to blow through our savings. Surely a CFO, of all people, would not make that kind of mistake.

"We should be fine."

CHAPTER 14

I WALKED INTO WEBB'S OFFICE to give him an update. Three weeks had passed since we put the IPO on hold.

"So where is the NASDAQ today?" he asked.

"It's up slightly. The index has been hanging around 3800. It almost hit 4000 on Monday."

"Really? It's bounced back faster than I expected."

The NASDAQ had recovered fifteen percent. I should have felt good about that, but now we had other problems.

"Sit down," he said. "I'll be with you in a second. I just want to see what this is."

I took a seat at the meeting table. Webb was opening a box that had come in the mail. The package was three feet long and nine inches wide by four inches deep. Webb cut through the tape quickly and reached inside.

"Splendid, just splendid! Look at this."

It was a cricket bat from a customer in the sporting goods business. Their logo was branded on the side. As I talked, Webb took practice swings.

"Which do you want first?" I asked. "The good news or the bad news?"

"Good news first, if you please. Always start with the good news." He must have played in school; he had a good swing. He knew how to grip and how to turn his wrists to maximize power transfer to the bat. He pretended to hit long balls out his plate-glass window and over the Capitol Building downtown.

"Gwen's getting some real traction with the new marketing program."

"Excellent." Webb shifted his stance to get more behind the swing.

"Conversion rates continue to improve as the call center reps gain experience. The cost of sale on each deal is now substantially lower than the field sales approach. Unfortunately, the channel works only for small deals, and we don't make money on small deals."

Webb stopped swinging and sat at the table. I had his full attention.

"What if we find a way to make money on small deals?"

"Then it will be a great channel, much cheaper than field sales."

Webb stared out the window in silence. He was like that sometimes. A random thought would hit him, and he'd stop talking, often for a couple minutes, like he was thinking through chess moves on a board. I had gotten used to it.

"We'd have to alter the product to make money on small deals," he mused. "It would have to be much simpler, much easier to deploy." Webb continued to stare at the sky. "Some of the engineers have been talking about the ASP model finally getting traction."

"ASP?"

Webb looked at me, thinking, not sharing his thoughts. "Nothing . . . nothing useful. So we have a good channel but nothing to sell through it. We'll have to keep working on that. Now, what's the bad news?"

He stood and started swinging again; this time he stayed close to the meeting table. The bat *whooshed* as it pushed the air in front to the sides.

"Two things. First, our pipeline is shrinking. We've lost ten percent of this quarter's deals in the last two weeks. At this point it may be difficult to meet the stretch goals."

"That sounds bad." He swung the bat hard and watched the imaginary ball sail over the table, through the roof, and out of the cricket field. "What does Henry say?" Webb continued to swing the bat around the table, too close to me. *Whoosh!* It made me nervous. The pen in my hand shook, so I set it on the table.

Ever since the IPO failed, I'd had trouble sleeping. I kept running through numerical scenarios for what the company would be worth when we finally did go public. I'd use those results to calculate my take and then take another look at my checking account. Each time I ran the numbers the outlook was worse. I had counted on a year-end bonus to tide us over, but with the softer pipeline, my projected bonus was shrinking.

Webb swung the bat again, hard, closer to the table this time.

"Could you do that farther away?" I asked.

"What? Oh . . . sure."

But he didn't move. Webb stayed in exactly the same spot and kept swinging the bat hard. What was he doing? Was he fucking with me? As a kid at Sunset High, I had been challenged many times, and I learned one rule early on: When someone threatened you, it was always best to hit him first.

"Henry's not worried," I said, my voice hesitating. I looked at my notepad but couldn't focus on the words. "He has several big deals . . . in the pipeline . . . that he says will cover any shortfall."

"Right, so what's the next bad thing?" Webb swung the bat to a quick stop over the center of the table, two feet from my head. I felt the movement of air from the bat against my face.

It was like a switch had been flipped. My hands clenched up, and I pushed the chair back. He wound up for another swing.

"Stop it!"

He stood up straight, a frown on his face. "What?"

"Stop swinging the bat." I stepped away from the table, arms hanging loose, fingers flexing.

He gave me a puzzled look.

"It's a warning, Webb. Don't swing that bat near me again."

"It's nothing, an office toy from a customer."

"No, it's not. You're using it to make me anxious. I feel threatened."

He let one hand fall from the bat and looked at me without understanding, as if I were a foreigner whose English was limited.

"Fine, fine. Don't get so bothered about it." He walked over and put the bat behind his desk.

I sat and drank from the water bottle. Webb looked out the window at Highway 360. When the bottle was empty, my heart rate had slowed enough to process what had happened. I had almost punched my boss, a career-limiting move in any circumstance, but he had touched a nerve. So long as our interaction remained in the realm of words and numbers, I could engage in the discourse at length, but when it became physical, I switched into stimulus-response mode, a survival mechanism that had served me well in the past.

I looked at Webb; he seemed willing to resume the discussion.

"The second bad-news item . . ." I reported. "The Chartwell deployment is in trouble again. In addition to the fourteen million they paid for the license, they have spent ten million on our consulting services and twenty million more with an offshore firm. The functional spec is still not finalized, and our project manager says it could be a complete disaster."

He turned toward me, nodded his understanding, and I left the room.

∘ ∘ ∘

A WEEK BEFORE THE END OF THE QUARTER I reviewed the sales pipeline with Henry Jiwanlal, Tommy King, and Matt Simon, our new controller. We met in my office.

"This is looking grim," I said.

Henry and Tommy wore their customary jeans and polo shirts. Matt sat ramrod straight in his chair. He wore a long-sleeved button-down shirt and had close-cropped, salt-and-pepper hair.

"You worry too much." Henry tried to convince me. "I have three big deals that could easily make the quarter." He was always optimistic; he never failed to live up to the nickname he and Tommy had earned: the Zealots.

"Those deals don't seem ready to close," I countered. "We haven't even exchanged legal contracts with the customers yet."

"We've been in worse shape and still made the quarter."

"What do you think?" I asked Tommy.

As usual Tommy hadn't said a word. He was fiddling with a Rubik's cube I kept in the middle of the table, creating multicolored patterns I hadn't seen before. "Your analysis is good," he said to Matt, and then turned to me. "And I concur with your assessment. It looks grim."

"That's bullshit," Henry responded. "When have you ever been optimistic about a quarter? Do you remember the time we needed five million to hit the stretch goal? Remember that? The scanned signature page came across before midnight, didn't it?" Henry continued with the story from the good ol' days.

I let him carry on for a few minutes and then brought the discussion to an end. "Go sell some software, will you? Do some big deals so we can get back to the IPO."

As they got up, I asked Matt to stay behind. We could hear Henry and Tommy on their way down the hall.

"Since when do you know fuck about pipelines?" Henry complained.

"You curse too much."

"Don't worry about it. Just stick to the fucking demos."

As their voices faded I turned to Matt. "This is shaping up like a train wreck." He nodded his concurrence. "I want you to run a cash flow outlook in case we hit the low scenario. We have to be ready with a plan if the worst happens."

* * *

I WENT HOME AT FIVE O'CLOCK that day and found Rose hunched over the dining room table. Hundreds of photos were scattered across the surface.

"Hey, babe," she said, turning to kiss me. "I didn't expect you home so soon."

"There wasn't much going on at work. Deal flow is a trickle."

"That doesn't sound good."

"It's not. Henry thinks some big deals will close, but I'm skeptical."

I eyed the chandelier we installed when we moved in. It cost three thousand dollars. Outside, a yard worker trimmed the hedges. The lawn service charged a hundred a week.

"What does that mean for us?" she asked.

"It means a smaller bonus than I thought. We might have to cancel our vacation."

Rose turned back to the pictures. "I keep thinking . . . maybe I should get a job, but what would I do?"

"You don't need to get a job. We'll make this work."

"But it bothers me that I'm not qualified to get a well-paying job."

She plucked a couple photos from a Disney trip and moved them to a group on the right.

"What have you got going here?" I asked.

"Scrapbooking. I hate this crap. Some women are so good at it. They produce works of art. Mine look like fifth-grade projects."

"Why are you doing it?"

"We have thousands of them." She nodded toward a stack of plastic storage boxes at the end of the table. They were filled with family photos. "We've got to do something with them. Hey—maybe I can get the girls to do it."

I helped her sort photos for half an hour, and then we started making dinner.

"Want some wine?" I asked.

"Yes, please."

I looked around the great room, the hardwood floors, the high ceiling, the plate-glass windows looking onto the pool and the lake. If we sold the place and downsized we could cut our mortgage and the associated living expenses.

I handed her a glass and Rose took a sip of chardonnay. "So . . . what does a bad quarter mean for the Connection's finances?"

"We may have to lay off some employees."

"Webb's not going to like that," she said.

"I expect not."

"Every time I talk to him at Connection Plus dinners, he's always so passionate about the employees."

"The new controller and I have done some analysis. We've laid out scenarios for best-case, most likely, and low scenario. To get to best-case, we have to close two out of three of Henry's big deals. If we don't close those deals, we'll either lay off employees or burn a lot of cash."

⁜ ⁜ ⁜

As it turned out, we missed achieving even the low scenario by a wide margin. I proposed downsizing the staff to Webb.

"Absolutely not!" he said. "We've never laid off a single employee and we're not starting now." We sat across from each other at the table in his office. His mouth was set, his eyes locked on mine. His look of determination, of sheer will, was still seductive.

"We added costs in anticipation of deals that didn't close," I said. "As a result we burned through ten million in cash in the second quarter. That will continue if we don't reduce our cost structure."

Webb's cell phone vibrated on the table. He ignored it.

"If it was just a one-quarter problem we could recover," I said, "but my analysis of the pipeline indicates that this slowdown will last three more quarters, and possibly much longer."

"How much do you think we need to cut?"

"Thirty percent of the positions immediately."

"That's ridiculous."

"I don't want to do it either, but—"

"We'll stop hiring."

"Then what will the recruiters do?" I countered. "Surely we should cut them."

"No. We'll work our costs down through attrition. Our attrition rates are high. The other software companies in town are always after our people. If we stop countering the offers they'll hire them away."

"Maybe some of them, but every tech company will face the same issue sooner or later. There will be no jobs anywhere. Our attrition rate will fall to zero."

"I don't wish to discuss it further. Find another way."

But Webb had a sharp business mind. It took him only one night to realize there was no other way.

* * *

OUTSIDE, the July sun baked everything: the lake, the plastic roof of the marina, the wooden walkways, and the few boaters who ventured out. It was over a hundred degrees and only slightly cooler in the bar. The hot air hung still and drained what little energy we had left.

That morning I had fired twenty-five finance employees in a group meeting and then met with each one briefly. I knew their stories, their personal situations. At first their tears moved me. I worried about how they would fare and gave the best advice I could, but by the end I was numb and wanted only for the day to be done.

"We're dead," Gwen said.

"We're not dead," Henry answered.

"It feels like we're dead. It feels like I cut my own heart out."

The five of us, the core team, sat in Carlos'n Charlie's, an open-air bar on the edge of the lake. We had furloughed four hundred employees in total, more than a third of the company, in one day. Afterward Henry suggested we change clothes and head out to Lake Travis, where we could drink without encountering anyone we knew. It was a weekday, and there were only a few other customers in the bar.

"Don't overdramatize it," said Henry. "As long as the core team is together, we can grow the Connection again."

"You're a moron, Henry," Gwen said. "We fired half my group today. I can't grow that back. Who would believe the recruiting pitch now? 'Come join us at the Connection. We're the future. We might be the next Microsoft, or, alternatively, we might fire you so we can make payroll.'"

Gwen cast an angry look at me, the grim reaper. She wore a black tank top, jeans shorts, and flip-flops. She put her chin on her knee and closed her eyes. Her blond hair hung below her shoulders.

We sat around a varnished wooden table. The waitress had come and asked for our order, but we were too lethargic to decide, so she had brought water.

"It had to be done," said Webb. "For the good of those who remain, we had to preserve the financial strength of the company."

"Of course you're right," said Tommy. "The numbers are the numbers, but what do we do now?"

"I don't know," said Webb. "I honestly don't know."

Webb was never at a loss for words. Even Henry was stumped. No one stirred. No one spoke. A lone drop of perspiration rolled down my side. I took a drink of the water. It was ice-cold and wet but didn't quench my thirst. A light breeze picked up off the lake and brushed across my arm.

I walked over to the wooden bar, where our waitress chatted with the bartender. She wore tight short shorts and a halter top, Hooters-style. Her smile popped automatically.

"What can I getcha?"

"Five top-shelf margaritas on the rocks. Patrón, please. We're desperate."

"Coming right up."

The bartender swung into action, and the drinks arrived in short order. Henry perked up and took a sip.

"Damn!" he said. "Just what the doctor ordered." He looked at Tommy. "Try that, Tommy. See if that doesn't wake you up." He glanced at Gwen, who was still slumped. "You too, Gwen."

It had the bite of a double and the tartness of fresh lime balanced with the sweetness of Cointreau.

"That *is* tasty," said Tommy.

"We need to do something together," Henry said to Webb. "Just the core team. We need to shock the system, like a heart attack victim in the ER, to become re-energized and renewed."

Webb still looked grim. He reached out for the margarita and took a large gulp. He blinked and swallowed. "What did you have in mind?"

Henry had a sly look on his face. Slowly a grin opened on bright white teeth. "I'm thinking Vegas."

Tommy sat up straight, his interest piqued. Gwen lifted her head and looked at Webb as he frowned.

"I'm not feeling much like Vegas," said Webb.

"It'll be the perfect thing," said Henry. "You'll see. Once we get there you'll fall right into it."

"I don't know."

"Absolutely. You can play high stakes at the craps table. Gwen can spend hours in the poker room, and the rest of us can hit the strip clubs . . . hard."

A small glimmer showed in Webb's eyes. "Vegas . . . ."

"Yes, sir. We can even bring Jack O'Shea along." Henry looked at me. "Even though the guy's married, he's an absolute chick magnet. It's fucking phenomenal."

"You curse too much," said Tommy, but he wasn't really complaining.

Over my glass I noticed Gwen looking at me. She picked up the margarita and sipped it. "All right," she said. "So we go to Vegas to have a good time. What happens when we get back?"

"We rebuild the company," said Henry. "Simple as that."

"It's not going to be simple," said Webb.

"Okay, you're right. It's not going to be simple. It's going to be hard as hell, and we'll have to work our tails off, but we are the core team. We can do anything. Am I right?"

He looked at Tommy. The other half of the Zealots was always the easy sell. A little grin came to Tommy's face. "You're right, Henry," he said. "We can do anything."

"Gwen? Joe? Am I right?" Henry raised his glass in the air as if to toast, a question on his face.

I still had the dream. It would take longer, but we could still do it. I hoisted my glass and saw Gwen smiling as she raised hers.

"What do you say, Webb? To the Connection? To the core team?"

Webb turned his violet eyes to the group. He looked at each of us in turn, as if to determine whether we were sincere, and then slowly raised his glass.

"We few . . ." Henry proposed.

And together we answered, "We happy few."

• • •

ALL I NEEDED was a kitchen pass to Vegas for a couple nights.

Rose was in the family room, folding clothes and watching the news. She wore an old T-shirt and gym shorts. She had on scant makeup, her hair pulled under a baseball cap with the ponytail flipped out the back. The kids were playing at a neighbor's house.

"Hey, babe?"

"Yeah?"

"What do you think of me going to Vegas for a couple nights with the core team?"

She stopped folding and gave me a skeptical look. "When?"

"Tomorrow. We just laid off four hundred people. Everybody's feeling low, and I want to be supportive."

She shook her head as I talked. "You're asking an awful lot."

"Not really. You took that trip to San Miguel. I supported you then."

Rose didn't say anything. She held a clean pair of little girl's shorts in her lap. Her face screwed up and her lips started to quiver.

"What's the matter?"

She stood and fought for control. "You brought us here from Dallas. I had a lot of friends in Dallas. So did the kids." She used the back of her hand to wipe away a tear.

I took a step toward her, but she put a hand out to stop me.

"You said we'd be millionaires. Four or five in the bank by now. Easy."

"We've got to get through this rough spot first. It's going to work out. You'll see. The dream is still alive."

"Dream? Some dream. More like a nightmare."

"You've got to have faith. Just because we hit a little bump in the road—"

"Bump in the road! This isn't a bump. The Connection just drove off a cliff!"

That shut me up, but she wasn't finished.

"I guess 'layoffs' means no bonus this year. Right?"

"Probably not," I admitted.

"So what about the money?" Her voice rose higher. "We've got the big mortgage, the car payments. You're the CFO. How do you make the numbers work?"

"We've got a cushion."

"Not much!" She threw the shorts on the floor and continued to shout. "You've already drawn down the 401(k). What's next?"

I was silent. I had hoped she wouldn't notice the loan against the retirement fund, but Rose was too quick for me. She must have become concerned and gone online to check the balance.

"Go ahead," she said. "Go to Vegas, but while you're there you'd better win big." She picked up the shorts and started folding again, faster than before. As I turned toward the patio door, she called after me, "Better yet, ask Webb for a raise."

I walked out into the staggering heat. Screw her. Sure, she worked hard to take care of the kids, but I was working harder, working until my brains were scrambled to provide for the family. I was stressed over the money too, plenty stressed. She got her party trip to San Miguel, and I was damn sure going to take mine.

CHAPTER 15

WE WERE BOOKED on the five o'clock Southwest Airlines nonstop. I found the gang drinking Coronas at Ray Benson's Roadhouse bar in the terminal. From the small bandstand a folk group sang "Whiskey in the Jar." Henry and Tommy hadn't shaved; they both wore Hawaiian shirts with shorts and sandals. Webb was unshaven as well and wore a polo, old jeans, and penny loafers with no socks. They were with a tall redhead in a black top with spaghetti straps and low-cut jeans. She had her back to me and was talking to the bartender; there was something familiar about the shoulders. She turned around with a margarita, and I did a double take.

Gwen took a sip, saw the surprise on my face, and said, "New times. New look."

"What'll you have?" the bartender asked.

I was distracted. It took a moment for his question to register.

"Dos Equis, lime."

The red hair was tucked behind her right ear; on the left side it lazily curled to a wavy finish that grazed her shoulders. The blue of her eyes was gone, replaced by a deep green, and her lips were a glossy rose. The heels made her taller, a hair shy of six feet.

"You look nice," I said.

Henry glared at me like I was stupid. "Nice? She looks fucking great," he exclaimed. "She's going to crush them in the poker room. You should see her, Joe. She plays that dumb-blonde routine—oh, I guess I should say dumb-redhead routine—and they lose track of the cards."

"I can imagine that," I said.

Gwen smiled at me. She took the lime out of my bottle and squeezed it, then jammed it in the narrow opening. It didn't want to go through, but she forced it.

"Oh, I'm harmless," she said. "You should play with me."

The memory of our tussle outside the elevator in New York was fresh, my frantic hands exploring her body. I'd have to be careful in Vegas.

"Thanks," I said. "I'd better stick to blackjack. It's safer."

"Suit yourself."

"Drink fast, folks," said Henry. "We've got an airplane to catch."

* * *

VEGAS WAS VEGAS, with drinks, gambling, wine with dinner, and afterward more gambling and more drinks. We met Jack O'Shea in the lobby of the MGM. Henry was right: Jack was a chick magnet and had already convinced three young teachers from Phoenix to join our party. He could stay only one night in Vegas and wasn't wasting any time.

All the while I told myself I wasn't going to the strip club with the guys. If you're married to a woman who enjoys sex as much as Rose, going to a strip club is like watching black-and-white television.

But after a half dozen drinks, and constant encouragement from Henry, I found myself in a stretch limo. Webb came also, as did the three teachers, but Gwen stayed behind to play poker.

As we stepped out of the limo at the Club Paradiso, Webb handed me a thick roll of hundreds. "Here," he said. "Keep this safe for me."

Webb tipped the bouncer a hundred, and he opened a cordoned area for us with a sectional couch big enough for a dozen people. A cute waitress in fishnet stockings, short shorts, and a sleeveless top dedicated her efforts to quenching our thirst.

The place was dark, with a topless woman on the center stage and three others on outlying platforms. The main dancer had tattoos on her shoulders and upper arms and climbed the pole to a heavy-metal tune. By then it was midnight, and the club was full of revelers like us.

The routines varied from woman to woman, but they all ended with the dancer wearing nothing but high heels and a G-string. Several dozen trolled the lounge for lap-dance customers. At any given moment a third of them were topless, dangling breasts in front of a man's face. It didn't take long for them to start wandering into our area. An Asian doll with an enhanced chest eased into my lap. She jumped up immediately.

"What's that?" she complained, and fingered the thick cylinder to make sure it wasn't offensive.

Without thinking I answered, "A roll of hundreds."

Within minutes seven of them were on me, urging me to join them in the VIP room. They were of all colors and shapes: one perched on each leg, three dancing in front, and another two behind the couch, massaging my chest. Two of the standing girls shed their tops to show me how their boobs could do the shimmy. Someone was digging at my pants pocket for the roll.

Webb stood to the side, shaking his head. He signaled our bouncer, and in seconds the girls had been scattered.

He laughed uncontrollably and took a full minute to catch his breath. "Have you ever tossed a bit of bread in a pond and seen the

minnows attack? That's precisely what you looked like with the dancers. They were going to rip you apart."

"I never should have mentioned the money."

"Agreed. Now hand me the roll." I fished it out and he peeled off
five hundreds. "Here, spend that wisely."

Webb turned back to the bouncer and pointed out a few different
girls in the bar. I drained my drink. The Bombay Sapphire on ice had
gone down too easily, so I switched to beer. Henry sat next to me, the
white of his grin glowing against his dark skin.

"Isn't it great?" He looked out over the expanse of the club. On
the main stage a topless black Amazon crawled to a cluster of cheering
cowboys. "It's not just the spectacle of half-naked women dancing for
money, although I'm not complaining about that part. It's really the
pageantry, the strategic layout of the separate stages, the careful selection of the music. It's a show, a highly choreographed performance."
Henry had a gleam in his eye, but he wasn't looking at a particular
girl. It was the whole experience that excited him.

"Yeah, it's great." I couldn't muster the same enthusiasm.

"You sound depressed. What's up?"

"Nothing."

"Come on. We're supposed to be having a great time. It's the
money, isn't it? You're worried about the IPO."

It was Henry's job to be empathetic. Once he knew the customer's
real need he could shape his pitch.

"Well, Rose is certainly bothered about the money."

"Tell her not to worry. So long as there is a core team, the money
will come."

"You don't seem to care that much."

"About what?"

"Money."

He shook his head. "I want us to have it because we deserve it, and because Tommy needs it, but I don't need money."

"But if you're rich you can do anything you want."

"What else would I want? I already have everything: you, me, Tommy, Webb, and Gwen. The core team, pursuing the goal, engaged in battle. That's all I need."

He was serious. He didn't look at me when he said it. Henry looked toward the stage, but his eyes didn't move with the girl; he was someplace else.

"It sounds like you've already got what I want," I said.

"What's that?"

"Freedom."

Henry looked back at me. We were both buzzed by then, but sometimes there comes a point, even in a drunk conversation, when you feel like you're close to making a connection, like something important is being discussed.

"No, dummy," he said. "Freedom doesn't come from money or other people. Freedom comes from within, but I'm not talking about that. I'm talking about living on a higher level than the individual. That's what the core team is: a group of highly intelligent people with extraordinary skills, bound together in pursuit of a nearly impossible goal. Nothing is more important than that."

Henry locked eyes with me. He wasn't smiling. It was as if he were fighting for a cause and wanted me to believe in it as much as he did.

"Do you understand?" he asked.

"No."

"The core team is everything. It's the beginning and the end. *Nothing* is more important to me."

"I can sense your passion, but it's not the same for me. My family is more important." As soon as the words were out of my mouth, it occurred to me that the core team was Henry's family. There was no one else.

He didn't say anything, just kept looking at me with a somber face, but after a while a smile came back to his lips. "We've got to lighten this up. Where the hell are the strippers?"

Just then a dancer walked up.

"Well, *hello*," Henry said, and stood to shake her hand. "What's your name?"

"Elsie."

I stood with them.

"My goodness, you're tall," she said to me.

"Please," Henry said. "Sit down. Sit down. Let's get you something to drink."

We sat in the corner of the sectional couch, with me in the middle.

She had the body and costume of a professional cheerleader, with white tight-fitting shorts, a blue halter top knotted in front, and short white boots. She had big blond hair and a round face with bright teeth. She leaned across me to talk with Henry.

"You men look so serious. I thought you could use some company."

"Much too serious," Henry said. "Much too serious, and it's all his fault."

Elsie picked at my wool sweater. "Oh, this has to go. It's too scratchy."

Henry waved the bottle girl over, and Elsie ordered champagne. I had made up my mind not to take any lap dances and moved forward to stand.

"Where you going, big boy?" Henry said. "Just sit your ass down."

Soon they were chattering like old friends and kept reaching across my lap to make their points.

She was intelligent, articulate, and had studied three years at Spokane College. She was in no particular rush to dance. In fact, she seemed quite content to laugh at Henry's jokes and gossip with us about the other girls who worked at the club. Elsie was all girl and

all fun. She was completely in the moment. She leaned against me as we talked. She playfully pushed on my shoulder and then absently let her hand fall on my leg.

Henry grabbed my arm drunkenly and pointed toward Jack O'Shea.

"Look at that. Jack's girls are getting lap dances."

Sure enough, O'Shea grinned wildly as three strippers moved in close to the teachers.

Henry started to tell me a story about Jack. After a minute I noticed Elsie talking to herself in a low singsong voice as her eyes darted around the room. It was a recital of something, but she said it so quickly I couldn't make sense of it.

"What's that, Elsie?"

With our attention secured, Elsie stood before us in her cheerleader get-up.

"It's a monologue," she said. "Do you want to hear it?"

"Oh, absolutely," said Henry. "We must hear it."

She spaced her feet shoulder-width apart and stood up very straight. "It's something I learned in a play we did one time at school."

"Please," Henry implored her. "Proceed when you're ready."

Elsie smiled, opened her eyes wide, and began:

> Be kind and courteous to this gentleman;
> Hop in his walks and gambol in his eyes.

I gave Henry a clueless look, and he said in my ear, "I never heard a stripper do Shakespeare before."

Elsie continued.

> Feed him with apricocks and dewberries,
> With purple grapes, green figs, and mulberries;

The honey-bags steal from the humble-bees,
And for night-tapers crop their waxen thighs
And light them at the fiery glowworm's eyes,
To have my love to bed and to arise;
And pluck the wings from painted butterflies
To fan the moonbeams from his sleeping eyes:
Nod to him, elves, and do him courtesies.

Henry whispered again. "It's Titania, from *A Midsummer Night's Dream.*"

Elsie plopped down and sipped the champagne, quite pleased with her performance. She sat sideways on the couch, facing me.

"Shakespeare?" I posited, as if hazarding a guess.

She nodded.

"*A Midsummer Night's Dream.*" I didn't dare name the character. I had no idea who Titania was.

Elsie beamed and threw her arms around my neck.

"You were brilliant," I said.

"I can't believe you know it. No one has ever recognized that monologue."

"What does it mean?"

She came in close to whisper. I smelled roses and baby powder. "Something about taking care of a man."

At that moment I thought about wrestling with Gwen in the hallway of the Hilton in New York. My resolve to forgo a lap dance was weakening. What would be the harm? After all, Elsie was an honest girl trying to make a living.

She read my mind and jumped up, spread my legs wide, and stepped in between. I looked to my right, but Henry had vanished. Two strippers were dancing for Tommy at the same time. Jack O'Shea laughed as the strippers rubbed themselves all over the girls.

Shania Twain sang "Man! I Feel Like a Woman!" and Elsie yanked my sweater over my head. She damn near pulled my T-shirt off at the same time.

She shed her costume in seconds until all that was left was a sequined thong and her boots. She knelt in front of me and slowly crawled her way to blow in my ear. Nipples brushed against my lips as fingers ran through my hair. She turned over and lay on my chest, her ass doing a slow churn in my lap. She stroked my legs while I ran my fingers along the outside of her thighs, up around her rib cage, and down her taut tummy. I traced the outline of her thong with my thumbs. She gradually slid down the length of my front until she knelt before me, facing away, the back of her head turning on my crotch as she watched me upside down. She flipped over again, pressed her full breasts into my loins and ground them in circles, smiling at me. The song ended then, not a moment too soon. She stood up, and I shifted on the couch, trying to get comfortable.

"Whew," she said. "I need to take a break." She sat and lit a cigarette, not bothering to get dressed. "You're a big guy," she said with a wink, a practiced gesture sure to score tips from all her customers.

The bottle girl fixed new drinks, and we talked. Elsie was perfectly at ease, drinking champagne, her breasts in full view, within arm's reach, the nipples still erect.

She explained her history. She had started dancing as a part-time thing in college, but when she realized how much money could be made, she quit school altogether.

We kept going like that: talking through a few songs, her doing a dance for me, then grabbing another drink. After an hour it was time for Elsie to take her turn on the center stage. I told her I'd be leaving before she finished. She was disappointed and told me to wait while she ran to the dressing room.

I tried to count the drinks I'd had since we took off from Austin, but got lost at ten. Somewhere in the back of my mind I knew it was time to go, because in the front of my mind, I kept thinking about how nice it would be to come live with Elsie.

She came back and gave me a business card that read, "Elsie Summers, Marketing." On it was a phone number. I was surprised that Elsie was her real name, and even more surprised that she had given me a card.

I gave her the five hundred dollars. Elsie tiptoed to nibble on my ear, reached around to grab my bottom, and then ran backstage. I knew it wasn't real, but it felt good anyway. I hadn't worried about money for hours. The argument with Rose was long gone.

CHAPTER 16

THE NEXT MORNING I slept until ten and woke with a Vegas hangover. I called Rose to check in. The kids were playing in the pool and took turns drying off so they could talk to Daddy. After a quick breakfast I decided to try swimming laps in the hotel pool to clear my head.

The MGM pool area is six acres of lush tropical plants. Set among the palm trees are five pools, four bars, dozens of cabanas, and several thousand chairs.

I walked by the big party pool first. Half the chairs were occupied by men and women in their twenties and thirties. Women in skimpy suits layered on lotion and lay out in full view of direct rays.

There were five lanes in the exercise pool, all of them occupied, so I sat under an umbrella to wait. A waitress came by and took my order for a Diet Coke.

Most of the swimmers were amateurs, but there was a serious athlete in the third lane. She wore her hair under a swim cap, and it took a few laps for me to recognize Gwen. She swam freestyle, with the long and powerful strokes of a trained swimmer. After a few more laps she glided to a stop at my end and reached for a water bottle on

the side of the pool. She wore dark swim goggles and a modest neon-yellow bikini top. I waved from twenty feet, and she spotted me.

"Give me ten minutes," she called, "and I'll join you."

After a glance at her watch she grabbed a kickboard and headed down the lane, her shoulders rotating side to side. Using only her legs, she moved as quickly as the unhindered pretenders beside her. As if to show off, she finished the workout with two laps of butterfly. The stroke has always fascinated and eluded me: the funky rhythm and the *whoompf*-splash-*whoompf*-splash do not look or sound quite human. Her thunderous kick propelled her upper body out of the water, allowing her to gulp air as her arms whipped to the front. When finished, she pulled off the goggles and rested her arms on the side of the pool, her lungs heaving.

Hopping out, she peeled off the cap and shook the red hair free as she walked. She wore a practical bikini bottom. It was the first time I had seen so much of her. Her body was strong but still feminine. The muscles in her thighs and calves were taut, her upper arms pumped from pulling the water.

She stopped at the chair next to mine.

"It's a great pool area, isn't it?" she asked, still breathing hard.

"They claim it's the best in Vegas."

She wiped her arms and legs with a towel and sat down.

"You boys have fun at the gentlemen's club last night?" She smiled her crooked smile and wrapped her arms around her knees in the chair. The skin of her legs was smooth and tan.

I nodded. "A little too much fun. I'm paying for it today."

"Are you going to work out?" she asked.

"I'd better. Maybe it will clear my head."

"Before you go, will you put some sunscreen on my back?"

I hesitated, but only for a second. "Sure."

Gwen lay on her stomach, snapped open the strap of her top, and held her hair off to the side.

I squirted cream into my hands and rubbed it into her skin, starting at the shoulders. Her back was already warm from the sun, and I applied the sunscreen liberally all across the strong muscles, down the small of her back to the top of the bikini.

"That okay?"

"Perfect. Go swim. I'm going to catch a nap."

I swam for thirty minutes. I tried to draw out my strokes, to pull the water efficiently like Gwen, but my style was no better than that of the other amateurs in the pool.

When I got out Gwen was asleep. I sat quietly, careful not to wake her while I toweled off. She was still on her stomach. Her arms were tucked to her sides along her legs. Her mouth was open, and she breathed slowly and evenly, the red curls spread across her shoulders. I watched the rise and fall of her back.

A loud couple walked by; they drank red, slushy cocktails from plastic cups.

Gwen began to wake up. Her eyes blinked but stayed shut. Her mouth moved and she licked her lips.

Behind me someone collided with a pool waiter, and a tray of drinks crashed to the deck.

Gwen pushed off the chair and yawned.

"What was that?"

Her breasts were in full view. They were small and firm, the areolas dark brown, the nipples erect.

"Uh, Gwen?" I indicated her condition with a nod of my head and then averted my eyes.

"Oh, shit. Don't look!"

Of course, by then it was too late. "Sorry."

It took her a few seconds to locate the top and fasten it.

"You can turn around now. Christ, that's embarrassing."

"Don't worry about it."

She looked sheepish for a few beats but then quickly recovered.

"Well, it's not like you haven't seen boobs before. Hell, you probably saw hundreds last night."

"That's a high estimate, but there were quite a few."

I tried to sound nonchalant, but I was turned on sitting so close to Gwen and seeing her half-naked. My mind flew back to the hallway in New York. Trying to pull it together, I surveyed the chairs and umbrellas surrounding the pool.

The moment of awkwardness left Gwen. After the workout and the nap she talked with ease. We discussed the upcoming presidential election, her poker adventures from the night before, and gradually came around to the Connection. As we talked about work I listened to her words and tried to ignore her body.

"This trip was a good idea," she said. "After the layoffs we needed to blow off some steam. It's going to be tough sledding when we get back to work."

"You think so?"

"Oh, yeah. Morale has never been worse. It's going to be nearly impossible to rally the troops."

"Henry doesn't agree. He is confident the Connection will turn quickly."

"The Zealots never lose their passion. Sure, we all joined hands and sang 'Kumbaya,' but that isn't going to make it any easier."

"You're starting to depress me."

"I'm just trying to be realistic. Think about it. We built a rocket ship . . . convinced everyone we were going to the moon, and then when times got tough, we jettisoned a third of them like a spent fuel stage."

I sipped my Coke and looked across the pool at the palm trees. Rockets are prettier going up than coming down. This turnaround could take a lot longer than I thought. My money situation would get

dicey. Rose was right; I should talk to Webb about a raise, or a loan to carry us through to the IPO.

"This could be the beginning of the end," she said.

"Now you've gone from realistic to pessimistic. Every business can be turned around so long as you don't run out of cash."

"You're probably right. In any case, that's enough serious talk. I didn't come here to fix the business. I came to have fun and fleece old guys in the poker room."

Gwen sat upright in the chair and reached into her bag for a T-shirt. "One thing I know for sure is that I won't win any money sitting by the pool. Are you gambling today?"

"I think I will. Despite your negativity, I'm feeling lucky."

· · ·

I COULDN'T LOSE THAT DAY. I won betting on baseball in the sports book. I won playing roulette. I joined a couple from Toledo at a black-jack table. They claimed martinis were their lucky drink. Why not? Four martinis and three hours later I was two thousand richer. I went to Wolfgang Puck's for dinner and ran into Henry and Tommy. They were heading over to the Hard Rock, but I begged off, not wanting to interrupt a winning streak. I wandered around the casino for a couple hours, not winning or losing much until I tried Let It Ride. I bet fifty bucks a hand and after six hands was dealt a full house. The payoff was twenty-five hundred dollars.

The world was a good place after all! There were four yellow chips in my pocket, each worth a thousand. I wanted to celebrate and went in search of my companions. As I rounded the far corner of the casino I passed the poker room.

It wasn't really a room, more of a large area cordoned with a

three-foot wooden rail. There were twenty or so tables, each big enough for ten players and a dealer, and every seat was taken.

Gwen sat at a table with nine men of all ages. She wore a white satin strapless party dress with a pleated bust. For jewelry she wore single-pearl earrings and a black onyx bracelet. They were between deals, and she joked with the men. A couple of the players were cautious and ignored her. The rest were engaged, thrilled by the banter and distracted by the long expanse of skin between her shoulders and the top of the dress. She looked busy, so I kept walking.

I searched for the others awhile but then gave up and stopped at the Crazy Horse bar for a Maker's Mark. The shelves were reserved for different liquors: expensive scotch lined the bottom shelf, liqueurs were on two, and vodkas on three. The colorful bottles were reflected in the mirror behind the shelves. Casino sounds were constant: chips being counted, slot machines, an occasional laugh.

It would be nice to celebrate with Gwen. If she were there I would study her face, her eyes, her hair, and the white satin dress with no straps. There was an awful lot of skin—skin that I had massaged with sunscreen that very morning. After an hour I looked up and there she was, smiling at me in the reflection of the mirror.

"I saw you in the poker room," I said. "You were leading the lambs to slaughter."

She smiled bigger and shrugged. "Sometimes it works."

The white party dress had a midlength skirt and a black tieback waistband. She wore black pumps with open toes.

We had a nightcap, and I recounted my gambling adventures. She laughed at my description of the Toledo folks and whistled at my Let It Ride win. When the drinks were empty, Gwen stood up.

"Don't walk me to the elevators," she said. "We both know that's trouble."

She leaned in to give me a kiss on the cheek. Her hand held my wrist and lingered there for just a moment. I wanted to touch her also, but resisted.

When she was gone, I ordered one more round and thought about that night at the Hilton. What would have happened if I had gone to her room? Would we have had an affair? No. I could never betray Rose . . . never break my marriage vows. Did I want to have sex with Gwen? Hell, yes. Would I ever? No. No. Never . . . out of the question. I was happily married, at least, most of the time.

I was crossing the slot machine field, heading back to the elevators, when a redhead in a white outfit caught the corner of my eye. At first I thought it was Gwen, but then I realized the woman was shorter and wore a miniskirt. We were heading in the same direction, and she hurried to intercept me at the end of a row.

"Where you goin'?" she asked. She was not on MGM's payroll but she was still working and wore sufficient makeup to play the part. Her red hair was short and curly, and she had a cute figure inside the tight skirt and halter top. With bright blue eyes and a big smile she continued the pitch. "You want to go have some fun?"

"No, thanks." I started to step around her.

She grabbed my arm and moved in close. "Are you sure?"

The slots were mostly empty. In the distance a cheer went up from a winning table. She had done a good job with the makeup, and her hand felt nice on my arm. I closed my eyes for a long second and saw Gwen lying on my king-size bed in her party dress.

"No, thank you." I moved insistently away.

She gave up and continued her search.

Back in my room I brushed my teeth and drank a bottle of water. I congratulated myself on turning down the prostitute. I took off my shoes and shirt and lay back on the bed in T-shirt and jeans. I tried to count the number of drinks I'd had that day but lost track again.

What kind of a CFO was I? I was starting to doze when there was a knock on the door.

It was too early for housekeeping. Then I remembered the prostitute; maybe she had promised the elevator security guy a cut of the action. I walked to the door and looked through the peephole to see red hair. I opened the door and there was Gwen, with green expectant eyes and her crooked smile.

She opened her mouth to speak. "I just thought . . ."

I grabbed her wrist and pulled her into the room. As the door closed I kissed her. We frantically clutched at each other. As the kiss continued she breathed through her nose, and the sound fueled my lust. I grabbed the front of the dress and yanked it down to free her breasts. I leaned down, buried my face in her chest, and tasted her nipples, inhaling the scent of her flesh. She ran her fingers through my hair and pulled my head into her. I knelt, and my hands felt the backs of her thighs and crept up to grasp her bare buttocks. I looked up to her face. She smoothed my hair with her fingers and smiled just a little.

Standing up, I pulled the dress above her waist and lifted her in the air. Gwen wrapped her legs around me as I carried her to the bed. I put her down, and she grabbed at my belt while I reached under the skirt. I found the sides of her lace thong and dragged them off, throwing her pumps on the floor. I pulled at my pants to free myself while Gwen reached in her clutch for a condom. I leaned into her, desperate to connect.

When we did I looked at Gwen, her eyes closed with head arched back against the bed, mouth open as she inhaled sharply.

"Oh, yes," she whispered. "I've been waiting . . . such a long time."

I began to thrust, the skirt around her waist, her legs spread wide. My arms were straight to the bed. She pulled back her hair and opened her eyes. We stared at each other, expressionless, focused on

the sensations, the building pressure. At the end I lunged into her, and Gwen pulled on my back as she ground against me. I watched as she broke my gaze and turned her head to experience the waves, breathing quickly. I kissed her mouth, eyelids, and down to her neck, burying my face in her hair. We separated to lie side by side, exhausted.

· · ·

AT FIVE A.M. I woke up, still drunk, needing to relieve myself. Gwen was in the same spot, asleep, naked except for the satin dress bunched around her middle. I zombie-walked around the bed and into the bathroom, then came back out to turn off lights, remove my pants, and fall back on the bed to sleep.

· · ·

SOMETIME AROUND NINE a heavy rush of noise subsided in my brain, and I neared consciousness. I was a mess: my throat parched, eyelids sealed shut, head pounding with each heartbeat. Even my joints ached.

I'd had dreams before about cheating on Rose with an old girlfriend and felt the heavy weight of guilt, only to be relieved upon waking that I was innocent. With my eyes still shut, a hazy recollection of the night assembled itself. Suddenly a vision of Gwen and me on the bed appeared, and for an instant I thought it was a dream. I sprang to a sitting position and opened my eyes to see her sleeping form. With head in hands, I tried to comprehend.

Quietly I stepped into the bathroom, shut the door, and turned on the bright light. The fan kicked on automatically. I turned on the faucet and ran my fingers under the water before splashing my face.

In the mirror my golden eyes were slits, bloodshot, with puffy bags. I stood to my full six-four and surveyed the suspect: sandy curls messed up by the bed, overgrown whiskers. I had the same solid frame and physical strength, but something was missing. Gone was the innocence, the suspect guilty as charged.

I set about my daily ritual: shaved, brushed teeth, showered the hair back in shape, and pondered a question: Is infidelity a black-and-white matter, or are there shades of gray? Look at it from one side and it's quite clear: You either did it or you didn't. Look at it from another angle and there are degrees of severity.

If I had paid for sex the night before, and the prostitute had left my room afterward, as she surely would have, it would have seemed less of a violation. If I sent Gwen away right then, blamed it all on alcohol, then perhaps there was an additional line I would not cross. Under that scenario I could tell myself, "On a scale of one to ten, my transgression was only a three, at most a four."

Back in the room sunlight crept in around the edges of the heavy curtains. Asleep, Gwen lay on her side facing me, wearing one of my T-shirts. Her hair was pulled back and she had taken off her makeup. As I sat on the bed she stirred and slowly awakened, her fists rubbing out the sleep. When she sat up, I saw that her eyes were a pale gray. She smiled and waited. I leaned in to kiss her, and she stopped me. "Wait; let me go to the bathroom."

I lay in bed and knew that I would make love to her again. She walked out nude, her breasts high and firm. She was a natural brunette, with pubic hair that was closely trimmed. We made out slowly, exploring each other's bodies, our fingers tracing contours of arms and waists and hips. When the tension began to build we stroked the sensitive spots until we were ready. She sat astraddle me with her hands on my chest, rocking slowly for the longest time, savoring the

sweetness, until I could wait no longer and urged her on. She moved with earnest concentration and soon cried out, shaking and settling to lie flat on my chest. I ran my hands down her sides and up her back until her breathing returned to normal.

My flight was at one, so I had to hustle. Rather than go back to her room, Gwen lay naked on the bed and watched me scurry around.

Jack had left Vegas the day before, and the rest of the team was staying for one more day, but Rose and I had agreed on two nights.

Gwen stood with me in the taxi line of the MGM, in her white satin dress and no makeup. I wasn't worried about anyone seeing us together; the others would sleep until two.

Hungover revelers with sagging faces lined up with their luggage. The doormen hustled bags into the trunks of cabs and pocketed two-dollar tips. A huge fan pushed hot, dry air across the guests.

"This has to be a one-time thing," I said.

I didn't know what she expected. I had an empty feeling, like someone close to me had died.

"That's funny." She gave me a sad smile. "It sure felt like two times to me."

"I'm serious. I can't lose my family."

She looked out from the overhang to the traffic on Tropicana Avenue. She had put in her contacts, so the green eyes were back to go with the red curls.

"You don't have to worry," she said. "I'm not going to stalk you or leave love notes in your e-mail in-box."

She stepped in to hug me.

I didn't know what else to say.

"There was a lot of sexual tension between us," she said, trying to make it easier for me. "Maybe with that out of the way, we can settle for being professional colleagues."

"We have to."

"Will you kiss me?"

I was at the front of the line, and the cab pulled up. I leaned in to give her a kiss and started to pull away, but she held me, not wanting it to end. So I stepped closer and wrapped her in my arms and kissed her with all the passion I had.

As the cab drove out she looked satisfied and stood tall with her shoulders back. I turned around and watched through the rear window as she strode confidently into the hotel.

· · ·

ON THE FLIGHT HOME I was miserable. Weary travelers sat all around me; those in the window seats leaned against the fuselage; those in the middle sat with their heads back, snoring. I was as tired as they were, but guilt is a powerful stimulant.

Rose and I had been married for ten years, and I had never cheated. How could I take it back? I couldn't. What could I do to make it right? Nothing. There was no do-over.

What was the next best thing? To never repeat. To live faithfully with the woman I loved . . . till death do us part, from *this* day forward.

Guilt of that kind can only be truly assuaged with one action: confession. But to confess was to risk the loss of everything, the sound of Rose's laughter, the children's belief that our marriage was perfect. No . . . living with guilt was the better course.

I carefully planned the lies. I had won four thousand dollars gambling, which made this my best Vegas trip ever. I was thrilled to be home, eager to see Chandler and Callie, and longing to hug and kiss Rose. These things were expected of me; delivering anything less would raise questions.

Lying successfully is about acting, about putting on a show. It's not just the lines you have to rehearse, but also the delivery, facial expressions, and mannerisms.

. . .

I LOUNGED AROUND the kitchen while Rose made dinner. We drank wine as she sautéed shrimp in olive oil and garlic. The sound of oil popping mixed with the stovetop fan. Nickelodeon entertained the girls in the family room. Rose came to me, grabbed my shirtfront, and shook it playfully.

"I'm sorry I gave you such a hard time about the money," she said.

"Forget it, babe."

"You've always provided for me and the kids. I know we're going to be okay no matter what happens. Even if we have to downsize, it's not a big deal."

"Thanks, honey."

She tiptoed to kiss me hard on the lips. "I love you."

"I love you too."

. . .

LATER THAT NIGHT, after we made love, I walked into the master bath to take a long, hateful look at the dickhead in the mirror.

CHAPTER 17

A T THE END OF THE REGULAR BOARD MEETING AGENDA the directors asked me to stay behind for an executive session. Henry, Tommy, and Gwen walked out, leaving me, Webb, and the outside directors. I had no idea what there was to talk about. We had stabilized the company, but there was no growth, no IPO in sight.

With fewer people in the room the projector fan sounded noisy. Webb turned up the lights and started the discussion. "You've all seen the numbers. To be candid, the picture is bleak. With that backdrop, what does everyone think?"

Mike Franzinni, the director from Central Texas Ventures, was the first to speak. "Now that the market has collapsed our IPO is a year away, at least. Do you agree?" he asked me.

"Yes. We don't even know if we've hit bottom yet."

"My guess is at least two years," said Webb.

On Mike's left sat Dan Chiu, his junior partner at CTV. Dan had spent most of the meeting with his nose buried in a laptop. Although I couldn't see the screen, I knew he was tweaking an Excel spreadsheet. Dan always created his own projections to double-check my numbers. He looked up from the laptop and asked me, "How much cash do we need to run the business?"

The Connection had been profitable for years, with plenty of cash and no debt. The recent losses and subsequent layoffs had consumed twenty million dollars, but we still had a balance of eighty million in cash.

"With the cost cuts we should be cash-flow positive in the third quarter," I said. "Theoretically we don't need any cash to run the business."

"But you'd want a cushion, just in case things get worse."

"Thirty million should be plenty."

"More than plenty," said Mike. "You could make it with twenty."

Mike's hands and fingers made a steeple. He sat stone-faced and shifted his gaze from me to Webb and back to me again.

"What exactly is the point of this conversation?" Webb asked Mike.

Mike studied the notepad in front of him and started carefully. "The company has become boring, Webb. It was exciting for a while but now it's boring. Growth may be nonexistent for a long time. CTV has been invested five years already. If we have to wait two more years—possibly longer—for a liquidity event . . . well . . . it's running to the end of our comfort zone."

"That is an interesting summary of the facts." Webb continued to interrogate Mike. "I agree with those facts. What precisely do you propose we do?"

Mike collapsed the steeple and leaned back in his chair.

"We have several alternatives. One is to begin an acquisition campaign, which could lead to a good growth story. The problem with that approach is that we only have fifty to sixty million in extra cash, which is not enough. If we want to grow through acquisitions we're going to need a lot more capital, and that means selling more stock, which will dilute existing shareholders."

"I'm not interested in diluting my position," said Webb.

"That doesn't surprise me," said Mike. "A second alternative would be to sell the company. Even with the recent losses we could get three to four hundred million."

"That's idiotic," said Webb. "We'd be selling at the bottom."

"I'm not surprised to hear you say that either. In fact, I agree it's a bad time to sell, but that means we're left with a boring company."

Mike paused then, as if to let the point sink in.

"If we're not going to invest in acquisitions," said Dan, "and we only need thirty million to run the business, then the fifty million is excess capital."

Until then, Gregor Smolnik had not participated in the conversation. He was sitting back with hands folded on his enormous belly, but when Dan mentioned excess capital Gregor took notice. He sat up and straightened his glasses. He cleared his throat and looked at Webb. "Maybe we should pay a dividend."

Now I understood. The entire dialogue had been rehearsed so that Gregor could suggest a cash dividend be paid to CTV.

Gregor continued. "If we pay a dividend of a dollar for each preferred share, CTV will receive twelve million dollars." He turned to Mike and asked, "Would that make the company interesting again?"

"Yes. It certainly would."

I ran through the math in my head. CTV had originally invested six million in the company and had twelve million shares. A one-dollar dividend would yield them a two hundred percent return—not a home run, but certainly respectable, and they would retain their equity position.

In my own case I had an option to buy a million shares. All employees were granted options in Class B shares, which were not eligible for dividends. All employees except me, that is. My option was to buy Class A shares. This was one of the points I had won from

Gregor when negotiating my deal. Even though my grant had not yet vested, the way my deal was structured, I would receive the dividend. And a million-dollar dividend would float Rose and me for several years; that money would give us plenty of time to jump-start the Connection's revenue and go public. Thinking through it, I loved the idea and wished I had thought of it myself.

"Of course, you won't receive the dividend," Gregor said to me, with a hint of a smile on his face, "but perhaps we could arrange a little bonus."

"Why won't I receive the dividend?" I asked, my blood pressure rising.

"Employee stock doesn't have dividend rights," Gregor announced, his smile spreading ever so slightly.

I shook my head.

"Joe has Class A shares," Webb reminded him. Gregor looked at Webb, then back at me, his pasty, fat face turning a light shade of pink.

I shrugged and tried a conciliatory tone. "Gregor is correct in that none of the other employees would receive a dividend. Maybe we could pay them a special bonus."

"What's all this talk about a special bonus?" Mike Franzinni asked. "Are we required to pay employees something when we pay a dividend?" he asked Gregor.

"No. Not at all."

"Then why would we pay them a special bonus?" Mike challenged me.

"Some employees have worked here a long time." I pressed the point. "They're going to be angry if a dividend is paid without consideration to them."

"B shares are not entitled to dividends."

"Yes," I admitted, "but there is an issue of fairness. For a few extra million we could pay a nice bonus that would satisfy everyone."

"They're not entitled to dividends," Mike repeated. He was normally congenial in the boardroom, but his tone had become sharp, the friendly demeanor gone. "They didn't invest any money."

"They put in sweat equity," I explained, trying to defend Henry, Tommy, Gwen, and hundreds of others.

"They were paid a salary for that!" Mike glared at me. "You're the CFO. You're supposed to be protecting the shareholders' interests, not pandering to employees."

The exchange unnerved me, and I sat back in my chair as he continued to glare. Mike Franzinni had always been a champion of mine. Now he clearly thought I was being stupid.

"Stop talking," insisted Webb. "Everyone, please stop talking. Let me think." He let us wrestle with our thoughts while he, by turns, looked at each person in the room. He then got up and walked to the window in silence.

He had freeze-framed the conversation again to be alone with his thoughts. What were the chess moves going through his mind? I was dying to know—would he go for the dividend?

Mike was used to Webb's periods of silence; he watched Webb for a few seconds and then patiently looked down at his hands.

After a couple minutes Gregor got nervous and fidgeted with his papers. When he started to speak Webb put out his palm, signaling him to remain silent. Webb continued to stare at nothing and think.

In another minute he sat down and summarized his thoughts. "This dividend concept is clearly complicated. I want everyone to think about it, and we'll resume the discussion at our next meeting."

There was no other business, so everyone began packing to leave. Mike and Dan were moving toward the door when Webb stopped them.

"I just remembered something. Joe, I need to talk to the board about one more thing. Could you give us a minute?"

I had asked Webb for a raise the day before. It occurred to me that he needed to clear that with the other directors, so I hustled out of the room. On the way Mike Franzinni shot me another angry look. After I left, the board remained in closed-door session for an hour.

CHAPTER 18

J ACK O'SHEA picked up the stress ball on my desk, trying to be nonchalant. He was dressed in his version of business casual: dark slacks, short-sleeved country club shirt, and four-hundred-dollar Italian loafers. I had never seen his forearms before. The muscles were big and toned from working out, the veins thick.

One of the things the board decided in their closed-door session was to fire the most expensive sales guys. Jack had been let go that day and stopped by my office on the way out.

"To tell you the truth," he said, "it's a mutual parting of the ways. The CRM market is a corpse, and if I can't sell it, I can't make money."

Software sales guys can't live on their base salary; it's enough to pay the light bill, but not enough for the cars, the trips, the expensive toys for the spouse. To afford those things they need a fat commission check.

"Anything I can do?" I asked. "References?"

"There sure is." He tried to stay calm, but his voice gave him away. "You can kill that scumbag Gregor Smolnik."

"What's up with Smolnik?"

"He's screwing me out of my commission." Jack passed the stress ball back and forth between his hands, squeezing the life out of it with every turn. "I generally don't get worked up about stuff, but when you try to take my money, it pisses me off."

"What's he doing? Specifically."

"Webb told me to deal with Gregor on my termination agreement, so I did. Now the bastard won't pay me the commission I'm due. A hundred and fifty thousand. On the SolarNext contract."

"We signed that deal months ago."

"Fifty percent of the commission is held back for six months. Gregor says I have to be on active payroll to receive a commission. Since I'm being fired, he claims I'm not entitled to the holdback."

It sounded like the same kind of bullshit Gregor tried to pull with my employment contract, but it wasn't my place to intervene.

"So what are you going to do?" I asked him.

"I'm going to work it out with Gregor, even if it takes a five iron to his fat head."

We chatted awhile longer, and I walked him to the door. Just as Jack was about to leave he turned to say, "Hey, I heard you had a ball in Vegas. You dog."

"Oh, yeah, I won big at Let It Ride."

He gave me a knowing smile, an Irish twinkle in his eye. "So the gambling was good. Good for you."

When Jack had gone I played our conversation over in my head. There was something out of place, something that made me anxious. Did he know about Gwen and me? Did he see us together in the taxi line at the MGM? No . . . Jack had left Vegas after the first night. Or did he? Yes . . . I was sure he left after one night.

· · ·

THE NEXT MORNING Zola Conti sent me a text while I was at home getting dressed:

"Meet me at Starbucks before you come in."

It was unusual. I replied: "Why?"

Her response was quick: "Just meet me there!"

Thirty minutes later I grabbed a grande latte and sat at one of the tables outside. Customers streamed in and out. A mourning dove called from across the parking lot: *Oo-wah-hooo, hoo-hoo.* The thermometer had already crested eighty, and the forecast was for a high of a hundred and eight.

I kept wondering why Zola wanted to meet.

She wore beige pants, a pink sleeveless top, and high-heeled platform sandals. As she crossed the parking lot, she passed two men, both of whom looked over their shoulders to check out the rear view. She came straight to my table.

"Want some coffee?" I asked, half out of the chair.

"No, no. I don't want any. This is the only place I could think of to meet before work."

She sat down and fiddled with her keys. Her round face expressed concern. The Starbucks door was ten feet away. Every time the door was opened from the inside she jerked to see whether it was someone she knew.

"Zola, what's the big secret?"

"I don't know how to ask you this." She looked at me with troubled brown eyes.

"Hell, just ask me." I shook my head at all the drama.

She switched chairs to be next to mine so she could whisper, "Are you sleeping with Gwen Raleigh?"

I didn't see it coming. A flash of panic swept over me, a sudden realization that the world was not as I perceived. All the sound shut

off. The dove in the nearby tree was mute. My vision tunneled until there was only a small circle with Zola's face in the middle.

"What? No! Why ask such a silly question?"

"Two different girls called me last night."

My hand shook as I reached for the coffee. It tasted bitter.

Zola knew I was lying.

"Who?"

"Recruiters. They both got laid off. The rumor is all over the Connection."

I fell back in the chair. My hands dropped to the sides. Zola let me process the information, and I felt only dread.

I mentally walked through my alternative courses of action; there were no good ones. Go home and confess . . . capitulation. I had been churning with guilt ever since Vegas, and there was a part of me that wanted to confess, to unload the secret.

But I resisted the notion. I couldn't see how it would help matters. It might give me emotional relief, but that wouldn't save my marriage. Besides, there was a chance that Zola was exaggerating, a chance that I could pass it off as a rumor. My other option was to go to work and ignore it—walk the halls as if the rumor didn't exist, bluff my way through. I couldn't come up with a third option.

"Is there something I can do?" she asked. Zola was always asking what more she could do, but she couldn't change the past.

On the other hand, if I was going to bluff my way through, maybe Zola could help.

"Yes. This is just a silly rumor someone started because Gwen and I happened to be in Vegas at the same time. If anyone else mentions it, just say it's a bunch of bullshit and they should focus on work instead of gossip."

Zola's eyes remained sad as she slowly nodded her head. "Okay, I can do that."

My one proactive step was to talk with Gwen. How could she pretend to protect our secret? She'd obviously confided in someone, or maybe two persons or more. Secrets were hard to keep at the Connection. It was a tight group. It would take only one person; the rumor would traverse the network in hours.

I dialed her cell from the Lexus.

"Hi, Joe, what's up?" She was businesslike, nothing unusual.

"Who did you tell?" I demanded. The other end of the line was silent. "Come on, who did you tell? Rumors are all over the place. Why did you do that?"

"I didn't tell anyone."

"Why are there rumors?"

"I don't know. I didn't tell a single person."

"Don't be ridiculous. You talked to somebody."

"No, I didn't," she insisted.

"You're lying to me."

Gwen was quiet. She didn't say anything for a long time; then finally she repeated herself: "I didn't tell anyone."

I hung up.

. . .

CONTRARY TO MY FEARS I received no angry or suspicious looks all day. No one cornered me with an accusation. Nobody giggled when I passed in the hallway. By the end of the day I convinced myself it was an unproven rumor that would die a quick death.

But when I pulled into my driveway and pressed the garage door transmitter, the feeling of dread returned. How could I have betrayed my wife? How could I have been so thoughtless and dishonest? My fingers drummed the steering wheel as the garage door closed behind me.

Walking into the house I knew something was wrong; no children came running to welcome their daddy.

The great room was empty, everything in its place: no furniture upturned, no pictures torn from the wall, no windows broken. The room was in shadows, with only the natural light from the windows. I placed my briefcase on the table behind the sofa and turned.

Rose stepped out from the side hallway that led to the half bath. She held one arm behind her back.

"Hi, babe," I said. "Where are the kids?"

"Next door." Her voice was shaky. "Tell me it isn't true. Just tell me it isn't true."

"What?"

"Tell me you didn't screw that woman!"

"What? I—"

"Don't mess with me, Joey. Just tell me it isn't true."

"I . . . I . . . I don't know what to say."

I looked out the window at the patio, knowing that I couldn't lie to her any longer, and that she already knew it was true.

As I turned back my eyes detected a dark object moving toward me with speed. I raised my hand and ducked, but not far enough. The full bottle glanced against my forehead and left a ringing sound. After bouncing off me it crashed into the stone fireplace, shattering in an explosion of glass and wine. I staggered backward and swayed, nearly falling.

Rose stared at me with all her Mexican fury.

"You fucking *pendejo*!" She stomped her foot and looked for something else to throw.

"Baby, I'm sorry."

"Don't say it. Don't say a fucking word."

I started to walk toward her.

"Stay right there. Don't come over here." She pointed, her hand shaking. "Not only did you cheat on me, you let the whole goddamn company know. I had to find out from the spouses' group. Four of them came to see me. They were so worried."

I was riveted, my eyes frozen to her.

She started to lose it. "They were worried because they knew how much I loved you and that we were a happy family." She reached out to steady herself on an armchair and collapsed into it.

I took three steps toward her but then stopped as she shook her head. "*No! No!*" she screamed, and kicked out viciously, her shoes striking me in the knees and sending me back. "Get the fuck out of here. I don't want you. Get out. Get out. . . ."

Every time I approached she screamed and tried to kick me. I wanted to stay, but the only way to help was to leave, so I got in the car and drove away.

A few miles down Bee Caves Road I realized there was blood on my shirt. I looked in the rearview; the right side of my forehead and face were a mess. I didn't care. My lies were discovered and my marriage devastated. Compared with that, the blood was nothing.

∘ ∘ ∘

THE NEXT DAY I expected the office to be a nightmare, but strangely it wasn't. No one seemed particularly surprised to see the fat bandage on my forehead.

In the morning Webb asked to see me in his office. He waved me over to the meeting table, grabbed two bottles of water from his personal fridge, and sat down to look at me. My clothes were presentable, but I hadn't slept at all.

"I'm terribly sorry," he said. "I hope you two can work things out quickly."

"It's a temporary separation." I tried to sound confident. "She'll give me another chance." But I wasn't sure. Rose was a strong-willed woman. She might never let me back. The thought of separation from Rose and the girls left me empty. . . .

"Joe?"

"What? Sorry, I'm distracted."

"No wonder. I was saying I asked Gwen to take a long holiday to let things settle down. Hopefully by the time she returns, your relationship with Rose will have mended. I need both you and Gwen to help fix the company. That's my top priority. Are you ready to work?"

"I guess so."

What else would I do? There wasn't much to my life other than family and work. Having screwed up the family part, I had only the work.

"Right," he said, changing his tone to be upbeat. "Hard work will keep your mind sharp." Typically meetings with Webb were quick, to the point, but he kept me more than an hour and created a list of follow-ups.

When we were finished, I stood to go.

"I'm surprised that everyone knows," I said. "It's as if my life has been broadcast on cable news."

Webb looked up, processing my comment, and then he shook his head slightly, as if a certain fact of life, while not pleasant, had to be endured. "There are no secrets here. Even after cutting a third of the company, the Connection is still strong. Three different employees told me this morning that Rose kicked you out for sleeping with Gwen. I suspect Rose called a friend from the spouses' group. After that, the rumor network took over."

. . .

I left Rose several voice mails that day, but she never called back. In the afternoon I sent her an e-mail: "Rose, please talk to me. How are the kids? Love you, Joe."

Two hours later I got a reply: "The kids are fine. Leave me alone. Fuck you."

I stayed at the Courtyard Marriott downtown. I had hoped to be home in a few days, but one day stretched into a week and then two weeks. Each night I ran on the trail around Town Lake. It was nine miles around the farthest loop. I'd complete the run in just over an hour and finish exhausted and thirsty. After cleaning up I'd head back out in search of a solitary meal.

Sleep eluded me, and I began to haunt the streets of Austin until three or four a.m., after the clubs had closed. I walked long miles every night: across the darkness of Zilker Park, way down Lamar and Congress in South Austin, east to I-35 and beyond. I walked in places white-collar guys aren't supposed to go. I had a few encounters with strangers, mostly the police. They couldn't fathom a tall, sober man loping along in East Austin at three a.m. Once a couple of panhandlers tried to talk me into a larger donation, but when I turned into the light and stepped up close, they changed their minds.

Late at night, after even the homeless have settled down to sleep, animals of the city come out of their hiding places to forage. Feral cats clang around in Dumpsters, skunks wander across unlikely roads, and stray dogs bark at the yipping coyotes down by the river. I saw them all on my lonely vigils.

As I walked I thought about my beautiful girls: Rose, Chandler, and Callie. I thought about how stupid and selfish I had been.

I crafted ways to get her back: flowers, love letters, presents. She would find them all contemptible. I settled on the simple approach of

one e-mail a day with the same message: "Rose, I'm sorry. I love you and want to come back. Joe."

Finally, after two weeks, she called me.

"The kids are driving me crazy. 'When is Daddy coming home? When is Daddy coming home?' I told them we had a fight. Now they're frantic, and it's driving me crazy."

My hand shook so hard I almost dropped the phone. I was afraid my voice would crack.

"How can I help? I want to come home. You know that."

"So you've told me. You can come home."

"Thank you." I held my breath, waiting for the conditions.

"But I'm only letting you back in the house because of the girls. Do you understand that?"

"Of course, I was thoughtless. I'm sorry. Thank you for giving me a second chance."

"I'm not giving you a second chance. You're sleeping in the guest room."

"What? Oh . . . okay."

"I'm never going to have sex with you again."

I was so relieved to be coming home I would have settled for a cot on the patio.

The kids were thrilled to see me. The tension between Rose and me was highly charged, but the girls pretended nothing had changed. I told them a Sheila story every night for a week.

The guest suite hung off the back of the great room and had its own bath and a separate entrance to the pool. At night I lay in bed awake, tried not to dwell on my mistakes, and listened for the sound of her. Almost every night Rose stepped out to sit on the patio and smoke.

* * *

AFTER I HAD BEEN HOME A COUPLE WEEKS, I was in the guest room bed one night, trying to sleep. Cicadas screamed outside the window. The air-conditioning unit kicked on, and cool air blew through the ceiling vent. My eyes were adjusted to the dark, so I saw movement as soon as the door cracked. Rose stepped in tentatively.

"Are you awake?" she whispered.

"Yes." My heart skipped.

She crept into the room and slipped into bed, wearing bikini briefs and a bra. I didn't dare say a word.

"I don't want to make love. I want to try sex." She stated it factually, drawing a clear distinction.

I kept silent and watched her, enthralled. Slowly my hand reached and touched her shoulder, which she took as agreement.

As she stripped she gave me a warning: "No kissing. I don't want you to kiss me."

It started off well. We were so accustomed to each other's physical desires that it was automatic. I thought it was working. She started to get into it, the excitement building, the pace increasing. Then suddenly she went slack, and her hands fell back to the bed. She stopped moving against me and closed her eyes.

I froze. "What's wrong?"

"I don't know. It felt good, but I keep thinking. . . ."

For a moment I didn't know what to do.

She encouraged me. "Just finish it. Go ahead."

I thrust into her one more time. It was madness, like trying to make love to a blowup doll. I rolled off and realized she was crying, soft sobs that choked her breathing and shook her chest. She turned away. I gently touched her back and traced the profile of her side. I wanted to hold her in my arms, but when I reached, she scooted out of bed and left the room.

Some couples spend their whole lives together and never break their marriage vows. The stories of their unions appear in the obituaries when one of them dies.

> Tom and Cynthia Snow were married in 1946, the year
> after he returned from serving in the Pacific. Tom was an
> insurance agent in Cedar Park for thirty-five years until he
> retired in 1983. Cynthia was a schoolteacher and raised their
> five children. Tom died on June 23 at the age of eighty. He
> is survived by Cynthia, his wife of fifty-four years, and . . .

It's one of those mistakes you can regret all you want, but you can't undo.

CHAPTER 19

O N September 7 the nasdaq closed at 4098. It had traded above 4000 for the prior two weeks. The next day Webb called me into his office and closed the door. I was excited to tell him something.

"Hugh Crandall called this morning," I said, sitting at the table. Webb remained standing.

"Again? What did he want?"

"He thinks the market will be receptive to ipos by year end. I've run some numbers. Assuming we level out and start growing again, we could be public in the first or second quarter."

"What sort of valuation?"

"Hard to say. Not as high as before."

"I doubt we'll grow anytime soon. In any case, we've decided *not* to do an ipo." He said the letters "ipo" with distaste, as if the term itself were offensive.

"I don't understand. You said we'd go out when the nasdaq got up to 4000."

"I said we'd think about it. We have thought about it. I've thought about it, and we're not going public."

I had heard Webb speak in this tone before. Once his mind was made up it was hard to change.

"Until when?"

"Never."

What was he talking about? Of course we were going to do an IPO; that was a key element of the dream.

Black and white chess pieces, carved in stone, were displayed in a glass trophy case next to the wall. Webb opened the case, idly picked up a chess piece and looked at it, then set it down quickly and turned to me.

"You've been a great asset to the Connection," he said, and then walked to look out the window. "How do I begin?" He turned back toward me. "The challenge is . . . a big part of the reason we hired you was to get us ready to go public."

"And to help build a great company," I reminded him. "Build something special."

"Of course. That too. But the primary driver was the IPO. The board feels, and I have reluctantly agreed, that since we are not going public we can no longer afford to retain you."

"What?"

"I'm afraid we're going to have to let you go."

"What?" I blinked, swallowed, and slid my chair back from the table.

"It has nothing to do with your performance. As I mentioned, you've been a great asset to the company."

"You're firing me?"

"It's really a cost thing, since we're not going public."

"I broke my back getting this company—your company—ready for an IPO."

"We all feel bad that that hasn't worked out."

I tried to process the information. It didn't seem possible. I had lived and breathed the Connection for twenty months. I had sacrificed

everything. Then I remembered the conversation about dividends at the board meeting.

"Does this have something to do with my shares . . . the fact that they're vesting in a few months?"

"Not at all. It's a cost thing."

"I dragged my family here for you. That was a big change. There were challenges."

"And we want to help you with the transition."

"Like vesting my option grant? You mean that kind of help?"

"Gregor is handling the details." Apparently Webb felt his part of the process was complete. "I can't afford to get involved. If I stick my nose in one, I'll have to do them all."

Webb shared a few more meaningless nice words and then indicated the meeting was over. I numbly walked to my office, stunned. Six months before, the picture of the dream had been large, clear, and brightly colored, but it had grown dim and smaller, and now it had been switched off. Gone.

· · ·

Gregor Smolnik waddled into my office an hour later, his shoulders pulled back to support his great belly, stains under his arms, fish eyes looking at me through cheap glasses. He wore a barely suppressed smile. "You never know what a day is going to bring, do you?"

I got up from my desk and walked toward him. He didn't pretend to want to shake my hand, just sat down at the round table and started looking through his folders.

"Let's see here," he said. "I know I've got your separation agreement. I saw it this morning." He gave me a pained expression, breathing heavily. "There have been so many lately."

"Are you going to vest my shares?"

Gregor frowned as a fat finger pushed the bridge of his glasses higher on his nose. "Your shares haven't vested yet. The schedule calls for half to vest in January. With today being your termination date, you won't have any shares."

A couple of engineers walked loudly by the door to my office. I got up to close it.

"Webb said you were going to help me out. I thought you might bridge me to the vesting date."

Gregor's lips stuck out, and his eyebrows bunched together; then his face brightened. "I know what Webb meant. He wanted to give you a big severance payment, so I included fifty thousand dollars."

Gregor had put on weight. He had to be over three hundred pounds. I thought about how good it would feel to drag him through the hall by his necktie. It wouldn't be easy, but I could manage it. Gregor would flail and choke at the same time. He'd lose a shoe about halfway and put his hands out in vain as I kicked him into the elevator.

He knew as well as I did that my agreement called for severance of a year's pay, two hundred and fifty thousand dollars.

"Do you mean in addition to the year of base salary?" I asked.

He got the confused look on his face again. "I'm afraid you don't understand your contract. You're not entitled to severance if you're terminated 'for cause.'"

My blood pressure started to increase. My eyes narrowed, and I cracked my knuckles before clearing my throat. "There is no 'cause' here."

"Well, sure there is. You didn't perform your duties as specified in the contract. It clearly spells out that you were to take the company through an IPO, and you didn't do that successfully."

"That's absurd."

"It's not absurd!" Gregor had the contract in his hand and shook it at me, his face turning red. "I've been through this with conferring

counsel, and he agrees. Now, you need to sign this separation agreement to get the fifty thousand."

"You can take the fifty thousand and shove it. You're going to pay the full two hundred and fifty, or I'm going to sue you for that amount, plus a million more for 'pain and suffering.'"

"I don't think any reputable firm will help you." Gregor put all the papers back in the folder.

"I won't be hiring a local firm. I'll use the big boys who wrote the contract in the first place."

He stood up to go. "If you're going to be a hard case about it, I'll talk to Webb. Maybe we can increase the severance a little."

"I'll give you today. Tomorrow you'll be talking to attorneys, and the price will go up."

At the threshold to the door Gregor turned and gave me the same smirk he did when he came in.

"You shouldn't get so worked up. You're luckier than some."

An hour later one of Gregor's associates called. While they believed Gregor's initial position was correct, they were willing to agree with my interpretation to avoid an expensive dispute resolution process. After withholding taxes I left the Connection with one hundred and seventy thousand dollars.

As I was packing my things I noticed an envelope in the snail mail in-box. Physical mail was a rare occurrence, so I opened it. It was an official notice that Chartwell Insurance was suing the Connection for fifty million dollars in direct damages and two hundred million in consequential damages. If the lawsuit were successful it would bankrupt the company. As my last official act I sent an e-mail to our in-house counsel, letting him know the good news.

* * *

"GREAT," SAID ROSE. "They fired you? That's just great!"

"Thanks for being so understanding."

We were in the kitchen. It was eleven thirty in the morning, and I had opened a beer.

"What are we going to do for money now?"

"I told you. They paid me severance, a year's salary."

"How long will that last?"

"It would last almost a year, except . . ."

"Except what?"

"We owe fifty thousand in real estate and income tax, due early next year."

"Great."

"Look . . . babe . . . I'll find a new job. Don't worry about that."

She looked at the granite countertop, the custom cabinetry, and the plantation shutters. "Maybe we should sell the house to cut back on costs."

I had already looked into that. "We can't. The Austin real estate market has fallen so much the house isn't worth the balance of the mortgage."

There was a mixture of anger and fear in her eyes. "Damn it . . . Joey . . ."

"I'll find a job."

"It won't be easy. A lot of companies have been furloughing people. Nobody will be hiring."

"I'll find one."

"You'd better."

"I will."

"Some dream. The Connection."

. . .

I COULDN'T SELL THE HOUSE, but I could unload the Lexus. It had been my first truly nice car, but a luxury sedan seemed all wrong for the ex-CFO of a failed software company. I traded it for a marigold Jeep Wrangler, which cut the lease payment in half. For some reason it lifted my spirits to manually shift gears in the noisy, soft-top ride.

After we cut all the costs we could, I analyzed our personal finances; it wasn't pretty. We had enough cash for five to six months. I needed a job, and soon.

Two weeks later I had a solid opportunity. I had interviewed the day before for a CFO job at a privately owned consulting company. I called the recruiter from my home office.

"Jane Davis."

"Hi, Jane. It's Joe Robbins. How are you?"

There was a long pause on the other end of the line.

"Oh, hi, Joe."

"So, what is the next step on the Brightcove Consulting job? I'm ready to start right away."

"Well, usually these things take some time, you know. They'll want to interview some other candidates first, to get a feel for the market."

That didn't sound too good. One of our air-conditioning compressors had gone out the week before, and the replacement cost eight thousand dollars. My cash cushion was disappearing faster than I expected. The sooner I could start the new job, the sooner our financial situation would improve.

"Did they give you any feedback on where I stand?"

"Hey, you know, I got a lead on a CFO position in Houston that you might be interested in."

"I'm pretty set on staying here in Austin."

"You shouldn't be put too many constraints on your job search. It's a tough market."

"What was the feedback, Jane?"

"Oh, I've got another call. Hang on a minute."

She put me on hold, and I looked out the window. Chandler rode her bicycle on the street outside. It was too small, and I had promised a new one for her birthday. She had her heart set on a Specialized model that cost five hundred dollars.

Maybe Brightcove had been spooked by my compensation history. They were targeting a base salary of one seventy.

Jane came back on the line. "You still there?"

"Yes. What did Brightcove say about the interview?"

"To be honest, they're thinking of going in a different direction."

"Is it the base salary? I told you I was flexible on compensation."

"It's not the money. They're looking for someone with more passion for the role. They thought you were a bit nonchalant."

"Nonchalant?"

"Yes. You know. They thought you were just in it for the paycheck. They want someone who is really interested in their business."

"Interested in consulting? Is anyone really interested in the consulting business?"

There was another long pause, and then Jane continued. "I'll let you know if something else comes up that might be a good fit for you."

We said our good-byes and hung up.

Not enough passion? Hell, I needed the money. How much more passion did they want?

* * *

ON THE HOME FRONT I was making more progress. Eventually Rose invited me back into the bedroom. She had physical needs, as did I. At first she took enjoyment from the sex. She knew how to receive pleasure, so it was easy, but after a couple of weeks her motions became

perfunctory. It was as if she viewed the sexual act as something she must do, as opposed to something she desired. I believed in time as the ultimate healer and was content to be patient.

In the last week of September, Zola came over to the house; she had big news to share. I fixed tart margaritas, and we sat and watched the kids swim in the pool. The brutal summer heat had nearly broken, and by six o'clock it was nice on the patio. Zola wore jeans shorts and flip-flops with a short-sleeved shirt knotted at the bottom. Rose wore similar attire. I was in cargo shorts and a polo shirt.

Chandler showed off by doing cannonballs off the rock wall at the back of the pool. Callie held the water cannon and squirted her sister in midair.

"So what's the news?" I asked Zola.

She reached into a small handbag and retrieved a piece of paper.

"I don't understand it," she said. "I had one of the engineers write bullet points for me."

I took a minute to read it.

"This is amazing."

"What?" they asked, in unison.

"They're recapitalizing the company."

"What does that mean?"

"Hang on. Let me read it again."

It was a two-step recapitalization. The preferred shares held by Central Texas Ventures were being paid a special dividend of three dollars per share; CTV held twelve million shares, so the dividend totaled thirty-six million dollars. Class A shares (those owned by Webb) and class B shares and options (those held by employees) were not being paid the dividend.

In the second step, the company was buying back all of CTV's preferred shares at two dollars per share (another twenty-four million

dollars), and offering to buy all class B shares at $1.60 per share. Options would be cashed out at $1.60 less their strike price.

A couple pieces of additional information were given. First, the lawsuit brought by Chartwell Insurance was described in detail in the offering document. Second, the risk associated with the lawsuit had been factored into the determination of fair value for the stock.

Employees weren't required to sell their shares; however, they would clearly be tempted. If the Chartwell lawsuit bankrupted the company, employee options would be worthless. The offer represented an opportunity for them to get some cash.

There were two notable exceptions to the buyback: apparently Gregor Smolnik and Slim Bohls would retain their class B shares. From my recollection, Gregor had about one percent of total shares, and Slim had two percent, which meant that Webb would now own ninety-seven percent of the company.

"There is also a rumor," Zola said, "that Gregor Smolnik is being paid a special bonus of three million dollars."

"For past board services rendered," I speculated.

We talked about the transaction for another minute, but Rose and Zola tired of it and began gossiping about people at the Connection.

The transaction meant nothing for me personally—my option had terminated unvested—but I was curious. I did some quick math in my head: Henry, Tommy, and Gwen would each walk away with about two hundred thousand dollars. There were about a hundred others who would receive less than fifty thousand, a far cry from the millions they expected six months before.

It was all perfectly legal. Essentially, Webb had bought out Central Texas Ventures for sixty million dollars, which yielded them a ninefold return on their money, and he was using the fair value of the company,

under the cloud of a lawsuit from Chartwell, to consolidate his control by buying out everyone else.

But twenty-two-year-olds don't read contracts, and dreams die hard. Someone had asked them whether they wanted to get rich; they had responded with enthusiasm and worked eighty-hour weeks to make it happen. They wouldn't realize that Webb was taking a hell of a risk using most of the company's cash for the buyback; he could easily wind up with nothing. Instead, they would focus on the sixty million going to CTV, essentially to people who were already rich, and they would know that Webb still had the big house on the lake. Dreams die hard.

I walked Zola out to her car. After she opened the door she turned to me, concern in her almond-shaped eyes. "How are you and Rose getting along?"

I looked back at the house, imagining Rose sitting on the patio with the kids.

"There is still a lot of tension between us, but we're going to be fine. Why do you ask?"

"Oh, nothing . . . just rumors."

"Rumors?"

She looked in her purse and pulled out the keys. "Forget it. I shouldn't have said anything."

"What kind of rumors?"

Zola looked at my face for a while, as if she were trying to make a decision. "Just that you two are still . . . having troubles. It's nothing. Probably came from the spouses' group. All the Peyton Place stuff comes from them."

"Yeah . . . sure."

She sat in the car and started the engine. "Oh . . . I forgot to tell you. Henry and Tommy were fired. They're starting their own company."

. . .

I ARRANGED TO MEET HENRY AND TOMMY the next night at Guero's on South Congress for Tex-Mex. There was a long line, so we sat outside at a picnic table in the holding area and drank Tecates with lime. Two sprawling live oaks provided shade for dozens of waiting customers. Under the small bandshell a country group played Johnny Cash tunes for tip money.

"It's not that big a deal," Henry said. "The CRM space is dead anyway."

Tommy had scrounged chips and salsa from the bar, and was scooping up sauce to cram in his mouth. "What are you talking about?" he said. "We didn't make any money. That's a big deal. Why should Gregor Smolnik get three million dollars? Why should Slim Bohls keep his shares? That asshole."

"We can make our own money," Henry said, as if that aspect were of little consequence. "What pisses me off is that the board talked Webb into breaking up the core team."

He stared at me with furious eyes, his lips a thin straight line, the muscles in his cheeks working as he ground his teeth.

It was curious to me that Henry blamed the directors and not Webb, when Webb was perfectly capable of making his own decisions, but as I pondered Henry's predilection his eyes gradually softened and turned sad. It wasn't in his nature to stay mad for long. Then his face changed again as he began looking through the crowd.

"We can't dwell on that," he said. "We've got new worlds to conquer." He nibbled on a chip and eyed a couple of college girls in skirts and cowboy boots.

"What's Webb going to do?" I asked.

"He's going to try to apply the ASP model to the CRM space," Henry answered. Seeing that I didn't follow, he elaborated. "ASP stands for

application service provider. Basically, the Connection will run the CRM software in its own data center and provide the functionality to customers as a service. The big advantage of the ASP approach is that it eliminates implementation challenges like those we ran into with Chartwell."

I vaguely remembered Webb mentioning ASP months before in his office.

"The problem is," Tommy added, "the customer's data has to reside on the Connection's servers, outside of the customer's firewall, and nobody will agree to do that. Customers will insist that their data remain behind their firewall."

"I told Webb it won't work," Henry said. "But you know Webb; once his mind is set he has to see it through, even if it destroys the company."

Henry studied the college girls, who had settled at the next table and were sipping on longneck Coronas. The silver-haired bandleader encouraged the crowd to sing the chorus to "Ring of Fire."

"Does this have something to do with Gwen's marketing program?" I asked.

Tommy nodded as he finished chewing a mouthful. "Webb's going to drop the price of the solution dramatically and try to sell it using direct marketing and inside sales."

"Correct," said Henry absently, not focusing on the girls, or anything. "And with an inside sales channel you don't need business development or presales teams, so the Zealots are unnecessary."

Tommy looked at me through half-closed lids while his tongue fished bits of chip from his teeth. The buzzer vibrated on the table, indicating they had room for us.

Henry looked at the buzzer. "It doesn't make any fucking difference." He sounded resigned. "With the Chartwell lawsuit the Connection is broken." But after only a moment, his spirits turned

again to the positive. "You wait and see, Joe. Webb will come around, and when he does, our business will be ready."

We went inside for dinner and they walked me through their ideas for a technology start-up.

As we stood to leave Tommy turned to me, his face worried. "Have you heard from Gwen?"

"No. I haven't seen Gwen since the day . . . uh . . . since the day Rose found out about the two of us. That was almost two months ago."

"She left town the next day, and no one has seen her since."

I had no desire to meet with Gwen, not since she divulged the secret of our fling in Vegas, but still, it was strange that she was incommunicado. Webb had sent her on a long vacation; maybe she had found a reason to never return.

CHAPTER 20

THE NASDAQ TRADED DOWN FIVE HUNDRED POINTS in September and closed at 3523 on October 4. That night Rose and I were going to dinner with Henry at Siena; Tommy was visiting his mother in San Marcos, and Henry didn't want to eat alone. He called me with an update in the late afternoon.

"Are you signed up for the Connection Alumnae email grouplist?" he said.

"No."

"It's a little creepy. A lot of employees are really pissed over the restructuring and they send nasty emails about the directors. It's like they're stalking them."

"You're kidding."

"Apparently someone found out the directors are having their final dinner as a formal board tonight. Guess where they're going . . . Siena."

"Shit. That's just what we need."

"Do you want to go somewhere else?"

I didn't relish running into the board of directors, but at the same time, I didn't want them dictating where I chose to eat.

"Screw that. Siena's is a good place. Let's stick with the plan."

. . .

ROSE AND I ARRIVED at seven. Siena is an Italian restaurant off Highway 360 not far from the Pennybacker Bridge. As we crossed the parking lot Rose walked to my left and swung her arms. Her right arm swung forward, and I noticed an emerald bracelet on her wrist. When the arm swung back I looked at it again. The bracelet was stationary.

"Is that a tattoo?"

She stopped in the middle of the lot and looked at her arm, then turned it over. The green ink bracelet was a quarter inch wide with gold beading along the edges and an opening on the underside of her wrist.

"I forgot to mention it," she said, like she had forgotten to pick up the dry cleaning. As an afterthought, she added, "Do you like it?"

"What the hell? You get a second tattoo and don't even tell me?"

"It's a small tattoo."

"It's permanent!"

She walked on briskly, and I hurried to follow. "It's not a big deal," she said. "The girls thought it was pretty."

"Oh, good, maybe we should have them tattooed."

Rose turned to me, hands on hips. "I see. It's okay for you to have an affair, but if I get a tattoo, it's unacceptable."

We were sliding backward quickly. Two patrons on their way in looked at us strangely, and I lowered my voice. "I didn't say that. You surprised me. That's all. It's your body. You should make the decisions regarding your body."

My concession speech saved us from Armageddon, and we continued into the restaurant. As we approached the door, someone behind the bushes stepped around the left corner of the building. I looked over, but they had already disappeared.

Siena is built in the Tuscan style, with stucco walls, a red tile roof, and a heavy wooden door. Inside is a foyer with restrooms on

the left and the restaurant to the right. Past the maître d' station is a semicircular bar with stools and hundreds of wineglasses hanging from overhead racks.

It was early. The restaurant wasn't yet full, but the bar was busy. A bartender popped the cork on a bottle of champagne and poured for a young couple. I scanned the room and saw Henry sitting at the bar, a glass of red wine before him. He stood to greet us.

"The grouplist was right," he said. "The big boys are here." His head turned slightly over his right shoulder, and I looked. Webb Elliot, Gregor Smolnik, and Mike Francinni were standing together around the curve of the bar.

Webb noticed us and gave a little wave. Gregor broke from the other two and headed our way.

"Okay," I said, "here we go."

Gregor wore a suit coat and a white shirt with no tie. He had to step to the side to make room for a passing couple. As he reached us he stopped, said hello to Rose, and turned to me. "Sorry about the little dustup over your severance, but we got it all sorted."

"Sure."

"Please excuse me. I'm going to the washroom."

Henry watched Gregor walk into the foyer, where he had to step aside again to make room for someone. "I feel sorry for Gregor," Henry said. "He doesn't seem to enjoy life. You know?"

The bartender came and took our order for wine. By that time Webb and Mike had walked over.

"Joe, it's good to see you," Webb said, pumping my hand. He was back in sell mode. "You look fantastic. How are you?"

"Fine, fine. You remember Rose."

"Of course. How are you, Rose?" Webb kissed her cheek and took her hand. When he pulled back I noticed she was blushing. He glanced down at her wrist. "Is that a new tattoo?"

Henry ignored Webb and typed something into his cell phone, while Mike edged over to me.

"How's the job search going?" Mike asked me.

"Okay. The market's a little slow right now, but I'll find something soon."

"You should come see me. We have a few opportunities in the portfolio."

Mike and I chatted about the opportunities and set an appointment to discuss it further. The five of us talked for a few more minutes, trying to get past the awkwardness, and then Webb and Mike left to sit at their table.

"Well, that was weird," Henry said.

"Painful," I said, as I watched them walk away. I was jealous. They were the privileged, the moneyed, the gainfully employed. What did that make me? Borderline desperate.

"So where is Tommy?" Rose asked.

"Visiting his mother in San Marcos," Henry said. "She's in a nursing home. Alzheimer's. She's had it for years."

"That's awful," Rose said, and they started to talk more about it.

After all the hand shaking I wanted to wash up, so I walked through the foyer to the men's room. Inside a Muzak cover of "Here Comes the Sun" played from the ceiling speakers. The floor and wall tiles were black. There were two urinals and one stall. I stepped up to the sink, turned on the spigot, and frowned at myself in the mirror. A few hairs stuck up on the back of my neck.

On the way in I had noticed a big black dress shoe with a black sock under the side of the toilet stall. Instead of being flat on the floor, facing forward, as would be the case with a man about his business, this foot was lazily off to the side, like the man had leaned back to rest. I edged back and looked at the foot again. It had not moved. The black tiles around the foot looked odd, like they were wet.

I didn't remember seeing Gregor come out of the restroom, and my first thought was that an obese man could have a heart attack anywhere. I walked to the front of the stall and knocked. Silence.

"Gregor. You in there?"

No answer. I could see the door wasn't latched.

"Hey, Gregor, are you all right?"

With apprehension, I reached to the top and pushed on the door. Inside, Gregor Smolnik sat calmly, but he was a mess. He was calm, but he was also very dead. His shirtfront bore a deep red stain from blood that had flowed from a clean line. The line ran across his throat from one side of his fat head to the other. His eyes were open slightly and looked out through the big lenses, his massive hands folded in his lap. A cardboard sign that read "SCUMBAG" in a large, bold font was viciously pinned to his stomach.

I stared at Gregor. Blood from the wound had splattered his pants, the sides of the stall, and the tiles around his feet. My knees wobbled. My eyes lost focus, and I swayed.

The men's room door opened, and Henry entered. "Hey, what's up?" I didn't answer, and he walked over to look in. "Oh, fuck. Oh, shit."

Henry's face drained of blood. His eyes began to roll back, the lids twitching. I grabbed his arm as he fainted and let him down to the floor gently.

I looked back to Gregor, still dead, a thick smell emanating from the mass of blood. Nausea threatened, but I managed to suppress it. I had seen dead people before. There was Amanda Sorenson, and before that Ted Thompson up in Dallas. I closed my eyes and saw Ted lying on the floor with holes in his chest, but then I shook my head and opened my eyes again.

Stay focused.

My hand shook as I called 911. Lieutenant Rico Carrillo's number was stored in my phone, so I called him as well.

I stood by the restroom door and barred entry until the police arrived. In a couple minutes Henry came to, and I sent him to tell Rose what had happened. It was hard to process that Gregor was dead, that he had been so horribly murdered. I had talked to him only minutes before his death. Once the police took over the scene Rose, Henry, and I sat silent, in shock. My stomach hurt from the mix of hunger and stress.

◦ ◦ ◦

CARRILLO WAS DRESSED in khaki pants, a light blue checked shirt, and a dark sport coat. He had grown a thick mustache. It had traces of white to match those on his temples. The black heterochromia in his almond-colored iris was distracting.

"Mr. Robbins, I'm sorry to meet you under these circumstances."

"Me too."

The lieutenant looked at me without speaking; his eyes studied the features of my face and then looked down to my shirt, arms, and hands. I wasn't quite sure what to say.

"How have you been?" I asked.

"Too busy, too busy. With the budget cuts there aren't enough resources to go around."

We were in Siena's kitchen, which Carrillo had shut down and commandeered as a temporary office. He sat at a cleared prep table with his laptop, and I sat opposite. The air smelled of garlic and cooked meat. The hum of a large freezer provided the only background noise.

I had drunk a glass of water to settle my stomach, but was still hungry and had developed a headache.

"Do you mind emptying your pockets on the table?" Carrillo asked.

"What?"

"It's routine. Of course, I can't force you to, but if you don't mind?"

Carrillo smiled at me simply. He wasn't trying to be cute; he was doing his job. I was at the scene of the crime, and he wanted to know more about me. If I had a bloody knife in my back pocket he would have his murderer, but he didn't expect that. He wanted to hear my answer. If I declined he would put me at the top of the suspect list.

I put my wallet, keys, and change on the table and turned my pockets inside out.

"I understand you found the body. What did you see?"

"By the time I got there Smolnik was dead. I didn't see anything."

"Did you touch or move the body at all?"

"No."

"Did you notice anyone leaving the bathroom?"

"No."

"Did you see anything unusual?"

"Well, there was the sign. That was pinned on Smolnik's stomach. It said, 'SCUMBAG.'"

"What about it?"

"I heard someone call Gregor a scumbag once . . . actually twice."

"Who?"

"Jack O'Shea. One of the top salesmen at the Connection."

I told Carrillo that Jack had called Gregor a scumbag in my office on the day he was fired, and that he had used the word at the Connection ball eighteen months earlier. Carrillo typed notes quickly into his laptop.

"Did you notice anything else?"

I shook my head no, but then remembered.

"Wait. There was something else, but not in the bathroom. It was earlier. When Rose and I were walking into the restaurant I saw someone step around the corner behind the bushes."

"Did you recognize them?"

"No. By the time I looked in that direction they were gone. I only saw the person as a moving shape out of the corner of my eye."

"Was it a man or a woman?"

"A man, I think. But honestly, it could have been a woman. I didn't see them clearly."

"Okay. We'll look into that."

He asked me more questions, and in the process I described the downfall of the Connection and the role Gregor had played in the restructuring.

Carrillo was most interested in the money.

"Let's go back to the IPO process. . . . When you said that some employees stood to make millions before the market fell in April, how many employees are we talking about?"

"Who could have made a million dollars?"

"Yes."

"About a hundred."

"A hundred?" Carrillo's eyes opened wide, and he blinked several times. He sat back in his chair and frowned at his laptop.

"What's wrong?"

He shook his head. "Nothing to do with you. It's my problem. We don't have resources to look at a hundred suspects properly. We're going to have to narrow down the list somehow, but never mind about that. Tell me more about the . . . what did you call it, cap something?"

"The cap table. It's short for capitalization table. It lists all the owners of the company, including the option holders."

"Can you share it with me?"

"I don't have it. As I mentioned, I'm no longer with the Connection. You'll have to get it from the company."

"Okay." He brushed his mustache with his fingers. "I'm sure we can get it from Mr. Elliot. When we do, will you walk me through the cap table? To make sure I understand how it works?"

I sensed a trap of some kind. Carrillo struck me as crafty. Surely he knew that Webb, or any of a dozen others, could help him interpret the cap table, but I was the one who had found the body. He wanted to keep me close.

"Am I a suspect?"

"How much would you have made? In the IPO."

"Twenty million or so."

The lieutenant whistled through his teeth. It was multiples of what he would make in his entire career.

"That's a lot of money. You *are* a potential suspect, until we can prove otherwise."

At once my stomach hurt again. A suspect? In a murder investigation?

"Do I need to hire an attorney?"

"Only you can decide that."

Carrillo studied my face again. I honestly don't know what he saw there. I didn't want to be a suspect in a murder case. I didn't want to be involved in any of this.

"You know," he said, "this case may have nothing to do with Connection Software. I have heard from some of the others that many people didn't care for Mr. Smolnik. Maybe he had enemies. On the other hand, if it does have something to do with Connection, who is to say the murderer was only mad at Mr. Smolnik? Why not the other board members? Why not Webb Elliot? Why not members of the senior management team?"

The acid jumped in my stomach.

"You think I could be in danger?"

Lieutenant Carrillo shrugged. "I'll be in touch with you shortly . . . about the cap table."

. . .

AT HOME, we were starving and sat at the kitchen counter to eat sandwiches. The girls were long since asleep.

"Why does Lieutenant Carrillo want to see you?" Rose asked.

"He said he wants my help in deciphering the ownership structure of the Connection, but I think . . . ."

I stopped talking and took a bite of the sandwich. Rose looked at me with suspicion.

"You think what?"

"Well, he also called me a potential suspect."

"A suspect? Why would he suspect you?"

"We stood to make twenty million in the IPO, and then the board restructured the company. And, of course, they fired me."

Rose eyed me with suspicion again. She put the sandwich down.

"Come to think of it, you always said you despised Gregor Smolnik."

"Good lord. You don't actually think I killed Smolnik, do you?"

"I don't know what to think anymore. You've changed so much since we came here."

I had lost her trust completely. Ten years of marriage had come down to this.

"Did you kill him?" she asked.

"No."

"Promise?"

"Jesus, Rose, that's enough."

She took another bite and looked at me thoughtfully.

"Okay," she said. "I don't think you're a murderer. You haven't sunk that low."

I got up to get another beer from the refrigerator.

"I am a little worried, though," I said.

"Worried? About what?"

"Carrillo thinks there's a good chance someone at the Connection killed Gregor, and I think he's right."

"So . . ."

"So he also thinks I might be in danger."

"You? Why would anyone be angry at you?"

"Someone from the Connection has gone crazy. I was on the core team. Who knows if or how the murderer will strike again?"

Rose didn't say anything. I told her what I was really thinking: "I'm going to see if I can help Carrillo."

"Help him? How?"

"By asking some questions. See if I can figure out who might have wanted to kill Gregor Smolnik."

"What?" Her voice got louder and higher.

"It's not like I've got anything better to do."

"What are you talking about? You need to find a job! That's what you need to do. You're not a detective."

"I know a lot of the players in the company. I worked there eighteen months."

Rose shook her head. "What are you thinking?"

"Nothing. I just thought I could ask a few questions."

"You need to find a job. We need the cash flow."

"I know that. I'll get a job. Trust me."

"You'd better."

"I will."

CHAPTER 21

CARRILLO CALLED THE NEXT DAY to set up an appointment. We met at the Radisson on Cesar Chavez, next to the Congress Avenue Bridge.

"I'm in the fortunate position of having a very capable team," he said. "They do all the legwork while I drink coffee at the Radisson and interview the bigwigs: directors, CEOs. . . ."

"Unemployed chief financial officers."

"It's a lot less intimidating than the real office. Besides, they know me here."

Rico walked straight to a corner table on the upper tier of the dining room. The lighting was adequate, the tablecloth checkered, and there were few customers. He waved a middle-aged waitress over.

"Dee, this is Mr. Joe Robbins. He's an associate."

"What'll you have, Joe?" Dee didn't bother pulling the order pad from the pocket of her apron.

"Diet Coke."

The soda and Carrillo's coffee were back in less than a minute. He spent most of that time staring at me, the black heterochromia sparkling in the restaurant light. I fidgeted in my seat.

"You've had a little trouble with the police before, haven't you, Mr. Robbins?"

"I'm not sure what you mean."

"That problem with Ted Thompson up in Dallas. Fancy gunplay."

"No charges were filed against me in that."

"And much earlier on . . . a few misdemeanor charges. Sunset High must have been a rough place."

"Those charges were all dropped. I was just a kid then."

"Sure. Sure. Kids having fun, but then there was that break-in at the neighbor's house."

"That guy was abusing his dogs. Besides, they never figured out who did it."

"I talked to the officer on the case. He's convinced it was you. Said he thinks you picked the lock with one of those kits you can buy in the mail."

Rico Carrillo was good. He came to his meetings prepared.

"I thought we were going to discuss the Smolnik murder," I said.

"I like talking about old times. Don't you?"

"Not particularly."

He leaned back in the chair and took a long sip of coffee.

"All right . . . let's fast-forward to the present. Tell me about your relationship with Mr. Smolnik."

"He did work for the Connection. Gregor was a competent attorney, certainly, but a bit of a jerk."

"A scumbag maybe?"

"I didn't make that sign."

"Some people say you were quite mad at Smolnik after you were fired."

"Who? Who said that?"

Carrillo's tight grin told me he wouldn't answer all of my questions.

"Mr. Robbins, are you an electric shaver man or a razor man?"

"Excuse me?"

"When you shave in the morning? Do you use a razor or an electric shaver?"

What the hell was he getting at now?

"A razor. I've always used a razor."

"Like a straight razor or a contemporary razor?"

I remembered the clean line across the bottom of Gregor's throat.

"Is that how he was killed? With a straight razor?"

"I'm asking the questions now."

"A safety razor. Gillette TRAC II, if you must know."

Carrillo studied my face. He had asked thousands of questions in situations like this. I was telling the truth, but would he know that just by looking at me?

"Let's review the cap table," he said.

He opened his laptop, and we went through the table. I gave him approximate values of a few grants, assuming the Connection had a market value of two billion dollars. I offered to build him a spreadsheet, and he promised to send me the soft copy. He was particularly interested in a value of a million dollars.

"Do you think one of these people would kill someone over a million dollars?" I asked.

Carrillo looked at me like I was clueless, completely out of touch.

"I've seen murders committed over a hundred dollars. The dollars are so big here they're almost irrelevant."

"So why don't you consider all the option holders suspects?"

"I can't. We don't have the resources. I've assigned a sergeant and six detectives to the case for two weeks. That's half my team."

Carrillo's team would be very busy. It would take time to track people down and meet with them. If the murder had been committed by a random Connection employee, they might need a lot more time to narrow the list.

"Why only two weeks?" I asked.

He offered me a stick of chewing gum.

"Thirty or so murders will be committed in Austin this year. My

department is responsible for homicides, suicides, and accidental or suspicious deaths. We get one or two new cases every week. If we don't make progress on the Smolnik murder in two weeks, we'll have to move on to the next one."

It made sense. It wasn't a business, but they still had resource constraints that had to be managed. You worked the cases you could solve to get the highest return.

I couldn't resist asking questions. I had two good reasons for wanting the murder solved. First, Carrillo thought I was a suspect; finding the murderer would eliminate that suspicion. Second, solving the case would remove any danger for me. But there was something else, an intense curiosity. Did someone from the Connection really kill Gregor Smolnik?

"Did you learn anything useful at the crime scene?" I asked.

He had just put the gum in his mouth and taken the first big chews on it, no emotion on his face.

"Do you watch a lot of television?" he asked.

"Sorry. You piqued my interest last night when you said I might be in danger."

He considered my request as he got the gum under control.

"All right, I'll tell you some things. Our forensics team didn't find any footprints behind the bushes because of the bark mulch. Other than that clue from you we haven't gotten anything useful from any-one. Oh, and the murder weapon *was* a straight razor."

I knew nothing about the process of crime investigation, but with more than a hundred suspects the case seemed daunting.

"Do you think you'll solve the case?"

"You're asking a lot of questions," he said, running short on patience. "Usually I'm the one who gets to ask the questions, but since I raised the 'danger' flag last night I'll tell you how it works. We'll ask a thousand questions, trying to get one person to tell us something

they saw or heard, or one person to say something stupid they didn't want to say. If we can get that one break, we have a real good chance of solving the murder."

"And if you don't get the break?"

"The team will move on and the case will go on the unsolved pile. It will sit there and wait for a random break."

At that moment, I thought about Amanda Sorenson. It had been eighteen months since her suicide, and no one had ever discovered the motive. That was what Carrillo had done with her case: he had put it on the unsolved pile to wait for a random break, and it was still waiting.

I sat up straight, rubbed my hands together, and asked Carrillo one more question. "What would you say if I told you I want to do some digging on this case myself? To see if I can find anything useful for you."

"Why in the world would you do that?"

"You obviously view me as a suspect. Plus, you said I might be in danger."

"That's really not a good idea."

"Look. I'm not trying to do your job, but I may be able to help. I know all the key players, and they might tell me something they won't tell you."

Lieutenant Carrillo frowned. He had summoned me to the Radisson to learn more about me, to keep me close, and I was proposing to get closer than he intended.

"I'm not going to give you a badge or anything, if that's what you're thinking."

"No."

"You're a private citizen, Mr. Robbins. I can't stop you from asking people questions, but don't do anything illegal, and if you find anything, be sure to let me know."

. . .

CARRILLO SENT ME THE SOFT COPY of the cap table that night, and I immediately started transforming the problem into an analysis. I needed some sort of framework to help me think about it.

I spent two hours on the Internet reading about crime investigation and got the idea to build a spreadsheet to incorporate probabilistic values of the three main factors in proving a crime: motive, opportunity, and means.

To begin, I loaded the names of employees with option grants into a spreadsheet. Next I calculated the "in the money" value of option grants if the Connection was worth two billion. Using Carrillo's logic that we couldn't look at everyone, I arbitrarily truncated the list by hiding grants worth less than a million dollars. That left me with one hundred and three names.

At the top, I labeled three columns "Motive," "Opportunity," and "Means." My idea was to load probabilistic values for each column by every name.

In the world of probability, a zero means no chance and a one means certainty. If a person had a clear motive to commit the crime I would assign a motive probability of one next to that name. If someone had an ironclad alibi, as Henry did, I would assign an opportunity probability of zero.

By multiplying the three cells, I calculated a combined probability for each name. Any name with a combined probability of zero would be deemed innocent. Names with a combined probability at or close to one would be the most likely suspects.

To begin, I loaded probabilities of one in all three columns for every name. As I got real data I would change the values in the spreadsheet.

I thought about the "means" factor. How did the murderer manage to cut Gregor's throat and put him in the stall without creating a

huge mess all over the men's room? Gregor was heavy, so it must have been a strong person. I was certain I could manage it myself, if I were good with a razor. I went through the list of names, trying to guess who could do it. But what if the murderer had a gun? A small person could hold a gun on Gregor, tell him to close his eyes, and then slash open his throat. That path of logic suggested that anyone with a gun and a razor had the means to commit the crime.

Next I tried brainstorming for suspects who were not equity holders. I remembered Jack O'Shea's anger at Gregor in my office. Salesmen worked for commission and did not receive equity, but Jack was clearly a potential suspect.

I typed in a few more names but deleted most of them as improbable. Two names I came up with were Randy Harlan and Slim Bohls. Randy had been livid the day he was fired, but why would he be angry at Gregor? He was capable of stealing, but could he commit murder? I kept him on the list. Slim Bohls was a weird character, but I couldn't think of a possible motive. He had kept his shares in the buyback, as did Gregor. If anything they were in the same predicament, so I deleted Slim's name.

I looked at the spreadsheet. It seemed hopeless. It was simply an analytical expression of what Carrillo already knew: There were too many suspects.

One thing was certain: Working with a spreadsheet wasn't going to solve the crime. I had to get out and ask some questions. I decided to use Randy Harlan as a warm-up to hone my interviewing skills. I would meet with Jack O'Shea second, as he was the more likely suspect. I sent them both innocuous e-mails to see whether they wanted to "catch up."

* * *

MEANWHILE, I still needed a job. The next day I went to see Mike Franzinni to discuss opportunities. Central Texas Ventures leased the twenty-ninth floor of the Bank of Texas building on Sixth Street. Mike was in a corner office.

The crime was less than two days old, so the conversation naturally started there.

"Do you think Gregor's murder was somehow related to the Connection restructuring?" I asked.

Mike shook his head in doubt.

"Let's face it," he said. "Gregor was a pain in the ass for a lot of people. I could name ten guys in town who thought he screwed them at one time or another. Besides, we didn't do anything underhanded at the Connection. It was a simple recap. The IPO just didn't work out. You were there. You saw that."

I didn't want to argue. I was there with my hand out, looking for a job. I steered the conversation onto that track, and Mike described several companies that sounded promising. But as we talked about them it became obvious the companies needed more time before they were ready for a full-time CFO.

"I'm sorry," he said. "This was a wasted trip for you. You'd be over-kill for these start-ups at this point. As soon as any of them needs some high-quality talent, even on a part-time basis, I'll be sure to call you."

"No worries. I appreciate your giving me the time. If you hear of anything else that's interesting, please let me know."

"Count on it."

I stood up to go.

"Hey," he said. "Let me walk you around the balcony as a consolation prize. We have a terrific view up here."

They had the penthouse floor, and the balcony surrounded all four sides of the building. Far below us, sunshine bounced off the surface

of Town Lake, tiny cars maneuvered their way through the streets, and in the distance the city faded into the hill country.

"Do you really think someone from the Connection killed Gregor?" he asked. For the first time ever I saw doubt in Franzinni's eyes.

"Yes. Maybe. I don't know. But to be on the safe side, don't turn your back on anyone."

                              ⁕ ⁕ ⁕

THE NEXT DAY I met with Randy Harlan. I had heard he never found work after the Connection, and was surprised when he suggested lunch at Barton Creek Country Club.

At the back of the men's locker room was a small café where male members could have a quiet lunch. Randy was dressed in an expensive golf shirt and stylish shorts. He looked relaxed and fit.

"Did you hear about Gregor Smolnik?" I asked.

"What a horrible way to go." Randy got a sick look on his face. "I never dealt with Gregor that much. I know a lot of people didn't like him, but I wouldn't wish that knife-across-the-throat thing on anybody."

"It was a straight razor."

"Was it?" He grimaced at the thought. "Well, that wouldn't make it any better."

If Randy was lying, he was really good at it.

"I didn't realize you were a member here," I said, looking around the room. There were three other groups of men in similar attire as Randy. They talked about business and sports.

"Yeah . . . I joined six months ago. I'm out here like four or five times a week. The pro has me shooting in the low nineties. My goal is to shave ten more strokes from my handicap."

The waiter brought our lunch. I had a hamburger, fries, and a Diet Coke. Randy had a salad with grilled salmon and a glass of pinot grigio.

"Are you working these days?" I asked.

"Heck, no. I'm retired. I guess we haven't talked in a while, have we?"

"I haven't seen you since you left the Connection."

"Jeez, that was a bad day." Randy looked at the other tables in the room and lowered his voice. "These guys don't know I ever worked at the Connection. All they know is I'm a private investor."

"Private investor?"

The Randy Harlan I knew punched the clock like most people. The only investing he did was move money between 401(k) funds.

"I'll tell you what happened. After you guys fired me I took the hundred grand and gambled it all in the high-tech stock market. It was found money as far as I was concerned, so I could afford to take big risks. I bought out-of-the-money call options on the highest-flying names I could find: Webvan, Freemarkets, Internet Capital, and eToys. There were dozens to choose from."

"That's insane."

"Yeah, insanely successful. As the market climbed the option values doubled and tripled in no time. Every time an option expired I put all the winnings right back in the game. When the market rocketed in November and December I was doubling my money every week. By the time the index hit five thousand in March I had ten million dollars."

"Damn."

"It was pure luck. I was in fantasyland. In mid-March I read an article that said the NASDAQ was going to hit ten thousand by year end. I had an epiphany: The party was over. I pulled out everything. Now I'm in T-bills."

I almost choked on the burger and had to reach for the Coke in a hurry. That strategy could work only in a superhot speculative market. The probability was infinitesimal, and it had worked for Randy Harlan, a thief. There he was. He had made ten million and was doing what I wanted to do, working on his golf game or whatever the hell else he felt like doing.

Randy started in on the salad, but he didn't eat efficiently and quickly, like a workingman born and raised in Buda, Texas. He ate like the other guys in the clubhouse: Pick up a modest piece, chew it carefully, swallow, engage in some conversation, and proceed with the next bite. He signaled the waiter to bring a refill on the wine.

I couldn't imagine any reason for Randy to kill Gregor Smolnik. On the way out he asked me about the girls.

"They're fine. Busy as ever with school and a million activities."

"They sure are beautiful children."

"Thanks, Randy. How are the twins?"

We stood in the sun just outside the pro shop. The landscape crew was blowing leaves off the sidewalks. Randy looked at his golf shoes.

"Okay," he answered. "My ex moved to Beaumont. She had custody and the judge allowed it. She's such a bitch. The only reason she did it was to jerk me around because I got rich *after* we finalized the divorce."

"Sorry to hear that."

"The boys stay with me one weekend each month, and I drive there for special occasions. You know . . . birthdays and things like that."

As I pulled out of the parking lot in the Jeep and shifted into third, I wondered how Randy's marriage had fallen apart. Having all the money and no one to share it with wasn't the endgame I had in mind.

Heading down the long hill toward Barton Creek I conducted a mental postanalysis of the meeting. I had learned a couple things. First, I could assign to Randy a zero probability for motive. Second, I had no idea what I was doing. In retrospect, interviewing Randy was

a waste of time. However, Jack O'Shea and I were meeting the following week, and that was more promising. Jack had a clear motive, and he hated Gregor Smolnik.

. . .

MEANWHILE, the job search was going nowhere. I had to face reality and admit that to find work I might have to look outside of Austin. I called my mentor at Liberty Air to see whether they could take me back. He told me they had launched another efficiency program and were looking to cut executives, not add them.

After hanging up I recognized a strange new pattern. The nearer I came to a real job opportunity, the more anxious I became; when an opportunity fell through I felt a sense of relief. The truth was, the prospect of suiting up to work in an office held no appeal whatsoever.

Great. I was desperate for cash. What was I going to do? Work outdoors?

. . .

JACK O'SHEA AND I MET FOR BREAKFAST at La Madeleine at the Village at Westlake Hills shopping center. It was a popular spot for entrepreneurs and venture capitalists to interview potential management hires.

"Christ," Jack said. "I'm spending my life in this place. I know the employees by name."

There were five other one-on-one meetings in progress in the room.

"I bet I've met thirty guys," he added. "They all have a great idea and want me to sell the product but can't identify a hundred-million-dollar market. I need a big market to generate big deals and big commission checks. They don't get it. If I can't make money, I'm not interested."

A waitress named Jacqui brought our breakfast. I had worked out that morning and was starving. I had a three-egg omelet with cheese and spinach. Jack had a croissant. I maneuvered the conversation around to Gregor Smolnik.

"Can't say I'm sad to see Gregor go," Jack admitted. "He was a scumbag." Realizing what he said, Jack opened his eyes wide and looked around to see whether anyone was listening. "Shit. That Lieutenant Carrillo's hauled me into his office three times now. He's got me down as a suspect."

"You're kidding."

"No. Apparently someone told him I used to call Gregor a scumbag. Unfortunately, I don't have an alibi. My wife, Sheri . . . you've met Sheri, haven't you? Blond curls? Kinda hot? Well, she was down in Cabo with some girlfriends spending money, and I was home alone watching baseball."

"Did you ever get your commission on the SolarNext deal?"

"No. I had to hire a lawyer, but with Gregor out of the way, Webb might actually—Hey . . ."

He stopped talking and tried to read me; sales guys are good at reading people. He grinned.

"You think I'm a suspect too, don't you?" he asked. "That's hilarious."

"What's so funny?"

"You don't know me as well as you should. A good CFO knows all sales guys are coin-operated. The only thing I care about is making money. That's it. How do I make money by killing Gregor Smolnik? Okay, there's the one fifty on the SolarNext deal, but the risk is huge compared to the return. If I get caught I go to prison, and I can't make any money in there."

"So you didn't kill him."

"Hell, no. I focus on the money. Emotion gets in the way. If I was

the type to get emotional I would have gone off on Webb Elliot when he was sleeping with Sheri last year."

"What?"

"You bet. They were doing the nasty while I was on the road selling software. But I didn't get upset, and you know why?"

"Why?"

"Well, for one thing, I was cheating on her too. We have a pattern of that. But the main reason was, if I got mad at Webb it would have screwed up the Chartwell deal, and that deal paid me seven hundred thousand dollars."

The world according to Jack O'Shea: It's all about the money, literally.

"What about the scumbag sign?"

"I must have told a hundred people Gregor was a scumbag, multiple times. It was the perfect way for someone to point the finger at me."

∘ ∘ ∘

I PULLED UP MY SPREADSHEET that night and looked at the names. Many of them were largely unknown to me. I knew their faces but not much about their personalities. The guys who knew the list really well were Henry and Tommy.

The next day I took them through the list and asked about anything unusual. The one data point that struck me as having real value was about Sanjay Kumar, the engineer who loved to play poker. Apparently Sanjay's love of the game had blossomed into a full-blown gambling addiction, and the rumor was he had a large debt to pay. I decided to interview Sanjay, but it would have to wait until after my follow-up meeting with Lieutenant Carrillo the next day.

∘ ∘ ∘

"Yes, it's an interesting spreadsheet," Carrillo said.

I couldn't tell whether he was serious or merely humoring me. We were in the Radisson at his unofficial office. I had walked him through the logic of multiplicative probabilities across means, motive, and opportunity.

"I think the framework is good," I said, "but as you can see, there are a lot of missing pieces of data. If someone on your team could provide the results of your investigation . . . you know . . . from alibi checking and so forth."

"Police detectives can build spreadsheets too," he said.

The lieutenant was chewing gum again, but didn't offer any to me this time.

"You don't think I'm adding value."

"Mr. Robbins, what did you do with the straight razor?"

"Pardon?"

"The murder weapon. What did you do with it?"

A ripple of panic swept through me and began to swell. Carrillo thought I was the murderer. Did he have enough evidence to arrest me?

"I didn't kill Gregor Smolnik."

"You were the only one with access to the body. The razor, Mr. Robbins. What did you do with the razor?"

Wait a minute. He couldn't find the murder weapon. That was the flaw in the theory of me as murderer. On the night of the murder there was no time for me to dispose of the weapon. If I were the murderer then the razor would be hidden in the men's room at Siena.

"You don't think I'm a suspect because you can't find the razor."

"Yet," he said. "We haven't found it yet."

But his expression said otherwise. Carrillo no longer considered me a likely suspect.

Dee brought a refill on my Diet Coke. "Here you are, Joe."

"Thanks, Dee."

"I will tell you one thing about your spreadsheet," he said. "You can keep your motive probabilities high. Just about everybody we talked to thinks the board screwed them, and quite a few blame Webb Elliot as well. I'd be a little worried if I were him."

I wasn't surprised to hear those findings. Dreams die hard.

Carrillo chewed his gum. Again my attention was drawn to the almond-colored eye with the flaw.

"Am I in danger?"

"Nobody seems to hold a grudge against senior management. I think you're okay."

That much felt good. We sat silently for a long moment. There didn't seem to be anything else to cover, but I didn't want the meeting to end. So far I had contributed nothing of value to the investigation, but it was still a lot more interesting than staring at income statements and balance sheets.

"Is there anything I can do?" I asked.

"It's not that I don't want the help. We certainly need it. The team has worked around the clock on this thing for two weeks. We've contacted almost everyone on your list and tried to verify alibis, but we haven't gotten that break we talked about."

"You're putting it on the unsolved pile."

"Not exactly, but I am cutting the team down to two detectives. They'll continue to work loose ends for another two weeks." The lieutenant looked at the laptop and paged through his notes. "Let's see. Maybe you can help after all. There are some people we haven't been able to reach."

He mentioned a few names that I knew nothing about, then Sanjay Kumar.

"I don't know where Sanjay is . . . haven't seen him since I left the company, but I did hear he has a large gambling debt he may not be able to pay."

"Interesting. Okay. We'll look into that." He typed in a few words. "What about Gwen Raleigh? What do you know about her?"

"I haven't seen Gwen since early August."

"Apparently no one has, but several people suggested you have a personal relationship with Ms. Raleigh. Is that true?"

Lieutenant Carrillo was good, and his team was good. They had covered a lot of ground. There was no point in lying to him.

"We had a brief affair, but that was back in July."

"I see. I'm concerned for her safety. What with the murder and her missing at the same time . . . it might be a random coincidence, but then again . . . ."

It looked for a moment as if the heterochromia in his eye grew larger, but when I looked more closely I wasn't sure.

"I want to be able to reach you," he said. "Please let me know if you leave town, and be sure to tell me if you hear anything about Ms. Raleigh."

. . .

I TOOK THE LONG WAY HOME, drove North on MoPac, across 183 a few miles, and then down Jollyville Road to an apartment complex. I walked up a flight of exterior stairs and knocked on Sanjay Kumar's door. There was no answer. I leaned way over the edge of the second-floor landing rail to look in the window. The sun was bright against the glass. Inside I could just make out a television and couch. I had the sudden and crazy urge to break into his apartment, but I didn't have the means, and, of course, that would violate Carrillo's "don't do anything illegal" rule.

CHAPTER 22

A FEW DAYS LATER, I was in the HEB pushing a cart through the cereal section when I ran into Becky Julliard, the spouse of a Connection employee. Rose kept up her Connection Plus friendships, and I knew an event was planned for the following night. I mentioned the dinner, and Becky told me they'd had to cancel due to low interest from spouses; the Connection was growing weaker.

The next day I was in our home office wrestling with bills online when Rose laid her hands on my shoulders and asked, "Have you got some cash?"

"Yes, why, do you need some?"

"No, you've got to pay the babysitter tonight."

"Are we getting a babysitter?" I asked. I had a scheduled dinner with my CFO network group but thought Rose would stay home.

"You're still going to that CFO thing, aren't you?" she asked.

"Yes, what are you doing?"

"I've got a Connection Plus event, dummy." On the way out of the room she added, "I talked to Becky this morning. She's expecting a great turnout."

Rose was lying. I lost focus on the screen in front of me. In my mind I saw a tilted picture frame on a wall—something was out of place. I leaned back in the chair.

Why had she lied to me? I wanted to ask her about the discrepancy, but my CFO training wouldn't let me. I tried to think; there must have been a dozen logical reasons for her deception, but I could manage to conjure only one. She would have a justification; I had cheated on her, why shouldn't she cheat on me? I was conscious of my paranoia, but the awareness itself offered no relief.

Out of my paranoia, an even more sinister thought emerged. I mentally rearranged the data a couple different ways, and a sinking feeling came over me. I took a deep breath and slowly exhaled.

No. It was an absurd thought. Rose would never . . . .

But my paranoia slowly evolved into obsession. As far-fetched as the notion was, it would not be banished by logic alone. To verify or alleviate my suspicions, I needed proof. I could not clandestinely follow Rose in the marigold Jeep. I needed to project where she might be, get there first, and wait.

I sent an e-mail to the CFO network sponsor to tell him I wouldn't be able to attend the dinner. On the computer I switched to Mapsco and studied a detailed street map of Austin until I was sure of the right location.

* * *

I LEFT THE HOUSE around six. On the way out I grabbed the Steiner 7x50 binoculars from the hall closet and tucked them under my windbreaker. I drove east on Bee Caves to Westlake Drive, turned left down the hill to Redbud, then across Town Lake. At Lake Austin Boulevard I turned right and looked for the sign, but missed it and had to U-turn back to Kyle Road.

I pulled into a lot next to a large field to wait for sunset. Teenage kids played pickup soccer. Nearby, grackles held a squawking contest. After thirty minutes it was almost dark. I walked a hundred yards

from the lot to an apartment complex whose buildings sat atop the hill above Lake Austin. The spot I was looking for was on the edge of the lake behind the apartment buildings. It took two passes to orient myself. No one saw me as I walked through the open stairwell of one of the buildings to the back side of the complex. There was a small clearing between the trees that lined the lake, and a path down to a small boat dock. The apartments at the rear of that building had a clear view of the lake and my target house on the other side.

Both sides of the lake were lined with bluffs; the apartment buildings were a hundred feet above water level, and the house across the lake was slightly lower. I walked down the path until I was eye level with the house and edged into the brush on the left to sit on a boulder. By that time it was completely dark.

Above me the balcony door to an apartment was open, and the sounds of zz Top drifted down with the faint smell of marijuana. The apartment dweller laughed occasionally, like he was watching television.

I trained the binoculars on the house, a hundred and fifty yards away. Spots lit the exterior, but inside it was dark, the only light provided by a large aquarium and the kitchen appliances. It was a white house of modern design with a flat roof and lots of right angles. Across the entire length of the main level was floor-to-ceiling glass. The glass wall opened onto a balcony that overlooked the lake. Beneath the balcony was an elaborate pool. I had visited the house twice before and stood outside on the balcony to look down at the lake. That was how I knew the opening in the woods existed next to these apartments.

The darkness inside the house was welcome news. I must have been wrong. I hoped I was wrong.

Nearby a solo cricket sounded, and every so often a fish jumped in the lake. I sat for thirty minutes. My backside grew sore, and I shifted to different positions.

I kept thinking about the new tattoo I had seen on Amanda Sorenson's hip the night she committed suicide.

A short while later a light came on in the house, then a second, and finally the entire main floor was illuminated. I pointed the Steiners at the entrance hallway and adjusted the focus. After a few moments Rose walked into Webb Elliot's house.

She was alone. She wore a black miniskirt, a jean jacket over a bright yellow blouse, and high heels. After dropping her purse and jacket casually on a side table, she walked the long hallway by the living room to the open kitchen. She opened a cabinet door, took out a bottle, drank two large shots in quick succession, and put the bottle away again. She took some wine from the refrigerator, poured a glass, and sat on the couch to look out the window.

My heart raced, creating a pain behind my eyes. I wanted to call and tell her to get out of there, but at the same time I had to know more.

Five minutes later Webb walked in. He must have come straight from the office, because he wore his standard designer jeans and dress shirt. She called out and walked to him. They kissed immediately, a deep, passionate kiss. His arms pulled her to him. My ears filled with the sound of my heart pounding.

They walked into the kitchen, where he poured more wine, and they talked. She stood next to him, grinning, pulling playfully on his belt, leaning in for another kiss every few minutes. He said something, and she stood up straight to pay attention. She gave a little nod, after which he walked to a cabinet in the living room and reached in to turn something on. I thought it must be a sound system.

Rose had followed, and when Webb stood up, she slowly removed her shirt and bra while he watched. They stood in front of the couch, in clear view of the window. He playfully slapped at one of her breasts. She laughed. Webb leaned to kiss them each in turn, and she pulled his head into her.

My eyes were glued to the binoculars. I wanted to throw them down the hill but could not.

Webb was facing away from me with Rose on his other side. I know that she unzipped him then, and got him ready, because soon after she squatted down, still standing on high heels, and pulled on his waist as she gave him oral sex.

I vomited off the side of the boulder. I wanted to disappear, to dissipate into atoms that would merge with the dirt and rotting leaves around me, to exist no more.

I made a noise, a loud noise, a cough followed by a heavy intake of air. I thought the apartment dweller upstairs would hear me, but when I looked that way, he only laughed again at his movie.

I turned back to Webb's house and saw that they were removing their clothes. I was stunned at their brazen sexual display, but after looking around I realized that a boater on the lake could not see into the house, and on this side, the clearing where I sat was the only break in the woods that afforded a view.

Over the next fifteen minutes they tried various positions. Each time they shifted he seemed to be explaining something, and she gave an enthusiastic nod. They started with Rose lying on the couch, one leg high in the air. Then they switched and he lay on the couch while she rode him. In their last position she stood and leaned forward with her arms on the back of the couch while Webb took her from behind. At the end he pulled out to finish. Afterward, she walked into the kitchen naked and used a hand towel to wipe her back, still wearing the high-heeled shoes. They picked up their wineglasses and walked into a room at the back of the house.

I put the Steiners to the side and sat with my head down. A roller coaster of images and voices threatened to make me sick again. My stomach ached, and my mouth tasted of vomit. Rage boiled within me and twice I stood to go, but then sat down again. To achieve my

intentions I needed to think clearly, to plan steps, and to act rationally up to a point.

I stayed for ten minutes, but they didn't reappear, so I hiked out to the Jeep.

Back at home, I paid the babysitter, checked on the sleeping kids, and set about my other work. A special key, taped to the back of a drawer in my desk, partially opened a safe on the top shelf of the master room closet. I dialed in the combination, which only I knew, to complete the sequence and open the door. Rose wanted nothing to do with guns, and I didn't want anyone else fooling with it. I took out the Smith & Wesson 686, its holster, and a box of .38 Special hollow-points. I took the whole lot out to the garage and hid them under the front seat of the Jeep.

In the family room I searched for her cigarettes. She would pick someplace high where the kids never looked. On my third try I felt above the cabinets over the stove and found them. I sat on the patio and smoked and waited for Rose.

I had never wanted to know anything about guns, but experience taught me they serve a purpose. Ted Thompson, one of our neighbors in Dallas, was an abusive husband who refused treatment. One night we heard him going for his wife, Nicky. After calling the police I went over there. I broke open the front door and interrupted him in mid-slap. When Ted came at me, I hit him hard until he stopped coming.

A few days later Ted threatened to kill me and my family, and the police took him away. I thought he might come back; that's when I bought the gun and spent every weekend for a month learning how to use it. I listened to the instructor carefully and practiced on the range until I was an accurate shot up to thirty feet.

We had a dog then, and one night at two o'clock he started barking. When he stopped so abruptly, I knew something was wrong and crept

out of the bedroom into the hall, the Smith & Wesson ready. Sensing motion ahead I flipped the light switch, and Ted fired a shot that tore by my shoulder. The instructor taught me to aim for the triangle at the top of the torso and to keep firing until the threat was eliminated. I pulled the trigger three times, and Ted went down for good.

I watched Ted Thompson bleed to death on the floor of my hallway. I had stuffed tea towels in the holes in his chest to stem the bleeding. Beads of sweat popped on his forehead, and his eyes lost focus as he spoke his last words: "Tell Nicky. Tell Nicky. I'm sorry."

After that, I vowed never to use a gun unless my family was threatened. It seemed to me that Webb Elliot had destroyed most of what I had.

An hour later, Rose came home. The patio door was open, and she must have smelled the smoke, because she stuck her head out the door.

"Joey?"

"Present."

She walked out slowly, not sure what to make of the situation.

"What are you doing?"

"Care for a cigarette, honey?"

"Have you started smoking again?"

We were both quiet then. Somewhere off in the woods a small creature shrieked as a bigger creature tore its flesh.

"I saw you. I watched your show tonight, on the lake. You and Webb."

"Jesus!" Her hands flew to the front of her mouth.

"Are you his mistress now? Or just his fuck buddy?"

"I didn't want . . . I didn't think you . . ."

The love of my life was standing in the light cast by the picture window. She was disappointed that she'd been caught, but not remorseful.

My lip trembled. "I . . . I thought we were trying to work on our marriage."

She stepped in front of my chair and looked down at me, defiant. "We worked on it. I worked on it . . . for ten years . . . and then you screwed someone else."

I wanted to maintain control, but the emotion rushed at me, like a wild animal that sees prey within reach and strikes.

"Damn it! He fired me."

I had no sense of getting up, but then I was standing, moving toward her. Rose stepped backward and fell onto a lounge chair.

"You . . ." I said. "You . . . you've . . . damn . . . we . . . ."

"Go ahead and hit me! That's what you want, isn't it? Find out how it makes you feel."

My fingers trembled and balled into a fist. The urge was there. I wanted to, but there remained enough will to resist the primal instinct. I knew it was time to go. She wasn't my target. Webb Elliot could sell anything to anybody. He was the mastermind behind my misery.

"I'm leaving."

"Fine. Go."

. . .

I DROVE OUT TO BEE CAVES and headed toward town. On the way images of Webb kissing and having sex with my wife flashed intermittently with the streetlights. If only I had never left Liberty Air. We'd still be in Dallas, eating in fine restaurants, following the pro teams, and enjoying family life. I cursed this place in the hill country, and I cursed Webb Elliot, the man who brought me here. The curves in the road and the limestone rock were the same as my first day at the Connection, but I had no more hopes for the future, only a plan to rectify the recent past.

I drove by the house first, looking for a place to pull over that was not easy to see. The Westlake police are keen and notice everything.

A quarter mile past Webb's place, three cars were parked in a little pull-off next to a gated community. There was room for a fourth. I loaded the gun, fit the holster to my belt, and hoofed it back to his driveway. The iron bar fence was eight feet tall with fake spikes on top, easy to scale. I walked to the house and took the footpath around and down to the pool deck level.

Walking up the exterior steps I looked through the huge windows and saw Webb sitting in the living room, talking on his cell phone. When he hung up and turned to the laptop on the side table, I walked to the sliding glass door and into the house.

Webb noticed immediately. He was startled and stood to see who it was. He recognized me and took a step back. At first he didn't see the Smith & Wesson.

"What . . . what are you doing here?" He knew why I was there, but not what I planned to do.

"I'm here to kill you."

The large aquarium divided the huge room.

The training had been quite clear: Hold the gun in two hands, focus on the sight, put it in the middle of the notch, and point it at the target. In the closed room the shot roared like a cannon. Water, glass, and fish bounced on the bamboo floor and began to spread. Webb stumbled to the hallway and walked backward away from me.

"Please don't—"

"When you fuck people over, there are consequences."

The mess of the aquarium wasn't enough. I fired two shots side by side at the big center glass pane. A jagged fracture inched its way toward the upper left corner. One more shot—*boom!*—and the entire window started falling in large chunks on both sides of the frame. My ears rang from the explosions.

Webb backed farther away and put up his hands to ward off bullets. I followed him step for step. Modern art graced the hallway.

"Don't . . . don't . . ."

He bumped into a side table and stumbled to the floor. A large Chinese vase overflowing with dried fronds stood on the table. I put a bullet through the vase and it shattered, showering him with bits of pottery and dust.

The Smith & Wesson 686 holds six bullets, and I had one left, plenty to get the job done. Webb shrank into a ball, his eyes shut, hands covering his face.

"No . . . No . . . Please . . . ."

"It's over," I shouted. "I'm ending you."

But the loud noises and flying debris had unnerved me. I pointed the gun at his face, but my index finger was outside the trigger guard.

They would catch me. Rico Carrillo or somebody like him would put together the evidence and track me down. I thought about Chandler and Callie. Even if I couldn't have Rose I could still have them, but in prison there would be no time for Sheila stories.

As I looked at Webb's face, my hand shook, and all I could see was Ted Thompson, his life leaking out on my hallway floor. I lowered the Smith & Wesson to the side.

Webb opened his eyes and slowly comprehended. As I walked past him toward the door, he said, "You're not going to kill me?" It was half question, half joyful noise.

"I guess not."

On my way back to the Jeep I gradually regained full awareness and went through the possibilities. I could still go to prison for a long time: breaking and entering, destruction of property, attempted murder. I wasn't too concerned about it, though; Webb Elliot would avoid scandal if possible.

I drove back to Bee Caves Road with no idea where to go. It was midnight. I pulled into an office parking lot and turned off the Jeep. I was a mess of frazzled nerves and jumbled emotions. The urge to

kill Webb recurred periodically, like aftershocks from an earthquake. Mixed with the anger and despair was shame: a certain knowledge, buried deep, that I had tipped the first domino.

The idea of hanging around Austin held no appeal whatsoever. There was one place I could go where people wouldn't judge me, where I could defer judging myself. After an hour I pulled a business card from my wallet. I made a phone call and put together a plan. I had six hours to kill, so I crawled in the back and tried to sleep.

CHAPTER 23

A T TEN A.M. my flight touched down in Vegas. Elsie Summers met me at the gate with a monster hug and a kiss on the lips. She wore jeans and sneakers and a burnt-orange, deep-vee cashmere sweater.

On the way to the garage she kept her arm around me, with her hand in my rear pocket. In the car on the way to the Bellagio she leaned over to give me a wet kiss and put her hand on my leg. She continued to play those games while we checked into the hotel, working her, and me, into a near frenzy. As soon as the door to our suite closed she pulled at my shirt and belt.

The first time we did it was fast.

Her breasts were as I remembered: natural, full, with large nipples. Her pubic hair was trimmed close to fit inside a G-string. She was in shape from all the dancing, but not so lean that she didn't have a full curve to her hips.

Elsie started on top, wanting to control the pace, and pressed down on my chest with her hands, her breasts swinging free. She laughed about it, making it funny and fun at the same time. She reached back to slap her ass and giggled. After a while she gave in to the pleasure and let it wash her away.

When I thought she'd had her fill, I grabbed her around the waist and turned us over so I was on top. The frustrations of the previous day caught up with me, and I hammered away at Elsie until I was finished, collapsing on her with my nose in a pillow while she stroked my back. Soon the perspiration dried, and we both fell asleep.

When we woke up, I ordered champagne, and the party started. Over the next forty-eight hours we consumed Vegas. We went to a Hard Rock show, a circus show, and a comedy show. We bought a vacation wardrobe for me and party clothes for Elsie. We gorged ourselves on food and wine. At Club Paradiso, Elsie had lap dances from all her friends.

All the while I drank: beers in the sports book, margaritas on the Strip, cocktails before dinner, and plenty of wine. We played the silly, fun games of roulette and Pai Gow, and we bet the ponies, Elsie cheering like crazy whenever our horse had a chance.

Money meant nothing to me. I couldn't reason why it should. I made stupid bets based on hunches and generally lost. I stayed away from games requiring calculation, which was good, because after the first few hours I was in a permanent state of fuzziness.

On Monday at noon we ventured down to the buffet.

"You should try the barbecue spare ribs," she said, taking a bite from a full plate. "They're delicious."

I was drinking a Bloody Mary. Elsie had champagne.

"Maybe after I finish my juice."

She wore her hair up in a high pony and was bright-eyed after six hours of sleep and a morning romp. She wore a long-sleeved teal T-shirt, with dangling earrings and a bright red Swatch. Elsie was twenty-eight but could pass for early twenties.

The waitress came by and topped off the coffee.

"Another Bloody, sir?"

"Please."

Elsie finished chewing a mouthful of green beans amandine. "You know," she said, "I don't plan to stay in Vegas forever."

"That sounds wise. This town runs some people into the ground." My stomach rumbled. I glanced at the spare ribs on her plate; they were beginning to spur my appetite.

"I've been dancing for six years now. I figure I'm good for another three years, four at most, and then I'm out."

Elsie sipped the champagne and buttered a roll.

"What will you do then?"

This was a side of Elsie I had not seen before. Most everyone spends time thinking about the future, but up until then, Elsie had lived only for the moment.

"By then I'll be thirty-one or thirty-two and ready to get married. It's best not to marry too soon . . . before you've run the wildness out. When I stop dancing, I'll move to San Diego, marry the best man I can find, and start having babies."

It was hard for me to picture. I could see Elsie dancing on the pole or doing Jell-O shots at the Hard Rock, but I couldn't see her pushing a stroller around the neighborhood.

"Really?"

"Oh, yeah. Don't get me wrong. This is great." She twirled her fork in the air to indicate the entire room. Around us were a hundred people, sitting at tables of two, three, and four, eating their fill, sipping on their first drink, laughing and smiling as they began another day in the land of the endless party.

"But I have a plan," she said.

"What's the plan?"

"Every year I save fifty thousand from my dancing income. The rest goes to living expenses and partying, and there is plenty left over for partying. By the time I'm done, I'll have five or six hundred thousand to start the family."

She went on to explain that a hardworking stripper in the right club could make a hundred and fifty a year. It was a tough job, but if you stayed away from the coke, and other temptations, you could save a bundle.

She drained the champagne and looked at her watch.

"You need to get some food so we can check out."

"Where are we going?"

"We're moving to my apartment. Tomorrow's Halloween. I'm throwing the party this year and I need your help to get ready."

. . .

I INSPECTED HER BAR and found it lacking. I drove her Maxima to the liquor store and picked up six bottles of booze, a mixed case of wine, and three cases of beer. Elsie focused on food, decorations, and tidying up the apartment.

She had a one-bedroom in an old-style complex on Driftwood Street. The building was U-shaped with two floors and twenty units in total. It was secured by a bougainvillea-draped wall and gate that faced the street. Elsie had lived there for years and was friends with most of the tenants.

She invited an eclectic group of casino dealers, waitresses, bouncers, and strippers. They wore outrageous costumes. Bush and Gore were both in attendance, dressed as Siegfried and Roy. Two dancers came as Elvis, shirts unbuttoned to their navels. Elsie was Madonna, complete with black stockings and the cone bra. I was a pirate, with eye patch, headscarf, purple bloomers, and a plastic sword.

Everyone brought a contribution, and soon there was a wide assortment of recreational drugs to match the booze in the kitchen. I was invited to try this and that, but politely declined. Alcohol was the only medicine I required, provided it was consumed in the proper quantities.

A bouncer named Tim and I decided the party was too slow, so we doled out tequila shots, making sure we got our fair share. It was Gran Patrón Platinum. Soon after, things started moving right along.

About midnight a contingent removed their clothes and headed to the hot tub. A few others went into the bedroom and closed the door. Elsie had disappeared, and a thin friend of hers, wearing a sheer black blouse with no bra, sat down and gave me an openmouthed kiss. She invited me upstairs to her apartment for a special massage. I declined, and she immediately went after a baccarat croupier sitting across the room.

I called a cab. I wanted to go downtown to gamble with the regular folk. He let me out on Fremont Street during the middle of the light show. I wandered into Binion's to try craps but had a hard time focusing on the dice. Up the street I found a Cajun-style slot parlor that sold hurricane smoothies in the shape of a football. For two dollars more they gave me extra shots of Everclear. I walked around downtown for a while, a pirate, football in hand, indestructible and indecipherable.

I turned down one street and vaguely noticed there were only three of us, me and the two guys asking politely for money. I put the football down, intending to negotiate, and remember only white flashes. Sometime later a policeman nudged me awake with his foot and suggested it was time to move on. The polite bandits had left my wallet and credit cards behind; maybe they figured the three hundred in cash was fair enough. I caught a cab back to Elsie's place and passed out on the sofa, the party long since over.

Six hours later I awoke with a hangover to win the prize. It hurt the most right behind my eyes, and for ten minutes I didn't dare open them. When I did it was agony. I shut them immediately and tried to go back to sleep. No success. With eyes as slits I felt my way to the kitchen and drank two glasses of water. There was a soreness in my right ear that didn't fit; it wasn't standard-issue hangover. The guest

bathroom mirror showed a thin trail of dried blood down to my collarbone, a good-size knot on my forehead, and a small cut above the eyebrow. With a wet washcloth I started to clean up.

A cute blonde with long hair walked in wearing a pair of Elsie's gym shorts and nothing else. She had pointy boobs, tattoos on her feet, and sat on the toilet while smoking a cigarette. She looked at me briefly, without interest. When finished she hopped up and walked out.

I am too weak to be an alcoholic; I cannot stand the physical pain and the psychological trauma.

* * *

THAT AFTERNOON Elsie and I sat on the couch and compared notes from the party. She thought my little altercation downtown was hilarious.

She nibbled on dry Cheerios and drank coffee, wearing an oversize Washington Redskins sweatshirt.

"I don't think you're cut out for this lifestyle," she said.

"What makes you say that?"

For the first time in days I held a Diet Coke that wasn't bolstered with Jack Daniel's.

"Well, for one thing, you have no sense of balance. For example, last night you should have stopped drinking and gone upstairs with Linda when I sent her your way. If you had done that, you'd be sober enough to party again today."

"Linda?"

"The skinny girl . . . you know . . . with the see-through blouse? From what I understand she could show you a few tricks."

"My loss."

Elsie sipped her coffee and continued with her appraisal. "The other big problem is you have kids. I know you and your wife are at war right now, but that *does not* let you off the hook as a dad."

She sat with bare legs folded up and under the sweatshirt. The stragglers from the party were gone, and the place was spotless. Elsie's eyes were clear and unwavering. It felt like I was back in school, and the professor was trying to convey important knowledge.

"You really are going to have a family in San Diego, aren't you?" I asked.

"Yes, I am, and I'll tell you another thing: I don't know exactly what you're looking for, but it's not here in Vegas. Don't get me wrong. This has been a blast, and you are welcome anytime, but right now you need to get back to Austin."

Elsie was a stripper with a plan and knew more about her future than I knew about mine. That was Wednesday, November 1. We agreed I would fly home on Friday, which gave us two more nights.

. . .

THE NEXT MORNING I was awakened by a call on my cell. All that week I had ignored Austin. It was time for re-entry, so I answered the phone.

"Where are you?" Zola asked.

"Vegas."

"Great. You need to get back to Austin right away."

"What is it? The kids?"

"No. It's Mike Franzinni. He's dead. He jumped off the penthouse balcony of the Bank of Texas building."

It had happened the day before. Zola filled me in on what she knew from the Connection network, which wasn't much.

In the afternoon Rico Carrillo called.

"What the hell are you doing in Vegas?"

"Uh, gambling?"

"Damn it. I told you to call me if you left town."

I could see him staring at me, the black flaw sparkling in his almond iris. I didn't like it. "Something came up."

"It certainly did. Another one of your directors is dead. How soon can you get your butt back here?"

"I have a flight in the morning."

"Meet me at the Radisson . . . two o'clock."

That night I grilled mahimahi out by the pool, and we split a bottle of chardonnay. We spent a quiet, peaceful evening together, a pair of lovers, both comfortable that we were separating in the morning.

Elsie took me to the airport. She leaned up for a kiss, and with a devilish grin reached around to grab my ass.

. . .

ON THE FLIGHT HOME I started to work through two problems. The first was money. After I subtracted the cost of the Vegas trip, the cash would last through March, but I would be short for the IRS payment in April. Without additional income I would have to file for bankruptcy in the first quarter. No brilliant solutions came to me; my only plan was to keep looking for a job.

My second problem was a place to stay. Although my "vacation" had quelled the violent urges, I was not prepared to live with Rose again. On this problem I had a breakthrough. A wealthy fraternity brother of mine had attended law school at UT and fallen in love with Austin. He returned to watch Longhorn football games and maintained a condo for those visits. I knew he didn't use the place much and thought he might lend it to me.

My stomach was queasy, and I had a small headache, but I attributed those symptoms to the long-term effects of too much booze. I went to sleep to the noise of droning aircraft engines.

. . .

"WHAT THE HELL WERE YOU DOING IN VEGAS, Mr. Robbins?"

I met Carrillo on the deck of the Radisson, which overlooked Town Lake and the hike-and-bike trail. A crew team rowed past with the coxswain urging them on. The voices of runners on the trail below rose up and over the railing to us.

"Maybe you could call me Joe. We seem to be meeting a lot."

"Don't change the subject."

I hadn't lied to him yet, and it didn't seem like the time to start. "I've been having some marital issues. I needed a break."

"You should have told me you were leaving. I still consider you a possible suspect."

"Suspect for what?" I hoped he didn't mention an assault on Webb Elliot.

"There's a growing list of possibilities."

My headache from the airplane was worse, and there was a scratch in my throat. The coffee felt good going down, but I was tired and wanted Carrillo to get to the point.

"Do you think Mike Franzinni was murdered?" I asked.

"Do you?"

"I have no idea. You have all the data."

"Where were you two nights ago?"

"In Vegas. I've been there for a week."

Carrillo sat back in his chair and watched the traffic on the Congress Avenue Bridge, a big frown on his face.

"I was staying with a friend," I said. "I'll give you her contact information."

The frown softened, and Carrillo nodded his head that this was acceptable. It appeared my interrogation had concluded for the moment.

"At first we thought it was suicide," he said, "but there is something funny about the surveillance video. You can see Franzinni walking into his corner office at eight fifteen p.m., but he never walks out. There is no image of him walking onto the balcony. The next live image is of the receptionist opening the office on Thursday morning."

A car screeched out on the bridge. A second later somebody yelled out their window.

"So you think someone tampered with the surveillance system."

"We don't know yet."

I thought about the lonely fall of Mike Franzinni: the office windows flying by, the frantic grasping at nothing, the feel and sound of rushing air, the sudden end of everything. He had been so proud of the view.

A few months before I had read an article in CFO magazine about video surveillance, and the conversation triggered a question.

"Is it an analog or digital surveillance system?"

"I have no idea."

"Digital surveillance is just coming onto the scene. A high-end group like Central Texas Ventures might have adopted it early. I don't know much about those systems, but it's possible someone could have hacked into it from the outside."

"Hold on. Let me check." Carrillo called a team member and spoke for a minute. "It's a digital system, but the security company says it can't be hacked."

"I'd like to get Tommy King's opinion on that, if you don't mind."

"That might be useful."

As Carrillo typed, my mind drifted back to Franzinni. As soon as Zola had told me he was dead, I was sure it was a second murder. A suicide would have been too much of a coincidence.

"If the murderer is after board members," I said, "Webb Elliot could be in danger."

"It's interesting you should say that. There was a report of gunfire and glass breaking from one of his neighbors last week."

I tried to keep a straight face while he looked at me.

"Do you know anything about that?" he asked.

"No." For the first time I lied to Carrillo, but I couldn't avoid it without incriminating myself.

"Are you sure?"

"What does Webb say?"

"He believes the glass was broken by vandals. He says there was no gunfire."

I took a sip of the coffee, relieved to see my hand didn't shake. We sat in silence.

"This is going to be a big case for Austin now, isn't it?" I asked.

"Huge. The mayor wants it solved right now. Even the governor is asking about it."

"Which governor?"

"The one who's trying to get into the White House."

"If you'll give me the data on the investigation, I'll load it in the spreadsheet . . . see where it takes us."

"I'll think about it."

Carrillo actually looked worried. There were bags under his eyes that had not been there before. I thought I'd ask the question before he did.

"Any news on Gwen Raleigh, or Sanjay Kumar?"

Carrillo shook his head. "I'm very concerned about Ms. Raleigh. Don't leave town again without telling me."

"Sure thing."

"By the way, are you all right? You look exhausted."

"Vegas can do that to you."

* * *

I FELT TERRIBLE. The headache had tripled in size and intensity. My throat was worse, and I was beginning to feel nauseous.

My fraternity brother had happily agreed to let me use the condo. He said I'd be doing him a favor. I was dying to get to bed with what I thought was a cold, but on the way to the car, I got a call from Webb Elliot. He implored me to meet him right away at Mozart's, a coffee shop on Lake Austin Boulevard.

"Why on earth would I meet with you?"

"Give me ten minutes. It involves an opportunity to make money."

The sound of his voice brought on violent urges, and my first instinct was to tell him to stick it, but Webb always knew the soft spots. I did need money, and the call itself was so audacious it made me curious. I agreed to meet.

Mozart's is on the edge of Lake Austin, just upriver of the dam that separates Lake Austin from Town Lake. It was one of those stunning November days when people sit on the deck in the sunshine to linger over coffee and watch the boat traffic.

I arrived before Webb and bought the largest cup of decaf they had. The headache was borderline debilitating, and the only thing keeping me going was hot liquid on my throat.

Webb didn't look the same. He wore the same uniform of jeans and dress shirt, but he hadn't shaved, his hair was uncombed, and he kept jerking his head to look behind him. I was at a table for two in the sun. When he sat down, I had the desire to strangle him and told him so.

He looked over his shoulder again and shifted his chair to more easily observe people traffic.

"Oddly enough," he said, "you're the only one I trust."

I sipped my coffee and didn't say anything. He leaned toward me.

"I know you won't kill me, because you had the chance and didn't take it."

"You're having sex with my wife. . . ."

Webb held up his hand, signaling me to stop until a customer passed by.

"I might change my mind," I said.

"If it helps at all, I haven't seen her since that night."

Actually, it did help. It improved my outlook marginally to think the affair had ended, but I wasn't going to share that with Webb.

"I don't even know why I do these things," he said, by way of explanation. "I ran into Rose with a few other girls at a bar. It was when you were staying at the Courtyard Marriott. We chatted awhile, and I gave her my card. I told her to call if she ever needed to talk with someone. She called. One thing led to another."

"If I could snap my fingers and erase you from the world I would, but it's not that simple."

Webb looked genuinely hurt. I didn't care.

"That whole sequence of events was so bloody complicated," he said. "Starting with Gwen . . . ."

"What do you mean, 'starting with Gwen'?"

Webb frowned, like he wasn't quite sure what he meant. "Well, your affair with Gwen started the whole thing."

The events were connected, but it was strange how he put it.

"Where is Gwen?" I asked.

"I don't know. I thought she'd go to South America. She's mentioned that before, but I haven't heard from her in months."

The whole conversation was irritating, and the coffee was nearly gone. "Why did you ask to meet?"

Webb leaned closer and whispered, "Someone has threatened to kill me."

"Who?"

"I don't know. They did it by anonymous e-mail."

A boat motor backfired, and Webb jumped in his seat. His face went white, and it took a few moments for him to realize it wasn't a gun.

"What did Carrillo say?" I asked.

"I haven't told him. I don't trust the police to solve this. Whoever is committing these murders is from the Connection. You know the level of intelligence involved. We hired a dozen people with perfect SAT scores. The police have no idea how the murderer cornered Gregor in the bathroom of Siena, or how he threw Franzinni off the building without being detected. Besides, the e-mail said if the police find out I'll be killed."

"Tell me about the e-mails."

"Each one has come from a different anonymous address. The first one made contact and threatened to kill me. The second laid out the basic scheme. And the third conveyed wiring instructions for a million dollars."

"Are you going to wire the money?"

"Yes, tomorrow."

I considered Webb's dilemma with the police. In the same situation I would have done the same thing. Money was not a scarce resource for Webb. If a million dollars could remove the threat he would gladly pay up.

"So where do I come in?"

Our table was in the middle of the deck area. Webb's head was on a swivel, trying to keep tabs on all the customers. Finally he couldn't take it any longer and moved to a booth next to the rail overlooking the lake. He signaled me to follow him.

"I want to hire you to find the killer. I'll pay you two hundred and fifty thousand dollars to find him—that is, before he kills me."

"I'm not a detective. I'm a CFO."

"I know you're working closely with Carrillo. That will give you an advantage."

"I don't think he would describe it that way."

"Regardless, at least you're talking to him. Plus, you've got street smarts and determination. You showed me that when you tracked down Randy Harlan with the fraud. And there's something else too:

You're not afraid. Like that time you almost hit me because of the cricket bat in my office. I don't have anyone else to help me on this. It's strange, but I have a sense that with you helping I'll stay alive."

"Once you make the wire payment you might be all clear."

"Maybe, maybe not. In any case, I'll pay you fifty thousand up front for your trouble."

A breeze blew across the lake and chilled my arms. I'd seen that look on Webb's face before, when he knew he was close to a deal.

"I want five hundred thousand, with a hundred grand up front."

"Done," he said, and put out his hand.

I didn't bother to shake it, but told him I'd start nosing around the next day.

· · ·

I FELT UNSTEADY walking up the steps and across the street to the parking lot. The nausea had almost won at Mozart's. I made it across the lot but then vomited all the coffee onto the empty space next to the Jeep. A passing couple looked at me with disdain; they must have thought I was drunk.

I drove to my friend's condo on Spyglass, just south of downtown. I kept my composure long enough to get the key from the manager and walk to the door.

Inside I checked my cell phone and retrieved a voice mail from Elsie. She said that Linda, the skinny woman who French-kissed me at the party, had a bad case of the flu. In Vegas, Elsie and I had practiced safe sex. I was safe from STDs but not from the flu.

I collapsed on the couch. For the next twenty-four hours I was in a semicomatose state. I dragged a plastic garbage can next to the couch and threw up repeatedly. Mostly I slept. I tried several times to drink water but couldn't keep it down.

I heard my cell phone ring, but it was miles away on the kitchen counter. Finally I crawled over to retrieve it and laid it on the couch next to me, too weak to check voice mail.

When it rang again I tried to say "hello" but managed only an awful croak.

"Joe, is that you?" It was Zola.

Another croak. I summoned saliva. "Yes."

"What's wrong?"

"Flu."

"Where are you?"

I explained, and thirty minutes later Zola arrived. She moved me from the couch to the bedroom, gave me a sponge bath, and put me in clean clothes. She went out for supplies and plied me full of flu medicine. On the third day I was able to keep down some soup, and from there it was all about rest.

That night we watched the election returns and both fell asleep about midnight. I woke up at three a.m., Zola leaning on my shoulder, the tired news anchors still trying to make sense of the numbers. Al Gore had conceded the election and later withdrew his concession. All eyes were on Florida. I left Zola on the couch and got in bed. When I woke in the morning all eyes were still on Florida.

The next day I dressed and walked out to my Jeep. I backed out of the garage and into the driveway and everything started to go blurry. Zola came running with an angry look on her face. She helped me back inside and onto the couch, where I spent most of the next two days.

It was a comfortable place to be sick. The condo had an efficient floor plan and was well furnished. The main room consisted of a small but fully equipped kitchen, large living space, and office area. The master bedroom had its own full bath, walk-in closet, and balcony entrance. There was a small guest room with bath where Zola slept. The best feature was a huge covered balcony that afforded a view of

the greenbelt and downtown. Below the balcony, about a hundred feet away, were the clubhouse and pool area.

After a week Zola and I walked down to the pool deck and sat in the sun. We talked it over, and she agreed that I was well enough to take care of myself.

Zola had no logical reason to help me. She was no longer my executive assistant. In fact, she was unemployed herself, having been caught by a subsequent wave of layoffs at the Connection. There was no hint of romance; she had made no such move since I rejected her initial advance my second week on the job. As far as I could tell, Zola helped me only because she was born with the ability and the desire to heal others in their time of trouble.

I didn't think about Zola for long, because there was work to do, but I did record a mental note that I owed her a debt. Someday, I would find a way to pay it off.

CHAPTER 24

I HAD LOST A FULL WEEK. On Sunday, I called Lieutenant Carrillo. I was eager to find out what he had learned about Franzinni's murder. He shared precious little information. No, they hadn't made any arrests. No, neither Sanjay Kumar nor Gwen Raleigh had been located.

While recuperating I'd had a lot of time to think about Webb's financial offer. The initial hundred thousand had already cleared my account, so I knew he was serious. The more I thought about it, the more I wanted the full half million.

I called Webb to check in. He had wired the million dollars to the murderer and heard nothing since. As a precaution he had moved into the Four Seasons, figuring it was safer than living alone in his house.

That night I had a date to take Chandler and Callie out for dinner and a movie. I stood outside the front door, hesitating, thinking perhaps I should ring the bell to my own house. Rose walked by, and I rapped on the window.

As she opened the door I looked at her. After two weeks of Vegas and the flu I had lost awareness of how physically attractive she was. It startled me. I wasn't angry anymore. The spark I had

for her was still there, but it was buried under all the crap. I didn't
know how to feel.

"I don't know what to say," she said.

"I was thinking the same thing."

At that moment Callie spotted me; she came running with open
arms.

"Daddy, Daddy."

I picked her up, and she hugged me tightly around the neck.

"I missed you so much," she said.

"I missed you too, sweetie."

I looked over her shoulder at Rose. Rose blinked fast a few times
and then turned to walk into the kitchen.

"When are you coming home?" Callie sat sideways against my
chest with one arm behind my shoulder.

"I'm not sure. Not just yet." I held her in my left arm while my
right hand played with her tennis shoe.

"Mommy said the two of you had another fight."

"Yes, that's true. We did have a fight."

"Chandler and I fight all the time, but then we make up and
everything is okay again."

"Yes, you two are good about making up."

"What did you fight about?"

"It's hard to explain, and we have to hurry or we'll be late for the
movie." I lowered her to the floor. "Go get your sister."

After the movie, but before leaving the house, I rummaged around
in the workshop to find a special kit I had purchased long ago. It was
the kind of thing most middle-school kids only dream about, but I
had actually bought one. When you're thirteen there is plenty of time,
and I had practiced until I could do it blindfolded. That night, back
in the condo, it took me an hour to refresh the technique; by then I
had picked the lock on the front door a dozen times.

. . .

On Monday I got up before six. Henry and Tommy were coming for breakfast. I had invited them so I could talk to Tommy about hacking into a security system, but first I wanted to return to Sanjay Kumar's apartment. Sanjay had disappeared, but maybe his apartment would tell me something.

I'm not sure why I took the step and broke Carillo's "don't do anything illegal" rule. Certainly the money was a factor, but there was also a sense that I had been blowing in the wind for most of the year; I had to do something proactive.

I arrived at Sanjay's apartment complex at six thirty. It was still sleepy; the only apparent life was a pair of joggers who were heading out as I drove in. I knocked on Sanjay's door out of caution more than expectation. It took me less than a minute to get in. I walked through the apartment: one bedroom, living space, kitchenette, and other basics. For furnishings he had an entertainment system, wide-screen television, and Scandinavian couch and table. On the bureau in the bedroom were pictures of family back in India. The bed was made up and the closet organized.

I didn't know exactly what to look for—something that was out of place perhaps. There were no messages on the answering machine, and the prior outgoing call was a month old. I stood in the living space and tried to figure out what was wrong. It looked like an engineer's apartment but didn't smell abandoned. The air wasn't stale, and the morning light that shone through the window carried no dust.

I opened the refrigerator to inspect the contents: milk, orange juice, a carton of eggs, and some fruit. I cautiously sniffed the milk—still fresh. The expiration date was for a week later.

There was a toaster and a coffeemaker on the counter. I looked closely at the coffeemaker. The pot was clean, but there were drops of

water on the inside. The warming pan held the slightest trace of heat. Sanjay had spent the night, eaten breakfast, and left before dawn. He was hiding out right here in Austin.

I drove south toward the condo and picked up breakfast supplies on the way.

. . .

I SLICED POTATOES and sautéed them with onions, mushrooms, and red peppers. At the same time I fried a pound of spicy sausage. When those were ready I scrambled eight eggs with chopped tomatoes and Gouda cheese. Henry kept an eye on the biscuits in the oven while Tommy made coffee.

I served it on the round oak dining table. Henry and I together ate less than half the eggs, but Tommy had no trouble finishing off the batch. Afterward we cleaned up the dishes, and I stepped out to the balcony. Elsie had smoked in Vegas and I had joined her; now it was a habit again.

The three of us looked over the live oak forest to downtown. The condo was part of a development on the high end of Spyglass Drive. We could hear traffic on MoPac Expressway two blocks to the west. There were a number of apartment complexes and condominiums in that area, but it retained a natural feel because of the strict zoning requirements.

It was misty and low sixties. We could see as far as the Capitol Building but not the UT campus. Down at the clubhouse the property manager talked to the pool service guy.

"This is a cool place," Henry said. "You should stay here."

Until that moment I hadn't thought of it as anything other than a temporary shelter. As bad as things were with Rose, in the back of my mind, my home was still with her and the kids.

Inside we poured more coffee, and I asked Tommy about hacking into a digital video surveillance system.

"Sure," he said, "that could be done. It depends on whether the system is connected to the supplier's overall security network, and I'll bet it is."

"How hard is it to do?"

"For you or Henry, impossible, but a real hacker could do it in a few hours."

"Would any of the Connection engineers know how to do it?"

We were at the dining table; Tommy picked up a leftover biscuit and took a bite. "I see where you're going with this. You think Franzinni's murderer hacked into the surveillance system and you want to narrow the suspect list to the engineers who could do it."

I got my laptop from the desk and opened it on the table. Tommy studied the list of a hundred names while Henry looked over his shoulder.

"We didn't hire people for hacking skills," Tommy said. "Our engineers are technical enough, but many of them don't have the personality. It takes a certain amount of ego to break rules and laws just for the fun of it." He started fiddling with my spreadsheet as Henry leaned in for a closer look.

"Some of the guys dabble in hacking a little," Tommy added. "I've done some myself, in fact. You know . . . just the odd job here and there, to boost my salary and approve bogus expense reports."

He said it with such a straight face that I believed him, until Henry grinned and said, "He's fucking with you."

"You curse too much."

"Don't worry about it."

"Joe, look, here's what I did. I put in a new column and checked twenty-three names that could hack into a security system." Tommy smiled. "For the sake of completeness I also checked my name."

"What about Gwen?" I asked.

"No way," said Henry.

"Hold on a second," said Tommy. "I didn't think about Gwen."

"She's not a coder," Henry objected.

Tommy sat back in the chair and looked at Henry. "Back in the old days everyone wrote code, except you. Your code was useless. One thing I'll say about Gwen: When she sets her mind on something, she's obsessive. I think she could do it."

"Yeah, maybe you're right." Henry looked at the data again. "Hey, one of these cells is wrong. Tommy should be a zero on opportunity for the Smolnik murder. He was in San Marcos with his mother."

"I haven't focused on that column," I said. "I was hoping Carrillo would share the results of the investigation with me, but he hasn't."

"You know, those boys are real thorough," said Tommy. "To verify my alibi they went over to the nursing home, interviewed the receptionist, and double-checked the logbook."

I looked at the list and noticed Tommy had checked Sanjay's name. "Do you think Sanjay Kumar could murder someone?" I asked them.

Henry swallowed and looked serious. "I can't imagine anybody murdering anybody. I still have nightmares of Gregor Smolnik with his throat cut."

"You never know," said Tommy. "Sanjay worked for me. He's temperamental, and ruthless. You have to be ruthless to win at poker."

Henry looked at his watch. "We need to go. We have work to do."

"It's not like we have a paying job," Tommy responded, not moving from the chair.

"You have to treat a start-up like a job; otherwise you never get anything done." Henry pulled on Tommy's arm until he reluctantly got up. As they moved toward the door Henry thought of something else.

"You should come camping with us," he said. "Tomorrow we're

going to San Marcos so Tommy can visit his mother, and then we're camping next to the river."

"I don't know. . . ." I felt a need to make progress on the investigation.

"Have you got something better to do?" Henry asked.

I looked at the two of them standing at the door of the condo. The Zealots: Henry Jiwanlal and Tommy King. I had been in Austin for nearly two years, and they were the only friends I had. I rationalized that I could use the time to ask them more questions about the suspect list.

"Sure, I've got some gear at the house. I'll pick it up tomorrow."

"Great," said Henry. "We can fill you in on our new start-up. It's coming together fast. We're going to need your help soon, and we're going to need Webb and Gwen. We're putting the core team together again."

"Do you really think that's possible?" I asked.

"Definitely. The core team's not temporary." He smiled. "It's 'to the ending of the world.'"

. . .

AT MIDNIGHT I sat crouched behind the red-tip photinias across from Sanjay Kumar's apartment building. I had been there three hours. My excitement level was high for the first ninety minutes, but I was past that and into the storied boredom of a stakeout.

I stood to stretch my legs and thought again about the conversation with Henry and Tommy that morning. I was amazed at Henry's simple faith that the core team would be reassembled. He was so excited about their start-up that I was reluctant to tell him there was no way I would ever work for Webb Elliot again. Doing a onetime project with an up-front payment of a hundred thousand, which I

desperately needed, was one thing; going into the office every day to work for Webb was unthinkable.

A man approached from a hundred yards. It was cloudy, and he skirted the brightness of the streetlights, but there was enough ambient light for me to recognize him. It was Sanjay.

He hesitated a building away, perhaps trying to spot someone like me, but there was no way he could see through the bushes. He walked to the building and up to the second floor. I hustled over just in time to start up the stairs as he was fiddling with his key.

"Sanjay."

He jerked and turned to see me. He took three steps, put one hand on the rail, and hurdled over and down into the bushes below. He was lucky he didn't break a leg.

Sanjay was a sprinter. By the time I got back to the driveway he had a twenty-yard head start and was extending it. There was a high fence behind all the buildings, so the only way out was through the entrance of the complex. He gained distance on me for the first quarter mile but then began to slow. By the time we reached Jollyville Road I was gaining on him.

He turned right on Jollyville about a hundred yards in front of me. I had done a lot of distance running that summer and was hitting my stride. Over the next half mile I cut his lead by two-thirds. We had covered a mile in six minutes. Judging from his pace he was about done.

He looked over his shoulder to judge the gap and turned right into the next complex. I was twenty seconds behind, but when I made the turn, he was gone. He had ducked around one of the first buildings, either the one on the left or the right. He couldn't go far, because the same high fence enclosed that complex as well.

I had a fifty-fifty chance. I turned around the building on the right, ran up to the fence, and stopped to listen. I kept breathing but tried to do it as quietly as possible. We were between the first and second

buildings, and there were plenty of bushes and stairs for him to hide behind, but he had to breathe. If he was nearby, he was holding his breath and would be able to do so for only a short while.

I heard a gasp, and he bolted ten feet from me, back toward the driveway. Before he got there I tackled him.

He went crazy, kicking and thrashing out with his arms, wiggling back and forth with his shoulders and hips. Finally I had to hit him, a full-on slap on the cheek with my open palm. It stunned him.

"Damn it, I want to talk to you."

I stood and brushed off my jeans, still breathing hard. He stopped struggling but stayed down and cowered, his hands over his face. "Are you going to kill me?"

"No. I want to talk to you. Why would I kill you?"

He slowly pushed off the ground with his hands, shook his head, and stood up. Sanjay was just under six feet and thin. Most of the lights were out in the apartments around us, making it hard to see.

"Wait," he said. "Is it you? Is it Joe Robbins?"

"Yes. Who did you think it was?"

"Thank God. I thought you were the mob, come to kill me."

It was the gambling debt. He told me the story as we walked back to his building. It had started slowly and then, like many before him, he had developed a taste for the life of a high roller in Vegas. When his savings were nearly depleted he ran into a guy in a bar who knew about the Connection IPO. The guy's people loaned Sanjay money against his stock position. When the IPO cratered, his loan balance was a hundred thousand. For a while he used his salary to cover the interest, but then he got laid off. When he fell behind on his payments the balance continued to grow, and the mob threatened. He had been hiding for five weeks, since just after Gregor Smolnik was murdered.

"Why haven't you talked to the police?"

"Joe, man, I haven't talked to anybody. My cell was cut off. They're

threatening to evict me. I have been living on the mercy of people I know from Hyderabad, my home city."

"Did you kill Gregor Smolnik and Mike Franzinni?"

"God, no. How can you ask that? That's insane."

Sanjay had fallen a long way from the star engineer who helped win the Chartwell deal. Still, I couldn't see him as a murder suspect. Why would he kill two people for vengeance when he had so many other problems?

"You need to call the police tomorrow. Hiding has made you a top-tier suspect."

I gave Sanjay forty bucks and made him promise to contact Carrillo in the morning.

"What should I do about the mob?" he asked.

It wasn't my problem. We were standing under the streetlight outside his building. His voice was low, and he had already started looking over his shoulder.

"Try Webb Elliot. Maybe he'll refinance your gambling debt. I don't know."

As I drove on MoPac, a thunderstorm approached from the southwest and put on a brilliant lightning show. I made it into the condo garage just before the rain began to pour.

◦ ◦ ◦

IN THE MORNING I slept late and left Carrillo a voice mail about nine thirty. He called me back in ten minutes, and I gave him a briefing on my footrace with Sanjay.

"Why didn't you hold on to him?"

"I can't do that. It's not like you gave me a badge or anything." I walked onto the balcony and lit a cigarette. It was still raining. If it didn't stop soon the campout would be called off.

"How did you figure out he was crashing at his place?"

"A guess. I started thinking about his gambling debt and how he would live with no money. Has he contacted you yet?"

"He's meeting with two detectives now."

"I don't think he's the guy. He's so busy being scared he doesn't have time to plot a murder."

"I'll see how the detectives do." Carrillo didn't sound impressed with my assessment. "Why are you still working on this?" he asked. "I told you there was little danger."

"You also told me I'm a suspect. I'd like to remove that cloud."

We talked about Tommy's assessment of who could hack into the security system, and I promised to e-mail the names.

"Won't that allow you to narrow the list of suspects?" I asked.

"It will be helpful. Thanks."

It was the first recognition from Carrillo that I was adding some value. I allowed myself an instant of self-praise.

"Is there anything else I can do?"

"Not unless you've heard from Ms. Raleigh."

"Sorry. Oh, if it stops raining I'm going camping near San Marcos, just for the night."

. . .

WE RODE DOWN I-35 in Henry's F-250, with two kayaks tied down in the bed of the truck. We took the first exit for San Marcos, cut west for a mile, and then turned on a side street that led to the Hill Country Retirement and Nursing Center. It was a one-story redbrick place with narrow vertical windows and a flat roof, big enough for twenty rooms. Out front was an asphalt parking lot with a half dozen cars and four bare crepe myrtle trees. To the side was a small pond with a perpetual fountain spewing water in the middle.

"Do you want us to come in?" Henry asked.

"No," said Tommy. "She gets upset if too many people are around."

The clouds had broken up and were scattering. I stepped out to have a smoke and watched through the front door as Tommy lumbered in, chatted with the receptionist, and continued down the hall.

"How often does he come here?" I asked.

"Couple times a week." Henry looked at the building. "It's kind of a dump. Tommy doesn't care about money for himself, but he was really hoping the IPO would come in so he could move her to a nicer place in Austin."

When Tommy returned we drove ten miles on the east side of I-35 to the Riverbend Campground. It was the ugliest campground I had ever seen. It occupied twenty acres, two-thirds cleared and the rest densely wooded with Spanish oaks and pecan trees. A dirt road ran around the field to connect campsites. The facilities were run-down, particularly the restroom, and the field was infested with rocks and fire ants. The positive aspects were the uncrowded conditions (I counted three other groups), a boat ramp directly into the river, and kayak rentals.

We picked a shaded site next to the river. I had been camping before but was a complete amateur compared to Henry and Tommy. They had all kinds of gear. Tommy erected an eight-person tent, set up sleeping cots inside, then moved on to put up hammocks and two gas lanterns. Meanwhile Henry lit the charcoal and set about grilling marinated steaks.

We had a feast: Greek salad, baked sweet potatoes, fresh bread, grilled meat, and red wine. For dessert we ate cobbler and drank coffee. By that time the stars were out. We built a campfire, and they pitched me their new business venture.

"Have you ever tried to rent a house for a vacation?" Henry asked.

"Once . . . for a beach trip."

"How was the experience of trying to find the right place to rent?"

I recollected hours on the phone and being nervous about the condition of the property. "It was a pain. It took a lot of time, and we wound up with a mediocre house."

"Exactly. It's painful. There are about a dozen Web sites that try to make that process easier and they do a decent job, but they all have the same problem: They don't have enough properties in their network to be useful to all vacationers."

The fire popped, and a burning ember jumped out past Tommy's chair. He leaned over to stomp it with his boot. Smoke from the fire drifted over me, and I dragged my chair fifteen degrees around the circle.

"These little guys make a solid profit," Henry said, "but they don't know how to grow their business. Our idea is to get financial backing and do a roll-up of the vacation rental sites. We're going to call it Travel Quest."

The appeal was obvious. The vacation rental market generated billions of dollars annually, and the existing distribution method was inefficient. Rolling up these sites could create a large and profitable business. I thought they had a great idea and told them as much.

"Have you had any luck raising capital?" I asked.

"Not yet," said Tommy.

Henry elaborated. "We lack the fine polish, you know. We need the blue-blooded unassailable confidence that attracts money. We need charisma. In short, we need Webb." He looked at Tommy. "And he's going to come."

Tommy was skeptical. "Webb will do what Webb wants to do—like always."

"Yes, and he'll want to join Travel Quest because it's a great idea."

Henry walked to the picnic table and poured some bourbon in three plastic cups.

Tommy took a sip of the bourbon and looked at me. "Do you remember when you caught Randy Harlan stealing, and Webb let him keep the money?"

"I never understood that," I said.

"It didn't make sense to any of us," said Tommy.

"He called it 'severance pay.'"

Henry put another log on the fire, causing a small explosion of sparks and flame. Down on the river the water gurgled as it passed around rocks and fallen branches.

"Maybe Webb felt he owed Randy," said Henry, "or that employees would react poorly if he was tough with Randy. We may not understand his logic, but Webb always has a reason."

"It's like I said," Tommy added. "Webb does what Webb wants to do."

Henry poked at the fire with a long stick, rearranging the logs into what he considered the optimal configuration.

"He's got a strong will," Henry said. "I'll give you that, but I still say he's going to join Travel Quest as an equal partner."

They both sat and stared into the fire for a while. Somebody laughed at one of the other campfires.

"There's only one person I ever met with a stronger will than Webb," said Tommy.

"Who's that?" I asked.

"Gwen. Did you know that after you and Gwen had your falling-out, she told Webb she was leaving for good? We haven't heard from her in over three months."

I thought about Gwen, how she had looked standing in the cab line with no makeup and her white satin dress, giving me that crooked smile. That started me thinking about other times with Gwen and the core team, which in turn took me all the way back to the day we drank champagne on top of the bluff.

"Henry, do you remember when I first started at the Connection, when we had the champagne toast? You and Webb said something that day: 'We few, we happy few.' Then we all said it together at Carlos'n Charlie's. What is that? Some kind of slogan?"

Henry had sunk down into a comfortable reverie, warmed by the alcohol and the fire. On hearing my question he popped his eyes open and perked up in the chair. Tommy looked interested too, like he knew something good was about to happen.

"Do you want to hear it?" Henry asked, but he wouldn't have taken no for an answer.

He stood up from his chair and walked, as onto a stage, to a spot fifteen feet back from the fire. He faced us both, legs together, back straight. He was a trained actor, a graduate of Carnegie Mellon's celebrated School of Drama, and he introduced the monologue formally: "From Shakespeare's *Henry V*, the Saint Crispin's Day speech.

> "From this day to the ending of the world,
> But we in it shall be remembered—
> We few, we happy few, we band of brothers;
> For he today that sheds his blood with me
> Shall be my brother; be he ne'er so vile,
> This day shall gentle his condition;
> And gentlemen in England now abed
> Shall think themselves accursed they were not here,
> And hold their manhoods cheap whiles any speaks
> That fought with us upon Saint Crispin's day."

After he delivered the monologue, it took Henry a little while to transform back into an entrepreneur on a campout in the twenty-first century. He sat down again and spoke to me.

"That is the spirit upon which the Connection was founded. That is the spirit behind the core team." Henry turned to Tommy and said, "And when he feels the spirit again, Webb Elliot will join us."

Tommy stared into the fire. He drained the bourbon. "Yes. I hope you're right. I hope he joins us."

. . .

THE NEXT MORNING I woke soon after sunrise and walked down to the river. The path cut through eighty-foot cypress trees with massive trunks. The San Marcos is aquifer-fed, warmed by the earth so the water runs a constant seventy-two degrees year-round. It's not a large river, in most places no more than twenty feet across. In many parts the bottom is sand and gravel, which gives the water a light blue, crystal quality. When heavy rains fall, as they had in the prior two days, the river runs higher.

When I came to the edge, I saw Tommy on the opposite bank casting a fly reel. It was a thing of beauty to watch. His forearm worked the rig smoothly, without haste. He rocked it back and forth six or eight times until he placed the fly over the spot where he thought the bass was hiding. After three casts the fish hit and Tommy reeled him in. He put him on a string with another four and hopped across the rocks to my side.

He held up the string of fish and smiled like a little kid.

"There's something about it . . . nature. I never get tired of it." He walked past me and then stopped. "Have you ever had fried fish for breakfast? With corn bread and jelly?"

"Can't say that I have."

"You're in for a real treat."

. . .

AFTER BREAKFAST I rented a kayak, and we put in at the boat ramp and began to paddle. For the most part, that section of the San Marcos is calm, and there is time to enjoy the view. The land is privately owned. Some of it is ranchland, a quiet home for cattle that graze close to the banks and watch people pass by in their watercraft. Some of it is residential, weekend cottages outfitted with backyard grills and ropes for swinging over the river. The water from the river gives life to tall trees on the banks: willows, cypress, and giant live oaks.

For a few exciting stretches the river narrows to ten feet across, and boulders lie beneath the surface, forcing the water to hurry and roil loudly. The rapids are not particularly dangerous if you know the way, but when the water is high, as it was that day, it pays to stay alert.

After two hours we stopped to eat a sandwich and rest on a grassy spot in the shade.

"There's one last stretch before the end that can be tricky," Tommy said, "particularly when the river is this high." He bit into the second half of Henry's sandwich.

"It's not that bad," Henry said, downplaying the danger as he chewed on a carrot.

"The river is about twenty-five feet wide," Tommy explained. "There is a sudden drop over a rock ledge and some felled trees in the middle that churn up the water. Stay to the left and paddle hard straight through the falls. You'll come out easy on the other side."

"Just follow us," Henry added. "You'll be fine."

"Stay to the left," I repeated, to confirm the directions. They both nodded.

After another twenty minutes of paddling I heard the sound of rushing water ahead. Tommy and Henry were thirty feet in front of me, and they began to paddle harder. All I could see downriver was calm water with a high bank at the end, indicating that the river turned sharply, but I couldn't tell which way. Tommy and Henry drifted a

little to the right. I stayed left of them so I could get to that side of the falls more quickly. As we drew closer, the falls grew louder, and I could see the river turned to the right. Once we made the turn, I saw the falls. There was a ton of water kicking up where a big tree was wedged between rocks in the middle of the river.

I was keenly focused on staying to the left. Out of the corner of my eye I saw movement. I looked to see Tommy waving wildly at me from the right. He was indicating I should come that way. Then he and Henry were shooting through to the right of the tree. The rapids had picked me up by then, and when I tried to pull right the current turned me sideways just as I shot over the falls on the left.

I was immediately thrown from the kayak. My body was turned over by the falls, and I lost the paddle. I took a deep breath before going under, and then it was all cold wet darkness and a rushing sound in my ears. My head bumped on the ground, and I was turned over again. Each time I started to come up, a hydraulic current pulled me back into the falls. As I hit the bottom and tried to push off, the water rolled me back to the top again. I was stuck in the falls, being tumbled over and over. I panicked as the cycle repeated itself: eight, ten, a dozen times.

I was in the washing machine for more than a minute and becoming more desperate. My oxygen ran out, and my brain slowed. There were no options. It gradually dawned on me that death comes quickly, with little warning. My head popped free in the air, and I opened my mouth to breathe but was pulled back under and inhaled water.

Suddenly I felt something poke me in the side. I reached out with my hand, but by that time I'd turned upside down. I had a vague sense of the cycle of tumbling, and the next time around, I felt the branch again and grabbed on. I stopped tumbling. The water crashing on my back forced the last bit of air from my lungs. Someone grabbed me

by the shoulder. Before I passed out there was a sensation of being dragged through the water.

I coughed. I coughed again and spit up water. One more cough was followed by a half breath. I was on my back on the bank. Tommy knelt beside me, his face very close to mine, soaking wet. When he saw I was alive, he leaned back to breathe himself and then pulled me up to a sitting position.

"Come on, buddy. Breathe. That's it. Just take it easy and keep breathing."

It took a few minutes to rebuild the oxygen in my blood. Until then I couldn't think clearly.

Henry paddled over with Tommy's kayak in tow, a look of crisis on his face. Tommy hovered, watching me carefully. Finally he let me sit on my own, his hand on my shoulder.

"The whole river shifted on us," he said, still panting. "It must have been that new tree. When we turned the corner, I knew it was wrong. That's why we went to the right."

Henry got out of his kayak and came over to make sure I was okay. "You scared me, Joe. Really. I thought you would drown."

"I should never have waved at you," Tommy said. "It was a stupid thing to do. You would have been okay on the left if you were straight, but when you tried to come with us you got pulled sideways."

Henry got real excited then. "Damn, I've never seen anybody move so fast. Tommy snapped that fucking branch and forced his way through the water to you."

I smiled, happy to hear his curse words.

"Every so often," Henry said, "one of your legs or arms went flailing past in the churn, and he started jabbing the branch at you."

We sat on the bank of the river to recover. After fifteen minutes we were able to start laughing about it. After a while longer we were

ready to go in search of my kayak and paddle. As screwed up as my life had become, at that moment I was insanely happy to be alive, lying on a muddy bank of the San Marcos River.

For as long as I wake up in the morning, I will be grateful to Tommy King for pulling me from the river and teaching me how to breathe again.

CHAPTER 25

I SIPPED THE WINE. Everything tastes better after almost drowning; coffee is richer, food is ambrosia, the smell of fresh air is life itself.

Down at the clubhouse a swimmer exercised in the lap pool.

I had returned to the condo after the campout and sat on my balcony to sip wine and enjoy a clear view of downtown. Nearby a neighbor played Spanish classical guitar while someone else grilled chicken. It was just cool enough for a sweater.

The lap pool was a hundred feet away and parallel with my line of sight, so that the swimmer swam away from me, flipped, returned toward me, flipped, and repeated the cycle. The swimmer had long legs and strong shoulders that rocked side to side with the motion of pulling water from far above. The turns were sharp, automatic; the legs flipped high and smacked the water on re-entry. She was a brunette.

I went back inside and watched the news. The presidential race had come down to a few thousand votes in Florida. The players continued to jockey for position; it looked like the whole thing might be decided by the courts. Thirty minutes later I was back on the balcony for a smoke and noticed the swimmer was still doing laps, not exactly a casual workout.

Curiosity got the better of me, and I walked down to the clubhouse. The lap pool was twenty yards long and located on one edge of the large deck. The main pool was the same length but much wider, and surrounded by lounge chairs.

I turned one of the chairs around and sat to study the swimmer in the cascading light from the clubhouse. I watched as she finished, recognizing the shoulders. After a final lap she stopped at the edge of the pool. Using her chest and arm muscles she hauled herself out in a single motion. She walked over, and I handed a towel to Gwen Raleigh.

"I didn't think you'd ever notice," she said, breathing heavily. "I've been swimming for an hour."

"You could have knocked."

As she dried her face, I saw that her eyes were a dark brown.

"I wasn't sure you wanted to see me," she said. "So I told myself, 'If he comes, then it's fate.'"

I hadn't seen or spoken with Gwen since Rose and I first separated. Given everything that had transpired—the fissures in my marriage, the murders, and nearly drowning—the fact that she had told someone of our affair in Vegas seemed a minor thing.

Up in the condo I made her a sandwich. Gwen had dyed her hair back to the natural color and let it grow longer still. She had spent a lot of time outdoors, and the sun had bronzed her face, bringing out a smattering of freckles under her eyes and across the top of her nose.

While she ate we shared news of what had happened while she was gone. Gwen hadn't been to South America at all.

"I knew it was time for me to leave the Connection for good," she said. "So after shutting down my apartment, I drove west. I wanted to reflect on ten years with the core team and decide what to do next, but people kept calling me: Webb, Tommy, Henry, and others. With someone calling every day, I couldn't attain the mental distance I sought. So finally, I threw my phone away.

"I spent most of August and September camping in the national parks up in the Rockies, until it got too cold, and then I explored small towns on the Northwest Coast."

"There's a Lieutenant Carrillo of the Austin Police Homicide Unit who is anxious to see you."

"So I gather."

I had asked Jack O'Shea and Sanjay Kumar the question point-blank; it seemed fair that I do the same with Gwen.

"Did you kill Gregor Smolnik and Mike Franzinni?"

She sat back in the chair with scrunched eyebrows and an intense stare. Then her face relaxed, and she laughed out loud.

"What a silly question," she said.

"That's not an answer."

She stopped laughing. "Why would I kill those two?"

"Maybe they stole your dream when they restructured the company."

Gwen shook her head. "That was just the last step. As soon as we pulled the IPO I had my doubts, but when we did the layoffs, I knew the big-money dream was over."

"You still haven't answered the question."

She was put out by my directness, and for a moment I thought she was going to dodge the question again, but then her eyes relaxed.

"I didn't kill those two and have no idea who did."

It was a relief to hear the words. "I believe you," I said, "but you'd better call Carrillo tomorrow morning. He may not be so trusting."

Gwen nodded.

"Why did you come here, to my place?" I asked.

The balcony door was open and the cool air mixed well with the malbec. Goose bumps had grown on her arm. I wanted to lean across and rub them away.

"I realized that of all the people in Austin, the one person I wanted to see most was you."

"Where are you staying?"

Her expression told me it was an open question. I offered to put her up in the spare bedroom until she made other arrangements.

. . .

LYING IN MY BED in the dark, looking at the stationary ceiling fan, I hoped she would come. Nearly drowning had something to do with it; I wanted to feel a lover's skin on my skin.

If it happened this time I wouldn't call it cheating. I wasn't sure where Rose and I stood; our last two encounters had been polite, but distant. We had crossed a new threshold. Marriages dissolve that way; one broken vow begets another, and so on, until there is little left of what once was.

I had nearly fallen asleep when Gwen climbed between the sheets, wearing only a T-shirt.

"If you don't want me to stay, I'll go."

She didn't touch me. Instead she lay on the far side of the bed, waiting. When I didn't respond she took off the shirt, and I pulled her to me. Her lips were hungry, her body nervous and excited.

The next morning I slept in and woke to the smell of freshly brewed coffee. I found Gwen on the balcony, reading the paper. She stood and wrapped her arms around my neck. Her eyes were gray and lit up after we kissed.

I didn't want her to be guilty of the murders. She had the same motive as everyone on the list, and she was capable, so on an intellectual level I knew it was possible, but on an emotional level I wanted to believe her. However, Carrillo didn't operate on an emotional level. He believed in what he could prove. He would want to verify her exact whereabouts on the key dates, and something told me he wouldn't interview her at the Radisson.

After breakfast we made plans to meet later, and she left to go see Carrillo.

I got out my laptop and looked at the suspect analysis spreadsheet. I had convinced myself, based solely on intuition, that Sanjay Kumar, Gwen Raleigh, Randy Harlan, and Jack O'Shea were all innocent. There were twenty other people whom Tommy King thought were capable of hacking into CTV's security system. I scanned down the names. I knew a few of them slightly, but none well.

The murderer was probably on that list. Rico Carrillo's work to verify alibis would narrow the field of suspects considerably, perhaps to two or three names, or even just one. It would be best to focus on those few people, but Carrillo wouldn't share the data with me.

My eyes lingered on Gwen's name. Could she slit a man's throat with a straight razor? Tommy King had said that when Gwen was determined she could do anything.

* * *

THAT NIGHT we ate at Eddie V's, a seafood place at the corner of Fifth and San Jacinto. Gwen wore a red loose-fitting dress with a drawstring neck. Her strong arms and shoulders were bare.

Carrillo had grilled her for two hours, and they were to meet again the next day, but she seemed unconcerned.

On our way out I noticed Slim Bohls sitting at the bar, looking at us. I hadn't seen him in more than a year, hadn't even thought about him. It felt awkward not to acknowledge him, so we walked over.

Instantly I recalled my distaste for his fast talking and the square chin. The tarnished copper pompadour was still a key part of his look. He wore a black cowboy shirt with silver buttons. Gwen shook his hand.

"Hi, Slim," she said with no enthusiasm.

He didn't let go immediately.

"Gwen, it's good to see you as a brunette again. That red is a beautiful color on you."

"Oh, thanks."

She was eager to get away, so we left shortly. On the way back to the condo I asked her about the tension with Slim.

"Slim came on to every woman at the Connection," she said, "but he gave everyone the creeps. All the girls called him the Slime Ball."

It was pitiful; he obviously craved company but had none of the requisite social skills.

Back at the condo we sat on the couch and watched television.

It started with my hand on the red dress, just above her knee. Slowly, over the course of ten minutes of watching the show, the fingers worked their way farther up her legs until she crossed them.

She wore amber crystal earrings that turned dark next to her hair. I leaned over to smell her. My hand accidentally grazed the top of her breasts. She pretended to watch the show intently as I tasted her earlobe. My hand felt its way under the dress and moved persistently up the leg to her panties, where it pressed its case, trying to spark interest. She was warm and moist.

"Are you trying to seduce me?" she asked, her lips full, breathing faster.

"Definitely. Is it working?"

"Definitely."

I got up to draw the curtains over the balcony door and turn off the television. When I got back she had pulled down the top of her dress and removed her bra. I knelt in front of the couch and kissed her small breasts, savoring the taste and smell of her. She pulled up on my waist, encouraging me to a standing position, and opened my belt and zipper. She unbuttoned my shirt and pulled down my boxers. She kissed my chest while my fingers combed through her hair. Her kisses ventured lower and lower. I listened and watched as her lips

and tongue prepared me, around and around, back and forth, again and again. In a few short minutes I was almost too ready.

We stripped out of the rest of our clothes, and I carried her into the bedroom. I couldn't get enough of her. My fingertips skimmed the surface of her body long after we were finished. Later, we lingered in bed, with a soft light from the bedside lamp casting shadows. Gwen doodled with a finger on my chest and became pensive.

"When I was camping, I had a lot of time to think about my years with the Connection. It seemed strange that my twenties went by so quickly. It was a whirlwind, with no time to think about the larger context. Out in the wilderness the pace slowed to a crawl. I went days at a time without speaking to anyone. There was plenty of time to be calm, and I began to reflect on everything that had happened."

The windows were open, and two blocks away light traffic rushed by on MoPac. For the most part she stared at a blank spot on the wall, but intermittently she looked at me to make sure I was paying attention.

"What I wanted to tell you," she said, "is that I may have remembered something significant."

I gave her a gentle hug of encouragement.

"The only truly bad thing that ever happened at the Connection was Amanda Sorenson's suicide. You remember when we tried to revive her. It was awful. Even now, when I close my eyes, I can instantly summon the picture of her lifeless body.

"At first it was just a passing thought as I sorted through memories from ten years of history, but after a while, I began to ponder it longer and longer, at night, when I was alone in my tent or a hotel room. And I may have come upon something."

"What?" I turned on my side and leaned on an elbow. "What was it?"

"I remembered the rumors about Webb."

"What rumors?"

"When we first started to sell bigger deals, after three years or so, we didn't have to worry about cash flow and we started hiring a lot of kids right out of school. We hired a lot of women too, to help us recruit engineers."

"The cheerleaders."

"Right. Webb always went through women in a hurry. I never felt a chemical attraction to him personally, but a lot of women wanted to date Webb even before we achieved success.

"But afterward, once we were beyond the start-up phase, he was more than just a rich Englishman. He was the CEO of a software company. Inside the Connection he was like a king or something. He dated a new girl every month, and then the rumors began. With a guy in that position, rich, charismatic, handsome, and with a penchant for big parties, rumors tend to spiral into the absurd.

"There were all kinds of crazy rumors. He's bisexual. He's a drug lord on the side. He's working for the CIA. I knew most of the rumors were baseless nonsense, but there was one that sounded plausible."

"What was it?"

"That he made videos of himself having sex with women."

"What do you mean? Like sex tapes? Like that actor . . . Who was it? Rob Lowe?"

"Yes, like that."

"I don't understand. Do you think the rumor about sex tapes had something to do with Amanda Sorenson?"

"You know Webb dated her," she said.

"Yes, he told me that himself."

"Well, maybe there was a video."

It still didn't make any sense to me. "Even if there was a video, she would have been complicit in its creation."

"I know," she said. "I kept hitting that point as I thought about it."

"Webb would be careful about something like that. He calculates things. He doesn't want anything to screw up his long-term image."

"I agree with you. It doesn't necessarily mean a thing, but once I hit on it, I kept thinking about it. I wanted to tell someone, and I'm glad I told you."

It had been a bothersome loose-end for her. Once she shared it with me, she relaxed and quickly fell asleep. After I turned off the light, her breathing slowed until it was barely audible.

I had dismissed her data point as irrelevant, but as I lay in the dark, it wouldn't go away. I thought hard about what she had said and tried to match it with other pieces of data I had from long ago. Every time my eyes closed, a vision came of Amanda Sorenson hanging from the balcony of the Driskill, a lifeless blonde in an azure dress.

CHAPTER 26

Zola Conti had her last bite of salad and sat back in the chair. "You've already thanked me a hundred times for nursing you. So why am I here?"

Her lips turned up in an innocent smile that showed lots of teeth. There was a good chance I was about to ruin her day, so I hesitated.

In the morning Gwen had left for another meeting with Carrillo, and I called Zola to invite her for lunch. We met at Shady Grove on Barton Springs Road, south of the lake. It was a warm, sunny Friday, and we had come early to beat the crowd. I chose a table outside, where we could talk in relative privacy. We sat beneath tall pecan trees and removed our sunglasses.

I had rehearsed the conversation and decided to push Zola hard and fast.

"Do you remember my second week at the Connection, when you wore a low-cut blouse and kept dipping to give me a view of your boobs?"

Zola turned a shade darker. "Shoot. That was a long time ago. I thought we were going to forget that."

"You told me that office romance had not worked out for you in the past."

She raised an eyebrow. "Did I say that? It's been so long I can't remember."

"Did you have an affair with Webb?"

She bunched the cloth napkin in her hands and then straightened it out again. "A lot of girls slept with Webb. Not just me."

I didn't want to take it to the next step, but there was no choice. "There was a video made of you and Webb having sex. Wasn't there?"

She dropped the napkin and sat up straight, her hands grabbing the armrests of the chair. She looked right at me, and I could almost hear her mind clicking through the steps. "This is about Amanda Sorenson, isn't it?"

I nodded slightly, and she drew a quick breath. I had maneuvered Zola to be seated with her back to the other customers so they couldn't see her face. She continued to stare at me silently. Behind her and to the sides was restaurant noise but it slowly faded as I focused all my attention on Zola. Her eyes began to tear up, and she reached for the napkin once more.

"Tell me all about it, Zola. I want to know everything."

The waitress delivered my beer and picked up the remaining dishes. She saw Zola crying and shot me a hard look, which I ignored. Zola sobbed quietly into the napkin. I felt like a heel for not arranging the meeting in complete privacy.

After a few minutes she regained her composure.

"When it started it seemed like a game," she said. "Webb set up a couple of cameras around the room and gave me instructions on what to do next, what to say, and how to say it."

I had a flashback of Rose giving Webb a nod while standing naked in his living room. She gave him the same nod each time they shifted from one position to another.

"The next time I came to Webb's house we watched the video on his television while we drank wine and ate expensive hors d'oeuvres.

Parts of it looked very amateurish, so bad it was funny, and we laughed ourselves silly. But it also turned us on to watch, and we started all over again. This went on a few times, and then I noticed something: The videos got dramatically better."

"What do you mean?"

"You know. It was like . . . the quality improved. There were more camera angles and zoom shots, and the film was edited so the stupid parts were cut out. It was like there was a movie crew in the room, but no one else was there.

"After another three or four sessions Webb broke it off. He had always been up front about it. He told me he wasn't interested in a long-term relationship. I was naive, like most girls who date him must be. I thought I could change his mind."

"Did he give you a copy of the videos?"

"Oh, no, I didn't want a copy after the affair was over. He told me he destroyed them . . . just like he said when he had me sign the paper."

"What paper?"

"He explained everything to me at the beginning. After we had sex the first time, Webb told me he wanted to make the videos, and that it would be fun, but that I had to sign a paper first that said I wouldn't try to sue him or get a copy of the videos."

"Jesus . . . Zola . . . you signed a release?"

I had said it too harshly, and she started to tear up again.

"I'm sorry," I said, and reached out to touch her elbow.

"You don't understand," she said, "what it's like to be me and get the kind of attention that Webb can show a person. I didn't care about the paper or the videos. I just wanted to be around him, to be a part of him."

"That's okay. It doesn't matter." Truthfully, I had felt Webb's magnetic draw myself when he convinced me to join the Connection.

"Anyway, that wasn't nearly the worst part," Zola said angrily.

"Go on. Tell me the rest."

"About a month after Webb ended the relationship, I got a call from Slim Bohls. He asked me out for a drink, said he wanted to talk about something important. I didn't really know Slim at the time, but I knew he was a friend of Webb's, so I agreed to meet him.

"At first Slim tried to flirt with me. I think he was trying to see if he could spark any genuine interest. He kept talking about how long he and Webb had known each other, since the beginning of the Connection. When I didn't respond, he told me he made the videos at Webb's request and he wanted to show me how.

"I think I knew all along where things were headed with Slim, but I couldn't figure a way out of it, so I agreed to go to his apartment. I thought that maybe, if Slim had a copy, I could steal my video. When I got there the first thing Slim did was take me onto his balcony. He had a clear view of Webb's house across the lake."

"Wait a minute. You can see Webb's house from Slim's balcony?"

"Yes."

I remembered the laughter from the apartment dweller above me on the night I had watched Rose and Webb from the bank of Lake Austin.

"That bastard," I said. My hands had been rubbing together. I cracked a couple of knuckles.

"Slim had the equipment set up in his living room, with separate monitors showing live feeds off of eight cameras hidden in Webb's house. He showed me how he used remote controls to change the camera angle, zoom in or out, and aim the microphone to record what he called the 'close-up sounds of flesh against flesh.'

"After he showed me the production setup he pushed a button, and one of the graphic scenes of Webb and me began playing on his

wide-screen television. I was supposedly panting in ecstasy, and Slim played the clip loud so that someone in the next apartment could hear it. That was really embarrassing, and I begged him to stop."

I imagined Slim's face and pompadour, badgering Zola with his fast talk, drawing her in for the close. I wanted to be in that scene so I could make him stop.

"Then Slim told me the video turned him on. He said I was beautiful and he wanted to date me. I told him that was out of the question, but he said it didn't matter too much whether I liked him. He said if I didn't have sex with him he would post the video on the Internet, like they did with that actress."

"Pamela Anderson."

Zola nodded and took a drink from the water glass.

The waitress tried to walk up with the check, but I waved her off. My gaze drifted to the lunch-hour traffic on Barton Springs Road. I didn't want to hear the rest.

"So I told Slim I was going to Webb . . . to tell him the whole thing. He said Webb didn't give a shit about me anyway, and in any case, if I went to Webb he would put the video on the Internet. Slim told me there was plenty of footage for him to edit a special cut where you could recognize me but not Webb."

Zola stopped and took another drink of water. She folded her hands in her lap and looked at me.

"So I had sex with him. We did it six times. I went over to Slim's place, and he put on one of the tapes, and we re-enacted everything that Webb and I did on the television."

Zola got real fidgety, kept wringing her hands in her lap and breathing funny. Her face screwed up, and I thought she was going to cry. I reached over and took her hand in mine, and she managed to calm down.

"I haven't told anybody before," she said, and began sobbing quietly again.

I had all the data I needed.

"You don't have to tell me anything else."

"No, I want to. He's a disgusting man. He smoked a lot of pot and always wanted me to smoke it with him. He played the same kind of music every time, Southern rock—old stuff: Charlie Daniels, Allman Brothers. . . ."

"zz Top," I offered.

"Yeah . . . he loved zz Top, always wanted to do it with certain songs playing. After those six times he got tired of me, or maybe he got scared that I would go to the police. He told me he didn't want to see me anymore, like we had been dating or something."

I closed my eyes and took a deep breath to calm myself. My hands clutched the sides of the chair. Finally, after a year and a half, I knew why Amanda Sorenson committed suicide. But I wanted to hear it from Slim Bohls's lips. I wanted to see his face up close right before I smashed it.

I opened my eyes. Zola's makeup was a mess. The lively spark she brought into the Shady Grove was extinguished. Some people who live through something like that crawl into themselves and never make it out again. As an executive assistant Zola had always been cheerful, buoyant, but maybe her attitude was just a veneer, her peppiness a way of coping. Slim Bohls had stolen from her. He had taken her freedom.

I wasn't sure of the legal definition. I didn't care. So far as I was concerned, Slim's extortion for sex amounted to rape.

"I'm sorry that happened to you," I said. "You didn't do anything to deserve that."

"I've always been afraid to tell anybody."

"I'm going to stop it. I'm going after the videos."

"Are you going to hurt Slim?"

"Maybe."

I didn't have a plan at that point. The situation was complicated by Rose's affair with Webb. I might have gone straight to the police if it hadn't been for that. Whatever I decided to do, it was best if Zola wasn't involved.

"Please don't mention this to anyone," I said.

I watched as Zola got up and walked out of the restaurant. She seemed older, her sexy sway replaced by a hesitant step, the shoulders slumped, the high heels out of place.

Often when you take a specific action it's out of necessity, for survival. It's not particularly right or wrong; it just is. When you get up in the morning and go to work, you don't do it because it's the right thing to do; you do it because you need a paycheck to feed, clothe, and shelter yourself and those who depend on you. You take the money you make and shop for groceries and cook dinner because you have to eat to survive.

On a rare occasion you are presented with a crystal-clear right thing to do. It is so right that to not do it is wrong. Those are the easy ones, in terms of making the decision, because you know you can't ignore them. I wasn't exactly sure how to bring it about yet, but the Webb Elliot and Slim Bohls Production Company was about to go out of business—permanently. And I was going to hurt Slim Bohls; that was a certainty.

. . .

BACK AT THE CONDO I spent a couple of hours on the Internet, learning what I could about home video technology. I had a Diet Coke and

sat on the balcony. As the shadows of the live oaks moved across the ground, I put together the rough outline of a plan.

About three o'clock Rico Carrillo called. He got right to the point.

"How come you didn't tell me Ms. Raleigh was back in town?"

"What are you talking about? I was the one who told her to call you."

"So you have seen her."

"Well . . . yes . . ."

I stopped midphrase. Did Carrillo suspect Gwen and I were involved together in the murders? Did he already know Gwen was staying at the condo?

"Were you going to say something else," he asked, "or leave me with dead air?"

"I have seen her. She's staying here with me, at my new place."

"So, are you two back together again?"

"Uh . . . no . . . she needed a place to stay."

"I see."

"Why did you call?"

"Just checking to see if you've learned anything new."

"No. Nothing new. How's the investigation going?"

"It's going fine. Are you sure there isn't anything else you need to tell me?"

What was he getting at? I had the distinct impression the only reason he called was to see what I would say about Gwen.

"Nothing at the moment."

He let silence fill the space between us for long seconds, seven or eight, until I had to say something.

"Is there anything I can do to help?" I asked.

"Maybe there is. Meet me tomorrow morning at the Radisson, nine thirty."

⁘

I CALLED ROSE and offered to watch the kids for the evening; she was happy to get the break. Next I called Gwen to tell her not to wait up.

At the house Rose was dressed casually in tight jeans and a form-fitting pink crewneck sweater, all set to go see a movie. I was confused by how great she looked. How could she look as good as ever after all we'd said and done? She told me we needed to talk when she returned.

Later, when I was helping the girls get ready for bed, Chandler was moody. We were in the bathroom they shared, and she kept fabricating problems.

"Mommy didn't wash my pajamas."

"Callie stole my toothpaste again."

"Where are the pink towels?"

I did my best to smooth over the grievances. Meanwhile, Callie had only one request.

"'Sheila Learns to Swim,'" she said. "I want to hear 'Sheila Learns to Swim.'"

"I don't want to hear any more stupid Sheila stories," Chandler complained.

"Why not?" Callie asked.

"Because they're stupid and they're not true, and *you* make them up." She cast an angry look my way and stomped into her room.

Callie was crestfallen.

"Don't worry, honey," I said. "Chandler just needs some time alone. She'll join us for the next Sheila story. Come on. Let's get you settled in bed."

She climbed under the covers, and I helped her put the stuffed animals in all the right places.

"Can you close the closet door, Daddy?"

"Sorry, I forgot." I jumped to solve that problem and then lay on top of the bedspread.

As I tried to recall the story, Zola's face popped into my head. She was at the Shady Grove, her mascara running. I blinked her away and Rose's image appeared, kicking at me with her feet. Next up was Amanda Sorenson performing ballerina steps on the Driskill balcony rail.

I stammered through a few introductory words, tried to start over again, and then stopped.

"Do you want a tissue, Daddy?" Callie reached for the box on her nightstand. "Don't worry," she consoled me. "I'll tell the story tonight."

In that story, Sheila is three and walking to the beach with her mother and brother, Tim, when a neighborhood dog knocks Sheila off a wooden bridge into a swash. Her mother, Mary, dives in after her but the current is fast and pulls Sheila rapidly toward the point where the swash meets the ocean. It is only by mimicking Tim's swimming motions, motions she had closely watched on other days, that Sheila gets to the shore before being carried out to sea.

In the crucial scene, Callie broke off the narrative to demonstrate the free-style stroke in bed. Then she concluded the story: "That is how Sheila learned to swim, and that is the end of the Sheila story."

"That was a great Sheila story," I said, relieved that Callie had bailed me out.

"Next time, you tell the story," she said. "I like it better the way you tell it."

I tucked Callie in and kissed her good night. As I walked out of her bedroom and passed Chandler's room, a shadow stepped away from the door and slipped into bed. I leaned my head into the room to hear Chandler sniffling. I sat on the bed and rubbed her back.

"I'm sorry, Daddy," she said. "I won't skip the story next time."

"There's nothing to be sorry about, sweetie."

"You're not coming home soon, are you?"

It had been nearly three weeks since I discovered Rose's affair and left for Vegas.

"I don't know. I want to come home, but Mommy and I still have some things to work out."

"Please work them out . . . for Callie and me. Please."

"We'll try, honey. We'll try."

"I see Mommy cry sometimes. She tries to hide it, but I can always tell."

"You're a wonderful girl, Chandler. You and Callie are both wonderful."

For a few minutes she told me about her recent activities at school and then gradually drifted off.

· · ·

WHEN I WAS SURE THEY WERE BOTH ASLEEP, I went out to the workshop to pick up a couple of things to help with my plan and then sat on the patio and watched the stars. It was about sixty degrees, and I wore a dark pullover, jeans, and running shoes. High overhead a commercial jet flew south. A light breeze blew up from the lake, carrying with it the scent of cedars.

Rose came out at ten thirty and sat in a chair next to me. I offered her a cigarette, and we smoked together, using an empty jar for an ashtray.

"Listen, Joey," she said. "I'm finished with Webb Elliot."

No one else ever called me Joey, not my family or my friends. She'd christened me with that nickname soon after we started dating.

"That's what he told me."

"You talked to Webb?" she asked.

"It was a business thing, related to the Connection."

She frowned at that answer, but it wasn't what she wanted to talk about, so she let it go. She exhaled smoke and flicked an ash into the jar.

"I'm sorry I slept with Webb. It was a stupid thing to do. I made a few dumb decisions."

"He seduced you."

She raised an eyebrow at me, as if I were off-track.

"Please give me some credit. Sure, Webb is handsome and rich and he made the offer, but I could have resisted. I didn't want to resist. I wanted to hurt you, of course, but that was only part of it. After you cheated on me I felt completely free to do anything I wanted, and I went a little crazy with that freedom."

She could have blamed it all on Webb, and I would have gladly allowed it; instead, she claimed responsibility.

I felt the need to move and walked to the pool to put my hand in the water. I waved it back and forth and let water wash between my fingers.

"I wanted to take initiative," she said. "Having an affair with Webb was stupid, but I don't regret wanting some independence."

"I wanted to fix our marriage," I protested. "I wanted to win your love again."

"That's not my point," she said. "I'm not playing the blame game now. I'm trying to explain something."

"I don't understand you. I don't understand at all."

If she had asked me to come home the next day, I would have done it. After everything, I still wanted her; I still wanted us to be a family.

"Do you remember what the priest said?" she asked.

"What priest?"

"The meeting my father arranged, before we married."

An image of a fortyish man in slacks and a short-sleeved collared shirt came into view. We had met in his office at the church. I was twenty-four at the time, and Rose was twenty-one. She had graduated

the week before, and we were engaged. Her father thought we should have a discussion with someone before we married.

There was nothing spiritual about it. The priest had married hundreds of couples and had firsthand experience of the marriages that worked and those that didn't. We wanted to marry right away, but the priest was concerned that we were too young, that we hadn't seen enough, or done enough, to be ready for a lifelong commitment.

He kept coming back to the same question: "What's the rush?"

His counsel was to postpone a few years so we could try other things, live in different cities, work on our careers, date other people, or, failing that, just live together. He was in favor of any plan that allowed us to mature before making that decision.

We ignored his advice and married almost immediately. Twelve months later Chandler was born. Rose was going back to the question the priest had posed ten years before.

"We're not ready to be together again," she said. "I'm not ready."

I thought about Gwen staying at the condo, sharing my bed. It hurt to admit it, but maybe Rose was right.

It was almost eleven o'clock, and I needed to get moving. Rose walked me to the door. She was on the verge of giving me a peck on the cheek, but I needed to ask a question first.

"You made a sex tape with Webb, didn't you?"

Her eyes grew wide. She folded her arms, took a step back, and looked down.

"How did you figure that out?"

"It's not important. Other women did the same thing, but this *is* important: Have you ever heard from a guy named Slim Bohls?"

"No," she said.

"Good . . . that's very good."

"What's this all about?"

"Slim helped Webb make the videos."

"Oh, shit. That was one of my dumb decisions."

"We've both made our share."

"Webb said he would destroy the video. Do you think he did?"

"I don't know. Do you want me to ask him?"

She didn't answer right away. Instead, she adopted a studious look. Would she trust me?

"Yes."

I had a somber task in front of me, but that one word put a spring in my step as I walked to the Jeep.

CHAPTER 27

I ARRIVED AT SLIM BOHLS'S APARTMENT complex at eleven thirty. I parked next to the soccer field, just as before. The Smith & Wesson was taped under the passenger seat of the Jeep, and I left it there. I had certain things to accomplish with Slim, but they didn't include murder.

I grabbed the stuff from home and walked to Slim's building, then around to the spot where I had watched Webb and Rose from the riverbank. Across the lake, Webb's house was dark. Clouds had rolled in and covered all the stars.

I looked up and saw the lights were out in Slim's apartment. It was Friday night, and I guessed that he wasn't home; if he was sleeping, I'd wake him abruptly.

About half the tenants in Slim's building were awake. Jazz music played from an open balcony door. A ground-floor tenant let his cat out for a walk.

The buildings of the complex lined the bank of the river. The bank made a sharp turn so that the building to the left was nearly perpendicular to Slim's.

I went around to the front and walked up one flight. I pulled on thin latex gloves, the kind that home repair stores sell for painting projects. Within a minute I had picked the lock and was inside.

The door opened into a space about fifteen by twenty feet. A small kitchenette was separated from the living room by a countertop. To the left of the entrance was a hallway that led to the bedroom. I walked through the rooms; there was no one in the apartment.

The living room was divided roughly into a workspace and an entertainment zone. The work area included a large desk with eight small monitors mounted on a rack to the right and a large twenty-four-inch monitor on the left. On the desk were two keyboards, a large fluorescent lamp, an ashtray, and three empty beer bottles. In the entertainment area a regular-size couch and coffee table faced a large television and sound system on the back wall.

The balcony sliding door was to the left of the entertainment zone. I stepped outside. There was a clear view down the path to the boat dock and across the lake to Webb's house. A satellite dish was mounted at one end of the balcony rail.

With a small flashlight I looked under the desk to find a Power Macintosh G4 with a supplemental external hard drive. From my Internet research I knew the Power Macintosh was popular with low-budget video production outfits. Slim would need the extra storage capacity to manipulate the videos. There was also a Pioneer DVD burner for storing the finished product.

Along the opposite wall of the living space was a large book cabinet that held a couple hundred DVDs. The collection was mostly action films, although the lower shelf included several dozen pornographic movies.

At the bottom of the cabinet was a locked drawer, and I got my kit out again to open it. Inside were ten DVDs and a large scrapbook. The side label of each DVD contained a woman's first name. Among them were Zola, Rose, and Amanda. On the front cover of each was a picture of a couple engaged in a graphic sex act. In each of these photos the woman's face was clearly visible but not the man's. I took

all the DVDs from the drawer and flipped through the scrapbook; it contained a half dozen eight-by-ten photos from each DVD episode, presumably Slim's favorite shots.

Turning to the entertainment center, I loaded Zola's DVD and pressed play. I turned the volume low so I could hear Slim's keys in the door if he returned. It started with a few minutes of small talk and then jumped into the sex. I played a minute of the first scene, fast-forwarded a bit, and played another minute. I stopped and listened whenever there appeared to be conversation. The dialogue was meaningless banter that led into the next graphic scene.

Slim was good at managing the hidden cameras remotely, and at editing. The scene cuts were smooth, and he used different angles and zoom perspectives to maximize the sensationalism of the couplings.

I finished Zola's DVD and loaded the one of Sheri O'Shea, Jack O'Shea's wife. I watched Sheri's video more quickly and learned nothing new. I loaded the third video and fast-forwarded through most of it. I wanted to verify there were no players other than the women and Webb; the presence of another man would complicate the problem.

Each video marched through a similar pattern of positions. First the woman stood like so while Webb did this, and then she stretched across a bed while Webb did that. The women appeared to enjoy it. They were acting but they weren't being forced. It was all consistent with Zola's story. After the third one I scanned them at high speed. What was titillating became comical as two nudes ground against each other and then hurriedly flipped this way and that.

When it was Rose's turn I sat down to calm the pounding in my ears. I listened to their conversations, but it was all the same chatter. Amanda Sorenson's video was depressing. She was a very young woman, trying to act mature.

I put all the DVDs and the scrapbook into a large heavy-duty trash bag. Then I turned to the computer under the desk. I booted

the system, figured out how to access the stand-alone hard drive, and deleted every video file. I unplugged all of the hardware, disassembled the Mac and external box enough to remove the hard drives, and lined everything up on the floor in the kitchenette.

I guessed that Slim would have duplicate copies of the videos and searched for a hiding place. I checked the living area and kitchen quickly and went to his bedroom. It took only a minute to find the framed opening to a crawl space in the ceiling of the closet. Using a chair I scrambled up and found his stash, including copies of the DVDs and a couple ounces of marijuana. In a small black carry bag in his room I found a laptop that was password protected. I threw the DVDs and the laptop in the trash bag and flushed the pot down the toilet.

After a thorough second check of the apartment I carted everything to the Jeep, including the hardware. It took three trips.

Returning to the apartment, I turned out the lights and waited for Slim's return. The difficult question was what to do with him. I wanted to beat him to a pulp, drag him to the lake, and hold his head underwater until no more bubbles surfaced. I got impatient and stepped onto the balcony for a smoke.

It was after two o'clock when Slim came home; he was alone.

He let the door close and flipped the light switch. He turned toward me and looked surprised.

"What are—"

I punched him. I hit him hard, a straight right to the side of the nose; he went down instantly.

His hands covered his face, blood trickling through his fingers. I kicked him in the ribs, and he scrunched up into a ball of pain and coughed, his eyes closed.

I thought about Zola crying into her napkin at the Shady Grove. I wanted to kick him a lot harder. I wanted to keep kicking him and feel the ribs crunching against my shoe, but instead I pulled his desk

chair over and sat down. There was more work to do, and I needed to stay focused. I gave him some time to bleed, catch his breath, and get scared. After a few minutes Slim got to his knees and then stood.

"I've already got the DVDs from the cabinet," I said. "I also took the Mac, the external drive, and your laptop. Now I want the backup copies."

He'd been drinking and looked shaky, like he might throw up, but he tried his luck anyway by saying, "I don't have any."

I stood up and threw a right hook to his body. I put a lot into the punch and connected well. Slim doubled over and sank to the floor again.

I sat and watched as he writhed and gasped. When he could breathe, he stammered, "In the closet . . . crawl space."

"I already found those. I want the off-site stash."

"I don't have anything else."

He faced away from me, curled up. I grabbed him by the shoulder and dragged him to a standing position. I slapped him hard across both cheeks. Blood from his nose got on my hand.

"Tell me where it is!"

His body shook, and he started crying, a high-pitched sob that let out slow and was followed by a big intake of breath through his mouth.

"Don't hit me again," he pleaded. "There's nothing more."

I believed him. He didn't have the strength to continue lying. I stopped hitting him but continued to hold him up by his shirtfront.

"None of this would have happened if you hadn't raped those women."

He looked quickly at me. A different kind of fear registered in his eyes.

"I know all about it," I said. "Tell me who you raped."

He looked like he was thinking too hard, so I pulled my hand back to slap him.

"Not your wife!" he quickly replied.

"Good boy, but I already knew that. And I know some of the others also. Now tell me the truth."

"It was four in all."

"Which four?"

"Danielle . . . Angie . . . Zola . . . and Joan."

"That was good. You're not lying, are you?"

"No. No. I'm not lying."

"I want everyone's complete name, first and last."

It took him a while, but he remembered all the names, both the ones he'd raped and the others. I wrote the names down, except Rose, and put the paper in my pocket.

I offered him the chair, and he fell into it.

"Tell me about Amanda Sorenson." I walked behind Slim and began massaging his shoulders, the fingers of my hands inches from his neck.

He got nervous, his fear of the police perhaps greater than his fear of me.

"There's nothing to tell."

My fingers closed around his throat. I felt him swallow and start to gasp as I slowly tightened my grip.

"Wait."

I loosened my hands enough for him to speak.

"I asked her," he confessed, "but she said no. She was so unreasonable."

He was complaining about a woman who refused his demands for sex. Why should such a man be allowed to breathe?

Would they catch me? I thought. *If I took his life?*

I lost track of what I was doing. I saw Amanda Sorenson go from the first ballet position to a plié and then step off the balcony rail into air. My vision went black, and I heard nothing. Unconsciously my fingers tightened, making a smaller and smaller circle.

You'd be doing the world a favor. It needs to be just a little tighter, and all will be well.

From within the darkness my hands felt something scratching. It was Slim desperately clawing for survival. Slowly I relaxed my grip and let him breathe.

He filled his lungs again and again until the spasms subsided.

"Go ahead," I said. "Tell me the rest."

"She knew she was in a difficult position," he said. "She was one of the 'good girls.' I think taping sex with Webb was the worst thing she'd ever done. I sensed her struggle with the decision and pressed her on it. That's when she cracked. I had no idea she would do that."

For the first time Slim exhibited something like remorse.

"I don't know whether to give you to the police," I said, "or kill you." I let the question linger. "I'll have to think about it."

This was my dilemma: I didn't want anyone else to know about the sex videos, because I wanted to spare the women embarrassment—and because of Rose's participation. I wanted all evidence of her involvement to vaporize. I was also skeptical about turning the DVDs over to the police; I didn't trust their custody processes. Videos of a rich businessman fornicating with attractive women would be a huge draw for someone in the evidence room. How many people had access? Would they all resist the temptation to take a look?

At the same time, Slim Bohls belonged in jail; there was no question about that.

Sometimes, when there are no good options, it pays to defer the decision. Perhaps a better path would reveal itself. I decided to mull it over for a few minutes.

Slim's face was a mess. Blood had run down the right side of his mouth to below his chin. The pompadour hung badly to one side. But his mind was still working, and the beginnings of a tiny smile formed on his lips.

"I could help you," he said.

There was no trusting the Slime Ball. If he had something to tell me it was more for his benefit than mine, but he put out the bait and I took it.

"Don't be ridiculous. How can you help me?"

"I know something . . . about your girlfriend . . . that you should know too."

Slim's smile grew, and his nearly black eyes turned sly. That look, together with his square-jawed face and wild hair, gave me an idea of how Zola felt when he held the leverage over her.

"What do you know about Gwen?"

"Let me clean my face," he suggested, "and I'll tell you."

I let Slim walk to the bathroom. I turned my back on him without concern; from my search I knew he didn't have a weapon, and if he tried to leave it would give me an excuse to pummel him again.

I stepped out to the balcony for another smoke. I was exhausted. The Slim Bohlses of the world suck all the joy from around them. They're a moving pestilence that leaves behind a trail of misery.

When I pulled the pack out of my pocket, one of the cigarettes fell on the wooden deck. As I bent to pick it up, I heard a hard *thwap* sound, followed closely by a *thunk* over my head. I stood and looked to the other side of the sliding door. At first I didn't comprehend what it was and had to step closer. There, stuck firmly in the exterior wood paneling, was an arrow. I looked in the direction from which it had come and saw movement on a dark balcony of the next building, about forty yards away.

I crouched and then crawled under a round table on the balcony at the same moment Slim walked out.

He saw the arrow immediately.

"What's that?"

"Get down!"

He looked at me cowering on the floor and laughed. He opened his mouth to say something, and I heard the hard *thwap* again.

The next instant Slim Bohls had eight inches of an arrow sticking out of his chest. He took a small step backward but remained standing. He looked down at the arrow and made a fish motion with his mouth, but no noise came. Slim turned toward the door to the apartment. The arrow point and two inches of shaft, covered in blood, extended from his back. A tiny red geyser erupted from the wound, propelled by the beating of his heart. He made it three steps and struggled with the fourth.

I crawled into the apartment behind him to escape the archer. Slim sank to one knee, and the other leg tried to take a step on its own. He put a hand out to steady himself and slowly settled on the carpet. With the next few heartbeats the flow of blood slowed to a trickle.

His mouth kept working.

"What is it?" I asked. I crawled around to his side, my head only a foot from his. "What is it, Slim?"

He never got any words out, and slowly all the air leaked from his lungs. His eyes remained open, devoid of emotion.

My mind stopped. I stared at his black eyes. There was no way for the archer to shoot me from that angle, but I froze in shock. I sank to the floor and imagined the horror in the night beyond the balcony. After a minute I crab-walked to the front door and turned out the lights. I sat on the floor in darkness, my back against the door, until I could think again.

There was nothing to be done for Slim Bohls. I was certain of that. I walked cautiously through the dark apartment to the balcony and looked to the neighboring building. There was no movement from where the arrows had been shot. The murderer had fled the scene.

I made a decision and walked out of the apartment. On the way to the Jeep I nervously watched the shadows. I drove back down Lake

Austin Boulevard, left on Redbud Trail, across the bridge, and into the forests of West Lake Hills. I pulled over at a wide spot in the road and hid all the stuff behind a boulder. Then I drove back to Slim's complex and parked right next to his building. Once in his apartment I called 911 and waited for Lieutenant Carrillo.

. . .

THE PATROLMEN ARRIVED in five minutes. Of course they saw the huge mess of blood on the carpet, but after a minute, they also noticed the cuts on Slim's face where I had hit him. They had plenty of questions, but I told them only that I wanted to talk to Carrillo. While I waited for him I thought about what to say.

Carrillo wore jeans and a store-brand sweater. I told him what happened on the balcony and let him point out the missing parts.

"I notice you have some scuff marks on your hand."

I turned my hand over and examined the small breaks on the top knuckles and the scratch marks from Slim's fingers.

"Yeah, Slim and I had a disagreement. Unfortunately, it came to blows."

"It looks like he lost."

"Slim wasn't much at fisticuffs."

Carrillo stared at me intensely. I looked away from his flawed eye to Slim. He was still on the floor, about six feet away, in the same position.

"You'd better start talking, Robbins."

I sat on the couch. Carrillo had pulled up the same chair I'd used earlier and sat across the table from me. I pulled my right leg onto my left knee and nervously picked at the hemline of my jeans.

"Why don't you call me Joe? Can I call you Rico?"

"Stop fucking around and tell me what the fight was about."

"I didn't like the way he treated a friend, a woman."

"Who?"

"Zola Conti. She used to work for me at the Connection."

"What did he do?"

"They went on a date, and he treated her poorly, badgered her for sex. Women call him the Slime Ball."

The door to the balcony was still open, and the night air had cooled into the forties. Rico closed the door and asked a policeman to turn up the heat.

"Why did you come over so late?" he asked me.

"I was mad. I just heard about it today."

"How do I know you didn't kill him?"

"Come on, Rico. That doesn't make sense. Why would I beat him up if I was going to shoot him with an arrow? Why would I call you? For Pete's sake, the first arrow was four feet from me."

He shifted in his seat, bags under his eyes from his having been woken in the middle of the night.

"I see all these monitors, but there's no computer. How come there's no computer?"

"I have no idea."

He knew I was lying but wasn't sure what to do with me.

"I'm tired," I said. "I need sleep. We have an appointment in the morning. We can go through it all again."

"Do you mind if I search your car?" he asked.

I had thought about this part of the conversation ahead of time and tried to play it cool.

"I could say no. Make you get a search warrant."

"Yeah, you could do that. It would take me a few hours to get one. In the meantime you can wait right here." He thought he had me. I could see it in the confident turn of his lips.

"Walk out with me," I said. "Take a look if you want."

He looked in the glove box, the backseat, and the rear cargo area. He appeared satisfied, and then Rico made his only mistake: He let me go.

"You know, Joe," he said, "you're awfully close to the action on this case. I hope you don't get hurt."

I watched him walk back into the apartment, and then drove to a spot past my hiding place, where I waited for fifteen minutes. When I was sure no one was following, I doubled back, picked up the stuff, and drove to the condo. Gwen was asleep in the bedroom, and I closed the door to keep from waking her.

Being an attorney, my fraternity brother kept a good shredder in his office. I shredded the DVDs, the pictures from the cases, and the scrapbook. I divided the shredded material into five different trash bags. I wasn't sure how to ruin a hard drive but invented my own technique. Out in the garage I used a special screwdriver to remove the covers and then took a blowtorch and heated the platters until they started to warp. I loaded all the stuff in the Jeep again and drove around South Austin, parceling everything into five different Dumpsters.

It was six o'clock by the time I returned to the condo. I took a long look at Gwen as she slept, wanting nothing more than to crawl in with her, but instead I took a shower and drove a half mile to the IHOP for breakfast and coffee.

CHAPTER 28

THE FOUR SEASONS LOBBY overlooks beautiful landscaping and pecan trees on the edge of Town Lake. I took a seat in an armchair and ordered more coffee. I had called Webb on the house phone to tell him Slim Bohls had been murdered.

Fifteen minutes later Webb sat across from me, his shirttail loose and hair out of place. It was Saturday; weekend visitors ate scones and muffins around us.

I gave Webb a quick summary of the murder and let him absorb the initial shock. He had known Slim a long time. After a few minutes, he tried to sort out a motive.

"Slim left the company three years ago," he said. "Why would anyone want to kill him?"

"You let him keep his stock in the buyback," I reminded him. "That could have made someone jealous."

"Slim gave me stock in his company, so I let him keep his in the Connection. Do you really think someone murdered him over that?"

"Who knows?" I paused. "But if they did, we have to assume you're still at risk."

Webb's eyes opened wide, and he looked in all directions, scouting for danger.

"Or maybe there was a different reason," I said.

His brows stitched together, and he looked puzzled. He knew I didn't make that comment randomly. I let him stew on it.

"What do you mean?"

"I know about the videos Slim made for you, the sex tapes. I've seen them all."

He closed his eyes, breathed out slowly, and massaged his temples. He coughed once and reached for the coffee.

I needed to know what Webb's involvement was in Slim's coercion scheme.

"Did you know he raped four of the women?" I asked. I watched closely for his reaction; it was perfect surprise and disbelief.

"That's insane. What makes you say that?"

"He used the videos to blackmail them for sex. One of the women told me about it, and Slim confessed to me last night before he was killed."

Webb spilled a little coffee on his jeans but didn't notice. He narrowed his eyes. Slowly he shook his head, as if by sheer will he could change the past, but I nodded in answer.

"How?"

"Slim said he would put their sex tape on the Internet if they didn't agree."

"That little fuck," he cursed. "He swore to me he destroyed all the copies."

For the next several minutes he heaped guilt onto Slim, attempting to exonerate himself. I let him start to feel better, then I lowered the boom on him.

"That's why Amanda Sorenson killed herself. When she didn't agree to have sex, Slim pressured her again and again. That was her answer."

Webb sat back in the gold-colored chair, his arms on the rests, mouth turned down, looking at me. We were in the middle of the lobby with guests all around us. Slowly his eyes began to fill; tears

formed at the inside corners and spilled over. They ran down around his nose and onto his lips. Webb didn't try to wipe them away.

A waiter stopped at the table, but Webb did not see him. I reached over to take the check. Webb continued to stare at me and cry silently, as if I had told him of the sudden death of a family member.

. . .

WHEN HE WAS READY, we drove to his house on the lake. I wanted all the copies of the DVDs, and he put up no resistance. While he went to fetch them, I surveyed the new window and aquarium. Everything looked as it had before I blew up the place, even the Chinese vase with the dried fronds.

He returned with the DVDs.

"I will destroy them all except this one," I said, holding Amanda's video toward him. "If I ever hear of you making tapes again, I'll send this to the police with a long explanation."

Webb nodded, and I gestured that he should sit on the couch. I needed to ask him another question.

"Last night Slim was going to tell me something about Gwen, but he never got the chance. I think you know what it is."

At first he looked at me, and then gradually his gaze turned out the window.

"I don't know what . . ." But his expression changed. He knew what it was.

The house was silent except for the soft hum from the aquarium.

"Would it hurt you to tell the truth?" I asked. "For once . . . tell me the truth."

Webb was startled. It was an absurd context: He sat on the leather couch where he'd had sex with my wife, and I sat on a matching side

chair. Maybe the absurdity affected him. I don't know, but he decided to tell me.

"Gwen is a beautiful and intelligent woman," he said, "but also quite independent. When we first met ten years ago, I fell in love with her instantly. She never responded."

Webb pressed his lips together and looked resigned. He stared into the sky at nothing, as if he were remembering something he lost, the one big deal he never closed.

"I was hurt," he said. "I was hurt and wanted to hurt her back. I learned her weakness and used it against her."

His lips turned up into a smile. He chuckled and shook his head.

"Gwen can't resist a challenge," he said. "It's simple, but still she can't see it. She is so confident that she will always win."

I shifted in the chair. My finger picked at the leather on the armrest.

"I used it mostly for business purposes," he explained. "Like the direct-marketing-to-inside-sales program."

He looked at me to make sure I was following him.

"I told her it was a bad idea . . . that the program would fail, knowing full well when I said it that she wouldn't rest until it was successful." He looked down at his hands. "Occasionally I exploited her weakness outside of work." He sat up straight and combed his hair over with his fingers. "Do you want some water or something?"

"What was Slim going to tell me?"

Webb raised his eyebrows and scrunched his lips in a pained expression. He turned the violet eyes on me.

"It was soon after you started with the Connection. You may not remember it. We were at the Connection Ball, on the mezzanine floor of the Driskill."

I had a vague recollection of Gwen in a navy dress talking to Webb across the room.

"Gwen mentioned in passing that you were good-looking. I told her to forget about you. I said you were so happy in your marriage that no other woman could ever have you."

He shrugged his shoulders and cast his hands out to the sides.

"That was all it took," he said, as if the puppeteer had no choice but to pull the strings.

I walked onto the balcony to smoke a cigarette and look at the calm water. Somewhere in the neighborhood a fireplace was burning wood. I had a sudden urge to get in the Jeep and drive far away, not to Vegas, but to a place in the mountains where there were no people, nothing but trees, and streams, and honest carnivores. I stubbed the cigarette out in an expensive plant and left.

. . .

I NEEDED TO CONFRONT GWEN, but Rico and I had an appointment to meet at nine thirty, and he would be suspicious if I didn't show, so I drove straight to the Radisson. The Four Seasons is only a block away, and I had a sensation of ping-ponging back and forth in the city.

He looked as tired as I felt.

"Did you get any sleep?" he asked.

"Yeah," I lied, "a little. What about you?"

"Couple hours. Sometimes it gets like that." Rico was freshly shaved and had changed into a white button-down and dark slacks with loafers.

Most of the guests had gone through the buffet already, and we nearly had the place to ourselves. I'd had my fill of coffee so asked Dee for a Sprite.

"I got some data from the crime scene," Rico stated. "It seems there is a lot you haven't told me."

"Like what?" I tried to sound innocent.

"We found traces of marijuana in the crawl space and the bath-room, like someone knew we were coming and flushed it. Also, it's possible the door lock was picked."

"I didn't smell any pot when I was there."

"Mr. Bohls had several cracked ribs."

I stayed silent. I wasn't sure how bad it was going to get.

Rico shifted in his chair and leaned over the table as far as he could. His right eye was still the same almond color, but the black flaw in the left was larger; it covered a third of the iris.

"If you don't open up you'll be charged with assault. You may not have killed him, but you'll still go to jail."

So I told him most of it: the story from Zola the day before, how it all hinged on amateur pornography with Webb Elliot. I told him about the blackmail scheme Slim ran for sex, and how that led to Amanda Sorenson's suicide. I didn't mention anything about destroy-ing evidence, and I didn't mention Rose.

"Fine," he said, sitting back in his chair. "I understand. I want the DVDs and the computer. We can forget about the marijuana. Homicide doesn't care about that."

"They were gone when I got there. Maybe Slim got rid of them."

Rico gave me a tense smile. "You don't get it."

His left iris was now completely black; the heterochromia had blotted out the normal color.

"There's something wrong with your eye."

"It happens when my systolic blood pressure rises above one forty. There's nothing I can do to stop it."

He let me stare at the deformity. It was unnerving.

"You're going to pay," he said. "You screwed up somewhere, and I'll catch you. I'll impound your car right now. We'll go over every inch of Slim's apartment and your condo and your house and we will find something."

I thought about the DVDs from Webb that were in the Jeep. I needed Rico on my side.

"I want to go off the record. You're not wearing a mike, are you?"

"Shit. I should have dragged you into the office—given you the scare treatment."

"You've scared me. I admit it. I destroyed the DVDs last night after Slim was killed. Why expose them now? Slim can't be prosecuted, and there is no evidence Webb was involved in the rapes. Zola Conti told me that making the videos was consensual."

He leaned back in his chair, no longer threatening me.

I put my elbows on the table, my hands going into sell mode. "Listen, I was concerned about turning the sex tapes over to the police. These are innocent women. They were manipulated. Tons of stuff in police custody goes missing every year."

"Sometimes that happens," he admitted, "on rare occasions. Still, you destroyed evidence. That's a serious crime."

"Do you have kids, Rico?"

"What is this? You're asking me questions again?"

"Please."

"Two boys, one girl."

"How old is your daughter?"

He knew I was setting him up, but Rico was a good listener.

"Sixteen."

"Amanda Sorenson was twenty-two. That's only six years' difference. She did ballerina steps on the balcony rail before she jumped. Kids make bad decisions sometimes. Her parents had to come here to claim her body. They've suffered enough. I couldn't give that video or any of the others to anyone."

He folded his arms.

"Here, look at this," I said. I gave him the list of four rape victims and the other women who had done sex tapes with Webb.

He studied the list carefully until the heterochromia had returned to normal size. He nodded his head.

"Well," he said, "if the DVDs are destroyed, they are destroyed. There's not much I can do about it now."

For all I knew he agreed with my logic for destroying the DVDs. He didn't bring it up again. Instead we talked about the investigation of what was now possibly a triple murder. Soon he started looking at his watch.

"We're going to have to reconvene. I have more questions for you, but my boss called a last-minute meeting to discuss the Bohls murder. How about lunch?"

"Sure."

He started to get up but then hesitated and sat down again.

"Have you picked up on the common MO in the three murders?" he asked.

"No, they all seem quite different."

"They're outrageous. Each one was executed with incredible risk. First, the murderer kills Smolnik in the men's room of a crowded restaurant. At any moment someone could have come in. Then he throws Franzinni off the balcony, which required hacking into a security system *and* escaping from the building while the corpse was lying in the street. Finally, he fires an arrow into Bohls's chest from forty yards with you just four feet away.

"Any of these murders could have been done with much less risk. The murderer is compelled to show how good he is, how smart he is, that he's better than anyone else."

"There were a lot of intelligent people at the Connection."

"I'm sure you're right, but we'll catch him, and soon."

An entirely new thought occurred to me, something that could dramatically change the analysis.

"Could more than one person be involved?"

Rico frowned. "A conspiracy? I doubt it. Conspiracy to commit murder is unusual in white-collar situations. There is no statute of limitations on murder, which means you have to trust the other person not to tell anyone for the rest of your life. It's rare except in organized crime and gangs."

He stood up.

"No," he said, "we're looking for one man." As he turned to leave, he paused and added, "Or woman."

After Carrillo left I had another Sprite and stared at the lake, not wanting to go back to the condo.

CHAPTER 29

WHEN I ARRIVED Gwen was sitting on the balcony with the newspaper. She heard the door and came bounding in wearing jeans and a T-shirt.

"God, baby, are you all right? I heard about Slim Bohls." She pressed herself against me, arms around my back, her face turned against my chest. After a moment she looked up, showed me her crooked smile, and kissed me. I wanted to respond, to pull her into the bedroom for a carnal escape, but my lips betrayed me.

She pushed back, her brown eyes searching mine.

"I figured it out, Gwen. I was a sucker for a long time, but even a dumb ass like me can figure things out if I get enough clues."

She wasn't sure yet what I was talking about.

"It started early, didn't it?" I asked angrily. "The inadvertent kiss in my office that night, the late-night drinks in New York, the heart-to-heart talk, groping in the hallway—but it didn't quite work that time."

"It started that way," she explained, her voice concerned. "But it's not like that now."

"Let me finish. The trip to Vegas, the new hairdo and green eyes, the peep show at the pool, the white satin dress, even the prostitute with the red curls. How much did you have to pay her?"

"You talked to Webb, didn't you? That asshole."

She turned away and took a slow step, then turned back, her eyes seeking forgiveness.

"At the beginning it was the challenge," she said. "I was attracted to you, and part of the attraction was your inaccessibility. So I did. I deliberately seduced you, but now—"

"You destroyed my marriage! You schemed . . . and set traps . . . and kept coming until you got your way."

Gwen's face went from endearing to angry. Her eyes flashed as she blurted, "Nobody made you fuck me! You did that on your own."

She had me there. She was a beautiful temptress with honey-dipped words, but that didn't absolve me.

"Whatever," I said.

She instantly regretted her attack and took a step closer. She tried to hug me, but I pushed her away.

"Joe, I've fallen for you. I swear it; I'm in love with you."

I shook my head.

"You're right," she confessed. "I seduced you. But damn it, now I get all churned up when you walk in the room."

"It's over." I dismissed her, tired of the argument, tired of everything.

"No. We can make it work. You've got to admit . . . it's good. We're good together."

"It would never work," I said. "You don't understand. Relationships are difficult. Things go wrong. You hurt each other and have to find the way back. With us, any time something went wrong, I would always look to the lies at the start. It would become a gulf between us."

"No." Her eyes begged. She shook her head, not willing to accept it.

"It's over. Pack your stuff."

As Gwen pulled her belongings together, I shredded the remaining DVDs.

In a half hour she was ready to go. She had changed into white jeans and a flowered top, and pulled her hair into a pony. She had two suitcases, a laptop bag, and a small purse.

Gwen tried to smile. "Will you kiss me?"

"No," I said, and it shook her up. I was on the couch. She sat down in a chair and looked at me simply. Both corners of her mouth turned down. Her chest heaved, just twice, and one big tear trickled from her eye. I watched it fall down her lovely cheek, the smooth, tanned skin. She looked in her purse for a tissue and came up empty. I jumped up and grabbed some off the counter.

"Let me carry your bags," I offered, trying too late to be a gentleman.

"No, thank you." She'd had her moment of weakness, but only a moment. "If you can't kiss me, I don't need you to lug my shit." Somehow she picked up everything and made it to the car in one trip. I watched her drive away through the window above the sink.

The door to the balcony was open, a highway for the fresh smell of a pleasant day. I walked out and lit another cigarette. A lot of people criticize smoking, and for good reason: It's a nasty, smelly habit and causes terrible health problems. Even so, one thing you can say for cigarettes is they never desert you. When your lovers disappoint you, and your own failings bring life down to its worst, the pack is still there, waiting for you with open arms, giving you something to do, allowing you to feel.

CHAPTER 30

RICO CARRILLO and I were to meet for lunch at El Arroyo on west Fifth Street. I arrived early and sat on the outdoor brick deck, under the shade of massive live oaks. The waitstaff chatted in advance of the lunch crowd. I ordered lemonade and snacked on tortilla chips and spicy salsa.

Rico arrived late and hurried over.

"How was the emergency meeting with your boss?" I asked.

He grimaced and tried to imitate a New England accent. "'Lieutenant Carrillo, you are badly behind the power curve on this case. It behooves you to solve it *before* everyone associated with the company is butchered on the streets of Austin.'"

"He sounds kind of highbrow."

"Captain Eldridge has a PhD in criminology from the University of Pennsylvania."

"Well, then, we're in fine shape."

We ordered the special tacos of the day. Rico looked around at the nearby tables, assessing the patrons. This wasn't his usual spot, but I had bribed him with lunch if we could go to a new place.

"Let me ask you something," he said. "Do you think any of the rape victims killed Slim Bohls?"

"No. If they were going to kill Slim, they would have done it when he first blackmailed them. Why wait until now? Plus, the whole arrow-in-the-chest thing, it doesn't strike me as a feminine murder method."

"I agree. We are ignoring them and focusing on the shareholder list. We haven't had a chance to check alibis for last night yet, but we may have enough to solve the case already."

"Why do you say that?"

"Your list of potential hackers was a breakthrough. As it turns out, twelve of the people on that list, including Tommy King and Henry Jiwanlal, were on a pub crawl together the night Mike Franzinni was killed. That alibi, cross-referenced with the hacker names, leaves us with very few suspects."

"A pub crawl doesn't sound like much of an alibi. Everyone gets drunk. Someone could slip out for an hour and never be missed."

"Every person at the crawl has at least two others who corroborate their presence the entire evening. Plus, like Henry Jiwanlal and Tommy King, every person has an alibi for the Smolnik murder. The point is, we're down to a couple names."

"Who are they?"

"I can't tell you that."

"One of them is Gwen, isn't it?"

"Ms. Raleigh's whereabouts cannot be verified for much of her trip. She claims she was camping in remote places."

"I can't see Gwen murdering someone."

"You haven't seen the things I've seen. Sometimes I think you're naive."

The waitress brought our food, and I started on the borracho beans and guacamole.

"Naive, huh?"

Rico looked at his plate, trying to decide whether to eat or talk.

"I shouldn't tell you this, but I will anyway. I'm sure you know Ms. Raleigh is athletic. We learned this morning that she was an expert archer in prep school."

"You mean like in competition archery?"

Rico nodded.

"Was Slim killed with a competition bow or a hunting bow? What do they use for hunting? I don't even know. A crossbow? A compound bow?"

"Slim was killed with a crossbow. I'm told it's not difficult to make the switch from one to the other."

Rico took a bite of his taco and watched me carefully. I tried to picture Gwen standing in the shadows of the balcony, aiming a crossbow at Slim Bohls. The image wouldn't come.

"Who is the other suspect?" I asked.

"Sanjay Kumar."

I didn't believe Sanjay was the murderer either. If this was the conclusion, we must be analyzing the problem incorrectly.

"Maybe we've got the wrong motive," I said. "The more I think about it, the more I believe money may not be the motive. These are all high-potential people. They were upset about the changes at the Connection, but that wouldn't drive them to murder. They will adjust, adapt, and move on to the next thing."

Rico was shaking his head at me.

"Now you're being naive again. It's not just blue-collar folks who get upset over money. Some people go crazy when they think they've been screwed."

We ate our food in silence. Somewhere between the first and second taco I realized I had missed something in the conversation. Rico was innocently eating his rice. Why was he still talking to me? I had no new information to give him.

"Why did you tell me about Gwen being a suspect?" I asked.

Instead of answering, Rico took the last bite of his taco and chewed slowly.

"You want me to tell her," I said. "Don't you?"

Rico never talked while eating. He carefully wiped his hands on a napkin.

"If Ms. Raleigh flees it will make things easier. We will undoubtedly catch her." He picked up his iced tea, took a sip out of the straw, and looked around the restaurant. "This is a nice place. I'm going to come back."

"She's not with me anymore. She left my place this morning."

He shrugged. "It doesn't really matter. I'm sure her story will fall apart when we talk with her again tomorrow."

Rico started to get his things together to go. I signaled the waiter for the check.

"You don't mind if I run, do you?" he asked. "I've got another meeting."

"Sure."

"Thank you, Joe. I appreciate your help on this case, but I think your involvement is about over. We should be wrapping things up quickly."

He put his sunglasses on and stood.

"Wait," I said. "How come you haven't focused more on me as a suspect?"

Rico removed the glasses and looked at me with sympathy.

"I never saw you as a suspect in the Smolnik murder. You're too practical. You would never take that kind of risk."

He was right about that. I thought the murderer took an insane risk with Smolnik.

"Plus," he added, "as far as the Connection goes, I always saw you as the novice, stumbling outside your comfort zone, being rolled around in the dirt by the brainy types."

* * *

BACK AT THE CONDO I collapsed on the couch and turned on the television. A tennis match was in progress. I mentally recounted the week's events: almost drowned on Wednesday, reunited with Gwen on Wednesday night, learned of Zola's rape on Friday, witnessed Slim's death on Friday night, and broke up with Gwen that morning.

I fell asleep, and the events became jumbled in a dream.

Gwen was practicing archery with a longbow. She wore a prep-school skirt and a long-sleeved white shirt. Slim Bohls was strapped to the target, his pompadour blowing in the breeze, and his black eyes searching for escape. Then it was me strapped to the target, and Gwen pulled back the arrow, a tear running down her face. Suddenly her face changed into Rose's face, and she continued crying as she made to let the arrow fly. At the last instant Tommy King knocked her down, and Henry Jiwanlal untied me. Webb stood at the podium of a graduation stage and read the names of those with honors. At the end Henry took the stage and repeated a line from the St. Crispin's Day monologue, over and over, but his words were all static. I kept trying to hear his words and in my frustration woke up.

The television announcer analyzed the latest volley. My head ached from lack of sleep. I sat on the couch and tried to remember the dream. Standing up, I went to the computer and searched for the line Henry had repeated. In a couple minutes I had it:

For he today that sheds his blood
with me shall be my brother.

If anyone could pull off a conspiracy it was Henry Jiwanlal and Tommy King.

I shook my head to sweep the crazy notion out with the cobwebs. Tommy had saved my life a few days before. They had moved on from the Connection; they were heavily involved in a start-up and wanted Webb to join them.

I got a water bottle from the fridge and walked out to the clubhouse patio to sit in the warm sun. The waterfall at the edge of the pool cascaded down three granite steps. The scent of cedar mixed with that of chlorine.

What if I suspended disbelief and assumed that Henry and Tommy were guilty? How would they do it?

On the night Gregor Smolnik was murdered, how would Henry have known to pick Siena as the venue for dinner with Rose and me? That was easy: the Connection alumnae e-mail grouplist had broadcast the location; Henry could have invited us to dinner, and then offered later to change restaurants on the bet that I'd want to stick to the plan. Timing the murder of Smolnik from outside the restaurant would be nearly impossible, but perhaps plausible if someone inside gave you a signal. I remembered Henry talking at the bar with Rose when Gregor Smolnik left us for the restroom. Henry could have signaled Tommy with a text message. High-tech professionals were always bending over their cell phones; I wouldn't have noticed. The figure I saw outside Siena on our way in could have been Tommy, waiting for the signal.

Henry had been horrified and fainted when he saw Gregor's corpse in the men's room. Could that have been a performance? After all, he was a trained actor.

But Tommy had an alibi for that night; he was visiting his mother in San Marcos an hour away. I decided to put that inconsistency on the side and think through the other murders.

The murder of Mike Franzinni would have been challenging but feasible for the Zealots to accomplish. A dozen drunk engineers on

a beer binge would be hard-pressed to certify who was in which bar at what time. Henry and Tommy could have walked to the Bank of Texas building on Sixth Street, thrown Mike over the side, and been back at the pub for the next round. Tommy could have hacked his way in earlier and planted a virus to freeze the cameras at a certain time.

Slim Bohls's murder was even easier to imagine. With Tommy's affinity for outdoor activities—rock climbing, fishing, kayaking—how far was the stretch to bow hunting? The motive for murdering Slim Bohls was less clear, although he had retained his shares in the Connection and also slighted Tommy in a romantic pursuit long ago.

The line of reasoning led me back to Tommy's alibi on the night of Gregor Smolnik's murder. That killed the whole concept. He had visited his mother, talked to the receptionist, and signed the logbook. Those facts had all been verified by the police. I myself had witnessed how the process worked at the nursing home on our way to the campground; Tommy had walked in, chatted with the receptionist, signed the logbook, and gone back to see his mother. I replayed the visual sequence in my mind. Had he signed the logbook? I couldn't remember.

For fifteen minutes I sat and watched the water splash off the last granite step into the pool. The logbook kept pestering me, and I decided to drive to San Marcos.

* * *

OUTSIDE THE NURSING HOME I nervously smoked a cigarette before walking in. The lobby area was a square, about twenty feet on each side. The furniture was flowery and at least a decade old. The walls were decorated with cheaply framed landscapes.

The receptionist sat in a small office behind a window. She was trying to decipher something on the computer and didn't notice me standing at the counter.

"Do you mind if I flip through the logbook?" I asked. "I'm trying to remember the last time I came for a visit."

Finally she looked up. "Who are you here to see?"

"Mrs. King."

"Tommy King's mother? I didn't know she had any other family."

"She's my aunt. Tommy's my cousin."

"Go ahead. Look through it." She turned back to her screen and hesitantly pecked a few keys.

The logbook was a simple affair, with seven-by-nine-inch lined pages.

"Do you have any of the older ones?" I asked. "It's been a while."

She frowned. I had presented a problem she wasn't sure how to solve.

"How far do you need to go back?"

"About six months."

"Oh, that book probably goes back to last year. A lot of folks come in so often they don't even sign it."

I started scanning the pages. She was right; there were days with only an entry or two, some with as many as five or six. The earliest dates in the book were more than a year old.

Gregor Smolnik had been killed on October 4 at just after seven thirty p.m. I flipped through every page. Tommy had logged a visit on October 4 from six fifteen p.m. to eight twenty-three p.m. It stood out because it was the only day he signed the book all year.

I stared at the page. Tommy's entry was the last one for October 4. The only other entry that day was for ten a.m. to eleven thirty a.m. I didn't want to believe it, so I examined every page in the book again, hoping to see another entry for Tommy, but the data was clear: Tommy signed the logbook only when he needed an alibi.

I looked at the receptionist, stunned. I'm not sure how long I watched her without speaking, but eventually she looked at me.

"Did you find what you were looking for?"

How should I answer the question? I didn't find what I wanted to find.

"I've forgotten my aunt's room number."

"Seventeen."

I signed in using the first name and date that came to mind: Davy Crockett, March 6, 1836, the final day at the Alamo.

I walked into the main building. It smelled of strong cleaning supplies, fresh laundry, and medical equipment. It was an old but well-maintained facility. There were only two short hallways, and I found Mrs. King's room easily.

The miniblinds were open to let in natural light. She was a strikingly attractive woman in her late sixties, with a central Texas accent and pale blue eyes. Someone had fixed her hair and dressed her in a festive sweater with brown slacks and slippers. She was studying a ranchland painting of mesquite trees, cactus, and longhorn cattle. I stayed for fifteen minutes and we talked about the painting, her pretty sweater, and whatever else came easily.

The conversation was tricky, because the frame of reference kept shifting, and my part changed with it. One minute I was Tommy's adult friend from Austin and the next minute I became a neighbor of hers when she was the mother of a fourth-grade boy.

"Tommy's much smarter than the other children," she said, "much faster and stronger too, but he's so quiet. That's why he doesn't have many friends in class, because he's so quiet."

"Yes, ma'am. Tommy's a nice boy."

"There's something about his mind. It's always racing ahead of everyone else in the room. I think he's quiet because he's constantly observing everything around him."

"He sure is smart."

"He's got this funny habit, when things are changing fast, like in a card game or something. He gets a studious look on his face, real serious for a ten-year-old, and when he makes a new decision, he smiles. No teeth show in that smile, but his lips turn up and form little dimples in his cheeks."

"He seems happy."

"I think that smile comes from the satisfaction of knowing he's made the right decision."

"Yes, ma'am."

On my way out, the receptionist didn't bother to look up.

· · ·

ON THE DRIVE BACK I tried to convince myself they were innocent. It was only one piece of data. In statistical analysis you're supposed to ignore the outliers.

I had no doubt that the Zealots had the means to commit the crimes. The flair and outrageousness of the methods would appeal to Henry's sense of elitism and desire for drama. He would not strike the fatal blow himself. His squeamishness at the sight of Gregor's corpse was genuine, but Tommy would strike the blow; as a naturalist, Tommy had killed many creatures. Henry would be the idea man, as always, and Tommy would supply the wherewithal to make it happen.

What about motive? Henry's motive would be revenge. He believed the board had carelessly destroyed a sacred bond. The core team was meant to exist "from this day to the ending of the world."

People make those statements all the time. They don't really believe them.

But Henry did believe them. I was certain of that.

Did Tommy believe? What did he say at Carlos'n Charlie's? "You're right, Henry. We can do anything." Tommy believed in dedication to Henry.

No . . . it couldn't be true. I owed my life to Tommy King.

I knew I should call Rico, but I didn't want to call him. There had to be another explanation. I had to get back to the condo first, to rest, and think it through again.

I had made the turn from I-35 onto Ben White Boulevard and was on the way to MoPac when I got a call from Gwen. The conversation was strained at first, but she finally decided to forge ahead.

"My cell battery's real low," she said. "If I cut out you'll know why."

"What's going on?"

"Henry and Tommy have invited the core team to toast their new company. They wanted me to tell you about it."

I almost missed the turnoff from Ben White to 360 north and MoPac.

"When is this supposed to happen?"

"Right now. It's a last-minute thing. They want us there before sunset."

"Where?"

"Do you remember the place where we went for the champagne toast? The bluff overlooking Lake Austin? Next to the Pennybacker Bridge?"

A sinking feeling came over me. Instead of turning off on MoPac I stayed on 360, toward Lake Austin and the bluff.

"Where are you now?" I asked.

"I'm crossing the bridge."

"Gwen, don't—"

But the sound in my ear went dead, a lost signal. I tried everyone's cell phone: Webb, Henry, and Tommy. No one answered. I called Rico Carrillo and left a voice message.

"I think I figured something out. Give me a call."

. . .

WEBB'S PORSCHE, Gwen's BMW, and Henry's truck were already parked in the little pull-off at the foot of the bluff. I sat in the Jeep, trying to figure out what the hell was going on. Outside, I started up the path and paused for a second. I remembered Rico's comment about me "being rolled around in the dirt."

I went back to the Jeep and took out the Smith & Wesson. It was fully loaded. I attached the holster to my belt and zipped my windbreaker enough to conceal it.

CHAPTER 31

A COLD FRONT was marching in from the north. Far to the south the sky was clear, but there was a dark and heavy cover over Austin. The temperature had dropped into the fifties, and a chill crept under my windbreaker.

I feared the worst as I climbed the dirt path through boulders and cedar trees to the top. I imagined bodies sliced in cruel ways and shot through with arrows.

But as I reached the top, some of the dread faded. It was set up like a cozy little campsite. A few cedar saplings had struggled their way through rock and dirt in the middle of the clearing on the bluff. Amid these, five folding camp chairs stood in a rough semicircle, as if around a fire. In the center Henry fiddled with a kerosene heater. He put a tank of fuel off to the side and pressed the starter button to ignite the internal flame.

A long folding table with a dark blue cover was set up for refreshments. Webb and Gwen chatted next to the table as Tommy opened a bottle of champagne. Gwen wore a brown suede jacket against the cold, but Webb was unprepared and wore only a white button-down. Tommy wore a plaid flannel shirt, and Henry was wrapped in a heavy parka.

I said hello to the others and walked to the edge of the bluff, twenty-five feet beyond the campfire. A hundred feet below, Lake Austin wove toward downtown on the left and west toward the fading sun on the right. There were no boaters. On the Pennybacker Bridge the weekend traffic was light. It was five thirty; only thirty minutes of daylight remained. I walked back to the table as Tommy poured champagne into flutes.

"We got the good stuff," Henry said. "Dom Pérignon."

Tommy pulled aluminum covers off plates of catered hors d'oeuvres: little roast beef sandwiches, shrimp skewered with toothpicks, stuffed mushrooms.

"Just like old times," Webb said, biting into an empanada and sipping on the champagne.

Gwen ignored the food and came to my side. "Can we talk? After this is over? I feel terrible about how we ended things."

"What?" I was distracted, scanning the ground around the chairs to see what else Tommy had brought along. There was a nylon camping bag about three feet long next to the chair on the right end of the semicircle. It looked too small to contain a crossbow. "Yeah, sure." I felt the hard outline of the gun through the windbreaker. Tommy looked at me and raised his eyebrows, as if to acknowledge an awkward situation.

"What's wrong?" Gwen asked me.

"Okay, everybody," Henry announced. "Please sit down so I can say something."

Webb drained his glass and did not move toward the chairs. "What's with all the mystery?" he asked, bouncing on his toes. "It's cold. Can we toast your endeavor and move on?"

Tommy tensed up with Webb's dismissal, but Henry smiled. He gestured toward the heater. "It's warm by the fire," he said. "We gave you ten years. Surely you can spare ten minutes."

Webb shrugged and moved toward the center seat in the semicircle.

Tommy was a step behind Webb and took him by the arm. "Here, you sit next to me." He guided Webb one seat over and then sat down at the end of the semicircle, the camping bag beside his chair. Webb was six feet tall and weighed one eighty, but he looked small sitting next to Tommy.

I let Gwen take the middle seat and sat on her left with my legs angled toward Tommy. The chair to my left was empty. Henry stood and faced us from the other side of the heater.

"What's going on?" Gwen whispered in my ear. She had picked up on the tension.

"Nothing." I leaned toward the heater and tried to act nonchalant.

Tommy watched me closely.

Henry presented his vision for Travel Quest. When Henry began a pitch you had no idea where he was going, but by the time he was finished you were convinced he had hold of the next big thing. The market for travel was huge. Travel Quest would revolutionize the buying experience. The value-add for consumers and property owners was ten times the value the Connection could ever create.

Once he was finished with the overture, Henry discussed the pipeline of companies they were targeting for acquisition. He described in rich detail the features they planned to add to the existing sites.

Out of context he would have looked comical, waving a half-full glass of champagne in his hand, his dark skin encased in a heavy parka, his face dominated by funny ears and black-framed lenses, but to be there in person and witness him sell was to see a thing of beauty. Webb began leaning toward him, eager to ask questions.

Henry summarized a meeting they had the day before in Dallas with a big venture firm. Their pitch had gone well, and the vcs proposed a funding round of twenty million to finance the first two acquisitions.

"Brilliant," said Webb. "That's excellent. You're moving quickly."

I knew Henry's goal for the meeting: Sign up the core team. But what would happen if we didn't agree? Would the Zealots turn on us? If they were truly the murderers they might do anything. I thought of a course of action that could get us off the bluff safely.

"Fantastic," I said. "You crushed them."

Gwen was silent, taking it in, trying to sort it out.

"We've made a lot of progress," Henry said, "but we're not done yet. That is why we asked all of you, the core team, to meet us today."

"I don't follow," said Webb, frowning.

"The venture guys want a full management group, not just Tommy and me. They want the core team."

Webb's eyebrows crunched together.

"I can do the pitch work," Henry said, "and Tommy can run the operation, but we need strong marketing, which is where Gwen comes in; we need a strong deal guy, which is where Joe comes in; and we need the overall leader, which is you, Webb."

Henry smiled. The pitch guy, having laid out the pitch, was optimistically awaiting feedback.

The point of the meeting started to dawn on Webb and Gwen.

Gwen said to me in a low voice, "If you and I aren't together, I'm moving to California."

"Just go along with it," I urged quietly.

"You chaps don't need me," Webb said, opening his arms, turning from Henry to Tommy and back again. "It's your idea. You should do it."

I watched Tommy closely as his hand slid down the right side of his chair toward the camping bag. What was he doing? My heart thumped as I pulled the zipper of my windbreaker down a couple inches. The conversation needed a push in the right direction.

"Count me in!" I said. "This will be huge. Webb, you should get in on it . . . you too, Gwen."

"Yes!" Henry smacked a fist into his other hand. He turned to Webb. "See? Joe gets it. He knows this rocket is going to the moon."

Tommy's hand pulled back into his lap.

"Henry," Gwen said, "I'm moving to California."

Henry frowned.

"That's okay," I said. "Gwen can telecommute. People do it all the time. She'll be traveling a lot anyway."

"Okay," Henry conceded. "I guess that could work."

Gwen gave me a puzzled look. Without sound she mouthed to me, *What?*

"Henry, Tommy, I'm flattered," said Webb. "Truly I am." Then he shook his head. "But I'm still running the Connection. That's a full-time commitment with the challenges we have."

"You need to give up on the Connection," Henry said. "With the Chartwell lawsuit the company is toast. Fold it up and join us."

"Actually, it appears we'll settle with Chartwell for a couple million, maybe less."

"What?" Tommy exclaimed. His eyes opened wide.

"It turns out Gregor Smolnik did a superb job negotiating the contract. We have favorable warranty language, and strict limitations of liability."

Just then my cell phone rang.

"Oh, shit, sorry; let me just . . ." I fished the phone out. It was Rico Carrillo. I ignored the call and acted like I was stuffing the phone back in my pocket but kept it in my hand.

"Each of us will get an equal share in Travel Quest," Henry explained, "not like the Connection. We'll all be equal partners."

"It's not that," Webb objected. "I want to do my own thing . . . with the Connection."

"You can't dissolve the core team." Henry was getting frustrated.

"It's not temporary. The Connection may have failed, but the core team goes on."

"Oh, no," Webb said. "Not again. Not the Shakespeare."

Tommy's left hand fished in his back pocket.

"Why are you being so selfish about this?" I asked Webb, grasping at straws.

"Yeah," said Henry. "It's not about the money."

"Of course it's about the money," Webb stated. He looked in frustration at Henry, then over at Tommy, like they were promising students who couldn't grasp an important law of science. "You always want to make it idealistic, but in the end, it's just about the money."

I thumbed the volume all the way down on my phone and felt around for the 9 button, hoping Tommy wouldn't notice.

"Now do you believe me?" Tommy asked Henry. "It's time for plan B."

"No," Henry objected.

"We agreed. If he didn't join we'd go the other way. Besides, we're out of time."

"What the hell are you guys talking about?" Gwen asked.

"Joe wants to do it," Henry told Tommy. "Webb will come around."

"Really?" said Tommy. "Joe wants to do it? Then why is he making a phone call?"

Everyone looked at me, and I fumbled the phone onto the ground.

"You went to San Marcos, didn't you?" Tommy asked as he stood. "The receptionist called me." He kept his eyes on me. "I've gone along with everything, Henry, but now it's too late. We need to make it easy for Carrillo."

Henry looked resigned. Webb and Gwen were totally confused. I slid my hand inside the windbreaker and touched the Smith & Wesson.

Tommy snapped one loop of a set of handcuffs on Webb's right hand and started to put the other around a cedar sapling behind his chair.

"What the bloody hell are you doing?" Webb yelled, and yanked the cuffed hand away.

Tommy slapped him hard in the face and secured the cuffs to the tree. He leaned down to the camping bag and pulled out a cricket bat. It was the same bat Webb had in his office long ago, with the sporting goods logo.

"You guys don't really want this," I said.

"God damn, Joe," Henry said. "Why did you have to keep digging?"

"Wait," Gwen said, looking at me. "Are you saying they killed . . . ?"

Webb struggled with the handcuffs, testing the strength of the sapling, but it held fast.

"Why?" I asked Henry. "Why did you kill them?"

"Because they broke up the team. We weren't just a bunch of players thrown together to make the board rich. We were building something great. It didn't matter if the Connection faltered so long as we kept the core team together, but Gregor and Mike screwed that up."

Tommy stood and lazily held the bat in two fingers. He didn't look like the Tommy I knew. His face was tense and determined. "It could have worked," he said. "We almost had it all, the revenge *and* some money."

"What about Slim?" I asked. "He didn't have anything to do with breaking up the team."

"Slim was my idea," said Tommy. "It's weird. In a way it's like hunting, but then it's not. I enjoyed killing Slim, not for the sport, but because he was an asshole that deserved to die."

"You almost shot me."

"I didn't expect you. I thought you were Slim. It was only at the last instant . . . well . . . my second arrow was true—straight to the heart."

Henry frowned and his shoulders slumped. "I never wanted this. You have to believe I never wanted it to go this far."

Tommy's face was grim.

Now I understood. Tommy knew I had solved the murder. He had told Henry he'd let him pitch the core team one more time, but Tommy had already made his decision.

"What are you planning to do?" Gwen asked, standing up.

Tommy's eyes were on me. He held the bat at his side.

Could I draw the gun before he could swing the bat?

"I'm sorry," Tommy said to Gwen. "Henry came up with a way to take advantage of the emotional complexities of you three."

"It was only a hypothetical scenario," said Henry, as if the architect couldn't be blamed for the finished structure.

Tommy had moved toward the heater. He twirled the bat in a slow circle.

I pulled the revolver from the holster but kept it hidden.

"Webb always wanted you, Gwen," Tommy explained. "So after we left the three of you up here, he must have beaten Joe to death with this bat."

He held the bat in the air like it was state's evidence.

I flipped off the safety.

Henry's face portrayed a hint of pride in his plan.

"Gwen," Tommy continued, "in a fit of rage you cut Webb's throat with the same razor you used to kill Gregor Smolnik."

With a sheepish look Henry pulled a straight razor out of his parka.

"After that," Tommy concluded, "you were so despondent over Joe's death you threw yourself off the cliff."

"It's tragic," Henry said, "almost Shakespearean."

"I can't let you do that." I drew the Smith & Wesson.

Tommy was so fast he almost got to me in time. I was lifting my arm up to aim when he took his first swing with the bat. He was close

enough to hit my hands. I drew them back but dropped the gun in the process. There was no room to back away, so I stepped forward and punched him hard in the side.

It didn't faze him. With a backhanded sweep of his arms he knocked me crashing over the heater. Henry had forgotten the fuel cap, and kerosene poured onto the ground.

I rolled and jumped to my feet to face Tommy on the run.

Gwen moved toward us, and Henry grabbed her. While they struggled the kerosene caught, and flames jumped eight feet high. To escape the heat Webb pulled back on the tree.

Tommy swung the bat at my head. I ducked it and stepped in to land another ineffective punch on his chest. We were only ten feet from the edge of the cliff.

Tommy stepped back and took a breath. He flipped the bat from his left hand to his right.

I was in a boxing stance, moving my feet. Several large boulders were on one side of us, the cliff at my back.

"Damn," he said. "I don't want to kill you."

"Then don't! Leave now. I won't follow you."

Over his shoulder the flames burned. Henry's arms held Gwen as she continued to struggle.

"Where would we go?" he asked.

"Anywhere! Canada! You could live forever up there."

"The police will catch us."

"Maybe not. Webb will send more money."

He started to lower the bat, considering my proposal.

"My mother," he said.

"I'll visit her . . . every week."

But that didn't work for Tommy King. He had already edged a step closer. He came at me and swung at my head again. I ducked, but

he tricked me; he checked the swing and came back with a half swing that rapped the side of my head and started a ringing noise in my ear.

The kerosene blaze burned lower.

I jumped at Tommy before he could finish me, straight punches to the middle, but he pushed me back so hard I fell to the ground. As I struggled to get up, he pounced. My back slammed against the dirt as his knees pinned me.

He held the bat in both hands and closed on my throat. I got two hands on the bat and tried to use it to leverage him to the side, but he was too strong. The bat began inching downward. I tried twice to shift my weight enough to throw him off, but he was too heavy.

Our faces were two feet apart, his lids open wide, his eyes committed.

"Tommy, don't," I pleaded.

I breathed through my nose as the bat reached my throat. I could feel the pressure increasing.

Suddenly there was more weight on him.

"You bastard!" Gwen screamed. Her fingers clawed at Tommy's face. "I'll scratch your eyes out."

Tommy stayed focused on choking me. Her nails cut deeply into the skin of his cheeks. She hooked a finger into his left eye and pulled.

"Aaagh!" Tommy yelled in pain and leaped off of me.

I turned on my side and coughed and gulped at air.

Gwen rode his back, her arms around his neck, and continued to scratch at his face. Tommy spun in a circle. He dropped the bat as he tried to get hold of her.

I rolled to my knees and slowly stood, catching my breath.

Henry was close to me, indecisive, the razor unopened in his hand. He took a step toward me, and I shoved him hard in the chest. He stepped backward and nearly fell.

Tommy finally grabbed Gwen's lower leg and threw her like a doll. Her head thumped against a boulder, and she collapsed on the ground.

"Gwen!" Henry cried, and stumbled toward her.

The flames had died away, and in the fading light I saw Webb on his cell phone, still cuffed to the tree.

Tommy shook his head and looked for me. I was ready for him and landed a left hook to the side of his face. His head was huge and hard. He turned back at me, and I threw a straight right at his nose. Blood started to flow, but he wasn't the least bit stunned.

"Oh, God," Henry wailed. "Tommy, I think she's dead."

I took two steps back, vaguely aware the edge of the cliff was nearby. Tommy started taking big bear swipes at me. I couldn't let him get close; if he wrapped me in those massive arms he would literally squeeze me to death. I evaded him and counterpunched when I could. Over the next few minutes I scored five or six shots to his head, and he moved more slowly.

"Stop," Henry shouted from the boulder. "Stop it."

Tommy knew he was losing the fight. Our arena was an open space between the boulders and the cedars next to the edge of the cliff, about twenty feet square. He kept the pressure on me, but after each attack he paused to look at the boulders on one side and the cliff beyond. I detected a pattern. He was maneuvering our positioning so I would be cornered between the boulders and the edge of the cliff.

I ducked a swing and threw another right hook at his temple. He staggered back and blinked hard. One or two more of those and I could knock him down, watch him until the police came. He moved to my left and made me step back against the boulder. I pushed off and stepped toward the edge; a quick look told me there was four feet of leeway.

Tommy rushed to push me off the cliff.

It's called tomoe nage, a basic Judo move. Instead of waiting to be pushed I stepped toward Tommy and grabbed his shirt at the left shoulder. I fell backward, ahead of him, and wedged my foot low on his waist. As we rolled and I hit the ground, I pushed my leg hard into him, and Tommy flipped over me into the open air.

He scrambled, but there was nothing to grab except me. He clasped my right forearm tightly as his center of gravity sailed to the edge of the cliff. I flipped his way, and Tommy fell hard to the ground on his back and shoulders. His upper body stopped, but his lower torso and legs kept falling; they were over the edge and pulled his head and shoulders with them. Tommy's grip was tight on me; his weight yanked me to the edge. There was a deep crack in the rock, and I wedged my other arm into it to keep from falling.

Tommy fell another couple feet before he stopped as deadweight hanging in the air. His three hundred pounds pulled every muscle in my arms and chest. The pain was excruciating, but the only alternative was to tumble to the bottom with Tommy.

I wrapped my hand around his forearm to weld us together as a unit.

He flailed in the open air for a handhold on the cliff wall, but it curved in at the top, and there was nothing he could reach. My head hung over the edge. He dangled below me while his bloodied face studied the rock for any kind of grip.

"Hang on, buddy," I said. "I've got you."

But I didn't have him. He had me. The burning of my muscles swept right through the biceps, triceps, pectoral, and down the other side. I heaved and grunted as I tried to pull him up. He rose a half inch before settling back down. My arms stretched further, and I began a slow downward progression, millimeter by millimeter. In a matter of seconds my arm would be ripped from the crack, and we would free-fall.

Tommy stopped all movement and adopted a look of heavy concentration. Our eyes locked together. Just like his mother predicted, a little smile came that pulled dimples into his cheeks.

"Good-bye, Joe," he said, and let go of my forearm. I held my grip another second before his arm slipped through my fingers and Tommy fell.

The cliff was a hundred feet high. An outcropping of rock protruded from the wall eighty feet down. Tommy's body slow-rolled lengthwise one rotation, smacked headfirst into a large boulder, and spun wildly into the lake. An angry red stain marked the rock. He landed facedown and didn't move, an ugly dark liquid pouring out of his skull to mix with the green water.

"Tommy!"

Henry had run up just after the splash. Below, the force of blood flowing into the lake told the story.

"Tommy! Oh, Tommy," he cried. Henry fell to his knees and wept.

I rolled back from the edge and scrambled to stand using elbows and stomach muscles. My arms were nearly useless.

I stumbled to search for the Smith & Wesson in the dirt.

"What happened?" Webb asked.

"Tommy fell."

I reholstered the gun and rushed over to Gwen. She lay on the ground next to the boulder, a crumpled mass. I gently straightened her shoulders and legs. There was a steady pulse in her throat. She had a lemon-size bulge on the side of her skull and blood in her hair. I took my handkerchief and pressed it against the wound. The blood had begun to coagulate. I leaned over to listen for her breath; it was slow and raspy. After I tilted her head back and lifted her chin to clear the airway she began breathing more easily. Out of the corner of my eye I saw Henry walking toward Webb.

"Henry," Webb called, panicking. "What are you doing?"

Henry held the straight razor open in his hand. Webb stepped to the other side of the tree and strained on the chain of the cuffs.

"Henry, stop." I said. I drew the Smith & Wesson and held it in two hands, the standard grip. I walked toward Webb.

Henry kept coming. He was so intent I wasn't sure he heard me. "Henry!"

He stopped and saw the gun. Slowly his face adopted a sad grin.

"Fucking Joe Robbins," he said. "Where the hell did you come from?"

He took a few more steps, grabbed a chair that stood between him and Webb, and threw it aside.

The cedar sapling leaned with the force of Webb pulling on it.

"No!" I yelled.

Henry turned and faced me.

"Why the hell are you here?" he asked. "Why did you come? To the Connection?"

I didn't think he was serious, but he waited for my answer.

"Really," he said. "Why?"

"I came to get rich."

He laughed and shook his head. "That didn't work out too well, did it?" He looked at Webb, then back at me.

"Don't you see?" he said. "It's better this way. After this last thing, you can kill me and be done with it. But Webb has to die."

"Shoot him," Webb told me. "Shoot him now."

"Shut up," I said.

Henry laughed again, a weary, resigned laugh.

"Back away!" I shouted.

"Webb lured us into it," Henry explained. "Sold us on it. I can't allow him to break it up. We can all die together . . . today."

"No. No more killing."

"You never really got it because you came for the money. When we started out it wasn't about money. We were going to change the world. We still could have, but they got to Webb, and he changed. Now I must end it."

"No."

Henry shook his head and tried a different tack. "He manipulated you and Gwen like children. He screwed your wife. He deserves to die."

An image of Webb going at it with Rose against the back of his couch flooded my mind, but only for an instant. I walked around to the side of them to have a clear shot at Henry with little risk of hitting Webb. My hands started to shake.

"Nobody deserves to die," I said. "Gregor didn't. Franzinni didn't. Tommy didn't."

"I must," Henry said, pleading with me. "The team must die together."

He flicked the straight razor and I almost missed him. Webb put out his hand and grabbed at the blade to keep it from his body. As Henry turned, my first shot hit the shoulder of his parka and left a bright stain.

Webb cried out in pain, his white sleeve splattered with red.

Henry staggered forward and fell on him. They were together, scrambling, until Webb pushed Henry away and then fell back, his neck exposed. Henry stood and drew his arm to swipe at Webb's throat. As his arm struck down, the Smith & Wesson exploded in my hands, and I shot him in the back. I had aimed for the triangle of his upper torso.

"Henry!"

I ran to pull him off the dirt and into my arms. There was no exit wound. The hollow-point bullet had done its work, mushroomed and bounced through vital organs.

Henry coughed blood and seemed to glaze over. I thought he was going to pass out, but he rose to consciousness and looked at Webb. Webb stared back, horrified.

"Do you remember what our world was like?" Henry asked. "Eh? Webb? Our awesome feats? Our derring-do?" He coughed again, and Webb said nothing. A thin line of blood trickled from Henry's mouth and down his dark skin. He smiled and carried on.

"Do you recall our fearsome battle cry? Back then we said, 'We few, we happy few.'"

Henry closed his eyes and said nothing more. He died in my arms a minute later.

I helped Webb stop the bleeding from the razor slash and watched over Gwen until the EMS arrived.

· · ·

IN ANOTHER HOUR they had bundled us up and driven us away. Gwen had a severe concussion. Webb needed thirty stitches. Henry and Tommy were pronounced dead.

Rico caught up with me at the hospital. He went out of his way to keep me from being charged. Webb's statement helped, as did the crossbow in the backseat of Henry's truck.

"It's a good thing you brought the gun," Rico said.

"Yeah, I guess."

The doctor prescribed pain pills and rest for my strained muscles. In another couple hours I was released and went home to drink a double whiskey and sleep.

That was the first time I had the nightmare: the bluff, the hanging women, the Smith & Wesson, and the river of blood.

CHAPTER 32

IT WAS THANKSGIVING DAY.

"We want an original Sheila story, Daddy," Chandler insisted, "not one of the old ones."

"Yeah, Daddy," Callie added. "Tell us a new story!"

We were in Callie's bed, the girls nestled in to my sides. My sore arms held them close.

"I'm too tired to make up a story."

"New story!" Chandler demanded, and Callie joined in. "New story! New story!"

"Okay, okay. I'll do my best."

I closed my eyes to concentrate and made up a story called "Never Give Up."

When the story begins, Sheila's father loses his job.

Callie looked at my face. "You lost your job. Didn't you, Daddy?"

"Shhh," Chandler said. "Don't interrupt."

As the story progresses, Sheila asks her mother, Mary, why people lose their jobs. After some thought, Mary answers, "It's just life. Life often presents challenges, but you can never give up, Sheila. Never give up."

Then, several weeks later, as Sheila is riding her bike she is surprised

by a sudden rainstorm. She falls down a waterfall and is knocked unconscious.

I stopped talking. I had a sudden vision of Tommy falling off the bluff, banging into the rock, and landing facedown in the lake. What bizarre story was I trying to tell?

"What's the matter, Daddy?" Chandler asked. "Are you all right?"

I blinked and nodded. "Yes, I'm fine. I'm figuring out where the story goes from here."

I forged ahead, telling how Sheila regains consciousness to find water crashing around her. She sits on the edge of a sheer drop-off, frightened and scared. Her situation is hopeless, until she remembers what her mother told her: "Never give up." She hears it again. "Never give up." Even though she has a broken arm, and multiple cuts and scratches, Sheila fights her way through ferns and roots and dirt to the path at the top of the waterfall.

I had recovered and proceeded with the ending.

"Sheila stood on the path in her muddied clothes, soaked and bloody, her left arm broken, scratches covering her legs, neck, and face. She was colder and dirtier than ever. But she was triumphant."

"I knew it!" said Callie. "I knew she would make it."

"Please," I said, "no more interruptions. We're almost to the end."

From there the wrap-up was easy.

"Three days later, Sheila's arm in a cast, the family took a walk to retrieve her bike. As they came down the path the woods opened up, and they saw the hill where Sheila had fallen.

"'Look, there it is.' Her brother, Tim, pointed to a flash of red lying in the weeds halfway down the now dry gulley.

"'Where did you land when you fell?' her father, Roger, asked.

"Sheila pointed to the spot where the cliff fell out of view. Her mother gasped.

"'Good heavens,' Roger said. 'How did you ever manage to climb up?'

"'I remembered what Mommy told me.'

"Mary knelt with a worried look and held Sheila by the shoulders. 'What was that, darling?'

"'Never give up. You told me to never give up.'

"Mary hugged her daughter to her chest.

"And that's the end of the Sheila story."

Chandler and Callie were dug in, their bodies warming mine.

Callie let out a big sigh. "That was a scary Sheila story, Daddy."

"I would never give up," Chandler said. "If I fall down a hill like that I will never give up."

"Me neither," Callie said.

"I know you won't," I told them. "You will never give up."

Chandler cocked her head, a question on her face. "What about you and Mommy?" she asked. "Have you two given up?"

Callie looked at me with wide, anxious eyes. What was I to tell them?

"No, girls," I said. "Mommy and I are taking a break. That's all. Marriage is hard work, and sometimes couples need a little break before they get back together."

For the time being that answer was good enough.

                           * * *

"DID I LIE TO THEM?" I asked Rose, after relating the story.

We were on the back patio, watching the moon compete with the stars for attention. The only sound was the wind in the trees. She sat on a lounge chair with her legs folded, arms around her knees. I offered her a cigarette, but she declined; the girls had caught her in the act, and she had promised to quit, so I put the pack away.

"I don't think you lied to them," she said. "That's how I think about it. We're taking a break."

"How long is the break? I'm ready to move back tomorrow."

I had to wait a long time for her answer. Finally she stood and wrung her hands. "I don't know. I'm still trying to figure out what to tell you."

"It was my fault." I got up and grabbed her by the shoulders. "We can start over, right where I messed things up." Her arms felt good in my hands. Light cascaded from the picture window onto the patio. I could see her brown eyes as they focused on mine, but she didn't kiss me.

"We can't start over in the same place," she said. "I still love you, but . . . we can't pretend nothing happened. I have an image of us in my mind. We're skating on ice, and for a long while the ice is strong and smooth; then there is a huge crack and we fall through."

"I don't get it. What does that mean?"

"We can't jump on the ice and start skating again. It means we have to do what the priest said. We can't rush it."

The pack called to me, and I fished it out of my pocket. I sat on the edge of the hot tub and lit a cigarette.

"Damn it," she said. "Give me one of those things."

We sat together in the night, indulging an unhealthy habit, trying to sort out our lives.

"I need to figure out who I am," she said. "I had Chandler when I was twenty-three, and ever since I have relied on you totally. I want to be my own person too."

"I want you to be your own person. Can't we be together at the same time?"

"It doesn't work that way. I'm not ready to commit. I need to try other things, see other people."

"What kinds of things?"

"I signed up to take the LSAT, like those kinds of things."

"Law school?"

"Why not?"

"See other people?"

"You should too. Look, we were married for ten years; then all hell broke loose. Before we get together again, we need to be sure."

I looked at Rose in the moonlight. She was more beautiful than the first time I ever saw her. Even back then I knew I was lucky. Could I win her again? I could see her as a law student, dressed smart casual, freshly done highlights. Ambitious, intelligent men would chat her up between lectures.

"It's not that simple," I objected. "We don't know how that turns out. You might fall in love with someone else. There are better men out there than me."

"We'll have to take that chance. It's the only way to know for sure."

She had worked it all out; she didn't want a divorce, but didn't want to live together either. She proposed a marital purgatory. It wasn't what I wanted, but it was better than the worst-case scenario.

I was tired. The sprained muscles had taken a toll, and I was starving myself of sleep to stay away from the nightmare. I wanted more than anything to climb into my own bed and sleep in peace for twelve hours, but it wasn't to be.

* * *

EARLIER IN THE EVENING I had shared with Rose some of what happened on the bluff, but not everything. The story of Slim Bohls's murder and the subsequent deaths of Henry and Tommy had been widely reported, but the press hadn't uncovered my role.

As I stood at the door to leave, she put her hands on my chest and leaned in to give me a warm kiss. I inhaled her scent. My thumbs hitched under the back of her jeans, and I pulled her body into mine. She broke it off and cupped my face in her hands.

"I know you killed them, Joey," she said. "Your face looks like it did with Ted Thompson, and your eyes are full of guilt." I tried to turn away, but she held me fast. "I'm glad you killed them," she whispered. "If you hadn't, they would have killed you." Her eyes glistened. "I couldn't bear a world without you."

CHAPTER 33

T HE NIGHTMARES WOULD END, I told myself. Even without Rose, in time, they would end.

I fell into a routine. In the morning I stretched, walked to the greenbelt a block away, and ran nine or ten miles. Sometimes I ran the path along Barton Creek, under Highway 360, then north a ways and back. Other days I ran into Zilker Park and around Town Lake. Back at the condo I worked with free weights, and then sat by the pool until I grew hungry. At night I listened to my neighbor's Spanish guitar, sipped Knappogue Castle, and smoked too much.

. . .

WEBB PAID ME OFF at Ringside, the bar at Sullivan's Steakhouse on Colorado. A jazz combo played a mellow cover of "I Get a Kick Out of You." Webb wore pressed khakis, a dress shirt, and brown oxfords. I wore faded jeans, an REI sweatshirt, and goatskin cowboy boots. The boots felt better than wingtips or loafers: solid, functional, comfortable.

Webb sipped on ice water while I drank a Mexican martini. He had a reservation for dinner with a group and kept looking at his watch.

"This is for you," he said, handing me a white envelope. "Your bonus."

Inside was a cashier's check for four hundred thousand dollars, my biggest payday ever.

I studied the four and all those zeroes. Were the numbers red for a reason? Where would Henry be now if I had let him kill Webb? Did I do it for the money?

I realized Webb was talking, giving me an update on the Connection.

". . . gaining momentum with the hosted model. Of course, we rely heavily on the old maintenance revenue now, but with Chartwell settling the dispute, and subscription revenue climbing, we can have another go at the IPO in a few years. You should join us."

"What?"

"I'm serious. Mike Franzinni was the one who insisted I fire you. He thought you had gone soft, but we both know that's not true. Don't we?"

"Do you ever think about them? Henry and Tommy? Do you?"

Webb looked at his watch again and checked over his shoulder to see whether his party had arrived.

"They were good at selling software," he said, "but let's face it: They went completely mental, truly psychotic. You know that."

He looked at me, the violet eyes sparkling, ready to close a deal.

"What do you say? Ready to come back to the Connection?"

"I don't know. . . ."

"Hugh Crandall sends his regards. He claims the valuation multiples on recurring revenue are headed to the stratosphere. I'll give you the same equity deal as before. Plus, I'll double your salary. With no board to answer to, I can pay whatever I want."

A half million in salary was enough to cover everything: the house, Rose and the girls, and my separate living costs.

To hell with it. I wouldn't work for Webb for a million-dollar base, or anyone else for that matter. I was through with punching the clock.

I shook my head.

"I guessed as much," he said. "I don't think you're fit for the corporate world any longer."

"No?"

"You're an action junkie now. You won't tolerate staring at spreadsheets late into the night, but you do have certain skills. Maybe you should freelance."

"Certain skills?"

"You sort things out, fix problems, and you're not afraid to color outside the lines."

"Those skills sound vague."

"Trust me. CEOs have situations where they need an unorthodox action junkie: turnarounds, ugly crises, issues that need to be dealt with quietly."

"Freelance," I said, testing the sound of it.

"I'll be glad to act as a reference."

His group walked in the door, and Webb put a twenty on the bar to cover the drinks.

"By the way," he said, "thank you for sending Sanjay Kumar my way. I refinanced his loan with the mob. In exchange Sanjay will work at half salary until he pays off the debt."

Webb walked to his group and slapped a suited Asian on the shoulder, already working on his next big deal.

Freelance. It was an interesting concept, but the check in my hand meant I didn't need to work at anything for a while.

I thought about the million dollars Webb had wired the Zealots. Rico Carrillo never found out about that. I don't know how Tommy worked it, but I do know his mother moved into an upscale facility

out by Lake Travis. I drove there one day to visit. It compared to the old place like the Four Seasons compared to the Radisson. She showed me the Western landscapes in her room, and we talked about whatever came easily.

. . .

ON THE DAY GWEN LEFT TOWN, we met for breakfast at Magnolia Cafe on Lake Austin Boulevard, an old cottage transformed into a diner. We sat at a wooden table and were served huevos rancheros by a tattooed waiter with green hair and a ring through his lip.

Gwen wore a ball cap to cover the spot where they shaved her head. She had cut her hair short, in a pixie, and her eyes were gray again.

She made a pitch for us to be together but knew I wouldn't go for it.

"You and Webb," I said. "You're out of my league."

"I've changed my ways," she said. "From now on I'm throwing right down the middle of the plate, no curveballs, no changeups."

"I hope you find what you want."

"You're always welcome in California." The left side of her lips turned up, and her eyes smiled.

She was headed out to the land of glitter, trying to break in using her intellect, courage, and looks. I expected she would do well.

"By the way," she said, "I never told anyone about our affair, in Vegas."

I had always assumed Gwen spilled our secret to someone. I had told no one. Who else was there?

"It was Webb. He paid a dozen people around the MGM to keep an eye on us. One of the bellmen saw us in the taxi line that morning, with me in the satin dress."

"How do you know?"

"I asked Webb about it. He lied to me, of course, but I can tell when he's lying. It took three days of asking around at the MGM before I found the right bellman. For a hundred bucks he told me the truth."

"Why did Webb do that?"

"Who knows? Webb does what Webb wants to do."

On our way out we paused in the small parking lot.

"Thank you," I said, "for saving my life."

"Does that entitle me to a kiss?"

I stepped closer and reached out. She wrapped her arms around my neck, and we came together for a last embrace.

Gwen walked to the BMW, shoulders squared back, head high, confident.

· · ·

THE ROUTINE CONTINUED: the workouts, the nightmares, drinking on the balcony.

I had plenty to think about on my balcony: Rose and the kids, my affair with Gwen, the failed road show, Webb's manipulations, Henry's passion, and a vivid recollection of Tommy saving my life. Anything was better than going to sleep, where a straight razor and a free fall awaited me.

People call CFOs bean counters, but I count a lot of different things. As a kid I counted everything that could be counted: steps to the second floor, trees in the yard, houses on our street.

Six people had died violently since I joined the Connection, and I couldn't make sense of it.

Webb called Henry and Tommy psychotic, but they didn't start out that way. They were idealists who thought we could build something great together. Who knows? Maybe we could have, but that wasn't Webb's game.

And contrary to what Webb said on the bluff, he wasn't in it for the money either. Webb had to be the man behind the curtain, to see the future and convince all the forces to move toward his vision. When the future changed and Webb saw that modifications were needed, he instantly changed all the tactics and resources. Henry and Tommy couldn't accept that change; they were, after all was said and done, the Zealots.

Each night, as I sat on the balcony, I counted the number of times I poured the Knappogue Castle. Drinking alone adds up to no good, but I had no friends in town. That was what I needed, some new friends, but it was easier to restock on liquor, pick up something to grill, and drink on my balcony.

One night, I recalled our camping trip to the San Marcos River. It had been only a couple of weeks; I could still remember our conversations in detail. At the campfire, after Henry gave the St. Crispin's Day speech, we played a game of charades, like kids. On one of his turns Tommy hunched over and clumped around in an obvious portrayal of Quasimodo. Henry pointed and kept saying, "What the fuck is that? What the fuck is that?" and I was laughing so hard I couldn't catch a breath.

Another night on the balcony, after I'd had a few, I heard a pounding noise. Rubbing my face, I walked inside and opened the door to find Zola Conti. She wore hip-hugger jeans, ankle boots, and a black leather jacket.

"Were you sleeping or something? I knocked three times." She walked past me into the room. "What have you got to drink?"

She turned her nose up at the whiskey, so I opened a bottle of sauvignon blanc, and we sat on the couch. I hadn't seen Zola since I had shattered her protective cover at the Shady Grove. I couldn't tell what sort of inner stresses remained, but outwardly she was energetic.

"Of course I'm glad the Slime Ball is dead," she said. "He was an asshole, but what happened to my video with Webb?"

"It's gone. I destroyed it . . . and all the copies."

She leaped off the couch and threw her arms around me.

"Joe Robbins, you're my hero!"

After Zola finished beaming, she became practical again.

"What have you got to eat around here?"

She jumped up to take charge of the kitchen. Rummaging through the refrigerator, she threw away half the contents but scrounged an apple, an orange, and some Havarti. She sliced and arranged everything on a plate with crackers.

Sitting at the kitchen table, we nibbled, drank the wine, and I filled her in on the rest. When I got to the part where Henry and Tommy died on the bluff I left out the details, but Zola was quick.

"So you killed them," she said, looking right at me.

"Well . . . uh . . . yeah."

After a few moments she put her hand over mine and squeezed. The hooded brown eyes studied my face. Her lips pressed together in an expression of thought.

"What you need is a vacation," she said, like a doctor giving a prescription.

I looked out to the balcony, hankering for a smoke. "I'll just chill out here. I don't want to go by myself."

"Who said anything about going alone?"

CHAPTER 34

TWO DAYS LATER we checked into the Royal Caribe, an all-inclusive resort near Playa del Carmen, forty minutes from Cancún. The open-air lobby was covered with a giant thatched roof and decorated with tropical plants and flowers. A light breeze greeted us at the entrance as a waiter pushed rum drinks into our hands. Zola had booked one room for the two of us, even though I assured her I didn't care about the cost. She maintained it was more convenient, and with two queen-size beds there was plenty of space.

The resort property was several hundred acres of landscaped tropical forest bordering the Caribbean Sea. Three beautiful pools with swim-up bars were at our disposal, or we could lounge on the beach under coconut palms. The resort catered to young couples and singles, with activities around the pool, and Jet Skis and sailboats on the beach.

Zola's favorite activity was water volleyball in the pool, where she made up for a lack of height with abundant enthusiasm. On the first day I watched from the safety of my sunglasses and pondered what to order from the pool waiter. On the second day one team was short a player, and Zola enlisted two other girls to drag me into the pool. I tried hard to stay depressed, but it was becoming more difficult.

On the third day I opened my eyes by the pool and turned to see Zola lying on her stomach in the chair next to me, reading a paperback, brown legs flipped up, feet swaying in the air. She wore a tiny bikini and lots of skin. Across the small of her back was a colorful butterfly tattoo, centered neatly between tribal designs.

"Did you get that when you were with Webb?" I asked.

"What?"

"Your tattoo. Did Webb suggest you get a tattoo?"

She put the book down. "He said it would 'commemorate our relationship.' How fucked-up is that? But I wanted to get one anyway."

Zola stood and backed next to me so I could get a good look at the tattoo. "I picked it out," she said with pride. "Those designs are Samoan. Do you like it?"

I could smell the suntan lotion.

"It's beautiful."

∗ ∗ ∗

HALF THE GUESTS WERE EUROPEAN, so roughly half the women on the beach sunbathed topless.

I was walking back from the beach bar with two frozen daiquiris. We were sitting next to a group of topless women, and I tried to locate Zola by her bikini top. The problem was, there was no bikini top.

Zola had reclined the chair three-quarters. She wore the bikini bottom, a straw hat, sunglasses, and a mischievous smile. Her breasts were large and young. She tanned easily and her skin had browned a few shades since we arrived, giving a sharp contrast to the bikini top outline. As she lay directly in the sun, her breasts had grown hot; light reflected off a tiny film of perspiration.

"I hope you don't mind." She giggled.

"Mind? Why should I mind?" A tremor shook the daiquiri as I handed it to her. I examined her breasts closely; if she was willing to show them I was willing to look. The areolas were dark, the nipples large and inviting.

After dinner that night, as we were about to go to bed, I stood on our balcony and looked over the pool, wearing shorts but no shirt. An evening wind blew through the date palms and cooled my skin. Zola came up behind and put her arms around my chest. She hugged me to her and kissed my back. Turning, I discovered she was naked.

"Please," she said, "don't say anything."

Without heels Zola was as tall as my chest. I leaned down to kiss her while running my hands down her back, past her buttocks to her thighs. She kissed hungrily, nibbling on my lips, running her tongue across the tops of my teeth. She kissed her way down my neck and pressed her lips to my chest. I reached up, felt the fullness of her breasts, and rolled my thumbs around the erect nipples. Her hands flew over my back, pulling me to her.

She stopped and looked at my face, her eyes needy. "You'd better carry me in soon, or I'll make a scene right here."

I reached down and lifted her legs from behind the knees. We kissed as I carried her into the room. I bumped into a chair, and we laughed as we collapsed on the bed. She leaped up and yanked away my shorts, her breasts bouncing as she worked. Zola straddled me immediately and bucked so wildly I had to hold her in place with my hands. She was frantic and quick.

After she came, she fell on top of me, a mass of quivering nerves and release. I played with the butterfly while her breathing slowed, and she fell asleep. I lay still, not wanting to wake her, and listened to the palm trees rustling outside.

A few minutes later she woke up, laughed lightly at herself, and kissed me, still hungry. She stayed on top but controlled her pace the

second time and focused on my pleasure. She dangled her breasts in front of me and then ground them into my chest. Gradually her pace increased, and the pleasure rose to a breaking point. As my wave of excitement crested, I felt a shell of tension crack and fall away.

Later we lay side by side on the bed, touching each other gently, growing accustomed to our nakedness.

My conscience gnawed away and kept me from relaxing.

"What's wrong?" she asked.

"I have a confession."

"Already?"

"I still love my wife."

Zola got up and pulled two bottles of water from the room fridge. She handed me one and stood next to the bed, a delicious nude.

"Any fool can see that, Joe Robbins."

I couldn't resist and reached out to touch the side of her hip to draw her to me, back into the bed. I took her in my arms and kissed her on the lips and the eyelids. She pulled back.

"I don't need a husband," she whispered. "I need a lover."

I kissed her chin, her throat, and the side of her neck.

"The last man I was with was Slim Bohls. Please help me forget."

"I will," I promised. "I'll help you forget."

* * *

WE ADOPTED A SCHEDULE of easy living at the resort: rise at nine; breakfast like royalty; spend the days swimming, sunning, and partying; clean up for dinner; and back in bed by eleven. At all hours we worked only to please each other.

But the nightmares remained.

As my lover, Zola claimed my waking hours; the nightmares claimed the rest. Before, Zola slept in the other bed, undisturbed, but

the first night she slept with me I woke with her shaking my shoulder, the sheet wet with sweat. She pressed a damp washcloth to my forehead and made me tell her the sequence of the nightmare. I suggested she sleep in the other bed, but she wouldn't have it.

The next day she told me to write it down.

I started by jotting notes on the pad provided in our room. I covered both sides of every page in half an hour. I bought five notebooks from the gift shop and began to fill them with longhand.

After another week we returned to Austin.

I spent the second half of December decorating the house, buying gifts for the kids, and otherwise engaged in holiday activities.

. . .

ON JANUARY 2, 2001, the NASDAQ closed at 2292—fifty-six points below where it was when I joined the Connection two years before.

Two days later, Zola and I returned to Playa del Carmen and rented an apartment on the beach.

We've been here a month and have taken to buying and cooking our own food. One day, while I was out, Zola threw away all my cigarettes. It was a not-so-subtle hint, but truthfully, I was glad she did it, for I had been trying to pick the right moment to quit.

I tried wakeboarding, but found, to my surprise, that it is actually quite difficult. As an alternative I bought a small sailboat, and on most days we take it out for a couple of hours. In the early morning and at dusk we take long walks on the beach.

While Zola sunbathes topless on the patio, I type away on the laptop I brought. Gradually, I have puzzled something out. They were my friends and I killed them; that much is true, but they had no right to take the life of Webb or anyone else, and I had a duty to protect the others if I could. When one human takes another human's life he

steals that person's freedom along with everything else. One thing I know for certain: Individual freedom trumps brotherhood and elitism and money, every time.

The nightmares have gone, and all that remain are the sun, life, and hopes for the future. I don't know what I'll do for money; maybe freelance. I like the sound of it.

Zola and I healed each other in Playa del Carmen, but I can tell the affair has about run its course. She is restless to get back to her life, and I am restless to get back to mine. Winning Rose again won't be easy, but there is really no rush. We have plenty of time, and I will never give up.

THE END

28189450R00200